Communications in Computer and Information Science   1863

Rationale

The CCIS series is devoted to the publication of proceedings of computer science conferences. Its aim is to efficiently disseminate original research results in informatics in printed and electronic form. While the focus is on publication of peer-reviewed full papers presenting mature work, inclusion of reviewed short papers reporting on work in progress is welcome, too. Besides globally relevant meetings with internationally representative program committees guaranteeing a strict peer-reviewing and paper selection process, conferences run by societies or of high regional or national relevance are also considered for publication.

Topics

The topical scope of CCIS spans the entire spectrum of informatics ranging from foundational topics in the theory of computing to information and communications science and technology and a broad variety of interdisciplinary application fields.

Information for Volume Editors and Authors

Publication in CCIS is free of charge. No royalties are paid, however, we offer registered conference participants temporary free access to the online version of the conference proceedings on SpringerLink (http://link.springer.com) by means of an http referrer from the conference website and/or a number of complimentary printed copies, as specified in the official acceptance email of the event.

CCIS proceedings can be published in time for distribution at conferences or as post-proceedings, and delivered in the form of printed books and/or electronically as USBs and/or e-content licenses for accessing proceedings at SpringerLink. Furthermore, CCIS proceedings are included in the CCIS electronic book series hosted in the SpringerLink digital library at http://link.springer.com/bookseries/7899. Conferences publishing in CCIS are allowed to use Online Conference Service (OCS) for managing the whole proceedings lifecycle (from submission and reviewing to preparing for publication) free of charge.

Publication process

The language of publication is exclusively English. Authors publishing in CCIS have to sign the Springer CCIS copyright transfer form, however, they are free to use their material published in CCIS for substantially changed, more elaborate subsequent publications elsewhere. For the preparation of the camera-ready papers/files, authors have to strictly adhere to the Springer CCIS Authors' Instructions and are strongly encouraged to use the CCIS LaTeX style files or templates.

Abstracting/Indexing

CCIS is abstracted/indexed in DBLP, Google Scholar, EI-Compendex, Mathematical Reviews, SCImago, Scopus. CCIS volumes are also submitted for the inclusion in ISI Proceedings.

How to start

To start the evaluation of your proposal for inclusion in the CCIS series, please send an e-mail to ccis@springer.com.

Ngoc Thanh Nguyen · Siridech Boonsang ·
Hamido Fujita · Bogumiła Hnatkowska ·
Tzung-Pei Hong · Kitsuchart Pasupa ·
Ali Selamat
Editors

Recent Challenges in Intelligent Information and Database Systems

15th Asian Conference, ACIIDS 2023
Phuket, Thailand, July 24–26, 2023
Proceedings

 Springer

Editors

Ngoc Thanh Nguyen (iD)
Wrocław University of Technology
Wrocław, Poland

Hamido Fujita (iD)
Iwate Prefectural University
Iwate, Japan

Tzung-Pei Hong (iD)
National University of Kaohsiung
Kaohsiung, Taiwan

Ali Selamat (iD)
Malaysia Japan International Institute
of Technology
Kuala Lumpur, Malaysia

Siridech Boonsang (iD)
King Mongkut's Institute of Technology
Ladkrabang
Bangkok, Thailand

Bogumiła Hnatkowska (iD)
Wrocław University of Science
and Technology
Wrocław, Poland

Kitsuchart Pasupa (iD)
King Mongkut's Institute of Technology
Ladkrabang
Bangkok, Thailand

ISSN 1865-0929   ISSN 1865-0937 (electronic)
Communications in Computer and Information Science
ISBN 978-3-031-42429-8   ISBN 978-3-031-42430-4 (eBook)
https://doi.org/10.1007/978-3-031-42430-4

This Springer imprint is published by the registered company Springer Nature Switzerland AG
The registered company address is: Gewerbestrasse 11, 6330 Cham, Switzerland

Paper in this product is recyclable.

Preface

ACIIDS 2023 was the 15th event in a series of international scientific conferences on research and applications in the field of intelligent information and database systems. The aim of ACIIDS 2023 was to provide an international forum for research workers with scientific backgrounds in the technology of intelligent information and database systems and their various applications. The conference was hosted by King Mongkut's Institute of Technology Ladkrabang, Thailand, and jointly organized by Wrocław University of Science and Technology, Poland, in cooperation with IEEE SMC Technical Committee on Computational Collective Intelligence, European Research Center for Information Systems (ERCIS), University of Newcastle (Australia), Yeungnam University (South Korea), International University - Vietnam National University HCMC (Vietnam), Leiden University (The Netherlands), Universiti Teknologi Malaysia (Malaysia), Ton Duc Thang University (Vietnam), BINUS University (Indonesia), and Vietnam National University, Hanoi (Vietnam). ACIIDS 2023 occurred in Phuket, Thailand, on July 24–26, 2023.

The ACIIDS conference series is already well established. The first two events, ACIIDS 2009 and ACIIDS 2010, took place in Dong Hoi City and Hue City in Vietnam, respectively. The third event, ACIIDS 2011, occurred in Daegu (South Korea), followed by the fourth, ACIIDS 2012, in Kaohsiung (Taiwan). The fifth event, ACIIDS 2013, was held in Kuala Lumpur (Malaysia), while the sixth event, ACIIDS 2014, was held in Bangkok (Thailand). The seventh event, ACIIDS 2015, occurred in Bali (Indonesia), followed by the eighth, ACIIDS 2016, in Da Nang (Vietnam). The ninth event, ACIIDS 2017, was organized in Kanazawa (Japan). The 10th jubilee conference, ACIIDS 2018, was held in Dong Hoi City (Vietnam), followed by the 11th event, ACIIDS 2019, in Yogyakarta (Indonesia). The 12th and 13th events were planned to be on-site in Phuket (Thailand). However, the global pandemic relating to COVID-19 resulted in both editions of the conference being held online in virtual space. ACIIDS 2022 was held in Ho Chi Minh City as a hybrid conference, and it restarted in-person meetings at conferences.

This volume contains 50 peer-reviewed papers selected for presentation from over 220 submissions. Papers included in this volume cover the following topics: data mining and machine learning methods, advanced data mining techniques and applications, intelligent and contextual systems, natural language processing, network systems and applications, computational imaging and vision, decision support, control systems, and data modeling and processing for industry 4.0.

The accepted and presented papers focus on new trends and challenges facing the intelligent information and database systems community. The presenters showed how research work could stimulate novel and innovative applications. We hope you find these results valuable and inspiring for future research work. We would like to express our sincere thanks to the honorary chairs for their support: Arkadiusz Wójs (Rector of Wrocław University of Science and Technology, Poland), Moonis Ali (Texas State

University, President of International Society of Applied Intelligence, USA), Komsan Maleesee (President of King Mongkut's Institute of Technology Ladkrabang, Thailand).

We thank the keynote speakers for their world-class plenary speeches: Saman K. Halgamuge from The University of Melbourne (Australia), Jerzy Stefanowski from Poznań University of Technology (Poland), Siridech Boonsang from King Mongkut's Institute of Technology Ladkrabang (Thailand), and Masaru Kitsuregawa from The University of Tokyo (Japan).

We cordially thank our main sponsors, King Mongkut's Institute of Technology Ladkrabang (Thailand), Wrocław University of Science and Technology (Poland), IEEE SMC Technical Committee on Computational Collective Intelligence, European Research Center for Information Systems (ERCIS), University of Newcastle (Australia), Yeungnam University (South Korea), Leiden University (The Netherlands), Universiti Teknologi Malaysia (Malaysia), BINUS University (Indonesia), Quang Binh University (Vietnam), Vietnam National University (Vietnam), and Nguyen Tat Thanh University (Vietnam). Our special thanks go to Springer for publishing the proceedings and to all the other sponsors for their kind support.

Our special thanks go to the program chairs, the special session chairs, the organizing chairs, the publicity chairs, the liaison chairs, and the Local Organizing Committee for their work towards the conference. We sincerely thank all the members of the International Program Committee for their valuable efforts in the review process, which helped us to guarantee the highest quality of the selected papers for the conference. We cordially thank all the authors and other conference participants for their valuable contributions. The conference would not have been possible without their support. Thanks are also due to the many experts who contributed to the event being a success.

July 2023

Ngoc Thanh Nguyen
Siridech Boonsang
Hamido Fujita
Bogumiła Hnatkowska
Tzung-Pei Hong
Kitsuchart Pasupa
Ali Selamat

Organization

Honorary Chairs

Arkadiusz Wójs — Rector of Wrocław University of Science and Technology, Poland

Moonis Ali — Texas State University, President of International Society of Applied Intelligence, USA

Komsan Maleesee — President of King Mongkut's Institute of Technology Ladkrabang, Thailand

General Chairs

Ngoc Thanh Nguyen — Wrocław University of Science and Technology, Poland

Suphamit Chittayasothorn — King Mongkut's Institute of Technology Ladkrabang, Thailand

Program Chairs

Hamido Fujita — Iwate Prefectural University, Japan

Tzung-Pei Hong — National University of Kaohsiung, Taiwan

Ali Selamat — Universiti Teknologi Malaysia, Malaysia

Siridech Boonsang — King Mongkut's Institute of Technology Ladkrabang, Thailand

Kitsuchart Pasupa — King Mongkut's Institute of Technology Ladkrabang, Thailand

Steering Committee

Ngoc Thanh Nguyen (Chair) — Wrocław University of Science and Technology, Poland

Longbing Cao — University of Science and Technology Sydney, Australia

Suphamit Chittayasothorn — King Mongkut's Institute of Technology Ladkrabang, Thailand

Ford Lumban Gaol — Bina Nusantara University, Indonesia

Tzung-Pei Hong	National University of Kaohsiung, Taiwan
Dosam Hwang	Yeungnam University, South Korea
Bela Stantic	Griffith University, Australia
Geun-Sik Jo	Inha University, South Korea
Hoai An Le Thi	University of Lorraine, France
Toyoaki Nishida	Kyoto University, Japan
Leszek Rutkowski	Częstochowa University of Technology, Poland
Ali Selamat	Universiti Teknologi Malaysia, Malaysia
Edward Szczerbicki	University of Newcastle, Australia

Special Session Chairs

Bogumiła Hnatkowska	Wrocław University of Science and Technology, Poland
Arit Thammano	King Mongkut's Institute of Technology Ladkrabang, Thailand
Krystian Wojtkiewicz	Wrocław University of Science and Technology, Poland

Doctoral Track Chairs

| Marek Krótkiewicz | Wrocław University of Science and Technology, Poland |
| Nont Kanungsukkasem | King Mongkut's Institute of Technology Ladkrabang, Thailand |

Liaison Chairs

Sirasit Lochanachit	King Mongkut's Institute of Technology Ladkrabang, Thailand
Ford Lumban Gaol	Bina Nusantara University, Indonesia
Quang-Thuy Ha	VNU-University of Engineering and Technology, Vietnam
Mong-Fong Horng	National Kaohsiung University of Applied Sciences, Taiwan
Dosam Hwang	Yeungnam University, South Korea
Le Minh Nguyen	Japan Advanced Institute of Science and Technology, Japan
Ali Selamat	Universiti Teknologi Malaysia, Malaysia

Organizing Chairs

Kamol Wasapinyokul   King Mongkut's Institute of Technology
                                 Ladkrabang, Thailand
Krystian Wojtkiewicz   Wrocław University of Science and Technology,
                                 Poland

Publicity Chairs

Marcin Jodłowiec   Wrocław University of Science and Technology,
                                 Poland
Rafał Palak   Wrocław University of Science and Technology,
                                 Poland
Nat Dilokthanakul   King Mongkut's Institute of Technology
                                 Ladkrabang, Thailand

Finance Chair

Pattanapong Chantamit-O-Pas   King Mongkut's Institute of Technology
                                 Ladkrabang, Thailand

Webmaster

Marek Kopel   Wrocław University of Science and Technology,
                                 Poland

Local Organizing Committee

Taravichet Titijaroonroj   King Mongkut's Institute of Technology
                                 Ladkrabang, Thailand
Praphan Pavarangkoon   King Mongkut's Institute of Technology
                                 Ladkrabang, Thailand
Natthapong Jungteerapanich   King Mongkut's Institute of Technology
                                 Ladkrabang, Thailand
Putsadee Pornphol   Phuket Rajabhat University, Thailand
Patient Zihisire Muke   Wrocław University of Science and Technology,
                                 Poland

Thanh-Ngo Nguyen	Wrocław University of Science and Technology, Poland
Katarzyna Zombroń	Wrocław University of Science and Technology, Poland
Kulwadee Somboonviwat	Kasetsart University Sriracha, Thailand

Keynote Speakers

Saman K. Halgamuge	University of Melbourne, Australia
Jerzy Stefanowski	Poznań University of Technology, Poland
Siridech Boonsang	King Mongkut's Institute of Technology Ladkrabang, Thailand
Masaru Kitsuregawa	University of Tokyo, Japan

Special Sessions Organizers

ADMTA 2023: Special Session on Advanced Data Mining Techniques and Applications

Chun-Hao Chen	National Kaohsiung University of Science and Technology, Taiwan
Bay Vo	Ho Chi Minh City University of Technology, Vietnam
Tzung-Pei Hong	National University of Kaohsiung, Taiwan

AINBC 2023: Special Session on Advanced Data Mining Techniques and Applications

Andrzej W. Przybyszewski	University of Massachusetts Medical School, USA
Jerzy P. Nowacki	Polish-Japanese Academy of Information Technology, Poland

CDF 2023: Special Session on Computational Document Forensics

Jean-Marc Ogier	La Rochelle Université, France
Mickaël Coustaty	La Rochelle Université, France
Surapong Uttama	Mae Fah Luang University, Thailand

CSDT 2023: Special Session on Cyber Science in Digital Transformation

Dariusz Szostek   University of Silesia in Katowice, Poland
Jan Kozak   University of Economics in Katowice, Poland
Paweł Kasprowski   Silesian University of Technology, Poland

CVIS 2023: Special Session on Computer Vision and Intelligent Systems

Van-Dung Hoang   Ho Chi Minh City University of Technology and
                                          Education, Vietnam
Dinh-Hien Nguyen   University of Information Technology,
                                          VNU-HCM, Vietnam
Chi-Mai Luong   Vietnam Academy of Science and Technology,
                                          Vietnam

DMPCPA 2023: Special Session on Data Modelling and Processing in City Pollution Assessment

Hoai Phuong Ha   UiT The Arctic University of Norway, Norway
Manuel Nuñez   Universidad Complutense de Madrid, Spain
Rafał Palak   Wrocław University of Science and Technology,
                                          Poland
Krystian Wojtkiewicz   Wrocław University of Science and Technology,
                                          Poland

HPC-ComCon 2023: Special Session on HPC and Computing Continuum

Pascal Bouvry   University of Luxembourg, Luxembourg
Johnatan E. Pecero   University of Luxembourg, Luxembourg
Arijit Roy   Indian Institute of Information Technology,
                                          Sri City, India

LRLSTP 2023: Special Session on Low Resource Languages Speech and Text Processing

Ualsher Tukeyev   Al-Farabi Kazakh National University,
                                          Kazakhstan
Orken Mamyrbayev   Institute of Information and Computational
                                          Technologies, Kazakhstan

Senior Program Committee

Ajith Abraham	Machine Intelligence Research Labs, USA
Jesús Alcalá Fernández	University of Granada, Spain
Lionel Amodeo	University of Technology of Troyes, France
Ahmad Taher Azar	Prince Sultan University, Saudi Arabia
Thomas Bäck	Leiden University, The Netherlands
Costin Badica	University of Craiova, Romania
Ramazan Bayindir	Gazi University, Turkey
Abdelhamid Bouchachia	Bournemouth University, UK
David Camacho	Universidad Autónoma de Madrid, Spain
Leopoldo Eduardo Cardenas-Barron	Tecnológico de Monterrey, Mexico
Oscar Castillo	Tijuana Institute of Technology, Mexico
Nitesh Chawla	University of Notre Dame, USA
Rung-Ching Chen	Chaoyang University of Technology, Taiwan
Shyi-Ming Chen	National Taiwan University of Science and Technology, Taiwan
Simon Fong	University of Macau, China
Hamido Fujita	Iwate Prefectural University, Japan
Mohamed Gaber	Birmingham City University, UK
Marina L. Gavrilova	University of Calgary, Canada
Daniela Godoy	ISISTAN Research Institute, Argentina
Fernando Gomide	University of Campinas, Brazil
Manuel Grana	University of the Basque Country, Spain
Claudio Gutierrez	Universidad de Chile, Chile
Francisco Herrera	University of Granada, Spain
Tzung-Pei Hong	National University of Kaohsiung, Taiwan
Dosam Hwang	Yeungnam University, South Korea
Mirjana Ivanovic	University of Novi Sad, Serbia
Janusz Jeżewski	Institute of Medical Technology and Equipment ITAM, Poland
Piotr Jędrzejowicz	Gdynia Maritime University, Poland
Kang-Hyun Jo	University of Ulsan, South Korea
Janusz Kacprzyk	Systems Research Institute, Polish Academy of Sciences, Poland
Nikola Kasabov	Auckland University of Technology, New Zealand
Muhammad Khurram Khan	King Saud University, Saudi Arabia
Frank Klawonn	Ostfalia University of Applied Sciences, Germany
Joanna Kolodziej	Cracow University of Technology, Poland
Józef Korbicz	University of Zielona Gora, Poland
Ryszard Kowalczyk	Swinburne University of Technology, Australia

Bartosz Krawczyk — Virginia Commonwealth University, USA

Ondrej Krejcar — University of Hradec Králové, Czech Republic

Adam Krzyzak — Concordia University, Canada

Mark Last — Ben-Gurion University of the Negev, Israel

Hoai An Le Thi — University of Lorraine, France

Kun Chang Lee — Sungkyunkwan University, South Korea

Edwin Lughofer — Johannes Kepler University Linz, Austria

Nezam Mahdavi-Amiri — Sharif University of Technology, Iran

Yannis Manolopoulos — Open University of Cyprus, Cyprus

Klaus-Robert Müller — Technical University of Berlin, Germany

Saeid Nahavandi — Deakin University, Australia

Grzegorz J. Nalepa — AGH University of Science and Technology, Poland

Ngoc-Thanh Nguyen — Wrocław University of Science and Technology, Poland

Dusit Niyato — Nanyang Technological University, Singapore

Manuel Núñez — Universidad Complutense de Madrid, Spain

Jeng-Shyang Pan — Fujian University of Technology, China

Marcin Paprzycki — Systems Research Institute, Polish Academy of Sciences, Poland

Hoang Pham — Rutgers University, USA

Tao Pham Dinh — INSA Rouen, France

Radu-Emil Precup — Politehnica University of Timisoara, Romania

Leszek Rutkowski — Częstochowa University of Technology, Poland

Jürgen Schmidhuber — Swiss AI Lab IDSIA, Switzerland

Björn Schuller — University of Passau, Germany

Ali Selamat — Universiti Teknologi Malaysia, Malaysia

Andrzej Skowron — Warsaw University, Poland

Jerzy Stefanowski — Poznań University of Technology, Poland

Edward Szczerbicki — University of Newcastle, Australia

Ryszard Tadeusiewicz — AGH University of Science and Technology, Poland

Muhammad Atif Tahir — National University of Computing & Emerging Sciences, Pakistan

Bay Vo — Ho Chi Minh City University of Technology, Vietnam

Dinh Duc Anh Vu — Vietnam National University HCMC, Vietnam

Lipo Wang — Nanyang Technological University, Singapore

Junzo Watada — Waseda University, Japan

Michał Woźniak — Wrocław University of Science and Technology, Poland

Farouk Yalaoui — University of Technology of Troyes, France

Sławomir Zadrożny   Systems Research Institute, Polish Academy of
                             Sciences, Poland
Zhi-Hua Zhou   Nanjing University, China

Program Committee

Muhammad Abulaish   South Asian University, India
Bashar Al-Shboul   University of Jordan, Jordan
Toni Anwar   Universiti Teknologi PETRONAS, Malaysia
Taha Arbaoui   University of Technology of Troyes, France
Mehmet Emin Aydin   University of the West of England, UK
Amelia Badica   University of Craiova, Romania
Kambiz Badie   ICT Research Institute, Iran
Hassan Badir   École Nationale des Sciences Appliquées de
                             Tanger, Morocco
Zbigniew Banaszak   Warsaw University of Technology, Poland
Dariusz Barbucha   Gdynia Maritime University, Poland
Maumita Bhattacharya   Charles Sturt University, Australia
Leon Bobrowski   Białystok University of Technology, Poland
Bülent Bolat   Yildiz Technical University, Turkey
Mariusz Boryczka   University of Silesia in Katowice, Poland
Urszula Boryczka   University of Silesia in Katowice, Poland
Zouhaier Brahmia   University of Sfax, Tunisia
Stéphane Bressan   National University of Singapore, Singapore
Peter Brida   University of Žilina, Slovakia
Piotr Bródka   Wrocław University of Science and Technology,
                             Poland
Grażyna Brzykcy   Poznań University of Technology, Poland
Robert Burduk   Wrocław University of Science and Technology,
                             Poland
Aleksander Byrski   AGH University of Science and Technology,
                             Poland
Dariusz Ceglarek   WSB University in Poznań, Poland
Somchai Chatvichienchai   University of Nagasaki, Japan
Chun-Hao Chen   Tamkang University, Taiwan
Leszek J. Chmielewski   Warsaw University of Life Sciences, Poland
Kazimierz Choroś   Wrocław University of Science and Technology,
                             Poland
Kun-Ta Chuang   National Cheng Kung University, Taiwan
Dorian Cojocaru   University of Craiova, Romania
Jose Alfredo Ferreira Costa Federal University of Rio Grande do Norte
                             (UFRN), Brazil

Mehmet Karaata — Kuwait University, Kuwait

Rafał Kern — Wrocław University of Science and Technology, Poland

Zaheer Khan — University of the West of England, UK

Marek Kisiel-Dorohinicki — AGH University of Science and Technology, Poland

Attila Kiss — Eötvös Loránd University, Hungary

Shinya Kobayashi — Ehime University, Japan

Grzegorz Kołaczek — Wrocław University of Science and Technology, Poland

Marek Kopel — Wrocław University of Science and Technology, Poland

Jan Kozak — University of Economics in Katowice, Poland

Adrianna Kozierkiewicz — Wrocław University of Science and Technology, Poland

Dalia Kriksciuniene — Vilnius University, Lithuania

Dariusz Król — Wrocław University of Science and Technology, Poland

Marek Krótkiewicz — Wrocław University of Science and Technology, Poland

Marzena Kryszkiewicz — Warsaw University of Technology, Poland

Jan Kubicek — VSB -Technical University of Ostrava, Czech Republic

Tetsuji Kuboyama — Gakushuin University, Japan

Elżbieta Kukla — Wrocław University of Science and Technology, Poland

Marek Kulbacki — Polish-Japanese Academy of Information Technology, Poland

Kazuhiro Kuwabara — Ritsumeikan University, Japan

Annabel Latham — Manchester Metropolitan University, UK

Tu Nga Le — Vietnam National University HCMC, Vietnam

Yue-Shi Lee — Ming Chuan University, Taiwan

Florin Leon — Gheorghe Asachi Technical University of Iasi, Romania

Chunshien Li — National Central University, Taiwan

Horst Lichter — RWTH Aachen University, Germany

Igor Litvinchev — Nuevo Leon State University, Mexico

Doina Logofatu — Frankfurt University of Applied Sciences, Germany

Lech Madeyski — Wrocław University of Science and Technology, Poland

Bernadetta Maleszka — Wrocław University of Science and Technology, Poland

Marcin Maleszka	Wrocław University of Science and Technology, Poland
Tamás Matuszka	Eötvös Loránd University, Hungary
Michael Mayo	University of Waikato, New Zealand
Héctor Menéndez	University College London, UK
Jacek Mercik	WSB University in Wrocław, Poland
Radosław Michalski	Wrocław University of Science and Technology, Poland
Peter Mikulecky	University of Hradec Králové, Czech Republic
Miroslava Mikusova	University of Žilina, Slovakia
Marek Milosz	Lublin University of Technology, Poland
Jolanta Mizera-Pietraszko	Opole University, Poland
Dariusz Mrozek	Silesian University of Technology, Poland
Leo Mrsic	IN2data Ltd Data Science Company, Croatia
Agnieszka Mykowiecka	Institute of Computer Science, Polish Academy of Sciences, Poland
Pawel Myszkowski	Wrocław University of Science and Technology, Poland
Huu-Tuan Nguyen	Vietnam Maritime University, Vietnam
Le Minh Nguyen	Japan Advanced Institute of Science and Technology, Japan
Loan T. T. Nguyen	Vietnam National University HCMC, Vietnam
Quang-Vu Nguyen	Korea-Vietnam Friendship Information Technology College, Vietnam
Thai-Nghe Nguyen	Cantho University, Vietnam
Thi Thanh Sang Nguyen	Vietnam National University HCMC, Vietnam
Van Sinh Nguyen	Vietnam National University HCMC, Vietnam
Agnieszka Nowak-Brzezińska	University of Silesia in Katowice, Poland
Alberto Núñcz	Universidad Complutense de Madrid, Spain
Mieczysław Owoc	Wrocław University of Business and Economics, Poland
Panos Patros	University of Waikato, New Zealand
Maciej Piasecki	Wrocław University of Science and Technology, Poland
Bartłomiej Pierański	Poznań University of Economics and Business, Poland
Dariusz Pierzchała	Military University of Technology, Poland
Marcin Pietranik	Wrocław University of Science and Technology, Poland
Elias Pimenidis	University of the West of England, UK
Jaroslav Pokorný	Charles University in Prague, Czech Republic
Nikolaos Polatidis	University of Brighton, UK
Elvira Popescu	University of Craiova, Romania

Piotr Porwik	University of Silesia in Katowice, Poland
Petra Poulova	University of Hradec Králové, Czech Republic
Małgorzata Przybyła-Kasperek	University of Silesia in Katowice, Poland
Paulo Quaresma	Universidade de Évora, Portugal
David Ramsey	Wrocław University of Science and Technology, Poland
Mohammad Rashedur Rahman	North South University, Bangladesh
Ewa Ratajczak-Ropel	Gdynia Maritime University, Poland
Sebastian A. Rios	University of Chile, Chile
Keun Ho Ryu	Chungbuk National University, South Korea
Daniel Sanchez	University of Granada, Spain
Rafał Scherer	Częstochowa University of Technology, Poland
Yeong-Seok Seo	Yeungnam University, South Korea
Donghwa Shin	Yeungnam University, South Korea
Andrzej Siemiński	Wrocław University of Science and Technology, Poland
Dragan Simic	University of Novi Sad, Serbia
Bharat Singh	Universiti Teknologi PETRONAS, Malaysia
Paweł Sitek	Kielce University of Technology, Poland
Adam Słowik	Koszalin University of Technology, Poland
Vladimir Sobeslav	University of Hradec Králové, Czech Republic
Kamran Soomro	University of the West of England, UK
Zenon A. Sosnowski	Białystok University of Technology, Poland
Bela Stantic	Griffith University, Australia
Stanimir Stoyanov	University of Plovdiv "Paisii Hilendarski", Bulgaria
Ja-Hwung Su	Cheng Shiu University, Taiwan
Libuse Svobodova	University of Hradec Králové, Czech Republic
Jerzy Swiątek	Wrocław University of Science and Technology, Poland
Andrzej Swierniak	Silesian University of Technology, Poland
Julian Szymański	Gdańsk University of Technology, Poland
Yasufumi Takama	Tokyo Metropolitan University, Japan
Zbigniew Telec	Wrocław University of Science and Technology, Poland
Dilhan Thilakarathne	Vrije Universiteit Amsterdam, The Netherlands
Diana Trandabat	University "Alexandru Ioan Cuza" of Iaşi, Romania
Maria Trocan	Institut Superieur d'Electronique de Paris, France
Krzysztof Trojanowski	Cardinal Stefan Wyszyński University in Warsaw, Poland
Ualsher Tukeyev	al-Farabi Kazakh National University, Kazakhstan

Olgierd Unold	Wrocław University of Science and Technology, Poland
Jørgen Villadsen	Technical University of Denmark, Denmark
Thi Luu Phuong Vo	Vietnam National University HCMC, Vietnam
Wahyono Wahyono	Universitas Gadjah Mada, Indonesia
Paweł Weichbroth	Gdańsk University of Technology, Poland
Izabela Wierzbowska	Gdynia Maritime University, Poland
Krystian Wojtkiewicz	Wrocław University of Science and Technology, Poland
Xin-She Yang	Middlesex University London, UK
Tulay Yildirim	Yildiz Technical University, Turkey
Drago Zagar	University of Osijek, Croatia
Danuta Zakrzewska	Łódź University of Technology, Poland
Constantin-Bala Zamfirescu	Lucian Blaga University of Sibiu, Romania
Katerina Zdravkova	Ss. Cyril and Methodius University in Skopje, Macedonia
Vesna Zeljkovic	Lincoln University, USA
Jianlei Zhang	Nankai University, China
Zhongwei Zhang	University of Southern Queensland, Australia
Adam Ziębiński	Silesian University of Technology, Poland

Contents

Data Analysis, Modeling, and Processing

Data Mining and Machine Learning

Forecasting and Optimization Techniques

Healthcare and Medical Applications

Speech and Text Processing

Computer Vision

Fast Camera Motion Compensation Based Kalman Filter and Cascade Association for Multi-object Tracking

Tung Thanh Do[1,2(✉)], Huy Quang Che[1,2], and Cuong Van Truong[1,2]

[1] University of Information Technolog, Ho Chi Minh City, Vietnam
19522491@gm.uit.edu.vn
[2] Vietnam National University, Ho Chi Minh City, Vietnam

Abstract. Numerous ways to improve the power of tracking algorithms have emerged in modern multi-object tracking problems. Tracking-by-detection, On the other hand, is one of the most precise approaches in the field, balancing the trade-off between precision and run-time. This method divides the tracking process into two steps: the detection process to localize objects in the image and the tracking process to assign identity for each response from the object detector. In this study, we optimize the tracking process by generalizing the BYTE technique (Cascade Association) and integrating camera-motion compensation to the Association stage. Our new tracker KCM-Track, sets a new state-of-the-art accuracy on MOT17 dataset in terms of the primary MOT metrics: MOTA, IDF1, and HOTA. On MOT17 test sets: **80.6%** MOTA, **79.7%** IDF1, and **64.6%** HOTA are achieved at **314** FPS for the tracking process.

Keywords: Multi-object tracking · Tracking-by-detection · Camera-motion-compensation · Data Association

1 Introduction

Various multi-object tracking methods have been introduced to recognize and estimate the spatio-temporal trajectories of several objects in the video stream. This increases the viability of MOT in real-world applications such as autonomous vehicles, traffic management systems, or video surveillance.

One of the most influential paradigms in multi-object tracking problems is tracking-by-detection [3,5,8,18,22]. The robustness of this method is mainly based on the accuracy of the object detector. To maximize the performance of this approach, we need to focus on optimizing the vital part of this method which heavily relies on object detection and tracking. Even though object detectors play a crucial role in this method, it is not easy to enhance the accuracy of this stage due to the complexity and the generalization of this problem. On the contrary, tracking is recognized as a postprocessing step and has a significant impact on overall accuracy. The simple and basic approaches in SORT [5] (based on intersect of union) or DeepSORT [18] (based on appearance similarity) is still the primary method at this stage.

© The Author(s), under exclusive license to Springer Nature Switzerland AG 2023
N. T. Nguyen et al. (Eds.): ACIIDS 2023, CCIS 1863, pp. 3–15, 2023.
https://doi.org/10.1007/978-3-031-42430-4_1

In the tracking stage, we have two small steps: motion model and data association. Based on previous motion cues, we need to predict the position of the current bounding boxes by motion model. Kalman filter [2] is one of the most common motion models in the tracking-by-detection paradigm. However, the Kalman filter is based on a constant-velocity model, so the IOU-based approaches that rely on the Kalman filter mostly fail when used in low frame rate circumstances, rapid motions, or camera motions. DeepSORT pioneered the application of re-identification to multi-object tracking by taking the object detector's responses through a feature extractor and then matching the tracks and detection boxes by appearance similarity. The appearance feature for matching helps reduce the IOU-based approaches' limitation and enhances the identity maintenance for each track. However, this method may be inadequate compared to the IOU-based method in crowded environments with many people overlapping and low visibility, leading to the trade-off between the tracker's ability to detect the objects (MOTA) and the tracker's ability to preserve the correct identities over time (IDF1).

ByteTrack [22], one of the current SOTA methods in multi-object tracking, use IOU-based tracking-by-detection approach to increase MOTA accuracy while keeping the high-speed inference time. The effectiveness of the BYTE algorithm has been shown when applied to 9 different trackers. However, for each different tracker, the confidence interval varies and has to carefully tune for each method. In this work, we generalize their method from a two-confidence interval to an n-confidence interval to best fit each type of detector.

In moving camera scene, the location of the detection boxes in the image plane might shift substantially, thereby making IOU-based techniques [5, 22] increasing ID switches or false negatives. In BOT-Sort [3], they use the global motion compensation (GMC) technique in the OpenCV [6] for calculating the affine matrix and applying this matrix to compensate for camera motion. However, the GMC approach is very resource-intensive and time-consuming, making it challenging to apply to low-computational-resource systems. As a result, we propose another technique that uses the information from BYTE algorithm's high-score bounding boxes [22] to adjust the low-score bounding boxes in the association step. Because this approach uses significantly fewer computational resources than the GMC, the run-time in the tracking stage is nearly the same while using this algorithm.

In this work, we propose a new tracker which achieve SOTA accuracy while maintain the high run-time speed in the MOT17 challenge by addressing the above limitations of IOU-based approaches and integrating them into the novel ByteTrack. In summary, our contributions can be given as follows:

- We generalize BYTE algorithm [22] from a two-confidence interval to an n-confidence interval and call it Cascade Association.
- We represent a new and straightforward method to compensate camera motion from information in the data association step for a more robust association in the tracking stage. We call it Kalman camera-motion compensation.
- We implement Cascade Association and Kalman camera-motion compensation to ByteTrack [22], experiment on the MOT17 dataset [12], and conduct ablation studies to prove the effectiveness of our proposed algorithm.

2   Related Work

2.1   Detection in Tracking-By-detection

MOT is merely an object detection problem with an identity where the accuracy mainly depends on the capability of the object detector. Many current SOTA methods use off-the-shell object detection methods to generate the bounding boxes for the objects in the image, [8, 22] using YOLOX detector [9], CenterTrack [24] using a modified model from CenterNet [25],... For older methods [5, 18], when applied with state-of-the-art object detectors, the accuracy in CLEAR [4], IDF1 [15] metric is competitive to the latest methods [3, 20, 22] in MOT.

2.2   Tracking in Tracking-By-detection

Motion Model. Kalman filter [2] is an extremely popular linear model to predict the position of future tracks because of its simplicity and efficiency. Although the constant-velocity assumption is not fit well in a real-world situation, it has been used widely since 2017 in SORT [5] until 2022 in by [3, 8, 22]. Many researchers employ more complex forms of the Kalman filter. For example, instead of estimating the bounding boxes' height and aspect ratio, [3] replaces the aspect ratio with the width to achieve better performance and verify it through many experiments. In many complex scenarios, such as non-static cameras, irregular movement from real-life situations may cause failure when using the Kalman filter. Many studies use more advanced techniques in Deep Learning to calculate the offset of each object by using the past information [19, 24]. This strategy is still not comparable to the Kalman filter IOU-based approaches due to the performance of the detection phase.

Data Association. This step in MOT is considered a linear assignment problem, starting from the SORT algorithm [5], which associates bounding boxes and tracks based on IOU. The following version, DeepSort [18], used cosine distance between apperance embedding features to match detection boxes and tracks. ByteTrack [22] uses high-score bounding boxes for matching and instantiating new objects and low-score bounding boxes for object matching. In addition, some methods modify the matching distance, such as CBIOU [20] extend the bounding boxes region to better match in the cases where the objects have an irregular shape and unpredictable movement.

2.3   Tracking with Camera Motion Compensation

The tracking-by-detection-based IOU and Kalman filter methods rely heavily on the assumption of linear motion. Therefore, significant camera motion may shift the estimated bounding boxes far away from the true position, which causes failure when calculating IOU between tracks and detection boxes. In BOT-Sort [3], they use the global motion compensation (GMC) technique to calculate the affine matrix and apply this matrix to compensate for camera motion. However, the GMC approach is very resource-intensive and time-consuming, making it challenging to apply to low-computational-resource systems. In crowed scenes, the estimation of the camera motion may fail due to a lack of background key points which can cause unexpected tracker behavior.

3   Proposed Method

In this section, we present our main contributions for the multi-object tracking-based tracking-by-detection methods. By integrating Cascade Association and camera motion-compensation based Kalman filter into ByteTrack [22], we present new state-of-the-art trackers, KCM-Track. The Cascade Association is presented in Algorithm 1 and the Kalman camera-motion compensation is presented in Fig. 1.

3.1   Cascade Association

We separate the high-score, and low-score detection boxes similar to the BYTE method [22], with the high confident boxes used to initialize new tracks and the low ones discarded. Nevertheless, we extend this method by increasing the number of confidence intervals rather than just one, implying that the high-score and low-score detection boxes may be divided into smaller groups. Then the matching process can begin from the highest to the lowest. The unmatched tracks from the higher confidence interval are matched with, the lower group again, which is why we name our association strategy Cascade Association.

In Algorithm 1, we take previous tracks, detection boxes, a set of predefined confidence intervals, and a high-score threshold as input. The Cascade Association returned activated tracks for evaluation, unactivated tracks for lost track removal, and unmatched detection for track rebirth. First, our algorithm separates the detection boxes into groups depending on their confidence value and predefined confidence interval. Using *match_dets_tracks* function, we conduct the matching process for each group to associate the tracks and detection boxes. After that, we store the unmatched detection boxes for track initialization if their confidence is higher than a high-score threshold (line 17 Algorithm 1).

3.2   Camera-Motion Compensation Based Kalman Filter

In the multi-object tracking-based tracking-by-detection methods, the IOU-based Kalman filter approach is one of the most popular due to its simplicity and effectiveness. This strategy, however, is based on a constant-velocity assumption, which creates many errors in a moving camera. Fig. 1 depicts the trouble caused by camera displacement. The camera is fixed in the first three frames (from $t = 1$ to $t = 3$). As a result, the Kalman filter fully captures the object's trajectory and matches it by applying the IOU-based technique. In the next frame ($t = 4$), the camera is shifted to the right by d, which alters the object's location in the image. The newly shifted position of objects is shown by red boxes, while the predicted boxes using the Kalman filter are represented by blue boxes. The IOU between the actual detection boxes and the predicted boxes decreased or equaled zero, causing the IOU-based matching technique to fail.

Algorithm 1: Cascade association

   Input   : A list of track $\mathcal{T}$, a list of bounding boxes $\mathcal{D}$, a list of confidence score
            $\mathcal{C}$, a list of matching threshold $\mathcal{M}$, high score threshold τ
   Output: A list of activated tracks $\mathcal{A}$, a list of unactivated tracks $\mathcal{U}$, a list of
            unmatched detection boxes $\mathcal{B}$

   // Split bounding boxes with confidence
   // interval
1 *Initialize det_array D and score_array S*;
2 **for** *conf in* **to** $\mathcal{C}$ **do**
3       $idx = \mathcal{D} > conf$
4       $d, s = \mathcal{D}[idx], \mathcal{C}[idx]$
5       $D = D \cup d$
6       $S = S \cup s$

   // Initialize step
7 *Initialize untracked track u_track = $\mathcal{T}$,*
8   *activated track ac_track = None,*
9   *refinded track re_track = None*
10   *and unmatched detection u_det = None* ;

   // Run matching from the highest confidence
   // interval to the lowest confidence interval
11 **for** *idx, dets in* D **do**
12      $at, rt, ut, ud = match\_dets\_tracks(dets, S[idx],$
13                              $u\_track, M[idx])$
14      $ac\_track = ac\_track \cup at$
15      $re\_track = re\_track \cup rt$
16      $u\_track = ut$
        // Keep high-score detection boxes for
        // trackers initialization
17   **if** $\mathcal{C}[idx] > \tau$ **then** $u\_det = u\_det \cup ud$;

18 **return** $u\_track, ac\_track, re\_track, u\_det$

The *match_dets_tracks* function is a matching algorithm from the SORT algorithm [5], which is an IOU-based matching strategy with the Hungarian algorithm [1]. However, we intentionally integrate our Kalman camera-motion compensation to mitigate the effect of large displacement in non-stationary camera.

The failure of this strategy is mostly due to a violation of the Kalman Filter's constant-velocity assumption. One way to mitigate this effect is to introduce the velocity of the moving camera when using the Kalman filter to make a prediction. This velocity can be calculated by following the global motion compensation (GMC) technique used in the OpenCV [6] implementation of the Video Stabilization module, similar to BOT-Sort [3]. However, this technique consumes a large number of computational resources.

As we may know, the closer the object is to the camera, the bigger it gets in the image. The bigger the object in the image, the less influence caused by the camera motion (object A in Fig. 1 still overlaps with its corresponding track box). Intuitively, our method use the "big" track boxes, which we can match with their corresponding detection boxes to achieve the camera velocity and guide the "small" track boxes. In more technical terms, we use the difference in velocity (also known as acceleration) of the matched track as camera velocity to re-update the unmatched track's location. The camera-motion compensation process is shown in Fig. 1. To get the camera velocity, we calculate the velocity offset between the newly updated state and the old state predicted from the Kalman filter for each matched track (line 7 to line 14 in Algorithm 2), then average the velocity offset (line 15 in Algorithm 2) to get camera velocity. Finally, we restore the unmatched track state and re-predict the new state using the camera velocity (line 16, 17, 18 in Algorithm 2).

4   Experimental Results

In this section, we conduct many experiments to verify the effectiveness of our method on the MOT17 dataset [12]. Our new tracker, KCM-Track, which is ByteTrack [22] with Cascade Association and Kalman camera-motion compensation.

4.1   Experiment on MOT17 Dataset

The studies were carried out using MOT17 [12] under the "private detection" procedure, one of the most widely used benchmarks in multi-object tracking for pedestrian detection and tracking in unrestricted contexts. The video sequences in MOT17 were captured using stationary and moving cameras, making them ideal for testing our camera-motion compensation algorithm. We use CLEAR metric [4], IDF1 [15] and HOTA [11] to evaluate the performance. The final result is shown in Table 1. The MOTA is higher than the baseline ByteTrack [22] by 0.4%, BOT-Sort 0.2% and 2.4% IDF1 which indicates the improvement in identity preservation. The HOTA accuracy does not surpass BOT-Sort [3], however, the estimated FPS increase significantly.

Algorithm 2: Matching detection boxes and tracks

---

1 **Function** match_dets_tracks(*dets, dets_score, tracks, match_thresh*):

    // Normal matching

2     $at = None$

3     $rt = None$

4     $dist = calculate\_dist(tracks, dets)$

5     $matches, u\_match, u\_dets = association(dist)$

6     $velocity = None$

    // Calculate the acceleration of activated
    // tracks

7   **for** *tracks, dets in matches* **do**

8   **if** *tracks is activated* **then** $new\_mean, old\_mean = tracks.update()$

9           $at = at \cup tracks$

10          $vel = vel \cup (new\_mean - old\_mean)$

11   ;

12   **else**

13          $tracks.reactivate()$

14          $rt = rt \cup tracks;$

    // Calculate camera velocity

15     $mean\_velocity = mean(vel)$

    // Update unmatched track with camera
    // velocity

16   **for** *tracks in u_match* **do**

        // Restore the track state before
        // prediction

17         $tracks.roll\_back()$

18         $tracks.predict(mean\_velocity)$

19     $u\_track = u\_match$

20   **return** at, rt, u_track, u_dets ;

Table 1. Result on MOT17 test set

Tracker	MOTA ↑	IDF1↑	HOTA↑	FP↓	FN↓	IDs↓	FPS↑
MOTR [21]	65.1	66.4	–	45486	149307	2049	–
CenterTrack [24]	67.8	64.7	52.2	**18498**	160332	3039	17.5
QuansiDense [13]	68.7	66.3	53.9	26589	146643	3378	20.3
CSTrack [10]	74.9	72.6	59.3	23847	114303	3567	15.8
TransTrack [16]	75.2	63.5	54.1	50157	86442	3603	10.0
TransMOT [7]	76.7	75.1	61.7	36231	93150	2346	9.6
ByteTrack [22]	80.3	77.3	63.1	25491	83721	2196	**29.6**
BOT-Sort [3]	80.5	**80.2**	**65.0**	35208	73244	**1212**	4.5
Our	**80.7**	79.7	64.6	37452	**69168**	2235	29 [1]

[1] The FPS is estimated because we do not have the same GPU and only modify the Data Association step, which runs on CPU.

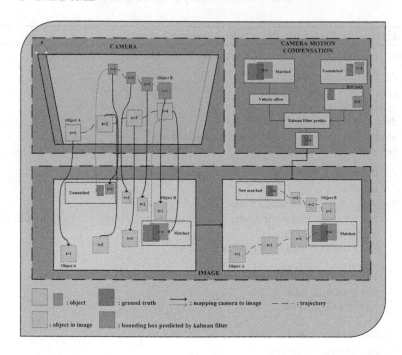

Fig. 1. The effect of camera motion and Kalman camera-motion compensation

4.2   Ablation Study

Experiment on MOT17 Validation Set. We follow [22] to split the MOT17 training set for training and validation. We evaluate the CLEAR metric [4], IDF1 [15] by using the source code of [22] for a fair comparison. The HOTA metric [11] is calculated using this GitHub repository[1]. By using more confidence intervals, we gain 1.2% MOTA, 1.9% IDF1 additionally, and by combining CA and KCM, we increase significantly 3.3% IDF1 and 1.2% HOTA. The results are shown in Table 2.

Table 2. Result on MOT17 validation set

	CA	KCM	MOTA	IDF1	HOTA
Baseline (ByteTrack)			76.6	79.2	67.8
Baseline (ByteTrack)	✓		77.8 (+1.2)	81.1 (+1.9)	68.5(+0.7)
Baseline (ByteTrack)	✓	✓	**78.4** (+1.8)	**82.5** (+3.3)	**68.9** (+1.2)

Run-Time Comparison. Due to the difference in GPU computational resources and only changes in the data association step, we measure the run-time

---

[1] https://github.com/JonathonLuiten/TrackEval.

of the data association stage on ByteTrack [22], BOT-Sort [3] and KCM-Track. The experiment is conducted on MOT17 validation using Intel(R) Core(TM) i9-10900X and 32GB Ram. The final results are shown in Table 3. The run-time between ByteTrack and our tracker is small and negligible, while BOT-Sort is higher than KCM-Track 15 times.

Table 3. The tracking time on MOT17 validation

	MOTA ↑	IDF1 ↑	HOTA ↑	Track time(s) ↓
ByteTrack	76.60	79.20	67.80	**6.96**
BOT-Sort	**78.46**	82.07	**69.17**	119.3
KCM-Track	78.40	**82.50**	68.90	7.66

Applications on Other Trackers. We apply CA and KCM on 8 different state-of-the-arts trackers, including JDE [17], CSTrack [10], FairMOT [23], TraDes [19], QDTrack [13], CenterTrack [24], Chained-Tracker [14] and TransTrack [16]. We only use the detection boxes generate by these tracker and intergrate our method to each tracker. The results is shown in Table 4. Even though when applying BYTE algorithm [22], there are a significant improvements, our method still can increase the performance of some trackers compared to BYTE, especially 1.3% MOTA on TransTrack, 2.3% IDF1 on QDTrack [13] and −104 ID switches on TraDes [19].

We apply CA, and KCM on eight different state-of-the-art trackers, including JDE [17], CSTrack [10], FairMOT [23], TraDes [19], QDTrack [13], Center-Track [24], Chained-Tracker [14], and TransTrack [16]. We only use the detection boxes generated by these trackers and integrate our method into each tracker. The results are shown in Table 4. Even though when applying BYTE, there are significant improvements, our method still can increase the performance of some trackers compared to BYTE, especially 1.3% MOTA on TransTrack, 2.3% IDF1 on QDTrack [13] and −104 ID switches on TraDes [19].

The Effectiveness of Kalman Camera-Motion Compensation. To prove the effectiveness of Kalman camera-motion compensation, we show the visualization of predicted bounding boxes by the Kalman filter in ByteTrack [22] and KCM-Track in Fig. 2. This is an image from the MOT17-13 video, and the camera is turning to the right. That is why, without Kalman camera-motion compensation, the bounding boxes in ByteTrack are shifted to the right while the bounding boxes in KCM-Track are fit to the pedestrian.

To show that our method can capture the camera direction, we plot $sign(x_{vel}) * e^{x_{vel}}$, where x_{vel} is the velocity of the camera in $x - axis$. In Fig. 3(a), MOT17-04 video is a static camera scene, the $sign(x_{vel}) * e^{x_{vel}}$ is around 1 and −1 which means x_{vel} is around 0. It is true because the camera is not moving. In Fig. 3(b), the MOT17-11 video is a moving camera scene with a man holding a camera while walking in the mall. This is why the $x - axis$ of camera velocity

Table 4. Results of applying CA and KCM to 8 different state-of-the-art trackers on the MOT17 validation set. In green are the improvements of at least (+0.5) point

Method	Association method	MOTA↑	IDF1↑	IDs↓
JDE [17]	–	60.0	63.6	473
	w/BYTE	60.6	66.0	360
	w/CA + KCM	61.1 (+0.5)	67.5 (+1.5)	286 (−74)
CSTrack [10]	–	68.0	72.3	325
	w/BYTE	69.3	73.9	285
	w/CA + KCM	70.3 (+1.0)	73.0 (−0.9)	290 (+5)
FairMOT [23]	–	69.1	72.8	299
	w/BYTE	70.3	73.2	236
	w/CA + KCM	71.2 (+0.9)	73.4 (+0.2)	198 (−38)
TraDes [19]	–	68.2	71.7	285
	w/BYTE	67.9	72.0	281
	w/CA + KCM	68.7 (+0.8)	73.3 (+1.3)	177 (−104)
QuasiDense [13]	-	67.3	67.8	377
	w/BYTE	67.9	70.9	258
	w/CA + KCM	68.4 (+0.5)	73.2 (+2.3)	239 (−19)
CenterTrack [24]	–	66.1	64.2	528
	w/BYTE	67.4	74.0	144
	w/CA + KCM	68.4 (+1.0)	74.3 (+0.3)	144 (−0)
CTracker [14]	–	63.1	60.9	755
	w/BYTE	65.0	66.7	346
	w/CA + KCM	65.2 (+0.2)	66.6 (−0.1)	293 (−53)
TransTrack [16]	–	67.1	68.3	254
	w/BYTE	68.4	72.4	181
	w/CA + KCM	69.7 (+1.3)	72.7 (+0.3)	172 (−9)

Fig. 2. Visualization of predicted bounding boxes by Kalman filter in ByteTrack and KCM-Track. The green boxes are ByteTrack, and the blue boxes are KCM-Track. (Color figure online)

follow a zigzag pattern, which is fit with left and right movement when a person is walking with a camera. It shows that our camera compensation method not only can capture the moving direction of camera but remains robust in a static scene.

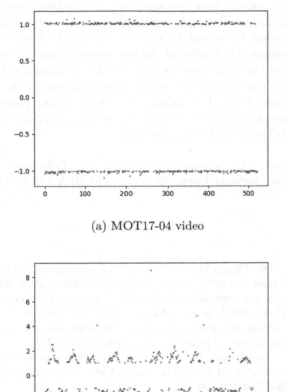

(a) MOT17-04 video

(b) MOT17-11 video

Fig. 3. The $x - axis$ velocity of camera on MOT17 videos.

5   Conclusion

In conclusion, we generalize BYTE Algorithm to form the Cascade Association algorithm and propose Kalman camera-motion compensation. We implement a new state-of-the-art tracker on the MOT17 dataset, KCM-Track. We also conduct many experiments to prove the effectiveness of our proposal and the generalization of our method when applying it to eight other trackers. In addition, the Kalman camera-motion compensation can perform in real-time compared to previous camera-motion compensation methods. Although our current method effectively incorporates camera motion into the tracking process, it relies on prior information for calculating the camera-motion. Consequently, in scenarios where only an object is present in a frame, the method may encounter limitations. To overcome this challenge, future research aim to employ advanced techniques that can mitigate camera motion. One such approach involves scanning the local region to identify a matching bounding box for the object without relying on a Kalman filter. This proposed technique holds promise for enhancing the robustness and accuracy of object tracking in scenarios where explicit camera motion information is not available.

Acknowledgement. This research is funded by University of Information Technology-Vietnam National University of Ho Chi Minh city under grant number D1-2023-14.

References

1. Kuhn, H.W.: The Hungarian method for the assignment problem. Naval Res. Logist. Q. **2**(1), 83–97 (1955). https://doi.org/10.1002/NAV.3800020109
2. Kalman, R.E.: A new approach to linear filtering and prediction problems. J. Basic Eng. **82**(1), 35–45 (1960). https://doi.org/10.1115/1.3662552
3. Aharon, N., Orfaig, R., Bobrovsky, B.Z.: Bot-sort: Robust associations multi-pedestrian tracking. arXiv preprint arXiv:2206.14651 (2022)
4. Bernardin, K., Stiefelhagen, R.: Evaluating multiple object tracking performance: the clear mot metrics. EURASIP J. Image Video Process. 2008 (2008). https://doi.org/10.1155/2008/246309
5. Bewley, A., Ge, Z., Ott, L., Ramos, F., Upcroft, B.: Simple online and realtime tracking. In: 2016 IEEE International Conference on Image Processing (ICIP), pp. 3464–3468 (2016). https://doi.org/10.1109/ICIP.2016.7533003
6. Bradski, G.: The OpenCV library. Dr. Dobb's J. Softw. Tools **25**, 120–123 (2000)
7. Chu, P., Wang, J., You, Q., Ling, H., Liu, Z.: Transmot: spatial-temporal graph transformer for multiple object tracking. In: 2023 IEEE/CVF Winter Conference on Applications of Computer Vision (WACV), pp. 4859–4869 (2023). https://doi.org/10.1109/WACV56688.2023.00485
8. Du, Y., Song, Y., Yang, B., Zhao, Y.: Strongsort: Make deepsort great again. arXiv preprint arXiv:2202.13514 (2022)
9. Ge, Z., Liu, S., Wang, F., Li, Z., Sun, J.: Yolox: Exceeding yolo series in 2021. arXiv preprint arXiv:2107.08430 (2021)
10. Liang, C., Zhang, Z., Zhou, X., Li, B., Zhu, S., Hu, W.: Rethinking the competition between detection and reid in multiobject tracking. IEEE Trans. Image Process. **31**, 3182–3196 (2022). https://doi.org/10.1109/TIP.2022.3165376
11. Luiten, J., et al.: HOTA: a higher order metric for evaluating multi-object tracking. Int. J. Comput. Vis. , 1–31 (2020). https://doi.org/10.1007/s11263-020-01375-2

12. Milan, A., Leal-Taixe, L., Reid, I., Roth, S., Schindler, K.: Mot16: A benchmark for multi-object tracking (2016). https://doi.org/10.48550/ARXIV.1603. 00831, arxiv.org/abs/1603.00831
13. Pang, J., et al.: Quasi-dense similarity learning for multiple object tracking. In: IEEE/CVF Conference on Computer Vision and Pattern Recognition (2021)
14. Peng, J., et al.: Chained-tracker: chaining paired attentive regression results for end-to-end joint multiple-object detection and tracking. In: Proceedings of the European Conference on Computer Vision (2020)
15. Ristani, E., Solera, F., Zou, R., Cucchiara, R., Tomasi, C.: Performance measures and a data set for multi-target, multi-camera tracking. In: Hua, G., Jégou, H. (eds.) Computer Vision - ECCV 2016 Workshops. LNCS, pp. 17–35. Springer International Publishing, Cham (2016). https://doi.org/10.1007/978-3-319-48881-3_2
16. Sun, P., et al.: Transtrack: Multiple-object tracking with transformer. arXiv preprint arXiv: 2012.15460 (2020)
17. Wang, Z., Zheng, L., Liu, Y., Li, Y., Wang, S.: Towards real-time multi-object tracking. In: Vedaldi, A., Bischof, H., Brox, T., Frahm, J.-M. (eds.) ECCV 2020. LNCS, vol. 12356, pp. 107–122. Springer, Cham (2020). https://doi.org/10.1007/978-3-030-58621-8_7
18. Wojke, N., Bewley, A., Paulus, D.: Simple online and realtime tracking with a deep association metric. In: 2017 IEEE International Conference on Image Processing (ICIP), pp. 3645–3649. IEEE (2017). https://doi.org/10.1109/ICIP.2017.8296962
19. Wu, J., Cao, J., Song, L., Wang, Y., Yang, M., Yuan, J.: Track to detect and segment: an online multi-object tracker. In: IEEE Conference on Computer Vision and Pattern Recognition (CVPR) (2021)
20. Yang, F., Odashima, S., Masui, S., Jiang, S.: Hard to track objects with irregular motions and similar appearances? make it easier by buffering the matching space (2022). https://doi.org/10.48550/ARXIV.2211.14317, arxiv.org/abs/2211.14317
21. Zeng, F., Dong, B., Zhang, Y., Wang, T., Zhang, X., Wei, Y.: Motr: end-to-end multiple-object tracking with transformer. In: Avidan, S., Brostow, G., Cissé, M., Farinella, G.M., Hassner, T. (eds.) Computer Vision - ECCV 2022. LNCS, pp. 659–675. Springer Nature Switzerland, Cham (2022). https://doi.org/10.1007/978-3-031-19812-0_38
22. Zhang, Y., et al.: Bytetrack: Multi-object tracking by associating every detection box (2022)
23. Zhang, Y., Wang, C., Wang, X., Zeng, W., Liu, W.: Fairmot: on the fairness of detection and re-identification in multiple object tracking. Int. J. Comput. Vis. 129, 3069–3087 (2021)
24. Zhou, X., Koltun, V., Krähenbühl, P.: Tracking objects as points. In: Vedaldi, A., Bischof, H., Brox, T., Frahm, J.M. (eds.) Computer Vision - ECCV 2020. LNCS, pp. 474–490. Springer International Publishing, Cham (2020). https://doi.org/10.1007/978-3-030-58548-8_28
25. Zhou, X., Wang, D., Krähenbühl, P.: Objects as points. In: arXiv preprint arXiv:1904.07850 (2019)

Image-Based Reliable Object Localization of UAV Cooperating with Ground Vehicle

Seokjun Lee[✉], Chungjae Choe, and Nakmyung Sung

Autonomous IoT Research Center, Korea Electronics Technology Institute, Seongnam, Korea
{sjlee88,cjchoe1,nmsung}@keti.re.kr

Abstract. Localization of target object in UAV becomes critical factor to accomplish missions successfully such as human rescuing, hazardous substance detection, and suspect tracking. To this end, a number of research have been conducted but there is inherent limitation due to camera distortion or diverse geographical features. In this paper, we utilize the location of ground vehicle and the distance from target object to estimate the location of target. The thorough experiments with real image data verifies that our algorithm can infer the target's location with error of 4.86 m ± 1.74 m. We believe that the proposed scheme can be used along with any previous works in complementary manner.

Keywords: Object Localization · UAV · Ground Vehicle Cooperation

1 Introduction

Recently, unmanned aerial vehicle (UAV) becomes mature enough to utilize in real industrial field. To this end, a number of global companies such as Amazon, DJI, Google, and Intel are actively release the commercial UAV and related services. For example, Google's Wing already have provided package delivery service using UAV from April, 2022 [1]. Due to this notable improvement of UAV, there have been many attempts to apply UAV in various fields. One of the most promising area is using UAV for search purpose such as human rescue, hazardous substance detection, and suspect tracking. To accomplish such mission successfully, object localization of UAV should be accurate and reliable.

There are extensive previous works for object localization in UAV such as using monocular camera [2–8], stereo camera [9], and even multiple UAVs [10, 11]. However, these methods inherently have limitation that as the distance of object between UAV increases, the location estimation prone to be wrong because of distortion of camera lens and diverse geographical features. To resolve this problem, we propose the reliable object localization technique by cooperating with ground vehicle.

Our intuition is that search mission is usually conducted with not only UAV but also ground vehicle such as police car, fire truck and robot. Thanks to the wide use of global positioning system (GPS) based navigation system, the location of ground vehicle can be easily acquired. And UAV naturally captures the ground vehicle in its camera frame

N. T. Nguyen et al. (Eds.): ACIIDS 2023, CCIS 1863, pp. 16–26, 2023.
https://doi.org/10.1007/978-3-031-42430-4_2

because it flies high for wide coverage. From this intuition, we use the ground vehicle as hint for object location. As the ground vehicle is more near by target object than UAV, the distortion and geographical issue can be minimized compared with UAV only solution. The proposed scheme first detects the target object and ground vehicle around it using Yolov7 [12] trained with vis-drone dataset [13]. Then measure the distance between target object and ground vehicle. Lastly, object location is estimated by using the GPS of ground vehicle and distance. Note that since our methodology exploits the known location of ground vehicle as additional hint, it can be applied any previous works which uses only UAV's GPS data.

Our contributions are as follows: i) we use the ground vehicle's location as a hint for object location estimation; ii) we propose the scheme to measure the distance between target object and ground vehicle under various environment such as camera tilting; ii) we conducted experiment with actual data to verify our system.

The rest of paper is organized as follows. Section 2 discusses about related previous works. Section 3 explains how to estimate the location of target object using ground vehicle's location. In Sect. 4, the experimental methodology and result is provided. Finally, Sect. 5 concludes this paper and suggests future work.

2   Related Works

Recently, the rapid innovation of vision technique using AI leads the active research on object detection with camera. The most widely used solution is Yolo series [12, 14–18] due to its high performance as well as minimized computation overhead of its tiny version. However, traditional schemes cannot directly applied to UAV because the camera view is completely different from ground. Some works [19, 20] tries to detect object in UAV using monocular or stereo camera. Beyond the object detection, location estimation of target object in UAV is more tricky due to camera tilting and mismatch between camera and world coordinates. To tackle this problem, a number of research have been conducted with various idea.

The most efficient way in terms of cost and power is using monocular camera for object localization. MultEye [2] is the scheme to detect, track, and estimate the speed for the ground vehicle from UAV's camera image. They designed a real-time system to track and speed estimation using a multiple sequential image under limited hardware resources. X. Zhao et al. [3] conducted research on the detection, tracking, and geolocation of moving vehicle from UAV using monocular camera. They proposed detailed geolocation method considering various factors such as pitch, roll, and yaw angles of camera. I. Kim and K. Yow [4, 5] developed an object localization method by estimating the depth of target object using sequential images. Although they showed acceptable performance in object tracking, the calibration phase is inevitable, which is not practical in search mission. S. Sanyal [6] proposed the object detection using YOLO and geolocation using UAV's GPS location and distance between target and UAV. The work includes the method to convert camera frame's coordinates to GPS coordinates. A. Kendall et al. [7] proposed a monocular vision based object tracking with low computation overhead. Especially, they did not use any external localization sensor such as GPS. This makes the solution impractical because UAV's accurate location cannot be acquired. H. R. Hosseinpoor et al. [8] suggested the method to geolocation and tracking the target object from

UAV using thermal camera. They calibrated the thermal camera for better performance. The object's location is reliably tracked by using extended Kalman filter (EKF).

| Object Detection | Distance Estimation | Localization |

Fig. 1. Overall system design.

For more accurate localization, research using stereo camera have been conducted. Eye in the Sky [9] suggests several techniques related with object tracking in UAV such as semi-direct visual odometry for camera calibration, depth estimation using multi-view stereo camera, and 3D object localization via ground plane estimation. Beyond stereo camera, another works tried to use multi-view image from multiple UAVs. Kim et al. [10] proposed a object localization method using two drones to support unmanned ground vehicle (UGV) that does not have GPS. Xu el al. [11] used more than three UAVs simultaneously to localize the ground target.

All of these works only utilized only UAV's information. Hence, they inherently have limitation that it is difficult to accurately locate the object far from UAV due to camera tilting and diverse geographical features. However, our work minimizes the effect of such factors by utilizing the location of ground vehicle nearby target object. Therefore, the proposed scheme can be applied to any previous works in a complementary manner.

3   Object Localization from UAV Aided by Ground Vehicle

In this section, we explain the system design followed by detailed methodology in subsections. The flow of the scheme starts from detecting the target object and ground vehicle around the target. By analyzing the image captured by camera in UAV, the bounding boxes of both target object and ground vehicle are estimated. In this phase, we used the Yolov7 [12] trained using Visdrone dataset [13]. Next process is to calculate the distance between target object and ground vehicle. By considering the camera and UAV position, the distance in image is converted to real distance. The closest vehicle is selected as anchor. Lastly, based on the GPS coordinates of selected ground vehicle and distance from object, the GPS location of target is estimated. Figure 1 shows overall architecture.

3.1   Object Detection Using Yolov7

Yolov7 is one of the most powerful and widely used object detector. We adopted Yolov7 for detecting target object and ground vehicle. Yolov7 is pre-trained by MS COCO dataset

[21] that consists of general images with more than 80 classes. Usually, Yolov7 is used by transfer learning from the pre-trained version. However, MS COCO dataset is inadequate for object detection in UAV. Figure 2 shows the comparison between MS COCO and Visdrone dataset, which indicates that the image from UAV is completely different with one in MS COCO dataset. To resolve this problem, we trained Yolov7 from scratch using Visdrone dataset [13]. The Visdrone dataset is one of the most widely used open dataset for training object detection in UAV. They provide not only image data but also video, single object tracking, and multi object tracking data with 10 categories of objects (pedestrian, person, car, van, bus, truck, motor, bicycle, awning-tricycle, and tricycle). We used image dataset (i.e., VisDrone2019-DET) with training (6,471 images), validation (548 images), and testing (1,580 images) data. Note that for practical usage, object tracking should be done, not detection because detection focuses on only a single scene whereas UAV should track the target object and ground vehicle in sequential images. Since the main goal of this paper is to prove the effectiveness of object localization aided by ground vehicle, the accurate object detection and tracking are not our scope. Therefore, we simply used state-of-art object detection method.

(a) Images in MS COCO dataset   (b) Images in Visdrone dataset

Fig. 2. Comparison of images in MS COCO [21] and Visdrone dataset [13].

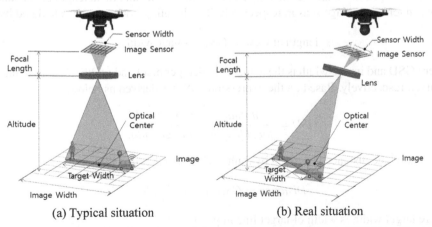

(a) Typical situation   (b) Real situation

Fig. 3. Typical and real situation when applying ground sampling distance (GSD) to estimate the distance between two points in image plane.

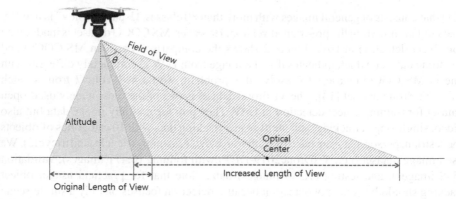

Fig. 4. The length of view in typical scenario and increased one when camera is tilted degree of θ.

3.2 Distance Estimation Between Target Object and Ground Vehicle

After detecting the target object and ground vehicle, distance between target object and ground vehicle is estimated. We exploited ground sampling distance (GSD) method for distance inference. GSD is the technique to calculate the centimeter per pixel (cm/px) to investigate the distance in camera image. As shown in Fig. 3(a), GSD is typically applied when the target line (blue line in figure) goes through the optical center and it is parallel to the horizontal axis of image while camera looks the ground directly, not tilted. In this scenario, the following proportion is established.

$$\text{length of view} : \text{sensor width} = \text{altitude} : \text{focal length} \tag{1}$$

where length of view is actual width of ground captured in image, sensor width the width of image sensor, altitude height of UAV from ground, and focal length the distance between lens and image sensor, respectively. The length of view can be calculated by

$$\text{length of view} = \text{GSD} * \text{image width} \tag{2}$$

where GSD and image width is the actual distance per pixel and width of camera image in pixel, respectively. Based on the expression, GSD is derived as below.

$$GSD = \frac{altitude}{focal\,length} * \frac{sensor\,width}{image\,width} \tag{3}$$

Finally, the distance is derived by multiplying length with GSD,

$$Distance = GSD * targetwidth \tag{4}$$

where target width is width of target line in pixel.

However, UAV usually rotates the camera for wider view, especially in search mission. Figure 3(b) depicts the practical scenario of distance estimation. In this environment, the proportion in Eq. (1) does not valid because proportion between length of view and sensor width is different from the one in typical scenario. Hence, when the camera is rotated, basic formula cannot be used to inference the target distance.

Figure 4 provides the detailed reason of this limitation. When the camera is not tilted, the original length of view is the width of blue area. But as the camera is tilted with degree of θ, the length of view increases as shown in red area in figure. Although the length of view changes, the sensor width does not change, which means that the Eq. (1) does not hold. Note that although the distance from lens to optical center (i.e., depth) also changes, it does not affect the Eq. (1) because the travel distance of light from lens to the region of target object in image sensor changes in the same proportion. To address this problem, we modified the GSD to consider various practical scenario.

Suppose that the camera is tilted with degree of θ and the ground is flat, as shown in Fig. 4. Since the length of view is proportional to the distance from lens to optical center, the projected length can be calculated as follows.

$$length\ of\ view_{projected} = length\ of\ view_{original}/\cos\theta \tag{5}$$

According to the Eq. (2) and (3), the generalized GSD with camera tilting is expressed as below.

$$GSD_{generalized} = GSD/\cos\theta \tag{6}$$

However, the camera equipped on UAV usually supports pitch and yaw movements. To calculate the length of view reflecting both movements, $\cos\theta$ should be calculated in 3-dimensional space. To this end, we used the 3-dimensional rotation matrix of x-axis (pitch) and z-axis (yaw),

$$R_x(\theta_x)R_z(\theta_z) = \begin{bmatrix} 1 & 0 & 0 \\ 0 & \cos\theta & -\sin\theta \\ 0 & \sin\theta & \cos\theta \end{bmatrix} \begin{bmatrix} \cos\theta & -\sin\theta & 0 \\ \sin\theta & \cos\theta & 0 \\ 0 & 0 & 1 \end{bmatrix} \tag{7}$$

where θ_x and θ_z are the degree of rotation for each axis respectively. Let the optical axis be the vector from lens to optical center and the optical axis without camera tilting be the original optical axis. After rotating the camera, the optical axis changes from original one. Suppose that there is two unit vectors on original optical axis and changed one each. Then their relationship can be expressed as follows.

$$\vec{V}_{projected} = R_x(\theta_x)R_z(\theta_z)\vec{V}_{original} \tag{8}$$

The $\cos\theta$ in Eq. (6) in 3-dimensional can be derived by calculating $\cos\theta$ between these vectors as below,

$$\cos\theta_{3d} = \frac{\vec{V}_{projected} \cdot \vec{V}_{original}}{(\|\vec{V}_{projected}\| \cdot \|\vec{V}_{original}\|)} \tag{9}$$

where $\|\vec{V}\|$ and $\vec{v} \cdot \vec{u}$ indicate the length of $\vec{v}$ and scalar product, respectively.

As shown in Eq. (1) and (2), all of above process focus on the image width. When the aspect ratio of sensor and image are the same, GSD for width-axis and height-axis would be the same. However, for general purpose, we divided the GSD in width and height axis.

$$\text{GSD}_{width} = \frac{altitude}{focal\ length} * \frac{sensor\ width}{image\ width} * \frac{1}{\cos\theta} \qquad (10)$$

$$\text{GSD}_{height} = \frac{altitude}{focal\ length} * \frac{sensor\ height}{image\ height} * \frac{1}{\cos\theta} \qquad (11)$$

Finally, the distance is calculated as follows,

$$Distance = \sqrt{(\Delta width * GSD_{width})^2 + (\Delta height * GSD_{height})^2} \qquad (12)$$

where $\Delta width$ and $\Delta height$ are the number of pixels between target object and ground vehicle in width-axis and height-axis, respectively.

3.3 Global Coordinates Estimation

Based on the GPS location of ground vehicle and the distance from the target object, we infer the global coordinates of target. By considering the heading of UAV and z-axis rotation of camera, the north direction in image can be easily measured. Let the object is φ degrees away from the vehicle in north-axis and its distance is d. The (x,y) denotes the UTM coordinates. Then the location of target in Universal Transverse Mercator (UTM) system can be derived as follows.

$$\left(x_{target}, y_{target}\right) = (x_{vehicle} + d * \cos\varphi, y_{vehicle} + d * \sin\varphi) \qquad (13)$$

4 Experiments

4.1 Experimental Setup

The proposed scheme is evaluated at server environment with specification of Table 1. For the object detection, we trained the YOLOv7 [11] with Visdrone [13] from scratch. To verify the effectiveness of our method, we collected the real image data using drone and ground mobility robot in factory environment whose size is more than 66,000 m². The images are recorded by 1 FPS (frame per second) in both UAV and robot, and the whole experiment duration is around 300 s. During the image collection, a number of employment and cars continuously moves through the factory. The collected images along with GPS data of drone and robot are recorded by robot operating system (ROS) to be replayed later for evaluation. The specification of camera on UAV is provided in Table 2. Note that the focal length is fixed as 4.4 mm during video recording.

4.2 Object Detection in UAV

The Visdrone dataset consists of 8,599 images with various size and ratio. To train the YOLOv7 with these images, we modified a code because the basic option '--rect' does not support asymmetric ratio. The training was conducted around 500 epochs and the best weight was used for experiment. Figure 5 (a) shows the performance of YOLOv7 on Visdrone test data (1,580 images). The pedestrian, people, and car classes are main target of our system, which shows mAP@0.5 of 0.612, 0.444, and 0.86, respectively. This indicates that UAV is able to detect target object such as person and ground vehicle successfully. Figure 5 (b) shows the object detection result for the image collected by authors. The green and white box represent the car and pedestrian, respectively. The detection result is acceptable for localization.

Table 1. Software and hardware specification of server

Item	Specification
CPU	Intel(R) Xeon(R) Silver 4210 CPU @ 2.20 GHz (40 processors)
GPU	NVIDIA GeForce RTX 3090 (4 cores)
OS	Ubuntu 20.04.4 LTS

Table 2. Specification of camera lens equipped on drone

Item	Specification	Item	Specification
Model	Q20KTIR	Focal Length (mm)	4.4 (wide) to 88.4 (tele)
Sensor Width (mm)	7.20	Image Width (pixels)	1920
Sensor Height (mm)	7.20	Image Height (pixels)	1080

(a) Precision-recall result of Visdrone da-   (b) Object detection result for our image
taset

Fig. 5. The performance of object detection using YOLOv7 trained with Visdrone dataset.

4.3   Localization of Target Object in UAV

We tested the performance of target object localization using real images collected by drone in our testbed. Drone records the video at 30 m high without camera tilting where a person and robot move under drone. The drone is controlled manually to track the person and robot. Note that video record using drone in South Korea is strictly restricted due to military issues. Therefore, we cannot take a image with camera tilting. The image is extracted one per second from recorded video along with location data of robot and drone.

First, we conducted experiment to obtain human's global coordinates using the robot's GPS and distance between them. To focus on the evaluation of proposed scheme itself, we assumed that the object detection is 100% accurately. To this end, the actual bounding box is generated manually. Figure 6 (a) shows the result of proposed method and original GSD method that exploits the drone's GPS data and width-axis GSD only.

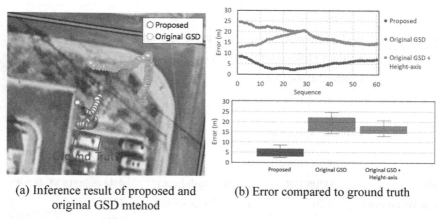

(a) Inference result of proposed and   (b) Error compared to ground truth
original GSD mtehod

Fig. 6. The result of localization using proposed scheme and original GSD method.

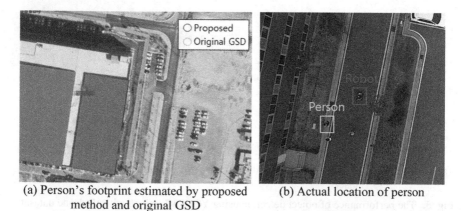

(a) Person's footprint estimated by proposed   (b) Actual location of person
method and original GSD

Fig. 7. The localization error of proposed scheme and original GSD method.

Unfortunately, due to various issues, the ground truth of human's path was not collected during experiment. However, as shown in the Fig. 6 (b) a person actually worked near by building, meaning that our scheme outperforms the original GSD.

For further verification, we defined a parked car as a target, whose accurate location can be extracted via map, to compare the our result with ground truth of car's GPS data. Figure 7 (a) shows the localization result of proposed and original GSD method. Our the result of scheme is much closer to the ground truth. Figure 7 (b) depicts the error according to the time, indicating that our algorithm (4.86 m $\pm$ 1.74 m error) outperforms the original GSD (18.89 m $\pm$ 3.32 m error). To validate the effectiveness of our idea, we applied height-axis GSD to the original method. The grey dot in Fig. 7 (b) indicates that height-axis GSD remarkably increases the accuracy as error of 16.24 m $\pm$ 2.12 m. However, after half of sequence, the performance is the same with original one because drone started to move horizontally at that time, minimizing the effect of height-axis GSD.

Although the experiment in real scenario was conducted in limited dataset, we believe that the performance of our mechanism will be uniform in various environments because the main idea is using robust GPS location of robot. By combining state-of-art object detection techniques, our algorithm can always locate the target object accurately.

5 Conclusion

In this paper, we proposed a scheme for reliable localization cooperating with ground vehicle to overcome the inherent limitation of previous works such as camera distortion or diverse geographical features. By using the location of ground vehicle and distance from target object, our method can minimize the effect of these factors. Through the experiment using real image data, we verified that our algorithm works well in real environment. We expect that our method can be applied to any previous works complementary to increase the localization performance by using additional hint (i.e., robot's location). There are still rooms to improve the accuracy such as considering the difference from optical center or using Kalman filter for sequential inference. In the future work, we will advance the scheme by adopting these factors.

Acknowledgement. This work was supported by Institute of Information & communications Technology Planning & Evaluation (IITP) grant funded by the Korea government (MSIT) (No. 2020-0-00959, Fast Intelligence Analysis HW/SW Engine Exploiting IoT Platform for Boosting On-device AI in 5G Environment).

References

1. Forbes.   https://www.forbes.com/sites/johnkoetsier/2022/08/30/inside-googles-plan-to-del iver-almost-everything-to-almost-everyone-via-drone/?sh=7f565043ee74, Accessed 09 Mar 2023
2. Balamuralidhar, N., Tilon, S., Nex, F.: MultEYE: monitoring system for real-time vehicle detection, tracking and speed estimation from UAV imagery on edge-computing platforms. Remote Sens. **13**(4), 573 (2021)

3. Zhao, X., Pu, F., Wang, Z., Chen, H., Xu, Z.: Detection, tracking, and geolocation of moving vehicle from UAV using monocular camera. IEEE Access **7**, 101160–101170 (2019)
4. Kim, I., Yow, K.: Object location estimation from a single flying camera. In: Proceedings of Ubicomm (2015)
5. Yow, K., Kim, I.: General moving object localization from a single flying camera. Appl. Sci. **10**(19), 6945 (2020)
6. Sanyal, S., Bhushan, S., Sivayazi, K.: Detection and location estimation of object in unmanned aerial vehicle using single camera and GPS. In: Proceedings of 2020 First International Conference on Power, Control and Computing Technologies (ICPC2T), pp. 73–78 (2020)
7. Kendall, A.G., Salvapantula, N.N., Stol, K.A.: On-board object tracking control of a quadcopter with monocular vision. In: 2014 International Conference on Unmanned Aircraft Systems (ICUAS), pp. 404–411 (2014)
8. Hosseinpoor, H., Samadzadegan, F., Dadrasjavan, F.: Pricise target geolocation and tracking based on UAV video imager. In: The International Archives of the Photogrammetry, Remote Sensing and Spatial Information Sciences, vol. XLI-B6, pp. 243–249 (2016)
9. Zhang, H., Wang, G., Lei, Z., Hwang, J.: Eye in the sky: drone-based object tracking and 3D localization. In: Proceedings of the 27th ACM International Conference on Multimedia (MM 2019), pp. 899–907 (2019)
10. Kim, J., Kwon, J., Seo, J.: Multi-UAV-based stereo vision system without GPS for ground obstacle mapping to assist path planning of UGV. Electron. Lett. **50**(20), 1431–1432 (2014)
11. Xu, C., Yin, C., Huang, D., Han, W., Wang, D.: 3D target localization based on multi–unmanned aerial vehicle cooperation. Measur. Control **54**(5–6), 1–13 (2020)
12. Wang, C., Bochkovskiy, A., Liao, H.: YOLOv7: trainable bag-of-freebies sets new state-of-the-art for real-time object detectors. arXiv 2022, arXiv:2207.02696 (2022)
13. Zhu, P., et al.: Detection and tracking meet drones challenge. IEEE Trans. Pattern Anal. Mach. Intell. **44**(11), 7380–7399 (2022)
14. Redmon, J., Divvala, S., Girshick, R., Farhadi, A.: You only look once: unified, real-time object detection. In: Proceedings of the IEEE Conference on Computer Vision and Pattern Recognition (CVPR), pp. 779–788 (2016)
15. Redmon, J., Farhadi, A.: YOLO9000: better, faster, stronger. In: Proceedings of the IEEE Conference on Computer Vision and Pattern Recognition (CVPR), pp. 7263–7271 (2017)
16. Redmon, J., Farhadi, A.: Yolov3: an incremental improvement. arXiv 2018, arXiv:1804.02767
17. Bochkovskiy, A., Wang, C., Liao, H.: Yolov4: optimal speed and accuracy of object detection. arXiv 2020, arXiv:2004.10934 (2020)
18. Li, C., et al.: Yolov6: a single-stage object detection framework for industrial applications. arXiv 2022, arXiv:2209.02976 (2022)
19. Cigla, C., Thakker, R., Matthies, L.: Onboard stereo vision for drone pursuit or sense and avoid. In: Proceedings of the 2018 IEEE/CVF Conference on Computer Vision and Pattern Recognition Workshops (CVPRW), pp. 738–746 (2018)
20. Grewe, L., Stevenson, G.: Drone based user and heading detection using deep learning and stereo vision. In: Proceedings of the SPIE 11018, Signal, Processing, Sensor/Information Fusion, and Target, Recognition XXVIII, pp. 110180X (2019)
21. Lin, T.Y., et al.: Microsoft COCO: common objects in context. In: Fleet, D., Pajdla, T., Schiele, B., Tuytelaars, T. (eds.) Computer Vision – ECCV 2014. ECCV 2014. Lecture Notes in Computer Science, vol. 8693, pp. 740–755. Springer, Cham (2014). https://doi.org/10.1007/978-3-319-10602-1_48

Images Retrieval and Classification for Acute Myeloid Leukemia Blood Cell Using Deep Metric Learning

Kaung Myat Naing[1] , Veerayuth Kittichai[2] , Teerawat Tongloy[1],
Santhad Chuwongin[1], and Siridech Boonsang[3](✉)

[1] Center of Industrial Robot and Automation (CiRA), College of Advanced Manufacturing
Innovation, King Mongkut's Institute of Technology Ladkrabang, Bangkok, Thailand
{62609004,santhad.ch}@kmitl.ac.th
[2] Faculty of Medicine, King Mongkut's Institute of Technology Ladkrabang, Bangkok, Thailand
veerayuth.ki@kmitl.ac.th
[3] Department of Electrical Engineering, School of Engineering, King Mongkut's Institute of
Technology Ladkrabang, Bangkok, Thailand
siridech.bo@kmitl.ac.th

Abstract. Deep metric learning-based image retrieval systems have recently been used in medical applications because they provide clinically relevant information-based similar images based on prior knowledge. Although train examiners and deep learning models successfully analyze leukocyte cells, there are still numerous difficult challenges due to biological variation, time constraints, and a variety of image-related aspects. In this study, we propose a deep metric learning model-based image retrieval and classification system for acute myeloid leukemia blood cells to address these issues and assist physicians. The proposed model utilizes the pre-trained ResNet-34 model as the backbone network, embedding loss with multi similarity miner, and M-Per-Class sampling strategy to learn an embedding function. The five embedding losses were also applied to compare the four performances in order to determine the best loss-based model. Based on the best loss-based model, the class-wise precision and sensitivity using a neighborhood size are also presented. The results show that the contrastive loss-based deep metric learning model achieved the highest precision of 94.90%, sensitivity of 94.85%, specificity of 99.64%, and accuracy of 99.32% in model comparison. Except for a few failures in small classes, the class-wise precision and sensitivity scores looked to be impressive in all classes. Therefore, this proposed system can highly be effective in screening and diagnosing of AML-related white blood cell stages that cause serious cancer.

Keywords: Acute myeloid leukemia (AML) · Images retrieval · Classification · Deep metric learning

N. T. Nguyen et al. (Eds.): ACIIDS 2023, CCIS 1863, pp. 27–39, 2023.
https://doi.org/10.1007/978-3-031-42430-4_3

1   Introduction

Leukemia is a type of blood cancer characterized by rapid production of abnormal white blood cells [1]. Acute myeloid leukemia (AML) is a specific subtype categorized based on characteristics of mature and immature white blood cells [2]. Early detection of leukemia is crucial for guiding treatment decisions. Identifying abnormal white blood cells can aid physicians in determining appropriate treatment options [3]. Flow cytometry and microscopic examination are commonly used methods, but they have limitations such as accessibility and subjectivity [4]. Improving blast cell classification is vital for efficient diagnosis and treatment planning.

Leukocyte (white blood cell) analysis has seen an integration of neural network technologies, with segmentation-based techniques and convolutional neural networks (CNNs) being effective for classification [5–7]. Object detection methods like SSD, YOLOv3, and R-CNN have been used for leukocyte cell recognition [8, 9]. However, challenges remain due to the use of various equipment, the uncertainty of the sample preparation process, data availability, dataset quality and the need for robustness to uncontrolled parameters. Metric learning-based image retrieval, specifically Deep Metric Learning (DML), has gained popularity for addressing image verification challenges [10]. DML combines feature extraction and metric learning and has been enhanced with the development of deep learning-based feature extractors [11]. DML has diverse applications in domains such as face verification, recognition, clustering [12], and person re-identification [13].

The goal of DML is to learn a function that maps images to an embedding space, where similar images are close together and dissimilar images are far away. In medical imaging applications, DML has been successfully employed. Sundgaard et al. developed an automatic diagnostic algorithm for otitis media classification using DML [14]. They used Inception V3 as the backbone network and evaluated different metric loss functions, achieving precision above 80% in each class and a test accuracy of 86% with triplet loss. Additionally, Zhong et al. proposed a content-based image retrieval (CBIR) model for analyzing chest radiograph images in COVID-19 decision-making [15]. They employed ResNet-50 as the backbone network, combined with hard-mining sampling and multi-similarity loss. The proposed model outperformed the baseline in terms of recall rate for the crucial task of COVID-19 screening. Inspired by these successful applications, we are motivated to explore the application of DML in leukocyte cell image classification. Observing that leukocyte cells exhibit distinct characteristics, the identification of leuko- cyte cell stages holds the potential to provide insights into patient health anticipation and treatment planning.

The contributions of this study are summarized as follows:

(1) We propose a deep metric learning system for image retrieval and classification, utilizing the ResNet-34 model as the backbone network. Through the incorporation of embedding loss, multi-similarity miner, and M-Per-Class sampling strategy, we learn an effective embedding function. A comparative analysis of five distance-based metric loss functions is conducted to select the most suitable model.

(2) The study focuses on the classification of 15 AML blood cell stages, considering their low biological variation. The proposed deep metric learning approach based

on the best loss-based model achieves high performance in image retrieval and classification of AML cell stages.

To the best of our knowledge, there isn't any clinical research using such deep metric learning for classification of the 15 classes of AML blood cell stages causing serious cancer. The rest of the paper is organized as follows. We discuss material and method in Sect. 2. We present our experimental results and discussion in Sect. 3 and conclude in Sect. 4.

2   Material and Methodology

There are three main sections in this part including dataset, model training, and model testing and evaluation using inference. Figure 1 shows the detailed experimental setup of deep metric learning based image retrieval and classification system for AML cell stages which includes AML dataset, training phase, and testing phase and evaluation.

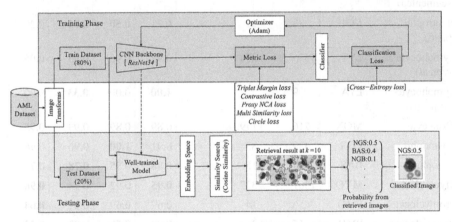

Fig. 1. Image retrieval and classification of AML blood cell images using DML.

2.1   Dataset

The data required for this study was obtained from The Cancer Imaging Archive (TCIA), which included AML cells images [16]. The original dataset consists of 18,365 images and the size of each single cell image has 400×400 pixels including background components such as erythrocytes, platelets, and cell fragments. We noticed significant class size imbalance in the dataset; the largest class, Neutrophil (segmented) has 8484 images while the smallest class, Lymphocyte (atypical), has only 11 images. In this study, we used 50% of the image data for the large four classes, which contained over 1000 images, to save training time and memory usage, as shown in Table 1.

In order to ensure consistent image resolution for training the deep metric learning model, the data needs to be converted before processing. The image transform techniques were applied to create customized training and testing datasets, which included resizing the input image to a specified size, randomly cropping a portion of the image and resizing it, and horizontally flipping the image with a given probability. The transformed image data was then converted into PyTorch tensors, and the final step involved normalizing the tensor image using the mean and standard deviation. For each class, the train-test dataset was randomly split, with 80% of the data allocated to the training dataset and the remaining 20% to the testing dataset. The identical train-test spits were used for all models, which can make the model performance comparison equally.

Table 1. Data utilization and class-wise performance comparison between the previous work and the contrastive loss-based DML model in terms of precision and sensitivity.

Class	Abb	Training (80%)	Testing (20%)	Precision		Sensitivity	
				[6]	Ours	[6]	Ours
Neutrophil (segmented)	NGS	3394	848	**0.99**	0.98	0.97	**0.98**
Neutrophil (band)	NGB	88	21	0.21	**0.50**	**0.72**	0.29
Lymphocyte (typical)	LYT	1575	394	**0.97**	0.96	0.95	0.95
Lymphocyte (atypical)	LYA	9	2	**1.00**	0.00	**0.33**	0.00
Monocyte	MON	716	179	0.89	0.89	0.93	**0.95**
Eosinophil	EOS	339	85	0.91	**1.00**	0.96	0.96
Basophil	BAS	64	15	**0.88**	0.85	**0.78**	0.73
Myeloblast	MYO	1307	327	**0.95**	0.92	0.94	**0.96**
Promyelocyte	PMO	56	14	0.67	**0.69**	0.31	**0.64**
Promyelocyte (bilobed)	PMB	15	3	0.00	**0.50**	0.00	**0.33**
Myelocyte	MYB	34	8	**0.75**	0.57	0.30	**0.50**
Metamyelocyte	MMZ	12	3	0.00	**1.00**	0.00	**0.33**
Monoblast	MOB	21	5	**0.33**	0.00	**0.50**	0.00
Erythroblast	EBO	63	15	0.82	**0.88**	1.00	1.00
Smudge cell	KSC	12	2	1.00	1.00	**1.00**	0.50
Total/avg		7705	1921	0.69	**0.72**	**0.65**	0.61

2.2 Training Phase

In deep metric learning, the selections of the appropriate function are key parameters in model training, such as the selection of loss function, backbone network, miner function, and sampling strategy. While there are various suggestions for loss functions [17] all parameter selections are important. To optimize the model's performance, this experiment conducted a comparison of five different loss functions. The detailed experimental setup is discussed further below.

Loss Function Selection

The defining of the appropriate loss function is a crucial factor to receive a successful solution in metric learning. Previous research has proposed various loss functions based on distances, regularizers, and reducers. This study applied cross-entropy loss for classification and employed five metric losses for embedding, as follows:

- Cross-Entropy Loss: Cross-Entropy computes the losses between input and target which are applied for various classification tasks. The formula of Cross-Entropy loss for the multi-class classification problem in this work is defined as follows:

$$L_{CE} = -\sum_{i=1}^{n} t_i \log p_i \tag{1}$$

where n is the number of classes, t_i is the true probability of class i and p_i is the predicted probability of that class by the model.

- Contrastive Loss: [18] proposed a Siamese network with contrastive loss to find out the positive or negative pairs in each training iteration. It is also known as the classic pair-based method and is designed to move closer together for the positive pairs and push away from each other for negative pairs over a given threshold. The loss computation is different according to the usage of metric: distance or similarity. Since this study was used as a similarity metric like cosine similarity, loss can be computed as:

$$L_{Contrastive} = [m_{pos} - s_p]_+ + [s_n - m_{neg}]_+ \tag{2}$$

where $pos\_margin = 1$ and $neg\_margin = 0$ were used in model training.

- Triplet Margin Loss: In [19], a triplet margin loss was proposed which consists of positive, negative and an anchor sample. This loss enforces the distance of the anchor-positive (d_{ap}) to be smaller than the distance of the anchor-positive pair (d_{an}) over a given margin. The triplet margin loss can be computed as follows:

$$L_{triplet} = [d_{ap} - d_{an} + m]_+ \tag{3}$$

where the desired difference (d_{ap}) and (d_{an}), $m = 0.1$ was used as default in this study.

- Circle Loss: [20] designed the circle loss which is named due to the result decision in a circular boundary. The advantages of circular loss are deep feature learning with high flexibility optimization and a more definite convergence target. This loss function is defined by:

$$L_{circle} = \log\left[1 + \sum_{j=1}^{L} \exp\left(\gamma \alpha_n^j \left(s_n^j - \Delta_n\right)\right) \sum_{i=1}^{K} \exp\left(-\gamma \alpha_p^i \left(s_p^j - \Delta_p\right)\right)\right] \tag{4}$$

where: $\alpha_p^i = \left[O_p - s_p^j \right]_+$; $\alpha_n^j = \left[s_n^j - O_n \right]_+$; $O_p = 1 + m$; $O_n = -m$; $\Delta_p = 1 - m$; $\Delta_n = m$;

in which m is the relaxation factor that controls the radius of the decision boundary and γ is the scale factor that determines the largest scale of each similarity score. Following the original paper, we set $m = 0.4$ and $\gamma = 80$ like a fine-gained image retrieval experiment.

- Proxy NCA Loss: [21] discussed the adaptation of Neighborhood Components Analysis (NCA) to minimize the total loss amongst a data point anchor and the two proxy points. In each training iteration, the loss was formulated over the proxy triplet (x, $p(y)$, $p(z)$) as follows:

$$l = -\log\left(\frac{exp(-d(x, p(y)))}{\sum_{p(z)\epsilon p(Z)} exp(-d(x, p(z)))} \right) \tag{5}$$

where x is the anchor data point and $p(y)$, and $p(z)$ are positive and negative proxy data points. Since this loss requires an optimizer, the embedding optimizer (Adam optimizer) was used as default and the required parameters were assigned as number of classes = 15, embedding size = 64 and softmax scale = 1.

- Multi Similarity Loss: [22] introduced the multi-similarity loss for the pair based metric learning to integrate pair mining and weighting schemes into one framework. The formula used in this loss by:

$$L_{MS} = \frac{1}{m} \sum_{i=1}^{m} \left\{ \frac{1}{\alpha} \log\left[1 + \sum_{k \in P_i} e^{-\alpha(s_{i,k}-\lambda)} + \frac{1}{\beta} \log\left[1 + \sum_{k \in N_i} e^{-\beta(s_{i,k}-\lambda)} \right] \right] \right\} \tag{6}$$

where $S_{i, k}$ means the cosine similarity between embedded features to measure the similarity between the selected pairs of images, P_i and N_i are the indices set of selected (same types and different type) pairs, m is batch size and α, β, λ are hyper-parameters. Following to the original paper, we set $\alpha = 2$, $\beta = 50$ and $\lambda = 1$.

Network Architecture and Training Details

As mentioned above, the dataset was split into 80% training and 20% testing using the class disjoint function. The ResNet-34 backbone architecture, pre-trained on ImageNet, was used as a feature extractor in model training. The last feature layer was followed by a multilayer perceptron to transform the features into the desired embedding size. The 1000-class output layer was replaced with a 64-dimensional embedding layer to serve as the embedder model. The embedding space was trained using a loss function that aimed to bring similar input classes closer and dissimilar ones farther apart. It is important to note that no classifier layer was included in the deep metric learning (DML) model training. Typically, the trained DML model works as a feature extractor, with the extracted feature vectors used to construct a K-Nearest Neighbor (KNN) classifier. However, in this study, a classifier layer was added to support the trainer. This classification layer computed the cross-entropy loss for classification, and the output vectors were set to the desired dimensions of the classifier, which in this case was 15. Thus, the deep metric learning model consisted of three consecutive steps: backbone, embedding, and classifier.

The choice of loss functions plays a crucial role in metric learning, but mining and sampling strategies can also impact the training process. The mining process helps identify the best samples for training. In this study, the Multi Similarity Miner was used as the default function to enable the application of various loss functions. It effectively selects pair-based losses for generating optimal pair mining candidates and triplet losses for the best triplet mining during training. The loss calculations are based on these pairs or triplets. The Multi Similarity Miner was proposed by Wang et al. [22], and an epsilon value of 0.1 was set as the default threshold for selecting positive and negative pairs.

Training with random sampling can lead to slow convergence and degrade model performance [22]. To overcome this issue, effective sampling strategies have been explored. In this study, the M-Per-Class Sampler [23] was applied with a batch size of 8 and 4 samples per class. Given the length of 7706 before the new iteration, the train split received 241 embedding batches. These mining and sampling strategies, along with the selection of loss functions, contribute to optimizing the training process and improving the overall performance of the model.

Using the default parameters mentioned above, the experiment is conducted by modifying the loss functions only. Each training experiment consists of 200 epochs, and the trained model is saved in two checkpoints – one based on the best accuracy during training and the other at the end of training. The Adam optimizer with default parameters ($\beta 1 = 0.9$, $\beta 2 = 0.999$, weight decay $= 0.001$, epsilon $= 10-8$) and learning rates (0.00001 for backbone and 0.0001 for embedding and classifier) is used. The embedding model outputs 64-dimensional embeddings, and the classifier produces a 15-dimensional feature vector. The training is performed using the open-source PyTorch Metric Learning Library [23] on Visual Studio Code, utilizing the NVIDIA GeForce RTX 2070 GPU. On average, each model takes approximately 9 h to train.

2.3 Model Testing and Evaluation

In deep metric learning, the inference process involves performing image retrieval and clustering on unseen images using a well-trained model. It is an essential part of model training as the trained model evaluates the error value and adjusts the weights during training. Unlike the training process, inference does not reevaluate the output results. Instead, it utilizes the learned parameters from the trained model to find the nearest images based on various saved data, such as the trained model, optimizer, and loss. Similar to the training phase, the train and test datasets are prepared for the inference. The inference model is constructed by loading the trained model and using a match finder function. The match finder function computes pairwise distances in the input embedding space to determine the matching pairs. The default parameters for distance computation are cosine similarity distance and a threshold value. Additionally, a KNN classifier is employed to create a train dataset index for similarity searches based on the chosen distance metric. In this work, the inference process is implemented using the recently developed PyTorch metric learning library [23].

The evaluation of deep metric learning involves assessing the retrieval images of the query using a specified neighborhood size, such as $k = 20$, after training the proposed model. The trained model provides the 20 nearest images for each query image. To compute the quality performances of the model, data management and analysis are performed, including precision, sensitivity, specificity, and accuracy calculations. Since there are 15 classes of AML blood cells, a 15×15 confusion matrix is used for evaluation. True Positive (TP), False Positive (FP), True Negative (TN), and False Negative (FN) values obtained from the confusion matrix are used to measure the model's performance. Unlike object detection and classification models, the deep metric learning model does not provide direct prediction scores due to the retrieval of k nearest images. The prediction scores for each class depend on the number of retrieved images for each corresponding class from the k nearest images. The class with the highest score is considered the predicted class for the query image. By counting the number of predicted results for each query image from the 15 classes of the test dataset, the confusion matrix is constructed. Performance evaluations for each class can be computed using the one-versus-rest approach in multi-class classification. Additionally, to address the class imbalance in the dataset, micro-averaging operation is applied to obtain the four conditions: TP, FP, TN, and FN [24].

3 Result and Discussion

This section is presented in two sections. The first section focuses on selecting the optimal loss-based model. We evaluate and compare the classification performance of each model using four performances on the test dataset. In the second section, we examine the precision and sensitivity of each class using the selected optimal model, providing a detailed analysis of its effectiveness.

3.1 Performance Analysis of Testing Dataset Using Five Proposed Models

We analyzed the classification performances of the image retrieval task for each loss function by comparing the four measurements. The trained five models were directly tested on a test dataset that consists of 1921 single cell images using a neighborhood size in inference. These performance computations were based on the overall measurement of 15 classes of AML blood cells across all images using a threshold of 50. For the four performances as reported in Table 2, what stands out in the table is that the contrastive loss achieves higher performance with respect to other loss functions. In particular, it achieves precision of 94.90%, sensitivity of 94.85%, specificity of 99.64%, and accuracy of 99.32% respectively. There is, however, no significant difference between the five loss-based models.

3.2 Analysis of Class-Wise Precision and Sensitivity Using a Contrastive Loss-Based Model

In this section, we further investigate how the contrastive loss-based model manages to classify the AML blood cell images using the neighborhood sizes (k values). The results

Table 2. The four performances comparison between the five loss functions with ResNet-34 backbone architecture. The bold means that the contrastive loss has the best performance score than the other four losses.

Methods	Precision	Sensitivity	Specificity	Accuracy
Triplet Margin Loss	94.58%	94.48%	99.61%	99.27%
Contrastive Loss	**94.90%**	**94.85%**	**99.64%**	**99.32%**
Proxy NCA Loss	93.91%	93.86%	99.56%	99.18%
Multi Similarity Loss	94.01%	93.96%	99.57%	99.20%
Circle Loss	94.01%	94.01%	99.57%	99.20%

described in the previous section; it is found that the contrastive loss-based model has the best performance than the other four models. In Fig. 2, we also showed UMAP's ability to visualize the space between different classes of AML blood cell images during the training process using the algorithm described in [25]. Within the model training, the UMAP was produced at the end of each epoch. The UMAPs in Fig. 2 are plotted at the initial epoch and the epoch which has the best trained accuracy. The figure also described the makers (dots) with different colors for the various classes of AML blood cells and each dot in the plots represents an AML blood cell image. They are clearly separated into 15 clusters (groups of dots) in the 2D plot due to the dimension reduction technique of UMAP. Therefore, we can infer that the proposed models are sufficient in model training as initially.

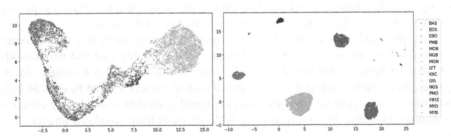

Fig. 2. The UMAP for contrastive loss-based model training with the first epoch and the best epoch.

In evaluation, the trained model's learning parameters were directly applied to the inference and tested on the test dataset without further training. The sensitivity and precision of class-wise comparisons were evaluated on every query image of the test dataset using the confusion matrix. These two performances were quantitatively calculated through the k returned images from the train samples. Table 1 presents the sensitivity and precision scores of each class for neighborhood size of 20. The proposed model achieves excellent performances in the commonly found physiological cell classes, including neutrophil (segmented), lymphocyte (typical), myeloblast, monocyte, and eosinophil (each above 94% in sensitivity and 89% in precision). The other classes are still challenging for the model performance and somewhat counterintuitive.

Furthermore, Table 1 presents a performance comparison between the best fold of the previous work utilizing the ResNeXt CNN and the contrastive loss based DML model in terms of sensitivity and precision. The DML model achieves higher precision than the previous work, while the previous work performs better in sensitivity. Despite using only 50% of the larger four classes in our model training and testing, the DML model produces comparable outcomes to the previous work and outperforms the other four folds of previous work in micro-averaging. The detailed analysis of the comparison results can be accessed in data availability. The precision score is a valuable measure in highly imbalanced class datasets, making it important for identifying all cancerous lesions. Thus, oncologists may prefer a model with a higher precision score as it reduces the occurrence of false-positive results.

From a morphological perspective, we analyzed the results of this research, as shown in Fig. 3. In AML blood smear samples, WBCs can be categorized into mature and immature cell types [6]. The mature cell types include neutrophils, lymphocytes, monocytes, eosinophils, and basophils. In our experiment, we observed that 57.14% of neutrophils (band) were misclassified as neutrophils (segmented), and the two test images of atypical lymphocytes were misclassified as typical lymphocytes. This indicates that our trained model can effectively distinguish mature leukocyte cells from other immature leukocyte cells. When considering the immature cell types, our model achieved outstanding results in diagnosing myeloblasts, promyelocytes, and erythroblasts, which are important indicators for suspected related diseases. Although our model incorrectly predicted the classes of other immature cell types, most of these misclassifications still fell within the immature cell category, except for monoblasts. Classifying monoblast cells is challenging since they bear morphological similarities to monocytes, which are the mature stage of monoblasts. This type of failure is the limitation of this study.

Using provided results in the above descriptions, we can summarize the outcomes of all trained models on the AML test dataset. We remarkably find that the methods perform a lot better in the image retrieval system of AML blood cell images. Taken together, these results suggest that the proposed trained model based on ResNet-34 with contrastive loss outperforms the other four comparable models and is highly effective in automatically retrieving and classifying AML diseases from blood cell images.

Query
Image

Nearest Images (*k*=9)

Classification
Results

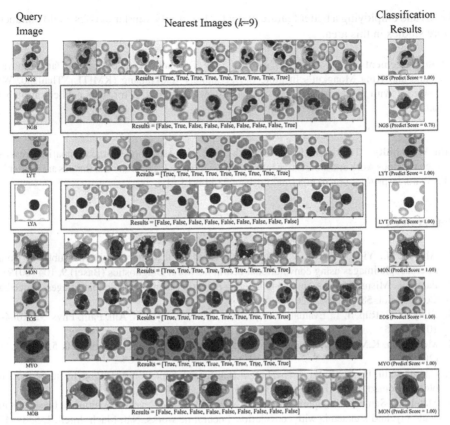

Fig. 3. The top-9 retrieval results of some class from the AML blood cell test dataset were learned by the proposed DML model with contrastive loss. The figure also includes sample images from five excellent performance classes and three failed classes with red color lines.

4 Conclusion

In this work, we proposed a deep metric learning model for analyzing AML blood cell images. Our experiments demonstrated the model's ability to handle various AML-related clinical problems and achieved satisfactory results in the automated classification of AML cell images. This model has the potential to develop as a diagnostic tool for retrieving and classifying AML cell images in medical treatment. We compared the performance of five metric loss functions: triplet margin, contrastive, proxy NCA, multi-similarity, and circle loss. The results showed that these loss functions, combined with the ResNet-34 backbone, achieved high performance in image retrieval and classification of AML blood cell images. Notably, the contrastive loss function outperformed the others in model comparison. We also reported the class-wise sensitivity and precision based on the contrastive loss. While most classes demonstrated remarkable performance, there were limitations in retrieving certain classes due to morphological similarities and the small dataset size. Addressing these limitations by improving images for small dataset classes and employing a better feature extractor to classify similar classes could enhance future studies in this area.

Acknowledgements. This work was supported by Thailand Science Research and Innovation Fund and King Mongkut's Institute of Technology Ladkrabang (KMITL), Thailand. We acknowledge with thanks to The Cancer Imaging Archive (TCIA) for their publicly available dataset.

Data Availability. The detailed analysis of the five loss-based models, the comparison results between previous work and contrastive loss-based DML model, and some test images are available at Figshare: https://doi.org/10.6084/m9.figshare.23544915.v1.

References

1. Ahmed, N., Yigit, A., Isik, Z., Alpkocak, A.: Identification of leukemia subtypes from microscopic images using convolutional neural network. Diagnostics (Basel) **9**, 104 (2019)
2. Patel, N., Mishra, A.: Automated leukaemia detection using microscopic images. Procedia Comput. Sci. **58**, 635–642 (2015)
3. Riley, L.K., Rupert, J.: Evaluation of patients with leukocytosis. Am. Fam. Phys. **92**, 1004–1011 (2015)
4. McKinnon, K.M.: Flow cytometry: an overview. Curr. Protoc. Immunol. **120**, 5.1.1–5.1.11 (2018)
5. Cao, H., Liu, H., Song, E.: A novel algorithm for segmentation of leukocytes in peripheral blood. Biomed. Signal Process. Control **45**, 10–21 (2018)
6. Matek, C., Schwarz, S., Spiekermann, K., Marr, C.: Human-level recognition of blast cells in acute myeloid leukaemia with convolutional neural networks. Nat. Mach. Intell. **1**, 538–544 (2019)
7. Jung, C., Abuhamad, M., Mohaisen, D., Han, K., Nyang, D.: WBC image classification and generative models based on convolutional neural network. BMC Med. Imaging **22**, 94 (2022)
8. Wang, Q., Bi, S., Sun, M., Wang, Y., Wang, D., Yang, S.: Deep learning approach to peripheral leukocyte recognition. PLoS ONE **14**, e0218808 (2019)
9. Kutlu, H., Avci, E., Özyurt, F.: White blood cells detection and classification based on regional convolutional neural networks. Med. Hypotheses **135**, 109472 (2020)
10. Yi, D., Lei, Z., Liao, S., Li, S.Z.: Deep metric learning for person re-identification. In: 2014 22nd International Conference on Pattern Recognition, pp. 34–39 (2014)
11. Lu, J., Hu, J., Zhou, J.: Deep metric learning for visual understanding: an overview of recent advances. IEEE Signal Process. Mag. **34**, 76–84 (2017)
12. Schroff, F., Kalenichenko, D., Philbin, J.: Facenet: A unified embedding for face recognition and clustering. In: Proceedings of the IEEE Conference on Computer Vision and Pattern Recognition, pp. 815–823 (2015)
13. Hermans, A., Beyer, L., Leibe, B.: In defense of the triplet loss for person re-identification. arXiv preprint arXiv:1703.07737 (2017)
14. Sundgaard, J.V., et al.: Deep metric learning for otitis media classification. Med. Image Anal. **71**, 102034 (2021)
15. Zhong, A., Li, X., Wu, D., Ren, H., Kim, K., Kim, Y., et al.: Deep metric learning-based image retrieval system for chest radiograph and its clinical applications in COVID-19. Med. Image Anal. **70**, 101993 (2021)

16. Matek, C., Schwarz, S., Spiekermann, K., Marr, C.: A single-cell morphological dataset of leukocytes from AML patients and non-malignant controls. The cancer imaging archive (2019)
17. Musgrave, K., Belongie, S., Lim, S.-N.: A metric learning reality check. In: Vedaldi, A., Bischof, H., Brox, T., Frahm, J.-M. (eds.) ECCV 2020. LNCS, vol. 12370, pp. 681–699. Springer, Cham (2020). https://doi.org/10.1007/978-3-030-58595-2_41
18. Hadsell, R., Chopra, S., LeCun, Y.: Dimensionality reduction by learning an invariant mapping. In: 2006 IEEE Computer Society Conference on Computer Vision and Pattern Recognition (CVPR 2006), pp. 1735–1742 (2006)
19. Weinberger, K.Q., Blitzer, J., Saul, L.K.: Distance metric learning for large margin nearest neighbor classification. In: Proceedings of the 18th International Conference on Neural Information Processing Systems, pp. 1473–1480. MIT Press, Vancouver, British Columbia, Canada (2005)
20. Sun, Y., et al.: Circle loss: a unified perspective of pair similarity optimization. In: 2020 IEEE/CVF Conference on Computer Vision and Pattern Recognition (CVPR), pp. 6397–6406 (2020)
21. Movshovitz-Attias, Y., Toshev, A., Leung, T.K., Ioffe, S., Singh, S.: No fuss distance metric learning using proxies. In: 2017 IEEE International Conference on Computer Vision (ICCV), pp. 360–368 (2017)
22. Wang, X., Han, X., Huang, W., Dong, D., Scott, M.R.: Multi-similarity loss with general pair weighting for deep metric learning. In: 2019 IEEE/CVF Conference on Computer Vision and Pattern Recognition (CVPR), pp. 5017–5025 (2019)
23. Musgrave, K., Belongie, S., Lim, S.-N.: Pytorch metric learning. arXiv preprint arXiv:2008. 09164 (2020)
24. Maslej-Krešňáková, V., Sarnovský, M., Butka, P., Machová, K.: Comparison of deep learning models and various text pre-processing techniques for the toxic comments classification. Appl. Sci. (Basel) **10**, 8631 (2020)
25. McInnes, L., Healy, J., Melville, J.: UMAP: uniform manifold approximation and projection for dimension reduction. arXiv preprint arXiv:1802.03426 (2018)

Superior Automatic Screening for Human Helminthic Ova by Using Self-supervised Learning Approach-Based Object Classification

Natchapon Pinetsuksai[1], Veerayuth Kittichai[2], Rangsan Jomtarak[3],
Komgrit Jaksukam[1], Teerawat Tongloy[1], Siridech Boonsang[4],
and Santhad Chuwongin[1(✉)]

[1] College of Advanced Manufacturing Innovation, King Mongkut's Institute of Technology Ladkrabang, Bangkok, Thailand
{63609007,komgrit.ja,santhad.ch}@kmitl.ac.th,
teerawat_tongloy@kkumail.com
[2] Faculty of Medicine, King Mongkut's Institute of Technology Ladkrabang, Bangkok, Thailand
veerayuth.ki@kmitl.ac.th
[3] Faculty of Science and Technology, Suan Dusit University, Bangkok, Thailand
Rangsan_jom@dusit.ac.th
[4] Department of Electrical Engineering, School of Engineering, King Mongkut's Institute of Technology Ladkrabang, Bangkok, Thailand
siridech.bo@kmitl.ac.th

Abstract. Human parasitic infections remain one of public health concerns for 1.5 billion people worldwide including Thailand. Conventional microscopic examination is a gold standard method and often used to identify the helminth ova and filariform larvae and also protozoa cyst in stool-dependent simple smear. The benefits of traditional techniques are diminished by time-consuming, complicated procedures, massive labor, and skilled and trained parasitologists. An automatically rapid screening of the most in need of treatment is considered to replace the conventional technique. Here, we aim to develop a deep convolutional residual network based self-supervised learning model to identify mostly common parasite ova in Thailand. Although small amounts of training data was used to train the proposed model, the result shows superior performance over 95% accuracy. As a result, low values of false positive and false negative based confusion matrix table found revealed the robustness of the proposed models. General accuracy of self-supervised learning based the area under a ROC curve proposed with greater than 94% is also support an outstanding model studied. Therefore, rank of 1% to 10% of fine-tuning data labelled used bring us about a comparable model to that of using a 100% labelled training data. These findings emphasize the transformative potential of the BYOL method for screening of parasitic infection, particularly in resource-limited settings where is a lack of supportive lab equipment and skilled parasitologists to manage a large amount of challenging data in the future.

Keywords: Helminthic eggs · Bootstrap Your Own Latent (BYOL) · Similarity loss · Self-supervised learning · Object classification

© The Author(s), under exclusive license to Springer Nature Switzerland AG 2023
N. T. Nguyen et al. (Eds.): ACIIDS 2023, CCIS 1863, pp. 40–51, 2023.
https://doi.org/10.1007/978-3-031-42430-4_4

1 Introduction

Human parasitic infections remain one of public health concerns for 1.5 billion people worldwide including Thailand. The parasite can cause asymptomatic to severe conditions in gastrointestinal tract diseases (including abdominal pain, diarrhea, loss of appetite and malnutrition), and also affecting school-aged absenteeism and developmental impairment in children. Specifically, more than 24% of the global population is affected by soil-transmitted helminth (STH) infection, which is commonly reported in Thailand. Such helminths (*Ascaris lumbricoides*, hookworm, *Strongyloides stercoralis*, Taenia species, and *Opisthorchis viverrini*) and pathogenic protozoa (*Entamoeba histolytica*, *Giardia intestinalis*, and *Blastocystis hominis*) [1].

Conventional microscopic examination is a gold standard method and is often used to identify the helminth ova and filariform larvae and also protozoa cysts in stool-dependent simple smears. Genus and species characterization of pathogenic parasites can be conducted based on their morphology and structure [2]. Nevertheless, shared common traits and background interference (tissue-debris and colors) during microscopic observation led to mistaken identification. The benefits of traditional techniques are diminished by time-consuming, complicated procedures, massive labor, and skilled and trained parasitologists. An automatically rapid screening of the most in need of treatment is considered to replace the conventional technique.

Pattern recognition dependent pixel-wise classification to recognize any object with its structure, size, shape, and unique morphology is possibly used to overcome the conventional method described above. This pattern recognition technique is based on artificial intelligence (AI), machine learning (ML), and deep learning (DL) to compile with a whole slide scanner to help transfer the public-health services. ML is a scientific study of algorithms that deal with input under independent two-processes including feature extraction by engineer and learning transference by convolutional neural network (CNN). Previous study was proposed by [3] to characterize eggs of helminths, namely capillaria species deposited in institutional collections, by using logistic model tree algorithm combining with the majority voting algorithm resulting in high metric values [4]. DL, a current next generation of ML that both feature engineering and CNN learning are operated within a computerized system, was used to study 34 human parasite species based on various algorithm versions of You Only Look Once (YOLO). There are not only the proposed trained-model used to deal with the largest datasets, but state-of-the-art model also revealed performance with superior to localize and classify the helminths and protozoa with greater than 95% of both recall and precision, respectively [2].

Practical ML and DL applications, including analysis of X-ray, CT scan, or MRI images, often rely on supervised learning and require ample, high-quality labeled data from trained medical professionals. Self-supervised learning prone to a promising approach due to the technique can learn a bunch of datasets needing small proportions of labels ranging 1% to 10% of total data. Several self-supervised learning applications in a medical sector mainly used for histopathological images of cancer types [5]. These proposed the technique to estimate and diagnose interstitial pneumonia with a progressive course and poor prognosis due to poor reproducibility by pathologists reported [3]. The research result gave the prediction of pneumonia and a finding suggestive of progressive disease with high accuracy and AUC at 0.86. In addition, the classification of benign and malignant cells in lung cytological images with a weakly supervised deep learning method was also provided outstanding with 91.67% accuracy which comparable to senior and junior cytopathologist who have 98.34% and 83.34%, respectively [6]. As a result, the types of explainable AI can collaborate with human.

In this study, our goal is to develop a self-supervised learning model based on deep residual neural networks to identify the most common parasite ova in Thailand. We aim to implement the Bootstrap Your Own Latent (BYOL) method in conjunction with our model, foreseeing them as invaluable tools for future parasitic infection screening, particularly in resource-limited areas.

2 Architecture

In Fig. 1, the green box represents the self-supervised learning (SSL) process based on the BYOL method. The Nvidia-DALI data loader aids the data input step. The pre-trained weights generated by this process are then used to fine-tune the selected classification model, utilizing new labels during downstream training.

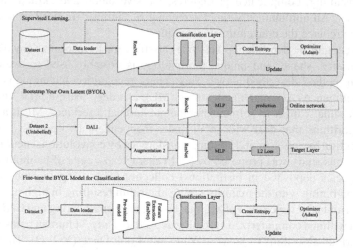

Fig. 1. Process Overview. The BYOL process (shown in the green box) generates a pre-trained weight file. These weights encapsulate rich, useful representations of the data, learned in an unsupervised manner by maximizing similarity between differently augmented versions of the same image. The obtained weights are then utilized in the fine-tuning of a new classification model (depicted in the yellow box), which further adapts these representations to the specific task of identifying parasitic ova. For comparative purposes, the traditional supervised learning method is also depicted (in the blue box), which relies on extensive labeled data to train the model from scratch.

In this study, we conducted two experiments. The first compared the performance of individual ResNet models with those fine-tuned using the pre-trained weights from the BYOL process. The second experiment sought to identify the optimal amount of training data needed in the downstream step for fine-tuning the ResNet models. We examined scenarios where 1%, 10%, and 20% of the labeled training data were used. The results from these experiments provide insight into the benefits of the SSL approach compared to traditional supervised learning (SL) models.

3 Materials and Method

3.1 Dataset Collection

The image data used in this study were obtained from a public dataset available at url[1] [7]. The dataset comprises 11 classes of parasitic ova, including *Ascaris lumbricoides, Capillaria philippinensis, Enterobius vermicularis, Fasciolopsis buski, Hookworm egg, Hymenolepis diminuta, Hymenolepis nana, Opisthorchis viverrini, Paragonimus spp., Taenia spp.,* and *Trichuris trichiura.* The microscopic images were captured at magnifications of 100x and 400x, resulting in a variety of image ratios. To concentrate on the key objects, the bounding box for each object was expanded by a factor of 1.2, and the images were cropped accordingly. These cropped images were then resized to a standard dimension of 608 × 608 pixels and saved in PNG format with square padding to maintain the aspect ratio. (See Fig. 2).

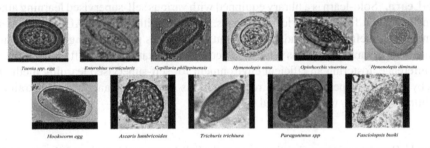

Fig. 2. Genus and species of 11-helminth classes used in this study.

In general, each class of parasites could be uniquely identified based on a combination of features such as the color of their egg-shell, the presence of certain organelles, and their size and shape [2].

Figure 3 provides an overview of the datasets used in the study. Dataset 1 (Training Dataset) consists of 8,800 labeled images and is used to train the Supervised Learning (SL) model. It is divided into four parts, representing 1%, 10%, 20%, and 100% of the original images. Dataset 2 (Pre-training Dataset) includes 8,800 unlabeled images and is used for pre-training the model based the BYOL method. Dataset 3 already obtained from previous dataset (Dataset 1) is also divided into four parts with class labels. They were used for fine tuning of SSL. Dataset 4 (Validation Dataset) contains 2,000 labeled images used for model validation during training. Dataset 5 (Testing Dataset) consists of 2,228 labeled images used to evaluate the quality performance of the proposed model.

---

[1] https://ieee-dataport.org/competitions/parasitic-egg-detection-and-classification-microscopic-images#files.

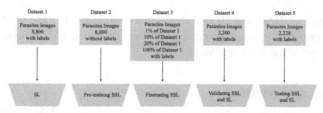

Fig. 3. Distribution of image datasets in Supervised Learning (SL), Self-Supervised Learning (SSL), and fine-tuning processes.

3.2 Self-supervised Learning and Model Training

Using Dataset 2, we applied the BYOL algorithm for self-supervised learning due to its superiority over contrastive models, a state-of-the-art method [8]. ResNet-50, ResNet-101, and ResNet-152 were utilized as our backbone models. The Uniform Manifold Approximation and Projection (UMAP) was employed to roughly evaluate the effectiveness of the pre-trained weight file. This technique visualizes datapoint clustering, where compact clusters within each class indicate successful pre-training, potentially enhancing downstream performance (see Fig. 1).

Solo-Learn. Solo-learn is a library equipped with various self-supervised learning algorithms beneficial for machine learning tasks. Coupled with Nvidia DALI, a data management tool, it efficiently handles data input, streamlines preprocessing pipelines, and manages hyperparameters. This synergy expedites computations for swift model training and inference, fostering an efficient environment for self-supervised learning methods, thereby ensuring superior learning representations and performance [9]. Our training condition of the SSL were described in Table 1.

Table 1. Hyperparameters and settings used in the Self-Supervised Learning (SSL) processes.

Parameter	Value
Data Format	Nvidia DALI
Dataset	Dataset 2
Batch Size	64
Tau base	0.99
Tau final	1.00
Learning rate	0.125
Maximum epochs	6000
Optimizer	Lars

Loss in BYOL. The loss for the BYOL method is determined using the mean squared error, calculated from the difference between the L2 normalized representations of the online and target networks (See Fig. 1) [8].

$$\mathcal{L}_{\theta,\xi} \triangleq \| \overline{q_\theta}(z_\theta) - \overline{z}'_\xi \|_2^2 \tag{1}$$

By examining the graph of training loss, we can initially determine if the model has reached saturation. As depicted in Fig. 4, the trend line shows an increase during the first 2000 epochs, followed by a fluctuating line between 2000 and 4000 epochs, indicating that the training had not yet reached saturation. Subsequently, we observed the model achieving a steady state during the training phase, specifically between 5000 and 6000 epochs. This observation was instrumental in helping us infer the optimal training duration (see Fig. 4).

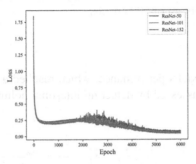

Fig. 4. Training loss of backbone ResNet-50, ResNet-101 and ResNet-152

Dimension Reduction. UMAP was utilized for dimension reduction to postulate if the pre-trained model can effectively segregate and cluster data-points per class.

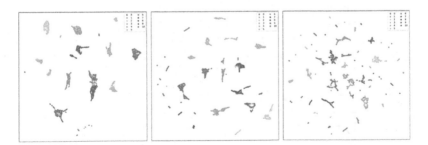

Fig. 5. UMAP of ResNet-50, ResNet-101, ResNet-152, respectively.

The UMAP analysis of ResNet-50 and ResNet-101 demonstrated more compact data-point clustering than ResNet-152 (see Fig. 5), indicating that these models might have comparable proficiency in feature detection and classification.

3.3 Downstream Task and Supervised Learning (SL)

For supervised learning, whole Dataset 1 was used to train the SL model. Also, we divided Dataset 1 into subsets constituting 1% (88 images), 10% (880 images), 20%

(1,760 images), and 100% (8,800 images) for training the SL model. Well-trained models were used to validate and testing by using Datasets 4 and 5, respectively.

In parallel, the downstream process utilized Dataset 3, comprising different proportions are likely to the subsets from Dataset 1. We fine-tuned models (ResNet-50, ResNet-101, and ResNet-152) with the BYOL pre-trained weight. In addition to Dataset 3, we also utilized Dataset 4 for model validation and Dataset 5 for testing the models performance.

Comparing the results from the SL and the fine-tuned models provided insights into the effectiveness of our approach, facilitating to determine the optimal learning condition and the suitable amount of training data. The details of our experimental configurations include a batch size of 32, the use of cross-entropy loss, an Adam optimizer, a learning rate of 0.0001, and a maximum of 500 epochs.

3.4 Evaluation Metric

The optimized trained model's performance, which reached a steady state in terms of loss during training, was assessed by detecting intestinal helminthic objects in the test image set (see Fig. 6).

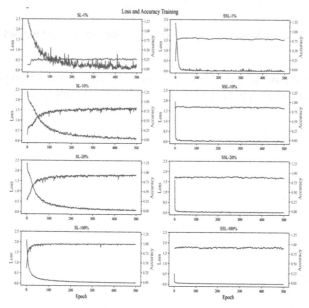

Fig. 6. Training accuracy and loss of ResNet-50, ResNet-101, ResNet-152 algorithms trained with varying amounts of data (1%, 10%, 20%, and 100%) in the self-supervised learning approach, compared with a supervised learning model.

The statistical metrics including precision, recall, specificity, F1 score, and general accuracy were assessed using the confusion matrix table [10]. The confusion matrix provided values for true positive (TP), true negative (TN), false positive (FP), and false negative (FN). From these values, statistical metrics such as

$$Precision = \frac{TP}{TP + FP} \tag{2}$$

$$Recall = \frac{TP}{TP + FN} \tag{3}$$

$$Accuracy = \frac{TP + TN}{TP + TN + FP + FN} \tag{4}$$

$$Specificity = \frac{TN}{TN + FP} \tag{5}$$

$$F1\ score = \frac{2 \times Precision \times Recall}{Precision + Recall} \tag{6}$$

In addition, Receiver Operating Characteristic (ROC) curve was plotted using the Scikit-Learn library in Python version 3.7.

4 Results

4.1 General Accuracies by Confusion Matrix Tables

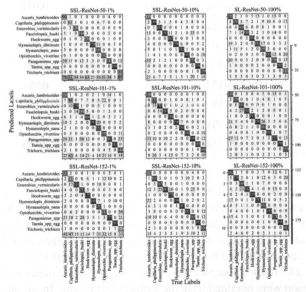

Fig. 7. Confusion matrix tables depicting the performance of various SSL ResNet models, differentiated by training data volume. Intensified color corresponds to higher TP values.

Accompanying the procedure in the material method section, the classification model and the pre-trained weight were fine-tuned by 11-helminthic labels. The quality performance of the trained models was initially assessed by using the confusion matrix table (see Fig. 7). In the confusion matrix table, the intensified diagonal pattern (from left to right) represented high degree of the TP values of each trained models found. Although all three trained-SL approaches seem to have a better pattern of TP values than the SSL approaches, the trained SSL has less training data than the SL and emphasize the remarkably cutting-edge technique of the SSL. As the results observed, the SSL-based ResNet-101 and SSL-ResNet-152 models outperform the SSL-ResNet-50 model.

Table 2. Evaluation metrics including recall, precision, accuracy, specificity and F1 score, respectively.

Evaluation metrics	Models	SSL		SL	
		1%	10%	20%	100%
Recall	ResNet-50	0.580	**0.785**	0.788	0.775
	ResNet-101	**0.666**	0.775	**0.804**	0.775
	ResNet-152	0.661	0.780	0.803	**0.819**
Precision	ResNet-50	**0.867**	0.923	0.898	0.875
	ResNet-101	0.855	**0.925**	0.913	0.875
	ResNet-152	0.852	0.906	0.908	**0.910**
Accuracy	ResNet-50	0.956	**0.977**	0.975	0.972
	ResNet-101	0.960	0.976	**0.977**	0.972
	ResNet-152	**0.962**	0.974	**0.977**	**0.979**
Specificity	ResNet-50	**0.991**	0.992	0.990	0.988
	ResNet-101	0.986	**0.993**	**0.991**	0.988
	ResNet-152	0.988	0.990	**0.991**	**0.991**
F1 score	ResNet-50	0.679	**0.849**	0.851	0.835
	ResNet-101	**0.744**	0.842	**0.863**	0.835
	ResNet-152	0.740	0.843	**0.863**	**0.877**

Although SL models appear to be superior to SSL, the SSL can be compared to the SL since all trained-SSL with merely 10% training data produced low FN and FP values. In SSL model, the performance of various training data based ResNet models is sporadic. In Table 2, For 20% of the training data, most statistical metrics at 97.7% accuracy, 99.1% specificity, and 86.3% F1 score were measured from both the ResNet-101 and ResNet-152 models, respectively. Only two statistical metrics of 80.4% recall and 91.3% precision were obtained from the ResNet-101 model. In summary, significant correlation between the small amounts of training data ranging 1% to 10% and ResNet-50 and ResNet-101 models was observed. During limitation of biological variation and quality of its labels, these uncontrolled factors might be solved by using only 1% of the training data and then results in 86.7% precision, 96.2% accuracy and 99.1% specificity, respectively. The result indicated that the SSL technique is moving forward to undergo the opened-world datasets which are mostly unlabeled as effective.

4.2 Performances of Various Models

An area under the ROC curve (AUC) calculated based 90% confident interval was revealed the generalized accuracy of the proposed trained model.

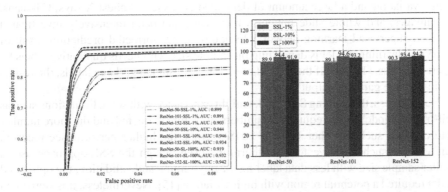

Fig. 8. Left: ROC curves assessing the general accuracy of supervised and self-supervised models. Right: Comparison of AUC between SSL and SL models, with an emphasis on the performance of models trained with small amounts of labeled data, ranging from 1% to 10%.

In consistent to those described as above, the AUC supported the performances of 10% of training data-based SSL-ResNet-50 (AUC = 0.944) and SSL-ResNet-101 (AUC = 0.946) model revealed outperform when comparing to others (see Fig. 8; Left). Interestingly, only 1% of training data reproduced the AUC equal to 89.9%, which suggesting high enough to employ the trained model in a real situation. The idea was supported by the result seen in Fig. 8 (Right). Also, the positive correlation between 10% of training data-based SSL-ResNet-101 model was shown (see Fig. 8; Right). Although the utilization of small neural network layers by the ResNet-50 model was trained with 1% data, the AUC still showed similar result to SL model. This indicated that the SSL technique is superior to the SL model.

5 Discussion and Conclusion

In this study, 11-common human-helminthic eggs in Thailand were automatic screening by using self-supervised learning approach. As workflow and architecture, our proposed algorithm contained two main components, namely online network that function to prepare feature extraction without class labelling and do data clustering-based similarity loss function. In our experiment, then, the result from previous section were used to do classification under labelling with multiclass-classification processes. Remarkably, the model trained with the advanced BYOL method outperformed the supervised learning model using ResNet. This was achieved even when a small fraction of the dataset, ranging from 1% to 10%, was employed for training and validation, highlighting the efficiency of the BYOL method in leveraging limited data resources. As mentioned as above, SSL approach for classifying our unseen image dataset is comparable to previous works based only on object detection [10–12], suggesting the superior model to supervised ones. This is because our SSL approach used trained data less than and equal to 10% of training data and reveal ranging of 87% to 99% accuracy, precision and specificity, respectively. According to the result mentioned as above, it can be assured that SSL is beneficial to solve the biological and medical tasks with still affecting by some serious issues such as high variation and a large amount of deposited data such as chest X-rays, CT-scans, MRI images, and whole slide images which these had been intensively investigated based on supervised learning network. In addition, the corrected prediction result of supervised learning model is depending on sample size with needs qualitative labels by expert clinicians [13, 14]. If the trained model was consumed garbage labels, the results would give the garbage output found.

Nevertheless, the training SSL model might experience with some limitations such as well-trained model could require the numbers of feature extracted and the more number feature vector such as either 1024 or 2048 vectors, the higher performance received than less one such as 64 vectors. Furthermore, even though the SSL approach uses a smaller sample size with less data labeling during training and validation, the optimized model required a potential region with high variation [15]. Nevertheless, this step could be fixed by implementing the augmentation function before doing training data. Lastly, computational speed still requires, specifically training with a large validation.

In conclusion, our study revealed the effectiveness of the SSL (BYOL)-based classification algorithm for solving the medical tasks even using small training dataset. Recognizing the prevalent human helminth infection in rural Thailand and Southeast Asia, the research result emphasizes the potential of transfer learning based BYOL method for screening of parasitic infection. Finally, this approach is particularly promising for future applications in remote environments, where it could address challenges like a shortage of lab equipment and expert parasitologists.

Acknowledgement. We are grateful to the National Research Council of Thailand (NRCT) [NRCT5-RSA63001–10] for providing the financial support for this research project.

References

1. Kache, R., Phasuk, N., Viriyavejakul, P., Punsawad, C.: Prevalence of soil-transmitted helminth infections and associated risk factors among elderly individuals living in rural areas of southern Thailand. BMC Public Health **20**, 1882 (2020)
2. Naing, K.M., et al.: Automatic recognition of parasitic products in stool examination using object detection approach. PeerJ Comput. Sci. **8**, e1065 (2022)
3. Uegami, W., et al.: MIXTURE of human expertise and deep learning-developing an explainable model for predicting pathological diagnosis and survival in patients with interstitial lung disease. Mod. Pathol. **35**, 1083–1091 (2022)
4. Zhong, A., et al.: Deep metric learning-based image retrieval system for chest radiograph and its clinical applications in COVID-19. Med. Image Anal. **70**, 101993 (2021)

5. Chen, R.J., et al.: Pan-cancer integrative histology-genomic analysis via multimodal deep learning. Cancer Cell **40**, 865–878.e866 (2022)
6. Xie, X., et al.: Deep convolutional neural network-based classification of cancer cells on cytological pleural effusion images. Mod. Pathol. **35**, 609–614 (2022)
7. Suwannaphong, T., Chavana, S., Tongsom, S., Palasuwan, D., Chalidabhongse, T.H., Anantrasirichai, N.: Parasitic egg detection and classification in low-cost microscopic images using transfer learning. arXiv preprint arXiv:2107.00968 (2021)
8. Grill, J.-B., et al.: Bootstrap your own latent-a new approach to self-supervised learning. Adv. Neural. Inf. Process. Syst. **33**, 21271–21284 (2020)
9. Da Costa, V.G.T., Fini, E., Nabi, M., Sebe, N., Ricci, E.: Solo-learn: a library of self-supervised methods for visual representation learning. J. Mach. Learn. Res. **23**, 1–6 (2022)
10. Kittichai, V., et al.: Classification for avian malaria parasite Plasmodium gallinaceum blood stages by using deep convolutional neural networks. Sci. Rep. **11**, 16919 (2021)
11. Butploy, N., Kanarkard, W., Maleewong Intapan, P.: Deep learning approach for ascaris lumbricoides parasite egg classification. J. Parasitol. Res. **2021**, 6648038 (2021)
12. Holmström, O., et al.: Point-of-care mobile digital microscopy and deep learning for the detection of soil-transmitted helminths and Schistosoma haematobium. Glob. Health Action **10**, 1337325 (2017)
13. Jiang, H., Zhou, Y., Lin, Y., Chan, R.C.K., Liu, J., Chen, H.: Deep learning for computational cytology: a survey. Med. Image Anal. **84**, 102691 (2023)
14. Jahn, S.W., Plass, M., Moinfar, F.: Digital pathology: advantages, limitations and emerging perspectives. J. Clin. Med. **9**, 3697 (2020)
15. Li, S., Du, Z., Meng, X., Zhang, Y.: Multi-stage malaria parasite recognition by deep learning. Gigascience **10**, giab040 (2021)

Cybersecurity and Fraud Detection

Obfuscated Malware Detection: Impacts on Detection Methods

Nor Zakiah Gorment[1,4] , Ali Selamat[1,2,3,5(✉)] , and Ondrej Krejcar[5]

[1] Malaysia-Japan International Institute of Technology, Universiti Teknologi Malaysia,
Jalan Sultan Yahya Petra, 54100 Kuala Lumpur, Malaysia
`aselamat@utm.my`

[2] School of Computing, Faculty of Engineering, Universiti Teknologi Malaysia, Johor Bahru,
81310 Johor, Malaysia

[3] MagicX (Media and Games Center of Excellence), Universiti Teknologi Malaysia,
Johor Bahru, 81310 Johor, Malaysia

[4] College of Computing and Informatics, Universiti Tenaga Nasional, Jalan IKRAM-UNITEN,
43000 Kajang, Selangor, Malaysia

[5] Center for Basic and Applied Research, Faculty of Informatics and Management,
University of Hradec Kralove, 50003 Hradec Kralove, Czech Republic
`ondrej.krejcar@uhk.cz`

Abstract. Obfuscated malware poses a challenge to traditional malware detection methods as it uses various techniques to disguise its behavior and evade detection. This paper focuses on the impacts of obfuscated malware detection techniques using a variety of detection methods. Furthermore, this paper discusses the current state of obfuscated malware, the methods used to detect it, and the limitations of those methods. The impact of obfuscation on the effectiveness of detection methods is also discussed. An approach for the creation of advanced detection techniques based on machine learning algorithms is offered, along with an empirical examination of malware detection performance assessment to battle obfuscated malware. Overall, this paper highlights the importance of staying ahead of the constantly evolving threat landscape to safeguard computer networks and systems.

Keywords: Obfuscated malware · Malware detection · Machine leaning algorithm

1 Introduction

Obfuscated malware is a type of malicious software that uses various methods of obfuscation to avoid detection [1] by antivirus software and security professionals. It disguises its code to evade detection by security tools, making it difficult to analyze and reverse-engineer.

In recent years, there has been a significant increase in obfuscated malware attacks, making it a challenging task for cybersecurity experts to detect and prevent such attacks since hackers use several techniques to obfuscate their malware code.

N. T. Nguyen et al. (Eds.): ACIIDS 2023, CCIS 1863, pp. 55–66, 2023.
https://doi.org/10.1007/978-3-031-42430-4_5

Based on the existing research works [2] for malware detection using machine learning algorithms, the two common malware detection issues are the increase of malware instants and undetected behavior of malware which led by obfuscation techniques as shown in Table 1.

Table 1. Malware detection issues which are led by obfuscation techniques.

Issue	Description		Year	No. of Citations	Reference
Malware variants	Failed to detect malware sample	Failed to detect new malware variants			
	√	–	2020	10	[3]
	–	√	2019	3	[4]
	–	√	2017	63	[5]
	√	–	2017	65	[6]
Malware Behaviour	Hiding technique features are found	Difficulties in malware detection			
	√	–	2021	6	[7]
	–	√	2019	8	[8]
	√	–	2019	56	[9]
	–	√	2021	8	[10]
	–	√	2017	43	[11]

As obfuscated malware continues to evolve and become more sophisticated, it is crucial for security professionals to keep pace with these changes by adapting their security strategies and using advanced tools and techniques to detect and prevent such attacks.

Consequently, via research and empirical analysis, our goals are to get a better understanding of obfuscation methods and provide an overall picture of their utilization. Thus, the following are our aims.

- We discovered common and cutting-edge obfuscation strategies.
- We gave a comparison on the impact of the deployed obfuscated malware detection approach.
- We investigated the limits that researchers confront and suggested viable solutions.
- We did empirical research to assess the efficacy of obfuscated malware detection using a machine learning technique and current technologies.

The rest of the research is broken down into the following sections: Sect. 2 offered basic study on obfuscation strategies, whereas Sect. 3 covers essential works related to the present status of obfuscated malware. Section 4 gives an empirical examination of the obfuscation technique's performance evaluation. Section 5 discusses the empirical analysis's findings. Finally, Sect. 6 summarizes the study project's findings and gives recommendations for future work.

2 Background Study

Malware is a form of program that has been developed specifically to harm or cause damage to computer systems, networks, or devices. There are various types of malwares, including viruses, worms, Trojans, ransomware, spyware, botnets, adware, rootkits, keylogger, and backdoor [12]. Malware behaves differently, and knowing how each one operates is crucial to building effective security solutions.

Malware authors employ obfuscation techniques to conceal the real nature of their code. The goal is to make identifying and removing malware more difficult for antivirus software and other security measures. Static and dynamic analysis [13] are two ways that can be utilized to identify disguised malware.

Static analysis entails inspecting the malware's code without running it. This can be accomplished by inspecting the malware's binary code or source code. This allows security researchers to discover patterns or signatures that indicate obfuscation. For example, they may seek code pieces that are repeated or appear to be created randomly.

The malware is dynamically analyzed by executing it in a controlled environment and analyzing its behavior. This may be accomplished in a virtual machine or sandboxed environment, which isolates the malware from the rest of the system. This allows security experts to determine the strategies employed by the malware to disguise itself. They may, for example, examine calls to encryption or compression methods.

Behavioral analysis and anomaly detection are two more ways used to identify disguised malware. Behavioral analysis is examining the malware's behavior as it interacts with the system, looking for patterns that indicate harmful behavior. Looking for signals that the system is performing improperly, such as unexpected network traffic or unusually high CPU utilization, is part of anomaly detection.

As a result, disguised malware necessitates a mix of tactics and experience. Security researchers must be able to recognize obfuscation indications and have the tools and methodologies to analyze the malware's code and behavior. As malware assaults get increasingly complex, security professionals must remain watchful and enhance their tactics for detecting and responding to these threats.

2.1 Obfuscation Techniques

In computer security, obfuscation methods are frequently employed to protect code from reverse engineering, alteration, or theft. The following are some of the most often used obfuscation strategies [12]:

Code Obfuscation. This entails changing the code so that it is difficult to read and comprehend. This makes it tough for attackers to find out what the code performs.

Control Flow Obfuscation. This entails changing the order in which the code is run, making it difficult to follow the flow of instructions. This makes it harder for attackers to decipher the program's logic and identify vulnerable weaknesses.

Variable Obfuscation. This entails modifying the names of the variables used in the program, making it difficult to comprehend what they are for. This makes identifying vulnerabilities that rely on specific variable names challenging for attackers.

Data Obfuscation. Encrypting, scrambling, or altering the data utilized in the program makes it harder to read or manipulate. This makes it harder for attackers to interpret the data and exploit weaknesses.

Anti-debugging Techniques. These are approaches for detecting and preventing code debugging. As a result, attackers have a more difficult time analyzing the code and identifying flaws.

Attackers find it difficult to reverse engineer, understand, and exploit code that has been obfuscated. They do, however, make it difficult for authorized users or developers to comprehend and maintain the code. As a result, obfuscation should be utilized sparingly and only when the advantages exceed the drawbacks.

3 Related Works

Obfuscated malware detection has been actively researched in the research community, with a range of strategies and algorithms offered to deal with it. Some related efforts on obfuscated malware detection are discussed further below:

3.1 Dynamic Malware Analysis

The execution of malware in a controlled environment to monitor its behavior [14] is referred to as dynamic malware analysis. To undertake dynamic analysis, many approaches such as code injection and sandboxing have been deployed. However, obfuscation techniques such as encryption and packing can circumvent these measures. To address this, researchers have developed methodologies such as behavior graph analysis, which generates a graph of the malware's behavior without relying on the code's contents.

3.2 Code Similarity Analysis

Code similarity study [15] compares known malware code against unknown code to detect similarities. Obfuscation techniques, on the other hand, can change the code to make it seem different from the original code, making it difficult to identify. Researchers have developed approaches to address this, such as function call graphs, which analyze the links between functions to detect commonalities.

3.3 Machine Learning-Based Detection

Machine learning-based detection uses algorithms to categorize malware based on a variety of characteristics, such as API calls and opcode sequences [16]. Obfuscation methods, on the other hand, can change these traits to avoid detection. Researchers have suggested strategies such as adversarial machine learning, which teaches the model to recognize obscured characteristics by creating adversarial samples, to address this issue.

3.4 Static Analysis

Static analysis is the process of analyzing code without running it [17]. Static analysis might be difficult to use when applying obfuscation techniques to detect the functionality of the code. Researchers have proposed numerous techniques to solve this, such as control flow analysis, which finds code that is never executed, and suggesting possible maliciousness.

Researchers must build advanced and robust detection systems as attackers continue to use more sophisticated obfuscation tactics. Meanwhile, current research efforts on Android platform obfuscation solutions, including KANDI, DroidPDF, Hybrid Obfuscation Technique, MGOPDroid, Framework of Paragraph Vector, and BLADE are presented in Table 2.

4 Empirical Analysis

Two empirical studies are presented in this section. The first empirical study assesses malware detection performance using a machine learning algorithm without filtering the obfuscated malware. The second empirical study evaluates the efficacy of existing anti-obfuscation techniques. The next subsection describes the experiments' chosen datasets and features. The setup of the experiment will be discussed shortly next. Finally, the experiment outcomes will be highlighted in Sect. 5.

4.1 Dataset

The first experiment uses the Obfuscation Elastic Malware Benchmark for Empowering Researchers (EMBER 2018) [26], which gathered features from 1 million Portable Executable (PE) files used for executables (.EXE,.SCR) and dynamic link libraries (.DLL) file formats. The PE files were scanned in or before 2018 and classified into eight categories of raw features that included both parsed and format-agnostic information. Parsed features are classified into five categories: general file information, header information, imported functions, exported functions, and section information, whereas format-independent features are classified into three: byte histogram, byte-entropy histogram, and string information.

The organization of the EMBER dataset will make it easier to assess models, categorize additional PE files, and expand the available feature set. EMBER was divided into two sections: 80% for training (800,000 training samples were collected, including 300,000 malicious, 300,000 benign, and 200,000 unlabeled samples) and 20% for testing (200,000 test samples were collected, including 100,000 malicious and 100,000 benign samples).

The second experiment employed the stated dataset for the n-gram technique, with 1576 samples split into 75% training and 25% testing.

Table 2. Comparative analysis on obfuscation techniques.

Year	Citation	Reference	Technique Used	Proposed Model	Challenges	Future Works
2022	3	[18]	Features of Multi-granular opcode	MGOPDroid	In some cases, static analysis is not reliable	A variety of obfuscation technologies will be uncovered, and static analysis will be improved
2021	7	[19]	Opcode Segments	BLADE	Classification techniques	Obfuscation methods will be explored
2020	8	[20]	Packer	DroidPDF	Packer	To improve the processing efficiency
2020	2	[21]	Reverse engineering & string encryption	Hybrid Obfuscation Technique	Obfuscated code	Customize the obfuscation method & improve the software protection
2019	6	[22]	Code obfuscation	Framework of paragraph vector	Obfuscation technique class level	To recognize an obfuscation approach, an engineering feature is necessary
2013	18	[23]	Vigenère ciphers based on ROL, ADD, XOR,	KANDI	–	–

4.2 Evaluation Metrics

In all investigations, TPR, FPR, FNR, ROC, Precision, Recall, F1-Score, and Accuracy were used to assess the performance of three various types of malware detection algorithms. A good and effective malware detection algorithm will have high TPR, Precision, Recall, F1-score, ROC, and Accuracy rates while having low FPR and FNR rates.

4.3 Experiment Setup

Several machine learning models were created using Python, which has a huge standard library of helpful codes and methods that may be used to build a machine learning model.

JupyterLab is used as an experimental development environment, exposing Jupyter notebooks, code, and data to users via a web browser, particularly for machine learning operations. Meanwhile, the Jupyter notebooks were ran using mamba and conda.

Support Vector Machine (SVM), Decision Tree (DT), and N-gram are three types of machine learning algorithms that were chosen for the first experiment based on past study findings of high-performance malware identification with a 100% accuracy rate. Our findings are compared to earlier findings, which are summarized in Table 3.

In the second experiment, only N-grams are employed as classifiers, with one-gram and bi-gram types chosen for malware identification prior to using anti-obfuscation algorithms. Figure 1a depicts the one-gram accuracy score, whereas Fig. 1b depicts the bi-gram accuracy score. Table 4 details the findings.

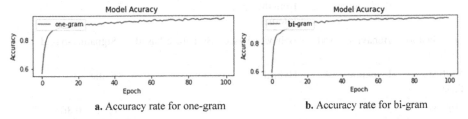

a. Accuracy rate for one-gram   b. Accuracy rate for bi-gram

Fig. 1a. Accuracy rate for one-gram **1b.** Accuracy rate for bi-gram

Opcode is utilized for obfuscation, with five forms of feature extraction: bigram opcode, intents, one-gram, permissions, and services extraction. Furthermore, as seen in Table 5, only one-gram approaches are used for anti-obfuscation.

5   Discussion

According to Table 3, the accuracy rates of all machine learning algorithms used to detect malware are insufficient to match the preceding research's 100% accuracy rate. The accuracy rate is jeopardized by the amount of the dataset. As a result, a little or insufficient dataset may result in a low malware detection accuracy rate. The experiment's accuracy rates for SVM, DT, and N-gram were 98.62%, 96.49%, and 97.43%, respectively, contradicting earlier results. SVM, on the other hand, outperformed the other two approaches and is likely to be utilized in a bigger experiment in the future.

Meanwhile, using the anti-obfuscation technique reduces one-gram accuracy from 91.4% to 91%, as seen in Tables 4 and 5. Consequently, we may conclude that disguised malware may influence the detection accuracy.

5.1   Limitations on Obfuscated Techniques and Methods

Obfuscation techniques and approaches are used to conceal or obfuscate a software program's functionality and code. While they can be useful in protecting intellectual property and avoiding reverse engineering, they are not without flaws.

Table 3. Comparison of three machine learning algorithm

Machine Learning Algorithm	Previous Research			Our Research		
	SVM [5]	DT [24]	N-gram [25]	SVM	DT	N-gram
Type of file	Win32-executable files	Internet files	Win32-executable files	Windows portable executable (PE) files		
Number of samples	1413	220	24	1 mil		
Dataset	CA Technologies VET Zoo & publicly available data sources	Clean and malicious data are scraped from the Internet	openmalware.org	EMBER 2018		
Classification Method	Behavior-based	Behavior-based	Signature-based	Signature-based		
Analysis Type	Dynamic	Hybrid	Static	Static		
TPR (%)	1	1	1	0.94	0.86	0.9
FPR (%)	0	0	0	1	1	1
FNR (%)	0	0	0	2.4	3.5	3.2
AUC (%)	100	100	100	99.93	99.64	99.81
F_1 (%)	100	100	100	98.24	97.45	97.68
p (%)	100	100	100	98.94	98.85	98.91
r (%)	100	100	100	98.46	96.08	97.04
Acc (%)	100	100	100	**98.62**	**96.49**	**97.43**

Table 4. The accuracy rate is low without using anti-obfuscation technology.

	One-gram	Bi-gram
Accuracy (%)	91.41	90.85

Performance Impact. Obfuscation techniques may have a major influence on program performance, frequently resulting in longer execution times and higher memory utilization. This might be a significant disadvantage in applications requiring high performance or low latency.

Limited Protection. Obfuscation methods can assist safeguard against inexperienced hackers or unauthorized users, but they may fall short against motivated and expert attackers. Advanced attackers may be able to circumvent obfuscation measures and get access to the underlying code and functionality.

Table 5. One-gram accuracy rate when anti-obfuscation method is implemented.

	Precision (%)	Recall (%)	F_1 (%)
Benign	83	84	84
Malicious	94	93	93
Accuracy	–	–	91
Macro Average	88	89	88
Weighted Average	91	91	91

Maintenance Issues. Obfuscation can make code maintenance and updating difficult for engineers. Debugging and troubleshooting can be difficult since code is frequently obfuscated throughout the development process. Longer development periods and higher expenses may arise as a result.

Compatibility. Some obfuscation techniques may be incompatible with specific computer languages or platforms, limiting their efficacy in specific situations. Developers may also need to thoroughly test the program to guarantee that it operates properly with obfuscation enabled.

Legal Issues. Techniques of obfuscation may breach intellectual property laws or software licensing agreements. Developers must guarantee that they have the legal right to utilize obfuscation techniques and are not infringing on others' intellectual property.

Obfuscation methods, in general, may be a useful tool for securing software and avoiding reverse engineering. However, before adding obfuscation in their apps, developers must carefully consider the potential restrictions and downsides.

5.2 The Impact of Obfuscation on the Effectiveness of Detection Methods

Obfuscation is the deliberate practice of making code or other information difficult to understand or decipher. This is sometimes achieved by hiding essential areas of the code using encryption or other means, making it more difficult for analysts to understand how the code works or what it does. The efficiency of detection systems can be significantly reduced through obfuscation. Here are some instances of how obfuscation may make discovery more difficult:

Obfuscated Code is More Difficult to Read and Comprehend. When code is intentionally obfuscated, comprehending what the code is doing becomes substantially more difficult. This can make identifying malicious behavior considerably more difficult, even if the methods used to detect it are effective under normal circumstances.

Obfuscation Can Hide Key Indicators of Malicious Activity. Many detection methods are centered on identifying certain patterns or signals of dangerous behavior. Attackers can make it more difficult to notice these indicators by obfuscating code, making it more difficult to recognize and respond to an attack.

Obfuscation Can Help Attackers Evade Detection. Attackers can use obfuscation to hide their activities from detection systems designed to identify malicious activity. By disguising their activities, attackers can make it far more difficult for these systems to recognize and block their actions.

Overall, obfuscation can help attackers evade detection and make it considerably more difficult for analysts to detect and respond to malicious behavior. While detection methods are regularly updated to work with obfuscation, this can be complex and time-consuming, and some types of obfuscation may be impossible to detect entirely. As a result, obfuscation is a key strategy for attackers and will very definitely remain so in the future.

6 Conclusion

To summarize, finding disguised malware is becoming an increasingly difficult challenge for cybersecurity organizations. Obfuscation techniques have evolved to make the detection of malicious code more difficult, making it easier for attackers to evade detection and remain undetected. However, with the use of advanced machine learning algorithms and other cutting-edge cybersecurity technologies, it is possible to identify obfuscated malware before it causes serious harm. Security professionals must stay up to date with the latest developments in obfuscation techniques and adopt proactive threat detection measures to protect their systems from the ever-evolving threat landscape. By taking a comprehensive, holistic approach to cybersecurity, organizations can minimize the risk of falling victim to obfuscated malware attacks and safeguard their valuable data and assets.

This study gave useful insight into the current issues and challenges associated with dealing with disguised malware. Furthermore, an empirical investigation was conducted to evaluate the current performance results created using SVM, DT, and N-grams, revealing that when the algorithm is trained using a bigger dataset, the accuracy rate drops from 100% to 98.62%, 96.49%, and 97.43%, respectively. In addition, an inadequate dataset, classification approach, analysis type, and obfuscated malware identification can all have an impact on malware detection accuracy. As a result, in the future, we will execute a substantial experiment on the chosen machine learning technique, with an emphasis on the development of obfuscated malware.

Acknowledgements. This work was supported in part by the Ministry of Higher Education through the Fundamental Research Grant Scheme under Grant FRGS/1/2018/ICT04/UTM/01/1; and in part by the Faculty of Informatics and Management, University of Hradec Králové, through the Specific Research Project (SPEV), "Smart Solutions in Ubiquitous Computing Environments", under Grant 2102/2023. We are also grateful for the support of student Michal Dobrovolny in consultations regarding application aspects.

References

1. Tahir, R.: A study on malware and malware detection techniques. Int. J. Educ. Manage. Eng. **8**(2), 20 (2018)

2. Gorment, N.Z., Selamat, A., Krejcar, O.: A recent research on malware detection using machine learning algorithm: current challenges and future works. In: Badioze Zaman, H., et al. (eds.) Advances in Visual Informatics, IVIC 2021, vol. 13051, pp. 469–481. Springer, Cham (2021). https://doi.org/10.1007/978-3-030-90235-3_41

3. Khariwal, K., Singh, J., Arora, A.: IPDroid- android malware detection using intents and permissions. In: 2020 Fourth World Conference on Smart Trends in Systems, Security and Sustainability (WorldS4), pp. 197–202. IEEE (2020)

4. Coban, O., Ozel, S.A.: Adapting text categorization for manifest based android malware detection. Comput. Sci. **20**(3), (2019)

5. Huda, S., et al.: Defending unknown attacks on cyber-physical systems by semi-supervised approach and available unlabeled data. Inf. Sci. **379**, 211–228 (2017)

6. Hashemi, H., Azmoodeh, A., Hamzeh, A., Hashemi, S.: Graph embedding as a new approach for unknown malware detection. J. Comput. Virol. Hacking Tech. **13**(3), 153–166 (2016). https://doi.org/10.1007/s11416-016-0278-y

7. Ibrahim, W.N.H., et al.: Multilayer framework for botnet detection using machine learning algorithms. IEEE Access **9**, 48753–48768 (2021)

8. Alkhateeb, E.M., Stamp, M.: A dynamic heuristic method for detecting packed malware using naive Bayes. In: 2019 International Conference on Electrical and Computing Technologies and Applications (ICECTA), pp. 1–6. IEEE (2019)

9. Kumar, R., Zhang, X., Wang, W., Khan, R.U., Kumar, J., Sharif, A.: A multimodal malware detection technique for Android IoT devices using various features. IEEE Access **7**, 64411–64430 (2019)

10. Mishra, P., et al.: VMShield memory introspection-based malware detection to secure cloud-based services against stealthy attacks. IEEE Trans. Ind. Inf. (2021)

11. Mira, F., Huang, W., Brown, A.: Improving malware detection time by using RLE and N-gram. In: 23rd International Conference on Automation and Computing (ICAC), pp. 1–5. IEEE (2017)

12. Gorment, N.Z., Selamat, A., Cheng, L.K., Krejcar, O.: Machine learning algorithm for malware detection: taxonomy, current challenges and future directions. IEEE Access (2023)

13. Singh, J., Singh, J.: Challenge of malware analysis: malware obfuscation techniques. Int. J. Inf. Secur. Sci. **7**(3), 100–110 (2018)

14. Sihwail, R., Omar, K., Ariffin, K.Z.: A survey on malware analysis techniques: Static, dynamic, hybrid and memory analysis. Int. J. Adv. Sci. Eng. Inf. Technol. **8**(4–2), 1662–1671 (2018)

15. Vinod, P., Jaipur, R., Laxmi, V., Gaur, M.: Survey on malware detection methods. In: Proceedings of the 3rd Hackers' Workshop on Computer and Internet Security (IITKHACK 2009), pp. 74–79 (2009)

16. Zhao, J., Zhang, S., Liu, B., Cui, B.: Malware detection using machine learning based on the combination of dynamic and static features. In: 2018 27th International Conference on Computer Communication and Networks (ICCCN), pp. 1–6. IEEE (2018)

17. Moser, A., Kruegel, C., Kirda, E.: Limits of static analysis for malware detection. In: Twenty-Third Annual Computer Security Applications Conference (ACSAC 2007), pp. 421–430. IEEE (2007)

18. Tang, J., Li, R., Jiang, Y., Gu, X., Li, Y.: Android malware obfuscation variants detection method based on multi-granularity opcode features. Future Gener. Comput. Syst. **129**, 141–151 (2022)

19. Sihag, V., Vardhan, M., Singh, P.: BLADE: robust malware detection against obfuscation in android. Forensic Sci. Int.: Digit. Invest. **38**, 301176 (2021)

20. Sun, C., Zhang, H., Qin, S., Qin, J., Shi, Y., Wen, Q.: DroidPDF- The obfuscation resilient packer detection framework for Android apps. IEEE Access **8**, 167460–167474 (2020)

21. Sultan, AB., Ghani, A.A., Ali, N.M., Admodisastro, N.I.: Hybrid obfuscation technique to protect source code from prohibited software reverse engineering . IEEE Access 8 187326–187342 (2020)
22. Park, M., You, G., Cho, S.J., Park, M., Han, S.: A framework for identifying obfuscation techniques applied to android apps using machine learning. J. Wirel. Mob. Netw. Ubiquit. Comput. Dependable Appl. **10**(4), 22–30 (2019)
23. Wressnegger, C., Boldewin, F., Rieck, K.: Deobfuscating embedded malware using probable-plaintext attacks. In: Stolfo, S.J., Stavrou, A., Wright, C.V. (eds.) International Workshop on Recent Advances in Intrusion Detection, pp. 164–183. Springer, Heidelberg (2013). https://doi.org/10.1007/978-3-642-41284-4_9
24. Sethi, K., Chaudhary, S.K., Tripathy, B.K., Bera, P.: A novel malware analysis framework for malware detection and classification using machine learning approach. In: Proceedings of the 19th International Conference on Distributed Computing and Networking, pp. 1–4 (2018)
25. Abiola, A.M., Marhusin, M.F.: Signature-based malware detection using sequences of N-grams. Int. J. Eng. Technol. (UAE) (2018)
26. Anderson, H.S., Roth, P.: Ember: an open dataset for training static PE malware machine learning models. arXiv preprint arXiv:1804.04637 (2018)

Estimating Post-OCR Denoising Complexity on Numerical Texts

Arthur Hemmer[1,2]([✉]), Jérôme Brachat[1], Mickaël Coustaty[2],
and Jean-Marc Ogier[2]

[1] Shift Technology, Paris, France
arthur.hemmer@shift-technology.com, jerome.brachat@gmail.com
[2] La Rochelle Université, L3i - La Rochelle Université, Avenue Michel Crépeau,
17042 La Rochelle, France
{arthur.hemmer,mickael.coustaty,jean-marc.ogier}@univ-lr.fr

Abstract. Post-OCR processing has significantly improved over the past few years. However, these have been primarily beneficial for texts consisting of natural, alphabetical words, as opposed to documents of numerical nature such as invoices, payslips, medical certificates, etc. To evaluate the OCR post-processing difficulty of these datasets, we propose a method to estimate the denoising complexity of a text and evaluate it on several datasets of varying nature, and show that texts of numerical nature have a significant disadvantage. We evaluate the estimated complexity ranking with respect to the error rates of modern-day denoising approaches to show the validity of our estimator.

Keywords: post-OCR correction · denoising · text complexity · invoices

1 Introduction

Optical character recognition (OCR) is the process of converting text from the visual domain into machine-readable text. It plays an essential role in bridging the gap between the physical and the virtual. Many businesses, governments and individuals rely on OCR to effectively manage documents of various types.

While OCR accuracy has improved greatly over the years, it remains an active area of research. In industries such as finance and insurance, high OCR accuracy has become crucial as it is used in fraud detection systems. These systems often work on semi-structured, scanned documents such as invoices, medical certificates, bank statements, etc. While the accuracy of modern-day OCR might be sufficient for information retrieval use cases, it falls short for these fraud detection use cases where wrong predictions can cause many false positives. These systems often rely on one or a few fields of highly specific nature from an array of documents. Small amounts of OCR noise occurring on these fields has a multiplicative, negative impact on the end-to-end accuracy of such fraud detection systems.

N. T. Nguyen et al. (Eds.): ACIIDS 2023, CCIS 1863, pp. 67–79, 2023.
https://doi.org/10.1007/978-3-031-42430-4_6

In order to combat noisy OCR output, one often uses OCR post-processing methods [1,22]. A classical approach combines a model of the typical errors that the OCR makes with a prior about the text that is processed consisting of a vocabulary with corresponding word frequencies. While this approach works well for natural language texts where the vocabulary is finite and well-defined, it is less effective for texts coming from business documents with numerical words such as dates, amounts, quantities, invoice numbers, etc. which are not contained in typical natural language vocabularies. An example of this is shown in Fig. 1, where a noisy reading of a dictionary word has few orthographically close corrections whereas numerical words cannot rely on this technique as all orthographic neighbours are equally likely. Most OCR post-processing approaches of aforementioned kind completely ignore these numerical words [6,25,26] or treat them as normal words [7], leaving them prone to errors.

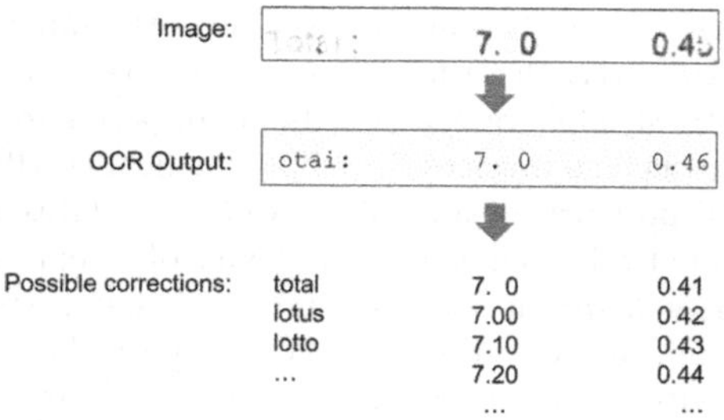

Image:	⌐ ²⁷ε⸢ ⸤	7. 0	0.4⸥
OCR Output:	otai:	7. 0	0.46
Possible corrections:	total	7. 0	0.41
	lotus	7.00	0.42
	lotto	7.10	0.43
	...	7.20	0.44
		...	...

Fig. 1. Visualisation of post-OCR correction process. Business information such as amounts are harder to denoise due to the possibility of all orthographic neighbors

A more modern approach to OCR post-processing is to consider it as a sequence-to-sequence ("Seq2Seq") problem, which is already widely researched for tasks such as translation and speech recognition. This type of approach has been boosted by deep-learning models and large parallel corpora. While these methods achieve state-of-the-art performance on OCR post-processing tasks [1,22], much like the classical vocabulary-based approaches, these language models are ineffective on numerical words [16,26]. Many methods do not make any distinction when considering numerical versus non-numerical words [7,11,19]. As such, some of them report that the majority of non-word errors come from tokens containing numbers [11]. In some cases, tokens containing punctuation and/or numbers are filtered out of the dataset entirely [6,25]. In other cases, the presence of non-alphanumeric characters is even considered as an important positive indicator for detecting erroneous words [6].

While the overall denoising performance has increased with these seq2seq approaches, we hypothesize that this improvement has been biased towards natural language, leaving datasets of more numerical nature untouched. The aim of this article is to quantify and compare the post-OCR denoising complexity of various datasets of both numerical and non-numerical nature. We do this by simulating textual noise and estimating the complexity by computing the performance of a simple denoising method under optimal conditions. Furthermore, we establish the real-world applicability of these estimates by comparing it to the performance of two cutting-edge post-OCR processing approaches under more realistic noise conditions. With these insights, we hope to shed more light on the strengths and weaknesses of modern-day post-OCR processing approaches and provide directions for future research. To summarize, in this paper we propose the following elements:

1. A formalization for estimating the OCR denoising complexity of a dataset
2. An evaluation of these estimates with respect to the performance from post-OCR processing approaches in more realistic settings

2 Related Work

Early work on estimating the denoising complexity of texts subjected to noise looked at the impact of the size of the vocabulary on the number of real-word errors [18], which are erroneous words that also occur in the vocabulary. They show that the fraction of these errors increases rapidly up to 13% for 100,000 words and then increases much more slowly to 15% for 350,000 words. While the conclusion states that smaller word lists are beneficial, this is only true for the real-word error rate. Hence, this conclusion was rightfully challenged [5] by showing that decreasing the size of the dictionary also increases the number of non-word errors, which are wrongly corrected words because the correct word was not in the vocabulary. The example they give is if *coping* were omitted from the vocabulary, the 4 misspellings of *copying* would be detected. However, the 22 correct uses of *coping* would be flagged as misspelled.

While these experiments look specifically at the impact of the size of the vocabulary, two important elements are not taken into consideration: the syntactic distribution of the words inside a vocabulary and the underlying noise model. For example, a small vocabulary consisting of words that are all within one edit distance from each other (numerical words) will be much harder to denoise than a large vocabulary where all words are within multiple character edits (natural words). As for the noise model, both [5,18] assume a uniform probability for each edit operation (transpose, add, remove, substitute) whereas there are factors that skew this distribution such as keyboard layout and phonological ambiguities. It should also be noted that this previous work was conducted in the context of human typing errors whereas it has been shown that human typing errors and OCR errors do not have the same characteristics [10]. Spelling errors typically generated by humans do not correspond to the noise that an OCR would introduce. For example, 63% of human misspellings occur in short words (of length 4 or less) whereas this is only 42.1% for OCR errors. To our knowledge, there is no prior work on estimating the denoising complexity of post-OCR processing approaches.

3   Background

The correction of spelling errors, whether they originate from humans or OCR software, has been a widely researched topic. Formally speaking, the goal is to find the original sequence w from a noisy observed sequence o, given a probabilistic model $p(w|o)$. As such, we denote the estimator of w as $\hat{w}$ such that:

$$\hat{w}(o) := \arg\max_w p(w|o) \tag{1}$$

While w and o can be any type of sequence (characters, words, sentences, paragraphs, etc.), it is typically considered at the character or word level due to limits in computational complexity. The parameters of this model have historically been estimated either by decomposing according to the noisy channel model or directly using more advanced sequence-to-sequence approaches, both of which are discussed separately below.

3.1   Noisy Channel Model

First works on error correction [3,13] estimated the parameters for $p(w|o)$ by applying the noisy channel model [23]. This works by applying Bayesian inversion to Eq. 1 and dropping the denominator as it does not impact the result of the arg max function. As this approach works on a word level, the arg max is taken with respect to a finite vocabulary $\mathcal{V}$ where $w \in \mathcal{V}$.

$$\hat{w}(o) = \arg\max_{w \in \mathcal{V}} p(o|w)p(w) \tag{2}$$

In this form, $p(o|w)$ and $p(w)$ are often referred to as the noise model and the language model (or prior), respectively. The noise model denotes the probability of observing a noisy sequence o from w. More often than not, there is not enough data available to directly compute $p(o|w)$. Instead, the noise is decomposed in individual character edits such as substitutions, insertions and deletions.

In the simplest case, the prior $p(w)$ consists of individual word probabilities. These can be estimated directly from the training data or come from auxiliary corpora. However, a single-word prior is restricted in the amount of information it can provide. To solve this issue, many approaches also take into account the surrounding context of a word where the language model becomes a word n-gram model or a more capable neural network-based language model. Using $\hat{w}_i$ to denote the i-th denoised word in a sequence gives us:

$$\hat{w}_i(o) = \arg\max_{w \in \mathcal{V}} p(o|w)p(w|\hat{w}_{i-1}, \hat{w}_{i-2}, \dots, \hat{w}_{i-n}) \tag{3}$$

While this enables a noisy channel denoiser to take into account the context of a word, it also introduces a new potential source of errors as the prior is conditioned on the previous estimates for $\hat{w}$ and not the true words w. An erroneous prediction for $\hat{w}_i$ can have a negative impact on the prior. *Beam search* [4] is often used to counter this problem. Instead of relying on a single prediction for each word, beam search keeps track of a top (fixed) number of candidates at each prediction step and computes the arg max for each of these candidates at the next prediction, and so on.

3.2 Sequence-to-Sequence Models

One can also use more capable methods to directly estimate $p(w|o)$ instead of decomposing it into a noise and language model. This approach is widely used in machine translation, where it is referred to as neural machine translation (NMT) when using deep-learning methods, and has also been shown to work well on text error correction [17,21,24]. It works by using an encoder-decoder [2] architecture, where the encoder takes the whole noisy input sequence and encodes it into a fixed length vector. A decoder is then conditioned on this vector and its own previous outputs to generate subsequent words in an autoregressive manner. This gives us the following estimator:

$$\hat{w}_i(o) = \arg\max_{w \in \mathcal{V}} p(w|o, \hat{w}_{i-1}, \hat{w}_{i-2}, \ldots, \hat{w}_{i-n}) \tag{4}$$

Similar to the n-gram approach, the autoregressive nature of these models is a potential source for errors. In the same manner, beam search can also be used for these direct estimators to overcome such errors.

4 Denoising Complexity

As discussed, there are various approaches to post-OCR processing. However, our hypothesis is that the frequency of numerals has a significant impact on the denoising complexity of a text, regardless of the used denoising approach. As such, we devise a simple method for quantifying the complexity of a text. We consider the noisy channel decoder from Eq. 2 under optimal conditions meaning that the denoiser has access to the true noise model and prior for a given text. For the prior, we use a unigram word frequency prior $p(w)$. The following subsection provides more details on the noise model before getting to the estimation of the complexity at last.

4.1 Noise Model

The noise model, $p(o|w)$, is a substitution-only noise model that we denote with π. While substitution-only is a simplification of reality where OCR errors can also contain insertion and deletion errors, it has been shown that the majority of errors consist of character substitutions [10]. Furthermore, we challenge this simplification in Subsect. 5.2, where we also include insertions and deletions in more realistic evaluation scenarios.

We compute the probability of obtaining word w from an observed word o under noise model π by taking the product of the individual character confusion probabilities. Here, w^i and o^i denote the character of token w and o at index $i \in \{1, 2, ..., n\}$ where n is the length of the token.

$$p_\pi(o|w) = \prod_{i=1}^{|w|} p_\pi(o^i|w^i) \tag{5}$$

where $|w|$ denotes the length of word w, and $p_\pi(o^i|w^i)$ the probability of observing a character o^i given a character w^i under noise model π. Since we are considering only substitutions, we will only consider o's that have the same length as w and vice versa. In other words, if $|w| \neq |o|$, then $p(o|w) = 0$.

Throughout the experiments we consider two noise models: a uniform noise model π_ϵ and a more realistic OCR noise model π_{ocr}. Given an alphabet $\mathcal{A}$ of possible characters, the uniform noise model π_ϵ has probability ϵ of confusing a character and probability $1 - \epsilon$ of keeping the same character. Within the substitution probability, each character has probability of $\epsilon/(|\mathcal{A}| - 1)$ for being substituted.

The second noise model, π_{ocr}, is estimated from the English part of the ICDAR 2019 OCR post-processing competition dataset [22]. The dataset contains a total of 243,107 characters from over 200 files from IMPACT[1]. The purpose of this noise model is to evaluate our estimator in a more realistic setting, as in practice OCR programs tend to have sparse confusion probabilities. For example, this means that when a mistake is made on a character such as "1", it is most often confused for visually similar characters such as "i", "t" and "l" and not so often by "8" or "Q".

4.2   Complexity Estimator

Finally, using the previously described noise model and noisy channel model, let us denote the denoising complexity of a dataset under noise model π as Θ_π. We define Θ_π by considering the accuracy of the optimal denoising algorithm under the noisy channel model with a unigram prior. The denoising complexity is estimated by taking the expectation of the number of errors according to the noise model.

$$\Theta_\pi = \mathbb{E}_{o,w\sim\pi}[\mathbb{1}\{w \neq \hat{w}_\pi(o)\}] \tag{6}$$

where we use $\hat{w}_\pi$ according to Eq. 1. We estimate it by sampling words $w \sim p(w)$ from our dataset and obtaining o by applying the noise model such that $o \sim \pi(w)$. An important advantage of our estimator is that it is computationally simple and highly parallelizable.

The intuitive interpretation of Θ_π is that it is the expected probability of picking an incorrect word given its noisy observation. It is the word error rate of a unigram denoising approach, but under optimal conditions. Having the true prior allows us to compare complexities between different datasets, as we rule out any variance that comes from having a sub-optimal estimate of the prior. In other words, having the optimal prior for a given dataset allows us to estimate and compare exactly our quantity of interest.

5   Experiments

Using our complexity estimator, we devise a ranking of denoisability of textual datasets of varying nature. Following this, we evaluate this ranking with respect to the performance of more advanced denoisers in a more realistic noise setting.

---

[1] https://www.digitisation.eu/.

In all experiments, we evaluate a total of five datasets. We chose two datasets of more numerical nature FUNSD [12] and SROIE [9], and three datasets of more alphabetical nature OneStopEnglish [27], KleisterNDA [8] and IAM [15]. Each dataset is tokenized using the SpaCy[2] tokenizer.

Table 1. The datasets used in the experiments along with relevant statistics

Dataset	Documents	$|\mathcal{V}|$	$|\mathcal{V}_\#|$	$|\mathcal{V}_\alpha|$	$p(\mathcal{V}_\#)$	$p(\mathcal{V}_\alpha)$	Document Type
FUNSD	149	5503	1477	3634	0.138	0.617	Forms
IAM	1277	11598	339	9776	0.007	0.841	Handwritten lines
KleisterNDA	254	12418	1988	9850	0.015	0.835	Legal documents
OneStopEnglish	453	15807	710	14791	0.016	0.847	Educational texts
SROIE	626	11397	7176	3838	0.246	0.480	Receipts

We use $\mathcal{V}$ to denote the vocabulary which represents the set of words present in a dataset. In addition, we use $\mathcal{V}_\#$ to denote the numerical vocabulary which is the subset of words containing at least one number, and $\mathcal{V}_\alpha$ to denote the alphabetical vocabulary which is the subset of words containing only letters. Note that $\mathcal{V}_\# \cap \mathcal{V}_\alpha = \emptyset$, but $\mathcal{V}_\# \cup \mathcal{V}_\alpha$ is not necessarily equal to $\mathcal{V}$ since we do not count punctuation and special characters in the alphabetical vocabulary. All datasets along with some descriptive statistics can be found in Table 1. We also included $p(\mathcal{V}_\#)$ and $p(\mathcal{V}_\alpha)$ which are the frequencies of the words in that vocabulary with respect to the whole dataset. As can be seen, FUNSD and SROIE have significantly higher frequencies of numerical words than IAM, Kleister-NDA and OneStopEnglish.

5.1 Denoising Complexity

Using previously described noise models and datasets, we estimate the complexity by sampling 10^6 words according to $p(w)$ and apply random substitutions according to the noise model to obtain observed word o. We then use the sampled (w,o) pairs to estimate the complexity according to Eq. 6. To estimate the complexity at varying degrees of noise, we gradually interpolate the noise from the character confusion matrix M_π with the identity matrix I using a parameter $\gamma \in [0, 1]$ such that $M_{noise} = \gamma M_\pi + (1 - \gamma)I$.

In our experiments we set $\epsilon = 0.07$ for the uniform noise π_ϵ. We chose this value because it aligns with the average confusion probability of the estimated OCR noise model. All results are computed for γ increments of 0.1 starting from 0.1 up to 1.0. We found that these increments gave us a good balance between computing time and visualisation value. For each noise model we also estimate the complexity on alphabetical words ($\mathcal{V}_\alpha$) and numerical words ($\mathcal{V}_\#$) specifically. The results can be found in Fig. 2.

---

[2] *en_core_web_sm* from SpaCy v3.4.4 from https://spacy.io/.

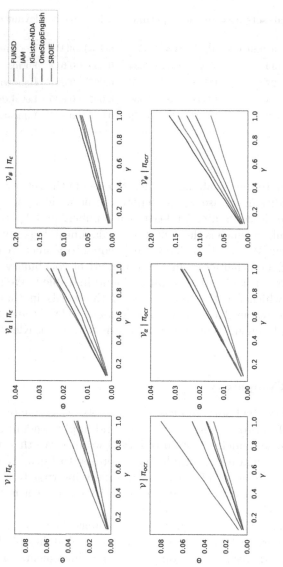

Fig. 2. Denoising complexity Θ for increased noise levels γ under noise models π_ϵ (left) and π_{ocr} (right).

Our primary observation is that the complexity ranking for $\mathcal{V}$ is preserved between the two noise models π_ϵ and π_{ocr}, and increases linearly with respect to γ. Under both noise models, the two datasets with the largest frequencies of numerical words (SROIE and FUNSD) have the highest complexity. Going from π_ϵ to π_{ocr}, their complexity increases, going from 0.047 to 0.084 for SROIE and from 0.042 to 0.071 for FUNSD, respectively. The steep increase in complexity for the numerical datasets can be mostly attributed to the higher average confusion probability for numbers for the OCR noise (0.14) compared to the uniform noise (0.07), combined with the significantly higher frequency of numerical words compared to the other datasets (see column $p(\mathcal{V}_\#)$ in Table 1). The other three, mostly alphabetical datasets show overall lower values for Θ, implying a lower denoising complexity. IAM and OneStopEnglish have close estimates under both the uniform and OCR noise models, though slightly higher for IAM in both cases.

Looking at the complexity estimates of the numerical vocabulary $\mathcal{V}_\#$, we observe them to be much higher than for the other vocabularies, even under the uniform noise model. Interestingly, the complexity ranking changes between the different vocabularies. Considering the complexity ranking of the numerical vocabulary, both OneStopEnglish and Kleister-NDA have similar or higher estimates than FUNSD and SROIE. A qualitative analysis of the results shows this to be due to the nature of numerical words in alphabetical datasets. In these datasets, numerical words used in natural language are often single numbers used for single counts (such as "Bob gave me 2 euros"), or numbers with low variation such as year numbers ("2007", "2008") and large rounded numbers ("10,000", "20,000", etc.). This is in contrast with FUNSD and SROIE, where numerical words consist primarily of amounts or dates which are longer, more diverse number sequences and thus slightly easier to denoise given that the numerical vocabulary does not cover all possible amounts. Note that while OneStopEnglish shows a high complexity for the numerical vocabulary, its overall complexity remains lower than FUNSD and SROIE, due to the lower frequency of numerical words in the dataset.

5.2 Applicability

The results from Subsect. 5.1 show us a relative denoising complexity for various datasets. However, when defining our estimator, we made several simplifying assumptions in order to compute this complexity. In this second part of our experiments, we wish to evaluate the applicability of our complexity estimate using a more realistic noise model as well as more advanced denoising methods.

First, we extend the noise model to also include insertions and deletions. The insertion and deletion probabilities for the OCR noise are estimated from the ICDAR 2019 OCR post-processing competition dataset [22]. To both the uniform and OCR noise models, we add the possibility for insertion and deletion with probabilities of 0.03 and 0.04 respectively.

Second, we evaluate the performance of 3 state-of-the-art denoising methods of the encoder-decoder architecture type. It consists of 2 transformer approaches ByT5 [28] and BART [24], and one Recurrent Neural Network (RNN) trained using OpenNMT [14]. ByT5 is a version of T5 [20] where the tokens are characters (bytes) instead of the usual SentencePiece tokens, which makes it more suitable for text denoising. Both transformer models were initialized from their publicly available pretrained weights (base) and were fine-tuned using an Adam optimizer with a learning rate of 0.0001 for 10 epochs. The RNN is trained on character sequences where the characters are separated by spaces and the words separated by "@". For coherence, we used the same hyperparameters as [17] for denoising OCR errors.

The data is preprocessed by concatenating all the datasets and splitting documents on spaces, of which the resulting token sequences are then used to create target sequences of at most 128 characters in length. The noisy sequences are generated by applying the noise model on the target sequences. To handle longer documents during evaluation, we split the input text again on spaces and denoise sequences of at most 128 characters at a time, after which they are concatenated again to form the final denoised prediction for a document. While it is technically possible for a word such as "article" to be noised into two separate words "art icle" and then split between evaluation sequences, we consider this to be rare enough as to not impact the results and at worst impact all denoisers equally. A separate model was trained for the uniform and OCR noise.

Finally, we compute the performance of each denoising method by computing the word error rate (WER) between the predicted output and the ground truth. In this case we use the non-normalized error rate which is the edit distance between the two tokenized sequences divided by the number of tokens in the ground truth sequence. We also include a baseline which is the WER that is computed from the original and unprocessed noisy sequence. This is to evaluate the relevance of our estimator.

The results are shown in Table 2. Our initial observation is that the baseline WER ranking does not follow the ranking of our complexity estimation, nor does it correspond to the WER of the other denoisers. Under uniform noise, SROIE and FUNSD show fewer errors than Kleister-NDA for the baseline. Under OCR noise, IAM has the lowest error rate, after Kleister-NDA and OneStopEnglish which have similar error rates.

We observe the error rates for the numerical datasets (FUNSD and SROIE) to be higher than the others for both BART and ByT5. While this is not the case for the OpenNMT denoiser, it should be noted that it has poor overall performance as it performs similar or worse than the baseline, with the exception being the Kleister-NDA dataset. As the Kleister-NDA dataset was significantly larger than the others, we suspect that the OpenNMT denoiser overfit on this dataset. Although BART achieves the lowest WER on Kleister-NDA, ByT5 has on average the lowest WER. Most notably, the gap in WER between the two numerical datasets FUNSD and SROIE is smaller for ByT5 under both noise models (uniform: +0.01, OCR: -0.01), whereas BART has consistently more difficulty with FUNSD (uniform: +0.05, OCR: +0.06). On the non-numerical datasets, Kleister-

NDA has consistently the lowest WER, with IAM and OneStopEnglish having nearly the same WER for BART and ByT5 under both uniform and OCR noise.

Compared to our complexity estimates, we do note some inconsistencies. First, FUNSD and SROIE are much closer in terms of their WER than their complexity estimates. For BART, FUNSD even has 5 and 6 percent points higher WER than SROIE under uniform and OCR noise respectively. While still close and much higher than the non-numerical datasets, we suspect this difference to come from the amount of training data which is three times higher for SROIE (96k tokens) compared to FUNSD (26k tokens). In addition, the receipts from SROIE are very homogenous and contain many longer recurring subsequences such as "gardenia bakeries (kl) sdn bhd (139386 x) lot 3" and "payment mode amount cash". Furthermore, this advantage for SROIE seems to be unique to BART, as the WER under OCR noise for ByT5 shows a higher value for SROIE than for FUNSD. We suspect that the sub-word token approach used for BART is better able to model these longer recurring sequences from SROIE compared to the character-based approaches.

Table 2. WER for the denoisers under the full noise model including insertions and deletions. ONMT = OpenNMT. **Bold** indicates the lowest WER for a given denoiser.

Dataset	Uniform				OCR			
	Baseline	BART	ByT5	ONMT	Baseline	BART	ByT5	ONMT
FUNSD	0.57	0.30	0.26	0.61	0.55	0.36	0.28	0.60
IAM	0.54	0.22	0.20	0.56	**0.48**	0.26	0.21	0.45
Kleister-NDA	0.61	**0.08**	**0.11**	**0.23**	0.55	**0.10**	**0.10**	**0.28**
OneStopEnglish	0.60	0.21	0.19	0.68	0.54	0.25	0.21	0.53
SROIE	**0.51**	0.25	0.25	0.55	0.57	0.30	0.29	0.52

6 Conclusion

We introduced a post-OCR error denoising complexity estimator, and evaluated its validity by comparing it to more complicated approaches in a more realistic setting. Furthermore, we also evaluated the complexity of specifically alphabetical and numerical words, to highlight the contribution of words of varying nature to the to the overall denoising complexity when they are sufficiently frequent. Future extensions of this work could look at the impact of using OCR word/character confidence distributions, which are sometimes available and exploited by denoising algorithms. Additionally, it would be interesting to research denoising approaches that specifically improve the denoising complexity of numerical datasets, as this would be most useful in industries relying on documents of primarily numerical nature.

References

1. Chiron, G., Doucet, A., Coustaty, M., Moreux, J.P.: ICDAR 2017 competition on post-OCR text correction. In: 14th IAPR ICDAR, vol. 1, pp. 1423–1428. IEEE (2017)
2. Cho, K., et al.: Learning phrase representations using RNN encoder-decoder for statistical machine translation. arXiv preprint arXiv:1406.1078 (2014)
3. Church, K.W., Gale, W.A.: Probability scoring for spelling correction. Stat. Comput. 1(2), 93–103 (1991)
4. Dahlmeier, D., Ng, H.T.: A beam-search decoder for grammatical error correction. In: Proceedings of the 2012 EMNLP, pp. 568–578 (2012)
5. Damerau, F.J., Mays, E.: An examination of undetected typing errors. Inf. Process. Manage. 25(6), 659–664 (1989)
6. Dannélls, D., Persson, S.: Supervised OCR post-correction of historical Swedish texts: what role does the OCR system play? In: DHN, pp. 24–37 (2020)
7. Dutta, H., Gupta, A.: PNRank: unsupervised ranking of person name entities from noisy OCR text. Decis. Support Syst. 152, 113662 (2022)
8. Graliński, F., et al.: Kleister: a novel task for information extraction involving long documents with complex layout. arXiv:2003.02356 (2020)
9. Huang, Z., et al.: ICDAR 2019 competition on scanned receipt OCR and information extraction. In: 2019 ICDAR, pp. 1516–1520. IEEE (2019)
10. Jatowt, A., Coustaty, M., Nguyen, N.V., Doucet, A., et al.: Deep statistical analysis of OCR errors for effective post-OCR processing. In: 2019 ACM/IEEE Joint Conference on Digital Libraries (JCDL), pp. 29–38. IEEE (2019)
11. Jatowt, A., Coustaty, M., Nguyen, N.V., Doucet, A., et al.: Post-OCR error detection by generating plausible candidates. In: 2019 ICDAR, pp. 876–881. IEEE (2019)
12. Jaume, G., Ekenel, H.K., Thiran, J.P.: FUSND: a dataset for form understanding in noisy scanned documents. In: 2019 International Conference on Document Analysis and Recognition Workshops (ICDARW), vol. 2, pp. 1–6. IEEE (2019)
13. Kemighan, M.D., Church, K., Gale, W.A.: A spelling correction program based on a noisy channel model. In: COLING 1990 Volume 2: Papers presented to the 13th International Conference on Computational Linguistics (1990)
14. Klein, G., Kim, Y., Deng, Y., Senellart, J., Rush, A.: OpenNMT: open-source toolkit for neural machine translation. In: Proceedings of ACL 2017, System Demonstrations, pp. 67–72. ACL, Vancouver, Canada (2017)
15. Marti, U.V., Bunke, H.: The IAM-database: an English sentence database for offline handwriting recognition. IJDAR 5(1), 39–46 (2002)
16. Mitchell, J., Lapata, M.: Language models based on semantic composition. In: Proceedings of the 2009 Conference on EMNLP, pp. 430–439 (2009)
17. Nguyen, T.T.H., Jatowt, A., Nguyen, N.V., Coustaty, M., Doucet, A.: Neural machine translation with BERT for post-OCR error detection and correction. In: Proceedings of the ACM/IEEE JCDL in 2020, pp. 333–336 (2020)
18. Peterson, J.L.: A note on undetected typing errors. Commun. ACM 29(7), 633–637 (1986)
19. Pham, D., Nguyen, D., Le, A., Phan, M., Kromer, P.: Candidate word generation for OCR errors using optimization algorithm. In: AIP Conference Proceedings, vol. 2406, p. 020028. AIP Publishing LLC (2021)
20. Raffel, C., et al.: Exploring the limits of transfer learning with a unified text-to-text transformer. J. Mach. Learn. Res. 21(1), 5485–5551 (2020)

21. Ramirez-Orta, J.A., Xamena, E., Maguitman, A., Milios, E., Soto, A.J.: Post-OCR document correction with large ensembles of character sequence-to-sequence models. In: Proceedings of the AAAI Conference on Artificial Intelligence, vol. 36, pp. 11192–11199 (2022)
22. Rigaud, C., Doucet, A., Coustaty, M., Moreux, J.P.: ICDAR 2019 competition on post-OCR text correction. In: 2019 ICDAR, pp. 1588–1593. IEEE (2019)
23. Shannon, C.: A mathematical theory of communication. Bell Syst. Tech. J. **27**(3), 379–423 (1948)
24. Soper, E., Fujimoto, S., Yu, Y.Y.: Bart for post-correction of OCR newspaper text. In: Proceedings of the Seventh Workshop on Noisy User-generated Text (W-NUT 2021), pp. 284–290 (2021)
25. Taghva, K., Stofsky, E.: OCRSpell: an interactive spelling correction system for OCR errors in text. IJDAR **3**(3), 125–137 (2001)
26. Thawani, A., Pujara, J., Szekely, P.A., Ilievski, F.: Representing numbers in NLP: a survey and a vision. arXiv preprint arXiv:2103.13136 (2021)
27. Vajjala, S., Lučić, I.: Onestopenglish corpus: A new corpus for automatic readability assessment and text simplification. In: Proceedings of the Thirteenth Workshop on Innovative Use of NLP for Building Educational Applications, pp. 297–304 (2018)
28. Xue, L., et al.: ByT5: Towards a token-free future with pre-trained byte-to-byte models. Trans. Assoc. Comput. Linguist. **10**, 291–306 (2022)

Reciprocal Points Learning Based Unknown DDoS Attacks Detection

Fu-An Ho[1]($\boxtimes$), Chin-Shiuh Shieh[1], Mong-Fong Horng[1],
Thanh-Tuan Nguyen[1,2], and Ying-Chieh Chao[3]

[1] Department of Electronic Engineering, National Kaohsiung University of Science
and Technology, Kaohsiung, Taiwan
{F111152122,csshieh,mfhorng}@nkust.edu.tw
[2] Department of Electronics and Automation Engineering, Nha Trang University,
Nha Trang, Vietnam
[3] ICP DAS Co., Ltd., Taipei, Taiwan

Abstract. In recent years, the increasing reliance on Internet services has made the Internet an integral part of our daily life. The COVID-19 pandemic has further accelerated this trend by driving the demand for online services such as remote work, virtual meetings, and online events. However, this increasing dependence on the Internet has also made us vulnerable to various cyber threats, particularly DDoS attacks, which have become a serious issue. For this reason, researchers have proposed numerous defense mechanisms to mitigate the risks associated with DDoS attacks, among which Machine Learning (ML) based Intrusion Detection Systems (IDS) have shown promising results. Nevertheless, most existing ML-based IDSs focus on known attack features, leaving them vulnerable to attacks that utilize unknown features. To overcome this limitation, researchers propose a new concept Open-Set Recognition (OSR), which explores new approaches that modify the Deep Learning method to identify unknown patterns. Therefore, we propose a novel IDS model based on OSR to detect Unknown DDoS attacks. The model detects unknown DDoS attacks with the U-Net + Reciprocal Points Learning (RPL). With a detection rate of approximately 99%, our model can successfully identify known and unknown DDoS attacks while maintaining an ability to manage imbalanced situations.

Keywords: Network security · Open-Set Recognition · Distributed Denial of Service · Machine Learning

1 Introduction

Distributed Denial of Service (DDoS) attacks pose a significant threat to the security of the internet, as they can disrupt and damage targeted systems. DDoS attacks work by using a network of compromised devices, also known as botnets,

This work was supported by National Science and Technology Council, Taiwan, grant No. MOST 111-2221-E-992-066- and MOST 109-2221-E-992-073-MY3.

to flood the target system with traffic. The traffic can be in the form of packets or requests, and it is designed to consume the target system's resources and bandwidth, making it unavailable to legitimate users.

To against DDoS attacks, Researchers have proposed various defense mechanisms designed to detect and prevent DDoS attacks. However, with the advent of the Internet and the shift towards remote work after COVID-19, there has been a notable rise in novel attacks. With the application of Machine Learning (ML) and Deep Learning (DL), attackers have nothing to hide under ML-based IDS. Nevertheless, ML-based IDSs also begin to have vulnerabilities, especially when ML-based IDS encounters attack features that have not been trained; the accuracy will drop dramatically. Therefore, our goal is to propose an IDS that can simultaneously detect known and unknown attacks.

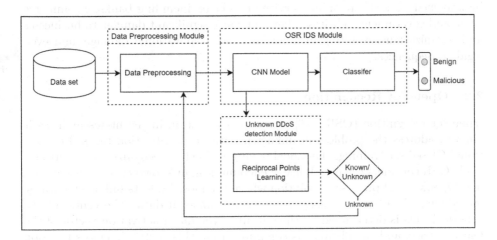

Fig. 1. OSR IDS Diagram.

We introduce the RPL Based OSR IDS model, which aims to detect both known and unknown attack features simultaneously using an existing IDS. The model is divided into three architectures: The Data Preprocessing Model, the OSR IDS Model, and the Unknown DDoS Detection Model, as illustrated in the (see Fig. 1) above. By utilizing these three architectures, our proposed model can effectively preprocess data, identify known and unknown DDoS attacks using OSR. Our approach provides an effective solution to detect DDoS attacks, making it a valuable tool for against cyber threats.

Our contributions mainly focus on the following:

– We propose a novel OSR IDS Model to detect the known and unknown DDoS attacks based on U-Net encode + RPL.
– The proposed model is capable of training on datasets with imbalance.
– The proposed model is capable of training on new attack features while preserving the accuracy.

2   Related Work

2.1   DDoS Attacks

In a DDoS attack, the attacker uses a network of compromised computers (often called a "botnet") to send large amounts of traffic to the target website or service, overwhelming its servers and causing it to crash or become inaccessible. The DDoS Attacks and Defense Mechanisms: Classification and State-of-the-Art [6], The authors provide an overview of DDoS attack types and defense mechanisms. The paper classifies DDoS attacks according to their characteristics and discusses defense mechanisms including filtering, rate limiting, and intrusion prevention systems. The goal of a DDoS attack is to overwhelm the target with traffic, resulting in a denial of service to legitimate users. DDoS attacks can be launched against any online service or website, including banks, e-commerce sites, and government websites. They can cause significant damage to businesses and organizations, resulting in financial losses, reputational damage, and even legal consequences.

2.2   Open-Set Recognition

Open-set recognition (OSR) [16] has gained attention in recent research, as it aims to address the problem of unknown data in classification tasks. In traditional Closed-set training, the model is only trained to recognize known classes, while OSR considers the possibility of encountering unknown classes during testing. OpenMax [2] proposes a solution where the model rejects unknown data by introducing an additional class to represent unknown data. The center of the spherical shell is determined by the output of the mean activation vector of the feature space, and the distance is computed from this center. The loss function used in OpenMax is also discussed. Classification-Reconstruction Learning for Open-Set Recognition (CROSR) [17] builds on the OpenMax approach by incorporating reconstruction into the model. The CROSR model uses a distribution-based approach to identify known and unknown data, and the reconstruction method is based on an encode/decode model that calculates the reconstruction error to distinguish unknown data. This approach improves the accuracy of OSR by considering the reconstruction error in addition to the distance-based approach used in OpenMax.

In recent research, several advanced approaches have been proposed to improve the performance of OSR learning methods for detecting unknown DDoS attacks. One such approach is Generalized Convolutional Prototype Learning (GCPL) [15], which standardizes the distance-based OSR learning method by using a prototype to constrain the distribution of deep features. Another approach is Spatial Location Constraint Prototype Loss (SLCPL) [14], which is based on GCPL but uses a different constraint term for the prototype loss function. Reciprocal Points Learning (RPL) [4], also based on GCPL, improves the prototype loss function by using reciprocal points for distance calculation. Moreover, the same research team has proposed an adversarial version of RPL called

ARPL [3], which uses a Generative Adversarial Network (GAN) [5] to improve the clarity of the deep feature distribution. These approaches have shown promising results in detecting unknown DDoS attacks and have the potential to improve the accuracy and effectiveness of IDS for DDoS attack detection

2.3   Unknown DDoS Detection

The detection of unknown DDoS attacks using ML techniques has been the focus of many recent research papers. For instance, in [10], the authors proposed using the Gaussian Mixture Model (GMM) to detect the deep features of DDoS attacks. Meanwhile, in [12], the authors used Dual Discriminators and GAN to detect unknown DDoS attacks. Another approach proposed in [11] is using One-Class SVM and Reconstruct Error to detect unknown DDoS attacks. These studies demonstrate that there are multiple methods available for detecting unknown DDoS attacks using ML, and the choice of method depends on factors such as the type of data available, the accuracy required, and the computational resources available. Therefore, ongoing research in this area is critical to developing more accurate and efficient approaches for detecting and mitigating the risks of Unknown DDoS attacks.

3   The RPL Based Unknown DDoS Detection Method

3.1   CICIDS 2017 Dataset

Most IDS research uses KDD99 [7], which was released in 1999 and does not include new network attacks like DDoS attacks. Therefore, although many studies still use KDD99 today, this study used the CICIDS 2017 [9] dataset to demonstrate our Unknown DDoS detection's efficacy (see Table 1).

The data collection period started at 9:00 a.m. on Monday, July 3, 2017, and ended at 5:00 p.m. on Friday, July 7, 2017. The traffic data includes protocols such as HTTP, HTTPS, FTP, SSH, and email and contains benign and malicious traffic. The CICFlowmeter [18] used Netflow protocol to extract features from the dataset, recording packets exchanged between end to end. The extractor has a maximum duration of 120 s and if exceeded, continues recording in the next line. A 5-s duration is used to determine the end of a traffic flow, with no transmissions signaling its end.

3.2   CICIDS 2017 Dataset Preprocessing

When selecting the dataset for training and testing the DDoS detection model, it is essential to consider various factors, such as the frequency and types of attacks, the availability of labeled data, and the representativeness of the data. In this study, we have chosen to use the CICIDS 2017 dataset for our experiments. Specifically, we have selected Wednesday as the training data and Friday as the testing data since DDoS attacks were found to be more prevalent on these days.

Table 1. CICIDS 2017 attack type information.

Date	Attack type
Monday	Benign (Normal human activities)
Tuesday	Brute Force FTP (9:20–10:20) Brute Force SSH (14:00–15:00)
Wednesday	DoS slowloris (9:47–10:10) DoS Slowhttptest (10:14–10:35) DoS Hulk (10:43–11:00) DoS GoldenEye (11:10–11:23) Heartbleed Port 444 (15:12–15:32)
Thursday	Brute Force (9:20–10:00) XSS (10:15-10:35) Sql Injection (10:40–10:42) Infiltration (14:09–15:45)
Friday	Botnet ARES (10:02–11:02) Port Scan (13:55–14:35) DDoS LOIT (15:56–16:16)

The (see Table 2) shows that. Benign traffic is the majority for the entire dataset, and there is also a considerable data imbalance between attack traffic, which increases the difficulty of IDS detection model training. To avoid this problem, well-organized data preprocessing is required. This study uses the following preprocessing method and discusses how to solve the imbalance problem.

Table 2. Distribution of the CICIDS 2017 Wednesday.

Labels	Data numbers
Benign	319186
DoS GoldenEye	159049
DoS Hulk	7647
DoS Slowhttptest	5707
DoS slowloris	5109
Heartbleed	11

As the network flow dataset may range from 0 to infinity, data normalization using the Min-Max algorithm is necessary. This linearly converts values to the range of [0,1] using maximum and minimum values, as represented by the following equation.

$$\overline{x}_n = \frac{x_n - min(x_n)}{max(x_n) - min(x_n)} \tag{1}$$

where x_n is the original value, $\overline{x}_n$ is the normalized value. Furthermore, the One-Hot encoding method distinguishes and marks the 6 labels. One-Hot encoding can avoid the linear dependence when the model training. The following (see Table 3) table shows the One-Hot encoding on training data.

Table 3. One-Hot encoding labels.

Labels	Encoding code					
BENIGN	1	0	0	0	0	0
DoS GoldenEye	0	0	1	0	0	0
DoS Hulk	0	1	0	0	0	0
DoS Slowhttptest	0	0	0	0	1	0
DoS slowloris	0	0	0	1	0	0
Heartbleed	0	0	0	0	0	1

3.3 Open-Set IDS Model Training

Here are two goals of training this model. **First,** Able to distinguish between benign and malicious features, or in common way we call it Close-Set recognition. **Second,** determine unknown attack features instead of identifying them as known attack features, or in common way we call it Open-Set recognition. Typical ML models only consider the first goal. Those studies have achieved satisfactory results. But for the second goal, since the identification of unknown features are not considered within the framework of the most ML model, which the general ML model cannot identify the second goal perfectly.

In the training procedure, the U-Net [13] model training to indicate benign and malignant traffic. This model employs an encode/decode architecture, which splits it into two parts. The encode part extracts the relevant data features through a convolutional layer. The decode part then restores the deep features of the predict data. Model accuracy is evaluated by comparing the predicted data to the true original data.

In CROSR [17], an encode/decode model is utilized to detect Open-set samples by combining the loss function of the encoder and decoder. Building on this approach, [11] applied the CROSR model to the task of detecting unknown DDoS attacks. Therefore, based on the successful results of previous studies, we chose to utilize the encode/decode model in our scenario. Specifically, we selected the U-Net architecture, which is a well-known and widely used encode/decode model. However, in our study, we focused solely on the encode part of the model, as we did not require reconstruction to improve the accuracy of our model for detecting unknown DDoS attacks.

Modifying the Loss function of U-Net is crucial for Open-Set recognition. In a common training process, the Loss function is mostly Softmax [8], the defection of Softmax can be expressed by

$$\sigma(z_i) = \frac{e^{z_i}}{\sum_{j=1}^{K} e^{z_j}}, \text{ for } i = 1, 2, \ldots, K \tag{2}$$

where the z_i is the Input vector of CNN output, the e^{z_i} is the standard exponential function for input vector, the K is the number of classes in the multi-class classifier, the e^{z_j} is standard exponential function for output vector.

But the characteristics of Softmax cause the model fails to recognize unknown features. Therefore, the Open-Set capable Loss function is required, which is the Reciprocal Points Learning (RPL) loss. It calculates the distance of deep feature space by Euclidean distance, and assume all known deep features has its own center, then calculate the reciprocal between the feature and center. Finally, push deep features far away from the reciprocal.

The RPL loss will be the combination of prototype loss and Open-Set loss. The prototype loss will be a variant of Softmax, it can be denoted as

$$L_c(x; \ \theta, o) = -\log \frac{e^{-d(\theta(x), o^i)}}{\sum_{i=1}^{K} e^{-d(\theta(x), o^i)}}, \text{ for } i = 1, 2, \ldots, K \tag{3}$$

where $d\left(\theta(x), o^i\right)$ is the Euclidean distance between $\theta(x)$ and o^i, the $\theta(x)$ is the denote as the embedding function which is the output of CNN and o^i is the center of each classis. For the Open-Set loss or constrain term can be denoted as $L_o(x; \theta, p)$

$$L_o(x; \ \theta, p) = \frac{1}{M} \sum_{j=1}^{M} d\left(\theta(x) - p_j^i\right), \text{ for } i = 1, 2, \ldots, K \tag{4}$$

where $d\left(\theta(x) - p_j^i\right)$ is the Euclidean distance between $\theta(x)$ and p^i, the $\theta(x)$ is the denote as the embedding function which is the output of CNN and p^i is the reciprocal of each classis, M represents the number of reciprocals for each class. The total loss will be the combination of prototype loss and Open-Set loss or constrain term. The equation can be denoted as $L(x; \theta, o, \ p)$

$$L(x; \ \theta, o, p) = L_c(x; \ \theta, o) + \lambda L_o(x; \ \theta, p) \tag{5}$$

where the λ is the hyper-parameter to control the constrain scale. With the Open-Set capable Loss function, the training data set can be used to train the OSR IDS model.

To provide a fair comparison between the different methods, it is important to use a common baseline model. In many previous OSR studies (see 2.2), LeNet [1] has been used as a baseline model for various classification tasks, including image recognition. It consists of several convolutional and pooling layers followed by fully connected layers, and has been shown to achieve good accuracy on various datasets. By using LeNet as a baseline, we can compare the performance of the OSR learning methods against a standard model and evaluate the effectiveness of these methods for the task of DDoS attack detection.

3.4 Unknown DDoS Detection

In order to detect unknown DDoS attacks, we developed the function to calculate
the probability of the target feature. The function uses Exponential to calculate
the probability, which is based on the Euclidean distance between the target
feature and the center denoted as $P(x)$

$$P(x) = e^{-\lambda d(\theta(x^i) - o^i)}, \text{ for } i = 1, 2, \ldots, K \tag{6}$$

where $d(\theta(x^i) - o^i)$ is the is the Euclidean distance between $\theta(x)$ deep feature and
o^i center, λ is the constrained term of probability, it adjusts the falling trend
of Exponential. Therefore, this function can adapt to a different distribution
(Fig. 2).

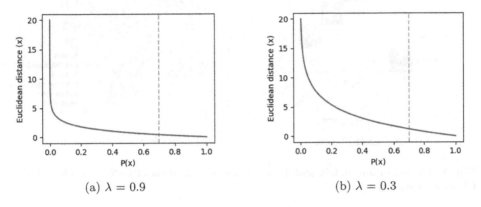

(a) $\lambda = 0.9$ (b) $\lambda = 0.3$

Fig. 2. The falling curve between different λ.

4 Experiments

4.1 Close-Set Evaluation

The experimental results in the Close-set show that, the training model has quite
good accuracy for known DDoS attacks, also achieved excellent results in various
indicators such as Precision, Recall, and F1 scores. The U-Net encode + RPL
is the proposed model, and the other three models are comparison to proposed
model.

The following figures (see Fig. 3) are the proposed model's confusion matrix
and deep features distribution. As you can see in the deep features distribution,
all the known features are clustered and separated, but only the Heartbleed
feature fails to achieve. This is due to the extreme imbalance of the Heartbleed
feature. Only 11 categories of data were labeled as Heartbleed compared to
the DoS Slow-httptest, which is the second least in the entire dataset and has
5109 data, so even though the proposed model is capable of imbalanced dataset
training when it faces quite an extreme situation, it still fails.

Table 4. The result of known DDoS attacks.

Method	ACC	Precision	Recall	F1
LeNet + SLCPL	0.9992	0.9992	0.9992	0.9992
LeNet + RPL	0.9886	0.9935	0.9886	0.9851
U-Net encode + SLCPL	0.9992	0.9992	0.9992	0.9992
U-Net encode + RPL	**0.9993**	**0.9993**	**0.9993**	**0.9993**

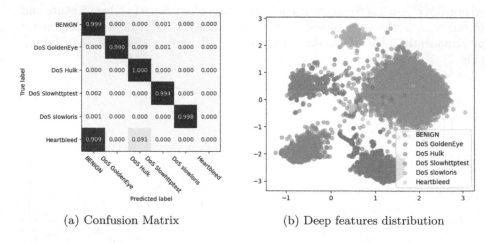

(a) Confusion Matrix   (b) Deep features distribution

Fig. 3. The confusion matrix and deep features distribution of U-Net encode + RPL Close-set learning.

4.2   Open-Set Evaluation

For the Open-set situation, if we feed an unknown dataset into the model directly, the accuracy will drop dramatically due to the characteristic of Close-set learning since there is no space for an unknown dataset in deep features distribution.

Table 5. The result of unknown DDoS attacks without OSR.

Method	ACC	Precision	Recall	F1
LeNet + SLCPL	0.8386	0.7121	0.8386	0.7683
LeNet + RPL	0.8297	0.7995	0.8297	0.8042
U-Net encode + SLCPL	0.8385	0.7539	0.8385	0.7869
U-Net encode + RPL	**0.8386**	**0.7771**	**0.8386**	**0.8034**

In the deep features representation shown in (see Fig. 4a), we observe that the unknown features are distinctly separate from the known features, indicating that they do not overlap. Additionally, (see Fig. 4b) displays the distribution of distances between features, further supporting the observation of minimal overlap between known and unknown features. We utilize equation (6) to calculate the $P(x)$ with a $\lambda = 0.3$. The classification of features as known or unknown is determined by the threshold value set for the $P(x)$, which in this case is 0.7. When the $P(x)$ exceeds this threshold, the input feature x is classified as unknown. The results of this classification can be seen in (Fig. 4c and Table 6).

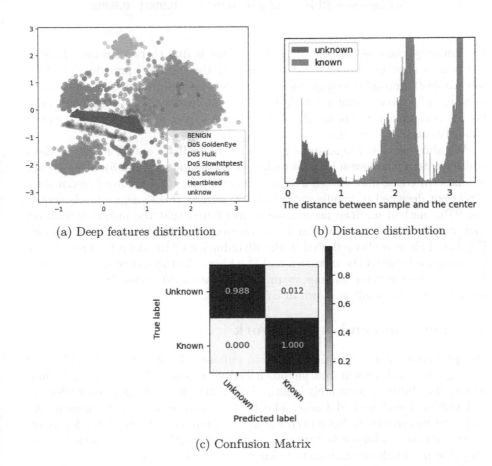

(a) Deep features distribution   (b) Distance distribution

(c) Confusion Matrix

Fig. 4. The visualization of the deep features distribution and distance distribution, and confusion matrix for U-Net + RPL Open-set learning.

4.3   Discussion

We evaluated the performance of our IDS model in both Closed-set and Open-set scenarios. Our experiments revealed that the model is capable of accurately detecting known DDoS attacks (see Table 4), even when the data is imbalanced. However, in cases of extreme data imbalance, the model tends to misclassify

Table 6. The result of unknown DDoS attacks with OSR.

Method	ACC	Precision	Recall	F1
LeNet + SLCPL	0.8393	0.8308	0.8393	0.7663
LeNet + RPL	0.9461	0.9473	0.9461	0.9466
U-Net encode + SLCPL	0.8408	0.8336	0.8408	0.7706
U-Net encode + RPL	**0.9901**	**0.9907**	**0.9901**	**0.9903**

the minority class as benign (see Fig. 3). This is due to two reasons. Firstly, the benign class accounts for the majority of the dataset approximately 64% (see Table 2). Secondly, benign traffic represents normal internet activity, which is inherently diverse, making it difficult for the model to distinguish between benign and malicious traffic. As a result, the model may incorrectly classify minority samples as benign.

We also conducted Open-set experiments to evaluate our OSR IDS model's ability to detect unknown DDoS attacks. As shown in (see Table 5), the presence of unknown DDoS data caused a drop in accuracy for the Closed-set model since it was not designed to handle such data. To address this issue, we implemented the RPL method on deep feature space and found that the unknown features were clustered near the center and did not overlap with the known classes (see Fig. 4a). This was also reflected in the distribution of the deep features, where the distance between the unknown and the known features were significant (see Fig. 4b). Based on these findings, we propose equation (6) to classify the unknown features, and the result is shown in (see Table 6).

5   Conclusion and Future Work

Our proposed framework utilizes OSR to enhance the detection capabilities of IDS against both known and unknown DDoS attacks. Our approach demonstrates the ability to accurately identify DDoS attacks while also being effective in handling imbalanced datasets. The RPL module separates the known and unknown features by U-Net's deep features. In unknown DDoS detection module restricts the unknown feature range and captures the unknown attacks. The proposed model shows promise in unknown emerging attacks.

However, we acknowledge that our current approach for detecting unknown DDoS attacks relies on manually adjusting the threshold of $P(x)$. To make our IDS more suitable for real-world scenarios, we aim to automate the threshold control process in future work. This will eliminate the need for human intervention and further enhance the effectiveness of our IDS in detecting unknown DDoS attacks.

References

1. Al-Jawfi, R.: Handwriting Arabic character recognition LeNet using neural network. Int. Arab J. Inf. Technol. **6**(3), 304–309 (2009)

2. Bendale, A., Boult, T.E.: Towards open set deep networks. In: Proceedings of the IEEE Conference on Computer Vision and Pattern Recognition, pp. 1563–1572 (2016)
3. Chen, G., Peng, P., Wang, X., Tian, Y.: Adversarial reciprocal points learning for open set recognition. IEEE Trans. Pattern Anal. Mach. Intell. **44**(11), 8065–8081 (2021)
4. Chen, G., et al.: Learning open set network with discriminative reciprocal points. In: Vedaldi, A., Bischof, H., Brox, T., Frahm, J.-M. (eds.) ECCV 2020. LNCS, vol. 12348, pp. 507–522. Springer, Cham (2020). https://doi.org/10.1007/978-3-030-58580-8_30
5. Creswell, A., White, T., Dumoulin, V., Arulkumaran, K., Sengupta, B., Bharath, A.A.: Generative adversarial networks: an overview. IEEE Signal Process. Mag. **35**(1), 53–65 (2018)
6. Douligeris, C., Mitrokotsa, A.: DDoS attacks and defense mechanisms: classification and state-of-the-art. Comput. Netw. **44**(5), 643–666 (2004)
7. Elkan, C.: Results of the KDD'99 classifier learning. ACM SIGKDD Explor. Newsl. **1**(2), 63–64 (2000)
8. Liu, W., Wen, Y., Yu, Z., Yang, M.: Large-margin Softmax loss for convolutional neural networks. In: Proceedings of The 33rd International Conference on Machine Learning, pp. 507–516 (2016)
9. Maseer, Z.K., Yusof, R., Bahaman, N., Mostafa, S.A., Foozy, C.F.M.: Benchmarking of machine learning for anomaly based intrusion detection systems in the cicids2017 dataset. IEEE Access **9**, 22351–22370 (2021)
10. Shieh, C.S., Lin, W.W., Nguyen, T.T., Chen, C.H., Horng, M.F., Miu, D.: Detection of unknown DDoS attacks with deep learning and gaussian mixture model. Appl. Sci. **11**(11), 5213 (2021)
11. Shieh, C.S., Nguyen, T.T., Chen, C.Y., Horng, M.F.: Detection of unknown DDoS attack using reconstruct error and one-class SVM featuring stochastic gradient descent. Mathematics **11**(1), 108 (2022)
12. Shieh, C.S., et al.: Detection of adversarial DDoS attacks using generative adversarial networks with dual discriminators. Symmetry **14**(1), 66 (2022)
13. Siddique, N., Paheding, S., Elkin, C.P., Devabhaktuni, V.: U-net and its variants for medical image segmentation: a review of theory and applications. IEEE Access **9**, 82031–82057 (2021)
14. Xia, Z., Wang, P., Dong, G., Liu, H.: Spatial location constraint prototype loss for open set recognition. Comput. Vis. Image Underst. **229**, 103651 (2023)
15. Yang, H.M., Zhang, X.Y., Yin, F., Liu, C.L.: Robust classification with convolutional prototype learning. In: Proceedings of the IEEE Conference on Computer Vision and Pattern Recognition, pp. 3474–3482 (2018)
16. Yang, J., Zhou, K., Li, Y., Liu, Z.: Generalized out-of-distribution detection: a survey. arXiv preprint arXiv:2110.11334 (2021)
17. Yoshihashi, R., Shao, W., Kawakami, R., You, S., Iida, M., Naemura, T.: Classification-reconstruction learning for open-set recognition. In: Proceedings of the IEEE/CVF Conference on Computer Vision and Pattern Recognition, pp. 4016–4025 (2019)
18. Zhou, Q., Pezaros, D.: Evaluation of machine learning classifiers for zero-day intrusion detection-an analysis on CIC-AWS-2018 dataset. arXiv preprint arXiv:1905.03685 (2019)

An Approach to Prevent DDoS Attack Using Real-Time Access Logs Analysis

Hanh-Phuc Nguyen[1]([envelope]), Thanh-Nhan Luong[2], Thi-Huong Dao[3], and Ninh-Thuan Truong[4]

[1] VMU - Vietnam Maritime University, 484 Lach Tray,
Le Chan, Hai Phong, Vietnam
phucnh@vimaru.edu.vn
[2] Haiphong University of Medicine and Pharmacy, 72A Nguyen Binh Khiem,
Ngo Quyen, Hai Phong, Vietnam
ltnhan@hpmu.edu.vn
[3] Hai Phong University, 171 Phan Dang Luu, Kien An, Hai Phong, Vietnam
huongdt@dhhp.edu.vn
[4] VNU University of Engineering and Technology,
144 Xuan Thuy, Cau Giay, Hanoi, Vietnam
thuantn@vnu.edu.vn

Abstract. Web applications are increasingly developing and occupying a dominant position in software systems, simultaneously shortening the distance in both space and time as well as bringing many other benefits to users. However, these applications always have the potential for dangerous cyber attacks. DoS and DDoS attacks arise thousands and millions of unnecessary requests, leading to overloading and causing serious consequences for the system. In this paper, we propose a real-time access log analysis method of a web system to detect user anomalies that may lead to DoS as well as DDoS attacks. Specifically, we concentrate on detecting and warning IP addresses that have a high number of requests over the allowed threshold of the system by constructing the formula to calculate the score of features of IP addresses. In addition, we have also carried out experiments with the proposed method on the *Shopbase* web system by supporting *ApacheSpark* and *Kubernetes* technologies in order to make visible the positive effect of the experiment in reality.

Keywords: DDoS attacks · log analysis · real-time · web application

1 Introduction

In the context of the growing Internet, the number of network users and software applications developed on the network platform is increasing. Web applications gradually rise to occupy the number one position in software applications. Because they are deployed in the Internet environment, web apps always have potential risks of unsafety on the network. In fact, cyber-attacks on web systems are increasingly diverse, sophisticated, and complex [8,12]. In order to meet the

© The Author(s), under exclusive license to Springer Nature Switzerland AG 2023
N. T. Nguyen et al. (Eds.): ACIIDS 2023, CCIS 1863, pp. 92–105, 2023.
https://doi.org/10.1007/978-3-031-42430-4_8

needs of users anytime, anywhere, vendors need to implement security methods while designing, developing as well as operating the system to ensure the security properties of the software systems.

DoS *(Denial-of-Service)* and DDoS *(Distributed Denial-of-Service)* [6,8] are the common types of cyber attacks that aim to make the server is flooded with more transmission control protocol/user datagram protocol (TCP/UDP) packets than it can process. This can lead to data corruption and resources may be misdirected or even exhausted to the point of paralyzing the system. The key difference between DoS and DDoS attacks is that the latter uses multiple internet connections to put the victim's computer network offline whereas the former uses a single connection. Nowadays, the prevention and warning of DoS and DDoS attacks pose a lot of challenges in the field of software security.

There have been many studies on the problem of DDoS attacks on web applications [1–5,7,13–15]. Currently, there is no method that can completely prevent DoS/DDoS attacks. Therefore, research problems in network security are often interested in detecting and preventing DDoS attacks, thereby reducing the risk of becoming a victim and mitigating the impact of a DDoS attack. For the problem of predicting a network attack, a number of machine learning techniques have been studied and applied in practice, many of which are used with decision trees [9–11]. Some of the methods mentioned in the studies are analyzing the information flow to detect signs of attacks, monitoring traffic to detect attacks early, creating an access management list to block the attacker's IP address... Our proposed method will analyze the web system's access logs to detect user anomalies that may adversely affect the system at runtime and lead to DDoS attacks. The paper's contributions include:

– *detecting and warning the IP addresses with the number of requests over the allowed-threshold that sent to the server in DoS attacks;*
– *creating the scoring formula for high-risk IP addresses in DDoS attacks based on some concrete criteria;*
– *constructing experimental software to illustrate the feasibility and effectiveness of the proposed method.*

The remainder of the paper is structured as follows. Section 2 provides some backgrounds of *ApacheSpark*, *Kubernetes* technologies, and the access log file. Next, Sect. 3 describes in detail the proposed approach. Followed by Sect. 4 that describes the implementation and experimental results. The next section summarizes the work that relates to this paper's research topic. Finally, Sect. 6 gives some conclusions and works in the future.

2   Backgrounds

2.1   Apache Spark

Apache Spark is an open-source data processing framework at scale. It provides an interface for programming parallel computing clusters with fault tolerance.

Apache Spark consists of two main components: *drivers* and *executors*. Drivers are used to convert user code into multiple tasks that can be distributed across worker nodes, and then monitor the execution of those tasks. The executor runs on the processing nodes and performs the tasks assigned to them. Spark can run in standalone cluster mode requiring only the Apache Spark framework and the Java virtual machine on each machine in the cluster, however, using cluster management tools between the two helps to take full advantage of the benefits of better resource utilization and allows on-demand allocation.

2.2 Kubernetes

We can use many ways to deploy Spark applications as Clusters. Kubernetes offers a solution very safe and effective implementation. It is also an open-source, portable, extensible platform for managing packaged applications and services, facilitating configuration, and automating application deployment. By providing a powerful framework for running distributed systems, Kubernetes can open a Container using its own DNS (Domain Name System) or IP address. If traffic to a container is high, Kubernetes can load balance and distribute network traffic for a stable deployment. To ensure speed, and utilize resources as well as used technologies, our application will have the model of a Cluster, with Drivers acting as Master nodes, and Executors acting as nodes. Each component will run on a separate machine, independent of each other based on the distribution of Kubernetes, where the Driver will be responsible for managing, connecting the components, and working together efficiently. This model also brings scalability to the whole application, if the data increases. An executor is a focal point to collect and they run concurrently, perform data preprocessing operations, and lean on the type of data the Driver wants. Then the Driver will go to collect what the Executor has processed to synthesize the next steps and give the results. This division of work helps data to be processed efficiently, taking full advantage of the cluster model and parallel processing of Executors to clean and shrink data for the driver to process. This process will be repeated for each batch of data received.

2.3 Access Log File

When participating in activities on the internet, some user information will be attached to the request to the server system providing the service. At that time, this information will be recorded in the access history data record of the server system that the user requests. In order to have information for the analysis of DoS and DDoS problems, when extracting information about the user's access history in the system, we are especially interested in the following aspects: *Connected IP address; Connection start time; Domain of the request; Connection protocol; Method of HTTP request; The path of the request; HTTP status code of the response; Size of data sent with HTTP request; Domain of the website associated with the requested resource; Agent performing access; Request processing time from receiving to returning results; Request Headers.*

3   The Method of Analyzing Access Logs in Real Time

The user's access history to the web application plays a critical role in detecting network attacks. In this paper, we propose a method to detect and warn of the threat of cyber attacks in real-time, especially for DoS and DDoS problems. The overview of the solving process encompasses three essential phases: *(1) collecting the user's access history; (2) analyzing the logs; and (3) notifying the administrator*, as shown in Fig. 1.

Regard to the first phase of the problem-solving process is to automatically collect the data throughout Kafka which is an event streaming platform. We can set the collection time for each log file that depends on the specific problem. The web app user data will do pre-processing and focus on only a few aspects that take into account as input for analysis (see Subsect. 2.3). The requirement for this process is that data is fully retrieved at the highest speed.

The final stage of the solving process is simply a decision to prevent access of the IPs in the BlackList or to notify about the threat of a network attack. At this time, the system is still completely up to the system administrator's discretion. Note that, for both DoS and DDoS issues, collecting log files or displaying information to users is similar and automated.

The most significant stage in our research is the data analysis method corresponding to DoS and DDoS problems. This phase receives input from the previous stage and provides messages to be made in the next stage. We will clarify both the ideas and analytical techniques for the problems in the following subsections. A factor determining our approach's effectiveness is the time aspect. The less time we take to detect, the less damage to the system's resources. Therefore, we aim to offer solutions to handle problems as soon as possible.

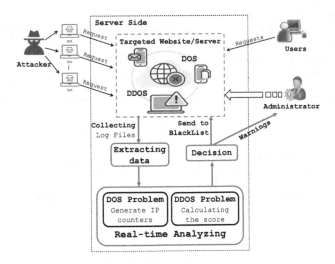

Fig. 1. The overview of the research problem-solving process.

3.1 DoS Problem

Concerning the DoS problem, our aim is to detect, warn and stop providing services for IP addresses with an abnormally high number of requests for a certain period of time (for three seconds). Our main idea to solve this problem is to generate IP counters that visit at a preset interval (every two seconds), then aggregate and filter out the IPs that exceed the threshold and put them in a BlackList to suspend services, as in Algorithm 1. After three seconds, these IPs will return to normal. This is to temporarily reduce traffic to the system so that the system can work better and meet the requirements of other normal IPs.

The number of hits of each IP will be recorded by the counters on the Executors, after the synthesis is complete, the data from the Executors will be sent to the Driver for processing as shown in Fig. 2. Here the Driver's job is just to filter out the IP addresses with the number of requests greater than the set threshold and add it to the BlackList. BlackList is the object used to store suspicious IPs, with the requirements set out as follows: (1) Has the property of the SET data structure, each Ip exists only as a single element in that list. (2) Has a feature to automatically delete data after a certain period of time. The truth is that the signs we recorded in this problem are only temporary signs to prevent the suspi-

---

Algorithm 1: Solve the DoS problem.

Input   : Log Files, threshold.
Output: Making decisions.
Data   : IPs - the set of IPs that make the request.

Procedure solveDoSProblem($s, threshold$)
begin
   $IPs \leftarrow s$;
   for *each* $IP \in IPs$ **do**
      $aggregateRequests(IP)$; //Aggregate the total number of requests by each IP for a period of 2 seconds.
      if $aggregateRequests(IP) > threshold$ **then**
         $blackList \leftarrow IP$; $warning(IP)$;

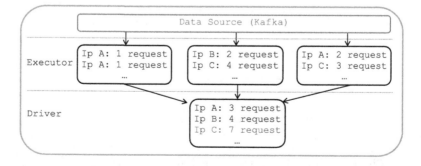

Fig. 2. The method of counting requests of IPs.

cious user from being able to continue using the system's resources much larger than normal. The action we want the web app system to take is not to process further requests from that user immediately after the time we detect (3 s) for everything is back to normal. (3) High speed of access, including read and write: Our analysis application is easy to write data to the Web Server (Openresty) and is easy to read out.

From the technical perspective, in order to meet all but the above requirements, our choice is *Redis*. As described in the supporting technologies section, here we use Redis' Caching feature, with the following mechanism: *On application side:* When an IP is detected to exceed the threshold, the application will immediately add a new key of the format "ipbl:$IP" to Redis with a value of 1 and a timeout time limit is 3 s; *On the Web server side:* Each request will be checked this condition. For each request, it will search for the value of the key "ipbl:$IP" on *Redis* with IP being the IP address of the client making the request, if it finds the value of this key, the request will be immediately denied.

3.2 DDoS Problem

Since an attacker can distribute the number of requests to the system from multiple devices for use in an attack, DDoS requires a much more complicated processing mechanism than the DoS problem. Therefore, instead of counting the number of requests of an IP address, we consider the IP address on different aspects as the foundation for giving DDoS attack warning. The solving process of preventing DDoS attacks is formalized in the Algorithm 2 in the three phases: *1) extracting crucial information from logs file every 5 s; 2) calculating the score; 3) comparing the score to the values and making a corresponding decision.*

Extract Data from Log Files. For the DDoS problem, we conduct preprocessing on log files that are collected every 5 s. We only take into account the

---

Algorithm 2: Solve the DDoS problem.

Input   : Log Files, *thresholds, weights*.
Output: Making decision.
Data   : IPs - the set of IPs that make the request.
            n - the number of IP addresses.

Procedure solveDDosProblem(*s, thresholds, weights*)
begin
  | $IPs \leftarrow s$; $n = |IPs|$;
  | **for** $i = 1$ **to** n **do**
  | | **for** $j = 1$ **to** 6 **do**
  | | | *convertingPoint*();
  | | | *scoreCalculate*($IP, thresholds, weights$);
  | | *makingDecision*(IP);

information **for each IP address** as follows: *1) Number of requests; 2) Number of requests with a high response time; 3) Number of requests per domain; 4) Number of requests with a status code equal to 429; 5) Number of requests with a status code equal to 429 per domain; 6) Number of requests with large body size;*

The gathering of user information is carried out automatically with the support of existing software such as Openresty, Nginx,... We have set up different counters in order to synthesize the information in log files and exploit the number of requests for criteria surrounding each IP address. To indicate anomalies in the number of accesses, we assemble data over a longer time range and evaluate changes in the data to find anomalies. Note that each counter corresponds to a criterion to be evaluated. Furthermore, the manner in which we select the

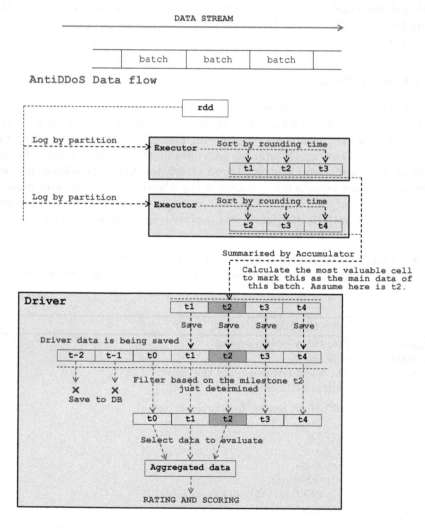

Fig. 3. The data preprocessing for DDoS attack detection.

threshold values plays a significant role in the results of our research. The process of analysis and synthesis is depicted in Fig. 3.

Calculating the Score. Before clarifying the scoring process for each criterion of each IP address, we will introduce some essential notions that are employed to constitute the scoring formula.

Threshold *is computed by the average of the number of requests over a given period, with the unit of measurement being requests per second (Reqs/s).*

Weight *is a value that represents the importance of a criterion in the set of considered criteria and gets a value in the range [0..1].*

We also introduce a special weight, namely *deadWeight*, which is applied when one criterion has a number of requests that greatly exceeded the threshold. In these circumstances, the system will send a notification regardless of any other criteria. Note that, each IP address has six criteria that need to be taken into account. Therefore, the sum of all the *weight* values of the criteria of an IP must add to 100% as non-functional constraints for six criteria as denoted in Table 1.

Without loss of generality, we assume that there are n IP addresses in one processing-log file that have been requested to the system, we calculate the score for all IPs following the formula:

$$S = \sum_{i=1}^{n} \sum_{j=1}^{6} cr_{ij} * w_j \tag{1}$$

where:

- S is the total score of all IP that has requested to the system;
- cr_{ij} is the *conversion score* of the IP has the request i with criterion j;
- w_j is the weight of the j criterion of an IP;
- j presents for the request of each criterion of an IP.

We will take into consideration the **threshold values** of the criteria **that represents the degree of influence on the outcome of the attack risk assessment.** *These values are selected through the experimental results that the system has carried out.* The thresholds and weights values of each evaluated criterion as denoted in Table 1 with seven rows, which includes six criteria to be evaluated as well as one exceptional case for **dead weight.** Based on the results of the experimental process, it is indicated that the number of requests sent to the system is the most significant factor leading to a high risk because of this is one of the main characteristics of DDoS attacks. The remaining factors have approximately equivalent roles except for the large body sizes criteria that have the least impact because many normal requests can also have large body sizes.

Next, we perform *conversion score* (cr_{ij}) (j is the ordinal number of the criterion under consideration in Table 1 and i is the ordinal number of the IP in the log file) for all criterion of an IP address by *calculating* the ratio of a criterion (r_{ij}) by *performing the division between the number of requests of criteria over the corresponding threshold value* (Table 2).

Table 1. The weight of criteria and respective thresholds of an IP address.

No.	Criteria	Weight	Threshold (Reqs/s)
1	Number of requests	30%	15reqs/s
2	Number of requests with a high response time	18%	3reqs/s (over 3 s)
3	Number of requests per domain	18%	5reqs/s
4	Number of requests with a status code equal to 429	14%	10reqs/s
5	Number of requests with a status code equal to 429 per domain	14%	3reqs/s
6	Number of requests with large body size	6%	4reqs/s (over 10MB)
7	The IP has a request with additional port information	deadWeight	

Table 2. The relationships between ratio and its corresponding conversion point

No.	Ratio (r_{ij})	Conversion point (cr_{ij})
1	$r_{ij} < 0.75$	0
2	$0.75 \leq r_{ij} \leq 1$	0.75
3	$1 < r_{ij} < 10$	1
4	$r_{ij} > 10$	5

Up to this moment, we have clarified all parameters that have been referenced in Formula 1 and finished the scoring process for all IP address that sent the request to the system. The final stage in solving approach is to take actions corresponding to the score value.

3.3 Decision

Decision-making is the final phase in the whole process of dealing with the problem of detecting and warning against cyber attacks. It is simply to compares the scores of the system with a decision table and takes the corresponding action that denotes various levels of attack risk as shown in Table 3.

Table 3. The relationship between the score of an IP and respective action

No.	Score	Action
1	$S \geq \gamma_0$	Block
2	$\gamma_1 \leq S < \gamma_0$	Jschallenge_4
3	$\gamma_2 \leq S < \gamma_1$	Jschallenge_3
4	$\gamma_3 \leq S \leq \gamma_2$	Jschallenge_2
5	$\gamma_4 \leq S < \gamma_3$	Jschallenge_1

For the DDoS detection problem, we use a scoring method based on a series of telltale signs that we have proposed, with each score we indicate the corresponding actions for the violation IPs such as Block, JsChallengeLv1, JsChallengeLv2... Based on experimental results, it is indicated that selecting a value of gamma γ_0 equal to 55 is the most efficient for our experimental system. The remaining parameters are separated by an interval of 5 units, respectively.

4 Implementation and Experiments

4.1 Implementation Environment

As stated above, *Kubernetes* is a portable, extensible, open source platform for managing containerized workloads and services, that facilitates both declarative configuration and automation. Our Spark applications are running on the Kubernetes Production cluster of the cross-border e-commerce platform Shopbase and successfully integrated to handle the aforementioned problems for this system[1]. From the technical perspective, the application architectures consist of components as shown in Fig. 4.

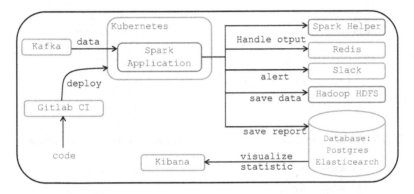

Fig. 4. The deployment architecture model

The architecture model includes many different modules, the functions of these modules can be summarized as follows: *Gitlab CI: automated application creation and deployment; Kafka: storing input data; Kubernetes: environment to deploy; Spark services: analytical applications; Spark Helper: pre-processing data; Redis: storing blacklist IP addresses; Slack: sending notification; Hadoop Hdfs: storing processing data; Database: storing output data; Kibana: synthesising data for threshold detection.*

---

[1] **The source code is available at:** https://github.com/GoogleCloudPlatform/ spark-on-k8s-operator/tree/master/charts/spark-operator-chart..

4.2   Experimental Results

The deployed system works stably and correctly detects according to the thresholds set in the configuration. Currently, the application has been integrated to operate with Shopbase's infrastructure. Figure 5 is an alert that detects an unusual increase by Slack during our application's run in a test environment. Figure 6 is an example of an Ip violating the DDoS rule.

Our application has a very fast processing speed, meeting the demand for real-time data processing. Alerts are sent in a timely and informative manner. The average amount of data received per second is 700 logs, and each batch of data with a period of 5 s will contain $\sim$ 3500 logs. The average processing time of each batch takes $\sim$ 2 s, much less than the maximum processing time of a batch of 5 s (the maximum time to avoid slowing down the Real-time processing). The number of logs per batch has sometimes reached 24000 logs when the system reaches the threshold of >4000log/s. Meanwhile, the processing speed of the application is still very fast due to a great load capacity. These results show that web apps that are actually deployed on a large web system with millions of users are still effective and have actually operated stably with non-functional goals achieved: *Performance, Scalability, Reliability, Resilience.*

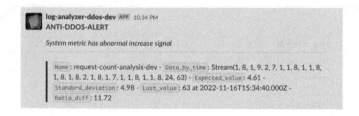

Fig. 5. An abnormal increase in access number detected to the system.

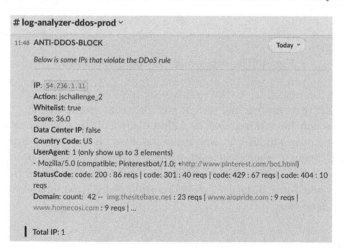

Fig. 6. The block message about an Ip violated the DDoS rule.

5   Related Work

Network security has received the consideration of many researchers, we present in this section the state-of-art of this issue and, especially, the solutions to the DDoS detection problem at the application layer of web services.

Zhao [15] designed a DDoS detection system that employs a neural network and is implemented in an Apache Hadoop cluster and HBase system. The system has a neural network architecture that can adapt to new types of DDoS attacks. A Hadoop and HBase cluster is established to process vast traffic, and then a neural network model is designed to detect DDoS attacks. The neural network chooses parameters from the Hadoop and HBase cluster modules, such as CPU usage, packet size, and the total number of TCP connections. Instead of using a single-factor detection approach, Zhao opts for a multi-factor detection approach to detect DDoS attacks, which can enhance the detection performance. In study [5], Heish suggests a neural network-based DDoS detection system that comprises five phases: packet collection, Hadoop HDFS, format conversion, data processing, and the neural network detection module. The author employed Hadoop's distributed file system to store traffic data and integrated the neural network into a big data platform, which uses seven parameters to detect DDoS attacks. This system is capable of analyzing high-speed and high-volume network traffic and the neural network is efficient in identifying packet features.

The article [7] discusses the increasing importance of network security due to the growing popularity and development of the Internet. Specifically, it focuses on the problem of Distributed Denial of Service (DDoS) attacks, which are easy to implement and can cause great losses, particularly in terms of server resources. The article proposes a method that uses LVQ neural network to detect DDoS attacks based on server anomaly detection. The method is trained on different DoS attack modes, achieving a high recognition rate and the ability to identify new types of attacks.

The problem of DDoS attack is divided into three crucial phases: *(i) DDoS detection; (ii) DDoS mitigation and (iii) IP traceback.* The authors [4] have analyzed in detail the mechanism of these three components and proposed a new method to protect DDoS attacks at the network and application layers. They first use any tool to determine the characteristics of the packets; then proceed to filter malicious packets by limiting their rate; finally, trace back their IP addresses. This helps to identify real IP addresses and reject spoofed IP addresses. Distributed Denial of Service (DDoS) in IoT networks, discussed by Ruchi Vishwakarm *et al.* [13], is an attack that objectives servers' availability by flooding the communication channel with impersonated requests coming from distributed IoT devices. In addition, the study also introduced different DDoS defense techniques and compared them to identify the security vulnerabilities as well as enumerated ongoing research problems about DDoS prevention and challenges that need to be solved in such a way stronger and smarter. In addition, Marta Catillo *et al.* [3] proposed a measurement-based analysis of the defense module, which was named mod_evasive, used for the Apache web server. The module blocked access from any *Ip* that attempts to make more than a given number of simultaneous requests or requests to the same page multiple times in less than a second against DoS attacks in order to ensure legitimate customer service. Their research results can be seen as suggesting settings for hardening web servers for each type of attack.

Andre Brandao *et al.* conducted automated log analysis to prevent network attacks and detect network intrusion [2]. This study proposes a log-based intrusion detection system (LIDS) to predict whether there is an attack or not. Logs from various sources are aggregated into one dashboard, and the most distinctive features are identified first. The proposed system shows its effectiveness through demonstration with the largest publicly labeled log file dataset KDD Cup 1999.

Methods of defense against DDoS attacks are generally classified into two categories: *(1) preventive and (2) reactive.* Prevention is the provision of contingency plans should attacks occur, meanwhile, the reactive is to detect the attack and respond to it to minimize the impact of the attack on the victim. The mechanism that we use to identify attacks is the scoring process and reconfiguring the system for IP addresses, thereby making decisions about the system's service providers are operating. Thus, the difference between our research to other studies is to construct the formula to calculate the weight of IP according to the criteria with the analysis process being carried out in real time, so the warning is detected early, leading to high efficiency in warning and anti-DDoS attack.

6   Conclusion and Future Work

In the context of cyber-attacks posing significant challenges to software security, we propose an approach to prevent DoS and DDoS attacks using real-time access logs analysis. We have extracted crucial information (criteria around an IP address) from log files and constructed a scoring formula based on these criteria. For specific value domains about scores that have been recommended throughout our experiments, we will make the decision to warn about the possibility of cyber attacks as soon as possible. Our research is particularly interested in real-time processing, including the time to collect the log files along with the time to handle them to find out the desired result. It is one of the essential conditions that help reduce the damage to the attacked system.

Furthermore, we have also implemented the proposed method by using *Apache Spark* and *Kubernetes* technologies. Besides the available components of these systems that support gathering and storing data, we have constituted some additional modules which encompass *Spark Application* (main processor), *Spark Helper* (preprocessing data), Hadoop HDFS (display output information) and **source code** (as input for Gitlab: automated application creation and deployment) are employed to solve the DoS and DDoS problems. Experimental results show the feasibility of the proposed method when operating the system in aspects of stability, low latency, and good load capacity. However, our research has just been implemented on only the Shopbase system due to the difficulty in the experiment and has not been compared with other methods. In the future, we will carry out these works to have a more extensive view of the effectiveness of the proposed method.

References

1. Alashhab, A.A., Zahid, M.S.M., Azim, M.A., Daha, M.Y., Isyaku, B., Ali, S.: A survey of low rate DDoS detection techniques based on machine learning in software-defined networks. Symmetry **14**(8), 1563 (2022)
2. Brandao, A., Georgieva, P.: Automatic log analysis to prevent cyber attacks. In: Sgurev, V., Jotsov, V., Kacprzyk, J. (eds.) Advances in Intelligent Systems Research and Innovation. SSDC, vol. 379, pp. 315–339. Springer, Cham (2022). https://doi.org/10.1007/978-3-030-78124-8_14
3. Catillo, M., Pecchia, A., Villano, U.: Measurement-based analysis of a DoS defense module for an open source web server. In: Casola, V., De Benedictis, A., Rak, M. (eds.) ICTSS 2020. LNCS, vol. 12543, pp. 121–134. Springer, Cham (2020). https://doi.org/10.1007/978-3-030-64881-7_8
4. Dayanandam, G., Rao, T.V., Bujji Babu, D., Nalini Durga, S.: DDoS attacks—analysis and prevention. In: Saini, H.S., Sayal, R., Govardhan, A., Buyya, R. (eds.) Innovations in Computer Science and Engineering. LNNS, vol. 32, pp. 1–10. Springer, Singapore (2019). https://doi.org/10.1007/978-981-10-8201-6_1
5. Hsieh, C.J., Chan, T.Y.: Detection DDoS attacks based on neural-network using apache spark. In: 2016 International Conference on Applied System Innovation (ICASI), pp. 1–4 (2016). https://doi.org/10.1109/ICASI.2016.7539833
6. Khalaf, B.A., Mostafa, S.A., Mustapha, A., Mohammed, M.A., Abduallah, W.M.: Comprehensive review of artificial intelligence and statistical approaches in distributed denial of service attack and defense methods. IEEE Access **7**, 51691–51713 (2019)
7. Li, J., Liu, Y., Gu, L.: DDoS attack detection based on neural network. In: 2010 2nd International Symposium on Aware Computing, pp. 196–199 (2010). https://doi.org/10.1109/ISAC.2010.5670479
8. Salim, M.M., Rathore, S., Park, J.H.: Distributed denial of service attacks and its defenses in IoT: a survey. J. Supercomput. **76**(7), 5320–5363 (2020)
9. Sangodoyin, A.O., Akinsolu, M.O., Pillai, P., Grout, V.: Detection and classification of DDoS flooding attacks on software-defined networks: a case study for the application of machine learning. IEEE Access **9**, 122495–122508 (2021)
10. Santos, R., Souza, D., Santo, W., Ribeiro, A., Moreno, E.: Machine learning algorithms to detect DDoS attacks in SDN. Concurrency Comput.: Pract. Exp. **32**(16), e5402 (2020)
11. Saranya, T., Sridevi, S., Deisy, C., Chung, T.D., Khan, M.A.: Performance analysis of machine learning algorithms in intrusion detection system: a review. Procedia Comput. Sci. **171**, 1251–1260 (2020)
12. Symantec, C.: Internet security threat report: Volume 24. Symantee Enterprise Security (2019)
13. Vishwakarma, R., Jain, A.K.: A survey of DDoS attacking techniques and defence mechanisms in the IoT network. Telecommun. Syst. **73**(1), 3–25 (2020)
14. Yavanoglu, O., Aydos, M.: A review on cyber security datasets for machine learning algorithms. In: 2017 IEEE International Conference on Big Data (Big Data), pp. 2186–2193 (2017). https://doi.org/10.1109/BigData.2017.8258167
15. Zhao, T., Lo, D.C.T., Qian, K.: A neural-network based DDoS detection system using hadoop and HBase. In: 2015 IEEE 7th International Symposium on Cyberspace Safety and Security, pp. 1326–1331. IEEE (2015). https://doi.org/10.1109/HPCC-CSS-ICESS.2015.38

A Novel Method for Spam Call Detection Using Graph Convolutional Networks

Trung-Kien Nguyen[1,2], Viet-Trung Tran[2(✉)], Huy-Anh Nguyen[1], and Khac-Hoai Nam Bui[1]

[1] Viettel Cyberspace Center, Viettel Group, Hanoi, Vietnam
[2] Hanoi University of Science and Technology, Hanoi, Vietnam
trungtv@soict.hust.edu.vn

Abstract. Unwanted calls from advertisers or phishers are a major nuisance for millions of mobile phone users. Manual blacklists are ineffective against this growing problem. A sophisticated approach is needed on the telephone operator side to detect spam calls based on malicious patterns. In this paper, we present a framework that uses network-relationship between mobile users for spam detection. Our framework has two main contributions: i) We propose an efficient and cost-effective method to construct a large, labeled spam detection graph by leveraging end-user collaboration; ii) We propose a graph neural network (GNN)-based model for the spam detection task. Our experiments show that our model outperforms strong baseline models in this research field.

Keywords: Spam call detection · Graph neural network · Telephony network data

1 Introduction

Malicious call seriously troubles our daily life. Mobile users not only feel annoyed by the advertising messages but also get scammed. Million people are suffocated by increasingly unwanted calls that are advertising or phishing every day. Recently, with artificial intelligence progress, it is unobstructed for the spammer to make a robot call that is able to make thousands of calls in some minutes. However, the classification models permanently deal with the ambiguity between spam calls and regular ones. Some kinds of adapters allow changing dynamic mobile numbers, and behavior to escape the normal rules that detect spam calls. In some cases, phishing call is the same behavior as normal ones on the other hand, with the development of internet-based services such as food shippers, logistic service, customer care services, and regular anonymous call increase extremely. Therefore, it is necessary to have a novel approach on the telephone operator side that is able to clarify automatically unwanted calls.

The previous works mentioned multiple approaches to the problem by applying some rules such as black/white lists, enforced caller introduction, and call

N. T. Nguyen et al. (Eds.): ACIIDS 2023, CCIS 1863, pp. 106–116, 2023.
https://doi.org/10.1007/978-3-031-42430-4_9

rate limiting [9,10]. MacIntosh et. al [8] based on the analysis of the VoIP signaling messages in order to assist service providers in detecting spam activity
targeting their customers. Lentzen et al. [5] proposed content-based detection
that uses a database of feature vectors, and new calls are compared with previous ones. Elizalde et al. [2] analyzed voice feature to filter spam voicemails.
A robust audio fingerprint of spectral feature vectors is computed for incoming audio data. On the other hand, Chaisamran et al. propose a trust-based
mechanism that uses the duration call and call direction between two users. The
trust value is adjustable according to the calling behavior. Furthermore, a trust
inference mechanism is also proposed in order to calculate a trust value for an
unknown caller to a listener.

Recent works focus on applying Machine learning (ML) models for spam
user classification. Specifically, Naive Bayes, K-Nearest Neighbors, SVM, Logistic
regression, and Random forest are well-known models, which are used to detect
email spam [4]. For instance, Li et al. [6] applied Random Forest, XGBoost,
RNN, and SVM with 29 features for mobile applications. These models bases
on behavior features of mobile numbers. It is effective to filter obvious cases, for
instance, robot calls. However, in the ambiguity cases that are mentioned above,
those aforementioned models are still difficult to classify ambiguity cases.

In this study, we propose a novel method that applies graph structure to
exploit the relationship between mobile users to detect spam users. In particular, regular users interact in some regular groups such as family, friends, companies, and customer services. On the other hand, abnormal users always have
weird relationships, which makes the calls become unacquainted numbers. In
this regard, representing the problem in graph structure is able to model the
telephony relationship effectively. Consequentially, Graph neural networks are
suitable to solve ambiguity cases. Accordingly, the Classification is based on
not only mobile number features but also their neighbors. Generally, the main
contribution of this study is two-fold as follows:

- We construct a telephony graph data set for spam call problems, which is
  able to exploit in more detail the relationship among users' relationship. To
  the best of our knowledge, this is the first study that represents telephony
  data as the graph structure for further exploitation.
- We present a classification model based on a graph neural network in order
  to improve the performance of spam user detection.

The rest of the paper is organized as follows: Sect. 2 presents the state-of-the-
art technique to filter spam calls in telephony networks. Section 3 describes the
data collection of telephone data and represents a telecommunication network
graph. Section 4 presents a GNN model for spam mobile user detection. Section 5
discusses the major results of the experiments. Finally, The conclusions and
future work are mentioned in Sect. 6.

2   Related Work

The problem definition and some basic approaches are introduced in [10]. Specifically, these works define some rules such as black/white lists, enforced caller introduction, and call rate limiting in order to deal with this problem. The work in [8] introduced a new method based on the analysis of the VoIP signaling messages which can assist service providers in detecting spam activity targeting their customers. The work in [5] proposed content-based detection that uses a database of feature vectors, and new calls are compared with previous ones. A robust audio fingerprint of spectral feature vectors is computed for incoming audio data. Elizalde et al. [2] proposed a new framework to analyze the voice feature to filter spam voicemails. On the other hand, Chaisamran et al. [1] propose a trust-based mechanism that uses the duration call and call direction between two users. The trust value is adjustable according to the calling behavior. Furthermore, a new trust inference mechanism is also presented in order to calculate a trust value for an unknown caller to a listener.

Recently, Machine learning (ML) models are applied to classify spam users. Accordingly, several well-known models such as Naive Bayes, K-Nearest Neighbors, SVM, Logistic regression, and Random forest are applied to detect email spam [4]. Specifically, the work in [6] uses ML models to Prevent Malicious Calls over Telephony Networks in which data is collected on mobile applications. Sequentially, The ML models (e.g., Random Forest, XGBoost, ANN, SVM) are evaluated with 29 features.

In this study, we present a novel method for spam call detection by applying a graph neural network (GNN). Specifically, we adopt Graph convolutional network (GCN), the most well-known GNN-based model [3] for learning our telephony network data, which is designed in a graph structure.

3   Graph Structure-Based Telephone Data Representation

3.1   Data Collection

In this section, we briefly about telephone network data flow and how we collect our dataset. This process is illustrated in Fig. 1.

Accordingly, we gather Call Detail Record (CDR) log from the Gateway Mobile Switching Center (GMSC) server. The log records consist of incoming calls, outgoing calls, transit calls, and SMS traffic. Initially, the CDR logs in the GMSC servers are passed through an Encryption Module that implements a symmetric-key algorithm - Data Encryption Standard (DES). The Encryption Module encrypts the mobile number in the CDR so that the data log is anonymous. Subsequently, our system stores CDR logs as raw data in the Big-Data module. We use a distributed file system (DFS) that is distributed on multiple servers to achieve high scalability and high performance.

Feature Engineer Module contains Extract-Transform-Load (ETL) batch jobs to synthesize features for each mobile number. Our research concentrated on the synthesis of two types of data tables, which are subscribers and relations,

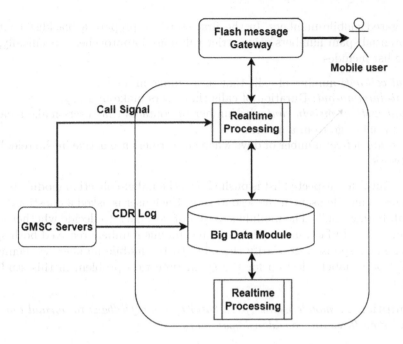

Fig. 1. Data collection flow

respectively. Specifically, *subscribers table* contains mobile numbers and their features. The users' features are sequentially described as follows:

– Ratio of average successful outgoing calls to incoming calls, the average number of outgoing calls per period (hour, day, year)
– Ratio of calls with short duration to the total number of calls.
– Ratio of the number of calls with a short time between calls (the time interval between two consecutive outgoing calls) to the total number of calls.
– Ratio of successful calls to total outgoing calls.
– Relation features are input to create a graph such as a ratio of calls to non-relational numbers (never called before) to total outgoing calls, rate of contact only call one time out of the total contact.

3.2   Collective Spam Labelling by End-Users

In this section, we describe the technique to label the data set into two classes, consisting of spam and regular user. End-users investigation is the feasible approach to label a call as spam. Our research processed three techniques, including flash messages, SMS messages, and customer-service calls. Overall, flash message techniques gave the best result. On average, 3% investigated users responded to the flash messages. While others are less than 1%. The reason is that end-users received flash messages as soon as terminated calls. It is comfortable for them to make the answers. Therefore, our research used flash messages to label the investigated mobile numbers. In the first step, we prepare a blacklist containing potential spam numbers using strict rule-based approaches. Specifically, the feature list includes:

- *total-call-out*: number of calls that users make in a day.
- *total-duration-out*: Duration of calls that users make in a day.
- *count-distinct-msisdn-contact*: Number of contacts that users make a call or send a message to in a month.
- *num-day-active*: number of days when subscribers are active in the telephony network.

Sequentially, the suspected list is pushed into the Label-collection module to send messages to mobile users in the second step. Each user is asked a question: "Does this call bother you?" The module is based on feedback to decide whether a call is spam or not. In fact, most of investigated mobile numbers received both spam and regular responses. To clarify the label to the mobile number, we define an assumption of label selection for the spam detection problem in this study as follows:

Assumption 1. *mobile users with a ratio of spam feedback to normal one that is more than three are considered spammers.*

3.3   Graph Construction

The main idea is that exploit the telephony graph in spam detection. For example, regular mobile numbers make a long-lasting relationship in their groups, and spam ones are not. Therefore, we aim to construct a telephony graph in which the nodes are mobile numbers, and the edges are the relationships between these numbers. In this regard, we formalize our telephony network graph $\mathcal{G} = (\mathcal{V}, \mathcal{E})$ as follows:

- $\mathcal{V}$ the vertex set consists of mobile-user nodes (subscriber data)
- $\mathcal{E}$ the edge set consists of the relation between mobile users. It is directed edges, from calling number to called number (relation data)
- Node features: user behavior and user profile
- Edge features: Call features between two numbers

To construct the graph, we implemented edges by random walk algorithm [7]. Starting with initial nodes that are spam mobile users located by the process in Sect. 3.2. Afterward, we inserted randomly nodes representing mobile numbers that received calls that have a duration of more than 0 s. The stop condition is that the inserted nodes reach a second in depth. Figure 2 visualize a telephony network as a graph structure.

4   Spam Call Detection Using GCN

In this section, we will discuss how we model the problem in terms of node prediction. Specifically, sub-sect. 4.1 discusses the problem definition of GNN

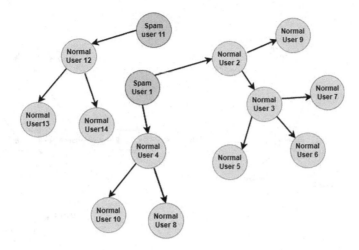

Fig. 2. A telephony network graph that is implemented by Random walk Algorithm

for spam call detection problems. The sub-sect. 4.3 describes the proposed GCN architecture to solve the problems, which is regarded as a node classification task.

4.1   Graph Neural Network for Spam Call Detection

Previous works used ML models for the classification such as SVM, Logistic regression, Random forest, XGBoost, and so on. The prediction of spam subscribers through subscriber features related to call and SMS message behavior. Specifically, those aforementioned ML models work well with a typical case like robot calls. However, the number of spam subscribers with similar behavior to normal subscribers is increasing, which takes the mobile network more complicated. For instance, sellers use the phone for the advertised goods and also use it for their daily life. Furthermore, there are legitimate subscribers with similar spam behavior such as shippers, and customer care subscribers. These subscribers also call many different customers. With the above cases, the classical classification models give low performances.

Alternatively, a new approach in this study is to model the relationship between subscribers in the graph structure. In particular, the classification of subscribers is not only based on its own features but also on the features of related subscribers. Consequentially, the spam call detection data can be represented as a graph structure (directed graph), and use the GNN-based model for the classification.

4.2   Node Embedding

Recently, there have been many studies on applying deep learning to graph data known as Graph Neural Networks (GNN). This section will introduce basic

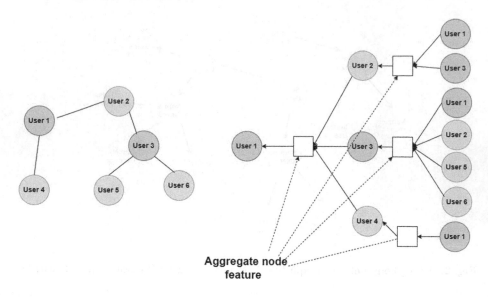

Fig. 3. Node Embedding in GCN

techniques suitable for spam detection problems. The Graph $\mathcal{G} = (\mathcal{V}, \mathcal{E})$ takes as input:

- A feature description x_i for every node i; summarized in a $\mathcal{N} \times \mathcal{D}$ feature matrix $\mathcal{X}$ ($\mathcal{N}$: number of nodes, $\mathcal{D}$: number of input features).
- A representative description of the graph structure in matrix form; typically in the form of an adjacency matrix $\mathcal{A}$.

For the node embedding, similarity in the embedding space approximates similarity in the graph. In this regard, produces a node-level output $\mathcal{Z}$ (a $\mathcal{N} \times \mathcal{F}$ feature matrix, where $\mathcal{F}$ is the number of output features per node). Graph-level outputs can be modeled by introducing some form of the pooling operation. A neural network layer can then be written as a non-linear function:

$$H^{(l+1)} = f(H^{(l)}, A) \tag{1}$$

$$f(H^{(l)}, A) = \sigma(AH^{(l)}W^{(l)}) \tag{2}$$

with $H^{(0)} = X$ and $H^{(L)} = Z$, L being the number of layers. Where $W^{(l)}$ is a weight matrix for the l-th neural network layer and σ is a non-linear activation function like the ReLU. Technically, the main idea is to generate node embedding based on local network neighborhoods. The Nodes aggregate information from their neighbors using neural networks. In this regard, the propagation process can be updated as follows [3]:

$$f(H^{(l)}, A) = \sigma(\hat{D}^{-\frac{1}{2}}\hat{A}\hat{D}^{-\frac{1}{2}}H^{(l)}W^{(l)}) \tag{3}$$

where $\hat{A} = A + I$, I represents the identity matrix, and $\hat{D}$ is the diagonal node degree matrix of $\hat{A}$. Network neighborhood defines a computation graph. Every node defines a computation graph based on its neighborhood as shown in Fig. 3.

4.3   Proposed Model

The proposed GNN model is shown in Fig. 4. Accordingly, the model contains two GCN layers and one dense layer

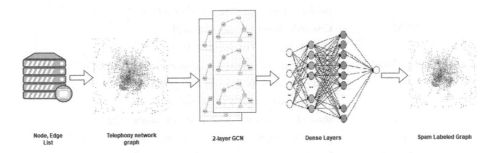

Fig. 4. The proposed GCN Architecture

The GCN model takes two inputs, the node features matrix and adjacency matrix, and gives the spam-labeled graph. Because the spam label node number is significantly smaller than the regular one, some techniques are applied to remove the imbalance of the data set, such as oversampling. Besides, the f1 score, precision, and recall are estimated to benchmark the classification GCN model.

5   Experiments and Results

5.1   Environment Settings

5.1.1   Base Model: We select Random forest, SVM, XGBoost, and ANN as the baseline models for the comparison, which follows the work in [6] for the Prevent Malicious Calls over Telephony Networks. Specifically, we applied the Sklearn library to build the Random forest, SVM, XGBoost, and ANN models. In particular, the hyperparameter configurations are shown in Table 1.

5.1.2   Hyperparameter Setting: We used the Pytorch library to implement the GCN model. The model includes two GCN layers and one dense layer. The number of epochs is set to 300. The hyperparameters of our model are shown in Table 2.

5.1.3   Dataset. The custom dataset includes 5.119 nodes(3.069 spam nodes and 2050 non-spam lab nodes) and 1.709 edges. A node contains 142 features and the edge contains 9 features, respectively. The training set contains 3.563 nodes(2.156 spam nodes and 1.407 non-spam nodes). The test set contains 1.556 nodes (913 spam nodes and 643 non-spam nodes).

Table 1. Based Model Hyper Parameter

Model	Hyper Parameter
Random forest	$test\_size\_equal$:0.3, $random\_state\_equal$:42
	max_depth:10.25, $min\_samples\_leaf$:9
	$min\_samples\_split$:6, $random\_state$:42
SVM	C:0.985, degree:3, gama:0.549
	kernel: linear, $random\_state$:42
XGBoost	$colsample\_bylevel$:0.45, $colsample\_bytree$:0.45
	$learning\_rate$:0.275, max_depth:5
	$random\_state$:42, sub_sample:0.6
	min_child_weight:0.12, $n\_estimators$:320
ANN	$drop\_out$: 0.36, $ann\_activation$: tanh
	Lr: 0.02, momentum: 0.86, optim: adam

Table 2. The hyperparameters of the proposed GCN model.

Hyper parameter	Value
$drop\_out$	0.36
$gnn\_activation$	tanh
gnn_hidden_dim	120
Lr	0.02
momentum	0.86
optim	adam
gcn_layer_number	2

Table 3. Model result

model	Accuracy	F1 score	Precision	Recall
Random Forest	0.9678	0.961	0.972	0.948
SVM	0.971	0.964	0.97	0.958
XGBoost	0.968	0.961	0.973	0.95
ANN	0.969	0.962	0.974	0.95
GNN	0.978	0.973	0.972	0.975

5.2   Main Results

Table 3 shows the results of the GNN model with baseline models on the test set.

The metrics are accuracy, f1 score, precision, and recall. As the result, the GCN model gives the highest Accuracy, f1 score, and recall. In particular, GCN f1 score achieves 0.973. Meanwhile, the highest baseline model f1 score is 0.964

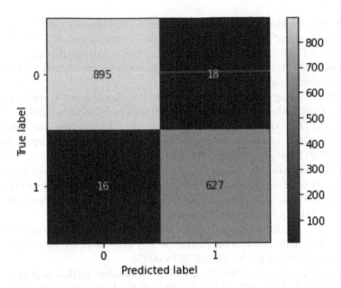

Fig. 5. GNN Confusion matrix

with SVM. The GCN accuracy and recall are 0.978 and 0.975, respectively. The GCN precision which is 0.972 is quite lower than other models. However, it is acceptable to filter positive labels. The confusion matrices of the proposed model are shown in Fig. 5.

6 Conclusions and Future Work

This paper proposes a new approach to the spam call detection problem using a graph convolutional network. Our contribution is two-fold. Firstly, we propose an efficient and cost-effective approach to building a large, labeled spam detection graph by leveraging end-user collaboration. Secondly, we propose to use a 2-layers Graph convolution neural network (GCN) as a classification model. Extensive experiments show that our framework can achieve a 0.973 f1 score, which is better than a robust baseline model. Regarding the future work of this study, we try to perform extensive experiments on a larger network graph. We also plan to experiment with multiple edge types with edge features better to model the complexity of relationships in the telephony network.

References

1. Chaisamran, N., Okuda, T., Blanc, G., Yamaguchi, S.: Trust-based voip spam detection based on call duration and human relationships. In: 2011 IEEE/IPSJ International Symposium on Applications and the Internet, pp. 451–456 (2011). https://doi.org/10.1109/SAINT.2011.84

2. Elizalde, B., Emmanouilidou, D.: Detection of robocall and spam calls using acoustic features of incoming voicemails. In: Proceedings of Meetings on Acoustics, p. 060004. ASA, POMA (2021), https://www.microsoft.com/en-us/research/publication/detection-of-robocall-and-spam-calls-using-acoustic-features-of-incoming-voicemails/

3. Kipf, T.N., Welling, M.: Semi-supervised classification with graph convolutional networks. CoRR abs/1609.02907 (2016). arxiv.org/abs/1609.02907

4. Kontsewaya, Y., Antonov, E., Artamonov, A.: Evaluating the effectiveness of machine learning methods for spam detection. Procedia Comput. Sci. **190**(C), 479–486 (2021). https://doi.org/10.1016/j.procs.2021.06.056

5. Lentzen, D., Grutzek, G., Knospe, H., Porschmann, C.: Content-based detection and prevention of spam over IP telephony - system design, prototype and first results. In: 2011 IEEE International Conference on Communications (ICC), pp. 1–5 (2011). https://doi.org/10.1109/icc.2011.5963108

6. Li, H., et al: A machine learning approach to prevent malicious calls over telephony networks. In: 2018 IEEE Symposium on Security and Privacy (SP), pp. 53–69 (2018). https://doi.org/10.1109/SP.2018.00034

7. Li, R., Yu, J.X., Qin, L., Mao, R., Jin, T.: On random walk based graph sampling. In: Gehrke, J., Lehner, W., Shim, K., Cha, S.K., Lohman, G.M. (eds.) 31st IEEE International Conference on Data Engineering, ICDE 2015, Seoul, South Korea, 13–17 April 2015, pp. 927–938. IEEE Computer Society (2015). https://doi.org/10.1109/ICDE.2015.7113345

8. MacIntosh, R., Vinokurov, D.: Detection and mitigation of spam in IP telephony networks using signaling protocol analysis. In: IEEE/Sarnoff Symposium on Advances in Wired and Wireless Communication, 2005, pp. 49–52 (2005). https://doi.org/10.1109/SARNOF.2005.1426509

9. Peterson, J., Jennings, C.: Enhancements for Authenticated Identity Management in the Session Initiation Protocol (SIP). RFC 4474 (2006). https://doi.org/10.17487/RFC4474, www.rfc-editor.org/info/rfc4474

10. Rosenberg, J.D., Jennings, C.: The session initiation protocol (SIP) and spam. RFC 5039, pp. 1–28 (2008). https://doi.org/10.17487/RFC5039

The Completion of a Smart Factory Research Project by Concluding a DAO

Dariusz Szostek[1,2,3,4] and Rafał Tomasz Prabucki[1,2(✉)]

[1] University of Silesia in Katowice, 40-007 Katowice, Poland
`dariusz.szostek@us.edu.pl`
[2] Multi-Agent Systems for Pervasive Artificial Intelligence for assisting Humans in Modular Production, Athens, Greece
`info@mas4ai.eu`
`https://www.mas4ai.eu/about/`
[3] University of Opole, 45-040 Opole, Poland
[4] Smart Human Oriented Platform for Connected Factories, München, Germany
`https://shop4cf.eu/`

Abstract. Managing smart factory science projects from the legal side generates challenges of a regulatory nature. The grant agreement may stipulate that the consortium of stakeholders will need to continue after the end of the project, but in such a way that it is possible to make decisions and benefit from the projec's results. Choosing a specific option implies that the consortium will have an entity. This raises considerable complications, as it requires consultation with the legal departments of the consortium partners and the construction of numerous links between the partners, mainly if the jointly developed solution consists of components produced by a different partner each time. The paper, therefore, put a creative solution - why not leave the nature of the social movement to the scientific project, and write the relationships between stakeholders and decision-making into the programming code? To answer this question, we present the state of the law related to DAOs and review the literature on whether the direction to apply this type of solution in smart factories is appropriate.

Keywords: smart factory · DAO · Blockchain · law as a code · legal entity · smart contracts

1 Introduction

1.1 Preliminary Issues

Decentralized autonomous organizations, that is, as the report of the World Economic Forum points out: "organizational structures that use blockchains, digital assets, and related technologies to allocate resources, to coordinate activities, and to make decisions" and are a solution from the sphere of blockchain-based innovations that gain users and become well-capitalized [15]. Decision-making is

N. T. Nguyen et al. (Eds.): ACIIDS 2023, CCIS 1863, pp. 117–128, 2023.
https://doi.org/10.1007/978-3-031-42430-4_10

one of the most vital issues of a DAO. As empirical evidence provided by science researchers studying matter, decision-makers in DAOs can make more rational, efficient, and effective decisions using a decision model to meet their requirements and priorities [1]. The ability to coordinate activity and allocate resources is the result of forming legal relationships between DAO participants (that is, the participants in the given DAO hold certain rights and obligations) [23]. The innovation of this solution stems from the use of blockchain technology, more precisely, the management of the originally digital organization through smart contracts stored on a public register (blockchain) [18]. As a machine will perform the recording, we will not deal with natural language in this solution. Therefore, legal relationships between participants will be expressed in an artificial language, not a natural one [25]. This issue has been identified as a significant deficiency in DAO research and is related to the problem of code as law or law as code, which will be explained further [8, 10].

The contribution of this work is based on two main aspects. The first one regards filling the research gap concerning the cybertext that characterizes DAOs. The second aspect relates to the issue of analyzing whether the specific nature of a DAO can be equated with an organization with no legal entity.

One of the ways to frame the DAO is to view this organization from the perspective of historical processes which, since Roman times, have developed different ways of managing economic and social interactions in order to run specific business ventures, as a particular partnership of profit-seeking actors [25]. However, the DAO, in its operating model, does not have to be similar to corporate governance, which, within the framework of known practices, we have developed over the years. An essential element of a DAO is decentralization. It makes it possible to create organizational governance solutions in a way that takes place in the governance structures of a state rather than a company, i.e., replicating democracy. This practice intends to achieve specific goals that are impossible in a non-blockchain environment with an implemented virtual machine, e.g., Ethereum [6]. The operation of DAOs based on the blockchain allows for new opportunities due to mechanisms that can create a new suitable environment for operations, such as those offered by individual legal systems due to freedom of business and contract [4, 14, 21].

DAOs are a new phenomenon. In the process of analyzing smart contracts created under innovative financial solutions in DeFi, like BendDAO, they are discussed in cases the business model fails [7]. They are also considered when analyzing the nature of code-expressed legal relationships between its participants, such as TheDAO and the programming error that allowed the funds raised by participants to be taken out [22]. This approach is correct - it was initially a digital organization. Therefore, as has been pointed out, it misses DAOs most important value, which is establishing by code the coordination of activities and allocating resources.

1.2 Research Methodology

The starting point for the analysis is a thought experiment. Researchers wishing to test the hypothesis:"The DAO can be a tool to manage the solutions developed in a certain scientific project, replacing contractual provisions with code." To this end, the researchers construct an imaginary situation - a thought experiment.

Proposition 1. *In a smart factory research project which is coming to an end, the consortium members cannot agree on a formula for operation after the grant agreement has ended. Therefore, this aspect cannot be overlooked. Obviously, it should be indicated under which formula. However, the project participants do not want to gain subjectivity or make any changes to the intellectual property. The main aim is to secure a way of voting on the activities, the project logo, and the participants' connection.*

This experiment is designed to stimulate the fundamental question for the lawyer about the search for a creative solution to a problem. An innovative approach will be taken into account using the idea of using DAOs together with the presentation of limitations, and the chosen direction will take the form of case-based [5]. Introducing the experimental function will be possible to be made with the support of contextual knowledge. It one will be constructed based on the classical methods used in legal sciences, namely the review of international sources. The authors used various search engines to obtain quite a few different results for DAO-related keywords.

2 Code vs. Law and the DAO

2.1 Cybertext Forming the DAO

The vast discrepancy in the pace of research on the representation of law as code and the emergence of blockchain technology and smart contracts resulted in more rapid developments in the form of page records in code and the development of the cryptolaw concept on private grounds. In this way, a trend has developed in which crypto-based systems are underpinning certain rules [24]. Since the first attempts, which were described in the UK in 1986, to turn the law into a logic programme, globally, little has changed in terms of legislation in this area [19]. It was only in a report to the New Zealand government that it was stated that law as code was the future [3]. It is important to note that there is a difference between the concept of code as law (code produces legal effects) and law as code; the law is defined as code. Blockchain technology makes it possible to transform law into code progressively [8]. As such, it is also often identified as a place of where artificial intelligence systems could be technologically controlled [20].

Regardless of legislators' actions, the open blockchain Ethereum has developed the languages that allow smart contracts to be written [11]. There are alternatives, such as The R3 - a consortium of 70 global financial institutions. They have a conceptual framework, Corda, for smart contracts in finance. We assume, however, that the permissionless blockchain consortium will be of interest for transparency, as the clout of the activity is also to achieve far-reaching clarity in the project [4,11,17,21].

A particular artificial language is chosen to be used as the DAO works in reliance on smart contracts (generally). For example, in Ethereum it is Solidity. Smart contracts are also possible in a concept such as Hyperledger. However, it is not an "open blockchain" solution. Ethereum is an open blockchain that uses Solidity, offers a virtual machine, and everyone can participate (which has its advantages and disadvantages). The smart contracts written on it that will enable the DAO to start operating are essential for the project. Ethereum will allow us to create an algorithm to operate tokens. The relationships between the parties to the organization registered in this way will be understandable to the machine. Writing up the rules in Solidity will provide us with all the benefits of automating the governing tokens (voting process), but it also has disadvantages. The resulting smart contracts are difficult to verify and challenging for non-programmers to understand. Furthermore, they need to be able to operate with abstract, ambiguous concepts. There is limited room for flexibility if one relies solely on programming code in the organization's operation [11,17,24].

Generally, smart contracts that make up a DAO are permissible in commercial dealings. There are no significant objections as long as the civil code of a specific country does not narrow down the question regarding the contract that the parties may enter into for some reason. The situation may become more complicated in the event of a dispute. Doubts may arise about the approach of the judge who, not understanding the content, may consider the smart contract to be a contract written in a foreign language and in this situation he can call in an expert, or in extreme cases he may consider that the contract should be concluded anyway. Since there is no objection for an agreement being a computer program, a contract written in a blockchain should not be negated either. Also, it is always possible to conclude a traditional contract by indicating elements written in code. This would also align with the concept of "law as code" [11].

2.2 The Problem with Naming Something "DAO"

Decentralization. As the introduction indicates, DAO is a problematic and complex term to define. Although the term itself is an acronym for the characteristics that this model of organization should have. Unfolding this compound term makes obtaining terminology relevant to the discussion possible. The first essential is 'decentralization.' From a legal perspective, as the UK Law Commission documents rightly point out, what this name refers to must be clarified. Indeed, it should be recognized that it is a non-sharp name, which, even in computer science, is indicated on two grounds - decentralization as software and network. In blockchain-related works, decentralization can have several meanings, even when limited to software (see Fig. 1). Thus, it is difficult to expect that 'decentralization' only indicates that it is an organization constructed based on smart contracts that run on the blockchain. Furthermore, decentralization in software terms can be graded. The existence of decentralization determines centralization, i.e., a single entity's assumption of authority over the system. In Blockchain-related works, it is noted that one must speak of complete decentralization or centralization. The e-mail service is cited as an example. Despite its technically decentralized nature, it is not seen in this way. Indeed, the market for this form of communication offers centralized solutions, an example of portals adapted to handle e-mails in the browser [12,16].

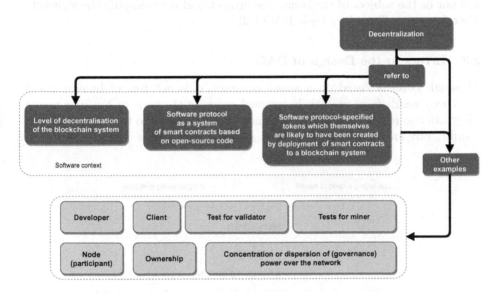

Fig. 1. Problems with the term "decentralization".

Autonomous. Another element is the word 'autonomous.' The time needs to be more problematic to suggest something more than only the automation of transactions. Generally speaking, human involvement still decides whether a transaction should or should not occur. Even with so-called 'oracles,' human in' element is still crucial. As human-machine interaction occurs in smart contracts (a virtual machine that executes programming code), there are signs that the future lies in combining the idea of DAOs with AI systems and that DAOs themselves may be their specific operating framework, in situations when human supervision additionally occurs. [11,12,17].

Organization. The final term to be considered is 'organization'. However, having pointed out the above doubts, one has to agree with the UK Law Commission that an organization operating as a DAO should not imply anything specific fair treatment. As indicated in the documents [12]:

The term DAO does not necessarily connote any particular type of organisational structure and therefore cannot on its own imply any particular legal treatment.

Therefore, the biggest challenge in terms of DAOs is to construct a suitable operating algorithm. It is he who will define the mechanism of operation. The nature of the organization determines its classification. The analogy is with a Sub-DAO, i.e., a DAO operating within a broader DAO structure. However, they will not be the subject of the issue. The project goal is to simplify the structure. Therefore, we will analyze basic DAO [12].

2.3   Errors in the Design of DAOs

Although DAO is based on a smart contract, it is not free of human errors. They may result from previously signaled errors in the code or business model. They can also result from hastily designed policies related to token issuance that insufficiently anticipated human factor issues in governance (see Fig. 2).

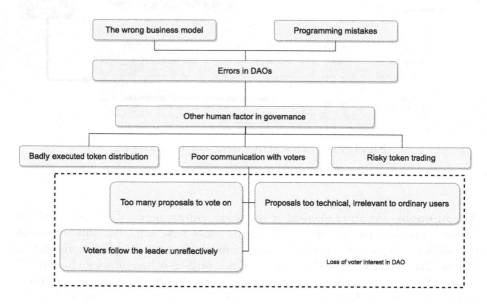

Fig. 2. Risks arising from human factor errors

The issue of token classification is a significant problem. It is important to stress that the essence of the innovation of an idea is not the token per se but the appropriate way to manage the organization using the token. Once again, therefore, the code that governs how the token is used is essential. Decision-making above the programmatically defined processes is generally effected through voting by tokens associated with or specified by the software protocol [12,15,17].

3 DAO for the Project and Legal Issue

3.1 Tokens

Based on the analyses carried out above, one would have to refer specifically to the issue of the project itself, i.e., a relatively simple, uncomplicated DAO formula. In order for this to be in accordance with the premise of 'law as code', all elements would have to be written into a contract beforehand. The issuing of tokens itself would, due to the number of partners and their assignment to the project through a prior grant agreement, have to be limited. The regulations defining tokens within cryptoassets are still being drafted. It must be assumed that, as this issue would have to be analysed after the entry into force of the regulation of the European Parliament and the Council on Markets in Cryptoassets, and amending Directive (EU) 2019/1937. The actual definition of cryptoassets in proposal is very broad:

> A token, generally a crypto-token, that has a unique identification number (or mechanism).

However, there are no specific regimes for NFT tokens. According to UK Law Commission documents, NFTs are [13]:

> A token, generally a crypto-token, that has a unique identification number (or mechanism).

As such, and with the specifics of the project, NFT tokens seem ideal for the chosen organization as well as the establishment of the voting mechanics (see Fig. 3).

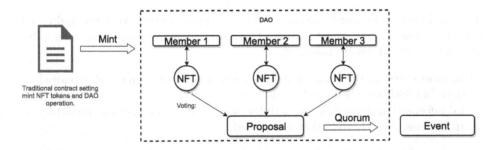

Fig. 3. Use of NFT tokens for DAO voting for a 3 members example.

The move away from one token, one vote paradigm towards one person, one vote model is relatively innovative. NFT-based voting can reduce the risk of plutocracy, which is typical of token-weighted voting. Another element to be established in the code is the quorum. In this case, we have to remember that we aim for a 'law as a code' model. When deciding on a DAO, which will be preceded by a contract that we classify as a kind of 'entityless' organization, we need to ensure that, in a given system, even such a form does not have any specific indications [12, 15].

3.2   Entityless

An unincorporated association will be formed when a group agrees to work for a common purpose other than business. Suppose the principles are accepted by these persons (the founding members), or there is an implicit but sufficiently explicit, clear agreement between them. In that case, there will be a contract creating an unincorporated association. In some jurisdictions, this is optional to be reported.

In our experiment, we suggest entering into a traditional contract. This could therefore be a contract that would establish a possible organization in a given system without legal personality. It would also make it possible to enjoy certain benefits associated with registration. Additionally, it will eliminate doubts about the motivation for setting up the DAO. It is worth noticing that there could some benefits for participants because as the UK Law Commission points out, where participants are not motivated by a profit motive or where the profit motive is secondary to the other purpose of participating in the DAO, the possibility of inferring a memorandum of the partnership will be low and they may instead be an unincorporated association, which seems to be a universal conclusion [12,15, 17]:

> (. . .) where participants do not have a profit motive or if a profit motive is subsidiary to some other purpose for participating in the DAO, the possibility of inferring a partnership agreement will be small, but they might instead be an unincorporated association.

3.3   Security of the Manufacturing Sector

The final issue to be taken into account is the project area. As it was indicated earlier, it concerns the smart factory. The smart manufacturing process is quite specific. As the literature notes [2]:

> In most cases, in the smart industry, we will not be dealing with personal data but with so-called machine data, which should be understood as digital information created by the activity of computers, IT systems, including those based on AI, and other networked devices.

Therefore, this is the ideal place for using more complex DAOs than those identified by the authors. It should be underlined, however, that only further development of DAOs, and tokens that operate by MiCA, can broaden the prospects for complex DAOs. The result of tokens in such a way that they can also be used, for example, in the Machine Economy or data monetization in the industrial area could accelerate the implementation of DAOs in this field. For now, however, the crypto-asset market is developing DAOs alone, which needs more certainty for such solutions [2,9,17,25].

What is an advantage in the case of the smart factory, unfortunately, is a disadvantage in the implementation of DAOs. The factory, as a collection of data and machines, is the ideal place for this new solution. However, it should be emphasized that the data in the factory is sometimes crucial from the point of view of business security and even EU cyber security. The best example is the Network and Information Security (NIS) Directive. It also covers some manufacturing industries.

This is therefore not an area where it would be possible to offer solutions that are not certain or that have not evolved enough to eliminate uncertainties in their use.

3.4   DLT in Smart Factory

Finally, it is important to note that factories - especially in Industry 4.0 model - are using DLTs. These are mainly data quality issues [26]. There are also case studies of more extensive implementations, such as the use of cryptoassets in the factory in terms of paying for electricity billing for using machines [27]. This also allows economists to sketch out future visions of how modern industry will evolve and DLT will be part of other developments in smart factories, such as AI implementations [28].

4   Conclusions and Guidelines for Further Research

The most critical problem in the indicated experiment is that legislators stimulated by similar situations in the crypto-asset market are only creating the legal

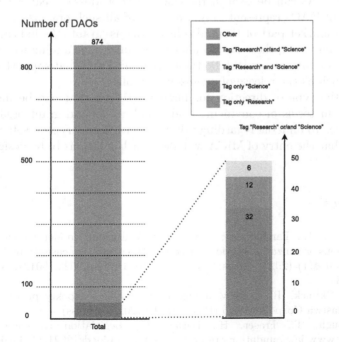

Fig. 4. Proportion of DAOs that are labelled "science" or "research"

framework for specific tools and solutions possible in this market. Therefore, the chosen model was intended to be simple in structure and preparation. However, there are possibilities to make it even more developed. As indicated, DAO will be more valuable for this type of initiative when the market is more developed and the DAO fits into a particular legal framework.

However, the application of the DAO could be applied to a smaller, less formal consortium, such as researchers aiming to write a monograph and wishing to popularise the conclusions contained in the monograph, e.g., by organizing a conference. For this purpose it would also essential to obtain a grant, set up a DAO, and allow the authors to act as a club-like consortium, where decisions will be made about, for example, adopting a monograph cover design, deciding whether to publish the monograph in an open-access format or whether to issue an NFT token for printed copies to certify the originality of the author's manuscripts. Such a DAO action is also an opportunity to gain experience (empire); empire translates into conclusions related to how to run this type of organization and into conclusions regarding the risks of making provisions between the parties through code. Let us assume that the trends, both technological and legal, will bring the expected results. All this can result in the establishment of a cadre of highly experienced practitioners who can set the standardization background for future scientific projects in this format. Most importantly, each activity of such a consortium is also an opportunity to gain experience for the members themselves.

A quick check also verifies whether and which DAOs related to 'research' or 'science' exist. As can be seen in the chart after a Messari search (see Fig. 4), these types of DAOs represent only 6 percent of all such organizations. On the cryptoassets market part of them also has a tag as 'grant'. As indicated by the UK Law Commission, these are peculiar to organizations aiming to give instant funds to community causes [12]. So these are grant DAO that support non-profit initiatives such as the release of open-source tools.

This is the type of direction for further research that can be measurable, albeit risky, in terms of convincing traditional actors and grant organizations, when it comes to an issue regarding other aspects of the cryptoassets market. It is possible that the entry of MiCA will allow such solutions to be designed more confidently.

References

1. Baninemeh, E., Farshidi, S., Jansen, S.: A decision model for decentralized autonomous organization platform selection: three industry case studies. Res. Appl. Blockchain **4**(1) (2023). https://doi.org/10.1016/j.bcra.2023.100127. Accessed 12 Feb 2023
2. Bar, G., Skibicki, R.: Dane w inteligentnej fabryce - aspekty prawne: Przegląd Ustawodastwa Gospodarczego (Bus. Law J.) (2023, inpress)
3. Barraclough, T., Fraser, H., Barnes, C.: Legislation as code for New Zealand. www.lawfoundation.org.nz/wp-content/uploads/2021/03/Legislation-as-Code-9-March-2021-for-distribution.pdf. Accessed 12 Feb 2023

4. Barrera, C., Hurder, S.: Cryptoeconomics: designing effective incentives and governance models for blockchain networks using insights from economics. In: Lacity, C.M., Treiblmaier, H., (eds.) Blockchains and the Token Economy. Theory and Practice, 1st edn. Palgrave Macmillan, Cham, Switzerland (2022)
5. Brożek, B.: Two Faces of Legal Reasoning: Rule-Based and Case-Based. https://www.tinyurl.com/57ppxv4y. Accessed 12 Feb 2023
6. Butterin, V.: DAOs are not corporations: Where decentralization in autonomous organizations matters. https://vitalik.ca/general/2022/09/20/daos.html. Accessed 12 Feb 2023
7. Chan, T., Low, K.F.K.: DeFi common sense: crypto-backed lending in Janesh s/o Rajkumar v unknown person ("CHEFPIERRE"). Mod. Law Rev. (2023, inpress)
8. De Filippi, P., Hassan, S.: Blockchain Technology as a Regulatory Technology From Code is Law to Law is Code arxiv.org/ftp/arxiv/papers/1801/1801.02507.pdf. Accessed 12 Feb 2023
9. Dhillon, V., Metcalf, D., Hooper, M.: Blockchain Enabled Applications: Understand the Blockchain Ecosystem and How to Make it Work for You, 1st edn. Apress, New York, USA (2017)
10. Ilyushina, N., MacDonald, T.: Decentralized aoutonomus organisations: a new research agenda for labour economics. J. Br. Blockchain Assoc. 5(1) (2022)
11. Kubiak-Cyrul, A., Potiopa, P.: Smart contract: perspektywy automatyzacji umów. In: Cyrul W., Kubiak-Cyrul A. (eds.): Od kodeksu do cybertekstu prawa, in press (2023)
12. Law Commision: Decentralised autonomous organisations (DAOs). Call for evidence. s3-eu-west-2.amazonaws.com/lawcom-prod-storage-11jsxou24uy7q/uploads/2022/11/DAOs-Call-for-Evidence-LC.pdf. Accessed 12 Feb 2023
13. Law Commision: Digital Assets: Consultation paper. s3-eu-west-2.amazonaws.com/lawcom-prod-storage-11jsxou24uy7q/uploads/2022/07/Digital-Assets-Consultation-Paper-Law-Commission-1.pdf. Accessed 12 Feb 2023
14. Lin, M., Kreutler, K., Macmillan, A.: Composable Expansion Packs for Decentralized Organizations. https://law.mit.edu/pub/composableexpansionpacks/release/1. Accessed 12 Feb 2023
15. Llyr, B., Slavin, A., Werbach, K.: Decentralized Autonomous Organization Toolkit. www.weforum.org/reports/decentralized-autonomous-organization-toolkit/. Accessed 12 Feb 2023
16. Narayanan, A., Bonneau, J., Felten, E., Miller, A., Goldfeder, S.: Bitcoin and Cryptocurrency Technologies. Princeton University Press, Princeton, USA (2016)
17. Mienert, B.: Dezentrale autonome Organisationen (DAOs) und Gesellschaftrecht, 1st edn. Mohr Siebeck, Tübingen, Germany (2022)
18. Santana, C., Albareda, L.: Blockchain and the emergence of decentralized autonomous organizations (DAOs): an integrative model and research agenda. Technol. Forecast. Soc. Change 182, 121806 (2022). https://doi.org/10.1016/j.techfore.2022.121806
19. Sergot, M.J., Sadri, F., Kowalski, R.A., Kriwaczek, F., Hammond, P., Cory, H.T.: The British Nationality Act as a logic program. https://dl.acm.org/doi/abs/10.1145/5689.5920. Accessed 12 Feb 2023
20. Sulkowski, A.: Industry 4.0 era technology (AI, BIG DATA, BLOCKCHAIN, DAO): why the law needs new memes. Kansas J. Law Public Policy, XXIX, 1 (2019)
21. Werbach, K.: The Blockchain and the New Architecture of Trust, 1st edn. MIT Press, Cambridge, USA (2018)

22. Werbach, K.: The siren song: algorithmic governance by blockchain. In: Werbach K. (ed.), After the Digital Tornado, 1st edn. Cambridge University Press, Cambridge, USA (2020). https://doi.org/10.1017/9781108610018
23. Wojdyło, K.: What is DAO from the legal perspective? In: Blockchian, smart contracts and DAO. http://wyoleg.gov/InterimCommittee/2019/S3-20190506DAOLegalPerspectives.pdf. Accessed 12 Feb 2023
24. Wood, G.: Ethereum: a secure decentralized generalized transaction ledger. EIP-150 revision. http://gavwood.com/paper.pdf. Accessed 12 Feb 2023
25. Wright, A.: The Rise of Decentralized Autonomous Organizations: Opportunities and Challenges. https://stanford-jblp.pubpub.org/pub/rise-of-daos/release/1. Accessed 12 Feb 2023
26. Isaja, M., et al.: A blockchain-based framework for trusted quality data sharing towards zero-defect manufacturing. Comput. Ind. **146**, 103853 (2023)
27. Roeck, D., Schöneseiffen, F., Greger, M., Hofmann, E.: Analyzing the potential of DLT-based applications in smart factories. In: Treiblmaier, H., Clohessy, T. (eds.) Blockchain and Distributed Ledger Technology Use Cases. PI, pp. 245–266. Springer, Cham (2020). https://doi.org/10.1007/978-3-030-44337-5_12
28. Sandner, P., Gross, J., Richter, R.: Convergence of Blockchain, IoT, and AI. Front. Blockchain **3**, 103853 (2020). https://doi.org/10.3389/fbloc.2020.522600

An Approach for Tamper-Proof QR Code Using Deep Learning Based-Data Hiding

Cu Vinh Loc[1(✉)], Tran Cao De[1], Jean-Christophe Burie[2],
and Jean-Marc Ogier[2]

[1] Can Tho University, Can Tho, Vietnam
{cvloc,tcde}@ctu.edu.vn
[2] La Rochelle University, La Rochelle, France
{jean-christophe.burie,jean-marc.ogier}@univ-lr.fr

Abstract. An application that significantly improves the traceability of the manufacturing sector and agriculture is the two-dimensional barcode (QR code). The QR code, however, is simple to copy and fake. Therefore, we suggest a novel strategy to prevent tampering with this code. The method entails two stages: concealing a security element in the QR code, and assessing how closely the QR code on the goods resembles genuine ones. For the first problem, error-correcting coding is used to encode and decode the secret feature in order to manage faults in noisy communication channels. A deep neural network is used to both conceal and decode the encoded data in the QR code. The suggested network has the ability to be resilient to actual distortions brought on by the printing and photographing processes. For the latter problem, we measure the similarity of QR codes using the Siamese network design. To assess if a QR code is real or false, the extracted secret feature and the outcome of the QR code similarity estimation are merged. With an average accuracy of 98%, the suggested method performs well and may be used to validate QR codes in practical applications.

Keywords: QR Code · Anti-forgery QR code · Data hiding · Watermarked QR code · QR code similarity

1 Introduction

The number of fake goods is increasing. Businesses in Vietnam and all across the world are having a lot of trouble with this. They impair customers' health in addition to doing significant economic damage. Products including pharmaceuticals, food, cosmetics, electronic components, etc. are frequently counterfeited. As a result, consumers have less faith in the commodity market's transparency, and firms' reputations suffer. For instance, the Market Management Department in Hanoi recently worked with regional functional organizations to destroy more than ten tons of illegally obtained commodities.

© The Author(s), under exclusive license to Springer Nature Switzerland AG 2023
N. T. Nguyen et al. (Eds.): ACIIDS 2023, CCIS 1863, pp. 129–141, 2023.
https://doi.org/10.1007/978-3-031-42430-4_11

The market for fake and counterfeit goods has continuously grown on the current market since March 2019, according to statistics provided by the Organization for Economic Cooperation and Development. Presently, counterfeit goods make up 3.3% of global trade. In 2018, counterfeit products cost the world economy $323 billion. According to the most recent estimates from the World Customs Organization, damage from counterfeit goods can reach $650 billion annually. When it comes to health-related products, counterfeit goods have unknown effects for customers in addition to having a negative impact on the company's brand and income. Therefore, businesses must use anti-counterfeiting solutions, particularly the use of widely available technologies like printing QR Codes [8,14,16], radio-frequency identification (RFID) [11,12], and anti-counterfeiting stamps (holograms) [1] on packaging to create a solution for anti-counterfeiting, all-encompassing security, and product traceability.

Today, these technologies are frequently applied to stop counterfeiting. The aforementioned methods have many benefits, but they also present certain challenges for consumers. For instance, organizations that want to utilize fake-proof stamps must go through numerous steps and wait a long time to obtain them. Despite falling costs, RFID technologies are still more expensive than alternative solutions. We must pay a charge to set up and utilize RFID, and we require specialist equipment to read data from the RFID card. QR codes are the alternative. This code is easy to use, and it may be obtained simply utilizing the built-in camera on a mobile device.

We provide a novel approach that makes the QR code challenging to copy or fake in order to address the shortcomings of existing techniques. In the event that the QR code is thought to be duplicated or forged, the user will have a method to verify its authenticity. There are two steps in the authentication process: From the QR code that is printed on the product, (i) the invisible hidden security feature is retrieved, and (ii) the resemblance of the obtained QR code to the real ones is assessed. To assess if the received QR code is authentic or false, these two features are merged. Additionally, as far as we are aware, the recommended approach has not been discovered in cutting-edge studies.

Anti-spoofing techniques are currently being presented in large numbers. However, these alternatives either cause users pain (for instance, NFC technology requires a specialized reader) or are simple for criminals to copy, like QR codes.

The paper is set up as follows. The next section reviews the previously published works. The proposed technique is described in Sect. 3. The experimental findings are highlighted in Sect. 4. In the section titled 5, the conclusion and potential changes are covered.

2   Related Work

The architecture of an anti-counterfeiting system for traceability using QR code has been proposed by Xie and Tan [16] in which the authors consider the problem of counterfeit detection for a product as the problem of copy detection for

QR code. The method of estimating the actual location of QR patterns in the obtained image of QR code has been improved to assess the performance of copy detection. Another approach using blockchain technology is depicted in the work [18]. The network of decentralized blockchain, smart contract, and distributed file storage system are utilized to develop the an anti-counterfeiting system for product verification. Tra and Hong [11] proposed an approach based upon RFID technique. This method consists of two protocols including tag authentication and database correction. The authors claim that their approach is secure against counterfeiting, and it is light enough to be implemented in the real-world applications. Another hologram-based anti-counterfeiting system [6] protects products against counterfeiting by combining detection with authentication. The anti-counterfeiting system based on Near-Field Communications (NFC) has been proposed by Yiu [17]. This approach is capable of keeping track the product origin and authenticity. The stored information to combat counterfeiting includes product genealogy, supply chain integrity, and transaction records.

The QR code is also applied in anti-counterfeiting, and this was found in several recent studies. Krishna and Dugar [8] make use of QR code to develop a system for product authentication. To enhance the security of the application, the information stored in the QR code is encrypted, and the encrypted data is verified at the server side. Wan *et al.* [14] proposed an approach in which the visual secret sharing and QR code are combined to enhance the security of QR code. The main idea of this method is to embed the secret data into the QR code. The decoding secret information is then used to determine whether the QR is genuine or not.

3   Proposed Method

Figure 1 shows the overall procedure of our method. The system consists of four basic operations: generating the QR code, encrypting it with a security feature, extracting the secret data from the watermarked QR code, and determining how closely the scanned watermarked QR code resembles the real ones.

3.1   QR Code Generation

The QR code is made up of black sample squares and dots on a white backdrop, and it can hold data like a URL, an event's time and location, a description, or a suggestion for a certain product. The benefit of this method is that it enables consumers to scan and read codes more quickly using tools like barcode readers or their phone's camera with applications for doing so. On the products we use, we might frequently see this code. Companies frequently include a QR code on their products so that consumers may scan it and obtain details about the item, including its type, composition, and related categories. Additionally, a very handy approach to make online payments is through the use of the QR code. The built-in library is used by us to create the QR code. The URL to access the credentials page is contained in the created code. This page contains the official

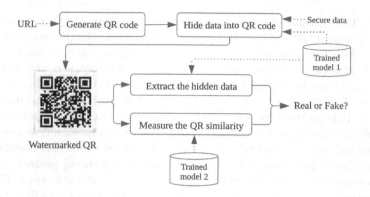

Fig. 1. The overall process of our approach in which the solid line is the main flow, and the dash line indicates input or reference data.

data used to track the product's origin as well as the software used to confirm the validity of the QR code that was scanned from the product using a mobile device.

3.2   Data Hiding Process

Information or data hiding techniques [10] are the process of hiding some of data into a digital media. This means that we can hide text or image into another digital media like texts, images, audio, or videos. The main purpose of these techniques is to provide data integrity, copyright protection, non-repudiation, covert communication, and authentication. Data hiding techniques comprise of digital steganography and watermarking. After hiding the information into a digital media, the following requirements need to be satisfied like imperceptibility, capacity, robustness, and security. In the context of our work, capturing the watermarked QR code affixed on the product is subject to various actual distortions. Thus, the robustness requirement needs to be a high priority. This is why we take advantage of digital watermarking technique in our work. The information used to hide in the QR code is considered as a secret message or secret feature. The QR code obtained after the hiding process is referred to a watermarked QR code.

There are several existing watermarking techniques proposed for hiding the secret information within the text images [13,15] and the images [7,19]. The methods for text images can not be directly applied for hiding the secret feature in the QR code. Meanwhile, the others meet the capacity requirement, but they are not robust against actual distortions caused by the process of print-scan and print-photograph. Thus, we have to propose a new method robust against these real distortions.

The proposed network is able to hide a secret message within the QR code in such a way that the perceptual difference between the input and watermarked QR code is minimal. The secret message is converted to a binary string of 100 bits. The bit sequence is then preprocessed to upsample to an image with the of size $400 \times 400 \times 3$ by using a dense layer. The preprocessing is performed because of the convergence of the network. The dimension of the input QR code is changed to the size of $400 \times 400 \times 3$. These two images are concatenated to form an image with the size of $400 \times 400 \times 6$. The network receives the six channel image as an input, and a three channel residual image as an output. In order to make the output image of the network (watermarked QR code image) visually similar to the input QR code image as much as possible and to make the secret message hidden within the QR code in imperceptible locations, we choose a combination of three losses for training the network as follows.

$$\mathcal{L} = \alpha_M \times \mathcal{L}_M + \alpha_R \times \mathcal{L}_R + \alpha_P \times \mathcal{L}_P \tag{1}$$

where $\alpha_M, \alpha_R, \alpha_P$ are loss weights, and $\mathcal{L}_M, \mathcal{L}_R, \mathcal{L}_P$ are cross entropy loss for the secret message, $\mathcal{L}_2$ residual regularization loss, perceptual loss respectively.

3.3   Data Extraction Process

The output QR code image of the data hiding process is the input of the data extraction process after feeding to the noise layer. This layer is intended to improve the robustness against the distortions caused by the process of print-scan and print-photograph. The noises added to this layer included JPEG compression, perspective warp, motion and defocus blur. For JPEG compression, we approximate the quantization step by the following equation.

$$q(x) = \begin{cases} x^3 & : |x| < 0.5 \\ x & : |x| \geq 0.5 \end{cases} \tag{2}$$

We randomly generate homography to simulate the geometric distortions caused by obtaining the QR code from various ways such as scanning the QR code by using scanner, or capturing the QR code by using mobile devices. Besides, we randomly perturb the four corner to create the perspective warp QR code image. In addition, we use Gaussian blur with its default derivation to simulate the motion blur.

The architecture of the data extraction network is described in the Table 1. We apply the ReLU activation function after each layer in the network except the last layer.

3.4   QR Code Similarity Measurement

We develop Siamese network to measure the similarity between the QR code captured from the product and the official ones. The proposed network contains three identical subnetworks which are used to generate feature vectors. The architecture of the network is partly based upon ResNet50 [4] where two fully connected layers are appended to the network. We apply batch normalization after each of the dense layers. With this approach, the network receives three

Table 1. The network architecture of data extraction process.

Layer	Kernel	Stride	Channels	In	Out	Input
Conv1	3	2	3/32	1	2	Watermark
Conv2	3	1	32/32	2	2	Conv1
Conv3	3	2	32/64	2	4	Conv2
Conv4	3	1	64/64	4	4	Conv3
Conv5	3	2	64/64	4	8	Conv4
Conv6	3	2	64/128	8	16	Conv5
Conv7	3	2	128/128	16	32	Conv6
FC0			20000			Flatten(Conv7)
FC1			20000/512			FC0
FC2			512/100			FC1

QR code images as an input in which two of QR code images are similar, they are considered as anchor and positive samples, and the third QR code image is unrelated, it is referred to negative sample. The main idea is for the network to learn to estimate the similarity between QR code images. The network then generates embeddings. The network output comprises of the distance between the positive and the anchor embedding, along with the distance between the negative and the anchor embedding. We utilize distance layer to estimate the distance, and this produces both values as a tuple. To train the network, we use a triplet loss [9], and this loss is computed by using the three embeddings returned by the Siamese network. The triplet loss is depicted by the following equation.

$$\mathcal{L} = max(\|f(A) - f(P)\|^2 - \|f(A) - f(N)\|^2 + margin, 0) \tag{3}$$

where $f(A), f(P), f(N)$, and $margin$ is referred respectively to anchor embedding, positive embedding, negative embedding, and a constant.

4 Experimental Results

To train the data hiding network, we choose 4,000 logos from Logo-2K+ [2]. Besides, we generate 100 QR code images, and each QR code image contains a randomly generated string of characters. We apply data augmentation on the generated QR images to create the diversity of 1,000 QR code images. This process is performed by applying random transformation such as image rotation. A total of 5,000 images are used to train the network. Figure 2 shows sample images from the various categories (Fig. 4(a), (b) and (c)) of the Logo-2K+ dataset. Besides, in order to evaluate the performance of the proposed data hiding network compared to the existing works, we separately train our network with the dataset named MIRFLICKR [5] comprising 25,000 images.

For similarity measurement network, we generate 100 QR code images, and the generated images are then fed to the data hiding network to carry the secret message with various lengths. After this step, we obtain 100 watermarked QR code images. These watermarked QR code images are printed at the default resolution by using the printer named Canon LBP 3300. The printed QR code images are scanned at the default resolution of 200 dpi by using the scanner entitled Toshiba e-STUDIO 856. Similarly, we capture the printed QR code images by using the camera of an iPhone 7. These QR code images are used to train the proposed Siamese network.

  (a) 24seven   (b) Ace   (c) Admiral   (d) QR code

Fig. 2. The sample images used to train the data hiding network.

The loss weights like α_M, α_R, and α_P are initially set to 0. After the network gets high accuracy during the training process, these weights are linearly increased. In case of similarity measurement network, the *margin* constant is assigned to 0.5.

4.1   Imperceptibility Assessment

The length of the secret message affects the quality of the watermarked QR code images. In addition, if the secret message length is large, this also reduces the accuracy of hidden data extraction. In general, there is a trade off between the accuracy of data recovery and the imperceptibility. The imperceptibility is measured by the difference between the QR code image and the watermarked QR code image. We adopt the peak signal to noise ratio (PSNR), the structural similarity index (SSIM), and the perceptual metric (LPIPS) to evaluate the quality of QR code images. For PSNR and SSIM, the higher the value is, the better the quality is obtained. The lower is better for LPIPS. For this experiment, we use the secret message of different lengths including the number of error correction bits. The error correction bits used in this work is BCH [3].

Table 2. The imperceptibility of the trained model with various secret message lengths.

Message length (bits)	PSNR ↑	SSIM ↑	LPIPS ↓
50	30.21	0.980	0.105
100	29.43	0.942	0.109
150	27.86	0.901	0.138
200	24.19	0.873	0.183

Table 2 depicts the quality of watermarked QR code images, and these results are averaged over 1,000 images. Figure 3 illustrates the QR code hidden the secret message with various lengths. By the experiments, we have observed that the long secret message will affect the quality of the watermarked QR code images. Specifically, the secret message of 150 bits or more in length will significantly degrade the watermarked QR code quality. The secret message up to 100 bits in length gives good quality to the watermarked QR code images, and it can be implemented in the real applications.

(a) 50 bits   (b) 100 bits   (c) 150 bits   (d) 200 bits

Fig. 3. The sample QR code hidden with various bit lengths.

4.2   Robustness Assessment

Due to the purpose of the work, we don't need the secret message to be too big. The secret message only needs to be of moderate length, but it has to ensure high accuracy when extracting. In order to prove the robustness of our approach, the proposed scheme has been experimented in the environment with and without distortions. For the watermarked QR code image without undergoing distortions, we have conducted to hide the secret message into 1,000 synthetic images of QR code, and the average result of hidden data recovery is 100%. For the watermarked QR code images subjected to distortions, we have tested our approach on 800 real images of QR code, and the results are detailed below.

Robustness Against Common Distortions. The watermarked QR code images are often subjected to JPEG compression which is widely used for size

Table 3. The minimum, maximum and average values of secret message recovery for JPEG compression distortion.

Secret recovery	Compression quality factor				
	10	20	30	40	50
Minimum	98.20%	100%	100%	100%	100%
Maximum	100%	100%	100%	100%	100%
Average (800 images)	99.91%	100%	100%	100%	100%

reduction or storing the scanned versions. Thus, we have adopted this distortion for proving the robustness of our approach. To conduct this experiment, the watermarked QR code images are sequentially compressed with a quality factor varying from 10 to 100 with a step of 10.

Table 3 presents the minimum, maximum and average values of watermark recovery on 800 testing images. The system has 100% ability to recover the hidden information for compressed watermarked QR code images with a compression quality factor of 20 or higher. We have observed that the watermarked QR code images compressed at the low compression quality factors are suffered from much of distortions caused by the coarse quantization of DCT coefficients.

Table 4. The minimum, maximum and average values of secret message recovery for scaling and rotation distortions.

Distortions	Minimum	Maximum	Average (800 images)
Rotation 5^0 (a)	100%	100%	100%
Rotation 7^0 (b)	100%	100%	100%
Rotation 10^0	97.50%	100%	98.92%
Scaling 0.3 (c)	98.25%	100%	99.47%
Scaling 0.5	100%	100%	100%
Scaling 1.5	100%	100%	100%
Scaling 1.7 (d)	100%	100%	100%
(a) + (c)	98.13%	100%	99.20%
(a) + (d)	100%	100%	100%
(b) + (c)	97.25%	100%	98.88%
(b) + (d)	100%	100%	100%

Besides, We also conduct experiments to test the robustness of our scheme on other common distortions like rotation, scaling, and their combination. For rotation, we perform the experiments with the rotation angles of 5, 7 and 10° whereas the scaling factor is taking values in the range [0.3, 1.7] with a step of 0.1. The results of robustness against these distortions are presented in Table 4.

Robustness Against Real Distortions. We study the robustness of our algorithm against print-scan and print-photograph distortions in possible conditions such as geometric transformation, rotation, color distortion, scaling distortion and the combination of rotation and scaling distortion. We print and scan the watermarked QR code images by using machines named Canon LBP 3300 and Toshiba e-STUDIO 856 respectively. After hiding the secret message, the watermarked QR code images are printed at the default resolution of 200 dpi. The printed versions of these watermarked documents are sequentially scanned with various resolutions of 200, 300, 400 and 600 dpi. For photographed QR code images, we use the camera of an iPhone 7, and a webcam to capture the images. These operations are conducted in the usual lighting conditions of the office. Table 5 illustrates the results of secret extraction in case the watermarked QR code images are distorted due to printing and scanning.

Table 5. The results of secret message recovery for print-and-scan distortions.

Secret recovery	Scanner resolution (dpi)			
	200	300	400	600
Minimum	98.24%	100%	100%	100%
Maximum	100%	100%	100%	100%
Average (800 images)	99.08%	100%	100%	100%

Table 6 depicts the results of watermark extraction in which the watermarked QR code images are captured from the printed version and the laptop display by using two different devices like webcam and iPhone 7. We illustrate the percentages of 100th, 500th, 800th and average values of the images which are taken over 800 watermarked QR code images. The results show that our approach is highly robust against a variety combination of camera and screen/ printer. We have observed that two-third of watermarked QR code images give an accuracy of 100%, and the lowest percentage value of watermark extraction is 96.88%. The overall percentage value of our method over 800 watermarked QR code images is 98.76%

Table 6. The results of secret message recovery for print-and-photograph distortions.

		100th	500th	800th	Average
Webcam	Printer	100%	100%	100%	99.38%
	Screen	100%	100%	98.25%	99.40%
iPhone 7	Printer	100%	100%	98.13%	97.75%
	Screen	97.25%	100%	100%	98.50%

4.3   Assessment of QR Code Similarity

We conduct to verify the trustworthiness of an QR code captured from the product by using the proposed network presented in the Sect. 3.4. Figure 4 demonstrates various QR code images in which Fig. 4(a) is the watermarked QR code image. This QR is hidden to carry the secret message, and it is considered as a genuine one. Figure 4(b) is the QR code image which is captured from the printed version by using an iPhone 7, and it is considered as a genuine one. The scanning and printing version (second round of printing) of the watermarked QR code image (Fig. 4(c)) is considered as a fake one (copied version). This implies that the counterfeiters scan the watermarked QR code affixed on a legitimate product package. The counterfeiters then print and continue to affix on their illegal products. Figure 4(d) is the code which is generated by using the popular QR code generation library, and it is also considered as a fake one.

Fig. 4. The various versions of the QR code images.

When users suspect a QR code affixed on the product, they can capture the QR code by using the common QR code scanning application integrated on the mobile phone. The captured QR code is then sent to the server side where the QR code detection application applies the trained model to infer the captured QR code. Table 7 illustrates the results of similarity estimation using various approaches like SSIM, earth movers distance (EMD), image match (IM), mean squared error (MSE), histogram (HIST), and our method. We apply the existing methods to compare the QR code obtained from the product with the legally watermarked QR code image. Meanwhile, our method uses the trained model for QR code inference. We have observed that the existing methods give results with slight difference between the various versions of the QR code. Thus, they yield low performance in detecting real or fake QR codes. On the contrary, our approach gives a relatively large difference, and the proposed method outperforms the existing ones. The threshold used to distinguish the difference between a copied QR code and a genuine one is set to 0.55.

Table 7. The similarity measure using different methods.

	SSIM	EMD	IM	MSE	HIST	Ours
Figure 4(a) vs (b)	0.99	0.0	0.36	6754.53	3.83	0.89
Figure 4(a) vs (c)	0.99	0.0	0.47	11039.81	12.67	0.47
Figure 4(a) vs (d)	0.99	0.0	0.56	798.51	2.56	0.29

In general, in order to verify a QR code obtained from the product, there are two conditions that need be satisfied. First, as the degree of similarity between the QR code captured from the product and the genuine ones has to be greater than 0.55. Second, the accuracy of extracting the hidden feature from the QR code is grater or equal to 95%. If the value of QR code similarity and the accuracy of hidden data recovery meet the mentioned thresholds, we conclude that the QR code image is real. Otherwise, it is probably be fake.

5   Conclusion

In order to confirm the authenticity of the QR code, we have introduced a novel method. An image perturbation is used to train the network for data concealment and detection, enabling it to be applied in the real world. We demonstrate the resistance of our method to the actual distortions brought about by the printing-and-scanning and photographic processes. In addition, we show that QR code similarity estimation outperforms more established techniques. However, in the future, we hope to enhance the suggested technique in order to conceal a secret message with more bits.

Acknowledgements. This study is funded in part by the Can Tho University, Code: T2022-126.

References

1. https://temchonggiavietnam.com/tem-chong-hang-gia/tem-chong-hang-gia-bo-cong-an/
2. https://github.com/msn199959/Logo-2k-plus-Dataset
3. Bose, R., Ray-Chaudhuri, D.: On a class of error correcting binary group codes. Inf. Control **3**, 68–79 (1960)
4. He, K., Zhang, X., Ren, S., Sun, J.: Deep residual learning for image recognition. In: 2016 IEEE Conference on Computer Vision and Pattern Recognition (CVPR) (2016)
5. Huiskes, M.J., Lew, M.S.: The mir flickr retrieval evaluation (2008)
6. Lancaster, I.: Anti-counterfeiting holograms (2009)
7. Luo, X., Zhan, R., Chang, H., Yang, F., Milanfar, P.: Distortion agnostic deep watermarking. In: Proceedings of the IEEE/CVF Conference on Computer Vision and Pattern Recognition (CVPR) (2020)
8. Malla, B., Dugar, A.: Product authentication using QR codes: a mobile application to combat counterfeiting. Wireless Pers. Commun. **90**, 381–398 (2016)
9. Schroff, F., Kalenichenko, D., Philbin, J.: Facenet: a unified embedding for face recognition and clustering. In: 2015 IEEE Conference on Computer Vision and Pattern Recognition (CVPR) (2015)
10. Shih, F.Y.: Digital Watermarking and Steganography: Fundamentals and Techniques, 2nd edn. CRC Press, Boco Raton (2017)
11. Tran, T., Hong, S.: RFID anti-counterfeiting for retailing systems. J. Appl. Math. Phys. **3**, 1 (2015)
12. Tuyls, P., Batina, L.: RFID-tags for anti-counterfeiting. In: Pointcheval, D. (ed.) CT-RSA 2006. LNCS, vol. 3860, pp. 115–131. Springer, Heidelberg (2006). https://doi.org/10.1007/11605805_8
13. Cu, V.L., Nguyen, T., Burie, J.C., Ogier, J.M.: A robust watermarking approach for security issue of binary documents using fully convolutional networks. Int. J. Document Anal. Recogn. (IJDAR) **23**, 219–239 (2020)

14. Wan, S., Yang, G., Qi, L., Li, L., Yan, X., Lu, Y.: Multiple security anti-counterfeit applications to QR code payment based on visual secret sharing and QR code. Math. Biosc. Eng. **16**, 6367–6385 (2019)
15. Xiao, C., Zhang, C., Zheng, C.: Fontcode: embedding information in text documents using glyph perturbation. CoRR (2017)
16. Xie, S., Tan, H.Z.: An anti-counterfeiting architecture for traceability system based on modified two-level quick response codes. Electronics **10**, 320 (2021)
17. Yiu, N.C.K.: An NFC-enabled anti-counterfeiting system for wine industry. CoRR (2016)
18. Yiu, N.C.K.: Decentralizing supply chain anti-counterfeiting systems using blockchain technology. CoRR (2021)
19. Zhu, J., Kaplan, R., Johnson, J., Fei-Fei, L.: Hidden: hiding data with deep networks. In: Computer Vision - ECCV 2018 (2018)

Data Analysis, Modeling, and Processing

Enhanced Energy Characterization and Feature Selection Using Explainable Non-parametric AGGMM

Hussein Al-Bazzaz[✉], Muhammad Azam, Manar Amayri, and Nizar Bouguila

Concordia University, Montreal, QC H3G 1M8, Canada
{h_albazz,mu_azam}@encs.concordia.ca,
{manar.amayri,nizar.bouguila}@concordia.ca

Abstract. In this paper, we propose an asymmetric generalized Gaussian mixture model (AGGMM) with simultaneous feature selection for efficient and interpretable energy characterization in the context of demand response and energy efficiency programs. The AGGMM captures the complex data distributions often encountered in smart meter data, while the simultaneous feature selection helps identify relevant features, leading to a more efficient and interpretable model. The mixture model parameters are optimized using a Bayesian Markov Chain Monte Carlo (MCMC) approach, which provides robust estimation and uncertainty quantification. To enhance model interpretability, we employ decision trees to define the cluster boundaries in terms of the data features using simple If-Then statements. We validate the proposed method on three real-life smart meter datasets, demonstrating its effectiveness in accurately characterizing energy consumption patterns and providing insights for utility companies to design and implement more effective demand response and energy efficiency programs. The results indicate that our method outperforms several state-of-the-art energy characterization frameworks, offering a powerful tool for smart meter data analysis and practical applications in the utility industry.

Keywords: Energy Characterization · Mixture Models · Bayesian Inference · Explainability · Feature Selection · Markov Chain Monte Carlo

1 Introduction

Recent power systems research clusters smart meter data at the household-level to understand residential energy consumption patterns and their impact on low-voltage networks. Publicly available datasets, such as the Irish smart meter trial [4–6], can be used to identify distinct energy behavioral groups. We extract and cluster smart meter data attributes to enhance LV network modelling and management for DNOs, focusing on assisting them in identifying suitable households for DR and EE initiatives.

Estimating parameters of models with latent variable is challenging, requiring appropriate algorithms. The expectation-maximization (EM) algorithm is a

© The Author(s), under exclusive license to Springer Nature Switzerland AG 2023
N. T. Nguyen et al. (Eds.): ACIIDS 2023, CCIS 1863, pp. 145–156, 2023.
https://doi.org/10.1007/978-3-031-42430-4_12

popular method for estimating probability density function parameters. However, its deterministic nature and susceptibility to overfitting and initialization conditions can prevent convergence to a global optimum. Bayesian inference techniques provide a robust theoretical framework for clustering algorithms and are extensively discussed in the literature. One popular approach for parameter estimation is the MCMC method, which approximates the posterior distribution of the model parameters, resulting in improved performance [3,10]. Previous research has employed the MCMC method to fit different mixture models to various real-world datasets [9, 14–17]. However, these studies did not take feature selection into account. Other researchers have attempted to fit the asymmetric Gaussian mixture model to different datasets and incorporated feature selection in their approaches [13]. However, the proposed model proposed in the aforementioned paper incorporated a base distribution that has a rigid bell shape. Additionally, a previous research paper have proposed a novel Bayesian framework for the asymmetric generalized Gaussian mixture model in [11]. However, the proposed model in the paper mentioned previously is a finite mixture and needs the number of clusters to be predetermined by the experiment. Our nonparametric model outperforms the models proposed in the aforementioned studies, as shown in the experimental results presented in this paper. Our model can fit asymmetric data with a variety of distribution shapes, including the Gaussian, the Laplacian, and the Uniform distributions. Furthermore, to address noisy, redundant, or uninformative features that can hinder clustering performance, we apply feature saliency, which decomposes the model into mixture-dependent and mixture-independent components, identifying relevant and irrelevant features [2].

The growing interest in machine learning algorithms with explicit representations of identified patterns has primarily focused on post-modelling explainability, which has drawbacks [1]. Our proposed model addresses these limitations by offering pre-modelling explainability, revealing insights into patterns, statistical properties, and defining data attributes. Our approach is based on model-based clustering, similar to the method proposed by [1].

In this paper, we have proposed an explainable non-parametric asymmetric generalized Gaussian mixture model with feature saliency (EXFSIAGGMM). The proposed model is validated using three real-world smart meter datasets. The performance of the proposed model is compared against three state-of-the-art clustering algorithms with feature saliency. The rest of the paper is organized as follows: In Sect. 2, we explain the mathematical representation of our proposed model and the model fitting process. In Sect. 3, we present the experimental results and their corresponding discussions. In Sect. 4, we present the conclusion.

2   Methodology

2.1   The Mathematical Representation of IFSAGGMM

The primary objective of feature selection is to identify the most informative set of features that effectively differentiate groups and mitigate the impact of noise.

In this section, we present the notion of feature saliency, which treats feature selection as a parameter estimation problem. Feature saliencies account for the potential existence of irrelevant features and assess the noise present in each feature, enabling the reduction of the effects of redundant features.

A feature is deemed relevant if it adheres to the mixture-dependent distribution AGGD; otherwise, it follows a mixture-independent background distribution and remains unrelated to the cluster labels. In this paper, we assume the background distribution to be a Gaussian distribution with parameters η and δ^2 representing the mean and the variance, respectively. We assume that the mean of the background distribution follows a Gaussian distribution as follows:

$$P(\eta) \sim \mathcal{N}(\mu_{\eta_0}, \sigma_{\eta_0}^2) \tag{1}$$

The variance of the background distribution is assumed to follow an inverse Gamma distribution as follows:

$$P(\delta^2) \sim \text{Inverse-Gamma}(a_{\delta^2}, b_{\delta^2}) \tag{2}$$

The feature importance within our proposed model is represented with an indicator variable that is of a standard basis and it is denoted by $\varphi = (\varphi_1, ..., \varphi_D)$. The component distribution is therefore defined as follows:

$$P(\mathbf{Y}_i|\theta_g) = \prod_{d=1}^{D} P(Y_{id}|\theta_{gd})^{\varphi_d} P(Y_{id}|\eta_d, \delta_d^2)^{1-\varphi_d} \tag{3}$$

where $\mathbf{Y}_i$ denotes the observation vector i. D denotes the total number of data dimensions, and θ_g represents the component g parameter set. the asymmetric generalized Gaussian distribution is defined as follows:

$$P(\mathbf{Y}_i|\theta_g) =$$

$$= \prod_{d=1}^{D} \frac{\lambda_{gd} \left[\frac{\Gamma(3/\lambda_{gd})}{\Gamma(1/\lambda_{gd})} \right]^{1/2}}{\left(\frac{1}{\sqrt{\varrho_{l_{gd}}}} + \frac{1}{\sqrt{\varrho_{r_{gd}}}} \right) \Gamma(1/\lambda_{gd})}$$

$$\times \begin{cases} \exp\left[-A(\lambda_{gd}) \left(\sqrt{\varrho_{r_{gd}}}(\mu_{gd} - Y_{id}) \right)^{\lambda_{gd}} \right] & Y_{id} < \mu_{gd} \\ \exp\left[-A(\lambda_{gd}) \left(\sqrt{\varrho_{l_{gd}}}(Y_{id} - \mu_{gd}) \right)^{\lambda_{gd}} \right] & Y_{id} \geq \mu_{gd} \end{cases} \tag{4}$$

where μ_g, λ_g, $\varrho_{l_{gd}}$, and $\varrho_{r_{gd}}$ denote the mean, the shape, the left precision and the right precision respectively. Subsequently, we define the proposed mixture model likelihood as follows:

$$p(\mathcal{Y}|\theta) = \sum_{g=1}^{M} p_k \prod_{d=1}^{D} \left[\omega_d P(Y_{id}|\theta_{gd}) + (1 - \omega_d) P(Y_{id}|\beta_d) \right] \tag{5}$$

where, $\mathcal{Y}$ denotes the dataset and θ denotes the mixture's full set of parameters. Subsequently, we introduce the latent variable $Z = (Z_1, ..., Z_N)$ to represent the membership of each observation. Assuming that Z_i is of a standard basis, then $Z_i = (Z_{i1}, ..., Z_{iN})$, and component g is responsible for generating the observation Y_i if $Z_{ig} = 1$. The likelihood function can be expressed as follows:

$$p(\mathcal{Y}|Z, \theta) = \prod_{i=1}^{N} \prod_{g=1}^{\infty} [p(\boldsymbol{Y}_i|\theta_g)]^{Z_{ig}} \tag{6}$$

Upon considering the entire dataset, the prior for Z can be established using the multinomial distribution. Let n_g represent the number of data points assigned to the g-th mixture component. Consequently, the prior for Z is expressed as:

$$p(Z|\boldsymbol{\pi}) = \prod_{i=1}^{N} \prod_{g=1}^{\infty} (\pi_j)^{Z_{ig}} \tag{7}$$

Following this, as we propose a Dirichlet Process Mixture Model, the mixing weights π_g are obtained from a Dirichlet Process using a stick-breaking construction:

$$\pi_g = V_g \prod_{l=1}^{g-1} (1 - V_l) \tag{8}$$

where $V_g \sim \text{Beta}(1, \alpha)$ represents the stick-breaking proportions. This prior on the mixing weights is inherently included in the prior for Z. The symbol α signifies the concentration parameter. Although there is no straightforward closed-form expression for $P(Z|\alpha)$, the Chinese Restaurant Process offers an alternative representation connecting the prior distribution of the latent variables Z with the concentration parameter, considering the stick-breaking construction as shown in Eq. 9.

$$p(Z|\alpha) = \prod_{g=1}^{\infty} \frac{n_g!}{(N - 1 + \alpha)!} \alpha^M \tag{9}$$

The conditional prior for a single indicator, $P(Z_{ig}|\alpha, Z_{-1})$, denotes the likelihood of assigning observation i to cluster g, considering the concentration parameter and the cluster assignments of all other observations (Z_{-1}). This conditional prior can be formulated as follows:

$$P(Z_{ig} = 1|\alpha, Z_{-i}) = \begin{cases} \frac{n_{g,-i}}{N-1+\alpha} & \text{if } g \text{ is an existing cluster} \\ \frac{\alpha}{N-1+\alpha} & \text{if } g \text{ is a new cluster} \end{cases} \tag{10}$$

where $n_{g,-i}$ indicates the number of data points assigned to cluster g while excluding observation i. The conditional prior accommodates the potential of observation i being allocated to either an existing cluster or a newly formed cluster. The conditional posterior probability ought to be proportional to the product of the likelihood and the conditional prior, resulting in the cases presented in Eqs. 11, and 12 as follows:

$$P(Z_{ig} = 1|\mathcal{Y}, \theta, Z_{-i})$$
$$\propto \left\{ \frac{n_{g,-i}}{N-1+\alpha} \prod_{d=1}^{D} P(Y_{id}|\theta_{gd}) \quad \text{if } g \text{ is an existing cluster} \right. \tag{11}$$

$$P(Z_{ig} = 1|\mathcal{Y}, \theta, Z_{-i})$$
$$\propto \begin{cases} \frac{\alpha}{N-1+\alpha} \int P(\mathbf{Y}_i|\theta_g) \\ P(\mu_{gd}|\mu_0, \sigma_0^2)P(\alpha_{gd}|a,b) \\ P(\lambda_{l_{gd}}|c,d)P(\lambda_{r_{gd}}|e,f)d\xi_g \quad \text{if } g \text{ is a new cluster} \end{cases} \tag{12}$$

In order to avoid the prior from overpowering the posterior distribution, Bayesian analysis typically employs non-informative or weakly informative priors. For Dirichlet Process Mixture Models, the Jeffrey's prior, a popular non-informative prior for the concentration parameter, corresponds to an Inverse-Gamma prior distribution with a shape parameter of $\beta_s = \frac{1}{2}$ and a mean parameter of $\beta_m = 1$.

$$P(\alpha^{-1}) \propto \alpha^{-\frac{3}{2}} \exp\left(-\frac{1}{2\alpha}\right) \tag{13}$$

To compute the conditional posterior for α, we begin by multiplying the likelihood and prior. This leads to a function resembling the Gamma function. Upon normalizing this function, we acquire the expression for the conditional posterior, which incorporates the Inverse-Gamma distribution along with the number of clusters and data points allocated to each cluster. The final expression is:

$$P(\alpha|\mathcal{Y}, Z) \propto \frac{\alpha^{-\frac{3}{2}} \exp\left(-\frac{1}{2\alpha}\right) \prod_{g=1}^{\infty} \frac{\alpha^{M_j}}{(M_j-1+\alpha)^{N_g}}}{\Gamma(\alpha)} \tag{14}$$

As the conditional posterior for α exhibits log-concavity, it can be efficiently sampled using the Adaptive Rejection Sampling (ARS) method.

2.2 Bayesian Optimization of Feature Importance

We first introduce a prior for ω using the Dirichlet distribution to ensure that the values lie within the range [0,1] and that $\sum_{d=1}^{D} \omega_d = 1$:

$$\omega = (\omega_1, \omega_2, \ldots, \omega_D) \sim \text{Dirichlet}(\alpha_1, \alpha_2, \ldots, \alpha_D) \tag{15}$$

For each hyperparameter α_d, we define a Gamma prior with shape and scale parameters k_d and θ_d.

$$P(\omega) \sim \text{Gamma}(k_d, \theta_d) \tag{16}$$

To compute the acceptance probability for all D ω's in a Metropolis-Hastings sampling process, we use the following equation:

$$\alpha(\omega^*, \omega^{(t)}) = \frac{P(\mathcal{Y}, \omega^*, \alpha)q(\omega^{(t)}, \omega^*)}{P(\mathcal{Y}, \omega, \alpha)q(\omega^*, \omega^{(t)})} \tag{17}$$

When using a Metropolis-Hastings algorithm for sampling, $q(\boldsymbol{\omega}^*, \boldsymbol{\omega}^{(t)})$ and $q(\boldsymbol{\omega}^{(t)}, \boldsymbol{\omega}^*)$ represent the proposal densities for transitioning between two points in the parameter space. They are used to propose new candidate samples in the MCMC process. A common choice for symmetric proposal densities is the Gaussian distribution. In this case, the new values $\boldsymbol{\omega}*$ is proposed from a Gaussian distribution centered around the current value $\boldsymbol{\omega}$ with a certain standard deviation, which controls the step size in the exploration of the parameter vector space.

2.3   The Parameter Set Learning of the Foreground Distribution

The Mean Parameters. In order to define the priors for the mean parameters, we must select an appropriate distribution that embodies our prior knowledge concerning the potential values of the mean parameters. A prevalent choice for the prior distribution of the mean parameters is the Gaussian distribution. We can represent the prior for the mean parameters as a Gaussian distribution with mean μ_0 and precision τ_0 as follows:

$$\mu_{gd} \sim \mathcal{N}(\mu_0, \rho_0^{-1}) \tag{18}$$

where the hyperparameters μ_0 and ρ_0^{-1} are shared among all components within a particular dimension. Furthermore, we assign the hyperparameter μ_0 a Gaussian prior with mean μ_{μ_0} and variance $\sigma_{\mu_0}^2$, expressed as follows:

$$P(\mu_0) \sim \mathcal{N}(\mu_{\mu_0}, \sigma_{\mu_0}^2) \tag{19}$$

The hyperparameters μ_{μ_0} and $\sigma_{\mu_0}^2$ for the Gaussian priors of the mean hyperparameter are assigned to the mean and variance of the observations, respectively.

Additionally, we assign the hyperparameter ρ_0 an Inverse-Gamma prior with designated shape and mean parameters. Denoting the shape parameter as a_{ρ_0} and the mean parameter as b_{ρ_0}, the Inverse-Gamma prior for the hyperparameter ρ_0 can be formulated as:

$$P(\rho_0) \sim \text{Inverse-gamma}(a_{\rho_0}, b_{\rho_0}) \tag{20}$$

In this implementation, the shape is assigned a fixed value, specifically $a_{\rho_0} = 1$. By setting the shape parameter to 1, we employ a relatively uninformative prior, implying that the prior will exert less impact on the posterior distribution, enabling the data to be more influential. Furthermore, the mean b_{ρ_0} is given a fixed value equivalent to the variance of the observations. The joint prior distribution for μ_{gd}, μ_0, and ρ_0 is formulated as follows:

$$P(\mathcal{Y}, \mu_{gd}, \mu_0, \rho_0) = P(\mathcal{Y}|Z, \theta) \times P(\mu_{gd}|\mu_0, \rho_0) \times P(\mu_0) \times P(\rho_0) \tag{21}$$

Consequently, the acceptance probability employed for the Metropolis-Hastings method to update the model parameter μ_{gd} is formulated as follows:

$$\alpha(\mu_{gd}^*, \mu_{gd}^{(t)}) = \frac{P(\mathcal{Y}, \mu_{gd}^*, \mu_0, \rho_0)q(\mu_{gd}^{(t)}, \mu_{gd}^*)}{P(\mathcal{Y}, \mu_{gd}, \mu_0, \rho_0)q(\mu_{gd}^*, \mu_{gd}^{(t)})} \tag{22}$$

The Shape Parameters. For the shape parameter b_{gd}, we presume an independent Gamma prior, expressed as:

$$P(b_{gd}) \sim \text{Gamma}(\alpha_{b_{gd}}, \beta_{b_{gd}}) \tag{23}$$

where $\alpha_{b_{gd}}$ represents the rate hyperparameter and $\beta_{b_{gd}}$ signifies the shape hyperparameter. For the shape hyperparameter $\beta_{b_{gd}}$, we presume an Inverse-Gamma prior, expressed as:

$$P(\beta_{b_{gd}}) \sim \text{Inverse-gamma}(\alpha_{\beta_{b_{gd}}}, \beta_{\beta_{b_{gd}}}) \tag{24}$$

where $\alpha_{\beta_{b_{gd}}}$ denotes the shape parameter and $\beta_{\beta b_{gd}}$ denotes the mean parameter. For the rate parameter $\alpha_{b_{gd}}$, we can assume an independent Gamma prior as well:

$$P(\alpha_{b_{gd}}) \sim \text{Gamma}(k_{\alpha_{b_{gd}}}, \xi_{\alpha_{b_{gd}}}) \tag{25}$$

where $k_{\alpha_{b_{gd}}}$ denotes the shape parameter and $\xi_{b_{gd}}$ denotes the scale parameter. We set $k_{\alpha_{b_{gd}}} = 1$ and $\alpha_{b_{gd}} = 1$ and the acceptance probability for this parameter is computed as follows:

$$\alpha(b_{gd}^*, b_{gd}^{(t)}) = \frac{P(\mathcal{Y}, b_{gd}^*, k_{\alpha_{b_{gd}}}, \tau_0) q(b_{gd}^{(t)}, b_{gd}^*)}{P(\mathcal{Y}, b_{gd}, k_{\alpha_{b_{gd}}}, \tau_0) q(b_{gd}^*, b_{jk}^{(t)})} \tag{26}$$

The Precision Parameters. As for the parameters $\varrho_{l_{gd}}$ and $\varrho_{r_{gd}}$, we assume Gamma priors with common hyperparameters: α_ϱ, β_ϱ.

$$P(\varrho_{l_{gd}}) \sim \text{Gamma}(\alpha_\varrho, \beta_\varrho) \tag{27}$$

$$P(\varrho_{r_{gd}}) \sim \text{Gamma}(\alpha_\varrho, \beta_\varrho) \tag{28}$$

The shape parameter α_ϱ of the Gamma priors for $\varrho_{l_{gd}}$ and $\varrho_{r_{gd}}$ follows an Inverse-Gamma prior distribution, with shape parameter a_{α_ϱ} and mean parameter b_{α_ϱ}, respectively.

$$P(\alpha_\varrho) \sim \text{Inverse-gamma}(a_{\alpha_\varrho}, b_{\alpha_\varrho}) \tag{29}$$

Furthermore, we assign a Gamma prior to β_ϱ with shape parameter a_{β_ϱ} and mean parameter b_{β_ϱ}, which is expressed as follows:

$$P(\beta_\varrho) \sim \text{Gamma}(a_{\beta_\varrho}, b_{\beta_\varrho}) \tag{30}$$

We propose using fixed values for the hyperparameters of the Gamma prior for β_ϱ as follows: $a_{\beta_\varrho} = 1$ and $b_{\beta_\varrho} = 1$. To compute the acceptance probability for the parameter $\varrho_{r_{gd}}$, we use the following equation:

$$\alpha(\varrho_{r_{gd}}^*, \varrho_{r_{gd}}^{(t)}) = \frac{P(\mathcal{Y}, \varrho_{r_{gd}}^*, \alpha_\varrho, \beta_\varrho) q(\varrho_{r_{gd}}^{(t)}, \varrho_{r_{gd}}^*)}{P(\mathcal{Y}, \varrho_{r_{gd}}, \alpha_\varrho, \beta_\varrho) q(\varrho_{r_{gd}}^*, \varrho_{r_{gd}}^{(t)})} \tag{31}$$

For the parameter $\varrho_{l_{gd}}$, the acceptance probability is computed as follows:

$$\alpha(\varrho_{l_{gd}}^*, \varrho_{l_{gd}}^{(t)}) = \frac{P(\mathcal{Y}, \varrho_{l_{gd}}^*, \alpha_\varrho, \beta_\varrho) q(\varrho_{l_{gd}}^{(t)}, \varrho_{l_{gd}}^*)}{P(\mathcal{Y}, S_{l_{gd}}, \alpha_\varrho, \beta_\varrho) q(\varrho_{l_{gd}}^*, \varrho_{l_{gd}}^{(t)})} \tag{32}$$

2.4   The Parameter Set Learning of Background Distribution

Given that we have assumed that the mean parameter η follows a Gaussian distribution with parameters mean η_0 and a variance σ^2, we assume that the parameter η follows another Gaussian distribution as follows:

$$P(\eta) \sim \mathcal{N}(\mu_{\eta_0}, \sigma^2_{\eta_0}) \tag{33}$$

we can use a normal distribution with mean 0 and a large variance, which makes it weakly informative:

$$P(\mu_{\eta_0}) \sim \mathcal{N}(0, \sigma^2_{\mu_{\eta_0}}) \tag{34}$$

For the hyperparameter $\sigma^2_{\eta_0}$, a suitable parameter would be the Inverse-Gamma distribution.

$$P(\sigma^2_{\eta_0}) \sim \text{Inverse-Gamma}(\alpha_{\eta_0}, \beta_{\eta_0}) \tag{35}$$

where α_{η_0}, and β_{η_0} denote the shape and scale parameters of the Inverse-Gamma distribution. Given the information within this section, we conclude the acceptance probability for this parameter as follows:

$$\alpha(\eta, \eta^{(t)}) = \frac{P(\mathcal{Y}, \eta^*, \mu_{\eta_0}, \sigma^2_{\eta_0})q(\eta^{(t)}, \eta^*)}{P(\mathcal{Y}, \eta, \mu_{\eta_0}, \sigma^2_{\eta_0})q(\eta^*, \eta^{(t)})} \tag{36}$$

As for the parameter $P(\delta^2)$, we recall proposing an Inverse-Gamma prior with hyperparameters a_{δ^2} and b_{δ^2}. We can use a uniform prior for a_{δ^2} as follows:

$$P(a_{\delta^2}) \sim \text{Uniform}(a_{\min}, a_{\max}) \tag{37}$$

Similarly, we can use a uniform prior for the scale parameter, reflecting weak prior knowledge about the scale:

$$P(b_{\delta^2}) \sim \text{Uniform}(b_{\min}, b_{\max}) \tag{38}$$

and therefore the acceptance probability is computed as follows:

$$\alpha(\delta, \delta^{(t)}) = \frac{P(\mathcal{Y}, \delta^*, a_{\delta^2}, b_{\delta^2})q(\delta^{(t)}, \delta^*)}{P(\mathcal{Y}, \delta, a_{\delta^2}, b_{\delta^2})q(\delta^*, \delta^{(t)})} \tag{39}$$

The algorithm begins by initializing the latent variable Z. It then proceeds to iteratively update the cluster assignments, mixture component parameters, and concentration parameter using a combination of Gibbs sampling, Metropolis-Hastings, and Adaptive Rejection Sampling methods.

3   Experimental Results

In this section, we validate our proposed model against three real-world smart meter datasets. Furthermore, the performance of our proposed model is compared against three state-of-the-art machine learning algorithms, namely: the

Table 1. Performance evaluation of the models utilizing the CER dataset

Performance measure	ExFSIAGGMM	ExFSIAGMM	ExFSIGGMM	ExFSIGMM
Silhouette	0.375	0.250	0.230	0.210
Davies-Bouldin	12.700	13.400	13.500	14.200

explainable non-parametric asymmetric Gaussian mixture model with feature saliency (ExFSIAGMM), the explainable non-parametric infinite generalized Gaussian mixture model with feature saliency (ExFSIGGMM), and the
explainable non-parametric Gaussian mixture model with feature saliency (ExF-
SIGMM). Drawing from four significant temporal intervals (indicated by $t \in$
$1, 2, 3, 4$, seven statistical feature are extracted following [12], namely: RAP_t,
Mean STD, Seasonal Score, WD-WE diff. Score.

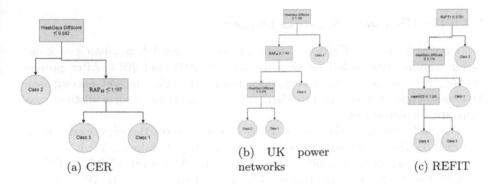

(a) CER

(b)   UK   power
networks

(c) REFIT

Fig. 1. Explainability figures of the three real-life datasets

3.1   The CER Dataset

We obtained our dataset from the publicly available Irish Social Science Data
Archive (ISSDA) [6], which contains smart meter records for over 6000 Irish
energy consumers between July 2009 and December 2010. After preprocessing,
we examined 3639 residential consumers assigned to one of six distinct tariffs
(E, A, D, C, B, and W) [6].

Table 1 highlights the superior performance of the ExFSIAGGMM model
when analyzing the CER dataset. With a notably higher Silhouette score of 0.375
and a lower Davies-Bouldin score of 12.700, ExFSIAGGMM outshines competing
models, which have Silhouette scores of 0.210–0.250 and Davies-Bouldin scores
of 13.400–14.200. These results emphasize the model's effectiveness in producing
well-defined, well-separated clusters, and its enhanced ability to discern meaningful patterns and groupings, leading to valuable insights within the data.

Additionally, given Fig. 1a, the resulting patterns obtained from our proposed
model are interpreted in simple IF-THEN statements. Consumption profile 2 has

Table 2. Performance evaluation of the models utilizing the London project dataset

Performance measure	ExFSIAGGMM	ExFSIAGMM	ExFSIGGMM	ExFSIGMM
Silhouette	0.440	0.310	0.290	0.270
Davies-Bouldin	0.770	0.840	1.070	1.550

Table 3. Performance evaluation of the models utilizing the REFIT project dataset

Performance measure	ExFSIAGGMM	ExFSIAGMM	ExFSIGGMM	ExFSIGMM
Silhouett	0.840	0.410	0.380	0.330
Davies-Bouldin	0.550	0.650	0.750	0.900

a "WeekDays DiffScore" that is larger than the value 0.602, Consumption profile 3 has "weekDays DiffScore" and "RAP_{t2}" that is greater than is less the value 0.602 and greater than the value 1.157 respectively.

3.2   The UK Power Networks Dataset

We employed the Low Carbon London project dataset [8], consisting of smart meter readings from 5,567 households between 2011 and 2014. After preprocessing, we analyzed 3,891 observations from 2013. The dataset encompasses Dynamic Time of Use and Standard tariffs, in addition to five distinct geodemographic categories.

The performance evaluation in Table 2 demonstrates the superiority of the ExFSIAGGMM model applied to the London project dataset. With a higher Silhouette score of 0.440 and a lower Davies-Bouldin score of 0.770, ExFSIAGGMM outperforms competing models, which have scores of 0.270–0.310 and 0.840–1.550, respectively. These results emphasize the model's enhanced ability to discern meaningful patterns and groupings, as well as its effectiveness in producing well-defined, well-separated clusters, leading to significant insights within the data.

In Fig. 1b, discovered patterns are explained using simple IF-THEN statements. Consumption profile 3 has "WeekDays DiffScore" < 1.108, Consumption profile 4 has "WeekDays DiffScore" and "RAP_{t2}" between 1.108 and 1.146. Patterns with "WeekDays DiffScore" > 1.108 and "RAP_{t2}" > 1.146 belong to Consumption profile 2 if "WeekDays DiffScore" > 0.478, and to Consumption profile 1 if "WeekDays DiffScore" < 0.478.

3.3   The REFIT Dataset

We utilized the REFIT project dataset [7] in this experiment. The performance evaluation results in Table 3 highlight the exceptional superiority of the ExFSIAGGMM model applied to the REFIT project dataset. With a substantially higher Silhouette score of 0.840 and a lower Davies-Bouldin score of 0.550, ExFSIAGGMM outperforms competing models, which exhibit scores of 0.330–0.410 and 0.650–0.900, respectively. These results demonstrate the model's effectiveness in producing well-defined, well-separated clusters and its ability to identify meaningful patterns and groupings within the dataset, thus offering valuable insights.

Similar to the previous experiments, we demonstrate the boundaries of the discovered patterns using our proposed clustering frameworks using simple IF-THEN statements as demonstrated in Fig. 1c.

4 Conclusion

In this study, we introduced the Explainable Non-Parametric Asymmetric Generalized Gaussian Mixture Model with Feature Saliency (ExFSIAGGMM), which leverages a hybrid hierarchical Bayesian sampling framework for robust parameter estimation and offers explainable results using simple IF-THEN statements. The ExFSIAGGMM model demonstrated superior clustering performance compared to three state-of-the-art clustering algorithms across three real-world smart meter datasets. This superior performance, combined with its ability to provide interpretable and meaningful results, establishes the ExFSIAGGMM model as a powerful tool for data-driven analysis, bridging the gap between complex statistical models and actionable insights, ultimately empowering practitioners to make informed decisions based on data.

References

1. Prabhakaran, K., Dridi, J., Amayri, M., Bouguila, N.: Explainable K-means clustering for occupancy estimation. Procedia Comput. Sci. **203**, 326–333 (2022). Elsevier
2. Law, M.H.C., Figueiredo, M.A.T., Jain, A.K.: Simultaneous feature selection and clustering using mixture models. IEEE Trans. Pattern Anal. Mach. Intell. **26**, 1154–1166 (2004)
3. Song, Z., Ali, S., Bouguila, N.: Bayesian learning of infinite asymmetric gaussian mixture models for background subtraction. In: Karray, F., Campilho, A., Yu, A. (eds.) ICIAR 2019. LNCS, vol. 11662, pp. 264–274. Springer, Cham (2019). https://doi.org/10.1007/978-3-030-27202-9_24
4. Cao, H., Beckel, C., Staake, T.: Are domestic load profiles stable over time? An attempt to identify target households for demand side management campaigns. In: Proceedings of the 39th Annual Conference of the IEEE Industrial Electronics Society (IECON), Vienna, Austria, pp. 75–86 (2013)
5. Haben, S., Ward, J.A., Greetham, D.V., Grindrod, P., Singleton, C.: A new error measure for forecasts of household-level, high resolution electrical energy consumption. Int. J. Forecast. **30**(2), 246–256 (2014)
6. Irish Social Science Data Archive, "CER Smart Metering Project" (2012). http://www.ucd.ie/issda/
7. Murray, D., et al.: A data management platform for personalised real-time energy feedback. In: Proceedings of the 8th International Conference on Energy Efficiency in Domestic Appliances and Lighting (2015)
8. (UK power networks), SmartMeter Energy Consumption Data in London Households, 2011–2014 [dataset] (2013). https://data.london.gov.uk/dataset/smartmeter-energy-use-data-in-london-households/

9. Fu, S., Bouguila, N.: A soft computing model based on asymmetric gaussian mixtures and Bayesian inference. Soft Comput. **24**(7), 4841–4853 (2019). https://doi.org/10.1007/s00500-019-04238-2
10. Elguebaly, T., Bouguila, N.: Bayesian learning of finite generalized gaussian mixture models on images. Signal Process. **91**(4), 801–820 (2011)
11. Vemuri, R.T., Azam, M., Bouguila, N., Patterson, Z.: Bayesian model and feature selection in asymmetric generalized gaussian mixtures. In: 2022 IEEE International Conference on Industrial Technology (ICIT), pp. 1–6. IEEE (2022)
12. Haben, S., Singleton, C., Grindrod, P.: Analysis and clustering of residential customers energy behavioral demand using smart meter data. IEEE Transactions on Smart Grid **7**(1), 136–144 (2015)
13. Song, Z., Ali, S., Bouguila, N.: Background subtraction using infinite asymmetric Gaussian mixture models with simultaneous feature selection. IET Image Process. **14**(11), 2321–2332 (2020). Wiley
14. Fu, S., Bouguila, N.: Bayesian learning of finite asymmetric gaussian mixtures. In: Mouhoub, M., Sadaoui, S., Ait Mohamed, O., Ali, M. (eds.) IEA/AIE 2018. LNCS (LNAI), vol. 10868, pp. 355–365. Springer, Cham (2018). https://doi.org/10.1007/978-3-319-92058-0_34
15. Fu, S., Bouguila, N.: A Bayesian intrusion detection framework. In: 2018 International Conference on Cyber Security and Protection of Digital Services (Cyber Security), pp. 1–8. IEEE (2018)
16. Fu, S., Bouguila, N.: Asymmetric gaussian mixtures with reversible jump MCMC. In: 2018 IEEE Canadian Conference on Electrical & Computer Engineering (CCECE), pp. 1–4. IEEE (2018)
17. Fu, S., Bouguila, N.: Asymmetric gaussian-based statistical models using Markov chain monte Carlo techniques for image categorization. In: 2018 17th IEEE International Conference on Machine Learning and Applications (ICMLA), pp. 1205–1208. IEEE (2018)

Hybrid Method for Short Text Topic Modeling

Jinyuan Chen and Bela Stantic[✉]

School of Information and Communication Technology, Griffith University,
Brisbane, Australia
Jinyuan.chen@griffithuni.edu.au, B.Stantic@griffith.edu.au

Abstract. The rise in social media's popularity has led to a significant increase in user-generated content across various topics. Extracting information from these data can be valuable for different domains, however, due to the nature of the vast volume it is not possible to extract information manually. Different aspects of information extraction have been introduced in literature including identifying what topic is discussed in the text. The challenge becomes even bigger when the text is short, such as found in social media. Various methods for topic modeling have been proposed in the literature that could be generally categorized as unsupervised and supervised learning. However, unsupervised topic modeling methods have some shortcomings, such as semantic loss and poor explanation, and are sensitive to the choice of parameters, such as the number of topics. While supervised machine learning methods based on deep learning can achieve high accuracy they need data annotated by humans, which is time-consuming and costly. To overcome the above mentioned disadvantages this work proposes a hybrid topic modeling method that combines the advantages of both unsupervised and supervised methods. We built a hybrid model by combining Latent Dirichlet Allocation (LDA) and deep learning built on top of the Bidirectional Encoder Representations from the Transformers (BERT) model. LDA is used to identify the optimal number of topics and topic-relevant keywords where the only need for human input, with the aid of ChatGPT, is to identify associated topics based on topic-specific keywords. This annotation is used to train and fine-tune the BERT model. In the experimental evaluation of posts related to climate change, we show that the proposed concept is applicable for predicting topics from short text without the need for lengthy and costly annotation.

Keywords: Topic Modeling · LDA · Deep learning · BERT · ChatGPT

1 Introduction

Social media have provided means for people to share their opinions and observations about different aspects and information deeply hidden in these data can

© The Author(s), under exclusive license to Springer Nature Switzerland AG 2023
N. T. Nguyen et al. (Eds.): ACIIDS 2023, CCIS 1863, pp. 157–168, 2023.
https://doi.org/10.1007/978-3-031-42430-4_13

be valuable for different stakeholders. However, due to the volume and complexity of social media data it is impossible and impractical to analyze all of the data manually. Therefore, it is necessary to use methods to extract the information. Identifying the topic in the text is one of the valuable aspects that can be extracted from the text and therefore topic modeling attracted significant attention in the literature, both related to natural language processing and machine learning. It is able to scan documents and, based on word patterns, identify word groups and similar expressions that best characterize a set of documents. The goal of topic modeling is to discover the hidden themes or topics present in a corpus of documents.

Broadly speaking topic modeling algorithms can be categorized into two main groups depending on the method applied: *Unsupervised learning* and *Supervised learning*. When trained on large, high-quality labeled datasets, supervised methods can achieve high accuracy on various tasks [6]. But obtaining labeled data can be time-consuming and expensive, especially when dealing with extensive collections of texts. While unsupervised learning algorithms do not require labeled data, which is making them more scalable and cost-effective, they can be inaccurate and identified topics are general not specific to a certain issue. In addition, unsupervised methods are sensitive to the choice of parameters including the optimal number of topics. The most popular techniques for topic modeling are different variations of Latent Dirichlet Allocation (LDA), an unsupervised learning method.

In this work, to overcome the limitations of both unsupervised and supervised methods we are proposing a hybrid method for topic modeling which combines supervised and unsupervised learning. We first preprocessed the data we collected from Twitter. Then, we identified the optimal number of topics and generated associated keywords for the optimal number of topics. Human involvement in the process of annotation was minimal, it was related to identifying the associated topics based on topic-specific keywords, with the aid of ChatGPT, and in this case, it took less than 30 min. This annotation is used to train and fine-tune the BERT model, which can be used for identifying topics and with all benefits of supervised methods. The remainder of the paper is organized as follows, in the next section considering we harness both unsupervised and supervised method topic modeling we elaborate on both. In Sect. 3 we present the proposed hybrid method for Topic modeling and in individual subsection we present steps of the proposed framework to be performed. Finally, in Sect. 4 we conclude the paper and suggest possible avenues for future work.

2   Literature Review

Topic modeling is a technique that can automatically analyze text and identify the underlying topic discussed in the text and cluster documents with the same topics. Various methods for topic modeling have been proposed in the literature that could be generally categorized as unsupervised or supervised learning methods. In the following subsections we will elaborate on topic modeling methods proposed in the literature.

2.1   Unsupervised Learning Methods

One of the first algorithms to implement topic modeling dates back to the 1990s. The early approaches to cluster and categorize large text datasets to topic modeling were based on Latent Semantic Analysis (LSA), also known as latent semantic indexing (LSI) [12]. Implementing LSA to identify latent document structures is based on Singular Value Decomposition (SVD) that captures a text corpus's underlying semantic structure by building a matrix of term-document frequency counts [17].

As for text classification and information retrieval, LSA is still an algorithm worth considering, but the topic modelling works implemented by LSA now have been largely replaced by other techniques such as Latent Dirichlet Allocation (LDA) [5]. LDA is a three-level hierarchical Bayesian model Fig. 1 [18], in which each item of a collection is modelled as a finite mixture over an underlying set of topics. Each topic is, in turn, modelled as an infinite mixture over an underlying set of topic probabilities. The output of the LDA model is a series of topics. Then the represented topic will be classified by a set of representative words, which can be used to label topics. For example, a topic distribution that is heavily weighted to terms like "soccer", "teammates", "score", and "goal" may be associated with the "sports" topic. Where M is the number of documents, N represents the number of words in a given document. The distribution of the 'θ' and 'β' represent the multinomial distribution. The parameters of the multinomial distribution are 'α' and 'ϕ'. Every row of data in 'θ' is a K-dimensional vector representing K^{th} topics in the corpus. 'Z' is one of a topic from 'θ'. while 'W' is the corresponding word in the topic 'Z'.

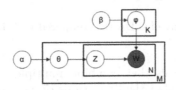

Fig. 1. The structure of Latent Dirichlet Allocation

Because of the simplicity and advantages of LDA, many models based on LDA, to suit different data, have been developed [1]. For instance, the method named *Sparse Topic-Latent Dirichlet Allocation* was the first LDA extension for unsupervised topic modeling without hierarchy regression [15]. In addition, several other models based on LDA have been proposed, for example, a Nonparametric Bayesian Model [3] and the correlated Topic Model [4].

2.2   Supervised Learning Methods

Supervised topic modeling, involves using the labeled dataset to train a model that could classify new unseen documents into topics. These methods require humans to annotate documents into corresponding topics. The topic model is trained with annotated data to categorize new documents accurately. Researchers have developed various supervised topic modeling methods for topic modeling. One such method is the supervised LDA algorithm (sLDA) initially proposed by [15]. This method uses labeled training data to train the model that is optimized for a specific task or application [7]. sLDA could be used with regression to multi-class classification [16], the differences between LDA and sLDA are displayed below in Fig. 2. For each D, the N_D words are generated by drawing a topic t from the distribution of documents and topics θ and then giving a word w from the topic-word distribution φ. The usability of sLDA is demonstrated in [9] where the intention was to check the key attributes influencing Airbnb user satisfaction and dissatisfaction by analyzing online reviews. Authors used LDA to extract positive and negative topics from reviews and combined the statistical results of sLDA to discover topics related to the satisfaction of Airbnb users.

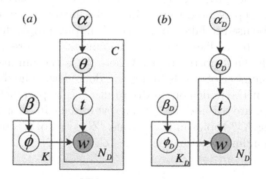

Fig. 2. Structure of sLDA (b) compared with LDA (a), [13]

There are also proposals that combine multiple methods and connecting individuals' strengths to offset the limitations of individual methods and therefore produce more accurate results than individual topic modeling methods. For example, an approach may combine probabilistic topic modeling methods like Latent Dirichlet Allocation (LDA) with clustering methods or word embedding techniques such as *Word2Vec* to enhance the accuracy and interpretability of the extracted topics. One such algorithm is the LDA-W2V method [11]. In addition, Topic Attention Model (TAM) for topic modeling combines a supervised recurrent neural network (RNN) with LDA [19]. TAM has two inputs, one of them is a sequence model and another is a bag-of-words topic model. So, the whole vocabulary is input for RNN, and the word embedding matrix was initialized by the word embedding learned from Word2Vec. In experimental evaluation authors demonstrated the dominance of the TAM method when compared to different unsupervised and supervised methods being applied individually.

3   Methodology

In this section, we present the methodology proposed to harness unsupervised learning as an annotation for supervised learning. The Framework and steps are shown in Fig. 3 and they are listed below:

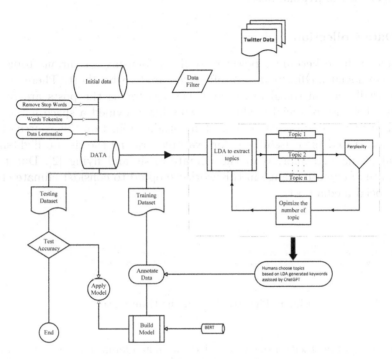

Fig. 3. Framework of Hybrid Model for Topic Modeling

- Data Collection: Collect Twitter posts relevant to climate change,
- Data Preparation: The first step task is to prepare the data, which involves preprocessing the text data, including cleaning, tokenization, and stop-word removal. In supervised topic modeling, the data preparation step is similar but also involves labeling the data with the corresponding topic or category.
- Unsupervised Topic Modeling: Dirichlet Allocation (LDA) is used to identify topics. These techniques generate a set of topics, each represented by a set of words that are highly correlated with each other.
- Identifying the optimal number of Topics.
- Human naming of topics based on the prevalence of words in individual topics. ChatGPT[1] can assist in identifying the most likely topic based on a set of words produced by LDA for an individual topic.

---

[1] https://openai.com/blog/chatgpt.

- Annotation: Assigning a label to the training dataset for each individual post, as identified by LDA and named by Humans assisted by ChatGPT.
- Building the model: based on the annotated training dataset. We harness BERT embedding with deep learning models for classification.
- Evaluation: apply the trained model to the test set and predict the associated topic of each individual post.

3.1   Data Collection

Social media have become a powerful tool for focusing on various topics and events. On social media, texts are often required to be short. Therefore, this work we will rely on social media and use Twitter as the posts are publicly available. The rise of social media platforms has provided a space for users to share their views on different topics. Many studies relied on this source of data and demonstrated their usefulness, for example, tracing the rise of 'flightshame' in social media and analysis of the climate crisis and flying [2]. Due to the significance of climate change in this work we opted to consider climate change related social media posts.

```
1  label,text,
2  PartyPolitics,scott morrison rule change government policy continue deal fallout hawaiian holiday pm visit
3  ClimatePolicy,lack expertise area im wonder much reduction emissions would obtain widespread adoption evs e
4  ClimatePolicy,70 per cent trade countries commit net zero prospect border tax introduce begin european unio
5  Bushfire,since government think get away announce notional bushfire recovery fund theoretical dont exist pa
```

Fig. 4. The structure of the training set

To access public Twitter data we relied on an academic-level Twitter application programming interface (API). The API has the option to filter posts by time, keywords, or a geographic area, on this occasion. Considering that we intended to look into opinions about climate change from the Australian public we applied geographic filter in the form 'location = "-26.117995,134.300207,2200km"'. In addition, we also apply keyword filtering and to avoid the sparsity of data, we selected several diverse keywords such as "Co2", "Climate change", and "emission". Because Twitter data is in JavaScript Object Notation (JSON) format, we stored the collected posts in the *MongoDB* database located in an in-house Big Data cluster. Out of the collected posts, considering that we were interested in topic modeling we randomly selected 4,502 posts of length more than 150 characters (Twitter has a restriction of 280 characters) and split the data set into 4,000 for training sets (the structure is shown in Fig. 4) and 502 for the test set, Fig. 5.

3.2   Data Pre-processing

Preprocessing is an important step in preparing text data for topic modeling. It is the process of cleaning and transforming original text data into a format

```
(NLP) [bob@bigdata TopicMOD]$ wc -l trainCAB.csv
4000 trainCAB.csv
(NLP) [bob@bigdata TopicMOD]$ wc -l testCAB.csv
502 testCAB.csv
(NLP) [bob@bigdata TopicMOD]$ ▊
```

Fig. 5. The number of records in training and test sets

suitable for further processing. In our dataset, the unstructured and noisy nature of Twitter data presents unique challenges for topic modeling and deep learning. To clean the text we have removed punctuations, special characters, Twitter handles, emojis, images, and URLs. Before performing tokenization, to reduce the number of tokens, we also performed lemmatization (grouping together different forms of the same word), and in addition, converted all letters to lowercase Fig. 6.

```
['scott morrison rule change government policy continue deal fallout hawaiian '
 'holiday pm visit families volunteer evacuation centre nsw today #auspol',
 'always look forward day try make magical spawn bullshit detest',
 'video move part develop story part andrew constance response need frame let '
 'say paint even darker picture mps right condemn pm know news']
[['scott', 'morrison', 'rule', 'change', 'government', 'policy', 'continue', 'de
al', 'fallout', 'hawaiian', 'holiday', 'pm', 'visit', 'families', 'volunteer', '
evacuation', 'centre', 'nsw', 'today', 'auspol']]
Lematized ['change government policy continue deal visit family voluntee
r today auspol', 'always look forward day try make spawn bullshit', 'video move
part develop story part response need frame let say paint even picture mp condem
n pm know news']
```

Fig. 6. Sample preprocessed, tokenized, and Lemmatized data

3.3 LDA

We used *Gensim*[2] to generate the LDA model. Gensim is an open-source Python library for natural language processing, specifically for topic modeling, document similarity analysis, and text summarization. Sample output from LDA-generated topics by Gensim is shown in Fig. 7.

```
Topic: 0 Words: 0.016*"bushfire" + 0.012*"news" + 0.011*"people" + 0.010*"make" + 0.009*"gover
 + 0.009*"could" + 0.008*"say" + 0.007*"thank" + 0.007*"covid" + 0.007*"emissions"
Topic: 1 Words: 0.017*"climatechange" + 0.009*"make" + 0.008*"fire" + 0.007*"look" + 0.007*"pe
 + 0.007*"increase" + 0.007*"smoke" + 0.007*"would" + 0.007*"like" + 0.006*"years"
Topic: 2 Words: 0.013*"people" + 0.012*"bushfire" + 0.011*"like" + 0.010*"make" + 0.009*"take"
09*"help" + 0.008*"right" + 0.006*"would" + 0.006*"good" + 0.006*"years"
```

Fig. 7. LDA Topic Distribution

The experiments were run on a CPU-based server (Intel(R) Xeon(R) CPU E5-2609 v3 @ 1.90 GHz, 12-Core Processor, 65 GB Memory), enhanced by a GPU (GeForce GTX 1080 with 8 GB of memory).

---

[2] https://pypi.org/project/gensim/.

3.4   Optimal Number of Topics

Usually, in order to evaluate works, 'Recall, Precision, and F-score' [10] are designed to be the metrics of classification tasks. In comparison, Perplexity is a vital metric to evaluate a language model. It is used to evaluate the predictive power of a language model, that is, whether the model can assign sequences in the test set to a distribution similar to the training set. Perplexity is a measure of how well a probability distribution or probability model predicts a sample (similar to entropy), the smaller value indicates the better performance of the model evaluation, it is shown in the formula below.

$$Perplexity = 2^{-\frac{1}{N} \sum_{i=1}^{N} \log_2 P(w_i)}$$

where N represents the total number of distinct words. $P(w_i)$ means the probability of the ith word from documents. To find the optimal number of topics we calculated perplexity for all options with the number of topics between 5 and 25. While testing different numbers of topics, we also looked into different values for learning_decay, learning_offset, and max_iter and performed experiments with all possible combinations. The max_iter is the maximum number of passes over the training data (aka epochs), learning_decay is a parameter that controls learning rate in the online learning method and to guarantee asymptotic convergence the value should be set between (0.5, 1.0]. The learning_offset (also called tau_0)is a parameter that down weights early iterations in online learning, it should be greater than 1.0. For topics, as mentioned earlier we considered the range from 5 to 25. From previous work, we concluded that for learning_decay the value should be between 0.7 to 0.95, and we tested all values with the step of 0.05. Similarly, we considered for max_iter and learning_offset values 10 and 20, shown in Fig. 8. We have noticed that the enforcing to calculate perplexity for every item did not improve the performance but just slowed down the experiment significantly. Therefore, we left the parameter evaluate_every=-1, which indicates to not evaluate perplexity for every item.

From the experiment results, where we tested all possible combinations of topics, learning_decay, max_iter, and learning_offset we found that the lowest perplexity is 912.86 when the number of topics is 16, learning_decay is 0.95, and both max_iter and learning_offset are equal to 20 (As it is shown and highlighted in Fig. 8). Therefore, we applied these values when generating keywords for 16 topics. We also identified that 12 keywords are sufficient to define the topics.

3.5   ChatGPT Annotation

The only involvement of humans in the annotation is to assign associated topic names for 16 topics produced by LDA. This can be assisted, and we also relied on ChatGTP 3.5[3] to identify associated topic names based on topic-specific keywords and to possibly cluster more LDA-identified topics into one, as it can be seen in Fig. 9. In our case, 16 LDA-generated topics were clustered into

---

[3] https://chat.openai.com/.

Topics	Decay	Perplexity Score			
		max_iter=10 offset = 20	max_iter=20 offset = 20	max_iter=10 offset = 10	max_iter=20 offset = 10
15	0.7	955.96	960.09	995.8	997.76
15	0.75	939.45	948.98	980.53	983.99
15	0.8	931.97	937.29	967.39	970.6
15	0.85	930.03	928.77	958.76	958.91
15	0.9	933.99	927.35	956.82	954.83
15	0.95	943.49	924.77	953.9	952.23
16	0.7	942.63	936.62	982.51	977.14
16	0.75	931.54	933.78	964.53	958.01
16	0.8	921.1	922.44	954	943.91
16	0.85	919.07	915.71	947.58	936.56
16	0.9	917.41	912.83	940.3	933.23
16	0.95	924.15	912.86	944.76	933.83
17	0.7	950.59	968.69	977.41	993.64
17	0.75	935.15	954.67	965.84	975.73
17	0.8	933.6	950.6	956.01	974.05
17	0.85	928.8	944.28	950.38	969.2
17	0.9	926.46	944.54	951.78	962.82
17	0.95	936.8	944.16	950.65	959.29

Fig. 8. Parameters for optimal number of topics based on lowest perplexity

5 categories and named appropriately based on keywords. It is important to mention that this task took only minimal effort and ensured that all training data (4000 posts) for supervised learning were labeled. In contrast, a similar task of annotation performed fully by humans in our previous project required 4,000 min (one minute per tweet) for annotation (about 66 h).

	Word 0	Word 1	Word 2	Word 3	Word 4	Word 5	Word 6	Word 7	Word 8	Word 9	Word 10	Word 11	ChatGPT
Topic 0	emission	year	plan	report	bushfire	reduce	change	government	action	energy	break	today	Others
Topic 1	watch	disaster	make	happen	team	bushfire	raise	police	relief	issue	agree	health	Bushfire
Topic 2	know	think	fund	tax	effect	bushfire	right	lie	work	build	history	burn	ClimatePolicy
Topic 3	time	people	bushfire	state	stop	year	say	love	come	leader	power	week	Bushfire
Topic 4	auspol	action	support	labor	story	need	come	morning	want	job	view	grow	PartyPolitics
Topic 5	need	know	lose	home	make	plant	work	forest	say	reason	response	understand	NatureBasedSolutions
Topic 6	emergency	tell	bushfire	service	destroy	stay	travel	road	thing	area	ask	farm	Bushfire
Topic 7	world	climatechange	level	policy	government	record	auspol	event	include	make	price	need	ClimatePolicy
Topic 8	country	leave	people	fight	warn	coal	emergency	govt	time	amp	auspol	action	Others
Topic 9	make	really	look	thing	think	energy	weather	problem	condition	year	know	issue	Others
Topic 10	read	vote	science	election	moment	fact	debate	look	denial	impact	say	link	PartyPolitics
Topic 11	bushfire	help	smoke	donate	affect	community	people	thank	bring	animal	money	city	Bushfire
Topic 12	forest	come	wait	school	tree	die	hope	sign	release	log	wake	mankind	NatureBasedSolutions
Topic 13	bushfire	season	start	firefighter	follow	time	day	news	volunteer	crisis	government	resource	Bushfire
Topic 14	risk	believe	increase	water	rain	force	opinion	wind	play	charge	try	use	NatureBasedSolutions
Topic 15	burn	people	away	cause	want	reduction	fuel	point	hazard	drive	life	year	Bushfire

Fig. 9. Suggestion by ChatGPT based on LDA-generated words and dominant keywords

After identifying suitable topics, based on keywords and assisted by Chat-GPT, these values were updated in the MongoDB database and resulted in the distribution shown in Fig. 10. It can be seen that most topics associate with 'Bushfire', followed by 'Others', and 'NatureBasedSolutions'. This is in line with annotation performed by humans on the same data set.

```
> db.trainCAB.aggregate( { $group : { _id:    { $substr: [ "$TargetLDA16", 0, 16]
}, total : {$sum:1} }), {$sort:{_id:1}})
{ "_id" : "Bushfire", "total" : 1781 }
{ "_id" : "ClimatePolicy", "total" : 495 }
{ "_id" : "NatureBasedSolut", "total" : 537 }
{ "_id" : "Others", "total" : 843 }
{ "_id" : "PartyPolitics", "total" : 343 }
>
```

Fig. 10. Topics generated by LDA named and clustered by humans based on keywords

3.6   Deep Learning Language Modeling

We have adapted the BERT model [8] to fine-tune our model with our LDA and ChatGPT assisted annotated data. The BERT model is deeply bidirectional and pre-trained using only a plain text corpus, which means it is designed to pre-train deep bidirectional representations from an unlabeled text by joint conditioning on both the left and right context. Bidirectionally trained models can have a deeper sense of language context and flow than single-direction language models and therefore can be fine-tuned with an extra additional output layer to create a domain-specific model. These bidirectional fine-tuned Transformer models can even surpass human performance in this challenging area.

We tested different BERT pre-trained models, as advised in [14], and concluded that in our case the 'bert-base-uncased' model performed the best, therefore we used it for training the model. The concept for fine-tuning of the model using problem-specific application data on top of the BERT pre-trained model is shown in Fig. 11[4]. The training was performed with a 'learning_rate: $4e^{-5}$' and 'num_train_epochs: 5'.

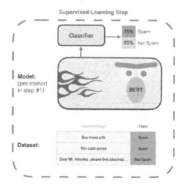

Fig. 11. Fine-tuning of pre-trained BERT model with annotated domain-specific data

The proposed concept takes a sample tweet text (pre-processed by removing URL, punctuations, and stop words as well as lemmatized to reduce the number

---

[4] http://jalammar.github.io/illustrated-bert/.

of tokens) as input and predicts the target label with fine-tuned trained model. It converts a sample tweet input into a feature tensor, which is next classified using a Neural Network to determine its target label. Considering the fine-tuning of the 'bert-base-uncased' model with LDA annotated data leads to more accurate and interpretable models. In the experimental evaluation of posts related to climate change, we showed that the proposed concept is applicable for predicting topics from short text without the need for lengthy and costly annotation.

4   Conclusion

Topic modeling is a useful technique that can automatically analyze text and identify the underlying topic discussed. It can be valuable for different domains, presenting potential advantages for diverse stakeholders. Various methods for topic modeling have been proposed in the literature. However, both main methods (unsupervised and supervised) have shortcomings. To overcome disadvantages this work proposes a hybrid topic modeling method that combines the advantages of both unsupervised and supervised methods.

We built a hybrid model by combining Latent Dirichlet Allocation (LDA) and deep learning built on top of the Bidirectional Encoder Representations from Transformers (BERT) model. LDA is used to identify the optimal number of topics and associated keywords. The only human input needed, with the help of ChatGPT, is to suggest to suggest topic names based on topic-specific keywords and possibly cluster more LDA-defined topics into one. This annotation is used to train and fine-tune the BERT model. In the experimental evaluation on posts related to climate change, we show that the proposed concept is applicable for predicting topics from short text without the need for lengthy and costly annotation. In this work, due to the harnessing of LDA, ChatGPT, and BERT, we completed the annotation of 4,000 posts in about 30 min while the same task required more than 66 h to be fully performed by humans. Testing the accuracy on test data revealed that the proposed concept achieves good accuracy and therefore the proposed concept is applicable for short text topic modeling.

As for future work, it would be interesting to further experiment with parameters for the LDA model to obtain better and maybe more keywords, which will possibly allow better classification and naming of underlying topics. In addition, it is also useful to experiment with deep learning parameters for fine-tuning and different pre-trained models. It is also necessary to devise the method to assess the accuracy of the hybrid method and experiment with other unsupervised topic modeling methods as well as explore the feasibility of applying the proposed method to other domains beyond climate change.

References

1. Albalawi, R., Yeap, T.H., Benyoucef, M.: Using topic modeling methods for short-text data: a comparative analysis. Front. Artif. Intell. **3**, 42 (2020)

2. Becken, S., Friedl, H., Stantic, B., Connolly, R.M., Chen, J.: Climate crisis and flying: social media analysis traces the rise of 'flightshame'. J. Sustain. Tourism **29**, 1450–1469 (2021)
3. Blei, D., Carin, L., Dunson, D.: Probabilistic topic models. IEEE Signal Process. Mag. **27**(6), 55–65 (2010)
4. Blei, D.M., Lafferty, J.D.: A correlated topic model of science (2007)
5. Blei, D.M., Ng, A.Y., Jordan, M.I.: Latent dirichlet allocation. J. Mach. Learn. Res. **3**(Jan), 993–1022 (2003)
6. Chen, J., Stantic, B., Chen, J.: Age prediction of social media users: case study on robots in hospitality. In: Jo, J., et al. (eds.) Robot Intelligence Technology and Applications 7, RiTA 2022. Lecture Notes in Networks and Systems, vol. 642, pp. 426–437. Springer, Cham (2023). https://doi.org/10.1007/978-3-031-26889-2_39
7. Chong, W., Blei, D., Li, F.F.: Simultaneous image classification and annotation. In: IEEE Conference on Computer Vision and Pattern Recognition, pp. 1903–1910 (2009)
8. Devlin, J., Chang, M.W., Lee, K., Toutanova, K.: BERT: pre-training of deep bidirectional transformers for language understanding. In: Proceedings of the 2019 Conference of the North American Chapter of the Association for Computational Linguistics: Human Language Technologies. NAACL-HLT, pp. 4171–4186 (2019)
9. Ding, K., Choo, W.C., Ng, K.Y., Ng, S.I., Song, P.: Exploring sources of satisfaction and dissatisfaction in Airbnb accommodation using unsupervised and supervised topic modeling. Front. Psychol. **12**, 659481 (2021)
10. Goutte, C., Gaussier, E.: A probabilistic interpretation of precision, recall and F-score, with implication for evaluation. In: Losada, D.E., Fernández-Luna, J.M. (eds.) ECIR 2005. LNCS, vol. 3408, pp. 345–359. Springer, Heidelberg (2005). https://doi.org/10.1007/978-3-540-31865-1_25
11. Jedrzejowicz, J., Zakrzewska, M.: Text classification using LDA-W2V hybrid algorithm. In: Czarnowski, I., Howlett, R.J., Jain, L.C. (eds.) Intelligent Decision Technologies 2019. SIST, vol. 142, pp. 227–237. Springer, Singapore (2020). https://doi.org/10.1007/978-981-13-8311-3_20
12. Landauer, T.K., Foltz, P.W., Laham, D.: An introduction to latent semantic analysis. Discourse Process. **25**(2–3), 259–284 (1998)
13. Ma, D., Rao, L., Wang, T.: An empirical study of SLDA for information retrieval. In: Salem, M.V.M., Shaalan, K., Oroumchian, F., Shakery, A., Khelalfa, H. (eds.) AIRS 2011. LNCS, vol. 7097, pp. 84–92. Springer, Heidelberg (2011). https://doi.org/10.1007/978-3-642-25631-8_8
14. Mandal, R., Chen, J., Becken, S., Stantic, B.: Tweets topic classification and sentiment analysis based on transformer-based language models. Vietnam J. Comput. Sci. **10**, 117–134 (2022)
15. Mcauliffe, J., Blei, D.: Supervised topic models. In: Advances in Neural Information Processing Systems, vol. 20 (2007)
16. Ramage, D., Hall, D., Nallapati, R., Manning, C.D.: Labeled LDA: a supervised topic model for credit attribution in multi-labeled corpora. In: Conference on Empirical Methods in Natural Language Processing, pp. 248–256 (2009)
17. Song, W., Park, S.C.: A novel document clustering model based on latent semantic analysis. In: Third International Conference on Semantics, Knowledge and Grid (SKG 2007), pp. 539–542. IEEE (2007)
18. Steyvers, M., Griffiths, T.: Probabilistic topic models. In: Handbook of Latent Semantic Analysis, pp. 439–460. Psychology Press (2007)
19. Wang, X., Yang, Y.: Neural topic model with attention for supervised learning. In: Conference on Artificial Intelligence and Statistics, pp. 1147–1156 (2020)

AWS: GNNs that Aggregate with Self-node Representation for Dehydrogenation Enthalpy Prediction

Geonyeong Choi[1], Hyunwoo Yook[2], Jeong Woo Han[2], and Charmgil Hong[1(⊠)]

[1] Department of Computer Science and Electrical Engineering, Handong Global University, Pohang, South Korea
{gychoi,charmgil}@handong.ac.kr
[2] Department of Materials Science and Engineering, Seoul National University, Seoul, South Korea
{hywook,jwhan98}@snu.ac.kr

Abstract. Although hydrogen is an ideal energy carrier, storing and transporting it in gas or liquid form is unsafe and inefficient. Liquid Organic Hydrogen Carriers (LOHC) are promising compounds that can efficiently accommodate hydrogen. However, choosing the optimal LOHC from millions of candidates is difficult because calculating dehydrogenation enthalpy, a key criterion, is computationally expensive. To address this, we propose a new graph neural network-based method called *Aggregate With Self-node representation* (AWS) that efficiently and accurately predicts dehydrogenation enthalpy. We improve existing graph neural networks and address cases where expressiveness is limited. We also present an ensemble scheme for weighting prediction results. Our experiments on real-world LOHC screening and benchmark datasets demonstrate the superiority of our method in chemical property predictions.

Keywords: Dehydrogenation Enthalpy · Property Prediction · Graph Neural Networks · Deep Learning Methods and Applications

1 Introduction

Imminent threats of climate change have forced humankind to harness renewable energy, such as hydroelectric, solar, and wind power. However, renewable energy has the disadvantage of unreliable production [21]. Consequently, many proposals have been made to overcome this drawback. One such option is to adopt hydrogen, an attractive, clean energy carrier that emits only water as its byproduct. Hydrogen produced from renewable energy is compressed and transported in liquid form [21]. However, storing hydrogen in liquid form requires high pressure and low temperature, and 0.3–3.0% of hydrogen losses in storage are inevitable due to boil-off [1]. Thus, another option for carrying hydrogen is to use Liquid Organic Hydrogen Carriers (LOHC) [21], safe and affordable molecules with which no hydrogen losses are expected from storage and transportation. Namely,

N. T. Nguyen et al. (Eds.): ACIIDS 2023, CCIS 1863, pp. 169–180, 2023.
https://doi.org/10.1007/978-3-031-42430-4_14

LOHC carries and emits hydrogen with the reversible processes of hydrogenation and dehydrogenation.

The discussion and discovery of the ideal LOHC among millions of LOHC candidates are still in progress [22]. There are several criteria for ideal LOHC, such as energy demand, toxicity, and material handling [21], and one of the criteria is dehydrogenation enthalpy, the difference in enthalpy between a hydrogenated molecule and a dehydrogenated molecule. Dehydrogenation enthalpy is closely related to the total energy for reactions, and optimal LOHC has an adequate dehydrogenation enthalpy of around $15\,\mathrm{kcal/mol^{-1}}$ [22] for an energetically efficient reaction. Dehydrogenation enthalpy can be calculated by the density functional theory (DFT) [23]. However, as DFT is very time-consuming considering millions of candidates for LOHC, many research has been done to avoid the time-complexity issue of DFT and achieve a prompt and precise estimation of molecular properties using data-driven approaches [15,24,31]. This work extends the endeavor and aims to build a new framework that effectively screens suitable candidate materials for LOHC.

Graph neural networks (GNNs) [12] are a type of deep learning architecture specifically designed to process data in the form of graphs. In recent years, GNNs have been shown to achieve state-of-the-art performance on complex data-driven problems, making them a promising approach in various real-world settings [32]. One area where GNNs have been particularly successful is in the field of molecular property prediction. Molecules, which consist of atoms and bonds, can be naturally represented and analyzed as graphs. Researchers have reported successful applications of graph-based approaches in molecular property prediction, including predicting properties such as solubility and toxicity [6,15,24]. In this study, we propose to utilize GNNs to model and predict dehydrogenation enthalpy for LOHC material screening. By using GNNs to model the molecular structure of potential LOHC materials, we can capture the complex relationships between atoms and bonds that contribute to dehydrogenation enthalpy. This approach has the potential to accelerate the discovery of new LOHC materials with improved dehydrogenation properties, ultimately contributing to the development of more efficient and sustainable hydrogen storage and transport technologies.

The following of the paper is organized as follows: Sect. 2 provides related background by introducing the problem of chemical property prediction and the basics of graph neural networks. Section 3 then proposes an improved GNN architecture called AWS, which addresses the shortcomings of state-of-the-art GNNs [27,29] by aggregating neighborhood nodes with self-node representations. Section 4 shows experimental results that AWS outperforms other GNNs in predicting dehydrogenation enthalpy and benchmark datasets. We further demonstrate the effectiveness of the ensemble methods via special weighting schemes that are determined by AWS and molecular representations.

2   Background

2.1   Chemical Property Prediction (CPP)

The problem of the LOHC material screening can be understood as a specific instance in chemical property prediction (CPP). Below we overview some of the existing approaches in CPP that are closely related to our work.

CPP Utilizing Molecular Features. The chemical properties of molecules are determined by their physicochemical structures. The quantitative structure-activity/property relationships (QSAR/ QSPR) modeling approaches [17] take *in-silico* approaches to predict chemical properties. OPEn structure-activity /property Relationship App (OPERA) [16] is a representative example that applies the weighted k-nearest neighbors algorithm on molecular features.

CPP Utilizing the SMILES Notation. Simplified Molecular Input Line Entry Specification (SMILES) is a set of strings that express atoms and bonds as characters. Early research like [4] successfully adopted SMILES in CPP. One caveat with SMILES is that a molecule may have multiple SMILES strings. Accordingly, trivial approaches may result in models with permutation-variant outputs. However, one issue with SMILES is that a molecule can have multiple strings, leading to permutation-variant outputs with trivial approaches. Graph Neural Networks (GNNs) solve this problem by utilizing connectivity between nodes, making them permutation-invariant. GNNs have also shown superior performance in CPP [25].

2.2   Graph Neural Networks

2.2.1   Definition

Suppose a graph $\mathcal{G} = \{\mathcal{V}, \mathcal{E}\}$ with node and edge sets $\mathcal{V}$ and $\mathcal{E}$. Each node $v \in \mathcal{V}$ has a node feature $x_v \in X$ (X denotes the node feature variable); and each edge $e_{uv} \in \mathcal{E}$ connecting nodes v and u has a edge feature $e_{vu} \in E$ (E denotes the edge feature variable). A GNN produces a node representation $h_v^{(k)}$ at its k th layer as:

$$h_v^{(k)} = COMBINE(h_v^{(k-1)}, AGGREGATE(\{h_v^{(k-1)}, h_u^{(k-1)}, e_{vu} : u \in \mathcal{N}(v)\}))$$

where $\mathcal{N}(v)$ denotes the neighborhood node set of node v, and $h_v^{(0)} = x_v$. At each layer for node v, GNNs aggregate the node representations with neighborhood nodes $\mathcal{N}(v)$ and update the node representation $h_v^{(k)}$ by combining the previous node representation $h_v^{(k-1)}$ and the aggregated neighborhood representations. Accordingly, as the number of layers increases, the receptive field (the node set that determines the node representation) becomes larger. In other words, $h_v^{(k)}$ captures the information over the k-hop neighborhood of node v.

2.2.2   Existing GNN Architectures

The operational specifications for the *message passing*, including the *COMBINE* and *AGGREGATE* functions, vary with GNN architecture. For example, *Graph Convolutional Networks* (GCN) [12] combine and aggregates node representations, executing graph smoothing by matrix multiplications $D^{-1/2}AD^{-1/2}$. However, such simplicity comes with constraints, as it is designed for a fixed graph and only allows for transductive learning, which can be a major limiting factor in various applications.

   GraphSAGE [7] was proposed to address the transductive issue of GCNs by sampling neighboring nodes and aggregating them using averaging. However, this method may lead to overlapping node representations if two neighborhoods produce proportionally identical aggregations, restricting GraphSAGE's expressiveness [29]. On the other hand, *Graph Isomorphism Networks* (GINs) [29] use summation for *AGGREGATE*, which generates distinct node representations for different neighborhoods. In this respect, GINs are *injective*, meaning that the model can discern multisets of duplicated elements. *Graph Attention Networks* (GATs) [27] use the self-attention mechanism [26] that GATs aggregate and combine node representations based on attention weights calculated from node features and their neighbors' neighborhoods.

   At the final layer K of GNNs, the *READOUT* function aggregate all node representations for the graph-level tasks.

$$h_{\mathcal{G}} = READOUT(\{h_v^K : v \in \mathcal{V}\}) \tag{1}$$

where the *READOUT* function can be any permutation-invariant function such as simple methods including summation (global add pooling, GAP) and averaging, or sophisticated methods including Graph multiset pooling (GMT) [2].

   In addition to studying the design and effects of the *COMBINE* and *AGGREGATE* functions, many researchers also investigate the architectural components of GNNs. One such component is the pre- and post-processing layers, which are essentially fully-connected layers that can be placed at the beginning and end of a GNN [32]. The pre-processing layer modifies $h_v^{(0)}$ for the first layer, while the post-processing layer modifies $h_v^{(K)}$ for the *READOUT* function. Skip connections, like residual connections and dense connections, improve GNN performance by allowing access to multiple layer representations [8,11,32]. Jumping Knowledge Networks (JKN) [30] concatenate node representations from all GNN layers, making optimal receptive fields available for decision-making.

3   Proposed Method

This section presents our proposed method, which addresses the limitations of GATs and GINs, which we will discuss further below. During the discussion, we will also explore the injectiveness of GINs, present an undesirable scenario, and propose a solution. Lastly, we will suggest a set of weighting schemes to enhance ensemble performances.

3.1   Motivation

3.1.1   Limitations of Graph Isomorphism Networks (GINs)

GINs are currently considered the state-of-the-art architecture among GNNs. This model, however, does not incorporate the self-node representation in its aggregation process. As a result, the aggregated node representations are independent of the self-node representation. The message passing of GINs can be written as:

$$h_v^{(k)} = MLP((1 + \epsilon)h_v^{(k-1)} + AGGREGATE^{(k-1)}(\{h_u^{(k-1)} + e_{vu} : u \in N(v)\})) \tag{2}$$

where $AGGREGATE$ function is a summation, ϵ is a learnable parameter, and MLP is a multi-layer perceptron. GINs do not utilize the self-node representation in their aggregation process, leading to aggregated node representations that are independent of the self-node representation. Consequently, the expressiveness of the aggregated node representations may be limited. Additionally, as demonstrated in [29], the aggregated node representations $\sum_{u \in \mathcal{N}(v)} f(u)$ should be *injective* where f is a function $f : v \to \mathbb{R}^n$. Unfortunately, GINs utilize the identity function ($f(u) = u$), which results in $\sum_{u \in \mathcal{N}(v)} f(u)$ not being *injective* (see Sect. 3.3.1).

3.1.2   Limitations of Graph Attention Networks (GATs)

Recent success with the self-attention mechanism across different fields [26, 27] has prompted GNNs to incorporate attention layers that integrate the neighbor node representations with the self-node representation. GATs, for example, utilize attention weights α_{vu} to aggregate neighborhood representations:

$$\alpha_{vu} = \frac{exp(a^T LeakyReLU(W[h_v^{(k-1)}||h_u^{(k-1)}||e_{vu}]))}{\sum_{i \in \mathcal{N}(v) \cup \{v\}} exp(a^T LeakyReLU(W[h_v^{(k-1)}||h_i^{(k-1)}||e_{vu}]))} \tag{3}$$

$$h_v^{(k)} = \alpha_{vv}(Wh_v^{(k-1)}) + \sum_{u \in \mathcal{N}(v)} \alpha_{vu}(Wh_u^{(k-1)}) \tag{4}$$

where W is a weight matrix, a denotes an weight vector and $||$ stands for concatenation.

GATs employ the self-node representation for aggregation and are *injective* since f is a mapping function with an attention coefficient α_{vu} and weight matrix W.

However, Eq. (4) presents an issue where a self-edge e_{vv} is necessary to compute α_{vv}, while the self-edge is unrealistic for a molecule that does not have self-bonding.

3.2   GNNs that Aggregate with Self-node Representation

We propose *Aggregate With Self-node representation* (AWS) that combines the advantages of GATs and GINs as below:

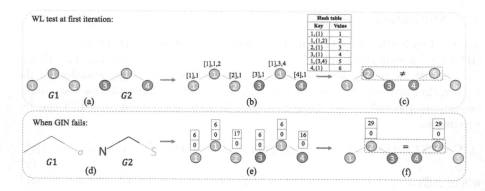

Fig. 1. Cases when GINs are not injective (a) Two graphs with four types of nodes. (b) Nodes with aggregated neighborhood nodes. (c) Types of nodes are reassigned by the hash table, and nodes with two neighborhoods do not have the same type. (d) Two molecules with the same node distribution as Fig. 1(a). (e) Two molecules with atomic features. (f) Two atoms with two neighborhood atoms have the same representations.

$$h_v^{(k)} = MLP(MLP(h_v^{(k-1)})\|(\sum_{u \in \mathcal{N}(v)} MLP(h_v^{(k-1)}\|h_u^{(k-1)}\|e_{vu}))) \qquad (5)$$

In AWS, we concatenate the self-node representation with the neighborhood node representations before the aggregation, and then concatenate it again with the aggregated node representations. This allows the model to choose information from both the self-node representation and the aggregated node representations. Unlike GINs, AWS uses an *MLP* to aggregate node representations, rather than an identity function. Moreover, the aggregated node representation is dependent on the self-node representation, similar to GATs. Importantly, AWS does not require a self-edge e_{vv} for the aggregation.

3.3   Discussion

3.3.1   Atomic Features and Expressiveness of GNNs
Richer atomic features can improve the predictive performance of GNNs beyond the basic atomic information (atomic numbers and chirality) [25]. Below, we demonstrate through a simple example that richer atomic features are indeed associated with injectiveness.

The Injectiveness and Atomic Features. The Weisfeiler-Lehman (WL) graph isomorphism test [28] checks whether two graphs are identical based on color refinement (Fig. 1(a–c)). It is an injective method and the most expressive GNNs can be as powerful as the WL test [29]. For this reason, [29] claims that GINs are considered as the most expressive GNNs. However, we found that GINs can be non-injective in certain cases, as illustrated in Fig. 1.

In the case of the WL test, the node representations of two graphs, $G1$ and $G2$ in Fig. 1(a), are determined by neighboring nodes and a hash table shown

in Fig. 1(b) and (c). After the first step of the WL test, the middle nodes of
$G1$ and $G2$ have different representations as they had different neighborhoods.
However, if GINs are as expressive as the WL test, the middle atoms in $G1$ and
$G2$ (Fig. 1(d)) should have different representations since they have different
neighboring atoms. In particular, if we consider only two atomic features are
available (as in [10,25]), the middle atoms yield identical representations as in
Fig. 1(f), implying that GINs may violate injectiveness if atomic features or
representations are too simple. Therefore, GINs cannot guarantee injectiveness
without increasing the number of atomic features. This example highlights the
importance of using a larger set of atomic features to improve the expressiveness
of GINs.

Types of Atomic Features Used in Our Solution. We use 15 atomic features, comprising nine *static* and six *dynamic* features, to learn injective representations related to the molecule's intrinsic properties. Static features, such as
atomic numbers, radius, volume, vdw radius, dipole polarizability, and *electroneg-
ativities* (*en_pauling, en_allen,* and *en_ghosh*), are position-invariant. Dynamic
features, such as *chirality, IsInRing, total degree, total valence electrons, IsAro-
matic,* and *the number of hydrogens,* are position-variant. We also add hydrogens
to the molecular graphs and use three bond features, including *bond type, stereo
configuration,* and *conjugation*. We use the Python libraries Mendeleev [19] and
RDKit [13] to obtain the feature values.

3.3.2 Post-hoc Performance Improvement via Ensemble

To address the issue of robustness in GNNs, ensemble approaches have been
applied [33]. Bui et al. [3] demonstrated that the simple averaging of multiple
results from GNNs could effectively solve the problem.

We take the average of predictions made by 25 GNNs and apply weights to the
predictions using a single weight matrix or MLP. However, since the networks do
not utilize the structure of molecules, we calculate weights based on molecular
structure using AWS. Molecular representation $h_{out} \in \mathbb{R}^{25}$ from AWS can be
used as weights for prediction results and directly multiplied with $y_{pred} \in \mathbb{R}^{25}$.

$$ASSIGN(h_{out}, y_{pred}) = h_{out}^T * y_{pred} = y_{pred}' \qquad (6)$$

where $y_{pred}' \in \mathbb{R}^1$. From Eq. (6), weights for some models can be very large and
cause overfitting since the range of weights is $\mathbb{R}$. Hence, we restrict the range
of weights to be between zero and one using the *softmax* function. We multiply
$softmax(h_{out})$ with y_{pred}.

$$ASSIGN(h_{out}, y_{pred}) = softmax(h_{out})^T * y_{pred} \qquad (7)$$

4 Experiments

We compare our proposed method with state-of-the-art GNN approaches and
demonstrate its effectiveness. We report and analyze the results on dehydrogenation enthalpy prediction, benchmark chemical property prediction datasets, and
evaluate ensemble models using weights determined by molecular structures.

4.1 Experimental Settings

The overall model structure is depicted in Fig. 2. It is composed of seven GNN layers with residual connections. The specific operations at each layers are determined with the type of GNNs. We use GNNs with Eq. (2) where the *AGGRE-GATE* function is the averaging (MEAN) or summation (GIN). We also use GNNs consisting of Eq. (4) as GATs and Eq. (5) as AWS. Three hidden layers are attached to the beginning and end of the GNN layers, and all node representations are concatenated at the end. To avoid overfitting and ensure injectiveness, global add pooling (GAP) is used for the *READOUT* function [2,14]. Additionally, 32 molecular features [13] are concatenated with the molecular representations from GAP. Finally, We use MLP with four hidden layers halving the hidden units and one hidden layer to make a final prediction.

For hyperparameters, we use 128 hidden units, batch normalization, and Gaussian Error Linear Unit (GELU) [9] as the activation function for every hidden layer. The checkpoint with the minimum validation loss is chosen, and the model performances are recorded on the test set. For the dehydrogenation enthalpy prediction and benchmark datasets, we use 3,000 epochs, a batch size of 250, and a learning rate of $1e-04$. In the ensemble experiments, we utilize 25 AWS models. The hyperparameters are chosen from epochs $\in \{10, 50, 100, 150, 200, \ 250, 300\}$, batch sizes $\in \{50, 250\}$, and learning rates $\in \{1e-03, 5e-03, 1e-04, 5e-04\}$.

We evaluate the performance using the mean absolute error (MAE) and coefficient of determination R^2.

4.2 Dehydrogenation Enthalpy Predictions

For the first set of experiments, we utilized 959 LOHC candidates with ring structures, and dehydrogenation enthalpy calculated by DFT. We divided the data into train, validation, and test sets in the ratio of 8:1:1 and performed 10-fold cross-validation with random splits. We compared the performance of GNNs with different architectures (*MEAN*, GIN, GAT, and AWS). We also used

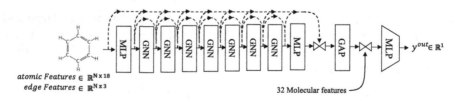

Fig. 2. Overall structure of networks

Table 1. Model performances with different GNNs architectures

Method	Dehydrogenation Enthalpy		ESOL		Freesolv		LIPO	
	MAE	R2	MAE	R2	MAE	R2	MAE	R2
MLP*only*	3.079 (0.515)	0.903 (0.040)	0.894 (0.090)	0.735 (0.040)	1.879 (0.202)	0.717 (0.092)	0.822 (0.033)	0.128 (0.096)
MEAN	2.378 (0.285)	0.944 (0.014)	0.853 (0.095)	0.757 (0.029)	1.543 (0.580)	0.802 (0.136)	0.655 (0.036)	0.420 (0.099)
GIN	2.449 (0.252)	0.941 (0.013)	0.898 (0.081)	0.732 (0.035)	1.434 (0.128)	0.821 (0.061)	0.669 (0.010)	0.403 (0.072)
GAT	2.444 (0.358)	0.930 (0.037)	0.842 (0.168)	0.739 (0.121)	1.488 (0.360)	0.828 (0.093)	0.683 (0.059)	0.369 (0.126)
AWS	**1.955 (0.231)**	**0.954 (0.017)**	**0.799 (0.091)**	**0.778 (0.040)**	**1.431 (0.188)**	**0.855 (0.043)**	**0.633 (0.016)**	**0.454 (0.028)**

molecular representations from atomic features with GAP and MLP (MLP*only*) having four hidden layers. The result of the experiment is shown in Table 1. We observed that models with GNN architectures performed better than MLP*only* on all datasets. This suggests that GNNs play a crucial role in producing accurate molecular representations for predictions. We also found that AWS had better performance than other models with GNNs architectures.

In addition, we predicted the dehydrogenation enthalpy of five representative LOHCs (Fig. 3) from [21] to demonstrate the effectiveness of our model. The results are shown in Table 2, where we report both the actual dehydrogenation enthalpy (Actual DH) from [21] and the predicted dehydrogenation enthalpy (Predicted DH) from GIN, GAT, and AWS. We observed that our model more accurately predicts the dehydrogenation enthalpy of all five molecules than other GNNs, suggesting that our model can be effective in screening LOHCs with dehydrogenation enthalpy. We have also shared the results to the domain experts in the process of LOHC screening, and confirmed that the test predictions of our model is similar to the actual dehydrogenation enthalpy within the confidence interval, indicating that our model's predictions are reliable.

4.3 Benchmark Datasets

On the benchmark test, we evaluated our model's performance using three molecular property prediction datasets: ESOL [5], LIPO [18], and Freesolv [20]. ESOL contains solubility data for 1,128 molecules in water, LIPO contains solubility data for 4,000 molecules in lipids, and Freesolv contains hydration free energy data for 642 molecules.

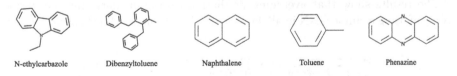

N-ethylcarbazole   Dibenzyltoluene   Naphthalene   Toluene   Phenazine

Fig. 3. Two-dimensional structures of five representative LOHC

Table 2. Actual and Predicted Dehydrogenation Enthalpy (DH) of standard LOHCs

Molecular name	Actual DH	Predicted DH		
		GIN	GAT	AWS
N-ethylcarbazole	53	61.012	61.219	**56.144**
Dibenzyltoluene	65.4	62.634	64.320	**66.355**
Naphthalene	66.3	65.674	68.025	**66.543**
Toluene	68.3	66.233	65.414	**66.940**
Phenazine	61.3	57.687	62.686	**60.360**

Table 3. Model performances with different ensemble methods

Method	Dehydrogenation Enthalpy		ESOL		Freesolv		LIPO	
	MAE	R2	MAE	R2	MAE	R2	MAE	R2
AVERAGE	1.661 (0.195)	0.966 (0.012)	0.758 (0.050)	0.802 (0.010)	1.310 (0.133)	0.864 (0.048)	0.615 (0.005)	0.488 (0.045)
1-Layer	1.738 (0.294)	0.964 (0.015)	0.774 (0.065)	0.795 (0.015)	1.290 (0.205)	0.809 (0.015)	0.614 (0.039)	0.476 (0.079)
MLP	1.691 (0.282)	0.967 (0.013)	0.750 (0.053)	**0.809 (0.015)**	1.262 (0.235)	0.866 (0.057)	**0.606 (0.024)**	**0.495 (0.075)**
GNN*weight*	**1.589 (0.254)**	**0.968 (0.013)**	0.833 (0.029)	0.758 (0.025)	1.335 (0.159)	0.853 (0.048)	0.626 (0.028)	0.444 (0.100)
GNN*softmax*	1.604 (0.246)	**0.968 (0.012)**	**0.744 (0.046)**	0.806 (0.007)	**1.194 (0.245)**	**0.882 (0.054)**	0.614 (0.003)	0.488 (0.045)

Table 1 presents the experiment results. We observed that AWS outperformed other GNNs and that, except for AWS, the best performing GNN varied depending on the dataset. This highlights the shortcomings of GNNs, such as the use of self-edges in GAT, can diminish the performance of the model. Our approach, on the other hand, compensated for these shortcomings in other GNNs and resulted in better performance on the datasets.

4.4   Ensemble Performances

We recorded performances by averaging prediction results (*AVERAGE*) and compared the performance to the other ensemble methods. The structure of the ensemble model is shown in Fig. 4. We use a single hidden layer (*1-Layer*), and MLP (*MLP*) with four hidden layers for the prediction, and we multiply weights (GNN*weight*) from AWS using Eq. (6), and weights with the *softmax* function (GNN*softmax*) using Eq. (7).

The results show that averaging prediction results outperforms the performance of using a single GNN in all datasets (Tables 1 and 3). The best performing

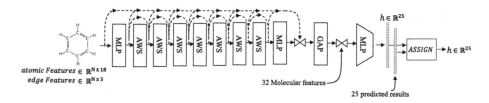

Fig. 4. Overall structure of ensemble models with weights determined by networks

ensemble method varies depending on the dataset. However, GNN*softmax* shows better performance than the *Average* method in all datasets and achieves the minimum MAE in ESOL and Freesolv datasets. From the experiments, we found that limiting the weight range improves the performance of ensemble models.

5   Conclusion

We proposed an enhanced GNN-based method, AWS, to predict the dehydrogenation enthalpy of LOHC candidates and demonstrated its superior performance compared to other GNNs. We confirmed improved performances of our model not only in predicting dehydrogenation enthalpy but also on various benchmark datasets, thereby demonstrating its ability in estimating other chemical properties. Also, in the case of ensembles, we found that utilizing outputs of multiple models with limited weight ranges could yield superior performance compared to simply averaging predicted outcomes. Moving forward, we plan to employ our model to predict LOHC criteria beyond dehydrogenation enthalpy, such as melting point and boiling point to screen millions of LOHC candidates.

References

1. Adametz, P., Müller, K., Arlt, W.: Energetic evaluation of hydrogen storage in metal hydrides. Int. J. Energy Res. **40**(13), 1820–1831 (2016)
2. Baek, J., Kang, M., Hwang, S.J.: Accurate learning of graph representations with graph multiset pooling. arXiv preprint arXiv:2102.11533 (2021)
3. Bui, A.T., et al.: Improving ensemble robustness by collaboratively promoting and demoting adversarial robustness. In: Proceedings of the AAAI Conference on Artificial Intelligence, vol. 35, pp. 6831–6839 (2021)
4. Cao, D.S., et al.: In silico toxicity prediction by support vector machine and smiles representation-based string kernel. SAR QSAR Environ. Res. **23**(1–2), 141–153 (2012)
5. Delaney, J.S.: ESOL: estimating aqueous solubility directly from molecular structure. J. Chem. Inf. Comput. Sci. **44**(3), 1000–1005 (2004)
6. Gasteiger, J., Becker, F., Günnemann, S.: GemNet: universal directional graph neural networks for molecules. In: Advances in Neural Information Processing Systems, vol. 34, pp. 6790–6802 (2021)
7. Hamilton, W., Ying, Z., Leskovec, J.: Inductive representation learning on large graphs. In: Advances in Neural Information Processing Systems, vol. 30 (2017)
8. He, K., Zhang, X., Ren, S., Sun, J.: Identity mappings in deep residual networks. In: Leibe, B., Matas, J., Sebe, N., Welling, M. (eds.) ECCV 2016. LNCS, vol. 9908, pp. 630–645. Springer, Cham (2016). https://doi.org/10.1007/978-3-319-46493-0_38
9. Hendrycks, D., Gimpel, K.: Gaussian error linear units (GELUs). arXiv preprint arXiv:1606.08415 (2016)
10. Hu, W., et al.: Strategies for pre-training graph neural networks. arXiv preprint arXiv:1905.12265 (2019)
11. Huang, G., Liu, Z., Van Der Maaten, L., Weinberger, K.Q.: Densely connected convolutional networks. In: Proceedings of the IEEE Conference on Computer Vision and Pattern Recognition, pp. 4700–4708 (2017)

12. Kipf, T.N., Welling, M.: Semi-supervised classification with graph convolutional networks. arXiv preprint arXiv:1609.02907 (2016)
13. Landrum, G.: RDKit documentation. Release 1(1–79), 4 (2013)
14. Lin, M., Chen, Q., Yan, S.: Network in network. arXiv preprint arXiv:1312.4400 (2013)
15. Mansimov, E., Mahmood, O., Kang, S., Cho, K.: Molecular geometry prediction using a deep generative graph neural network. Sci. Rep. 9(1), 1–13 (2019)
16. Mansouri, K., Grulke, C.M., Judson, R.S., Williams, A.J.: Opera models for predicting physicochemical properties and environmental fate endpoints. J. Cheminform. 10(1), 1–19 (2018)
17. Mansouri, K., Judson, R.S.: In silico study of in vitro GPCR assays by QSAR modeling. In: Benfenati, E. (ed.) In Silico Methods for Predicting Drug Toxicity. MMB, vol. 1425, pp. 361–381. Springer, New York (2016). https://doi.org/10.1007/978-1-4939-3609-0_16
18. Mendez, D., et al.: ChEMBL: towards direct deposition of bioassay data. Nucleic Acids Res. 47(D1), D930–D940 (2019)
19. Mentel, L.: Mendeleev documentation (2022)
20. Mobley, D.L., Guthrie, J.P.: FreeSolv: a database of experimental and calculated hydration free energies, with input files. J. Comput. Aided Mol. Des. 28(7), 711–720 (2014)
21. Niermann, M., Beckendorff, A., Kaltschmitt, M., Bonhoff, K.: Liquid organic hydrogen carrier (LOHC)-assessment based on chemical and economic properties. Int. J. Hydrogen Energy 44(13), 6631–6654 (2019)
22. Paragian, K., Li, B., Massino, M., Rangarajan, S.: A computational workflow to discover novel liquid organic hydrogen carriers and their dehydrogenation routes. Mol. Syst. Des. Eng. 5(10), 1658–1670 (2020)
23. Parr, R.G.: Density functional theory. Annu. Rev. Phys. Chem. 34(1), 631–656 (1983)
24. Simm, G.N., Hernández-Lobato, J.M.: A generative model for molecular distance geometry. arXiv preprint arXiv:1909.11459 (2019)
25. Sun, R.: Does GNN pretraining help molecular representation? arXiv preprint arXiv:2207.06010 (2022)
26. Vaswani, A., et al.: Attention is all you need. In: Advances in Neural Information Processing Systems, vol. 30 (2017)
27. Veličković, P., Cucurull, G., Casanova, A., Romero, A., Lio, P., Bengio, Y.: Graph attention networks. arXiv preprint arXiv:1710.10903 (2017)
28. Weisfeiler, B., Leman, A.: The reduction of a graph to canonical form and the algebra which appears therein. NTI Ser. 2(9), 12–16 (1968)
29. Xu, K., Hu, W., Leskovec, J., Jegelka, S.: How powerful are graph neural networks? arXiv preprint arXiv:1810.00826 (2018)
30. Xu, K., Li, C., Tian, Y., Sonobe, T., Kawarabayashi, K., Jegelka, S.: Representation learning on graphs with jumping knowledge networks. In: International Conference on Machine Learning, pp. 5453–5462. PMLR (2018)
31. Xu, M., Luo, S., Bengio, Y., Peng, J., Tang, J.: Learning neural generative dynamics for molecular conformation generation. arXiv preprint arXiv:2102.10240 (2021)
32. You, J., Ying, Z., Leskovec, J.: Design space for graph neural networks. In: Advances in Neural Information Processing Systems, vol. 33, pp. 17009–17021 (2020)
33. Zügner, D., Akbarnejad, A., Günnemann, S.: Adversarial attacks on neural networks for graph data. In: Proceedings of the 24th ACM SIGKDD International Conference on Knowledge Discovery & Data Mining, pp. 2847–2856 (2018)

Utilising Unet3+ for Tooth Segmentation on X-Ray Image

Huong Hoang Luong[1] , Hao Van Tran[1] , Bang Do Huu Dang[1] ,
Duy Khanh Nguyen[1] , Phuc Tan Huynh[1] , Dat Tuan Ly[1] ,
and Hai Thanh Nguyen[2(✉)]

[1] Information Technology Department, FPT University, Can Tho 900000, Vietnam
{haotvce150521,bangddhce150240,duynkce150519,
phuchtce150394,datltce150718}@fpt.edu.vn
[2] College of Information and Communication Technology,
Can Tho University, Can Tho 900000, Vietnam
nthai.cit@ctu.edu.vn

Abstract. Oral health has become increasingly important because it helps gain confidence in communication and work. Therefore, detecting and diagnosing teeth as early as possible is essential to reduce adverse patient effects and protect oral health. Nowadays the importance of the oral cavity is recognized as a vital part of the human body. However, it affects health status and causes mental and work productivity problems. This study proposes a model applying the Unet3+ model to classify and detect teeth in the jaw. The dataset consists of anonymized and deidentified panoramic dental X-rays of 116 patients at Noor Medical Imaging Center, Qom, Iran. The subjects cover various dental conditions, from healthy to partial and complete edentulous cases. The experimental results show Unet3+ model achieves promising results, with Accuracy being 94.80 and F1-score being 0.9533.

Keywords: Oral health · Unet3+ · panoramic dental

1 Introduction

According to the report [1], oral health is one of the most important predictors of general health, happiness, and quality of life. Dental diseases, including erosion, caries, and periodontitis, are linked to several mental problems, including severe mental illness, affective disorders, and eating disorders. As described in [2], Mental health can affect oral health and cause the following diseases: Periodontal disease, Tooth surface loss, Xerostomia, Dental caries, Chronic orofacial pain, and Soft tissue lesions.

Oral health also dramatically impacts physical health; oral health has been connected to cardiovascular disorders. The correlations between poor dental health and the prevalence of cardiovascular disease have been the subject of numerous investigations [3]. In specially, the researchers looked at 150,774 subjects [4]. Gastrointestinal cancer was analyzed according to periodontal disease and oral hygiene indicators: frequency of tooth brushing, dental visits for any reason, professional dental cleanings, and several missing teeth. Bacteremia and systemic inflammation, two established mediators of cancer development, are directly linked to poor oral hygiene. Regular tooth brushing was significantly linked to a lower incidence of gastrointestinal cancer [4].

Applying technology in medical examination and treatment in oral health care is widely applied. Because of that, tooth detection can help to treat the disease effectively but also helps to reduce treatment time and cost. Using the Unet model for automatic tooth segmentation to avoid tedious, challenging, and time-consuming is widely used nowadays [5–7]. Unet models have also developed many family models such as Unet++, RIC-Unet, Swin-Unet, and Eff-UNet used for medical image analysis [8–10]. Through the research results, we found that Unet3+ is most suitable for auto-segmentation on teeth [11] and decided Unet3+ is the critical technology in this research.

Unet3+ directly predicts teeth in input X-ray images by converting them into image arrays. It outperforms other modern models in the Unet family when there is enough data to train. Hyperparameters are optimized to maximize the model's Accuracy on the existing dataset. The results aid in tooth analysis for treatment decisions. We compare and evaluate the Unet3+ results with other Unet family models, such as Unet and Unet++.

This research article has used Unet3+ architectures to the pre-trained networks, with the major contributions as follows:

- Dental x-ray image segmentation has been extensively studied using Unet and Unet++ deep learning architectures. We propose the Unet3+ model and compare its efficiency with recent approaches, such as Unet and Unet++. Prior to training the model, the x-ray images undergo picture preprocessing, including transform size, color adjustments, contrast, and other image properties. Preprocessing can shorten the training time and improve inference speed.
- In addition to using image generation techniques, we produced more than 600 additional images from the original set of 116 images by modifying a few of the image's properties and parameters.
- Our study performs CCA analysis to visualize the proposed model's training results.

2   Related Work

Currently, in dentistry, tooth segmentation from X-ray images is mainly performed by doctors manually. However, tooth segmentation has been used extensively for therapy and data collection. According to [12], 80% of studies use images of the mouth, such as bite marks and periapical, to perform their experiments. Segmentation of teeth in panoramic images is the ultimate goal that we aim for; our work is to continue to exploit to increase accuracy metrics based on X-rays of panoramic images.

In 2019, using the 2-D Coupled Shape Model (the presented method is based on a 3-D coupled shape), Witz et al. [13] achieved an accuracy of 0.887 on a set of 14 test images. The linked shape model has been expanded to include single 2-D pictures for dental X-ray images. To depict the contour of objects and their relative transformation to the connected model's center, deformable 2-D model elements and the accompanying 2-D transformations have been introduced. Using a point distribution model (PDM) and principal component analysis, these 2-D model elements are created and represented as statistical shape models (PCA).

In addition, the researchers also used the wavelet transform architecture for processing bitewing X-ray images. For example, on a database of 681 teeth in 85 bitewing X-ray images, Salimzadeh [14] employed wavelet transformed to teeth segmentation and achieved an accuracy of 90.6% [14]. The suggested technique is based on separating dental contours across crowns through four phases, including morphological processing, region of interest (ROI) determination, edge detection using wavelet transform, and magic enhancement-fruit-separated teeth depending on dividing lines. The researchers point out that this approach may still be applied as a component of ADIS when necessary.

Besides, the Unet architecture is also a bright spot in tooth segmentation problems: 2022, Helli & Hamamcı [15] proposes a post-processing stage to obtain a segmentation map in which the objects in the image are separated and apply this technique to segment individual teeth using Unet. A dice overlap score of 95.4 ± 0.3% is obtained in overall teeth segmentation. The proposed post-processing stages reduce the mean error of tooth count to 6.15%, whereas the error without post-processing is 26.81% by using a relatively small training dataset with 105 images.

Moreover, recently, Unet3+ has been proposed to reduce network parameters to improve computational efficiency. We continue to propose a model to apply the Unet3+ model to classify and detect teeth in the arch to obtain more satisfactory results when the actual result is 94.80% accuracy 95.33% F1-score (the F1-score ratio is not reduced compared to the CNN mentioned above architecture).

3   Proposed Method

3.1   Overall of the Proposed Process

Prior knowledge of the data is beneficial when using techniques like segmentation, image preprocessing, data augmentation, accuracy metrics, and algorithms.

We collected 116 panoramic dental X-rays for Abdi's study, manually segmented by two dentists. First, the images were randomly selected for training and testing processes, with 105 for training and 11 for testing. The images for the training and testing processes in Fig. 1 were then randomly selected from the dataset; 105 images were randomly selected for training and 11 for testing. The Unet3+ model was chosen and optimized for the best output, compared with the original Unet model. The results were presented in tables and graphs using various metrics. In neuroscience research, Canonical Correlation Analysis (CCA) is a promising approach to detect joint multivariate interactions among several modalities, increasing correlation by identifying linear combinations of variables. Various CCA variants are used, including Kernel CCA, Restricted CCA, Deep CCA, and Multiset CCA [16].

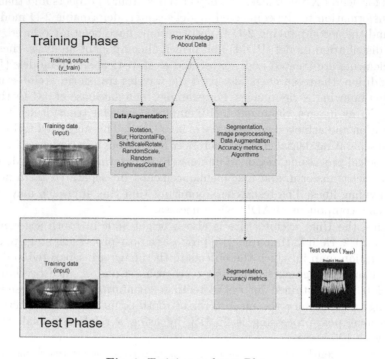

Fig. 1. Training and test Phases

3.2   Proposed Model (Fine-Tuned Unet3+)

To enhance the functionality of Unet and Unet++, Unet3+, a new semantic segmentation model, was created [11]. To improve performance, Unet++ uses skip connections, but it is unable to extract feature information from the complete input data. By utilizing connectivity and interconnection, Unet3+ resolves this issue while keeping spatial information even at higher encoder levels. As a result, Unet3+ is computationally efficient and has high-performance segmentation results, like Unet++. Figure 2 shows its structure. This includes downsampling and up-sampling as described in Fig. 3. Down-sampling decreases spatial resolution, enhancing it while preserving 2D representation. The output activation of the model will be transformed using the Sigmoid function to ensure that the output value is between 0 and 1 after going through the convolution and upsampling layers to decompress the data. After that, a threshold can be used based on model output values to distinguish between segmentation and non-segmentation regions. This is advantageous for segmentation because it enables the application of a threshold to distinguish between segmented regions and those not based on model output values. In addition, we altered hyperparameter configuration using formulas like ReLu and maximum pooling, improving precision and optimizing Accuracy for more reliable results.

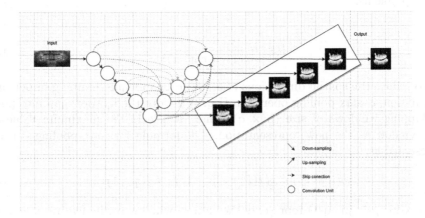

Fig. 2. Describe the working architecture and process of the model Unet3+ [17]

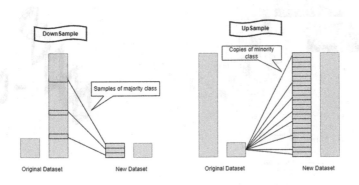

Fig. 3. Down-sample flow and Up-sample flow [18]

To improve x-ray image segmentation accuracy, we created a tailored model by altering hyperparameters and changing the input shape, number of layers, and parameters like stack and filter num. In addition, the deep supervision parameter was removed, and Fig. 4 shows the model design. These modifications improved model performance, producing impressive output results.

The ReLU activation function (Eq. 1) returns 0 if input < 0, and x if input $\geq$ 0. It is popular in deep learning and effective in various applications, including image classification, natural language processing, and reinforcement learning.

$$f(x) = max(0, x) \tag{1}$$

The Sigmoid (Eq. 2) function maps input x to a value between 0 and 1 using the exponential function of a math library, making it useful for binary classification problems.

$$f(x) = \frac{1}{(1 + exp(-x))} \tag{2}$$

To reduce the spatial dimensions of a feature map while retaining important information, a max pooling operation (Eq. 3) divides the feature map into non-overlapping windows of size (p × q). Then, it selects the maximum value of each window as the new representation. The formula for max pooling can be represented as:

$$y(i, j) = max(x(i : i + p - 1, j : j + q - 1)) \tag{3}$$

where x(i:i+p-1, j:j+q-1) represents the (p x q) window in the feature map and y(i, j) represents the new representation of that window.

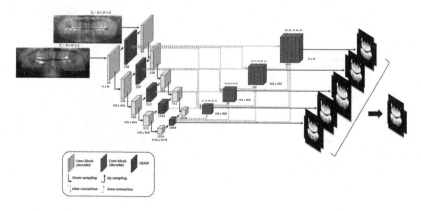

Fig. 4. Unet3+ architecture with image segmentation and hyper-parameters [17]

4   Experiment

4.1   Dataset

The dataset used in this study consists of 116 panoramic dental X-rays taken at the Noor Medical Imaging Center in Qom, Iran. The images have been thoroughly anonymized and deidentified to ensure patient privacy. The dataset covers a diverse range of dental disorders, including healthy patients, partially edentulous patients, and completely edentulous patients. In addition, two experienced dentists have manually segmented the mandibles in each patient. This dataset is the foundation for the study conducted by Abdi et al. [19]. Consequently, we obtained more than 600 images from the initial dataset.

4.2   Evaluating Method and Comparison

This study divides the data set into two sets-training and testing. Compare the results to Unet, Unet++, and Unet3+ using the accuracy metrics (Eq. 4), the F1-score (Eq. 5), Recall (Eq. 6), loss using Mean Squared Error (MSE) metric (Eq. 7 with y_{true} is actual label value. In contrast, y_{pred} is the predicted value) and Dice coefficient (Eq. 8). In which we focus on customization and use Accuracy as the primary metric. An indicator of the model's performance across all classes is Accuracy. When all classes are equally important, it is helpful. It is measured as the proportion of correctly predicted events to all predicted events. The formula for the accuracy metric is described below.

$$Accuracy = \frac{TrueNegative + TruePositve}{TruePositve + FalsePositve + FalseNegative + TrueNegative} \quad (4)$$

$$F1 - score = \frac{2 * Precision * Recall}{Precision + Recall} \quad (5)$$

$$Recall = \frac{TruePositive}{TruePositive + FalseNegative} \quad (6)$$

$$MSE = \frac{1}{n} \sum_{i=1}^{n} (y_{true} - y_{pred})^2 \quad (7)$$

$$Dice = \frac{2 * TruePositive}{(TruePositive + FalsePositive) + (TruePositive + FalseNegative)} \quad (8)$$

4.3   Scenario 1: Model Accuracy with and Without Using Data Augmentation

In Scenario 1, we look at how data augmentation affects the precision of our model Unet3+. In particular, we train our model on two distinct datasets, one with and one without data augmentation. Then, we compare the model's accuracy for each case using a different test dataset. As the model trained on the augmented dataset outperforms the model trained on the original dataset without augmentation, our results imply that data augmentation increases the model's accuracy as described by Table 1. These findings show how data augmentation can effectively boost machine learning model performance, especially in situations where the size of the initial dataset is constrained.

Table 1. The performance of Unet3+ with and without using data augmentation

Model	Accuracy	Loss
Without Data Augmentation	92.04%	0.55%
With Data Augmentation	94.80%	0.04%

4.4   Scenario 2: Performance Comparison with Unet Family

Unet3+ Model: 120 epochs, 8 batch sizes, and adjustable parameters are recommended. The activation is ReLU, output activation is Sigmoid, the batch norm is true, the pool is max, and unpool is false. By taking the maximum value in each local window, max pooling is a typical strategy used in CNNs to reduce the dimensionality of a feature map. Un-pooling, which is the opposite of max pooling, is used to up-sample a feature map by replacing the maximum values from the matching max pooling operation with zeros. When the pool and unpool settings in a research article are set to "max" and "false", respectively, the model uses max pooling to downsample the feature map but not employing any unpooling procedure to upsample. The feature map's dimensions may be decreased as a result, which may improve computing efficiency, but there may also be a trade-off in terms of performance. The number of filters is [64, 128, 256, 512], filter num skip is [128, 128, 1], and filter num aggregate is 32. Loss is tailored. Results are in Table 2 and Fig. 6.

Table 2. Results comparison Unet3+, Unet and Unet++

Model	Accuracy	F1-score	Recall	Loss	Dice co-eff
Unet	91.80%	95.71%	92.00%	0.08%	91.98%
Unet++	14.67%	23.80%	31.32%	0.23%	32.18%
Unet3+ (ours)	**94.80%**	**95.33%**	**95.48%**	**0.04%**	**95.30%**

4.5   Scenario 3: Layer Dense Addition to the Unet3+ Model

The neural network design was modified to include hyperparameters and a dense
layer [256], which considerably increased the model's accuracy Table 3. For the
best performance, network architecture components must be carefully chosen.
Even more precise outcomes might come from further investigation into dense
layer architectures. The results are presented in the Fig. 5.

Table 3. Results comparison Unet3+ with other layer dense

Model	Accuracy
Unet3+(Layer[256])	91.66%
Unet3+(Layer[256][256])	91.79%
Unet3+(Layer[256][256][256])	91.61%
Proposed Model(Unet3+ without dense layers)	**94.80%**

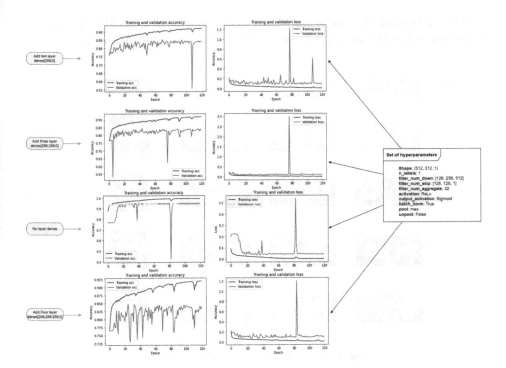

Fig. 5. Visualize Result of model training [17]

4.6   Scenario 4: Performance Comparison with State-of-the-Art Methods

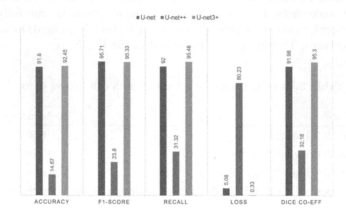

Fig. 6. Result Comparison Chart

After collecting the model training results, we choose to predict the photos in the test set in the subsequent phase. The outcomes are shown in Fig. 7.

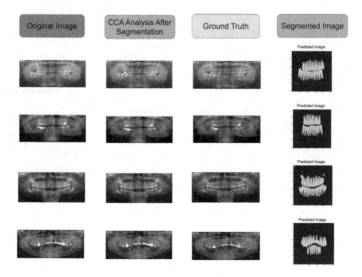

Fig. 7. Illustrating Segmentation Results

Table 4 shows the proposed model's performance in terms of Accuracy, Recall, loss, Dice coefficient, and F1-score under three conditions. Results indicate that the proposed method achieved positive outcomes in all three scenarios, with a prediction accuracy of 94.80%, Recall of 0.9548, loss of 0.04, Dice coefficient of 0.9530, and an F1-score of 0.9533 on the training set. In addition, compared to the previous Unet and Unet++, the proposed model outperformed both, achieving higher Accuracy, Recall, and F1-score.

Table 4. Performance comparison with state-of-the-art methods

Ref.	Architecture	ACC
Salimzadeh et al. [14]	WAVELET TRANSFORM	0.906
Helli & Hamamcı [15]	Unet (ReLU)	0.954 ± 0.003
Wirtz et al. [13]	2-D Coupled Shape Model	0.887
Gil Jader et al. [12]	Mask R-CNN	0.98
TL Koch et al. [20]	Unet (FCNs)	0.936
Yuya Nishitani et al. [21]	Unet (ReLU)	0.89
Proposed model	**Unet3+ (Fine-tuned)**	**0.9480**

5   Conclusion

Our selected Unet3+ architecture performs well in segmenting teeth in panoramic images in the field of dental radiology. Our proposed model achieved high Accuracy of 94.80%, a 95.48% recall rate, a 95.33% F1-score, and a 95.30% dice coefficient. Our study has shown that adding dense layers has not been effective with the Unet3+ model and that changing the hyperparameter set has significantly improved its accuracy. When using Data augmentation along with the best set of hyperparameters we have discovered, the Unet3+ model has demonstrated great efficiency in our research.

In the future, We plan to improve the model by refining data preparation, implementing visualization techniques, and augmenting the dataset. Our work contributes to the field's growth by offering new and improved dental X-ray image segmentation models. Further study and innovation are necessary to develop accurate and versatile segmentation techniques for various image formats.

References

1. Dattani, S., Ritchie, H., Roser, M.: Mental health. Our World in Data (2021). https://ourworldindata.org/mental-health
2. Hudson, J.: How mental health affects oral health. BDJ Student **28**(3), 21–23 (2021)
3. Aldossri, M., Farmer, J., Saarela, O., Rosella, L., Quiñonez, C.: Oral health and cardiovascular disease: mapping clinical heterogeneity and methodological gaps. JDR Clin. Transl. Res. **6**(4), 390–401 (2021)

4. Lee, K., et al.: Oral health and gastrointestinal cancer: a nationwide cohort study. J. Clin. Periodontol. **47**(7), 796–808 (2020)
5. Yang, S., et al.: A deep learning-based method for tooth segmentation on CBCT images affected by metal artifacts. In: 43rd Annual International Conference of the IEEE Engineering in Medicine and Biology Society (2021)
6. Sivagami, S., Chitra, P., Kailash, G.S.R., Muralidharan, S.: UNet architecture based dental panoramic image segmentation. In: 2020 International Conference on Wireless Communications Signal Processing and Networking (WiSPNET), pp. 187–191. IEEE (2020)
7. Ying, S., Wang, B., Zhu, H., Liu, W., Huang, F.: Caries segmentation on tooth X-ray images with a deep network. J. Dent. **119**, 104076 (2022)
8. Zeng, Z., Xie, W., Zhang, Y., Lu, Y.: RIC-UNet: an improved neural network based on UNet for nuclei segmentation in histology images. IEEE Access **7**, 21420–21428 (2019)
9. Cao, H., et al.: Swin-UNet: UNet-like pure transformer for medical image segmentation. arXiv preprint arXiv:2105.05537 (2021)
10. Baheti, B., Innani, S., Gajre, S., Talbar, S.: Eff-UNet: a novel architecture for semantic segmentation in unstructured environment. In: Proceedings of the IEEE/CVF Conference on Computer Vision and Pattern Recognition Workshops, pp. 358–359 (2020)
11. Huang, H., et al.: UNet 3+: a full-scale connected UNet for medical image segmentation. In: 2020 IEEE International Conference on Acoustics, Speech and Signal Processing (ICASSP), ICASSP 2020, pp. 1055–1059. IEEE (2020)
12. Silva, G., Oliveira, L., Pithon, M.: Automatic segmenting teeth in X-ray images: trends, a novel data set, benchmarking and future perspectives. IEEE Trans. Neural Netw. Learn. Syst. **107**, 15–31 (2018)
13. Wirtz, A., Mirashi, S.G., Wesarg, S.: Automatic teeth segmentation in panoramic X-ray images using a coupled shape model in combination with a neural network. In: Frangi, A.F., Schnabel, J.A., Davatzikos, C., Alberola-López, C., Fichtinger, G. (eds.) MICCAI 2018. LNCS, vol. 11073, pp. 712–719. Springer, Cham (2018). https://doi.org/10.1007/978-3-030-00937-3_81
14. Salimzadeh, S., Kandulu, S.: Teeth segmentation of bitewing X-ray images using wavelet transform. Informatica **44**(4) (2020)
15. Helli, S., Hamamcı, A.: Tooth instance segmentation on panoramic dental radiographs using U-Nets and morphological processing. Düzce Üniversitesi Bilim ve Teknoloji Dergisi **10**(1), 39–50 (2022)
16. Zhuang, X., Yang, Z., Cordes, D.: A technical review of canonical correlation analysis for neuroscience applications. Hum. Brain Mapp. (2020)
17. Mo, J., Seong, S., Oh, J., Choi, J.: SAUNet3+ CD: a Siamese-attentive UNet3+ for change detection in remote sensing images. IEEE Access **10**, 101434–101444 (2022)
18. Barros, T.M., Souza Neto, P.A., Silva, I., Guedes, L.A.: Predictive models for imbalanced data: a school dropout perspective. Educ. Sci. **9**(4), 275 (2019)
19. Abdi, A.H., Kasaei, S., Mehdizadeh, M.: Automatic segmentation of mandible in panoramic X-ray. J. Med. Imaging **2**(4), 44003 (2015)
20. Koch, T.L., Perslev, M., Igel, C., Brandt, S.S.: Accurate segmentation of dental panoramic radiographs with U-Nets. In: 2019 IEEE 16th International Symposium on Biomedical Imaging (ISBI 2019), pp. 15–19. IEEE (2019)
21. Nishitani, Y., Nakayama, R., Hayashi, D., Hizukuri, A., Murata, K.: Segmentation of teeth in panoramic dental X-ray images using U-Net with a loss function weighted on the tooth edge. Radiol. Phys. Technol. **14**, 64–69 (2021)

Group Trip Planning Approach with Travel Time and Ratio Constraints

Hung-Yu Huang, Eric Hsueh-Chan Lu$^{(\boxtimes)}$ ⓘ, and Chia-Hao Tu

Department of Geomatics, National Cheng Kung University, No. 1, University Road, Tainan
City 701, Taiwan (R.O.C.)
luhc@mail.ncku.edu.tw

Abstract. With the popularity of wireless communication technologies and smart
mobile devices, the researches and applications of Location-Based Services
(LBSs) have attracted the attention of many scholars and industries. Group trip
planning is one of active LBS topics. Although a number of related studies have
been proposed, few of them deeply discussed the group travel constraints and
preferences. In this paper, we address a novel group trip planning query based on
the travel time and ratio constraints of a group. To solve this query, we propose
an approach named *Group-Trip-Mine* to find the optimal group trip that best fits
for the group preferences under the group constraints. The experimental results
show that our proposed approach performs well under various group constraints
and is greatly better than the algorithm extended by the single-user trip planning
algorithm.

Keywords: Group trip planning · time constraint · ratio constraint ·
location-based service · data mining

1 Introduction

With the rapid development of economic and technological society, people often pay
more attention to leisure travel and other activities to regulate the quality of life. In
addition, due to the popularity of wireless communication technology and smart mobile
devices, the researches and applications of LBSs have attracted the attention of many
scholars and industries. Travelers can share travel information such as mood, travel,
location, trajectory and multimedia information through mobile devices, but travelers
cannot fully understand all the information in a limited time for an unknown city. Travelers hope to plan a trip that meets time and budget constraints based on their expectations. In terms of attractions, the activities, value-added, types, and the number of
people in different time periods will also change the level of preference for travelers.
The weather is unknown and changeable. The planned trip may become a different
result than expected due to weather conditions. Therefore, how to instantly recommend
the appropriate time and attractions to travelers especially a group of users is a rather
complicated issue. It must not only meet the needs of a single traveler, but also the
overall preferences and constraints of the group. Based on the above observations, we
find that the research on travel-related issues is quite interesting and changeable, and
has considerable commercial and academic value.

© The Author(s), under exclusive license to Springer Nature Switzerland AG 2023
N. T. Nguyen et al. (Eds.): ACIIDS 2023, CCIS 1863, pp. 193–204, 2023.
https://doi.org/10.1007/978-3-031-42430-4_16

In the past, many studies on recommended tourist attractions have been proposed. We roughly divide trip planning related research into two categories. One type is to find a travel path that takes the shortest distance or time in accordance with the constraints of Points-Of-Interests (POIs) proposed by the user, e.g., *Trip Planning Query (TPQ)* [9] and *Optimal Sequenced Route (OSR)* [16]. Another type is to find a travel plan with the highest preference score, in compliance with the time constraint proposed by the user, e.g., *Trip-Mine* [11]. However, previous related studies only considered a single traveler or a group of travelers as one. *Group Trip Planning (GTP)* [7] was first proposed to expand the single-person trip planning problem *TPQ* into a group trip planning problem. Since then, several related studies have been proposed. As far as we know, there has been no research about the difference in peer travel preferences. Therefore, it is a critical issue to plan group trip for travelers by considering their constraints and preferences.

In this paper, we address a new query called *Group Trip Planning with Travel Time and Ratio Constraints*. This query is used to plan a set of travel itineraries with a user-specified travel time constraint for a group of travelers, and let the group travelers travel together to achieve the ratio constraint given by the members. The goal of this query is to find a set of trips that are the most interest for all members of the group. In other words, let the travelers visit the attractions with the highest scores. In order to solve this query, we propose a method based on the extension of *Trip-Mine*, called *Group-Trip-Mine* to plan the group trip for travelers. As we know, *TPQ* and *Trip-Mine* are proven as NP-hard problems. *Group-Trip-Mine* based on *Trip-Mine* is also NP-hard. Therefore, our biggest challenge is to find the optimal solution as efficient as possible.

The following part is the organization of the paper. We show a review of the related work of trip planning problem in Sect. 2. In Sect. 3, we introduce the proposed approach *Group-Trip-Mine*. Section 4 evaluates the proposed method by the experiments and analyzes the results. In Sect. 5, conclusions and future works of the paper will be mentioned.

2 Related Work

Single trip planning query is only for single traveler. The definition is to select some appropriate POIs from a tourism environment, plan the best path based on different goals, and satisfy the different constraints proposed by the traveler. In 2005, *Trip Planning Queries (TPQ)* [9] question was proposed by Li *et al.* for solving single trip planning queries. Ahmadi *et al.* proposed a *Best-Compromise In-Route Nearest Neighbor Queries* [1]. The goal is to simultaneously minimize the total travel distance and the travel distance to the selected POI, and emphasize that the path usually cannot optimize both standards at the same time. Compared with the non-sequential *TPQ*, Sharifzadeh *et al.* proposed an *Optimal Sequenced Route (OSR)* query technique [16]. They used the threshold to filter out nodes that are unlikely to be the best path and then explored the shortest path from the starting point through all demand type nodes. Li *et al.* proposed a backward search and forward search method to solve the sequential path query of some interest point categories [13]. Liu *et al.* proposed the *Top-k Optimal Sequenced Routes (KOSR)* querying on large. The *KOSR* is the shortest path to find the top-k from a given source to the destination to visit a specific category point [10]. Traveler preferences for various attractions and acceptable travel time constraints are not considered by the *TPQ* and *OSR*. Such as time constraints, travelers can choose the attraction that they are most interested in to make the trip the most enjoyable under time constraints. In 2011, Lu *et al.* proposed the *Trip-Mine* [11] to efficiently explore the travel path that meets the time constraint of users and has the highest attraction score.

Group trip planning is to plan a set of travel routes for a group of travelers. Safar *et al.* proposed the *Group K-Nearest Neighbor (GKNN)* problem [14], the POI closest to the current location of all group members is found. Li *et al.* used the concept of *Voronoi* diagram to solve the problem of minimizing the minimum distance [12], which is to minimize the moving distance of all members. Further, Hashem *et al.* proposed a new method for *Group Trip Planning (GTP)* query [7]. The goal is to minimize the total travel distance of all members. The same research team proposed to simultaneously minimize the total travel distance and a maximum travel distance of group members [6]. The same team also proposed a *SubGTP (SGTP)* query [8]. Tabassum *et al.* introduced the concept of dynamic grouping for group travel planning queries and proposed *Dynamic GTP (DGTP)* queries [17]. Similarly, Samrose *et al.* proposed *Group OSR (GOSR)* technology [15] to solve the *Sequenced GTP Queries (SGTPQ)*. Ahmadi *et al.* proposed two algorithms for solving *SGTPQ*, namely *Progressive Group Neighbour Exploration (PGNE)* [2] and *Iterative Backward Search (IBS)* [3]. Barua *et al.* proposed a *GOSR* query with a weighted POI called *Weighted Optimal Sequenced GTP (WSGTP)* query [4].

The above researches only concern the completion of the request for visits, and try to find the minimum travel route to meet the demand, without considering the individual needs, preferences and maximum time constraint for travelers. Fan *et al.* proposed a new spatial social optimization problem called *Optimal Group Route (OGR)* [5], which is the best group route query for multi-person travel planning. The goal is to find the travel profit that can satisfy the total profit of all travelers. In terms of the existing research, we believe that it is more in line with the needs of most travelers in real life to be able to satisfy the proposed travel time of traveler and to maximize the preference of traveler for the travel process. However, in the *OGR* queries, the entire travel itinerary requires group action. We believe that some travelers may want to choose their favorite POI on certain trips. Therefore, group trip planning problem considering travel time and ratio constraints is a useful approach. Travelers can provide a travel ratio constraint. Group actions must be maintained at least to travel ratio time during travel. so as not to become a travel itinerary. In addition to guaranteeing a certain proportion of common travel itineraries, travelers can choose other POIs that they are more interested in, and consider the fun of group travel together, and also maintain their favorite attractions.

3 Proposed Method

We describe the entire algorithm in this section. Figure 1 shows the flow chart of *Group-Trip-Mine*. In this flow chart, we first use the Improved Trip-Mine to find Group-Based Attraction Sets. Then, we propose the Projection and Score Sorting methods to find top scores of Individual Attraction Sets. Besides, Time-Alignment method is proposed to find the group travel path that matches the top scores of time constraints and ratio constraints. If the solution cannot be found in Time-Alignment step, the score sorting step is performed and go back to the time alignment method, until a valid solution is found or no valid solution to satisfy the constraint can be found. *Trip-Mine* is the optimal travel path algorithm for solving single-person travel problems meeting the time constraint of traveler and the highest score based on the source, destination location and time constraint of traveler, score and stay time of attraction, and travel time between attractions. To solve the group travel problem by *Trip-Mine* expansion that solves the single-person travel problem, we make three corrections to *Trip-Mine*: 1) We put the candidate attractions that satisfy the travel ratio into the Group-based Attraction Sets, and this set of attractions no longer generates a longer set of attractions with other collections of attractions; 2) We only output the Group-based Attraction Sets that meet the time constraints and meets the Travel Ratio; 3) Since Score Checking in *Trip-Mine* is based on the current highest score of travelers in personal travel, the amount of calculation of Permutation is reduced. However, in the group travel algorithm, each preference score of travelers for the attraction is not necessarily the same. The Score Checking is not suitable for group travel algorithms, so the Score Checking method is omitted.

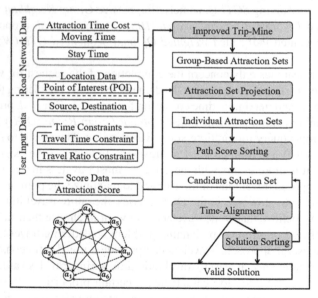

Fig. 1. Flow chart of *Group-Trip-Mine*.

3.1 Improved Trip-Mine

We put all location data, attraction time costs, user-given group travel time and ratio constraints into the algorithm. In *Improved Trip-Mine*, 1-sets of attractions with a length of 1 are generated first. They are sorted according to the time cost of the attraction, i.e., the sum of moving time and stay time. Attraction sets are combined with other candidate attraction sets into a set of 2 lengths of attractions. If the set of candidate attractions with higher time cost is placed in the front position. It happens to exceed the time constraint and is deleted at an early stage. There is no need to perform the steps of combining with other sets. This step can effectively reduce the number of operations. Low Bound (LB) checking and Travel Ratio Constraints checking two filtering strategies are executed when generating candidate attraction sets. In LB Checking step, the attraction set that may exceed the travel time constraints is filtered by a very small amount of calculations. In Travel Ratio Constraints checking, we find candidate attraction sets that exceed the minimum Travel Ratio Time. The minimum Travel Ratio Time is calculated by the travel time constraint multiplied by the Travel Ratio Constraints. We call this set as the Group-based Attraction Sets. The set of candidate attractions that meet Travel Ratio will no longer be combined with other attractions to generate longer candidate attractions. We stop this phase until the longer length of the set is an empty set.

3.2 Attraction Set Projection

We generate the Individual Attraction Sets for each Group-based Attraction set by projecting the Attraction score and the Group-based Attraction Sets obtained from the first part of the algorithm. We use LB Checking to initially filter the Individual Attraction Sets that may exceed the travel time constraint. Each base is one of its Individual Attraction Sets. Put the attraction of length 1 and not yet appearing on this base. The Individual Attraction Sets is generated that is one more than the length of the base. Suppose the set length is k, we place the n attractions that do not appear in this Group-based Attractions Set. The n new the candidate Individual Attraction Sets are generated. Next, we take two the candidate Individual Attraction Sets of length k and which have k-1 attractions of the same attractions. We combine each other to generate a candidate Individual Attraction Set of length $k + 1$. It is not possible to be combined in each two individual attraction candidate group of length k. This step is repeated to complete candidate Individual Attraction Sets of length $k + 2, k + 3$, etc. until the longer candidate Individual Attraction Sets can no longer be generated.

3.3 Path Score Sorting

The scores of candidate Individual Attraction Sets generated by Group-based Attraction Sets are sorted. Because each score of travelers for each attraction is not necessarily the same, the order of candidate Individual Attraction Sets under the same base is different for each traveler. All travelers choose their Top Individual Attraction Sets. The structure of Tree is used to record the number of components of this Individual Attraction Sets. Its Group-based Attraction Sets and Individual Attraction Sets score are recorded. Each Individual Attraction Sets is recorded by a separated Tree structure. We use the Linked list to link all child nodes. The child nodes with the top score in all Tree structures can be found through the Linked list, and get the top score for the Individual Attraction Set output.

3.4 Time-Alignment

We use the Time-Alignment to find out the Top Individual Attraction Sets that satisfy the travel time constraint and the ratio constraint. If a valid solution is not found at this step.

Then the score sorting step be executed. The Time-Alignment method is repeated until a valid solution is found or we can never find the solution with Travel Time and Ratio Constraints. The concept is to operate through the product of attractiveness. All possible attractive visit sequence results are listed, and a set of effective solutions are found by waiting for each other during the trip. The Time-Alignment can be roughly divided into four steps. All valid solutions in this attraction sets are generated. The first step is all possible visit orders for each attraction selected by the traveler are listed. Attraction set product operation means to multiply all the visit orders listed in the previous step. The Based Attractions Sequential step is to remove the product results of different group-based attractions in different trips of travelers. The reason is that the meaning of group-based attractions is that travelers in all groups must participate in the attractions together. In the case of different attractions, the travelers will wait for each other to cause a deadlock. The last step, Base Attractions Time Adjust, the Last Enter Time finding for group-based attractions must be find, and we align all the Attractions of traveler with the time of the last visit to this attraction. Travelers who could have started this group-based attraction must wait for the traveler to arrive at the slowest. Therefore, the waiting time of the group-based attractions is generated in this step. Travel time also is adjusted. If the adjusted total travel time is in line with the travel time constraint, then this attractive visit order is the last best solution.

As shown in Fig. 2, different colored arrows represent different travelers. Each solid arrow is represented as a group-based attraction, and the dotted arrow is represented as the attraction that the traveler can visit alone. The length of the arrow is represented as the Stay Time at the attraction. The middle blank is the moving time. Travelers who arrive at the group-based attractions first must wait for other group members. Members visit and leave the group-based attractions at the same time. We use the Base Attractions Time Adjust step to align the travelers to the same attraction to the last arrival time. After we align all the group-based attractions in sequence, we can find the length from the start to the end, for the total travel time of all the travelers who participate in the attraction and finally arrive at the destination. If a valid solution cannot be found by the combination of this attraction set in the Time-Alignment method, we use the candidate solution with the highest score to do the solution finding method. We assume that there are n travelers in the group. The n new Individual Attraction Sets be generated by the solution finding method. Each Group-based Attractions Set is mapped to a Tree structure. In each new Individual Attraction Set, the next highest score set for different travelers are found in their own tree structure. Then, we compare the newly generated Individual Attraction Set with other Individual Attraction Sets already in the tree structure of this Group-based Attractions Set. We only do sort score calculations for the Individual Attraction Set. The Individual Attraction Set with the highest score is found in the tree structure of group-based attractions, and it is compared with the highest score of the Individual Attraction Set of the other group-based attractions. We select the highest score and repeat the Time-Alignment step.

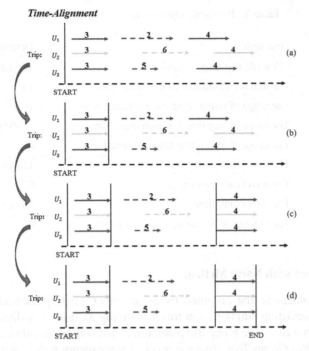

Fig. 2. Time-Alignment step.

4 Experimental Evaluation

We conduct a series of experiments with various simulation data to evaluate the performance of *Group-Trip-Mine*. In the experiment, we adjusted the parameters and output data to evaluate and analyze execution time and memory cost. We use Java 1.8 to implement our algorithm. For the experimental computer, CPU is Intel i7–4470 GHz and memory is 32 GB.

4.1 Experimental Data and Setting

To evaluate the performance and scalability of the algorithm, we design a simulation model to generate synthetic data. Table 1 summarizes the main parameters in the simulation model and their default values. We use a $|W| \times |W|$ network to simulate a trip map. All attractions are randomly generated in the map, and the number of attractions is determined by N_A. For each attraction, the scores of travelers and stay time are determined by an uniform distribution within the range given based on R_{RS} and R_{ST}, respectively. The moving time between attractions R_{TT} is determined by the Euclidean distance between the attractions. The travel time constraint is specified by the parameter C_{TT}. The travel ratio constraint is specified by C_{TR}. The ratio time can be independently fixed and controlled by T_{TR}. The number of members in the travel group is given by N_P. We adjust the two kinds of constraint settings and make detailed analysis of each output result in terms of execution time and memory cost.

Table 1. Parameter setting range and default value.

Parameter	Description	Default Value
$|W|$	$|W| \times |W|$ trip map network	100 km
N_A	The number of attractions in the network	15
R_{RS}	The range of rating score for each attraction	1–10
R_{ST}	The range of stay time for each attraction	15–90 min
R_{TT}	The range of travel time between locations	-
C_{TT}	The travel time constraint	150 min
C_{TR}	The travel ratio constraint	0.3
T_{TR}	The travel ratio time	45 min
N_P	The number of people in the travel group	4

4.2 Experiment with Naïve Method

Due to this problem is first proposed by us, no other existing method can be used directly, so the existing single-person travel planning algorithm is directly expanded into a method that can solve group trip planning, called Naïve algorithm. Figure 3 show that our algorithm *Group-Trip-Mine* has much better execution time and memory cost than the Naïve algorithm. The execution time and memory cost are improved about 81% and 89% compared with the Naïve algorithm, respectively. This shows the necessity of studying an algorithm for group tourism planning.

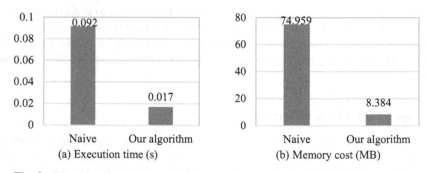

Fig. 3. Execution time (a) and memory cost (b) compared with the Naïve algorithm.

4.3 Impact of Travel Time Constraint

When we change the travel time constraint, the ratio time constraint will also be changed since the travel ratio is fixed. To avoid two parameters changes at the same time, we only change the travel time constraints but fix travel ratio time. Figure 4 shows the execution time and memory cost when changing travel time constraints. We observed that when the travel time is less than 150 min (the default value), the lower bound time of the generated Group-based Attraction Set is unchanged due to the fixed ratio time. The range of boundaries that can be generated becomes smaller than the previous experiment. On the other hand, when the travel time is greater than 150 min, the boundary range that can be generated becomes larger than the previous experiment for the same reason. The number of Group-based Attraction Sets and Individual Attraction Sets has also changed greatly or less, and increase the memory cost. In the case of a large amount of travel time, the execution time and the number of times of Time-Alignment are relatively moderate. We speculate that it may be that the number of candidate solutions is increased. An attraction set with a higher score but is not previously considered the candidate solutions is also found. When the attraction set that is spent less stay time is the Group-based Attraction Set, it is just given a higher score. It is a very favorable situation for finding a valid solution.

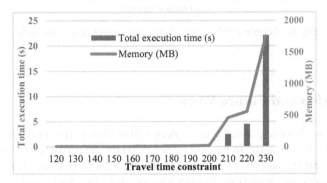

Fig. 4. Experimental results of changing travel time constraint.

4.4 Impact of Travel Ratio Constraint

Figures 5 shows the experimental results of changing the travel ratio constraint. When the ratio constraint is smaller, the time for the traveler to act independently and freely increases. Conversely, the greater the ratio constraint, the closer the group travel planning problem that the group must act together. All values are zero after the travel ratio constraint reaches 0.5. The reason is that in our definition of the travel ratio constraint, we only calculate the attraction time of the attraction as the ratio time. In order to achieve the travel ratio constraint, the sets need to add more stay time of attractions, but attractions will increase the movement time between more attractions. If the stay time is deducted and the remaining time is not enough to accommodate these movement times, there is no candidate set. However, this algorithm cannot generate any effective solution, resulting in a zero result. The design of our algorithm leads to an increase in the Travel Ratio Constraint that only reduces the arrangement of the permutations. Therefore, the higher the ratio, the better for our algorithm. When the Travel Ratio Constraint is low, the Group-based Attraction Set is generated less, and also project fewer Individual Attraction Sets. It can be seen that our algorithm is beneficial regardless of whether the Travel Ratio

Constraint is low or high. When the Travel Ratio Constraint is equal to 0.15, the number of Time-Alignment times is reduced. The possible reason is that the effective solution of the highest score can be found in advance at this ratio.

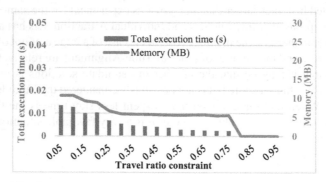

Fig. 5. Experimental results of changing travel ratio constraint.

5   Conclusion and Future Work

In this paper, we have addressed a new query called Group Trip Planning with Travel Time and Ratio Constraints. In this query, we consider the travel time constraint, ratio constraint, the preference scores of each traveler for each attraction, the movement and stay time between the attractions to plan a group trip. The purpose of the query is to find the optimal trip with the highest total score of the total preference of group meeting the constraints, and reduce the query time and memory cost as much as possible. To efficiently solve this problem, we have proposed a *Group-Trip-Mine* approach to reduce the execution time and the memory cost. The experimental results show that our proposed method has advantages in every travel ratio constraint given by the travel group. It is much better than the Naïve algorithm extended by the existing single trip planning algorithm. The execution time and memory cost decrease more than 80% compared to the Naïve method. It shows the necessity and importance of planning an algorithm for group travel planning. As far as we know, this paper is the first group travel planning query and approach that considers travel time, travel ratio, and traveler preference.

In the future, we think that this algorithm can be further improved. For example, in the path score sorting step, we can add more screening and optimization strategies. Furthermore, more pruning strategies can be designed when projecting Individual Attraction Sets. It is possible to filter the attraction sets that cannot be solution early. The output data generated by these two steps will greatly affect the number of combinations of the Time-Alignment steps. If we can filter from these two parts early, we can expect to greatly improve the overall performance of the algorithm and reduce the memory cost. Although this paper has considered the preference of traveler for attractions, time and ratio constraints, there are some important information that have not been considered. For the attraction, the opening time, cost, the upper limit of the number of people, the appropriate season, and so on may be considered. For the travelers, we may also consider budget constraints, group composition types, group preferences similarities and differences. For the road network data, the road segment properties and traffic flow at different time periods have not been considered. We further think that perhaps the route is not used when there are attractions in the road map, but the concept of activities. Some special events and celebrations are not necessarily held in a fixed place. When the event is held somewhere, the place will become an attraction during the event period. In the experimental part, we currently refer to *Trip-Mine* settings. In the future, we can add more realistic considerations in parameter setting to be closer to real life.

Acknowledgment. This research was supported in part by Higher Education Sprout Project, Ministry of Education to the Headquarters of University Advancement at National Cheng Kung University (NCKU), and Ministry of Science and Technology, Taiwan, R.O.C. under grant no. MOST 111–2121-M-006–009-.

References

1. Ahmadi, E., Costa, C.F., Nascimento, M.A.: Best-compromise in-route nearest neighbor queries. In: Proceedings of the 25th ACM SIGSPATIAL International Conference on Advances in Geographic Information Systems (2017)
2. Ahmadi, E., Nascimento, M.A.: A mixed breadth-depth first search strategy for sequenced group trip planning queries. In: 16th IEEE International Conference on Mobile Data Management, vol. 1, pp. 24–33 (2015)
3. Ahmadi, E., Nascimento, M.A.: IBS: an efficient stateful algorithm for optimal sequenced group trip planning queries. In: 18th IEEE International Conference on Mobile Data Management (MDM), pp. 212–221 (2017)
4. Barua, S., Jahan, R., Ahmed, T.: Weighted optimal sequenced group trip planning queries. In: 18th IEEE International Conference on Mobile Data Management (MDM), pp. 222–227 (2017)
5. Fan, L., Bonomi, L., Shahabi, C., Xiong, L.: Optimal Group route query: finding itinerary for group of users in spatial databases. GeoInformatica **22**(4), 845–867 (2018)
6. Hashem, T., Barua, S., Ali, M.E., Kulik, L., Tanin, E.: Efficient computation of trips with friends and families. In: Proceedings of the 24th ACM International on Conference on Information and Knowledge Management, pp. 931–940 (2015)
7. Hashem, T., Hashem, T., Ali, M.E., Kulik, L.: Group trip planning queries in spatial databases. In: Nascimento, M.A., et al. Advances in Spatial and Temporal Databases. SSTD 2013. Lecture Notes in Computer Science, vol. 8098, pp. 259–276 (2013). https://doi.org/10.1007/978-3-642-40235-7_15
8. Hashem, T., Hashem, T., Ali, M.E., Kulik, L., Tanin, E.: Trip planning queries for subgroups in spatial databases. In: Cheema, M., Zhang, W., Chang, L. (eds.) Databases Theory and Applications. ADC 2016. Lecture Notes in Computer Science, vol. 9877, pp. 110–122, (2016). https://doi.org/10.1007/978-3-319-46922-5_9
9. Li, F., Cheng, D., Hadjieleftheriou, M., Kollios, G., Teng, S.-H.: On trip planning queries in spatial databases. In: Bauzer Medeiros, C., Egenhofer, M.J., Bertino, E. (eds.) SSTD 2005. LNCS, vol. 3633, pp. 273–290. Springer, Heidelberg (2005). https://doi.org/10.1007/11535331_16
10. Liu, H., Jin, C., Yang, B., Zhou, A.: Finding Top-k Optimal Sequenced Routes--Full Version, *arXiv preprint* arXiv:1802.08014 (2018)

11. Lu, E.H.C., Lin, C.Y., Tseng, V.S.: Trip-Mine: an efficient trip planning approach with travel time constraints. In: IEEE 12th International Conference on Mobile Data Management, pp. 152–161 (2011)
12. Li, F., Yao, B., Kumar, P.: Group enclosing queries. IEEE Trans. Knowl. Data Eng. 23(10), 1526–1540 (2010)
13. Li, J., Yang, Y.D., Mamoulis, N.: Optimal route queries with arbitrary order constraints. IEEE Trans. Knowl. Data Eng. 25(5), 1097–1110 (2012)
14. Safar, M.: Group K-nearest neighbors queries in spatial network databases. J. Geogr. Syst. 10(4), 407–416 (2008)
15. Samrose, S., Hashem, T., Barua, S., Ali, M.E., Uddin, M.H., Mahmud, M.I.: Efficient computation of group optimal sequenced routes in road networks. In: 16th IEEE International Conference on Mobile Data Management, pp. 122–127 (2015)
16. Sharifzadeh, M., Kolahdouzan, M., Shahabi, C.: The optimal sequenced route query. VLDB J. Int. J. Very Large Data Bases, 17(4), 765–787 (2008)
17. Tabassum, A., Barua, S., Hashem, T., Chowdhury, T.: Dynamic group trip planning queries in spatial databases. In: Proceedings of the 29th International Conference on Scientific and Statistical Database Management. ACM. no. 38 (2017)

When are Latent Topics Useful for Text Mining?

Enriching Bag-of-Words Representations with Information Extraction in Thai News Articles

Nont Kanungsukkasem[1], Piyawat Chuangkrud[1,2],
Pimpitcha Pitichotchokphokhin[1], Chaianun Damrongrat[2],
and Teerapong Leelanupab[1,3]

[1] Faculty of Information Technology, King Mongkut's Institute of Technology
Ladkrabang (KMITL), Bangkok 10520, Thailand
{nont,piyawat,pimpitcha,teerapong}@it.kmitl.ac.th
[2] National Electronics and Computer Technology Center (NECTEC),
Pathumthani 12120 Thailand
chaianun.damrongrat@nectec.or.th
[3] The University of Queensland, Brisbane, QLD 4072, Australia
t.leelanupab@uq.edu.au

Abstract. The Bag-of-Words (BOW) model is simple but one of the successful representations of text documents. This model, however, suffers from the sparse matrix, in which most of the elements are zero. Topic modeling is an unsupervised learning method that can represent text documents in a low-dimensional space. Latent Dirichlet Allocation (LDA) is a topic modeling technique used for topic extraction and data exploration, with interpretable output. This paper presents a thorough study of potential benefits of applying LDA, as a feature extraction, to topic discovery and document classification in Thai news articles, comparing with TF–IDF and Word2Vec. We also studied how much of the top Thai terms extracted from LDA with the different numbers of topics can be interpretable and meaningful, and can be a representative of the corpus. Besides, a set of Topic Coherence measures were included in our study to estimate the degree of semantic similarity of extracted topics. To compare the performance and optimization time of classification of features from the different feature extraction methods, various types of classifiers, e.g., Logistic Regression, Random Forest, XGBoosting, etc., were experimented.

Keywords: Topic Modeling · Latent Dirichlet Allocation · Word Embedding · Bag of Words · Text Mining · Thai News

1 Introduction

In a Bag-of-Words (BoW) model, a text document is represented as a distinct vector of *weights* of tokens, indexed words or terms in a vocabulary. The weights from a term weighting indicate the importance of terms in a document and/or their discriminative power in differentiating one document from the others on

N. T. Nguyen et al. (Eds.): ACIIDS 2023, CCIS 1863, pp. 205–219, 2023.
https://doi.org/10.1007/978-3-031-42430-4_17

specific tasks, though it lacks perception of word morphology, grammar and word order. Examples of term weighting are raw or normalized term frequency (TF), variants of TF-Inverse Document Frequency (TF–IDF) and BM25 weighting. Generally used in natural language processing (NLP), information retrieval (IR) and machine learning (ML), the BoW model has several good reasons owing to its simplicity and robustness. Previous studies showed that simple systems, e.g., in IR and ML, using large amount of data could outperform complex ones using fewer data [8]. As a trade-off for performance, BoW-based systems sacrificed their computational cost due to high dimensional feature vectors regarding a large vocabulary. However, BoW does not consider similarity between words and co-occurrence statistics between words.

Word embedding is a dense continuous word representation, capable of capturing the syntactic and semantic relationship of words. Focusing on the sequential combination of words, word embedding models assume that the appearance of each word is only related with a limited set of words before it. Commonly available and notable pre-trained word embeddings include Word2Vec [11]. In this paper, we utilize Word2Vec as a representative approach from word embedding to reduce a document representation from based on words to based on sentences in a document.

Towards dimensionality reduction and semantic information extraction, topic modeling is one of the unsupervised learning techniques for document representation. Independent on any language, topic modeling can reduce a noisy BoW to a more compact representation based on topics. Regarded as the state-of-the-art topic modeling method, Latent Dirichlet Allocation (LDA) [3] showed better performance than Non-negative Matrix Factorization (NMF), Latent Semantic Analysis (LSA) and probabilistic LSA (pLSA) [16].

1.1   Goals of the Paper

The main goal of this paper is to conduct a comprehensive study of potential advantages of applying latent topics, as extracted features, to text mining tasks in Thai news articles. In general, Thai language is considered more complex to mine than others. This is due to the lack of word boundary defined in a Thai sentence, introducing ambiguity in word tokenization. Topic modeling is a language-independent technique that can reduce such complexity. However, there have been a few studies of topic modeling in Thai corpora [16]. This paper aims to answer the following research questions by conducting two sets of experiments regarding two text mining tasks (i.e., topic discovery and text classification):

Q1: How does LDA perform in discovering a set of k topics, represented by *top-ranked terms*? Are the top-ranked terms for each topic meaningful and interpretable, especially for the Thai language?

Q2: How can we define the number of k topics on modeling? Does topic coherence provide a rough estimate of the number of topics discovered by LDA?

Q3: Other than the benefit of meaningful and interpretable features from LDA in Q1, how much do the performance and computational trade-off of TF–IDF, LDA with three different numbers of k topics and Word2Vec gain or lose in *text classification*

1.2   Previous Work

Li *et al.* [9] proposed a new model for clustering short English texts from academic abstracts, represented by paragraph features of Word2Vec and topic features of LDA as well as their unique embeddings derived from the combination of the two features. They compared the performance regarding clustering performance with a traditional TF-IDF BoW model. Inspiring the work of Li *et al.*, a hybrid approach of Wang *et al.* [18] used both Word2Vec and LDA as document features. By ad-hoc varying the number of topics, Wang *et al.* however only studied on the aspects of topic distribution over terms and distance between discovered topics. Instead of using Word2Vec. Asawaroengchai *et al.* [2] added the contextual relationships among words to all topics in a semantic space by using N-gram as input to LDA. In comparison with a traditional LDA, their Topic N-grams model was evaluated on a BEST2010 Thai corpus. Nararatwong *et al.* [14] simply improved topic extraction of LDA in Thai tweets by adding a refined stop-word list as a text pre-processing step.

2   Experimental Design

2.1   Data Preprocessing

We conducted the experiment on Thai news articles from BangkokBiz news website[1], published in separate categories. We collected 30,092 news articles, excluding their headline, from seven main categories, i.e., Politics, Finance, World, Economic, Lifestyle[2], Business, and Royal from April 11, 2019 to March 30, 2020 by using Beautiful Soup library. The numbers of documents out of 30,092 in each category are 8,567, 7,379, 5,485, 3,853, 3,577, 864 and 367, respectively.

PyThaiNLP library for Thai text processing provides modules to support all four steps in data pre-processing, i.e., word tokenization, stopword removal, stemming and noise removal. The library provides many tokenization algorithms (i.e., newmm (default), longest, deepcut, attacut, icu and ulmfit) to choose. However, Chormai *et al.* [7] showed that deepcut was better than the others in term of segmentation quality but worse in term of computational time. We also confirm the Chormai's findings in our pilot study that newmm is inferior to deepcut. For example, "หัวเว่ย", which is transliterated from "Huawei", was erroneously tokenized to two separated tokens, "หัว" for "Hua" and "เว่ย" for "Wei", by newmm, but was correctly tokenized to "หัวเว่ย' by deepcut. Accordingly, we chose to use deepcut exploiting the convolutional neural network to tokenize our dataset after removing the characters that were not letters or vowels. Then, low-frequency tokens appearing less than five times were filtered out. Afterwards, we filtered out all function words in Thai and English by using two stopword lists as provided by PythaiNLP and Natural Language Toolkit (NLTK), respectively. The preprocessing of 30,092 articles resulted in a total of 5,898,527 tokens, approximately

---

[1]https://www.bangkokbiznews.com

[2]"Lifestyle" category includes contents from other subcategories, e.g., health and sport.

196 tokens on average per article. Out of these tokens, 29,537 were unique. The preprocessed articles were then randomly splitted into 70% for training and 30% for testing which is 21,064 documents with 29,220 unique tokens for training and 9,028 documents with 26,565 unique tokens for testing.

2.2   Feature Extraction

To answer Q3, we selected TF-IDF, LDA and Word2Vec for comparison. They were applied to extracting features from the preprocessed articles. We chose to use Scikit-learn to extract the articles into 29,220 TF–IDF (BoW) features. Then, we consider the final results from these features as a baseline for Q3. Accordingly, we chose to use Gensim that features both LDA and topic coherence. Practically, the proper numbers of topics and iterations have to be investigated by a preliminary experiment.

To answer Q1, the top-ranked terms of k topics must be interpreted to compare with the seven collected categories of the news articles to show whether the latent topics from LDA can represent all of the categories. Accordingly, we started our experiment with seven as the number of topics for LDA (LDA7), resulting in seven features for training a model. However, setting the number of topics to be the same as the number of categories of a corpus is not practical with other datasets as they are not pre-categorized. Besides, LDA is an unsupervised algorithm to find latent topics, by which we in practice do not know the actual number of topics. Then, we determined the number of topics using the topic coherence scores of the results from LDA with different numbers of topics ranging from 1 to 50. However, as LDA is a generative probabilistic model, the estimation is not always the same. Accordingly, for each number of topics, we experimented ten times to get its average coherence score.

Furthermore, we experimented all four topic coherence measures provided by gensim, i.e., UMass, UCI, NPMI and CV to answer Q2. When the number of topics, as suggested by the topic coherence, was not equal to seven or not the same as the number of seven main categories that we had collected, we would get two sets of the top-ranked terms from LDA. Otherwise, there would be only one set of the top-ranked terms to be further used for answering Q1 and Q2. Also, LDA with two different numbers of topics were then used to extract features for the next step to answer Q3. Gensim also features Word2Vec algorithm including both Skip-gram and Continuous Bag-of-Words (CBOW) models. As Mikolov et al. [11] suggested Skip-gram provided a better semantic accuracy than CBOW, we therefore applied Skip-gram as a training algorithm to Word2Vec and used default settings for the other parameters in our study.

We further set the dimensionality of the word vectors to 300 and set the context (window) size to five according to Mikolov et al. [12]. As the number of features extracted from Word2Vec is 300 (W2V), we also set the number of topics in LDA to 300 (LDA300) to get the same number of features from W2V in order to set a fair comparison between them. Accordingly, there were five sets of features for our comparative experiment.

2.3 Modeling and Evaluation

To answer Q3, we measure the performance and computational trade-off when applying different types of features (i.e., TF–IDF, LDA, Word2Vec) to a downstream task (e.g., multi-class text classification.) We therefore studied on various machine learning algorithms to classify Thai news articles into seven classes, labeled by the actual categories of our dataset. These algorithms included Logistic Regression (LR), Multilayer Perceptron (MLP), Decision Tree (DT), Support Vector Machine (SVM), Random Forest (RF), Adaptive Boosting (ADAB), GradientBoosting (GBM) [4] and XGBoosting (XGB) [6].

We performed the model optimization by tuning hyperparameters using GridSearchCV with $k=5$, to cross-validate each classifier with its set of permuted parameters to control its learning process. The best parameters of each classifier were maintained to fit the model on a training set, previously split by a simple hold-out method. Each trained model was subsequently validated on the remaining test set. All experimental runs were conducted on Google Cloud Platform by running on virtual machines with the specifications; zone: asia-southeast1-b, machine type: n2-custom (8 vCPU, 32 GB memory), boot disk: balanced persistant disk (50 GB) and OS: Ubuntu 18.04 LTS.

To evaluate the performance of a classifier with different sets of features, we employed two evaluation metrics; accuracy and macro F1. Those metrics are suitable for multi-class classification problem, and especially when we have an imbalanced dataset but all classes are equally important. Computational time for tuning hyperparameter by GridsearchCV was also reported to compare the time spent on fitting and tuning models by features from different extraction methods. Lastly, the trade-off between performance and time was computed by the fraction of the performance gain over Time Loss (TL). When considering the performance gain by Accuracy Gain (AG), we call it Accuracy-to-Time (AT) ratio defined as:

$$\text{AT-ratio} = \frac{\text{AG} + \epsilon}{\text{TL} + \epsilon} \tag{1}$$

where ϵ is a very small constant that is added to the denominator to avoid problems of division-by-zero and added to the numerator to avoid misinterpretation when the numerator is equal to 0. For example, when accuracy values of two experiments are the same number as the minimum accuracy of all experimental runs but with different time losses, the one with the lower time loss should be considered as a better one. Provided epsilon was not added to the numerator, two experiments would be considered the same because both of them would be equal to zero. Besides, the addition to both numerator and denominator also gives us the number 1 as a baseline, which is the number of the ratio when an experiment performs the worst but spends the least computational time, instead of 0/0. The epsilon was set to 0.001 in our experiment.

AG is calculated from the Accuracy metric (acc) and the minimum of Accuracy of all experimental runs[3]. The AG can be formalized as follows:

---

[3] As Accuracy is in percentage, we do not need any normalization like TL.

$$AG = acc - \min(acc) \tag{2}$$

TL is the difference between a computational time (t) and the minimum computational time of all experimental runs scaled by Min-Max normalization.

$$TL = \frac{t - \min(t)}{\max(t) - \min(t)} \tag{3}$$

When we consider the performance gain by F1 Gain (FG), we call it F1-to-Time (FT) ratio. It can be derived by simply replacing AG with FG in the AT ratio where FG can be calculated by the following equation from the macro-F1:

$$FG = F1 - \min(F1) \tag{4}$$

3   Results and Discussions

3.1   Q1 and Q2

In each of the seven topics extracted by LDA7, we retrieve the top ten terms and present them in Table 1[4]. By interpreting all terms together, we can assign a label to each topic. Labels are shown after the topic numbers in parenthesis, such as Finance, Economy, Politics, and so on. Ideally, these labels should be aligned with the categories we collected from BangkokBiz (see Section 2.1.) Some topics are duplicate. For example, topic 1 and 3 are both labeled with Finance, and topic 4 and 5 are also labeled with Politics. In contrast, some categories are missing and cannot be discovered by LDA7, i.e., Royal, Business and Lifestyle. However, for the "Lifestyle" category, it is instead actually labeled with its subcategory, "Health" and "Disaster". Topic 3 can be interpreted and assigned with three labels, i.e., Finance, Economy and World. In our view, the imbalance of our data might be one of the reasons of lacking the categories, "Royal" and "Business".

Table 1. Seven topics extracted by LDA7

Topic 1 (Finance)	บาท ล้าน เงิน ปี ทุน หุ้น ลด ค่า บริษัท ราคา
Topic 2 (Economy)	ประเทศ ปี งาน ไทย ทำ ธุรกิจ พัฒนา สินค้า สร้าง โลก
Topic 3 (Finance/Economy/World)	ตัว สหรัฐ ราคา ตลาด จีน ลด น้ำมัน ดอลลาร์ จุด เงิน
Topic 4 (Politics)	คน พรรค ทำ รัฐบาล เรื่อง เมือง ประชาชน ตัว เลือกตั้ง นายก
Topic 5 (Politics)	รัฐมนตรี ประชุม ข้อ คณะ พิจารณา เรื่อง กฎหมาย คดี งาน ประธาน
Topic 6 (Disaster)	น้ำ พื้นที่ ทำ เรียน ศึกษา เด็ก งาน ภัย รถ ปี
Topic 7 (Health)	โรค คน เชื้อ ติด ไวรัส ป่วย ระบาด ประเทศ บิน เดินทาง

As it is not practical to know the number of topics, we experimented on LDA with different numbers of topics ranging from 1 to 50 to find the potentially

---

[4]We provide a hyperlink for each Thai word leading to its meaning in English.

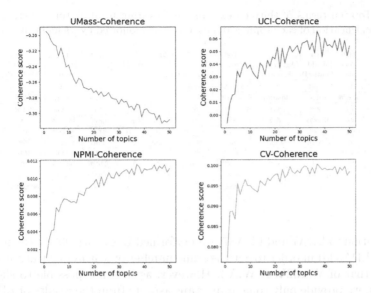

Fig. 1. The average coherence scores of LDA as evaluated by four different metrics i.e., UMASS, UCI, NPMI and CV, respectively.

optimal number of topics. The result plotted in Fig. 1 shows that topic coherence scores from UCI, NPMI and CV have the same elbow at 37 but 47 from UMass. According to the majority voting among studied topic coherence metrics, we chose 37 to be the potentially optimal number of topics for fitting LDA on our corpus. We later name this method LDA37 for feature extraction.

Again, we retrieved the top ten terms in each of the 37 topics extracted by LDA37. Table 2[4] demonstrates examples of the top ten terms in 13 out of 37 topics[5]. As we can see, they cover all the seven categories with a lot of subcategories. Even though there are only 367 documents in the "Royal" category which is only 1.2% of the total document in our corpus, LDA37 can extract the topic, "Royal", which is interpreted from top ten terms in topic 6. An example of all seven categories extracted from LDA37 is topic 1, 2, 3, 6, 8, 13 and 14 that can be interpreted easily to be the same as Finance, Lifestyle, Economy, Royal, Business, World and Politics categories, respectively.

Some topics from LDA37 are more specific than those from LDA7. For instance, topic 4 is about the protests and demonstrations in Hong Kong which happened around the time we collected the data, and topic 12 is specifically about COVID. Topic 12 is separated from topic 10 which is about "Health" unlike topic from LDA7 that has only one "Health" topic. Even though some topics are duplicate in broad interpretation, they are still different when we did deeper interpretation. However, a few topics are difficult, but possible, to be interpreted deeper by human.

---

[5] All 37 topics and 300 topics can be viewd via the provided link attached to this footnote.

Table 2. Top ten terms of thirteen example topics from total 37 topics extracted by LDA37. Identification of each topic is denoted by "T", followed by its identifier number.

T01 (Finance)	T02 (Lifestyle/ Travel)	T03 (Economic)	T04 (World/ Political)	T05 (Agriculture/ Farming)	T06 (Royal)	T07 (Econo-/ Finance)	T08 (Business)	T09 (World/ Lifestyle)	T10 (Health)	T11 (Development)	T12 (Health/ COVID-19)	T13 (World)
ล้าน	บิน	ปี	ฮ่องกง	น้ำ	ตำแหน่ง	สหรัฐ	ธุรกิจ	ร้อย	โรค	งาน	เชื้อ	ประเทศ
หุ้น	ท่องเที่ยว	เศรษฐกิจ	ตำรวจ	เกษตรกร	ราชการ	เดือน	บริการ	ปี	ป่วย	พัฒนา	ไวรัส	ปี
ปี	เที่ยว	ตัว	ทหาร	ข้าว	พระราชทาน	ตัว	ลูกค้า	ระบุ	ยา	ระบบ	ระบาด	ญี่ปุ่น
บาท	เครื่อง	ลด	ประท้วง	สัตว์	เสด็จ	จุด	ทำ	อันดับ	แพทย์	โครงการ	คน	ล้าน
ทุน	เดินทาง	กระทบ	ชุมนุม	สาร	ประกาศ	อังกฤษ	ตลาด	เมือง	อาการ	สร้าง	โรค	โลก
บริษัท	โดยสาร	ไทย	เจ้าหน้าที่	เกษตร	พศ	ระดับ	ออนไลน์	โลก	รักษา	ประเทศ	ติด	บริษัท
ราคา	สาย	ประเทศ	คน	ปลูก	ดำรง	ดัชนี	ดิจิทัล	สำรวจ	พยาบาล	ระดับ	โควิด	เอเชีย
ขาย	คน	ทุน	กอง	ผลิต	พระราชพิธี	การณ์	สร้าง	คน	สุขภาพ	นโยบาย	แพร่	อินเดีย
ซื้อ	ไทย	คาด	เหตุการณ์	พืช	king *	ร่วม	เติบโต	ตัวอย่าง	กัญชา	ดำเนิน	ประเทศ	เวียดนาม
กำไร	เส้นทาง	โลก	ทัพ	ปริมาณ	แต่งตั้ง	เกี่ยว	ยอด	อายุ	ติด	ทำ	สถานการณ์	สิงคโปร์

*พระบาทสมเด็จพระเจ้าอยู่หัว

In addition to LDA7 and LDA37, we performed LDA with 300 as the number of topics (LDA300) in order to get the same number of features or feature vector length as that of Word2Vec (W2V). However, as it is not possible to show all 300 topics, we provide only some important aspects from the results of LDA300 to compare them with those of LDA7 and LDA37. The results from LDA300[5] can cover all seven categories. However, as 300 is a lot higher than seven, the actual number of categories, and set without any theory support, many of the latent topics from LDA300 are too ambiguous to be interpreted and many of them can be interpreted to be the same topics. Additionally, nine topics have the exact same top ten terms with the same order.

In summary, the top-ranked terms of seven topics from LDA7 are the easiest to be interpreted and very meaningful, but cannot represent all seven categories of our corpus. Furthermore, the number of topics cannot practically known beforehand. So, we set a preliminary experiment on LDA with the different numbers of topics, compared their topic coherence scores and got 37 as the potentially optimal number of topics for our corpus. The top-ranked terms of 37 topics from LDA37 are interpretable though a bit difficult for a few topics, and meaningful enough to give the rough idea of the context possibly from the topics. They cover all seven categories and give us a lot of latent topics that is comparable to subcategories of our corpus. Accordingly, Q2 can be answered that we can define the number of topics by experimenting with various numbers of topics and we can use topic coherence scores to get a rough estimate of the number of topics. Besides, LDA with 300 was additionally performed. The top-ranked terms of 300 topics from LDA300 are difficult, if impossible, to be interpreted and some of them are not meaningful at all. As a result, we can answer Q1 that LDA with the potentially optimal number of topics gives us the best set of latent topics represented by top-ranked terms that is interpretable and meaningful.

3.2 Q3

Table 3 shows the performance (i.e., Accuracy and macro F1) and computational time of classification algorithms using five comparative sets of features. In Ta-

Table 3. Performance and computation time of each classification algorithm with different feature extraction methods.

	Accuracy (percent)					macro F1 (percent)					Computational time (seconds)				
	BoW	LDA7	LDA37	LDA300	W2V	BoW	LDA7	LDA37	LDA300	W2V	BoW	LDA7	LDA37	LDA300	W2V
LR	87.96	67.79	81.40	85.16	**88.37**	84.01	46.16	73.10	80.43	**84.49**	971	**30**	35	60	767
SVM	87.31	73.14	84.49	86.83	**88.72**	82.88	60.04	78.92	82.68	**84.47**	1226	**93**	137	718	607
MLP	88.21	72.15	83.27	86.15	**88.24**	**83.82**	58.67	77.15	81.02	83.74	1300	**53**	81	169	520
DT	74.52	70.46	76.72	74.49	**75.14**	**66.91**	55.78	66.45	67.82	65.77	160	**6**	20	91	300
RF	83.93	74.03	83.62	84.38	**86.66**	75.72	62.27	76.23	77.65	**81.54**	422	**108**	185	367	944
ADB	85.20	72.77	83.98	85.26	**87.11**	79.88	61.39	78.12	80.63	**82.27**	10493	**271**	854	4208	10596
XGB	87.87	74.90	84.37	87.13	**88.48**	83.45	63.23	78.52	82.93	**84.70**	16238	**3295**	7012	22109	46961
GBM	86.22	74.50	83.54	85.06	**87.43**	80.61	61.64	75.78	76.89	**81.78**	4839	**631**	1403	4576	29360

Note: The values in **bold** show the best among feature extraction methods and in underline show the best among learning algorithms.

ble 4, we calculate and report the trade-off between performance gain and time loss, shown by AT and FT ratios.

When considering among LDAs with the different numbers of topics (i.e., LDA7, LDA37 and LDA300), the features from LDA7 classified by DT (LDA7-DT) spent the least time for optimization. Additionally, when considering only features from LDA7, LDA7-DT was also the best in term of trading off according to both ratios. However, LDA7-DT performed the worst with 70.46% accuracy and 55.78% macro F1 among different feature extraction methods and different algorithms. Besides, DT performed the worst with four sets of features and the second worst with a set of features.

Among LDAs, the XGB classifier trained with LDA300 features (simply denoted as LDA300-XGB) showed the best performance with 87.13% accuracy and 82.93% macro F1 but the most computational time, 22108s. However, considering only features from LDA300, LDA300-LR gave the best results in terms of trading-off according to both AT and FT ratios. Even though almost all of the algorithms performed the best with the features from LDA300, they spent the most computational time in comparison with the other LDAs. Accordingly, when considering with trade-off, the set of features from LDA37 was the best for all classification according to AT ratio and the best for 5 algorithms and the second for 3 algorithms according to FT ratio. Besides, LDA37-LR was the best according to both AT and FT ratios.

Among all feature extraction methods in our experiment, LDA-DT was still considered the best in term of computational time but the worst in term of performance. However, even the performance of XGB-LDA300 was the best in LDA-based runs, it still performed worse than many of those based on BoW and W2V. Considering accuracy, the features from W2V classified by SVM (W2V-SVM) showed the best performance at 88.72% accuracy with only 60s optimization time. In contrast, considering macro F1, the features from W2V classified by XGB (W2V-XGB) showed the best performance with 84.70% micro F1 but with the longest optimization time at 46961s. When considering trade-off, the best among all feature extraction methods were the same as the best among LDAs. However, when we considered only the results with more than 80% in both accuracy and macro F1, LDA300-LR was the best in term of trade-off with 81.48 AT ratio and 160.30 FT ratio. Besides, comparing W2V-SVM with

Table 4. Accuracy-to-Time (AT) and F1-to-Time Gain (FT) ratios of each classification algorithm with different feature extraction methods.

	AT ratio					FT ratio				
	BoW	LDA7	LDA37	LDA300	W2V	BoW	LDA7	LDA37	LDA300	W2V
LR	9.41	0.67	**84.65**	81.48	12.02	17.62	0.67	**166.96**	160.30	22.34
SVM	7.27	19.08	**44.30**	11.85	15.25	13.65	48.94	**86.65**	22.66	27.86
MLP	7.19	22.26	**60.06**	41.40	17.21	13.23	62.94	**119.86**	78.40	31.55
DT	15.94	27.70	**70.07**	24.29	10.28	48.65	97.20	**158.21**	77.74	27.19
RF	16.48	19.95	**33.16**	19.23	9.04	30.09	51.00	**62.80**	36.40	16.92
ADAB	0.78	7.64	**8.55**	1.94	0.86	1.51	**23.06**	16.82	3.82	1.60
XGB	0.58	1.01	**1.11**	0.41	0.21	1.08	**2.42**	2.16	0.78	0.39
GBM	1.78	4.76	**5.15**	1.77	0.32	3.32	**10.89**	9.66	3.14	0.57

Note: The values in **bold** show the best among feature extraction methods and in underline show the best among learning algorithms.

LDA300-LR, the performance between these two were not much different but the computational time of W2V-SVM was slightly tenfold greater than that of LDA300-LR. Accordingly, LDA300-LR seemed be the best choice according to our cross comparison of performance and computational time from five sets of features classified by eight algorithms. It took not much computational time and gave only a bit lower performance than the best one and got the highest ratios among the other features with over 80% in both accuracy and macro F1.

In summary, on average, W2V was the best in term of performance but the worst in term of optimization time and the second worst in term of trade-off and LDA 7 was the best in term of optimization time but the worst in term of performance and in the middle among all features extraction methods in term of trade-off. Even though LDA300 was in the middle in both performance and optimization time, its ratios did not the show the best trade-off but LDA37's ratios did. However, when specifically considering only the performance with over 80% in both accuracy and macro F1, LDA300-LR performed fairly good with not much time and got the highest score from both ratios.

4 Document Representations

4.1 Term Frequency-Inverse Document Frequency (tf-idf)

tf-idf [10] is a traditional method for term weighting in a BoW model. tf quantifies how important a term t is in a document, and idf quantifies how common the term t is among the corpus. Then, tf-idf is simply the product of tf and idf. There are many variant of tf-idf, especially for the idf component.

idf_t uses logarithm to reduce the effect of a fraction of the total number of documents (N) over the number of documents that the term t occurs (df_t). Both numerator and denominator are added by 1 to avoid a division-by-zero problem. This experiment used tf-idf function in Scikit-learn with its default parameters. Therefore, the constant 1 is added more to the idf after applying logarithm to avoid $idf = 0$ due to the ignorance of the term that appears in all documents.

$$idf_t = \log_e \left(\frac{N+1}{df_t+1} \right) + 1 \tag{5}$$

4.2 LDA (Latent Dirichlet Allocation)

LDA is a type of statistical model for discovering latent topics from a collection of documents, by inferring the relationship between terms, documents and topics in a corpus. Blei *et al.* [3] introduced LDA as an unsupervised topic model. It has become one of the most widely used topic models.

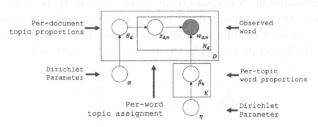

Fig. 2. The graphical model of LDA

The LDA model has the assumption that each of the n-th observed word $w_{d,n}$ in document d is generated by the other unobserved variables as shown in Fig. 2. In this representation, β_k denotes the word distribution of topic k, θ_d denotes the topic distribution of document d, and $z_{d,n}$ denotes the topic number of word n in document d. Each word is assigned as an index in the vocabulary, $w_{d,n} \in \{1, ..., V\}$ when a corpus of D documents contains V vocabulary words, and document d consists of N_d words, $(w_{d,1}, ..., w_{d,N_d})$. Additionally, η and α are Dirichlet parameters for β_k and θ_d, respectively. LDA also relaxes its assumptions to: *i)* the order of documents are not important. *ii)* the order of terms are not important. *iii)* the numbers of topics, K, is known and constant.

Given all words in all documents, the value of the unobserved variables in the model can be estimated by computing the posterior distribution to get the final results from LDA: β_k, each of which represents a latent topic $k \in \{1, ..., K\}$, and θ_d, each of which represents a proportion of topics per document calculated from $z_{d,n}$. Then, θ_d may be used as a representative or features of the document. The approximation of the posterior can be computed by inference algorithms, e.g., Gibbs sampling and Variational Bayes, to infer the variables.

4.3 Word2Vec

In NLP tasks, a BoW model shows only how frequent a word occurs in a document, but does not show similarity between words. Afterwards, Mikolov *et al.* [11] introduced two unsupervised models, Continuous Bag-of-Words (CBOW) model and Skip-gram models, both of which are architectures for computing representations of words in a continuous vector form by using neural networks. The goal of the architectures is the weights of hidden layer that need to be trained by backpropagation from a large dataset. Then, the weights become the continuous vector representations of words, called word embedding. The number of dimensionality used to represent each word (aka. the number of nodes in the hidden layer of the neural network) can be any number. The larger dimensionality values, the more fine-grained relationships can be captured. However, a lower dimensionality may capture more general features of words whereas a higher dimensionality may overfit to specific contexts. CBOW is a model architecture with the fake task to predict a middle word based on its surrounding words, but Skip-gram is a model architecture with the reverse fake task of CBOW, predicting the surrounding words based on a given word. In fact, the predictions from Skip-gram are not its objective but word representations that are useful for predicting the surrounding words. So, given a training data with T words, the objective of Skip-gram model is to maximize the average log probability:

$$\frac{1}{T} \sum_{t=1}^{T} \sum_{-c \leq j \leq j \neq 0} \log p(w_{t+j}|w_t) \tag{6}$$

where c is the context (window) size of surrounding words from the center word w_t. In theory, the probability in Equation 6 can be computed by a softmax function. However, when the size of the vocabulary is large, it is intractable to compute. Then, the approximation by a hierarchical softmax or negative sampling comes to make it feasible to compute [12]. The negative sampling is used by default in gensim with 5 noise words

4.4 Topic Coherence

Topic Coherence is an evaluation metric for topic modeling. To assess overall topics' interpretability, it measures the degree of semantic similarity between high scoring words in each topic. Topic Coherence can also be used to optimize the number of topics of topic models, which is generally needed to be specified by human topic ranking. Although there are many topic coherence measures, our experiment calculated topic coherence by functions in Gensim which cover 4 models, i.e., UCI, NPMI, UMass, and CV.

For UCI, topic coherence is quantified by calculating the pointwise mutual information (PMI) of each word pair from N top words inferring a topic (see in Eq. 7.) Each probability in PMI can be estimated from any external corpus as formalized in Eq. 8. Newman *et al.* [15] suggested that UCI achieved the best result when the external corpus was the entire Wikipedia articles.

$$C_{\text{UCI}} = \frac{2}{N \cdot (N-1)} \sum_{i=1}^{N-1} \sum_{j=i+1}^{N} \text{PMI}(w_i, w_j) \tag{7}$$

$$\text{PMI}(w_i, w_j) = \log \frac{p(w_i, w_j) + \epsilon}{p(w_i)p(w_j)} \tag{8}$$

However, Aletras and Stevenson [1] showed that the UCI coherence performed better with normalized PMI (NPMI) as purposed by Bouma [5]. When the PMI in the UCI coherence is replaced by the NPMI, Eq. 9, the *modified* UCI coherence is then called NPMI coherence.

$$\text{NPMI}(w_i, w_j) = \frac{\text{PMI}(w_i, w_j)}{-\log(p(w_i, w_j) + \epsilon)} \tag{9}$$

UMass coherence [13] is also based on co-occurrences of word pairs. However, instead of using the product of probabilities of two words as the denominator just as in PMI, UMass coherence uses the probability of one word (see Eq. 10.)

$$C_{\text{UMass}} = \frac{2}{N \cdot (N-1)} \sum_{i=2}^{N} \sum_{j=1}^{i-1} \log \frac{P(w_i, w_j) + \epsilon}{P(w_j)} \tag{10}$$

CV coherence was proposed by Röder *et al.* [17] and described in a systematic framework of coherence measures that combines the indirect cosine similarity with the NPMI and the boolean sliding window.

5 Conclusion

In this paper, we focused on the comparison of performance, computational time and their trade-off of classification when the input features were extracted from different methods, TF–IDF (BoW), LDA, Skip-Gram Word2Vec (W2V), which gave the different numbers of features (Q3). However, the number of topics from LDA, which was the number of input features for classification, needed to be calculated (Q2). So, we studied more on LDA about representation of Thai categories by top ten terms extracted by LDA whether they could be interpretable and meaningfulness. (Q1).

The results showed that LDA7 could discover topics with the top-ranked terms that were easy to be interpreted. However, such discovered topics could not represent all the categories in our corpus. Besides, setting the number by this way in practice is unfeasible as we do not know the number of topics in advance. In comparison, the top-ranked terms from LDA37, of which the number of topics was estimated by topic coherence score, could represent all categories of our corpus including many subcategories (Q1 and Q2).

For a fair comparison with Word2Vec having 300 features, we compared the results of LDA300 in a classification task produced by several learning algorithms with five sets of features. In our view, LDA300 with logistic regression seemed to be a pretty good choice when we considered performance, computational time, AT ratio and FT ratio. When we concerned about performance the most, W2V was the best choice to choose but had a trade-off for a lot longer optimization time. Comparatively, when we concerned about optimization time the most, LDA7 was the best choice to choose but demanded a trade-off for the worst performance. However, in our view, if we had to pick one set of features without considering a classification algorithm, we would pick the features from LDA with its potentially optimal number of topics (LDA37 in our experiment.) This selection was because the features was interpretable, could represent the corpus well and got the best trade-off for all classification algorithms according to the AT ratio, and received the best for five algorithms and the second for three algorithms according to the FT ratio.

Acknowledgements This work was supported by KMITL Research Fund under Research Seed Grant for New Lecturer with grant number: KREF186507.

References

1. Aletras, N., Stevenson, M.: Evaluating topic coherence using distributional semantics. In: IWCS 2013 (2013)
2. Asawaroengchai, C., Chaisangmongkon, W., Laowattana, D.: Probabilistic learning models for topic extraction in thai language. In: 2018 5th International Conference on Business and Industrial Research (2018)
3. Blei, D.M., Ng, A.Y., Jordan, M.I.: Latent dirichlet allocation. Journal of machine Learning research **3**(Jan) (2003)
4. Bonaccorso, G.: Machine learning algorithms (2017)
5. Bouma, G.: Normalized (pointwise) mutual information in collocation extraction. In: Proceedings of GSCL. vol. 30 (2009)
6. Chen, T., He, T., Benesty, M., Khotilovich, V., Tang, Y., Cho, H., Chen, K., Mitchell, R., Cano, I., Zhou, T., et al.: Xgboost: extreme gradient boosting. R package version 0.4-2 **1**(4) (2015)
7. Chormai, P., Prasertsom, P., Rutherford, A.: Attacut: A fast and accurate neural thai word segmenter (2019)
8. Lakshminarayanan, B., Pritzel, A., Blundell, C.: Simple and scalable predictive uncertainty estimation using deep ensembles. In: Guyon, I., Luxburg, U.V., Bengio, S., Wallach, H., Fergus, R., Vishwanathan, S., Garnett, R. (eds.) NeurIPS. vol. 30 (2017)
9. Li, C., Lu, Y., Wu, J., Zhang, Y., Xia, Z., Wang, T., Yu, D., Chen, X., Liu, P., Guo, J.: Lda meets word2vec: A novel model for academic abstract clustering. WWW '18 (2018)
10. Luhn, H.P.: A statistical approach to mechanized encoding and searching of literary information. IBM Journal of research and development **1**(4) (1957)
11. Mikolov, T., Chen, K., Corrado, G., Dean, J.: Efficient estimation of word representations in vector space. arXiv preprint arXiv:1301.3781 (2013)
12. Mikolov, T., Sutskever, I., Chen, K., Corrado, G.S., Dean, J.: Distributed representations of words and phrases and their compositionality. In: Burges, C., Bottou, L., Welling, M., Ghahramani, Z., Weinberger, K. (eds.) Advances in Neural Information Processing Systems. vol. 26 (2013)
13. Mimno, D., Wallach, H.M., Talley, E., Leenders, M., McCallum, A.: Optimizing semantic coherence in topic models. In: EMNLP (2011)
14. Nararatwong, R., Legaspi, R., Cooharojananone, N., Okada, H., Maruyama, H.: Solving the difficult problem of topic extraction in thai tweets. Journal of Telecommunication, Electronic and Computer Engineering **8**(6) (2016)
15. Newman, D., Lau, J.H., Grieser, K., Baldwin, T.: Automatic evaluation of topic coherence. In: NAACL HLT 2010 (2010)
16. Pitichotchokphokhin, P., Chuangkrud, P., Kalakan, K., Suntisrivaraporn, B., Leelanupab, T., Kanungsukkasem, N.: Discover underlying topics in thai news articles: A comparative study of probabilistic and matrix factorization approaches. In: ECTI-CON 2020 (2020)

17. Röder, M., Both, A., Hinneburg, A.: Exploring the space of topic coherence measures. WSDM '15 (2015)
18. Wang, Z., Ma, L., Zhang, Y.: A hybrid document feature extraction method using latent dirichlet allocation and word2vec. In: DSC 2016 (2016)

Assessing Data Quality: An Approach for the Spread of COVID-19

Dariusz Król[1]([✉])[iD] and Anna Bodek[2]

[1] Department of Applied Informatics, Wroclaw University of Science and Technology,
Wroclaw, Poland
dariusz.krol@pwr.edu.pl
[2] Faculty of Computer Science and Management, Wroclaw University of Science and
Technology, Wroclaw, Poland

Abstract. The work aims to develop a method for assessing the quality of publicly available data collections on the spread of the COVID-19 pandemic with daily infection statistics, recoveries and deaths. The World Health Organization, European Center for Disease Prevention and Control, Johns Hopkins University and Ministry of Health of the Republic of Poland provide this data as proof of concept. Metrics have been proposed that describe the most important quality features for this type of data collection - accuracy, completeness and consistency. Additional measures have also been defined based on anomaly detection, credibility and correlation between sets. A quality assessment method has been developed that uses specific metrics. The effectiveness of measures was tested on original and modified data. The findings showed that the measures were defined correctly. The method assigns lower-quality categories to datasets containing irregularities and higher for data with fewer errors.

Keywords: Big data analytics · Data quality · Data reporting ·
Knowledge engineering · Real world data · COVID-19

1 Introduction

Major institutions and companies generate, collect and process vast amounts of data on users or services provided daily. This data is used for trend prediction, cost analysis and other business purposes. The quality of this data is critical so that it is possible to make correct inferences, allowing you to make the most favourable business decisions. The same is true when we take into account epidemiological data. In this case, any decisions will not affect material profits but the lives of many people - appropriate restrictions make it possible to stop the development of diseases or reduce the number of patients in hospitals, which relieves public health care. The biggest problem in data processing in every field is their poor quality - missing records, errors, and anomalies. They affect various types of predictions, decisions and actions many institutions take. As a result of the COVID-19 pandemic, it was necessary to record all data on illnesses, recoveries or deaths because it is a rapidly spreading disease that affects the entire

N. T. Nguyen et al. (Eds.): ACIIDS 2023, CCIS 1863, pp. 220–233, 2023.
https://doi.org/10.1007/978-3-031-42430-4_18

society. For this reason, many datasets have been created that are publicly available and provide new data on the pandemic every day for different countries around the world - these include collections of the World Health Organization (WHO), European Center for Disease Prevention and Control (ECDC), Johns Hopkins University (JHU) and Ministry of Health of the Republic of Poland (MZ). Based on these data, many analyses, articles, and forecasts have been created. As part of the work, it was decided to check the quality of data provided by the institutions mentioned above - it is necessary to develop a quality assessment method for this type of collection. First, the data representation methods in selected sets were reviewed, statistical and graphical analysis of data on Poland was made, and a core set of metrics for data evaluation was proposed. Then a quality assessment method was proposed.

The work aims to develop a method for assessing the quality of data for publicly available collections on the spread of the COVID-19 pandemic with daily statistics of illnesses, deaths and recoveries.

2   Related Literature

In this section, we discuss relevant past studies. An example of an article that deals with the assessment of the quality of a collection is the work [1]. The authors undertake to develop a method for assessing the quality of Linked Open Data based on metrics. The proposed solution aims to increase the quality of data available on the Linked Open Data Cloud platform by evaluating them before posting them on the portal. The work considers the ISO/IEC 25012 standards and uses 3 out of 5 features: accuracy, completeness and consistency. Finally, 5 characteristics were developed, where the first 3 are the details of the accuracy:

- syntactic accuracy - data meets syntactic rules, syntactic accuracy of the entity and its properties,
- semantic accuracy - data correctly reflects real-world values,
- uniqueness – no redundancy of entities, classes, properties and their values for Linked Open Data,
- consistency – no contradictory information, there should be no contradictions at the schema level, format and data values are consistent with the schema,
- completeness – required classes and properties should be listed, as well as their values.

The work [7] assesses the quality of data from the Koblenz Network Collection using metrics. The measures were based on the features of the ISO/IEC 25012 standard - consistency, completeness, accuracy, and uniqueness. The criteria for selected datasets are semantic consistency, referential integrity, completeness of values and uniqueness. The final assessment of data quality consists in assigning, depending on the results of calculations, one of 4 categories:

- perfect quality – all indicators are 100%,
- good quality – none of the developed metrics is below the specified threshold,

- of sufficient quality – data should be cleaned up, but still of good enough quality,
- insufficient quality – data for which none of the other requirements is met.

The work [3] reviews quality assessment methods for public health information systems. While reviewing the papers, the authors came across 49 attributes used to describe the data quality. The most frequently used ones were completeness, accuracy and timeliness. There were also, among other things, credibility or coherence. Descriptive statistics are often used for quantitative data analysis - the percentage of complete, correct data based on whether they comply with quality standards. Graphical forms, graphs and statistical techniques such as correlation, chi-square and Mann-Whitney tests are used. Quantitative methods were most often used to assess variables. Specific rules and guidelines characterise the comprehensive data quality assessment method. However, the authors of the work rarely came across articles that precisely describe the procedures for data analysis and quality requirements. Therefore, it is necessary to establish consistent and understandable definitions of data quality and assessment methods for data from public health information systems.

The work [4] analyses the reliability of data from the pandemic's beginning from over 200 countries. The data under assessment came from JHU collection and concerned the daily number of infected and deaths. In addition, the authors used an additional variable describing the number of tests performed. The reliability of the given values was verified by checking their compliance with Benford's Law for Leading Digits. Their frequency in the first place in numbers is described by the Benford distribution [2]. As part of the work, static tests were carried out to confirm that the data for each country separately can comply with Benford's law. The selected tests are the Kolmogorov-Smirnov test, the chi-square test and the coefficient d^*-*factor* developed by the authors, which measures the Euclidean distance. Countries for which none of the tests confirmed compliance with the Benford distribution accounted for only 3% of all nations - the worst results were obtained for Iran, Latvia and Taiwan. Compliance with Benford's law in all tests has been demonstrated in the case of the United States, Germany and France, among others. The author repeated the research after 2 years of the pandemic in work [5], using additional data on the number of tests and vaccinations from the collections of JHU and Our World in Data. The article included data on almost 200 countries, and 4 statistical tests were performed (including 3 already used in work [4]). The data was modified due to their large amount, which may affect the frequency of the maximum numbers - it was decided to analyse not daily data but data divided into 5-day intervals. Seven countries ultimately failed to comply with the Benford Law requirements. The study emphasised that a deviation from the Benford distribution does not indicate fraud or manipulation but problems with the functioning of public health institutions.

A similar analysis was made in work [6], where Benford's law was also used to determine data accuracy for European Union countries. The data from the ECDC collection concerned the daily number of new cases and deaths from March to December 2021. As in the previously discussed work, the chi-square and Kolmogorov-Smirnov tests were used. Euclidean distance and mean absolute deviations were used for additional verification. As a result of the research, the data from almost all European countries in the selected period did not comply with Benford's law. The authors argue that this inconsistency does not necessarily mean the data is false. They indicate, however, that a high degree of vaccination of people may be associated with non-compliance with the discussed distribution.

Based on the literature review, we can conclude that in the case of COVID-19 collections, there are problems related to their completeness, consistency or reliability. Due to the lack of work assessing the most known COVID-19 collections, which are publicly available and updated daily, it was decided to analyse them. As part of the conducted research, metrics describing data sets will be defined based on the characteristics defined by the ISO/IEC 25012 standards and additional measures based on the frequency of anomalies, correlations between sets and reliability.

3   Data

This section will discuss the data analysed as part of the work. They come from international organisations and state institutions. They are used in many reports, analyses and research: (1) European Centre for Disease Prevention and Control, (2) World Health Organization, (3) Johns Hopkins University and (4) Ministry of Health of the Republic of Poland.

3.1   Statistical Data Analysis

Statistical analysis was conducted for selected data collections from March 4, 2020, to January 25, 2022. Basic descriptive statistics, including the mean, standard deviation and quartiles, were determined.

Table 1 presents the analysis for the daily infection variable. These sets contain the same number of values. The minimum values do not differ, while the maximum values are equal for ECDC and WHO. In the case of MZ, the maximum is slightly lower than the others. It can be noticed that the average for the MZ set was more than 20 cases lower than in other data sets. The mean values are the same in the ECDC and WHO data, but the standard deviation for the latter is more significant. This means that the WHO data is less clustered around the mean than in the first set - this is also confirmed by the coefficient of variation, which is greater than that of the ECDC. The median for WHO is also lower by over 160 infections compared to other collections.

Based on the analysis, including daily and total infections, recoveries and deaths, it can be concluded that the same variables between the sets differ very often regarding location and dispersion, despite the same number of available values. The datasets often differ in the values they provide. However, no relationship was found between the differences in statistics.

Table 1. Descriptive statistics of daily infections for selected datasets

Descriptive statistics		ECDC	WHO	MZ
Number of values		693	693	693
Average		6615.238	6615.238	6580.778
Standard deviation		8687.468	8735.675	8625.957
Coefficient of variation		131.325%	132.054%	131.078%
Minimum		0	0	0
Maximum		40878	40878	40876
Quartiles	Q1	333	324	333
	Q2	1515	1350	1516
	Q3	11107	10992	11008
Quarter range		10774	10668	10675
Skewness		1.424	1.433	1.422
Kurtosis		1.223	1.218	1.228

3.2 Visual Data Analysis

Before developing the metrics, the data were visually analysed to compare the data regarding the values provided. In Fig. 1(a) the data overlap to a large extent. More considerable differences are visible for WHO data in October and November 2020. The ECDC and JHU data also differ significantly from the other two sets at the end of November 2020.

Regarding daily data in Fig. 1(b), some differences are noticeable - WHO data for October and November 2020 differ from ECDC, JHU and Ministry of Health data. The graph shows that ECDC and JHU data at the beginning of March 2021 contain different values than other sources.

Data on the number of convalescents for each day are provided only by the Polish Ministry of Health. As seen in Fig. 1(d), these values were not recorded at the end of 2020. Daily increments of convalescents were determined based on the total number of convalescents in the JHU data. These values differ significantly between sets at the turn of 2020 and 2021.

Data on COVID-19 cases are collected differently, but the approach to collecting them is also often changed. Some countries compile death data based on deaths caused solely by COVID-19, while others also include cases where the person suffered from other conditions and the infection was not necessarily the cause of death. Data on positive cases can also vary significantly, as not all types of tests need to be included in the statistics. The analysis shows that data on the COVID-19 pandemic also vary for the same provider, depending on the data source. The reasons may be delays in data transfer to institutions developing data sets and different hours of data published by these organisations. Another reason may be the variety of data collection methods. JHU describes that the data may include confirmed cases and probable cases if reported.

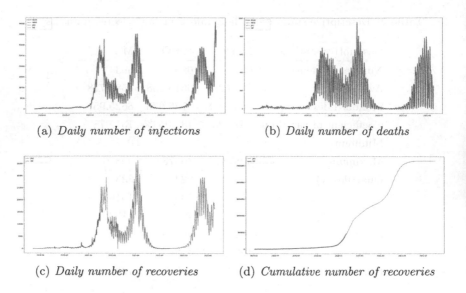

(a) *Daily number of infections*   (b) *Daily number of deaths*

(c) *Daily number of recoveries*   (d) *Cumulative number of recoveries*

Fig. 1. COVID-19 characteristics by selected data source

4   Measures and Method

This section describes the proposed list of measures and a new method for assessing the quality of COVID-19 data. They have been divided into two types - basic quality measures and measures specific to data relating to COVID-19. The second type will be introduced.

4.1   Quality Measures Specific to COVID-19 Data

The plausibility analysis was based on daily increments and cumulative data from 2020 only. According to some sources, Benford's law should only be applied to exponentially increasing data. Such data can be obtained mainly at the beginning of the pandemic - the introduction of vaccinations and additional legal regulations from a later period were aimed at reducing the number of cases, which could affect data distribution - and thus the distribution of the first digits in numerical values. For this reason, it was decided to analyse data only from the beginning of the pandemic. Only non-negative values are analysed.

Two statistical tests were used to assess the reliability of data - chi-square and Kolmogorov-Smirnov. A significance level of 5% was assumed for both tests. The measure, which describes the reliability of a given variable from a selected data source, uses test results as described in Table 2.

The data review and graphical analysis noted potential deviations in the daily data. For this reason, it was decided to develop a measure that would consider the number of anomalies in the data - their small number is synonymous with a better quality of the collection. The method developed in the work [8] is based

Table 2. Description of the metric describing the reliability of COVID-19 data

Metric	Condition
1.0	both tests confirm compliance with the Benford distribution
0.5	one test confirms compliance with the Benford distribution
0.0	none of the tests confirm compliance with the Benford distribution

on checking for violations in the growth rate limits in values. The value increase rate limit will not be exceeded when the following conditions are met:

$$(Y_{t_1} - Y_{t_2})/(t_2 - t_1) < SC_1 \tag{1}$$

and

$$\frac{(Y_{t_1+1} - Y_{t_1})}{(Y_{t_2} - Y_{t_1})/(t_2 - t_1)} < SC_2 \tag{2}$$

where:

t_1, t_2 - any two points in time for which $t_1 < t_2$,
Y_t - cumulative number of incidents on t,
SC_1, SC_2 - predetermined threshold values.

The authors of the work [8] did not provide any example values that can be used as threshold values, or a range for the quantities SC_1, SC_2. In addition, the content of the work does not specify points that would be considered anomalies in the event of failure to meet the conditions described above. Based on the formulas, it can be concluded that the Eq. 1 describes the average increase in incidents in the selected period. Equation 2, in turn, determines the increase in the value for adjacent points from the beginning of the series $(Y_{t_1+1} - Y_{t_1})$ relative to the average increase determined in the previous equation. It can be assumed that the outlier for Eq. 2 will be $t_1 + 1$. However, it is unclear how to determine an anomaly if only the first condition is not met. An attempt was made to apply this solution. However, the lack of suggestions regarding thresholds, freedom in determining the time interval and, above all, the lack of information about points considered anomalies, mean that the results may differ significantly depending on the assumptions made and the size. For this reason, it was decided not to use the above solution.

To determine outliers, Seasonal-Trend decomposition using LOESS (STL) was used, which allows the separation of the trend, seasonality and outliers from the time series. Anomaly detection is performed on daily increment data. Such data are characterised by the increasing amplitude of seasonality and the growing trend. For this reason, a more appropriate type of decomposition is multiplicative decomposition. The STL method uses additive decomposition. Therefore it is necessary to transform the input data using the natural logarithm according to the scheme presented below:

$$y_t = S_t \cdot T_t \cdot R_t$$
$$ln(y_t) = ln(S_t) + ln(T_t) + ln(R_t) \tag{3}$$

where:

y_t - measurement data,
T_t - trend component,
S_t - seasonal component,
R_t - noise component.

After STL decomposition, each component is converted to its original form using an exponential function. For example, a significant noise value for the ECDC daily data decomposition, is noticeable, which allows us to conclude that using the STL method, can effectively indicate significant anomalies in the data. There are also high values for data from the beginning of the pandemic - these deviations are not easily noticeable during graphical analysis.

The measure of the absence of anomalies is calculated as the quotient of the number of non-anomaly values to the number of all values available for the selected variable. The decomposition, and thus the measure, was used only for daily data - one of the works discussed in the literature review dealt with the decomposition of time series only for daily increments, and no other application of decomposition for any cumulative values was found anywhere else.

The literature review mainly showed the Pearson and Spearman correlation coefficients. However, the Ministry of Health collected variables we examined using the Lilliefors test. This test allows you to check whether the data can come from a normal distribution when the population's mean and standard deviation is unknown. The null hypothesis is that the test sample comes from a normal distribution. The results are presented in Table 3, and a significance level of 5%.

Table 3. Lilliefors test results for data from the Ministry of Health

Variable	Stat value	p-value
daily cases	0.22669	0.00100
daily recovery cases	0.24621	0.00100
daily deaths	0.26539	0.00100
total cases	0.32106	0.00100
total recoveries	0.25675	0.00100
total deaths	0.24809	0.00100

Variables from various sources were examined for correlation. Table 4 presents the Spearman correlation matrix between different sources for daily variables and total infections and deaths. All coefficient values are positive and high, so the same variables between different datasets are strongly related to each other.

Table 4. Spearman's correlation coefficient for selected variables

		ECDC	JHU	WHO	MZ
correlation of daily number of cases	ECDC	1.00000	–	0.98921	0.99933
	WHO	0.98921	–	1.00000	0.99008
	MZ	0.99933	–	0.99008	1.00000
correlation of total cases	JHU	–	1.00000	1.00000	1.00000
	WHO	–	1.00000	1.00000	1.00000
	MZ	–	1.00000	1.00000	1.00000
correlation of daily deaths	ECDC	1.00000	–	0.97077	0.99981
	WHO	0.97077	–	1.00000	0.97073
	MZ	0.99981	–	0.97073	1.00000
total death correlation	JHU	–	1.00000	1.00000	1.00000
	WHO	–	1.00000	1.00000	0.99999
	MZ	–	1.00000	0.99999	1.00000

4.2 Data Quality Assessment Method

The final quality score indicates whether the dataset is high or low quality. It was decided to set thresholds for each of the proposed measures - the values should not be lower than the specified values for the data feature to be considered good enough. For the correlation, it was decided to choose the value of 0.6 because, in this case, the variable is still highly correlated with the collections of JHU, ECDC, WHO and the Ministry of Health. The threshold for reliability is equal to 0.5, which means confirmation of the variable's reliability by at least one of the statistical tests. For the remaining metrics - completeness, consistency, accuracy, and lack of anomalies - a value of 0.9 was selected. These are some of the most critical features in the context of data quality assessment; hence their relatively high minimum value was chosen.

The quality assessment of a given collection is made based on the following formula:

$$Q_d = \overline{m}_d \cdot \frac{c_d}{M_d}$$

where:

d - data source,
Q_d - rating index for data on the COVID-19 pandemic for the d source,
$\overline{m}_d$ - average value of measures for source d,
c_d - number of measures not exceeding the threshold for the d source,
M_d - the number of all measures that can be determined for the d source.

The final data quality assessment is selected based on the determined Q_d indicator, depending on the value obtained. Table 5 shows the rating scale for the indicator values. The average of the $\overline{m}_d$ measures is also used to determine the score to reduce the score further if shallow metric values are obtained.

Table 5. How a score is assigned to a dataset based on the score value

Evaluation Indicator Value	Data Evaluation
$[1.0; 0.8)$	very good quality
$[0.8; 0.6)$	good quality
$[0.6; 0.4)$	medium quality
$[0.4; 0.2)$	low quality
$[0.2; 0.0]$	very low quality

5 Results

5.1 Multi-metric Performance Analysis

Before the final assessment, tests were performed on the effectiveness of the proposed metrics. The research to lower (downgrade) or improve (upgrade) the quality was conducted for data between 04/03/2020 and 25/01/2022. Tests were carried out for each of the designed measures. As data for modification, a set developed by the Polish Ministry of Health was used. The following changes to the source data were made to test the effectiveness of the measures:

– for precision measures
  • unique dates – adding 50 records with dates that already exist in the set
  • daily increment accuracy – change 100 values of each variable to random negative values
  • accuracy of the total number of cases – changing 100 values of each variable to values disturbing monotonicity (higher values precede lower values)
– for completeness measures
  • completeness of dates – delete 150 rows
  • completeness of daily increments and total cases – delete 50 values of each variable
– for consistency measures
  • daily and cumulative data consistency – 100 random daily values plus a fixed amount
– for reliability measures
  • reliability of daily and cumulative data – the first digits of the numerical data modified so that the digit 1 is 50% of the distribution
– for measures of the absence of anomalies
  • daily data anomalies – 100 random values increased by a fixed amount of 10000
– for correlation measures
  • correlations of daily and total data - values from the first 100 rows multiplied by a fixed amount of 1000.

See Table 6 showing the modified values for selected measures. From the table, we can understand how the measures are distributed within the acceptance range. For example, how random values disrupted the monotonicity of the sequence of the total number of incidents. Changing the value of daily increments significantly impacted the values of consistency measures, which is the expected result when comparing the values generated based on increments with the values of the total number of cases. Regarding credibility measures, the variables describing recoveries and deaths changed from 1.0 or 0.5 to 0.0. This means that after introducing the changes, no statistical test confirms compliance with the Benford distribution for these variables, which results in line with expectations. For the total and daily number of cases, the indicator's value did not decrease.

Table 6. Examination of selected measures after downgrading

Measure name	Before changes	After changes	Change
cumulative recovered accuracy	1.00000	0.62264	↓
cumulative deaths accuracy	1.00000	0.62264	↓
cumulative recovered completeness	0.38240	0.31024	↓
cumulative deaths completeness	0.38240	0.31024	↓
recovered sum consistency	0.85283	0.02264	↓
deaths sum consistency	0.87170	0.03396	↓
recovered reliability	0.50000	0.00000	↓
deaths reliability	1.00000	0.00000	↓
cumulative recovered reliability	0.50000	0.00000	↓
cumulative deaths reliability	0.50000	0.00000	↓

Table 7. No-anomaly and correlation measures for daily and cumulative data after downgrading

Measure name	Before changes	After changes	Change
recovered nonanomalous	0.91342	0.87590	↓
deaths nonanomalous	0.92785	0.85570	↓
recovered correlation	1.00000	0.40000	↓
deaths correlation	1.00000	0.40000	↓
cumulative recovered correlation	1.00000	0.20000	↓
cumulative deaths correlation	1.00000	0.20000	↓

Table 7 shows the no-anomaly and correlation measures for daily and cumulative data after downgrading. Initially, the number of anomalies was: 57 for cases, 60 for recoveries and 50 for deaths. As a result of the changes, the following anomalies were obtained: 76 for infections, 86 for recoveries, and 100 for deaths. Some of the added anomalies made the previous anomalies no longer detectable because the new values were much more outliers than the previous ones, and the time series began to have different properties. The minor difference in the infection and recovery data is also due to adding a fixed value of 10,000, which does not always result in a significant change in the context of these variables. These values reach much larger than the number of deaths. To test the correlation measure, the test data was modified so that the values from the pandemic's beginning had a different upward trend than the original values. This was done by multiplying these values by a fixed value of 1000.

Tests on the effectiveness of the measures were conducted for both reductions and improvements in the quality of the source data. Both studies showed that the measure values decrease or increase accordingly when the data is modified. Only as a measure of reliability after the deterioration of the case data, there was no difference from the original set - one of the tests was insensitive to the changes made. In the case of changes made to the other variables, the metric's value deteriorated as expected. Improving the data in terms of reliability also increased the measure ratios and reached 1.0 in all cases. It follows that this measure also shows correct results, although one of the tests, in some cases, turns out to be less sensitive to data deterioration.

5.2   Assessing the Quality of Data Collections

In the section, data quality assessments for selected sources were determined using the developed method. It was also checked whether this assessment changes in case of quality deterioration. Data quality was assessed for 4 sources analysed as part of the work - JHU, ECDC, WHO and the Ministry of Health. Table 8 shows the final assessment and indicator. Each set was of at least good quality - the MZ set turned out to be the worst because there are gaps in the daily data on convalescents, and the cumulative values have been discontinued.

Table 8. Data quality assessment for selected data sources

Data source	Rating indicator value	Overall rating
MZ	$0.84483 \cdot 27/32 = 0.71283$	good quality
WHO	$0.94733 \cdot 20/20 = 0.94733$	very good quality
ECDC	$0.94607 \cdot 12/12 = 0.94607$	very good quality
JHU	$0.91009 \cdot 13/14 = 0.84508$	very good quality

6   Concluding Remarks

A method for assessing the quality of publicly available data sources on the COVID-19 pandemic was developed as part of the work. WHO, ECDC, JHU and MZ provide the tested data sets. Based on the literature review, it was decided to develop metrics regarding the essential quality features, such as accuracy, completeness and consistency. Measures specific to data describing the pandemic were also proposed based on the correlation between sets, anomaly detection and reliability. The effectiveness of the defined measures was tested by making modifications to the source data.

Studies on the effectiveness of the developed measures showed that lower values were obtained after removing or modifying the values to incorrect values. It was also observed that the scores decreased evenly for different variables for which similar modifications were applied, which met the expectations. The proposed method evaluated selected public collections WHO, ECDC and JHU, classified as high-quality collections. In contrast, MZ data were classified only as good quality. An assessment was also made for modified data to check the method's effectiveness. Selected datasets edited to degrade the data quality received lower scores than the original data - they were assigned medium or low-quality scores. The indicators used to determine the quality category were the lowest for data with the most significant number of modifications. In the case of the MZ set, the result was lower than for the other sets due to deficiencies in the data on convalescents and cumulative data. Other collections do not provide this and therefore receive higher scores in the defined method. Introducing changes to the required data could positively impact the assessment for the MZ set and negatively affect those that do not present selected variables - for example, when users need data on convalescents.

When analysing the effectiveness of the measures, it was noticed that the metric of no anomalies did not significantly impact the results. These values were always above 0.8, and in a few situations, they were decisive for the assessment, particularly in the case of sets with massive deviations. In addition, when the sets were modified, these values often increased because the characteristics of the time sequence changed and negative numbers were not taken into account - the purpose of this was to make the measure of the absence of anomalies independent of the measure of the accuracy of daily increments because the latter already included values below 0. The likelihood values did not always change, as in the case of efficiency testing. Even though the case variables were significantly modified to diverge from Benford's distribution, one of the statistical tests still showed agreement with this distribution. As in the literature review papers, more statistical tests may be needed to increase the measure's effectiveness.

In future, we are planning to develop additional anomaly detection methods. Making the definition of the measure of the absence of anomalies consistent could better influence the assessment results. Another modification may be a change in the period used to determine the reliability of a variable. Due to constant modifications and the emergence of new data in known collections, additional measures may be defined for variables such as the number of tests or vaccinations. Also, a single rating indicator value may not be the best option, as all of the measures are not equally important in assessing quality.

Acknowledgments. Part of the work presented in this paper received financial support from the statutory funds at the Wrocław University of Science and Technology.

References

1. Behkamal, B., Kahani, M., Bagheri, E., Jeremic, Z.: A metrics-driven approach for quality assessment of linked open data. J. Theor. Appl. Electron. Commer. Res. **9**(2), 11–12 (2014)
2. Benford, F.: The law of anomalous numbers. Proc. Am. Philos. Soc. **78**(4), 551–572 (1938)
3. Chen, H., Hailey, D., Wang, N., Yu, P.: A review of data quality assessment methods for public health information systems. Int. J. Environ. Res. Public Health **11**(5), 5170–5207 (2014)
4. Farhadi, N.: Can we rely on COVID-19 data? An assessment of data from over 200 countries worldwide. Sci. Progr. **104**(2), 1–19 (2021)
5. Farhadi, N., Lahooti, H.: Forensic analysis of COVID-19 data from 198 countries two years after the pandemic outbreak. COVID **2**(4), 472–484 (2022)
6. Kolias, P.: Applying Benford's law to COVID-19 data: the case of the European Union. J. Public Health **44**, e221–e226 (2022)
7. Pucher, S., Król, D.: A Quality Assessment Tool for Koblenz Datasets Using Metrics-Driven Approach. In: Fujita, H., Fournier-Viger, P., Ali, M., Sasaki, J. (eds.) IEA/AIE 2020. LNCS (LNAI), vol. 12144, pp. 747–758. Springer, Cham (2020). https://doi.org/10.1007/978-3-030-55789-8_64
8. Wang, G., et al.: Comparing and integrating us COVID-19 data from multiple sources with anomaly detection and repairing. J. Appl. Stat. **50**(11–12), 2408–2434 (2023)

Improved U-Net Based on Dual Attention Mechanism for Glottis Segmentation and Dysphagia Auxiliary Diagnosis

Shih-Hsiung Lee[1]([✉])(iD), Jui-Chung Ni[2], Yen-Cheng Shen[2], Hsuan-Chih Ku[1], Chu-Sing Yang[2], Ko-Wei Huang[3], and Chun-Hao Chen[4]

[1] Department of Intelligent Commerce, National Kaohsiung University of Science and Technology, Kaohsiung City 824, Taiwan
{shlee,c108156120}@nkust.edu.tw

[2] Institute of Computer and Communication Engineering, National Cheng Kung University, Tainan City 701, Taiwan
q38031013@ncku.edu.tw, n26101850@gs.ncku.edu.tw, csyang@ee.ncku.edu.tw

[3] Department of Electrical Engineering, National Kaohsiung University of Science and Technology, Kaohsiung City 80778, Taiwan
elone.huang@nkust.edu.tw

[4] Department of Computer Science and Information Engineering, National Kaohsiung University of Science and Technology, Kaohsiung City 80778, Taiwan
chench@nkust.edu.tw

Abstract. In today's aging society, the proportion of elderly population is increasing year by year, and providing comprehensive care for the elderly has become an important issue. Among many aging diseases, dysphagia is a health threat that we often overlook, which if not detected and treated in time, can lead to aspiration pneumonia. Currently, the main detection method is usually through imaging of the throat and judgment by doctors. However, inexperienced doctors may make misjudgments. In order to avoid such situations, this study hopes to assist doctors in their diagnosis through effective image semantic segmentation technology. In the field of medical image semantic segmentation, the U-Net architecture has been proven to be a successful image segmentation architecture. The encoder-decoder technology in U-Net can effectively extract features and restore the original image. However, U-Net may lose important features during the downsampling process of feature extraction. Therefore, this study added a dual attention mechanism in the encoder, which effectively captures important features through position attention and channel attention in the image. In addition to the dual attention mechanism, this study added ResNet blocks in each encoder and decoder block to preserve feature information between downsampling and upsampling. Finally, this paper proves the effectiveness of these mechanisms through experiments and obtains good results.

Supported by National Science and Technology Council of Taiwan (under grant No. 111-2221-E-992-070-MY2 and 111-2221-E-006-124).

N. T. Nguyen et al. (Eds.): ACIIDS 2023, CCIS 1863, pp. 234–243, 2023.
https://doi.org/10.1007/978-3-031-42430-4_19

Keywords: Glottis Segmentation · Deep Learning · Dysphagia Auxiliary Diagnosis

1 Introduction

As everyone knows, elderly people must face some physical aging conditions, such as common chronic diseases like hypertension, diabetes, and osteoporosis. However, there is another condition that is often overlooked by the public, which is dysphagia. According to a survey by Taiwan's Health Bureau, dysphagia has a prevalence rate of 12.8% among the elderly population, which means that 1 out of 10 elderly people has mild or above chewing and swallowing difficulties. This number will continue to rise with Taiwan's aging population. Abnormal chewing and swallowing may also increase the risk of aspiration pneumonia in the elderly. Pneumonia has risen to the third leading cause of death in Taiwan's top 10 causes of death in 2016, and the number of cases is still increasing, especially among people over 65 years old. In recent years, aspiration pneumonia caused by chewing and swallowing difficulties in the elderly has become one of the threats to their health. Some causes of aspiration pneumonia are due to poor oral hygiene or decreased function of the chewing and swallowing muscles, which leads to many bacteria or pathogens in the oral cavity being inhaled or choked into the lungs with food, causing aspiration pneumonia. Therefore, dysphagia is a condition that cannot be ignored. In recent years, with the advent of the big data era, many medical institutions have digitized their data, which means that they now have a huge amount of data compared to before. In deep learning, learning from data is the core idea of this technology. After each round of learning, the model calculates the loss function, updates the weights in the model, and achieves an effective learning cycle to provide accurate information to assist in diagnosis. Hence, how to use the deep learning technology to increase efficiency of dysphagia auxiliary diagnosis is an important issue.

There have been remarkable advancements in semantic segmentation and instance segmentation for multi-object detection. In addition, the popularization of medical examinations such as X-rays and ultrasound has enabled the acquisition of large amounts of data. There are many domestic and foreign studies on the diagnosis of diseases using X-ray and ultrasound images, which extract small but important features directly from the images. Diagnosis is then performed using neural network models such as semantic segmentation and instance segmentation. These technologies bring many conveniences to doctors and can assist doctors with less experience. In the future, this may help reduce the serious shortage of medical manpower and allow people to enjoy higher quality medical services.

Many successful medical image segmentation papers from the past to the present have been based on modifications and variations of the U-Net [1] network architecture. This is because U-Net is a relatively simple and effective architecture, and its success is believed to be attributed to its encoder-decoder structure, which can effectively integrate and extract features that are difficult to perceive by the naked eye. In addition, using the skip-connection mechanism between the encoder and decoder can retain a large amount of original information, effectively preventing gradient vanishing and suppressing overfitting when the network structure is too deep. Therefore, based on the advantages and flexibility of U-Net, this paper uses U-Net as the base network architecture to improve and optimize the issue of glottis segmentation. Currently, many studies combine U-Net with ResNet [2]. This is because ResNet has a powerful function to prevent gradient vanishing, and its own training effectiveness is already quite good. Its residual block and shortcut structure, similar to the skip-connection effect of U-Net, both reuse the extracted feature information. These neural network modules can effectively utilize past information during training, without losing important features due to deep networks. In addition, we have found from past literature that combining U-Net with ResNet is feasible and has better results [3,4].

The attention mechanism [5] was proposed by Google. This technique can use three variables, query, key, and value, to identify the most helpful features for the result, in other words, to find the most important parts to pay attention to in the features. Based on this attention mechanism, Fu et al. proposed the dual-attention mechanism [6], which divides image features into two directions, including position attention and channel attention. The dual-attention mechanism can search for required features through these two attention mechanisms, and these two operate in parallel without interfering with each other's results. Therefore, this study incorporates the dual-attention mechanism into the skip-connection of U-Net to improve the generalization of feature extraction and increase the accuracy of the results.

In previous studies on dysphagia, most of the data types were based on asking patients to swallow fluorescent agents and then using advanced equipment such as X-Ray [7–12] or MRI [13] to record the entire swallowing process. Then, doctors would observe the patient's swallowing trajectory, the movement of throat muscles during the swallowing process, and the residual fluorescent agent near the pyriform muscle in the throat to assess the patient's swallowing disorder. Based on the doctor's judgment, the severity of the disorder is classified. In addition, some data was collected using ultrasound [14], which is similar to the above method, where the entire swallowing process is recorded using ultrasound, and then evaluated by a doctor.

In this study, the dataset was obtained by manually sampling using a laryngoscope on a mannequin. A dataset of 509 throat images with glottis was collected. The proposed improved U-Net model, combined with ResNet and dual-attention mechanism, will be used to segment the location of the glottis in the image and label them. The output of this study can assist less experienced doctors in preliminary screening, to prevent misdiagnosis and guide subsequent diagnosis and treatment accurately.

The rest of this paper is organized as follows. In Sect. 2, we introduce related work. Section 3 presents the proposed architecture in this paper. In Sect. 4, we discuss the experimental results and compare them with some existing methods. Finally, we conclude the paper.

2   Related Work

Some scholars have already conducted research on the segmentation model of the glottis, such as the study by Huijun Ding, Qian Cen, Xiaoyu Si, Zhanpeng Pan, and et al. [15]. The network architecture they used was the DA-U-Net based on U-Net. The DA-U-Net architecture replaces the convolutional layers of U-Net with dense blocks to obtain more feature information. Then, DA-U-Net also added color normalization (CN) to form a new CN-DA-Unet architecture. Adding color normalization is because most of the previous training and research used grayscale images. However, this paper used color images for training, so normalization can effectively reduce computation after preprocessing.

There is literature on the combination of U-Net, ResNet, and dual-attention for medical imaging, such as the architecture proposed by Ibtihaj Ahmad, Yong Xia, Hengfei Cui, and et al. in their paper [16]. This paper aims to use a segmentation model to label cancer cells in order to identify the type of cancer cells. They replaced the encoder part of U-Net with residual blocks, which preserve the original data with their feature access ability. They added dual-attention in the skip-connections to increase feature extraction ability before passing the data to the decoder. The decoder retains the original convolutional layers, and experiments showed that this method performs better than using only the dual-attention mechanism. The paper published by Xiangyu Zhao, Peng Zhang, Fan Song, Guangda Fan, Yangyang Sun, Yujia Wang, Zheyuan Tian, Luqi Zhang and et al. [17] aims to use a segmentation model to identify and label COVID-19 patients' chest CT slices, in order to locate the infected areas from the images for treatment and healthcare. The proposed architecture in this paper replaces the decoder part of U-net with residual blocks and utilizes a dual-attention mechanism for the skip-connections. The difference is that they adopt the attention mechanism using SENet, while retaining the original convolution layers for the encoder part. According to their experiments, this architecture can accurately locate the infected areas.

3   Proposed Architecture

From the literature review in the previous section [16,17], we found that residual blocks and dual-attention mechanisms can effectively improve the accuracy of the model. The key is how to effectively integrate the relationship between the two. First, we need to preserve the original appearance of the entire image. Therefore, in the U-Net-based architecture, we use the shortcut feature of the residual block for feature extraction in the encoder part, which preserves the original appearance while also extracting features. Then, the extracted features are sent to the next layer of residual blocks, until the final layer of the designed structure. The number of layers designed in this paper is four layers to achieve the best results and reduce the occurrence of overfitting. When designing a model for image segmentation, reducing the occurrence of overfitting is one of the important goals. This is because high accuracy results can generally be obtained based on the U-Net structure. However, under this result, the model is prone to overfitting. Therefore, this paper focuses on the design of the model's generalization ability, and the ability to adapt well to new data. Moreover, overfitting problems are prone to occur when the dataset is not large enough. Therefore, this paper added a dual-attention mechanism to the skip-connection layer in the middle of the U-Net, using position attention and channel attention to increase the model's accuracy and reduce overfitting. The spatial attention mechanism can extract the more important position features from the entire image, thereby enhancing the model's generalization ability. The channel attention mechanism strengthens the more important information during convolution operation, making it easier to increase the model's robustness during training. Finally, for the decoder part, we refer to the idea in [16]. We fully retain the features extracted by the encoder for the subsequent residual blocks, and add the enhanced features brought by the dual-attention mechanism. This completes the design concept of the entire architecture, reducing overfitting and increasing the overall generalization ability and accuracy of the model. The proposed model architecture is shown in Fig. 1.

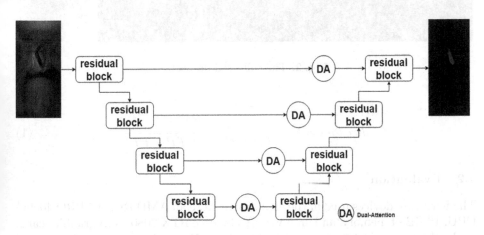

Fig. 1. The propposed model of improved U-Net based on dual attention mechanism and Residual block.

4   Experiment

4.1   Dataset

First, we used a laryngoscope as the device for collecting images, and simulated different glottis sizes by opening the glottis with varying degrees of force after entering the throat. We divided the 509 photos in the collected dataset into

448 training data, 50 validation data, and 11 testing data. For each evaluated model, we performed 10 epochs of training. The scoring standards used were the IoU (Intersection over Union) score and the dice loss. In the evaluation of the segmentation model, the IoU score is often used as one of the evaluation criteria. It represents the overlap ratio between the predicted image and the ground truth. In other words, the higher the value, the more accurate we can believe it to be. The dice loss formula (1) is also commonly used as the loss function in the training of the segmentation model. This loss function is derived from the calculation of the dice coefficient or F1-score, where TP represents true positive, FN represents false negative, and FP represents false positive. We can think of it this way: the lower the dice loss value, the higher the model's accuracy, as it is an inverse relationship. The collected dataset is shown in Fig. 2.

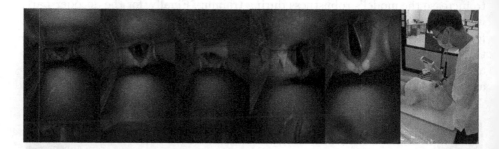

Fig. 2. The collected dataset.

$$dice\ loss = 1 - \frac{2 * TP}{(TP + FN) + (TP + FP)} \tag{1}$$

4.2   Evaluation

The hardware devices used in the experiment were an AMD Ryzen 5 PRO 4650G CPU, 16 GB of memory, and an NVIDIA GeForce RTX 2080 8 GB graphics card.

In the first experiment, we evaluated the U-Net architecture. U-Net showed a very high level of accuracy from the beginning, with a training IoU score as high as 0.995 and a validation score of 0.9969. However, as shown in Fig. 3, we discovered a significant overfitting phenomenon in U-Net, which is not desirable.

U-Net++ [18] is an enhanced version of U-Net that includes more nodes in the skip-connection layer to extract features for better accuracy. In the experiment, the training IoU score reached 0.9955, and the validation score was 0.9973. The experimental results show that the accuracy is indeed higher than U-Net. However, as shown in Fig. 4, the overfitting problem still exists.

We attempted to use DeepLabV3 [19], proposed by Google, for evaluation. This architecture introduces the concept of Atrous Convolution, which can increase the model's spatial generalization ability while maintaining the total

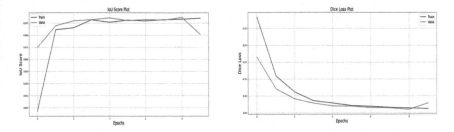

Fig. 3. IoU score and dice loss of U-Net.

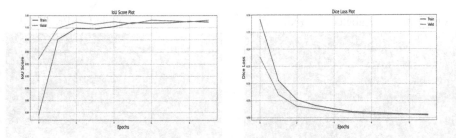

Fig. 4. IoU score and dice loss of U-Net++.

calculation amount of the kernel. Finally, DeepLabV3 achieved a training IoU score of 0.9927 and a validation score of 0.9949. Although the accuracy did not increase, the overfitting situation showed a tendency to decrease as shown in Fig. 5.

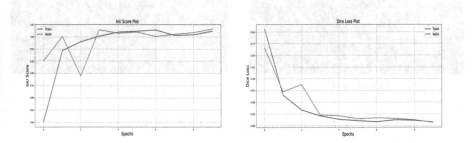

Fig. 5. IoU score and dice loss of DeepLabV3.

The architecture we proposed finally achieved a training IoU score of 0.9912 and a validation score of 0.986 in the experiment. Although the IoU score and dice loss performance were not the best, the overfitting situation disappeared as shown in Fig. 6. The dual-attention and residual blocks did play their roles. Table 1 gives a summary of each model. The Fig. 7 showed the segmentation result of each model.

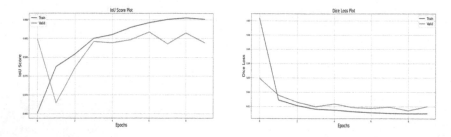

Fig. 6. IoU score and dice loss of proposed model.

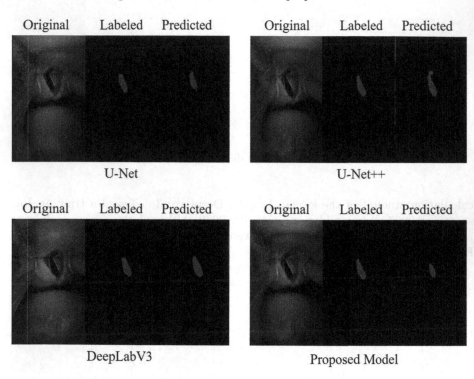

Fig. 7. The segmentation result of each model.

Table 1. The performance of each model.

	IoU (train)	IoU (validation)	dice loss (train)	dice loss (validation)
U-Net	0.995	0.9969	0.0063	0.0046
U-Net++	0.9955	0.9973	0.0053	0.0038
DeepLabV3	0.9927	0.9949	0.0057	0.0078
Proposed model	0.9912	0.986	0.0051	0.0076

5   Conclusion

The proposed architecture in this paper, as demonstrated by experiments, shows that the combination of U-Net, ResNet, and dual-attention mechanism is quite useful in addressing the issue of overfitting. Although the accuracy is not higher than other architectures, the difference is quite small. In the future, for detecting glottis, this paper will use features such as muscle movements during swallowing or whether the epiglottis covers the trachea completely to determine the severity of swallowing disorders, which can help doctors conduct preliminary screening, and prevent this disease in some countries or cities with less developed medical resources.

References

1. Ronneberger, O., Fischer, P., Brox, T.: U-net: convolutional networks for biomedical image segmentation. In: Navab, N., Hornegger, J., Wells, W.M., Frangi, A.F. (eds.) MICCAI 2015, Part III. LNCS, vol. 9351, pp. 234–241. Springer, Cham (2015). https://doi.org/10.1007/978-3-319-24574-4_28
2. He, K., Zhang, X., Ren S., Sun, J.: Deep residual learning for image recognition. In: 2016 IEEE Conference on Computer Vision and Pattern Recognition (CVPR), Las Vegas, NV, USA, pp. 770–778 (2016). https://doi.org/10.1109/CVPR.2016.90
3. Kaili, C., Zhang, X.: An improved Res-UNet model for tree species classification using airborne high-resolution images. Remote Sens. **12**(7), 1128 (2020)
4. Chu, Z., Tian, T., Feng, R., Wang, L.: Sea-land segmentation with Res-UNet and fully connected CRF. In: IGARSS 2019–2019 IEEE International Geoscience and Remote Sensing Symposium, Yokohama, Japan, pp. 3840–3843 (2019). https://doi.org/10.1109/IGARSS.2019.8900625
5. Ashish, V., et al.: Attention is all you need. In: Advances in Neural Information Processing Systems, vol. 30 (2017)
6. Fu, J., et al.: Dual attention network for scene segmentation. In: 2019 IEEE/CVF Conference on Computer Vision and Pattern Recognition (CVPR), Long Beach, CA, USA, pp. 3141–3149 (2019). https://doi.org/10.1109/CVPR.2019.00326
7. Wilhelm, P., Reinhardt, J.M., Van Daele, D.: A deep learning approach to video fluoroscopic swallowing exam classification. In: 2020 IEEE 17th International Symposium on Biomedical Imaging (ISBI), Iowa City, IA, USA, pp. 1647–1650 (2020). https://doi.org/10.1109/ISBI45749.2020.9098510
8. Ariji, Y., Gotoh, M., Fukuda, M., et al.: A preliminary deep learning study on automatic segmentation of contrast-enhanced bolus in videofluorography of swallowing. Sci. Rep. **12**, 18754 (2022)
9. Kim, J.K., et al.: Deep learning analysis to automatically detect the presence of penetration or aspiration in videofluoroscopic swallowing study. J. Korean Med. Sci. **37**(6) (2022)
10. Kim, H.-I., et al.: Hyoid bone tracking in a videofluoroscopic swallowing study using a deep-learning-based segmentation network. Diagnostics **11**(7), 1147 (2021)
11. Zhang, Z., et al.: Automatic annotation of cervical vertebrae in videofluoroscopy images via deep learning. Med. Image Anal. **74**, 102218 (2021)
12. Seong Jae, L., et al.: Automatic detection of airway invasion from videouoroscopy via deep learning technology. Appl. Sci. **10**(18), 6179 (2020)

13. Feng, S., et al.: Automatic hyoid bone tracking in real-time ultrasound swallowing videos using deep learning based and correlation filter based trackers. Sensors **21**(11), 3712 (2021)
14. Khalifa, Y., Donohue, C., Coyle, J.L., Sejdić, E.: Autonomous swallow segment extraction using deep learning in neck-sensor vibratory signals from patients with dysphagia. IEEE J. Biomed. Health Inform. **27**(2), 956–967 (2023). https://doi.org/10.1109/JBHI.2022.3224323
15. Ding, H., et al.: Automatic glottis segmentation for laryngeal endoscopic images based on U-Net. Biomed. Signal Process. Control **71**, 103116 (2022)
16. Ahmad, I., et al.: DAN-NucNet: a dual attention based framework for nuclei segmentation in cancer histology images under wild clinical conditions. Expert Syst. Appl. **213**, 118945 (2023)
17. Zhao, X., et al.: D2A U-Net: automatic segmentation of COVID-19 CT slices based on dual attention and hybrid dilated convolution. Comput. Biol. Med. **135**, 104526 (2021)
18. Zhou, Z., Rahman Siddiquee, M.M., Tajbakhsh, N., Liang, J.: UNet++: a nested U-net architecture for medical image segmentation. In: Stoyanov, D., et al. (eds.) DLMIA/ML-CDS - 2018. LNCS, vol. 11045, pp. 3–11. Springer, Cham (2018). https://doi.org/10.1007/978-3-030-00889-5_1
19. Chen, L.-C., et al.: Encoder-decoder with atrous separable convolution for semantic image segmentation. In: Proceedings of the European Conference on Computer Vision (ECCV) (2018)

The Application of Machine Learning Technique to Soil Salinity Mapping in South of Kazakhstan

Timur Merembayev[1]([envelope]) [ID], Ravil Mukhamediev[1,2][ID],
Yedilkhan Amirgaliyev[1][ID], Dmitry Malakhov[3][ID], Aleksey Terekhov[1][ID],
Yan Kuchin[1][ID], Kirill Yakunin[1,4][ID], and Adilkhan Symagulov[1,2][ID]

[1] Institute of Information and Computational Technologies,
Almaty 050010, Kazakhstan
timur.merembayev@gmail.com
[2] Institute of Automation and Information Technology,
Satbayev University (KazNRTU), Almaty 050013, Kazakhstan
[3] GIS and Remote Sensing Department, Institute of Zoology SC MES RK,
Almaty 050060, Kazakhstan
[4] School of Engineering Management, Almaty Management University,
Almaty 050060, Kazakhstan

Abstract. In this paper, we consider the problem of assessing the salinity of the lands of the Turkestan region using remote sensing data. We aim to analyze the applicability of machine learning methods to evaluate the salinity of agricultural lands in southern Kazakhstan based on remote sensing. The machine learning algorithm uses Sentinel 1 radar data as features and Model A results expert assessment of soil salinity as output or target values for Gaussian Process training. The Gaussian Process model demonstrates a high degree of agreement with an expert estimation on the test subset of data (the recall, precision, and f1 metrics have a value of 0.89). The results allow us to recommend this approach for further testing based on ground-based measurement data and other machine learning methods for mapping the salinity of agricultural lands. The examined process of categorizing salinity has the potential to enhance the effectiveness of addressing challenges related to automating the digital mapping of salinity across extensive regions.

Keywords: Soil salinity · Machine learning · Decision tree · Gaussian process · Synthetic Aperture Radar

1 Introduction

Irrigation salinization of arable lands and degradation of agricultural lands in the South of Kazakhstan is a systemic negative factor that most strongly affects four regions of Kazakhstan: Turkestan, Almaty, Zhambyl, and Kyzylorda. The main problem is water resources, which are formed by the region's transboundary

N. T. Nguyen et al. (Eds.): ACIIDS 2023, CCIS 1863, pp. 244–253, 2023.
https://doi.org/10.1007/978-3-031-42430-4_20

flow of large rivers (the Syrdarya, Ile, and Chu Rivers). Kazakhstan is located in the lower reaches of these river basins and is, therefore, very vulnerable. The growth of water consumption in the upper parts of the river basins and climate change create problems in the water supply in southern Kazakhstan. Ensuring water and food security in the south of Kazakhstan, where two of the three big cities of the Republic are located (Almaty and Shymkent), raises the task of developing technologies for monitoring the processes of salinization and degradation of agricultural land.

The article aims to describe one of the machine learning methods for soil salinity mapping based on expert assessment and high-resolution radar images. Machine learning methods (ML) are an important subsection of artificial intelligence (artificial intelligence - AI) and put into practice the ideas of AI to create learning systems [2,8]. Several serious results in solving problems of classification, clustering, and regression analysis in various scientific fields [7] led to the fact that ML methods were also used in salinity studies, starting around 2012 [1,10–12,14].

In [5] the salinity mapping problem is solved using radar images and machine learning algorithms. The Mekong Delta was studied in the research. The authors proposed a regression problem in which features generated from Sentinel-1 Synthetic Aperture Radar (SAR) C-band radar images were used as input variables. Soil conductivity measurements form the target column. The generation of features from radar images was carried out using the method of constructing the Gray Level Co-occurrence Matrix (GLCM) proposed in [4].

The similar research presents a method for mapping soil salinity in the 0–30 cm layer of irrigated arable land using multispectral data obtained from unmanned aerial vehicles (UAVs) [6]. The study was conducted in the southern region of Almaty, Kazakhstan. The authors proposes a data preprocessing method and compares several machine learning algorithms such as XGBoost, LightGBM, random forest, support vector machines, ridge regression, and elastic net. The XGB regressor exhibited the highest quality results with a coefficient of determination of 0.701, a mean-squared error of 0.508, and a mean absolute error of 0.514.

In general, this makes it possible to evaluate the applicability of machine learning methods for solving the problem of mapping the salinity of agricultural lands in the southern regions of Kazakhstan.

The work consists of the following sections. In the second part, we describe the salinity estimation ML method that uses Sentinel-1 satellite SAR radar images as input and expert assessments as target values. In the third part, we discuss the result obtained. In conclusion, we summarize the discussion and formulate tasks for future research.

2 Suggested Method

The methodological scheme of the study includes the following main elements (see Fig. 1):

1. Expert estimation. Estimation of salinity based on spectral indices. As a result, a map is formed with five salinity levels, which are then converted into binary values (there is salinity and no salinity).
2. Gaussian Process model. Classification model where the input data are radar images and the target values are binary estimates of salinity, formed by expert estimation.

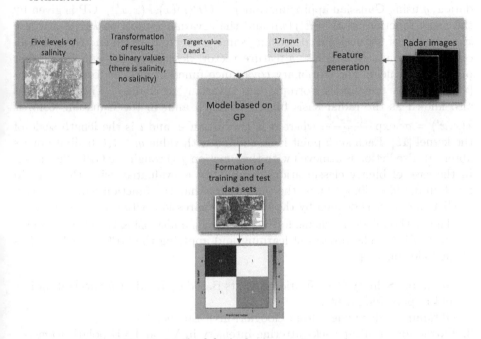

Fig. 1. Methodological scheme of research.

The results of the Gaussian Process (GP) model are evaluated using the confusion matrix and indicators of accuracy (precision), recall (Recall) and harmonic measure (f1-Score):

$$Precision : P = \frac{TP}{(TP + FP)}$$

$$Recall : R = \frac{TP}{(TP + FN)} \tag{1}$$

$$F1score : f1 = \frac{2 * P * R}{(P + R)}$$

True positive (TP) and true negative (TN) are cases of correct classifier operation, i.e., when the predicted class matched the expected one. Accordingly, false negatives (FN) and false positives (FP) are misclassification cases.

Precision, Recall, and f1-Score indicators, calculated on the test data set, allow us to assess the degree of agreement between expert estimation and GP model. The task at hand is a binary classification problem based on radar data. Build the GP model approach was used as described in [5]. The Gaussian Process Classifier (GPC) algorithm was used as a classifier. The theoretical description and practical results of using GPC for the binary classification problem are presented in [9]. The authors of this work studied various approaches to improve the accuracy of the GPC algorithm for binary classification. The Expectation Propagation approach is suitable for the binary classification problem.

The main task of GPC is to find a latent function f given the observation data x, y using Gaussian approximation $f = GP(m(x), k(x, x'))$. GP is given by the mean function $m(x) = E[f(x)]$ and the covariance function $k(x, x')$, where x is a vector of feature value describing some point from a field and the set of all considered points X, x' is also a feature vector, describing the same or another point from a field. The stationary covariance function has the form $k(x, x') = |x - x'|$. This function is isotropic and invariant to changes. The function is also known as the radial basis function (RBF) and, in the Gaussian form, is $k(x, x') = \sigma^2 \exp \frac{-(x-x')^2}{2l^2}$, where σ is the variance, and l is the length scale of the kernel [13]. Each such point is associated with value $y_i \in 1, 0$ (salinity or its absence). Prediction is achieved with the function f through the GPC algorithm. In the case of binary classification, the quality is evaluated using the sigmoid function $\sigma : \mathbb{R} \rightarrow [0, 1]$. Thus, the probability that the function will accurately predict the event is defined by the following expression: $P(y \vee x) = \frac{1}{(1+e^{f(x)})}$.

The methodological scheme for determining salinity using the GPC model is shown in Fig. 2. The process of learning and applying the GPC model consists of the following steps:

1. Obtaining Salinity Classification Results Based on Landsat-5 Spectral Indices and Expert Judgments.
2. Obtaining radar images from Google Earth Engine.
3. Extraction of linear backscattering intensity in VV and VH polarizations.
4. Texture analysis using the Gray Level Co-occurrence Matrix (GLCM) method.
5. Application of machine learning algorithms and evaluation of the quality of the trained model.
6. Application of the model to classify salinity and map new areas.

3   Data Analysis

Based on GP model results, we performed the marking of the territory shown in Fig. 3, for which we randomly selected 102 points on the map of the area and determined whether this location has salinity or not salinity. Thus, we formulated the problem of binary classification. Figure 3 and 4 show the selected points.

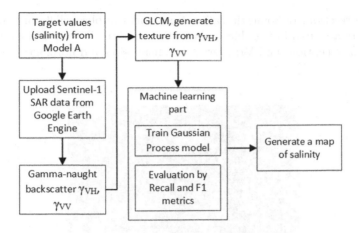

Fig. 2. Flowchart for learning and applying GP model.

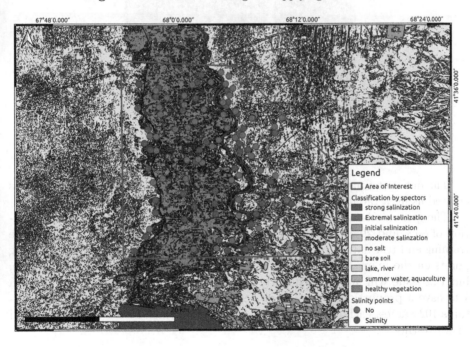

Fig. 3. Randomly marked 102 points in the selected territory.

To predict salinity (1) or its absence (0), we used the radar data from the Sentinel 1 satellite (image date: 07/04/2021). The resolution of radar images of this satellite is 10 m. The images were obtained using the Google Engine API [3] https://developers.google.com/earth-engine. Using the SNAP toolbox version 8.0.3 http://step.esa.int/main/toolboxes/snap/. The images of the desired area were processed. As a result, the primary scene corrections were performed, such as orbit correction, radiometric calibration, and Doppler relief correction. The images were acquired in two dual-polarization modes, VV (vertical transmission and vertical reception) and VH (vertical transmission and horizontal reception), see Fig. 5.

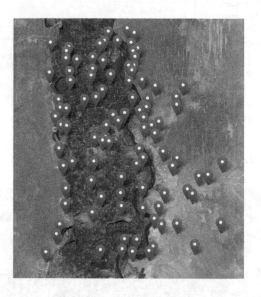

Fig. 4. Location of points.

The data set consisted of binary soil salinity values and 17 features and was created using a radar image and the GLCM method in Table 1.

The generated data set was divided into training and testing in the proportion of 80% and 20%, respectively. Figure 6 shows the class distribution for the training and test datasets. We balance two classes equally by randomly selecting points on the map. Therefore, the current dataset does not have an imbalance, but this issue will appear frequently in real samples. The distributions of both sets have a proportional share of objects of different classes. The data set contains 102 values, each described by 17 features, of which 81 are for training and 21 for testing.

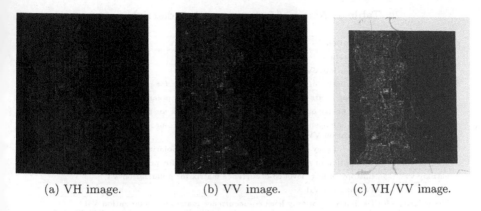

(a) VH image.   (b) VV image.   (c) VH/VV image.

Fig. 5. Composite of radar data with VH, VV, VH/VV bands.

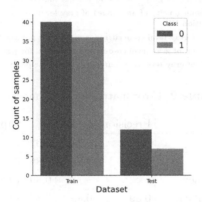

Fig. 6. Distribution of classes over samples for training and testing.

4   Results

The calculations were performed on a computer with the following characteristics: Intel Core i7 8700 3.2 GHz processor and 32 GB of RAM. The experiment used open source solutions: QGIS solution was used for GIS problems, geemap framework [15] was used for spatial data processing, skimage framework [13] was used for texture analysis of radar images using the GLCM method, and sklearn framework for building a machine learning model.

Table 2 shows the estimated accuracy of the trained model GPC on the test set. It can be stated that the model has high values on the test data set for the recall metric for class 0 (no salinity) and 1 (salinity present). This proves that the model can identify salinity zones from radar data (Fig. 7).

Table 1. Names of features and their description.

Name	Description
point_class	Binary class
gamma_vv	Polarization VV
dissimilarity_vv	Dissimilarity of gray level co-occurrence matrix for polarization VV
contrast_vv	Contrast of gray level co-occurrence matrix for polarization VV
homogeneity_vv	Homogeneity of gray level co-occurrence matrix for polarization VV
ASM_vv	ASM (homogeneity of an image) of gray level co-occurrence matrix for polarization VV
energy_vv	Energy of gray level co-occurrence matrix for polarization VV
correlation_vv	Correlation of gray level co-occurrence matrix for polarization VV
entropy_vv	Entropy of gray level co-occurrence matrix for polarization VV
gamma_vh	Polarization VH
dissimilarity_vh	Dissimilarity of gray level co-occurrence matrix for polarization VH
contrast_vh	Contrast of gray level co-occurrence matrix for polarization VH
homogeneity_vh	Homogeneity of gray level co-occurrence matrix for polarization VH
ASM_vh	ASM (homogeneity of an image) of gray level co-occurrence matrix for polarization VH
energy_vh	Energy of gray level co-occurrence matrix for polarization VH
correlation_vh	Correlation of gray level co-occurrence matrix for polarization VH
entropy_vh	Entropy of gray level co-occurrence matrix for polarization VH

Table 2. Error matrix for GPC models.

Class	Precision	Recall	F1	Support
0	0.92	0.92	0.92	12
1	0.86	0.86	0.86	7
Accuracy			0.89	19
Macro avg	0.89	0.89	0.89	19
Weighted avg	0.89	0.89	0.89	19

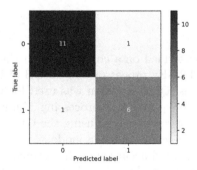

Fig. 7. Error matrix for the test set.

5 Conclusion

The paper analyzes the possibilities of using machine learning algorithms to assess soil salinity according to remote sensing data in Kazakhstan. Our attention was focused on two salinity classification models. The expert estimation represents the classification of the degree of salinity by spectral indices using the algorithm Decision Tree with an expert's participation to adjust the decision tree's parameters. Since expert evaluation is laborious and, in addition, data for calculating spectral indices is not always available, it is advisable to use a more stable and weather-independent data source such as radar images and train a model that could perform automatic salinity classification. To this end, the GPC model takes the output of an expert estimation as classification targets and performs binary classification using the radar data as input. GPC model uses the GPC algorithm. The result indicates that based on the GPC algorithm, the GPC model shows positive results: a recall of 0.92 for class 0 (no salinity) and a recall of 0.86 for class 1 (salinity).

The considered process of salinity classification can increase the efficiency of solving problems of automating the digitization of salinity over large areas. The expert estimation results can be replaced by field data or other objective salinity estimates, allowing the GPC model to be tuned with live data and more accurately estimate soil salinity over time. Due to the large area, including cultivated land, the method for determining soil salinity using the GPC model is very relevant since it significantly reduces the number of labor-intensive ground studies and provides a high speed of analysis.

At the same time, the described method for assessing soil salinity requires further research due to the high variability of parameters affecting soil salinity (terrain relief, weather conditions, irrigation methods, groundwater level, etc.). In future research, the authors intend to solve several problems:

1. Conduct laboratory measurements of the electrical conductivity of the surface layer of the soil and, based on received data, refine expert estimation and train the GPC model.
2. Assess the terrain's influence and nearby irrigation facilities' presence on the models' quality.
3. Perform a comparative analysis of the applicability of several machine learning models for both classification degrees of salinity and quantifying salinity based on electrical conductivity data.
4. Assess the applicability of high-resolution multispectral images obtained from UAVs to assess the salinity of local soil areas.

Acknowledgement. This research has been funded by the Science Committee of the Ministry of Education and Science of the Republic of Kazakhstan grant BR10965172 "Space monitoring and GIS for quantitative assessment of soil salinity and degradation of land agricultural in the South of Kazakhstan" and grant number BR18574144 "Development of a data mining system for monitoring dams and other engineering structures under the conditions of man-made and natural impacts".

References

1. Akramkhanov, A., Vlek, P.L.: The assessment of spatial distribution of soil salinity risk using neural network. Environ. Monit. Assess. **184**(4), 2475–2485 (2012)
2. Amirgaliyev, Y., Shamiluulu, S., Merembayev, T., Yedilkhan, D.: Using machine learning algorithm for diagnosis of stomach disorders. In: Bykadorov, I., Strusevich, V., Tchemisova, T. (eds.) MOTOR 2019. CCIS, vol. 1090, pp. 343–355. Springer, Cham (2019). https://doi.org/10.1007/978-3-030-33394-2_27
3. Gorelick, N., Hancher, M., Dixon, M., Ilyushchenko, S., Thau, D., Moore, R.: Google earth engine: planetary-scale geospatial analysis for everyone. Remote Sens. Environ. **202**, 18–27 (2017)
4. Haralick, R.M., Shanmugam, K., Dinstein, I.H.: Textural features for image classification. IEEE Trans. Syst. Man Cybern. **6**, 610–621 (1973)
5. Hoa, P.V., et al.: Soil salinity mapping using SAR sentinel-1 data and advanced machine learning algorithms: a case study at ben TRE province of the Mekong river delta (Vietnam). Remote Sens. **11**(2), 128 (2019)
6. Mukhamediev, R., et al.: Operational mapping of salinization areas in agricultural fields using machine learning models based on low-altitude multispectral images. Drones **7**(6), 357 (2023)
7. Mukhamediev, R.I., et al.: Review of artificial intelligence and machine learning technologies: classification, restrictions, opportunities and challenges. Mathematics **10**(15), 2552 (2022)
8. Mukhamediev, R.I., Symagulov, A., Kuchin, Y., Yakunin, K., Yelis, M.: From classical machine learning to deep neural networks: a simplified scientometric review. Appl. Sci. **11**(12), 5541 (2021)
9. Nickisch, H., Rasmussen, C.E.: Approximations for binary gaussian process classification. J. Mach. Learn. Res. **9**(Oct), 2035–2078 (2008)
10. Nosair, A.M., Shams, M.Y., AbouElmagd, L.M., Hassanein, A.E., Fryar, A.E., Abu Salem, H.S.: Predictive model for progressive salinization in a coastal aquifer using artificial intelligence and hydrogeochemical techniques: a case study of the Nile delta aquifer, Egypt. Environ. Sci. Pollut. Res. **29**(6), 9318–9340 (2022)
11. Phonphan, W., Tripathi, N.K., Tipdecho, T., Eiumnoh, A.: Modelling electrical conductivity of soil from backscattering coefficient of microwave remotely sensed data using artificial neural network. Geocarto Int. **29**(8), 842–859 (2014)
12. Vermeulen, D., Van Niekerk, A.: Machine learning performance for predicting soil salinity using different combinations of geomorphometric covariates. Geoderma **299**, 1–12 (2017)
13. Van der Walt, S., et al.: scikit-image: image processing in python. PeerJ **2**, e453 (2014)
14. Wang, J., et al.: Machine learning-based detection of soil salinity in an arid desert region, Northwest China: a comparison between landsat-8 OLI and sentinel-2 MSI. Sci. Total Environ. **707**, 136092 (2020)
15. Wu, Q.: Geemap: a python package for interactive mapping with google earth engine. J. Open Sour. Softw. **5**(51), 2305 (2020)

Principal Components Analysis Based Frameworks for Efficient Missing Data Imputation Algorithms

Thu Nguyen[1](✉), Hoang Thien Ly[2], Michael Alexander Riegler[1],
Pål Halvorsen[1], and Hugo L. Hammer[1]

[1] SimulaMet, Oslo, Norway
thu@simula.no
[2] Warsaw University of Technology, Warsaw, Poland

Abstract. The problem of missing data is common in practice. Many imputation methods have been developed to fill in the missing entries. However, not all of them can scale to high-dimensional data, especially the multiple imputation techniques. Meanwhile, the data nowadays tends toward high-dimensional. Therefore, we propose *Principal Component Analysis Imputation* (PCAI), a simple but versatile framework based on Principal Component Analysis (PCA) to speed up the imputation process and alleviate memory issues of many available imputation techniques while maintaining good imputation quality. In addition, the frameworks can be used even when some or all of the missing features are categorical or when the number of missing features is large. We also analyze the effect of using different formulations of PCA on the technique. Next, we introduce *PCA Imputation - Classification* (PIC), an application of PCAI for classification problems with some adjustments. Experiments on various scenarios show that PCAI and PIC can work with various imputation algorithms, including state-of-the-art ones, and improve the imputation speed significantly while achieving competitive mean square error/classification accuracy compared to imputing directly on the missing data.

Keywords: imputation · classification · dimension reduction

1 Introduction

Despite recent efforts in directly handling missing data [14,16,18], imputation approaches [3,30] remain widely used. This is because directly handling missing data can be complicated, and methods are usually developed for specific target problems or models. Meanwhile, imputation can be more versatile as it makes the data *complete*, i.e., no longer have any missing values. Therefore, it is easier to continue with other preprocessing steps, analysis, and data visualizations. Meanwhile, strategies for directly handling missing data are often more complicated and not that readily available.

While many techniques have been developed for missing data imputation [3,28,30], most of them are computationally expensive for big datasets. For

N. T. Nguyen et al. (Eds.): ACIIDS 2023, CCIS 1863, pp. 254–266, 2023.
https://doi.org/10.1007/978-3-031-42430-4_21

example, experiments in [17] show that under their experiment settings, for Fashion MNIST , a dataset of 70,000 observations and 784 features, MICE [3] and missForest [27] are unable to finish the imputation process within three hours for a missing rate (the ratio between the number of missing entries versus the total number entries in the dataset) of 20%. Since datasets nowadays are trending towards larger sizes, with hundreds of thousands of features [8], it is crucial to speed up the available imputation techniques. Taking into account resource consumption and availability, such speed up cannot be achieved by only providing more and better hardware but by the development of new methods.

To achieve this goal, this work introduces two novel frameworks based on Principal Component Analysis (PCA) to speed up the imputation process of many available techniques or the imputation-classification process for missing data classification problems. The first framework, **PCA Imputation (PCAI)** is proposed to speed up the imputation speed by partitioning the data into the set of fully observed features and the set of features with missing data. After that, the imputation of the missing part is performed based on the union of the PCA - reduced version of the fully observed part and the missing part. Interestingly, it turns out that the method has a great potential to aid the performance of methods that rely on many parameters, such as deep learning imputation techniques. Meanwhile, the second one, **PCA Imputation - Classification (PIC)** is proposed to deal with classification problems involving missing data where dimension reduction is desirable in advance of the model training step. PIC is based on PCAI with some modifications. Note that these frameworks are different from the methods developed for principal component analysis under missing data presented in [7,10], which are about how to conduct PCA when the data contains missing values.

In summary, the contributions of this article are: (i) we introduce **PCAI** to improve the imputation speed of many available imputation techniques; (ii) we introduce **PIC** to deal with missing data classification problems where dimension reduction is desirable; (iii) we analyze the potential strength and drawbacks of these approaches; and (iv) we illustrate via experiments that our frameworks can work with various imputation strategies while achieving comparable or even lower mean square error/higher classification accuracies compared to the corresponding original approaches, and alleviate the memory issue in some approaches.

The rest of the paper is organized as follows. In Sect. 2, we review two popular formulations of PCA. Next, in Sect. 3, Sect. 4, and Sect. 5, we introduce our novel PCAI and PIC frameworks, and study related works, respectively. After that, in Sect. 6, we demonstrate their capabilities via experiments on various datasets. The paper ends with conclusions, remarks, and future works in Sect. 7.

2   Preliminaries

Let $\mathbf{X} = [x_{ij}]$ where $i = 1, ..., n; j = 1, ..., p$ be an input data matrix of n observations, p features. In addition, assume that the features are centered and scaled. We review two popular formulations of PCA, which we refer to as **PCA-form1** and **PCA-form2**.

*PCA based on Covariance Matrix (**PCA-form1**).* Let Σ be the covariance matrix of $\mathbf{X}$. Next, let $(\lambda_1, \mathbf{v}_1), ..., (\lambda_p, \mathbf{v}_p)$ be the sorted eigenvalue-eigenvector pairs of Σ such that $\lambda_1 \geq \lambda_2 \geq ... \geq \lambda_p \geq 0$. Suppose that we choose the first r pairs for dimension reduction. Then the proportion of variance explained by these r pairs is

$$\frac{\lambda_1 + \lambda_2 + ... + \lambda_r}{\lambda_1 + \lambda_2 + ... + \lambda_p} \tag{1}$$

Next, let $\mathbf{V} = [\mathbf{v}_1, \mathbf{v}_2, ..., \mathbf{v}_r]$. Then, the dimension reduced version of $\mathbf{X}$ is $\mathbf{XV}$.

*PCA based on the Input Matrix $\mathbf{X}$ (**PCA-form2**).* The solution of PCA can also be produced based on the singular value decomposition of $\mathbf{X}$:

$$\mathbf{X} = \mathbf{UDW}^T \tag{2}$$

where $\mathbf{U}$ is an $n \times p$ orthogonal matrix, $\mathbf{W}$ is a $p \times p$ orthogonal matrix, and $\mathbf{D}$ is a $p \times p$ diagonal matrix whose diagonal elements are $d_1 \geq d_2 \geq ... \geq d_p \geq 0$. Suppose that r eigenvalues are used, then the projection matrix is $\mathbf{V} = \mathbf{W}_r$ where $\mathbf{W}_r$ consists of the first r columns of $\mathbf{W}$. Then the dimension-reduced version of $\mathbf{X}$ is also $\mathbf{XV}$.

3   PCA Imputation (PCAI)

To start with some notations, let $pca(A)$ be a function of a data matrix A. The function returns $(\mathcal{R}_A, V)$ where $\mathcal{R}_A$ is the PCA-reduced version of A, and V is the projection matrix where the ith column of V is the eigenvector corresponding to the ith largest eigenvalue. In addition, denote by $[\mathcal{A}, \mathcal{B}]$ the column-wise concatenation of two data portions $\mathcal{A}$ and $\mathcal{B}$ of relevant sizes. Next, suppose that we have a dataset $\mathcal{D} = [\mathcal{F}, \mathcal{M}]$ where $\mathcal{F}$ consists of data from fully observed features and $\mathcal{M}$ consists of data from features with missing values.

The framework is as depicted in Algorithm 1. We first conduct dimension reduction on the fully observed portion $\mathcal{F}$, which produces a reduced version $\mathcal{R}$ of $\mathcal{F}$. Then, the imputation of $\mathcal{M}$ is done on the set $[\mathcal{R}, \mathcal{M}]$ instead of $\mathcal{D} = [\mathcal{F}, \mathcal{M}]$ as how imputations are usually done (i.e., impute directly on the original missing data). In conducting dimension reduction, we expect to reduce the dimension of the fully observed portion so that the imputation of $\mathcal{M}$ can be faster.

For the choice of the PCA formulation, note that if the number of observations is larger than the number of features in $\mathcal{F}$, then the size of the covariance matrix is smaller than the size of $\mathcal{F}$. Therefore, one may expect using the formulation of PCA based on the covariance matrix (PCA-form1), to be faster. Meanwhile, if the number of features in $\mathcal{F}$ is larger than the sample size, then the covariance matrix of $\mathcal{F}$ is larger than $\mathcal{F}$. Therefore, in such a case, it is better to use the PCA formulation based on the data itself (PCA-form2).

Algorithm 1. PCAI framework

Require:
    - $\mathcal{D} = [\mathcal{F}, \mathcal{M}]$ where $\mathcal{F}$ is the fully observed portion and $\mathcal{M}$ is the portion with missing values
    - Imputer I , PCA algorithm pca
Procedure:
    $(\mathcal{R}, V) \leftarrow pca(\mathcal{F})$
    $\mathcal{M}' \leftarrow$ the imputed version of $\mathcal{M}$ based on $[\mathcal{R}, \mathcal{M}]$
    return Imputed version $\mathcal{M}'$ of $\mathcal{M}$

One may reckon that using $[\mathcal{R}, \mathcal{M}]$ instead of $[\mathcal{F}, \mathcal{M}]$ may lead to loss of information due to dimension reduction and therefore lower the quality of imputation. However, as will be illustrated in the experiments, the differences between the mean squared error of the imputed version versus the ground truth for these approaches are only slightly different, and many times, PCAI seems to be slightly better. This is possibly because PCA retains the important information from the data while removing some noise, and therefore helps to improve the imputation quality. However, PCAI also has some shortcomings. For problems where the sample size n is smaller than the number of features in the fully observed block q if PCA-form1 is used, the covariance matrix has the size of $q \times q$, which is bigger than the size $n \times q$ of the fully observed portion $\mathcal{F}$. This may make the PCA dimension reduction process become computationally expensive, rendering PCAI to be slower than imputing directly on the original missing data. This issue will be illustrated in the experiment section.

4 PCAI for Classification (PIC)

In this section, we discuss a straightforward application of PCAI in classification, with a slight modification for classification problems where it is desirable to conduct a dimension reduction before training a model, such as when the number of features is much larger than the sample size. To start, note that since PCAI conducts PCA on the fully observed portion $\mathcal{F}$, it reduces the dimensions for a portion of the data. Therefore, rather than imputing values using the PCAI framework and then conducting a dimension reduction step on $[\mathcal{F}, \mathcal{M}']$, one can perform dimension reduction on $\mathcal{M}'$ to get $\mathcal{R}'$, a PCA-reduced version of $\mathcal{M}'$. Then, one can use $[\mathcal{F}, \mathcal{R}']$ as reduced dimension data. As will be shown in the experiments, this speeds up the imputation and classification process significantly. This is the basic idea of our *Principle component Imputation for Classification (PIC)* framework.

PIC operates as shown in Algorithm 2. The procedure starts by performing PCA on the training fully observed portion $\mathcal{F}_{train}$, which gives the reduced version $\mathcal{R}_{train}$ of $\mathcal{F}_{train}$ and a projection matrix V. Next, we project $\mathcal{F}_{test}$ on V to get the reduced version $\mathcal{R}_{test}$ of $\mathcal{F}_{test}$. Then, we impute $\mathcal{M}_{train}$ on $[\mathcal{R}_{train}, \mathcal{M}_{train}]$ to get the imputed version $\mathcal{M}'_{train}$. Next, we impute $\mathcal{M}_{test}$ on $[\mathcal{R}_{test}, \mathcal{M}_{test}]$ to get the imputed version $\mathcal{M}'_{test}$. After that, if $reduce_{miss}$ is set to true, the algorithm performs dimension reduction on $\mathcal{M}'_{train}, \mathcal{M}'_{test}$. Then, we train the classifier on $[\mathcal{R}_{train}, \mathcal{R}'_{train}]$, i.e., the union of the reduced version of $\mathcal{F}_{train}$ and the reduced version of $\mathcal{M}_{train}$. For prediction of a vector $\mathbf{x} \in \mathcal{D}$, we can decompose $\mathbf{x}$ into $\mathbf{x} = (\mathbf{x}_{\mathcal{F}}, \mathbf{x}_{\mathcal{M}})$. After that, we can project $\mathbf{x}_{\mathcal{F}}$ on V to get a projection $\mathbf{r}$. Similarly, we can project $\mathbf{x}_{\mathcal{M}}$ on W to a get projection $\mathbf{r}'$. Finally, we can predict the label of $\mathbf{x}$ using the classifier C with input $(\mathbf{r}, \mathbf{r}')$.

Algorithm 2. PIC framework

Require:
- $\mathcal{D} = [\mathcal{F}, \mathcal{M}]$ where $\mathcal{F}$ is the fully observed portion and $\mathcal{M}$ is the portion with missing values
- $reduce_{miss} = True/False$: if $True$, perform dimension reduction on the imputed portions; if $False$, do not perform dimension reduction on the imputed portions
- $\mathcal{F}_{train}, \mathcal{F}_{test}$: the training and testing data of the fully observed portion $\mathcal{F}$,
- $\mathcal{M}_{train}, \mathcal{M}_{test}$: the training and testing data of the portion that has missing data $\mathcal{M}$,
- Imputer I, classifier C, PCA algorithm pca

Procedure:
 $(\mathcal{R}_{train}, V) \leftarrow pca(\mathcal{F}_{train})$
 $R_{test} \leftarrow \mathcal{F}_{test}V$
 $\mathcal{M}'_{train} \leftarrow$ imputed version of $\mathcal{M}_{train}$ based on $[\mathcal{R}_{train}, \mathcal{M}_{train}]$
 $\mathcal{M}'_{test} \leftarrow$ imputed version of $\mathcal{M}_{test}$ based on $[\mathcal{R}_{test}, \mathcal{M}_{test}]$
 if $reduce_{miss}$ **then**
  $(\mathcal{R}'_{train}, W) \leftarrow pca(\mathcal{M}'_{train})$
  $\mathcal{R}'_{test} \leftarrow \mathcal{M}'_{test}W$
  Train the classifier C based on $[\mathcal{R}_{train}, \mathcal{R}'_{train}]$
  Classify based on $[\mathcal{R}_{test}, \mathcal{R}'_{test}]$,
 else
  Train the classifier based on $[\mathcal{R}_{train}, \mathcal{M}'_{train}]$
  Classify based on $[\mathcal{R}_{test}, \mathcal{M}'_{test}]$
 end if
 return trained classifier C

Note that when the number of features in the missing portion $\mathcal{M}$ is large, one may be interested in reducing the dimension of $\mathcal{M}'$, and therefore, set $reduce_{miss}$ to $True$. However, when the number of features in the missing portion is small, one may want to keep it to $False$. Also, since PIC is a straightforward application of PCAI for classification, the choice of PCA formulation should be used is similar to PCAI, which is analyzed in the previous section.

5   Related Works

Various works have been published on missing data imputation to deal with different situations, and with the rapid growth of data size [17], various works have been done on PCA that are related to missing data, which mostly can be categorized into missing values imputation using PCA, or dimension reduction using PCA under missing values. Some typical works that make use of PCA for missing values imputation are probabilistic PCA for missing flow volume data imputation [20]; chunk-wise iterative PCA for data imputation on datasets with many observations [11]; [10] proposes a fast algorithm for PCA under missing data that helps in case of sparse, high dimensional data; and [2] proposed an imputation approach based on PCA and factorial analysis for mixed data. Next, PCA under missing values was first studied in [4], where only one component and one imputation iteration are used. After that, [1] proposes a method based on maximum likelihood PCA, where the method assigns large variance to missing values prior to implementing the method, which aims to guide the algorithm to fit a PCA model disregarding those points. Also, [23] introduces the EM algorithm for building a PCA model that can deal with missing data. More recently, [6] proposes new techniques for building a PCA model with missing data. In addition, [26] studies estimation and imputation in Probabilistic PCA when the data is missing not at random.

Different from the previous approaches, PCAI is a framework to speed up the imputation process, which can be used with various imputation methods, including the aforementioned PCA imputation algorithms and the state-of-the-art imputation algorithms such as softImpute [15], MissForest [27], GAIN [30]. In addition, note that since PCAI and PIC conduct dimension reduction on the fully observed portion $\mathcal{F}$, and not the missing portion $\mathcal{M}$ if $reduce_{miss} = False$, they can handle missing data, even if categorical features are present in the missing portion $\mathcal{M}$ when used with imputers that are capable of handling categorical/mixed data (MissForest [27], SICE [13], FEMI [21], etc.). In addition, even if there exist categorical and continuous features in $\mathcal{M}$; or $reduce_{miss} = True$ and there exist categorical and continuous features in $\mathcal{M}$, one can easily adjust the algorithm to conduct PCA on continuous features only. The previously mentioned PCA based approaches can, however, only be used for continuous data, because PCA requires the data to be continuous.

6 Experiments

6.1 General Experiment Settings

We compare the speed (seconds) and MSE of PCAI with **direct imputation (DI)**, i.e., use an imputation algorithm directly on the dataset. The imputation approaches used for comparison: softImpute [15,24], MissForest [27][1] and MICE [3,19], KNNI, GAIN [30] are implemented with default configurations. The codes will be available upon the acceptance of the paper. For PIC, we compare the five-fold cross-validation (CV) score (accuracy, speed) of PIC when dimension reduction is applied on the imputed missing part (**PIC-reduce**), when dimension reduction is not applied on the imputed missing part (**PIC**), and when PCA is applied to the imputed version on the full missing data (**DI-reduce**), and when no dimension reduction is applied to imputed data after direct imputation (**DI**). Here, the default PCA formulation is PCA-form1, unless specified otherwise. For all PCA computations, the number of eigenvectors is chosen so that the minimum proportion of variance explained is 95%.

Details of the datasets used in the experiments are available in Table 1. All experiments are run on an AMD Ryzen 7 3700X CPU with 8 Cores, 16 processing threads, 3.6 GHz, and 16 GB RAM. We terminate an experiment if no result is produced after 6,500 s of running or if there arises a memory allocating issue, and we denote this as **NA** in the result tables.

6.2 Performance of PCAI and PIC When the Missing Values in $\mathcal{M}$ are Randomly Simulated

Note that any datasets can be rearranged so that the first q features do not contain missing data and the remaining features do. Therefore, without loss of

---

[1] https://pypi.org/project/missingpy/.

Table 1. Description of datasets used in our experiments

Dataset	# Classes	# Features	# observations
Parkinson [25]	2	754	756
Fashion MNIST [29]	10	784	70000
Gene [5]	5	20531	801

Table 2. (MSE, speed) for PCAI and DI on the Parkinson dataset with $q = 700$.

Imputer	Strategy	missing rate		
		20%	40%	60%
softImpute	PCAI	(0.073, 0.860)	(0.185, 0.774)	(0.305, 0.875)
	DI	(0.072, 4.097)	(0.188, 4.043)	(0.308, 4.467)
MICE	PCAI	(0.091, 139.811)	(0.186, 85.241)	(0.369, 109.815)
	DI	NA	NA	NA
GAIN	PCAI	(0.254, 45.046)	(0.538, 43.938)	(0.779, 43.956)
	DI	(0.608, 69.839)	(1.097, 70.548)	(1.369, 70.293)
missForest	PCAI	(0.064, 188.324)	(0.163, 178.849)	(0.292, 138.085)
	DI	(0.058, 905.002)	(0.160, 692.150)	(0.258, 449.415)
KNNI	PCAI	(0.127, 0.355)	(0.299, 0.398)	(0.466, 0.416)
	DI	(0.113, 0.310)	(0.274, 0.337)	(0.426, 0.372)

generality, we assume that the first q features of each dataset do not contain missing data, and the remaining ones contain missing value(s). Then, we simulated missing data randomly on the missing portion $\mathcal{M}$ with missing rates 20%, 40%, and 60%. Here, a missing rate of 20% means that 20% of the entries in the missing portion $\mathcal{M}$ are missing. The results for such experiments are reported in Tables 2, 3, 4. Due to space limit, the results related to PIC on Fashion MNIST are reported in the supplementary materials.

From the tables, it is clear that the proposed frameworks reduce the imputation time significantly while maintaining competitive MSE/classification accuracy compared to DI, in most of the cases. For example, at the missing rate of 20% on the Parkinson dataset (Table 4), when using GAIN for imputation, the running time of PIC-reduce (91.086 s) is much lower compared to DI-reduce (130.349), the running time of PIC (89.984 s) is also much lower compared to DI (129.702). Another example can be seen from Table 2, for the Parkinson dataset, at 20% missing rate, when PCAI is applied to missForest, the running time reduces to 188.324 s, which is almost 1/5 of the DI (905.002 s). Next, on Fashion MNIST (Table 3), it is worth noticing that for MICE, DI cannot give the results due to memory issues but PCAI can alleviate this issue and deliver the results.

For KNNI, the running time for KNNI between the PCAI approach and direct imputation for Parkinson (Table 2) is not much different. However, for the Fashion MNIST dataset, KNNI using the PCAI framework obviously deliver a

Table 3. (MSE, speed) for PCAI and DI on the Fashion MNIST dataset with $q = 700$. MissForest results all are NA, and therefore are removed from the tables.

Imputer	Strategy	missing rate		
		20%	40%	60%
softImpute	PCAI	(0.032, 22.408)	(0.066, 22.797)	(0.109, 25.603)
	DI	(0.032, 67.627)	(0.064, 69.349)	(0.107, 77.233)
MICE	PCAI	(0.027, 2218.864)	(0.055, 1374.558)	(0.095, 1641.962)
	DI	NA	NA	NA
GAIN	PCAI	(0.053, 65.730)	(0.091, 68.752)	(0.137, 69.743)
	DI	(0.041, 97.898)	(0.079, 99.049)	(0.125, 96.317)
KNNI	PCAI	(0.055, 1607.850)	(0.115, 2033.153)	(0.180, 2272.370)
	DI	(0.049, 3042.752)	(0.102, 3659.300)	(0.161, 3959.832)

Table 4. Five fold CV results (accuracy, speed) of SVM on Parkinson with $q = 700$.

Imputer	Strategy	missing rate		
		20%	40%	60%
softImpute	PIC-reduce	(0.862, 1.026)	(0.862, 1.137)	(0.862, 1.161)
	PIC	(0.858, 1.008)	(0.858, 1.079)	(0.859, 1.112)
	DI-reduce	(0.861, 4.116)	(0.862, 4.424)	(0.861, 4.718)
	DI	(0.858, 3.775)	(0.858, 3.912)	(0.855, 4.248)
MICE	PIC-reduce	(0.859, 204.605)	(0.861, 256.340)	(0.861, 240.211)
	PIC	(0.858, 524.739)	(0.859, 694.667)	(0.859, 925.426)
	DI-reduce	NA	NA	NA
	DI	NA	NA	NA
GAIN	PIC-reduce	(0.857, 91.086)	(0.852, 102.861)	(0.848, 122.349)
	PIC	(0.851, 89.984)	(0.853, 104.773)	(0.853, 123.233)
	DI-reduce	(0.855, 130.349)	(0.851, 149.864)	(0.851, 181.135)
	DI	(0.846, 129.702)	(0.849, 152.031)	(0.852, 183.67)
missForest	PIC-reduce	(0.859, 204.850)	(0.861, 276.537)	(0.858, 153.783)
	PIC	(0.858, 202.939)	(0.861, 277.067)	(0.858, 153.463)
	DI-reduce	(0.861, 656.948)	(0.862, 729.872)	(0.861, 472.230)
	DI	(0.858, 655.750)	(0.861, 730.013)	(0.858, 472.388)
KNNI	PIC-reduce	(0.858, 0.533)	(0.861, 0.462)	(0.862, 0.625)
	PIC	(0.858, 0.513)	(0.861, 0.462)	(0.862, 0.607)
	DI-reduce	(0.862, 0.696)	(0.862, 0.642)	(0.859, 0.803)
	DI	(0.859, 0.438)	(0.859, 0.45)	(0.858, 0.552)

competitive result in a significantly shorter time. Specifically, KNNI at a missing rate of 20% on Fashion MNIST gives a result after only 1607.850 s, while DI takes up to 3,042.752 s. This is because Fashion MNIST (70000 observations) has much more observations than Parkinson (756 observations), and KNN needs to do a lot of pairwise comparisons. Therefore, PCAI and PIC would be extremely helpful for KNNI when the sample size and the number of fully observed features are large. Note that it does not require the number of features with missing data to be large or small.

From Table 2, we can see that PCAI generates a lot of improvements in MSE for GAIN, in addition to improvements in speed. This is possibly because PCA reduces the number of features while the sample size remains the same, making such a deep learning approach more applicable to the newly reduced data.

For PIC, the result for experiments related to PIC are provided in Table 5. From the tables, it is clear that PIC approaches reduce the imputation time significantly while maintaining competitive classification accuracy compared to PCA on $[\mathcal{F}, \mathcal{M}']$, in most of the cases.

Table 5. 5 - fold cross validation results (accuracy, speed) of SVM for different imputation-classification strategies on the Fashion MNIST dataset with $q = 700$, when the missing values in $\mathcal{M}$ are simulated at randomly given rates.

Imputer	Strategy	missing rate		
		20%	40%	60%
softImpute	PIC-reduce	(0.891, 285.707)	(0.890, 279.263)	(0.889, 353.506)
	PIC	(0.891, 593.652)	(0.891, 598.726)	(0.890, 609.252)
	DI-reduce	(0.892, 467.406)	(0.891, 458.625)	(0.891, 486.162)
	DI	(0.892, 710.019)	(0.892, 644.585)	(0.891, 630.044)
MICE	PIC-reduce	(0.892, 2379.869)	(0.892, 1884.385)	(0.891, 2851.581)
	PIC	(0.892, 2416.485)	(0.891, 1907.529)	(0.892, 2897.839)
	DI-reduce	NA	NA	NA
	DI	NA	NA	NA
GAIN	PIC-reduce	(0.892, 539.720)	(0.891, 580.754)	(0.891, 660.633)
	PIC	(0.891, 583.016)	(0.892, 608.384)	(0.891, 703.145)
	DI-reduce	(0.891, 1320.018)	(0.891, 1351.854)	(0.890, 1573.656)
	DI	(0.891, 846.002)	(0.892, 787.246)	(0.891, 863.685)
KNNI	PIC-reduce	(0.891, 3040.393)	(0.891, 4235.292)	(0.89, 6059.608)
	PIC	(0.891, 3110.041)	(0.891, 4279.305)	(0.889, 6088.542)
	DI-reduce	NA	NA	NA
	DI	NA	NA	NA

6.3 PIC Under Different PCA Formulations and Number of Missing Features

The missing data in these experiments are generated at random as in Sect. 6.2 and the five-fold cross-validation results of SVM on the Gene dataset with $q =$

15000, 20000, are shown in Table 6 and Table 7. From these tables, one can see clearly that for a dataset where the number of features is significantly higher than the number of observations such as Gene, PCA-form2, which is based on the input data ($\mathcal{F}$ specifically) gives much faster computations compared to PCA-form1, and also is faster than direct imputation-classification without PCA. In addition, when PCA-form1 is used, even though PIC and PIC-reduce are faster than PCA on directly imputed data (DI-reduce), they are still much slower than direct imputation - classification without PCA.

Interestingly, the accuracy of PIC and PIC-reduce are almost identical to PCA on directly imputed data, and are higher than direct imputation - classification without PCA. Next, note that the main idea of the proposed methods is to reduce the dimension of the $\mathcal{F}$ to speed up the imputation. Therefore, we have made no assumption about the number of features in the missing portion $\mathcal{M}$. In Table 6 and Table 7, $q = 15000, 20000$, which means 5,531 and 531 missing features in $\mathcal{M}$, respectively. This means PIC can handle datasets where $\mathcal{M}$ has many features.

Table 6. Five fold CV results (accuracy, speed) of SVM for softImpute based strategies on the Gene dataset when $q = 15000$.

	Strategy	missing rate		
		20%	40%	60%
PCA-form1	PIC-reduce	(0.994, 2250.451)	(0.992, 2412.082)	(0.992, 2415.434)
	PIC	(0.992, 2429.114)	(0.992, 2276.354)	(0.992, 2284.414)
	DI-reduce	(0.994, 5018.368)	(0.994, 4529.766)	(0.994, 3785.947)
PCA-form2	PIC-reduce	(0.995, 47.850)	(0.992, 56.638)	(0.992, 63.980)
	PIC	(0.992, 48.356)	(0.992, 57.113)	(0.992, 64.786)
	DI-reduce	(0.995, 99.698)	(0.992, 110.993)	(0.994,128.083)
No PCA	DI	(0.985, 71.884)	(0.985, 74.812)	(0.985, 92.309)

Table 7. Five fold CV results (accuracy, speed) of SVM for softImpute based strategies on the Gene dataset when $q = 20000$.

	Strategy	missing rate		
		20%	40%	60%
PCA-form1	PIC-reduce	(0.994, 2578.910)	(0.994, 4001.717)	(0.994, 3848.950)
	PIC	(0.994, 2583.717)	(0.994, 4144.157)	(0.994, 4057.188)
	DI-reduce	(0.995, 2891.994)	(0.994, 4476.563)	(0.995, 4332.869)
PCA-form2	PIC-reduce	(0.995, 8.666)	(0.995, 9.597)	(0.995, 10.639)
	PIC	(0.995, 8.566)	(0.995, 9.464)	(0.995, 10.491)
	DI-reduce	(0.995, 87.298)	(0.995, 78.814)	(0.995, 79.843)
No PCA	DI	(0.985, 74.06)	(0.985, 71.6)	(0.985, 84.963)

7 Conclusion and Remarks

We have presented two novel frameworks for datasets where many continuous features are fully observed, PCAI and PIC, that can speed up imputation algorithms significantly while having competitive accuracy MSE/accuracy compared to direct imputation and alleviate the memory issue for some imputation approaches such as MICE, KNN. In addition, the frameworks can be used even when some or all of the missing features are categorical or when the number of missing features is large. Note that when the sample size is significantly larger than the number of fully observed features, PCA-form1 should be used since, in such a case, the covariance matrix is much smaller than $\mathcal{F}$, making it faster than PCA-form2. On the other hand, when the number of fully observed features is significantly larger than the sample size, PCA-form2 should be preferred, as the covariance matrix is bigger than $\mathcal{F}$ itself in such a case. A limitation of the proposed framework is that if there are not many fully observed continuous features, then due to the computational cost of PCA, the proposed frameworks may not lead to any improvement in speed.

Even though PIC is only introduced for classification, the same strategy can be applied to a regression problem. We would like to explore that in the future. Moreover, since various dimension reduction techniques such as sparse PCA [12], incremental PCA [22], and truncated SVD [9] have been developed to suit different scenarios, it is worth investigating different dimension reduction techniques for PCAI and PIC. In addition, it would be interesting to explore if applying a PCA variant to the missing portion $\mathcal{M}$ would result in an even more efficient method for datasets with continuous features in the missing portion. Also, this paper so far has only investigated the performance of PCAI and PIC on randomly missing data. In the future, it is necessary to investigate the performance of these methods on missing not at random data or structurally missing data.

References

1. Andrews, D.T., Wentzell, P.D.: Applications of maximum likelihood principal component analysis: incomplete data sets and calibration transfer. Anal. Chim. Acta **350**(3), 341–352 (1997)
2. Audigier, V., Husson, F., Josse, J.: A principal component method to impute missing values for mixed data. Adv. Data Anal. Classif. **10**(1), 5–26 (2016)
3. Buuren, S.v., Groothuis-Oudshoorn, K.: MICE: multivariate imputation by chained equations in r. J. Stat. Softw. 1–68 (2010)
4. Dear, R.E.: A principal-component missing-data method for multiple regression models. System Development Corporation (1959)
5. Dua, D., Graff, C.: UCI machine learning repository (2017). https://archive.ics.uci.edu/ml
6. Folch-Fortuny, A., Arteaga, F., Ferrer, A.: PCA model building with missing data: new proposals and a comparative study. Chemom. Intell. Lab. Syst. **146**, 77–88 (2015)
7. Grung, B., Manne, R.: Missing values in principal component analysis. Chemom. Intell. Lab. Syst. **42**(1–2), 125–139 (1998)

8. Guyon, I., Li, J., Mader, T., Pletscher, P.A., Schneider, G., Uhr, M.: Competitive baseline methods set new standards for the nips 2003 feature selection benchmark. Pattern Recogn. Lett. **28**(12), 1438–1444 (2007)
9. Halko, N., Martinsson, P.G., Tropp, J.A.: Finding structure with randomness: probabilistic algorithms for constructing approximate matrix decompositions. SIAM Rev. **53**(2), 217–288 (2011)
10. Ilin, A., Raiko, T.: Practical approaches to principal component analysis in the presence of missing values. J. Mach. Learn. Res. **11**, 1957–2000 (2010)
11. Iodice D'Enza, A., Palumbo, F., Markos, A.: Single imputation via chunk-wise PCA. In: Chadjipadelis, T., Lausen, B., Markos, A., Lee, T.R., Montanari, A., Nugent, R. (eds.) IFCS 2019. SCDAKO, pp. 75–82. Springer, Cham (2021). https://doi.org/10.1007/978-3-030-60104-1_9
12. Jenatton, R., Obozinski, G., Bach, F.: Structured sparse principal component analysis. In: Proceedings of the Thirteenth International Conference on Artificial Intelligence and Statistics, pp. 366–373. JMLR Workshop and Conference Proceedings (2010)
13. Khan, S.I., Hoque, A.S.M.L.: SICE: an improved missing data imputation technique. J. Big Data **7**(1), 1–21 (2020)
14. Lipton, Z.C., Kale, D.C., Wetzel, R., et al.: Modeling missing data in clinical time series with RNNs. Mach. Learn. Healthc. **56** (2016)
15. Mazumder, R., Hastie, T., Tibshirani, R.: Spectral regularization algorithms for learning large incomplete matrices. J. Mach. Learn. Res. **11**(Aug), 2287–2322 (2010)
16. Nguyen, T., Nguyen, D.H., Nguyen, H., Nguyen, B.T., Wade, B.A.: EPEM: efficient parameter estimation for multiple class monotone missing data. Inf. Sci. **567**, 1–22 (2021)
17. Nguyen, T., Nguyen-Duy, K.M., Nguyen, D.H.M., Nguyen, B.T., Wade, B.A.: DPER: direct parameter estimation for randomly missing data. Knowl.-Based Syst. **240**, 108082 (2022)
18. Nguyen, T., Phan, N.T., Hoang, H.V., Halvorsen, P., Riegler, M.A., Nguyen, B.T.: PMF: efficient parameter estimation for data sets with missing data in some features. SSRN 4260235
19. Pedregosa, F., et al.: Scikit-learn: machine learning in Python. J. Mach. Learn. Res. **12**, 2825–2830 (2011)
20. Qu, L., Li, L., Zhang, Y., Hu, J.: PPCA-based missing data imputation for traffic flow volume: a systematical approach. IEEE Trans. Intell. Transp. Syst. **10**(3), 512–522 (2009)
21. Rahman, M.G., Islam, M.Z.: Missing value imputation using a fuzzy clustering-based EM approach. Knowl. Inf. Syst. **46**(2), 389–422 (2016)
22. Ross, D.A., Lim, J., Lin, R.S., Yang, M.H.: Incremental learning for robust visual tracking. Int. J. Comput. Vis. **77**(1), 125–141 (2008)
23. Roweis, S.: EM algorithms for PCA and SPCA. Adv. Neural Inf. Process. Syst. **10** (1997)
24. Rubinsteyn, A., Feldman, S.: Fancyimpute: an imputation library for python (2016). https://github.com/iskandr/fancyimpute
25. Sakar, C.O., et al.: A comparative analysis of speech signal processing algorithms for Parkinson's disease classification and the use of the tunable q-factor wavelet transform. Appl. Soft Comput. **74**, 255–263 (2019)
26. Sportisse, A., Boyer, C., Josse, J.: Estimation and imputation in probabilistic principal component analysis with missing not at random data. Adv. Neural Inf. Process. Syst. **33**, 7067–7077 (2020)

27. Stekhoven, D.J., Bühlmann, P.: MissForest-non-parametric missing value imputation for mixed-type data. Bioinformatics **28**(1), 112–118 (2012)
28. Vu, M.A., et al.: Conditional expectation for missing data imputation. arXiv preprint arXiv:2302.00911 (2023)
29. Xiao, H., Rasul, K., Vollgraf, R.: Fashion-MNIST: a novel image dataset for benchmarking machine learning algorithms. arXiv preprint arXiv:1708.07747 (2017)
30. Yoon, J., Jordon, J., Schaar, M.: Gain: missing data imputation using generative adversarial nets. In: International Conference on Machine Learning, pp. 5689–5698. PMLR (2018)

An Integration of Big Data and Blockchain for Strategic Analysis of Schools in Thailand

Pattanaphong Pothipasa[1] and Pannee Suanpang[2]($\boxtimes$)

[1] Sisaket Rajabhat University, Si Sa Ket District 3300, Thailand
[2] Suan Dusit University, Bangkok 10300, Thailand
pannee_sua@dusit.ac.th

Abstract. In the era of digital transformation, the information used for strategic management in schools needs to be utilized for maximum benefit, efficiency, and effectiveness. Further, it requires storage in a secure, transparent, and verifiable manner worldwide. Recognizing the importance of this research contribution, the researchers designed a strategic data storage and analysis system to be used in larger secondary schools by integrating big data, artificial intelligence, and blockchain technologies. The integrated system provides a platform to collect and analyze annual operational plans for schools by facilitating compatibility with text analytics and machine learning technologies of large, high-security schools in Thailand. The results showed that the plans and projects for each department in the school were encrypted at the time of login, and the system generated a starting block. Through each step of the corresponding analysis process, new blocks are created continuously, meaning each plan and project will generate a chain of blocks encrypted with the hash function until the plan and project are approved. Furthermore, the system has a high level of security and user satisfaction ($X^- = 4.00$, SD. 0.76)). Thus, the system could be implemented and adopted in schools to support educational management in the 21st century.

Keywords: Big data · Artificial intelligence · Strategic analysis · Text Analytics · Blockchain

1 Introduction

The digital transformation era has caused a significant change in every dimension of work, especially in the education sector. Regarding current research on intelligence education administration management [1, 2], many schools have been using advanced information technology, particularly the new age of artificial intelligence (AI) and big data, to support strategic management in schools and contribute to the comprehensive quality of teaching and learning [2, 3]. With the rapid development of information and communication technology, there has been a dramatic increase in the collection, storage, use, exploration, and access of data in the era of "big data" [1, 4].

The concept of "big data" has triggered a wave of technological innovation worldwide. Big data is defined as "a new generation of technologies and architectures designed to economically extract value from very large volumes of a wide variety of data, by enabling the high-velocity capture, discovery, and/or analysis" [5, 6]. Moreover, big data is characterized by the 6 Vs model, which includes volume, variety, velocity, veracity, value, and variability [5–7]. There are several activities involved in big data analysis, including the specification, capture, storage, access, and analysis of datasets to make content-supported decisions [5, 6, 8]. The benefits of big data include low cost, fast acquisition, processing, and analysis technology from a variety of large data with extraction [5, 9]. The integration of big data technology with blockchain technology supports data analytics for effective and safe business transactions [9, 10]. Blockchain technology decentralizes data to other parties in network systems, which can be applied in an array of industries such as finance, supply chain, healthcare, and education [12–14].

In recent times, blockchain technology has been implemented in school management to support academic research, reputation, e-portfolios, and intellectual property, as well as to connect lifelong learning and learning analytics platforms, credits, and school strategic development [15–17].

In the digital transformation era, especially during the post-COVID-19 period, school management has participated in these practices while adjusting to a world where technology plays a role in many areas of a country's development. For educational organizations in Thailand, policies are issued by the Ministry of Education at the secondary school level. In the fiscal year 2023, the Ministry of Education, under the administration of the Thai government, has adopted the policy and focus of the Ministry, which was announced in 2021 and designed to be compatible with the Thai government's 20-year National Strategy [5, 11, 18].

Recognizing this need, the researchers were inspired to develop a platform to help compile school-level strategies, Ministry of Education strategies, and national strategies by storing them in a large database management system called big data. Artificial intelligence technology was also utilized in text analytics and machine learning to help analyze the compatibility of these strategies with the Ministry of Education policy and the national strategy. In addition, the researchers incorporated blockchain technology to ensure security and transparency in school-level strategic planning.

This research aims to develop a platform that facilitates the effective management of action plans for large secondary schools in Thailand, ensuring consistency with national policies, Ministry of Education policies, and spatial context. The platform is based on artificial intelligence technology, text processing, big data databases, and blockchain technology, which provides maximum security, transparency, and traceability, making it a good example of how blockchain technology can be used for public administration. This research contributes to the Thai bureaucracy by facilitating the transition from traditional paperwork to electronic documents. It also adds to the existing research on the application of big data and information security technologies like blockchain at the strategic level in Thailand.

2 Review Literature

To obtain a platform for gathering, collecting, and analyzing high school strategic plans that align with the policies of the Ministry of Education of Thailand and the 20-year National Strategy of the Thai government, the research team has reviewed research and supporting data as follows.

2.1 The 20-Year National Strategy

The 20-year National Strategy is a plan for national development that provides a framework and guidelines for government agencies in all sectors to follow. It aims to achieve the vision of a stable, prosperous, and sustainable Thailand with development guided by the philosophy of the sufficiency economy, as expressed by the motto "Stable, Prosperous, Sustainable" [18, 19]. The objective of the strategy is to improve the quality of life of Thai people by promoting happiness, responding to national interests, and generating high income. It also seeks to create a stable society that is characterized by equality and fairness, and one that can compete effectively in the global economy.The 20-year National Strategy consists of 6 aspects comprising (1) stability, (2) competitive capability, (3) human resource development and enhancement, (4) opportunity and social equality, (5) growth in the quality of life that is friendly to the environment, and (6) balance and development of the public administration system.

2.2 Context of School in Research Area in Thailand

The research area is located in Sisaket Province, which is in the northeast region of Thailand. Several schools, particularly Sisaket Wittayalai School, participated in this research project. The reason for choosing Sisaket Wittayalai School is because the school has a prestigious reputation and is academically strong. Additionally, it is well prepared and has the potential to develop its systems. It is also a user of the integration of big data and blockchain system in the school's operations aiming to progress towards becoming a model school (Fig. 1).

Fig. 1. SisaketWittayalai School the research area [19]

Sisaket Wittayalai School is located at No. 319 Moo 5, Wan LukSuea Road, Nong Khrok Sub-district in Mueang Sisaket District, Sisaket Province, covering an area of 145 rai. Originally named Khukhan Province School, it was established on May 17, 1912, under the name "Khukhan Rat Rangrak" using the Sala Rong Thammarat of Maha-Phuttharam Temple (Wat Phra To). The school started with 3 classrooms, 28 students, and 3 teachers. Since then, SisaketWittayalai School has had 27 directors. Currently, SisaketWittayalai School provides education for Mathayom 1–6 students according to the Basic Education Core Curriculum B.E. 2551 (revised B.E. 2558). There are a total of 3,834 students (89 classrooms), 9 school buildings, and 15 compound buildings. Over time, SisaketWittayalai School has made significant progress in all aspects, making it a high-quality secondary school in Sisaket Province, Thailand [19].

2.3 Big Data in Education

The concept of big data has become a buzzword and gained popularity over the last decade [5]. However, there is still no official definition for big data, as different research studies have diverse definitions [5, 20]. Generally, big data refers to large data sets that require complex computational platforms to be analyzed [21]. It is compiled from the proliferation of data, both structured and unstructured, as well as increased computer processing power, data storage capacity, the use of computers to mediate transactions and social interactions, and the density of sensors, all at decreasing costs [5, 22].

Table 1. Big data system architecture [5, 23]

	Calculation model	Describe	Developers
Hadoop	Batch processing	The first open-source implementation of a MapReduce paradigm	Apache
Spark	Flow calculation	Apache distributed flow of computing	TApache
Samza	Batch processing	Support data memory and the latest analysis system	UC Berkeley AMP Lab

The big data system architecture shown in Table 1 consists of:

1) Hadoop uses the MapReduce distributed computing framework and the HDFS distributed file system developed based on Google File System (GFS) [5, 23].
2) Spark supports the analysis of in-memory data and recovery capabilities and is based on Hadoop with several architectural improvements [24].
3) Samza is a real-time distributed stream processing framework. Samza streams data processing, with each Kafka cluster connected to a Yarn cluster to process Samza jobs, which process real-time streaming data such as log services, real-time services, and data tracking applications [5, 25, 26].

The research paper by Cui et al. [20] analyzes the development of online education and the impact of combining online education with big data. The paper introduces innovative online education technology and its results, highlighting the opportunities and development of online education under the influence of the COVID-19 pandemic using big data technology. By analyzing big data technology, the paper demonstrates the potential of combining big data technology and online education and concludes that this innovative approach could be applied in other areas beyond education.

The paper also examines the impact of this combination on the online education industry and other industries. The paper concludes that the combination of big data and online education is innovative since the emergence of COVID-19, and it provides a comprehensive introduction to the concepts and methods of integrating online education and big data technology. The online education platform provides a suitable introduction to the research paper by Cui et al. [20]. The paper can be used to understand the issues and challenges faced by innovative online education in the context of the COVID-19 pandemic as well as to explore future possibilities based on this combination of technologies.

Several studies have shown that effective teaching behaviors play a crucial role in student learning and outcomes. To measure the extent of effective teaching behavior, academics have developed various tools. In this study, an open-ended questionnaire was used in a survey of a large group of students. The researchers employed machine learning tools to separate teaching behavior topics from the open-ended responses of the students. They then tested the validity of the results by comparing them with the theoretical self-driven coding results based on expert judgment. The researchers utilized latent Dirichlet allocation (LDA) topic model analysis along with the Visualization Tool (LDAvis) to analyze qualitative data collected from 173,858 secondary school students in the Netherlands [25, 26]. This approach enabled them to identify patterns and topics within the students' responses, providing insight into effective teaching behaviors.

Based on the data-driven machine learning analysis, the researchers identified eight themes of teaching behavior domains including clear descriptions, a supportive, student-centered learning atmosphere, a variety of lesson characteristics, teachers who arouse interest, follow-up comprehension, and others. Additionally, the researchers randomly selected 864 student responses from the same dataset and conducted theoretical content analysis to write their own code. This resulted in nine teaching behavioral domains and 19 subdomains. The results of the study suggest that the relationship between machine learning and human analytics is complementary. By combining the two approaches, researchers can gain a more comprehensive understanding of effective teaching behaviors. The use of machine learning tools provides an efficient and effective method for analyzing large datasets, while human analytics provides a more nuanced and detailed understanding of the data. Together, these approaches can improve the accuracy and validity of research findings in the field of education.

2.4 Blockchain

Blockchain is a technique for storing data in the form of blocks, which the hash and block system cannot handle; this makes the blockchain ideal for storing sensitive data. One of them is drug information. Therefore, research has been carried out on blockchain technology for medical use in terms of using it to store patient records utilizing smart contracts. For the goal of blockchain applications with pharmaceuticals, drug information from manufacturers can be viewed and purchased directly from buyers.

The research by Jaya et al. (2023) [25] builds upon blockchain research and innovation by applying it to drug data storage. The researchers implemented the Ethereum blockchain and found that the stored data could be integrated effectively into a smart contract. Smart contracts can support and facilitate transactions between producers and buyers while keeping information safe. Access rights in smart contracts can be used to maintain data integrity and security. Ultimately, privacy, decentralization, transparency, and authenticity in drug information can be ensured through the use of blockchain technology and smart contracts for every transaction.

In research by Wang et al. [26], the objective was to solve online learning problems in isolated areas, particularly the problem of sharing data. To address this issue, the researchers proposed an educational data management model based on blockchain technology. The model aimed to facilitate the sharing of data and resources for online learning using verification codes and third-party key mechanisms. Additionally, the study introduced a smart contract-based mechanism for sharing online learning data, and the system's efficiency was evaluated in terms of security analysis.

2.5   Text Analytics

Text analysis, also known as text mining, refers to a set of methods used to collect, process, and interpret unstructured text data [28]. These methods typically involve converting large amounts of text data into a structured format, which can then be analyzed to identify key facts, relationships, and patterns. Common examples of text analysis include response retrieval (such as Apple's Siri or IBM's Watson), sentiment analysis/opinion mining, text summarization, and the integration of structured data into databases, data warehouses, or dashboards for descriptive, inferential, or predictive analytics. Natural Language Processing (NLP) is a field of study that deals with the processing and analysis of text data using machine learning algorithms. NLP algorithms can handle vast amounts of textual information consistently and reliably as well as interpret concepts within complex contexts and decode linguistic ambiguity.

The study by McLaughlin et al. [28] aimed to provide guidance and explanations for text analysis. The study presented a methodological literature review that provided an overview of text analysis, including its brief history, contemporary techniques, and basic steps. The authors illustrated this approach with several examples of common text analysis techniques. The study also offered practical recommendations to support the use of text analysis in pharmaceutical education. These recommendations included clarifying the purpose of text analysis, ensuring that research questions were relevant and based on the literature, developing a processing strategy and creating a dictionary, exploring tools for analysis and visualization, being tolerant of errors, training, calibrating, and validating analytical strategies, and collaborating and preparing.

The authors also discuss the potential impact of text analysis, which provides a systematic approach to generating information from the textual content. The approach has several benefits, such as improving the efficiency of text analysis and explaining new knowledge. Despite recent developments in text analysis techniques, however, the study highlights the limitations of this approach. The authors suggest that efforts to improve the usability and accessibility of text analytics continue and pharmacy educators should position their work in the context of these constraints (Fig. 2).

Text analytics is a technology that combines machine learning suites with statistical and linguistic techniques to process large amounts of unstructured text or text without a

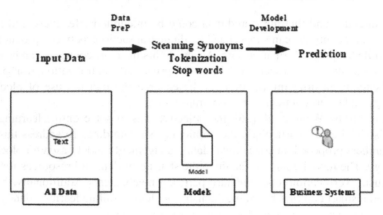

Fig. 2. Text Analytics Operations [29]

predetermined pattern. Its purpose is to gain insights and patterns that enable businesses, governments, researchers, and the media to leverage vast amounts of content to make critical decisions. Text analysis employs a variety of techniques, including sentiment analysis, topic modeling, named entity recognition, word frequency, and event extraction [29].

3 Methodology

3.1 Research Framework

In order to obtain a strategic analysis platform for high school administration that integrates blockchain technology within, the researchers designed the architecture of the system into three tiers, in line with the inputs of school administration, analysis process and plan management, and reports for executive level.

   The work of the system architecture starts from the department or the learning group adds the operational plan data into the system, which adds this data to create a new block into the system, when the data is saved in the database system. Central by stamping the Hash Key, such information is considered information that can guarantee the identity of the entity that enters the transaction, then will be analyzed for the consistency of the plan with the national strategy and the focus of Ministry of Education, where the information that has been processed from the beginning of the data entry until the consistency analysis will be presented to the school administrators in the form of Summary Reports (Fig. 3).

3.2 System Development Life Cycle

The researchers aimed to develop a platform that could collect and analyze high school strategic plans in accordance with the policies of the Ministry of Education of Thailand and the Thai government's 20-year National Strategy. To accomplish this, they employed a system development process known as SDLC. There are five steps as following:

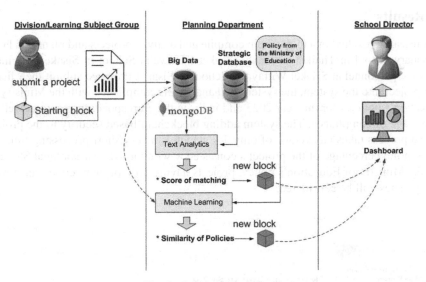

Fig. 3. Research Framework

1) System analysis: of an existing system the research team conducted a detailed feasibility study of the operational plan for Sisaket Wittayalai School. The details of this study are presented in the action plan at Sisaket Wittayalai School and was originally made into a booklet on paper [19]. Also, the research team reviewed relevant research pertaining to the school context, management structure, the 20-year National Strategy, Ministry of Education policy, big data research, blockchain research, and text analytics research.

2) System design: architecture design involved dividing the system into three parts: (1) divisions and subject groups, (2) the planning department, (3) school administrators as show in Fig. 4

3) System development: involved database design and the creation of a set of instructions for performing all three tasks. The system development part includes: (1) database design, (2) table design, (3) input form design, (4) blockchain module design, (5) design. Analyzing the consistency of the agency's work plan with the Ministry of Education's focus, (6) Designing a summary report.

4) System was then subjected to testing in the Sisaket Wittayalai School for 4 months (one semester November 2022-February 2023)

5) System evaluation: by teacher and staff at the school 30 people. The research team conducted an experiment to evaluate the efficiency of the developed platform in terms of user interface quality and system acceptance to support plan analysis, by testing with 30 system users. Usability, stability, accuracy and completeness, with an average score in all aspects at 4.00 as in

4   Results

This research resulted in a tool to help compile and analyze projects and plans at a large secondary school in Thailand, namely Sisaket Wittayalai School in Sisaket Province. After the personnel at Sisaket Wittayalai School in Sisaket Province submit their fiscal year project into the system, the system will analyze its compliance with the Ministry of Education's policies for the year 2023 and indicate the corresponding points as well as percentage of compliance. The system adding blockchain-based security to the project upload process takes an average of only 1 s, which is a very short processing time. In terms of the percentage of the project's consistency with the 20-year National Strategy and the Ministry of Education's policy, projects having 50% or more compliance with both policies will be considered.

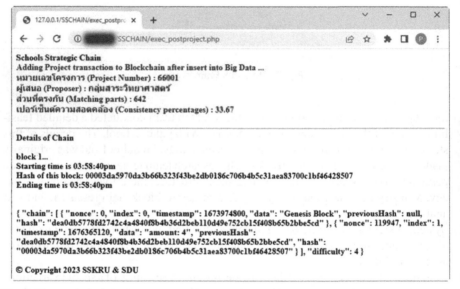

Fig. 4. Integration of big data and blockchain for strategic analysis of schools in Thailand result

Figure 4 Project information that has been analyzed for compliance with the policy of the Ministry of Education and recorded in the big data system will be encrypted with blockchain. The research team conducted an experiment to evaluate the efficiency of the developed platform in terms of user interface quality and system acceptance to support plan analysis, with 30 users. Work, stability, accuracy and completeness with an average score of 4.00 (Mean 4.00, SD. 0.76) as shown in Table 2.

The results of the evaluation of the efficiency and satisfaction of the system users presented in this research are shown in the table above. The research team found an average score of 4.0, which concluded that overall performance and user satisfaction with the developed platform were good.

After adding data to the big data database system, a list of projects will be created as a transaction in the blockchain system to ensure transparency and accountability for any additions, changes, or amendments made to the details of such projects.

Table 2. System Evaluation

Evaluation Indicators	Issue	Means	SD.
Usability	1.1 Easy to use	4.00	0.85
	1.2 Easy to access	4.00	0.77
Stability	2.1 Stability of the systems	4.00	0.65
	2.2 Network stability	4.00	0.87
	2.3 Run time error	3.50	0.55
Accuracy	3.1 System accuracy	4.50	0.89
Completeness	4.1 System completeness	4.00	0.98
	Overall	**4.00**	**0.76**

5 Conclusion and Discussion

This research developed a platform for collecting, archiving and analyzing the strategic plans for large secondary school in line with Thailand's Ministry of Education policy and the Thai government's 20-year National Strategy. The goal was to make the process of managing secondary schools in the age of competition more effective, given the limitation of budget.

To ensure consistency in each project at Sisaket Wittayalai School, the research team chose to use artificial intelligence technology, specifically text analytics, to assist in identifying the consistency of each project's message with the policy of the Ministry of Education. Compatibility was determined using machine learning, specifically supporting vector machines. To ensure transparency and accountability in the project submission, review, and revision processes, the researchers incorporated a blockchain mechanism after inserting project data into the big data DBMS.

The use of big data technology in this research aligns with the research guidelines of Cui et al. [20]. The use of text analytics in analyzing secondary school projects and the policies of the Ministry of Education aligns with the research guidelines of McLaughlin et al. [28]. The application of blockchain to the Ministry of Education's annual project proposals improves transparency, data security, and research consistency [26].

References

1. Deng, J., He, J., Dua, Z., Liu, Y.: Application research of advanced intelligent big data analysis based on intelligent sensor network in the design of personalized education management system and the construction of innovation system. Hindawi J. Sens. **7113098**, 1–8 (2022). https://doi.org/10.1155/2022/7113098.(2022)
2. Suksai, T., Suanpang, P., Tangchitcharoenkhul, R.: Digital leadership model for basic school administration to conform the policy of Thailand 4.0. Rev. Int. Geog. Educ. (RIGEO) **11**(9), 1120–1130 (2021). https://doi.org/10.48047/rigeo.11.09.96
3. Hao, J.: Design of intelligent educational administration system based on big data technology. In: 2021 3rdInternational Conference on Artificial Intelligence and Advanced Manufacture (AIAM2021), October 23–25, 2021, Manchester, United Kingdom. ACM, New York, NY, USA, p. 5 (2021). https://doi.org/10.1145/3495018.3495406

4. Li, L., Liu, X., Du, R.: Application of big data technology in evaluation of operating status of high-pressure hydrogenation heat exchanger. Chin. Pet. Process Petrchem. Technol. **20**(3), 17–23 (2018)
5. Suanpang, P., Jamjuntr, P.: The integration of a big data framework and a mobile application on the iOS platform to support smart tourism. Int. J. Mach. Learn. Comput. **10**(6), 714–722 (2020). https://doi.org/10.18178/ijmlc.2020.10.6.995
6. Team, O.R.: Big Data Now: Current Perspective from O'Reilly RaderSebastopol, USA: O' Rielly Media, CA, (2011)
7. Laney, D.: 3D Data Management Controlling Data Volume, Velocityand Variety, META Group research Note (2011)
8. Gandomi, A., Haider, M.: Beyond the hype: Big data conceptsmethods, and analytics. Int. J. Inf. Manage **35**, 137–144 (2015)
9. Ocheja, P., Agbo, F.J., Oyelere, S.S., Flanagan, B., Ogata, H.: Blockchain in education: a systematic review and practical case studies. IEEE Access **10**, 99525–99540 (2022)
10. Suanpang, P., Pothipasa, P., Netwrong, T.: Policies and platforms for fake news filtering on cybercrime in smart city using artificial intelligence and blockchain technology. Int. J. Cyber Criminol. **15**(1), 143–157 (2021). https://doi.org/10.5281/zenodo.4766539.(2021)
11. Bouras, M.A., Lu, Q., Dhelim, S., Ning, H.: A lightweight blockchain-based IoT identity management approach. Future Internet **13**(2), 24 (2021)
12. Gordon, W.J., Catalini, C.: Blockchain technology for healthcare: Facilitating the transition to patient-driven interoperability. Comput. Struct. Biotechnol. J. **16**, 224–230 (2018)
13. Ocheja, P., Flanagan, B., Ueda, H., Ogata, H.: Managing lifelong learning records through blockchain. Res. Pract. Technol. Enhanced Learn. **14**(1), 1–19 (2019)
14. Grech, A., Camilleri, A.F.: Blockchain in Education. Luxembourg, U.K.: 824 Publications Office of the European Union (2017)
15. Gräther, W., Kolvenbach, S., Ruland, R., Schütte, J., Torres, C., Wendland, F.: Blockchain for education: Lifelong learning passport. In: Proceedings of 1st ERCIM Blockchain Workshop, pp. 1–8 (2018)
16. Jirgensons, M., Kapenieks, J.: Blockchain and the future of digital learning credential assessment and management. J. Teacher Educ. Sustainability **20**(1), 145–156 (2018)
17. Suksai, T., Suanpang, P., Thangchitcharoenkhul, R.: A digital leadership development model for school administrators in basic education to fulfill the Thailand 4.0 policy. PSAKU Int. J. Interdisc. Res. **10**(2), 11–20 (2021). https://doi.org/10.14456/psakuijir.2021.2
18. Zcooby.com. (n.d.). Accessed 14 Feb 2023. https://www.zcooby.com/20_years_national_str ategy/
19. SisaketWittayalai School (2023). https://skw.ac.th/. Accessed 15 Feb
20. Cui, Y., et al.: A survey on big data-enabled innovative online education systems during the COVID-19 pandemic. J. Innov. Knowl. **8**(1), 100295 (2023). https://doi.org/10.1016/j.jik. 2022.100295
21. Li, J., Xu, L., Tang, L., Wang, S., Li, L.: Big data in tourism research: a literature review. Tour. Manage. **68**, 301–323 (2018)
22. Akoka, J., Comyn-Wattiau, W., Laoufi, N.: Research on big data-a systematic mapping study. Comput. Stan. Interfaces **54**, 105–115 (2017)
23. Price, K.H., Dunnigan, R.: Big Data Analytics: A Practical Guide for Managers. CRC Press Taylor & Francis Group, FL (2015)
24. Chen, J.,Tang,J, Jiang, Q, Wang, Y. and Tao, C. Research on architecture of education big data analysis system, *in proc. IEEE 2nd International of big data analysis*, Beijing, China, 10–12 March, (2017)
25. Gencoglu, B., Helms-Lorenz, M., Maulana, R., Jansen, E.P., Gencoglu, O.: Machine and expert judgments of student perceptions of teaching behavior in secondary education: added

value of topic modeling with big data. Comput. Educ. **193**, 104682 (2023). https://doi.org/10.1016/j.compedu.2022.104682

26. Wang, Y., Sun, Q., Bie, R.: Blockchain-based secure sharing mechanism of online education data. Procedia Comput. Sci. **202**, 283–288 (2022). https://doi.org/10.1016/j.procs.2022.04.037

27. Jaya, R.M., Rakkhitta, V.D., Sembiring, P., Edbert, I.S., Suhartono, D.: Blockchain applications in drug data records. Procedia Comput. Sci. **216**, 739–748 (2023). https://doi.org/10.1016/j.procs.2022.12.19

28. McLaughlin, J.E., Lyons, K., Lupton-Smith, C., Fuller, K.: An introduction to text analytics for educators. Curr. Pharm. Teach. Learn. **14**(10), 1319–1325 (2022). https://doi.org/10.1016/j.cptl.2022.09.005

29. TIBCO, What is text analytics? TIBCO Software (n.d.). https://www.tibco.com/reference-center/what-is-text-analytics. Accessed 26 Feb 2023

Federated Deep Reinforcement Learning - Based Bitrate Adaptation for Dynamic Adaptive Streaming over HTTP

Phuong L. Vo[1,2]([✉])[ID], Nghia T. Nguyen[1,2], Long Luu[1,2], Canh T. Dinh[3],
Nguyen H. Tran[3], and Tuan-Anh Le[4]

[1] International University, Ho Chi Minh City, Vietnam
[2] Vietnam National University, Ho Chi Minh City, Vietnam
{vtlphuong,ntnghia}@hcmiu.edu.vn, ITITIU18079@student.hcmiu.edu.vn
[3] University of Sydney, Sydney, NSW 2006, Australia
{canh.dinh,nguyen.tran}@sydney.edu.au
[4] Institute of Engineering and Technology,
Thu Dau Mot University, Binh Duong, Vietnam
letuanh@tdmu.edu.vn

Abstract. In video streaming over HTTP, the bitrate adaptation selects the quality of video chunks depending on the current network condition. Some previous works have applied deep reinforcement learning (DRL) algorithms to determine the chunk's bitrate from the observed states to maximize the quality-of-experience (QoE). However, to build an intelligent model that can predict in various environments, such as 3G, 4G, Wifi, *etc.*, the states observed from these environments must be sent to a server for training centrally.

In this work, we integrate federated learning (FL) to DRL-based rate adaptation to train a model appropriate for different environments. The clients in the proposed framework train their model locally and only update the weights to the server. The simulations show that our federated DRL-based rate adaptations, called FDRLABR with different DRL algorithms, such as deep Q-learning, advantage actor-critic, and proximal policy optimization, yield better performance than the traditional bitrate adaptation methods in various environments.

Keywords: bitrate adaptation · deep reinforcement learning · federated learning · dynamic adaptive streaming over HTTP

1 Introduction

Dynamic adaptive streaming over HTTP (DASH) is the primary method of video streaming on the Internet today. This standard is widely applied because of its

This research is funded by Vietnam National University HoChiMinh City (VNU-HCM) under grant number DS2020-28-01, and in part by the Vietnam National Foundation for Science and Technology Development (NAFOSTED) under Grant 102.02-2019.321.

N. T. Nguyen et al. (Eds.): ACIIDS 2023, CCIS 1863, pp. 279–290, 2023.
https://doi.org/10.1007/978-3-031-42430-4_23

flexibility and scalability. The video is chunked and encoded in different bitrates. Depending on the current network condition, the user's adaptive bitrate (ABR) function chooses an appropriate bitrate to request the video chunks [1–3].

The traditional ABR methods include throughput-based [1] and buffer-based methods [3]. The throughput-based method chooses the quality level of the next chunk using the estimated throughput (usually the mean) of the previously downloaded chunks [1]. The buffer-based method determines the quality level of the next chunk based on the current buffer level. BOLA is a well-known buffer-based method that optimizes the Lyapunov function to select a quality level for chunks [3]. Both throughput-based and BOLA are deployed as two main ABR methods in the reference video client Dash.js [4].

The ABR based on tabular Q-learning maximizing the user's QoE is studied in [5]. The states, including estimated throughput and buffer size, are discretized. The reward combines three objectives: high chunk quality level, low number of quality switches, and short rebuffering time. The success of deep Q-learning (DQN), which achieved human-level playing in the Atari game [7], has inspired the development of various deep reinforcement learning (DRL) algorithms and their applications in many fields. Recently, there have been several works [10–12] that applied several DRL algorithms to improve the performance of ABR. In work [10], the proposed Pensieve method has applied an asynchronous advantage actor-critic (A3C) algorithm to rate adaptation. The action is the quality level the client will request for the next chunk. The state combines different observations, such as estimated throughput, next chunk sizes, number of remaining chunks, buffer size, delay, *etc.* The reward is the utility penalized by quality switching and video rebuffering. Since A3C is a policy-based method, a neural network approximates a state to an action distribution, and the action corresponding to the maximum probability is chosen. Similar to Pensieve, D-DASH proposed in [11] uses DQN algorithm for ABR. The state space, action space, and reward function are similar to the ones in Pensieve. Two network architectures are used in [11], *i.e.*, multilayer perceptron and long-short term memory. The work [12] has applied several DRL algorithms to ABR, *i.e.*, temporal difference, A3C, DQN, and rainbow DQN. The DRL-based ABR methods achieve a higher QoE than the traditional methods.

The federated learning (FL) algorithms [14] in supervised learning emerge as promising algorithms that allow learning distributively. In each round, several random clients are selected to train in several epochs with their local datasets and send the weights of the trained models to the server. The server then averages the received weights and broadcasts the average weight to all clients. In FL, data is kept locally without being sent to the server, hence, preserving the user's privacy.

Inspired by the success of FL, federated deep reinforcement learning (FDRL) is the architecture combining federated learning and reinforcement learning [15]. Inherit from the categorization of FL algorithms [16], FDRL has two groups of algorithms: horizontal FDRL and vertical FDRL [15]. In horizontal FDRL, the clients have aligned the state space and action space. The clients explore different aspects of their environment but are unwilling to share their experiences with a central model. The horizontal FDRL framework helps to increase training samples and improve global model performance. In vertical FDRL, clients' training data may have different features. The state space and the action space of the clients are not aligned. Each client observes part of the global environment and can perform a different set of actions depending on their observed environment.

We propose a horizontal FDRL architecture for rate adaptation in which the clients experience different environments like network delay, throughput, buffer thresholds, *etc.* The contributions in this paper include the following:

1. We propose a federated deep reinforcement learning-based bite rate adaptation framework called FDRLABR. The global model can predict action in various environments.
2. We implement FDRLABR with different DRL algorithms run at clients, including value-based algorithm, *i.e.*, deep Q-learning (DQN), and actor-critic algorithms, *i.e.*, advantage actor-critic (A2C) and proximal policy optimization (PPO)[1].
3. We train and evaluate our proposed algorithms in an event-driven environment. The global model can predict the action for various environment datasets and yields a better QoE than the traditional methods such as BOLA and throughput-based.

To the best of our knowledge, this study is the first work that proposes a distributed DRL framework for bitrate adaptation in DASH.

The remaining paper has the following structure. Section 2 describes FDRLABR framework. Section 3 presents the performance of the proposed algorithms, and Sect. 4 concludes the work.

2   Federated Deep Reinforcement Learning-Based Bitrate Adaptation (FDRLABR)

Our proposed FDRLABR framework includes a global model at the server implementing federated updates and multiple local models at clients running DRL algorithms. Figure 1 describes the framework of FDRLABR. Both global and local models have the same neural network architecture. In each global round, the server randomly selects several clients and broadcasts its model's parameters to these clients. Each selected client performs local training for E episodes and sends back the weights of its model weights to the server. The server then averages the received weights and goes to the next round.

2.1   DRL Model for Bitrate Adaptation at Client

A DRL agent interacts with the environment and learns from experiences. At each time step, the agent observes state s, chooses action a, and receives a reward

---

[1] https://github.com/toiuuvagiaithuat/FDRLABR.

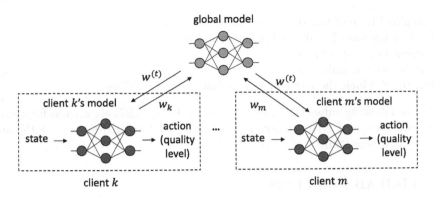

Fig. 1. The framework of FDRLABR.

r. The agent aims to maximize the cumulative reward [6]. Assuming that each time step begins when the client requests a video chunk and an episode is the set of all the chunks of a video. The reward function, states, and actions of the DRL model applied for bitrate adaptation are described as follows.

Corresponding to an observed state, the DRL agent decides which quality level of the chunk will be requested. The *action space* includes all the quality levels of the video. At time step n, assuming that the agent takes the action corresponding download chunk n at bitrate R_n, the received *reward* is the combination of three QoE metrics: the utility value corresponding to chunk's quality level, the quality difference between two consecutive chunks, and the rebuffering time in this time step. The following formula is the reward corresponding to chunk n:

$$r_n = q(R_n) - \alpha |q(R_{n-1}) - q(R_n)| - \beta \phi_n,$$

where,

- $q(R_n)$ is the utility function mapping bitrate R_n to a value. Logarithm utility function $q(R_n) = \log(R_n/R^{\min})$ is used as in [3,10], where $R^{\min}$ is the bitrate of the minimum quality level.
- $|q(R_{n-1}) - q(R_n)|$ represents the difference in the quality levels between two consecutive chunks.
- ϕ_n is the rebuffering time in time step n. If the download time d_n of chunk n is greater than the amount of video (in seconds) currently in the buffer, B_n, then the rebuffering time is $d_n - B_n$. Otherwise, there is no rebuffering. Hence, rebuffering time associated to chunk n is given by $\phi_n = \max(0, d_n - B_n)$.
- α and β are the coefficients associated with the quality difference and rebuffering time penalties, respectively. We use the values $\alpha = 2.6$ and $\beta = 1$, the same as [10].

A *state* is a vector of the following components:

- estimated network throughput for last 06 video chunks in seconds,

- download time of last 06 video chunks in seconds,
- next chunk sizes for all quality levels in Mb,
- current buffer size in seconds,
- number of remaining chunks,
- bitrate at which the last chunk was downloaded in Mbps.

In the following subsections, we will present FDRLABR algorithms for clients using two groups of DRL algorithms: a value-based algorithm, *i.e.*, DQN, and policy-based algorithms, *i.e.*, A2C and PPO.

2.2   FDRLABR with DQN

DQN is a value-based algorithm [7]. Q-network with parameter w estimates Q-values $Q(s, a; w)$ from an observed state s for each action a. An action is selected according to ϵ-greedy policy, in which the agent selects the quality level corresponding to the maximum Q-value with probability $1 - \epsilon$ and explores a random quality level with probability ϵ, in the training phase (see [7]). To make the algorithm more stable, DQN uses an experience replay memory to store the transitions *(state s, action a, reward r, next state s')* of previous steps. In addition, a target network parametrized by w^-, that periodically clones the parameters of Q-network, is used to estimate the target value $r + \gamma \max_a Q(s', a; w^-)$. Each training step updates w to minimize the difference between the Q-value $Q(s, a; w)$ and the target value with a random batch of transitions from the experience replay memory.

Algorithm 1 describes the steps of FDRLABR with DQN. The aggregation server collects the weights of Q-networks of the selected clients, averages them, and sends the average weights back to the selected clients of the next global round.

2.3   FDRLABR with Actor-Critic Algorithms

We apply two actor-critic algorithms for clients' ABR, *i.e.*, A2C and PPO. The first policy-based algorithm, REINFORCE [6], uses an actor network, parametrized by θ, to estimate the policy $\pi(a|s; \theta)$ directly. Actor-critic algorithms use a baseline to reduce the fluctuation of REINFORCE. The value function $V(s; \nu)$ is a common baseline, and a critic network, parametrized by ν, is used to estimate this baseline. Advantage actor-critic (A2C) or asynchronous advantage actor-critic (A3C) are well-known actor-critic algorithms. Using N-step update, the advantages are given by

$$A_n = R_n - V(s_n; \nu), n = 1, \dots, N.$$

where $R_n = r_n + \gamma r_{n+1} + \dots + \gamma^{N-n-1} r_{N-1} + \gamma^{N-n} V(s_n; \nu)$ (see Algorithm 2).

Both A2C and A3C use multiple copied environments in parallel to accelerate the training. In A3C, the actor corresponding to each environment runs on a separate thread and updates asynchronously [8], whereas A2C uses synchronous

Algorithm 1. FDRLABR with DQN.

1: Initialize w_k randomly, experience replay memory $\mathcal{D}_k = \emptyset$ for all client k.
2: **for** each global round $t = 1, \ldots, T$ **do**
3:     Server uniformly chooses a set $S^{(t)}$ of K clients.
4:     Server sends $w^{(t)}$ to all clients in $S^{(t)}$.
5:     **for** each client $k = 1$ in $S^{(t)}$ **do**   ▷ Local updates
6:         $w_k = w^{(t)}$.
7:         **for** each iteration n in each of E episodes **do**
8:             Take action a_n according to ϵ-greedy policy, observe reward r_n and next
    state s'_n.
9:             Append transition (s_n, a_n, r_n, s'_n) to $\mathcal{D}_k$.
10:            Update w_k by minimizing the loss function

$$\mathbb{E}\big(r + \gamma \max_a Q(s', a; w_k^-) - Q(s, a; w_k)\big)^2$$

    with a random batch from $\mathcal{D}_k$.
11:            If $n \mod C == 0$, $w_k^- = w_k$.
12:        **end for**
13:        Send w_k to server.
14:    **end for**
15:    Server updates the weights of the global model by averaging the weights received
    from clients:

$$w^{(t+1)} = \frac{1}{K} \sum_{k=1}^{K} w_k.$$

16: **end for**

---

updates on only one thread. We use A2C in the experiments, however, A3C can be implemented similarly. The objective function in A2C is given by

$$L(\theta) = \sum_{i=1}^{m} \sum_{n=1}^{N} \log \pi(a_n | s_n; \theta) A_n^{(i)},$$

where m is the number of parallel environments used in training.

PPO is also an actor-critic algorithm. To prevent the catastrophic drop in the performance of A2C/A3C, PPO constraints the change in policy between two consecutive training steps by introducing a new clipped surrogate objective [9]. PPO has shown a reliable performance and is used in many DRL applications. The surrogate objective of PPO is given by:

$$L(\theta) = \sum_{i=1}^{m} \sum_{n=1}^{N} \min \big(r(\theta) A_n^{(i)}, \text{clip}(r(\theta), 1 - \epsilon, 1 + \epsilon) A_n^{(i)}\big),$$

where ϵ is a small constant for clipping and $r(\theta) = \frac{\pi(a|s;\theta)}{\pi(a|s;\theta_{\text{old}})}$ in which θ_{old} is the parameters of the actor network of the previous update.

In FDRLABR with actor-critic algorithms, the server averages the weights of both actor and critic networks received from the selected clients in each global round. The detailed algorithm is described in Algorithm 2.

Algorithm 2. FDRLABR with actor-critic algorithms.

1: Initialize parameters θ_k, ν_k randomly for all clients k.
2: **for** each global round $t = 1, \ldots, T$ **do**
3:     Server uniformly chooses a set $S^{(t)}$ of K clients.
4:     Server sends $w^{(t)} = (\theta^{(t)}, \nu^{(t)})$ to all clients in $S^{(t)}$.
5:     **for** each client k in $S^{(t)}$ **do**   ▷ Local updates
6:         Update actor and critic networks

$$\theta_k = \theta^{(t)}, \quad \nu_k = \nu^{(t)}.$$

7:         **for** each iteration in each of E episodes **do**
8:             **for** environment i in m copied environments at client k **do**
9:                 Run policy $\pi(\theta_k)$ for N steps.
10:                Compute advantage $A_1^{(i)}, \ldots, A_N^{(i)}$.
11:            **end for**
12:            Update ν_k by minimizing

$$\sum_{i=1}^{m} \sum_{n=1}^{N} (R_n^{(i)} - V(s_n; \nu_k))^2.$$

13:            Update θ_k by maximizing the objective $L(\theta_k)$.
14:        **end for**
15:        Send $w_k = (\theta_k, \nu_k)$ to server.
16:    **end for**
17:    Server updates the weights of global model by averaging the weights w_k received from clients:

$$w^{(t+1)} = \frac{1}{K} \sum_{k=1}^{K} w_k.$$

18: **end for**

---

3 Performance Evaluation

3.1 Simulation Setting

We use an event-driven simulation that allows a video player to play a 240-s video in less than one second, similar to [10]. The maximum buffer size of the video players is 20 s. The video used in the simulation is Big Bug Bunny with seven quality levels 700, 900, 2000, 3000, 5000, 6000, and 8000 Kbps. The video chunk length is four seconds [2]. To show the effectiveness of FDRLABRs in different environments, we generate 100 agents with environments different in network bandwidth and round-trip-time.

Network Bandwidth. We use two real-trace datasets: a broadband dataset [18] and a 4G LTE Dataset [17]. The **broadband dataset** contains over 1 million throughput traces provided by US Federal Communications Commission (FCC). The data are from the "download speed" category of the September 2019 collection with 10-s granularity [18]. The **4G dataset** is collected by Irish mobile operators with five mobility patterns: static, pedestrian, car, bus, and train. It contains 135 traces, about 15 min per trace at 1-s granularity [17]. For each FCC or 4G dataset, we generate 2000 320-s traces, 1000 traces have mean throughputs greater than 2 Mbps, and the other 1000 traces have mean throughputs less than 2 Mbps. In each group of traces, we randomly select 80% for training and the remaining 20% for testing. Each client chooses a random trace in the training set for each episode in the training phase. In training, each agent randomly selects one of each bandwidth group for training.

We utilize Stable Baseline3 [19] library to implement DQN, A2C, and PPO for clients. Stable Baseline3 includes a set of reliable implementations of DRL algorithms and is used in many DRL applications. We use fully connected neural networks with 64 nodes for each hidden layer. We tuned the number of hidden layers for the algorithms. Table 1 lists some tuned hyper-parameters for three algorithms. The not-listed hyperparameters are used with the default values provided by Stable Baseline3. In FDRLABR with A2C and PPO algorithms, we use n-step update with five steps and one environment at each client.

3.2   Results

DRL algorithms are known to be very sensitive to different initial points [13]. We train the proposed algorithms with 500 global rounds in five runs. Figure 2 shows the convergences of the average rewards of 100 clients in five runs in the training phase of FDRLABR with DQN, A2C, and PPO algorithms. All the plots show that the more selected users per round (K) or the more local episodes the selected users run per round (E) yields a better convergence rate and higher rewards. This observation also agrees with the characteristics of FedAvg algorithm [14].

We evaluate FDRLABR algorithms with the best models. Table 2 compares the test results of FDRLABRs with other ABR methods, *i.e.*, throughput-based (THGHPUT) [1], buffer-based (BOLA) [3], and CONSTANT (which always chooses 5 Mbps) methods. The numbers in the table are the average values of 800 episodes corresponding to 800 test traces. FDRLABR algorithms yield higher average rewards than the other algorithms' rewards, except for FDR-LABR with A2C with $K = 10$ and $E = 10$. In some cases, FDRLABR with A2C results in lower rewards and much higher variations than FDRLABRs with PPO and DQN. This result shows that FDRLABR with A2C is not as stable as with DQN or PPO, which is also a drawback of A2C.

Figure 3 shows the convergence of FDRLABR with DQN, A2C, and PPO algorithms at clients in each group with $K = 5$ and $E = 10$. The rewards resulting from the high-bandwidth FCC and LTE groups have much lower variations than those from the low-bandwidth ones. In each quality level, the actual bitrates of the video chunks are much smaller than the encoding bitrate [2]; indeed, many

Table 1. Tuned hyper-parameters of DRL algorithms

Parameters	Values
FDRLABR w/DQN tuned parameters:	
q-network	[64, 64]
activation function	Tanh
learning rate	0.0005
batch size	128
target network update period (C)	25
exploration fraction	0.5
exploration final ϵ	0.05
discount factor (γ)	0.9
FDRLABR w/A2C tuned parameters:	
actor network	[64, 64, 64]
critic network	[64, 64]
activation function	Tanh
learning rate	0.0005
discount factor (γ)	0.9
FDRLABR w/PPO tuned parameters:	
actor network	[64, 64, 64]
critic network	[64, 64, 64]
activation function	Tanh
learning rate	0.0001
discount factor (γ)	0.9

chunks' bitrates are less than half of their encoding bitrates. Hence, the average reward of each episode in high bandwidth groups is very high. FDRLABR with A2C has the highest variation among the three FDRLABR algorithms, which is also shown in Table 3.

Table 3 shows the test rewards corresponding to four groups of test traces with $K = 5$ and $E = 10$. We see that the rewards resulting from the high-bandwidth traces are much higher than those from the low-bandwidth traces. In most cases, the rewards of FDRLABR algorithms are higher than those of the other algorithms.

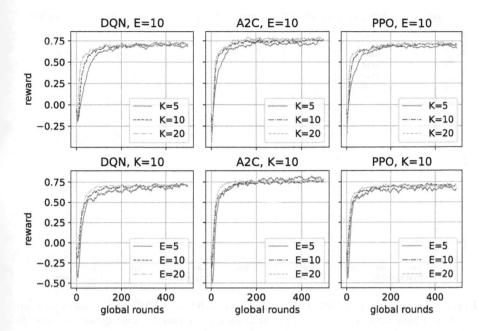

Fig. 2. Convergence of FDRLABR with DQN, A2C, and PPO when varying the number of selected users ($E = 10$) and varying the number of local episodes ($K = 10$).

Table 2. Rewards of ABR methods. FDRLABR's values are the average rewards and deviations in five runs.

ABR methods			Rewards		
Constant			−1.427		
THGHPUT			0.701		
BOLA			0.742		
FDRLABR	$K = 5\ E = 10$	$K = 10\ E = 5$	$K = 10\ E = 10$	$K = 10\ E = 20$	$K = 20\ E = 10$
w/DQN	**0.846±0.02**	**0.833±0.038**	**0.876±0.021**	**0.885±0.015**	**0.878±0.017**
w/A2C	0.792±0.127	0.823±0.03	0.735±0.125	0.817±0.024	0.83±0.031
w/PPO	0.812±0.034	0.822±0.016	0.856±0.023	0.834±0.034	0.855±0.025

Table 3. Average rewards of users in 04 group of environment trained with $K = 5$ and $E = 10$.

ABR methods	FCC high bw	FCC low bw	LTE high bw	LTE low bw
Constant	1.123	−4.244	0.536	−3.122
THGHPUT	1.239	0.409	0.852	0.305
BOLA	1.283	0.521	0.995	0.170
FDRLABR w/DQN	1.333±0.041	**0.687±0.033**	1.012±0.038	**0.403±0.041**
FDRLABR w/A2C	1.357±0.012	0.558±0.221	1.013±0.048	0.239±0.23
FDRLABR w/PPO	**1.362±0.005**	0.624±0.054	**1.024±0.01**	0.239±0.076

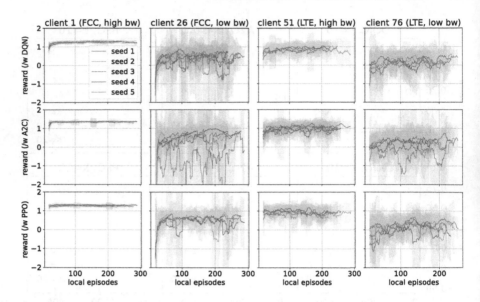

Fig. 3. Convergence of FDRLABR with DQN, A2C, and PPO at the users in each group of 5 runs with $K = 5, E = 10$. The lines are the running average of previous 20 values and the shade regions are the standard deviation.

4   Conclusions

We have proposed FDRLABR, a framework combining federated learning with different DRL-based bitrate adaptation algorithms. Three DRL algorithms are used at clients, *i.e.*, DQN, A2C, and PPO. The clients experience different network environments; however, the trained models yield a better QoE than the traditional methods.

References

1. Stockhammer, T.: Dynamic adaptive streaming over HTTP- standards and design principles. In: Proceedings of the Second Annual ACM Conference on Multimedia Systems, pp. 133–144 (2011)
2. Lederer, S., Müller, C., Timmerer, C.: Dynamic adaptive streaming over HTTP dataset. In: Proceedings of the 3rd Multimedia Systems Conference, pp. 89–94 (2012). https://ftp.itec.aau.at/datasets/mmsys12/ElephantsDream/ed_4s/
3. Spiteri, K., Urgaonkar, R., Sitaraman, R.K.: BOLA: near-optimal bitrate adaptation for online videos. IEEE/ACM Trans. Netw. **28**(4), 1698–1711 (2020)
4. dash.js. https://github.com/Dash-Industry-Forum/dash.js/
5. Claeys, M., Latré, S., Famaey, J., Wu, T., Van Leekwijck, W., De Turck, F.: Design and optimisation of a (FA) Q-learning-based HTTP adaptive streaming client. Connect. Sci. **26**(1), 25–43 (2014)
6. Sutton, R.S., Barto, A.G.: Reinforcement Learning: An Introduction. MIT press, Cambridge (2018)

7. Mnih, V., et al.: Human-level control through deep reinforcement learning. Nature **518**(7540), 529–533 (2015)
8. Mnih, V., et al.: Asynchronous methods for deep reinforcement learning. In: International Conference on Machine Learning PMLR, pp. 1928–1937 (2016)
9. Schulman, J., Wolski, F., Dhariwal, P., Radford, A., Klimov, O.: Proximal policy optimization algorithms. arXiv preprint arXiv:1707.06347 (2017)
10. Mao, H., Netravali, R., Alizadeh, M.: Neural adaptive video streaming with pensieve. In: Proceedings of the Conference of the ACM Special Interest Group on Data Communication, pp. 197–210 (2017)
11. Gadaleta, M., Chiariotti, F., Rossi, M., Zanella, A.: D-DASH: a deep Q-learning framework for DASH video streaming. IEEE Trans. Cogn. Commun. Netw. **3**(4), 703–718 (2017)
12. Liu, J., Tao, X., Lu, J.: QoE-oriented rate adaptation for DASH with enhanced deep Q-learning. IEEE Access **7**, 8454–8469 (2018)
13. Henderson, P., Islam, R., Bachman, P., Pineau, J., Precup, D., Meger, D.: Deep reinforcement learning that matters. In: Proceedings of the AAAI Conference on Artificial Intelligence, vol. 32, no. 1 (2018)
14. McMahan, B., Moore, E., Ramage, D., Hampson, S., y Arcas, B.A.: Communication-efficient learning of deep networks from decentralized data. In: Artificial Intelligence and Statistics PMLR, pp. 1273–1282 (2017)
15. Qi, J., Zhou, Q., Lei, L., Zheng, K.: Federated reinforcement learning: techniques, applications, and open challenges. arXiv preprint arXiv:2108.11887 (2021)
16. Zhang, C., Xie, Y., Bai, H., Yu, B., Li, W., Gao, Y.: A survey on federated learning. Knowl.-Based Syst. **216**, 106775 (2021)
17. Raca, D., Quinlan, J.J., Zahran, A.H., Sreenan, C.J.: Beyond throughput: a 4G LTE dataset with channel and context metrics. In: Proceedings of the 9th ACM Multimedia Systems Conference, pp. 460–465 (2018)
18. US Federal Communications Commission (FCC). https://data.fcc.gov/download/measuring-broadband-america/2019/data-raw-2019-sept.tar.gz
19. Raffin, A., Hill, A., Gleave, A., Kanervisto, A., Ernestus, M., Dormann, N.: Stable-Baselines3: reliable reinforcement learning implementations. J. Mach. Learn. Res. **22**(1), 12348–12355 (2021)

A Multi-criteria Framework Supporting Sustainability Assessment Considering SDG 7 Targets

Jarosław Wątróbski[1,2](✉) ⓘ, Aleksandra Bączkiewicz[1](✉) ⓘ, Robert Król[1] ⓘ,
and Iga Rudawska[3] ⓘ

[1] Institute of Management, University of Szczecin,
ul. Cukrowa 8, 71-004 Szczecin, Poland
{jaroslaw.watrobski,aleksandra.baczkiewicz}@usz.edu.pl
[2] National Institute of Telecommunications, ul. Szachowa 1, 04-894 Warsaw, Poland
[3] Institute of Economics and Finance, University of Szczecin,
ul. Mickiewicza 64, 71-101 Szczecin, Poland

Abstract. Reliable assessment of countries' performance concerning achieving the targets incorporated in Sustainable Development Goals (SDGs) requires appropriate methods considering multiple indicators. Sustainable development evaluation can be supported by engineering applications that automatize it and provide opportunities for comparative analysis of results. A combination of strategies involving developing clean energy systems and methodological frameworks for supervising and measuring sustainable energy systems could help evaluate regions regarding sustainable, clean energy systems, which contribute to improving air quality. This paper aims to present the framework based on multi-criteria decision analysis (MCDA) methods that can serve as a methodical engine for such applications. The proposed framework provides tools for comparative analysis and validation of results. Research confirmed results reliability and usefulness of the proposed framework in countries' assessment in compliance with SDG 7 targets.

Keywords: Clean energy systems · SDG 7 · Decision support systems · Multi-criteria assessment

1 Introduction

The fight against poverty, social inequalities, air pollution, and harmful climate change has been at the center of the sustainable development objectives of European policy for a long time. Human development and industrialization using conventional energy sources such as oil and coal contribute to polluting emissions into the atmosphere [8]. Developing affordable and clean energy systems contributes to reducing air pollution [16]. A combination of strategies focused on the development of modern and clean energy systems and the development of methods and frameworks to help supervise and measure sustainable energy systems in regions and countries could help identify regions in need of improvement in the development of clean energy systems, which in turn could improve air quality worldwide [8].

In order to encourage countries to undertake global efforts toward sustainable development, the United Nations (UN) adopted the 2030 Agenda for Sustainable Development in 2015. It provides a new policy framework supporting the evaluation of achieving 17 Sustainable Development Goals (SDGs) related to different aspects of sustainable development [5]. One of the seventeen goals of the 2030 Agenda is SDG 7, which covers targets related to providing access to modern energy services, enhancing energy efficiency, and increasing the share of renewable energy in energy consumption. Implementation of targets included in SDG 7 promotes accelerating the transition to affordable, reliable, clean, and sustainable energy systems and investment in clean energy technology [11].

Each SDG contains multiple indicators for monitoring sustainable development in given fields. In order to reliably evaluate countries in terms of the realization of targets of the 2030 Agenda, regular collection of performance data on indicators included in SDGs is necessary. Besides, there is a need for methods enabling appropriate aggregation of acquired results. This requirement is fulfilled by multi-criteria decision analysis (MCDA) methods that allow simultaneous consideration of multiple criteria, even conflicting ones [10].

MCDA methods, due to differences in assumptions and algorithms, can provide different outcomes, evident in differences in the resulting rankings of the regions or countries evaluated. It can confuse analysts and policymakers interested in the results of assessing the implementation of strategies toward sustainable energy systems. Therefore, performing a comparative analysis using several selected MCDA methods or their functions is advisable. Depending on the needs, such a procedure makes it possible to identify stable solutions that maintain high positions despite the change of methods and provides many solutions for further analysis by decision-makers.

This paper proposes a methodical framework based on MCDA methods to provide a methodical engine for engineering applications supporting the SDGs' realization assessment. The proposed framework consists of four MCDA methods: TOPSIS (Technique for Order of Preference by Similarity to Ideal Solution) [9], ARAS (Additive Ratio ASsessment) [7], CODAS (COmbinative Distance-based ASsessment) [1], and PROMETHEE II (Preference Ranking Organization Method for Enrichment and Evaluations II) [12]. These methods were chosen because of their popularity and the similarity of the assumptions considered when evaluating alternatives. A common feature of the first three methods, namely TOPSIS, ARAS, and CODAS, is that they measure the distance of evaluated alternatives from reference solutions. TOPSIS uses the Euclidean distance measurement of alternatives to the ideal and anti-ideal solution. CODAS, on the other hand, employs Euclidean distance as a primary and Taxicab as a secondary measure to measure the distance from an anti-ideal solution [1]. In ARAS, the utility of alternatives is calculated by comparing them to the ideal solution [7]. A reliable framework for multi-criteria assessment requires validation because different MCDA methods can give varying results due to different calculation techniques, for example, different normalization techniques. The validation is conducted using the reference model, enabling testing multiple cases [10]. The PROMETHEE II method, providing six different shapes of preference functions, was employed to validate and objectively compare the results received. PROMETHEE II was chosen as a validation method because of its properties considering the limitation of linear compensation of criteria and a quantified score for evaluating the alternatives relevant to sustainability assessment. PROMETHEE II is an outranking method. Therefore it is appropriate for assessing energy and environmental problems [12].

The rest of the paper is structured as follows. In Sect. 2 literature review is provided. Section 3 provides fundamentals and general assumptions of methods applied in this research. Section 4 illustrates the practical problem of multi-criteria evaluation of countries concerning SDG 7. Research results are presented and discussed in Sect. 5. Finally, the findings are summarized in Sect. 6, and future work directions are drawn.

2 Related Works

MCDA methods, due to differences in algorithms, can generate different results for the same problem. It implies that an essential step in multi-criteria evaluation is the validation of outcomes [4]. The importance and usefulness of validation are proven because the results obtained by single MCDA methods may lack sufficient accuracy and robustness [15]. For this purpose, recent literature suggests using additional methods to validate the results using objective consistency measures, such as correlation coefficients [4,7]. Other MCDA methods are often used as validation methods. Obtained results are compared with results generated by reference MCDA methods. For example, presented in [4], in a multi-criteria procedure for evaluating battery electric vehicles based on technical specifications, authors used methods such as SECA (Simultaneous Evaluation of Criteria and Alternatives), MARCOS (Measurement of Alternatives and Ranking according to COmpromise Solution), MAIRCA (Multi-Attributive Ideal-Real Comparative Analysis), COCOSO (COmbined COmpromise SOlution), ARAS (Additive Ratio ASsessment) and COPRAS (COmplex PRoportional ASsessment). For multi-criteria assessment of site location of solar-powered hydrogen production plants demonstrated in [15], authors of the paper compared rankings produced by WASPAS (Weighted Aggregated Sum Product Assessment), COPRAS, EDAS (Evaluation Based on Distance from Average Solution), and WSM (Weight Sum Model). In another research work presented in [7], material handling equipment was selected using two MCDA methods: ARAS and COPRAS. Obtained rankings were compared with six other MCDA methods: TOPSIS (Technique for Order of Preference by Similarity to Ideal Solution), SAW (Simple Additive Weighting), WPM (Weighted Product Model), WASPAS, MOORA (Multi-Objective Optimization on the basis of Ratio Analysis) and MULTIMOORA.

Considering the research work discussed, the authors created a framework supporting sustainability assessment considering SDG 7 targets, which consists of three MCDA methods: TOPSIS, ARAS, and CODAS, which makes it possible to compare the rankings provided by different methods based on measuring the distance from the reference solution. An additional contribution is adding the validation of the results using PROMETHEE II, which allows using six different preference functions with different indifference and strong preference threshold determinations, enriching the comparative analysis [12].

3   Methodology

This section provides the basics, assumptions, and mathematical formulas of MCDA methods employed in the framework supporting the sustainability assessment of SDG 7 introduced in this paper. Then, the procedure of assessment regarding the dataset and criteria is presented. The purpose of the presented framework is to provide a benchmarking environment for selected MCDA methods based on reference solutions, namely TOPSIS, ARAS, and CODAS. PROMETHEE II was chosen as the method for benchmarking because it provides six different preference functions, which provide opportunities to perform multiple comparisons of the obtained rankings using different methods. As a result, it is possible to check the reliability of the methods used in the study and select the method that gives the most convergent solution for the problem evaluated.

The TOPSIS Method. The TOPSIS method is presented based on [9].

Step 1. Normalize the decision matrix $X = [x_{ij}]_{m \times n}$ with m alternatives and n criteria, using chosen normalization technique. Normalized values are represented by r_{ij}.

Step 2. Calculate values of the weighted normalized decision matrix using Eq. (1), where w_j denotes criteria weights.

$$v_{ij} = w_j r_{ij} \tag{1}$$

Step 3. Determine the Positive Ideal Solution (PIS) v_j^+ and Negative Ideal Solution (NIS) v_j^- with Eq. (2). PIS is a vector with maximum v_{ij} values, while NIS contains its minimum values.

$$v_j^+ = \{v_1^+, v_2^+, \ldots, v_n^+\} = \{v_j^{max}\}, \ v_j^- = \{v_1^-, v_2^-, \ldots, v_n^-\} = \{v_j^{min}\} \tag{2}$$

Step 4. Calculate the distance from PIS D_i^+ and NIS D_i^- for each alternative as Eq. (3) shows.

$$D_i^+ = \sqrt{\sum_{j=1}^{n}(v_{ij} - v_j^+)^2}, \ D_i^- = \sqrt{\sum_{j=1}^{n}(v_{ij} - v_j^-)^2} \tag{3}$$

Step 5. Calculate the score for each alternative with Eq. (4). The best scored alternative has the highest C_i value.

$$C_i = \frac{D_i^-}{D_i^- + D_i^+} \tag{4}$$

The ARAS Method. The ARAS method is described based on [7].

Step 1. Normalize the decision matrix using chosen normalization method.

Step 2. Calculate the weighted normalized decision matrix applying Eq. (5), where w_j represents j-th criteria weights and r_{ij} are normalized values in decision matrix.

$$d_{ij} = r_{ij}w_j \tag{5}$$

Step 3. Calculate the optimality function S_i for each i-th alternative with Eq. (6).

$$S_i = \sum_{j=1}^n d_{ij} \tag{6}$$

Step 4. Calculate the utility value U_i for each i-th alternative according to Eq. (7), where S_o denotes the optimality function value for the optimal alternative. The best-ranked alternative has the highest U_i value.

$$U_i = S_i/S_o \tag{7}$$

The CODAS Method. The CODAS method is detailed based on [1].

Step 1. Normalize the decision matrix using chosen normalization method.

Step 2. Calculate the weighted normalized decision matrix as Eq. (8) shows, where w_j represents criteria weights and n_{ij} are normalized values in decision matrix.

$$r_{ij} = w_j n_{ij} \tag{8}$$

Step 3. Determine the anti-ideal solution according to Eq. (9).

$$ns_j = r_j^{min} \tag{9}$$

Step 4. Calculate the Euclidean E_i and Taxicab T_i distances from the anti-ideal solution for each evaluated alternative using formulas presented in Eq. (10), where N means size of sets.

$$E_i = \sqrt{\sum_{j=1}^N (r_{ij} - ns_j)^2}, \; T_i = \sum_{j=1}^N |r_{ij} - ns_j| \tag{10}$$

Step 5. Create the relative assessment matrix according to Eq. (11), where $k \in 1, 2, \ldots, m$ and ψ represents a threshold function to determine indifference between the Euclidean distances calculated for two alternatives by Eq. (12).

$$h_{ik} = (E_i - E_k) + (\psi(E_i - E_k) \times (T_i - T_k)), \tag{11}$$

$$\psi(x) = \begin{cases} 1 \ if \ |x| \geq \tau \\ 0 \ if \ |x| < \tau \end{cases} \tag{12}$$

τ represents the threshold parameter set by the decision-makers. The recommended value for this parameter ranges from 0.01 to 0.05. Thus, lower than τ difference between the Euclidean distances from the anti-ideal solution implies additional comparing of these alternatives with Taxicab distance.

Step 6. Calculate the preference value for each alternative using Eq. (13). The best scored alternative has the highest preference value.

$$H_i = \sum_{k=1}^{m} h_{ik} \tag{13}$$

The PROMETHEE II Method. The PROMETHEE II method is presented based on [12].

Step 1. Calculate the preference function value for each pair of considered alternatives in the decision matrix regarding evaluation criteria. The preference function is represented by Eq. (14)

$$P_j(a, b) = F_j[d_j(a, b)], \ \forall \ a, b \in A \tag{14}$$

where A represents the set of evaluated alternatives, $d(a, b)$ denotes the difference computed for pairwise comparison of two actions as presented in Eq. (15) for profit criteria B and cost criteria C.

$$d_j(a, b) = \begin{cases} g_j(a) - g_j(b) \ if \ j \in B \\ g_j(b) - q_j(a) \ if \ j \in C \end{cases} \tag{15}$$

PROMETHEE II provides six preference functions: Usual, U-shape, V-shape, Level, V-shape with indifference (Linear), and Gaussian. Depending on the type, the preference function requires providing some additional parameters. These parameters are p, q, or s, which are vectors with values for each criterion. The mathematical formulas for each preference function are detailed in [12]. In this research, the preference thresholds were determined based on the standard deviation σ_j of all performance values in the decision matrix for the j-th criterion. The indifference threshold was computed by $q = 0.5\sigma_j$ and the preference threshold by $p = 2\sigma_j$, as advised in [12]. The s value is determined as intermediate value based on p and q.

Step 2. Calculate the preference value between two alternatives a and b as Eq. (16) shows.

$$\begin{cases} \pi(a, b) = \sum_{j=1}^{n} P_j(a, b)w_j \\ \pi(b, a) = \sum_{j=1}^{n} P_j(b, a)w_j \end{cases} \tag{16}$$

where $P_j(a, b)$ is a concordance factor for two alternatives compared regarding j-th criterion with the chosen preference function, n denotes the criteria number, and w_j means the j-th criterion weight. a and b denote compared alternatives, and $\pi(a, b)$ expresses how much a is preferable to b in terms of all criteria. Each action is compared against $m - 1$ other actions in the set A. High values imply that decision-makers prefer this action more than another one.

Step 3. Calculate the positive Φ^+ and negative Φ^- outranking flows for each alternative using Eq. (17). The positive outranking flow demonstrates how much alternative a is preferable to other alternatives. The negative outranking flow shows how much other options are preferable over a.

$$\Phi^+(a) = \frac{1}{m-1} \sum_{i=1}^{m} \pi(a, b_i), \ \Phi^-(a) = \frac{1}{m-1} \sum_{i=1}^{m} \pi(b_i, a) \tag{17}$$

Step 4. Calculate the net flow Φ with Eq. (18). The alternative with the highest $\Phi(a)$ value is best scored.

$$\Phi(a) = \Phi^+(a) - \Phi^-(a) \tag{18}$$

4   MCDA Evaluation Regarding SDG 7 Targets

This research focuses on assessing 30 selected European countries towards affordable, reliable, and sustainable energy systems considering targets included in SDG 7. SDG 7 contains eleven targets, as displayed in Table 1.

Evaluated countries and data on their performance values regarding SDG 7 criteria assessment C_1–C_{11} are included in the decision matrix provided in Supplementary material on GitHub [3]. The data on SDG 7 for evaluated countries were collected from the Eurostat database for the recent available year 2020 [6]. The flowchart in Fig. 1 presents the methodology of subsequent stages of the proposed multi-criteria framework. Constructed decision matrix was normalized and evaluated by TOPSIS, ARAS, and CODAS methods. Since some negative criteria values appear in the decision matrix, Minimum-Maximum normalization was chosen as the normalization technique suitable for such cases [2]. Criteria weights were determined based on a decision matrix, using an objective weighting method called CRITIC (Criteria Importance Through Inter criteria Correlation) detailed in [13]. TOPSIS, ARAS, and CODAS rankings were then compared using the Weighted Spearman correlation coefficient represented by r_w. It is used to determine the convergence of compared rankings [14]. In order to benchmark and confirm the results' reliability, validation with PROMETHEE II was conducted. PROMETHEE II does not require normalization of the decision matrix and provides as many as six preference functions, making it suitable for validation purposes. In benchmarking, rankings were compared using Weighted Spearman correlation coefficient.

Table 1. Evaluation criteria incorporated in the framework based on SDG 7.

Criterion C_j	Criterion name	Unit	Aim
C_1	Primary energy consumption	Tonnes of oil equivalent (TOE) per capita	Max
C_2	Final energy consumption	Tonnes of oil equivalent (TOE) per capita	Max
C_3	Final energy consumption in households per capita	Kilogram of oil equivalent KGOE	Max
C_4	Energy productivity	Euro per kilogram of oil equivalent (KGOE)	Max
C_5	Share of RES in gross final energy consumption in general	[%]	Max
C_6	Share of RES in gross final energy consumption in transport	[%]	Max
C_7	Share of RES in gross final energy consumption in electricity	[%]	Max
C_8	Share of RES in gross final energy consumption in heating and cooling	[%]	Max
C_9	Energy import dependency regarding all types of energy products	[%]	Min
C_{10}	Population unable to keep home adequately warm	[%]	Min
C_{11}	Greenhouse gas emissions intensity of energy consumption	Index, 2000=100	Min

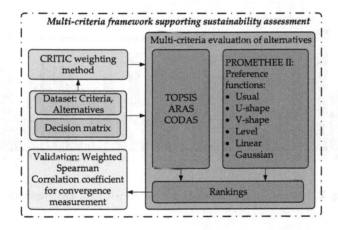

Fig. 1. A flowchart illustrating the methodology of the proposed approach.

5   Results and Discussion

This section provides the results of performed research. In the first stage, results of three selected MCDA methods based on reference solutions, including TOPSIS, ARAS, and CODAS, are provided and obtained rankings of evaluated countries concerning performances regarding criteria of SDG 7 are briefly discussed. Then correlations between TOPSIS, ARAS, and CODAS rankings are provided to examine rankings' consistency. In the next stage rankings provided by PROMETHEE II using different preference functions are compared using

r_w correlation coefficient. The last step of research includes benchmarking of TOPSIS, ARAS and CODAS rankings with rankings given by PROMETHEE II using different preference functions. Figure 2 displays rankings obtained for each evaluated country using TOPSIS, ARAS, and CODAS. Complete results, including preference values and ranks, are provided in the Supplementary material on GitHub [3].

The best scored countries are usually the most interesting for decision-makers. It can be noted that Iceland (IS) is the leader of each generated ranking. Norway achieved second place in all rankings (NO), and Sweden (SE) took third place. Among well-scored countries are also Denmark (DK) in fourth place, Finland (FI) in fifth place, and Austria (AT) in sixth place. On the other hand, the worst ranked countries are Bulgaria (BG), Cyprus (CY), and Lithuania (LT). The next step of the research was a comparative analysis of the MCDA methods used, conducted using the Weighted Spearman correlation coefficient. Correlation values between compared rankings are 0.9970 between CODAS and TOPSIS, 0.9716 between CODAS and ARAS, and 0.9658 between ARAS and TOPSIS. High correlation values close to 1 prove that consistency is high for all compared rankings. It evidences that obtained results are reliable because the change of the MCDA method does not cause significant changes in rankings.

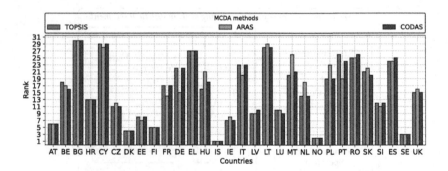

Fig. 2. Comparison of rankings generated with MCDA methods.

The final stage of the research was to validate the results obtained with the proposed framework using PROMETHEE II. For this purpose, the rankings of the assessed countries were determined using PROMETHEE II for its six different preference functions. The purpose of the validation was to verify the consistency of the rankings calculated by PROMETHEE II with each preference function with the rankings generated by the other MCDA methods included in the proposed framework. Validation with PROMETHEE II is objective because PROMETHEE II does not require normalization of the decision matrix, which could influence the results, and it provides six different preference functions allowing for a sufficient number of comparisons. The validation procedure used the same criteria weights as in the previous steps of the research, that is, those determined by CRITIC.

The first validation stage involves comparing rankings achieved with different preference functions of PROMETHEE II using correlation values of the r_w coefficient. High correlation values displayed in Fig. 3a prove high convergence between all PROMETHEE II rankings. It confirms that PROMETHEE II is a suitable method for validation because it gives stable results regardless of the applied preference function. V-shape and Level preference functions gave the most convergent rankings with the rest of the preference functions. The next validation step includes comparing TOPSIS, ARAS, and CODAS rankings with PROMETHEE II rankings. Comparative analysis of TOPSIS, ARAS, and CODAS rankings with reference PROMETHEE II rankings is displayed in Fig. 3b including r_w correlation values.

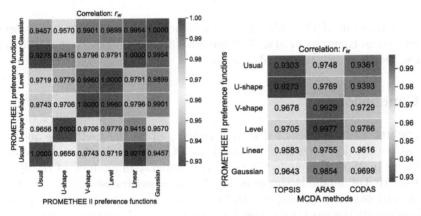

(a) Correlation of PROMETHEE II rankings.

(b) Correlation of PROMETHEE II and other MCDA rankings.

Fig. 3. Correlation of PROMETHEE II rankings.

Results confirm high consistency between rankings provided by TOPSIS, ARAS, and CODAS and rankings generated with PROMETHEE II using six preference functions. Preference functions giving the highest correlation with other compared rankings are V-shape and Level. ARAS showed the highest convergence with PROMETHEE II reference rankings. PROMETHEE II rankings are demonstrated in Fig. 4.

The best evaluated countries by most PROMETHEE II preference functions are the same as for TOPSIS, ARAS, and CODAS. The best ranked country in five of six PROMETHEE II preference functions is Iceland (IS). Using PROMETHEE II with four preference functions indicated Norway (NO) as the second country in the ranking, and five preference functions identified Sweden (SE) in the third rank. A comparative analysis of the MCDA methods incorporated in the proposed framework and validation with PROMETHEE II proved that the resulting rankings are reliable and make an important contribution to the assessment of European countries against the affordable and clean energy

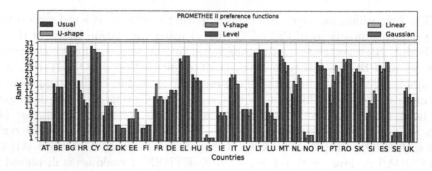

Fig. 4. Comparison of PROMETHEE II rankings.

targets included in SDG 7. The proposed framework demonstrated that among the best scored countries in SDG 7 frame are Nordic countries (Iceland, Norway, Sweden, Denmark, Finland) and Austria.

6 Conclusions

The research findings presented in this paper confirm the usefulness and reliability of the developed framework based on MCDA methods for evaluating the targets set by the UN included in SDG 7. Comparative analysis of results provided by MCDA methods employed in the proposed framework demonstrated high consistency of rankings, especially in the case of the top of the ranking, which is usually the most important for stakeholders. Validation performed with PROMETHEE II confirms the reliability of the achieved results. The main limitations of the research are related to the subjectivity of chosen MCDA methods, criteria weighting techniques, and normalization of the decision matrix.

Future work directions include applying other MCDA methods, weighting techniques to check their impact on results and research on other SDGs. Since the limitation of the study is the consideration of a single period (2020), further works will focus on methods that allow multi-criteria evaluation of sustainability problems with consideration of variability over time.

Acknowledgement. This research was partially funded by the National Science Centre 2022/45/B/HS4/02960 (J.W., A.B.).

References

1. Badi, I., Kridish, M.: Landfill site selection using a novel FUCOM-CODAS model: a case study in Libya. Sci. Afr. **9**, e00537 (2020). https://doi.org/10.1016/j.sciaf.2020.e00537
2. Bielinskas, V., Burinskienė, M., Podviezko, A.: Choice of abandoned territories conversion scenario according to MCDA methods. J. Civ. Eng. Manag. **24**(1), 79–92 (2018). https://doi.org/10.3846/jcem.2018.303

3. Bączkiewicz, A.: A Multi-Criteria Framework Supporting Sustainability Assessment Considering SDG 7 Targets (2023). https://github.com/energyinpython/SDG7-Sustainability-assessment

4. Ecer, F.: A consolidated MCDM framework for performance assessment of battery electric vehicles based on ranking strategies. Renew. Sustain. Energy Rev. **143**, 110916 (2021). https://doi.org/10.1016/j.rser.2021.110916

5. Elavarasan, R.M., Pugazhendhi, R., Irfan, M., Mihet-Popa, L., Campana, P.E., Khan, I.A.: A novel Sustainable Development Goal 7 composite index as the paradigm for energy sustainability assessment: a case study from Europe. Appl. Energy **307**, 118173 (2022). https://doi.org/10.1016/j.apenergy.2021.118173

6. Eurostat: Eurostat database (2022). https://ec.europa.eu/eurostat/data/database

7. Goswami, S.S., Behera, D.K.: Solving material handling equipment selection problems in an industry with the help of entropy integrated COPRAS and ARAS MCDM techniques. Process Integr. Optim. Sustain. 5(4), 947–973 (2021). https://doi.org/10.1007/s41660-021-00192-5

8. Jayachandran, M., et al.: Challenges in achieving sustainable development goal 7: affordable and clean energy in light of nascent technologies. Sustain. Energy Technol. Assess. **53**, 102692 (2022). https://doi.org/10.1016/j.seta.2022.102692

9. Liern, V., Pérez-Gladish, B.: Multiple criteria ranking method based on functional proximity index: un-weighted TOPSIS. Ann. Oper. Res. (4), 1–23 (2020). https://doi.org/10.1007/s10479-020-03718-1

10. Mousavi, M.M., Lin, J.: The application of PROMETHEE multi-criteria decision aid in financial decision making: case of distress prediction models evaluation. Expert Syst. Appl. **159**, 113438 (2020). https://doi.org/10.1016/j.eswa.2020.113438

11. Phillis, A., Grigoroudis, E., Kouikoglou, V.S.: Assessing national energy sustainability using multiple criteria decision analysis. Int. J. Sustain. Dev. World Ecol. **28**(1), 18–35 (2021). https://doi.org/10.1080/13504509.2020.1780646

12. Singh, A., Gupta, A., Mehra, A.: Best criteria selection based PROMETHEE II method. Opsearch **58**(1), 160–180 (2020). https://doi.org/10.1007/s12597-020-00464-7

13. Tuş, A., Aytaç Adalı, E.: The new combination with CRITIC and WASPAS methods for the time and attendance software selection problem. Opsearch **56**(2), 528–538 (2019). https://doi.org/10.1007/s12597-019-00371-6

14. Wątróbski, J., Bączkiewicz, A., Sałabun, W.: pyrepo-mcda-Reference objects based MCDA software package. SoftwareX **19**, 101107 (2022). https://doi.org/10.1016/j.softx.2022.101107

15. Xuan, H.A., Trinh, V.V., Techato, K., Phoungthong, K.: Use of hybrid MCDM methods for site location of solar-powered hydrogen production plants in Uzbekistan. Sustain. Energy Technol. Assess. **52**, 101979 (2022). https://doi.org/10.1016/j.seta.2022.101979

16. Zhao, Y., Tan, Y., Feng, S.: Does reducing air pollution improve the progress of sustainable development in China? J. Clean. Prod. **272**, 122759 (2020). https://doi.org/10.1016/j.jclepro.2020.122759

A Novel Software Tool for Fast Multiview Visualization of High-Dimensional Datasets

Luying Zhang[1], Hui Tian[2], and Hong Shen[3,4(✉)]

[1] School of Computer Science, Beijing Jiaotong University, Beijing, China
[2] School of Information and Communication Technology,
Griffith University, Gold Coast, Australia
[3] Faculty of Applied Sciences, Macao Polytechnic University, Macao, China
hshen@mpu.edu.mo
[4] School of Computer Science and Engineering,
Sun Yat-sen University, Guangzhou, China

Abstract. Scatterplot is a popular technique for visualizing high-dimensional datasets by using linear and nonlinear dimension reduction methods. These methods map the original high-dimensional dataset onto scatterplot points directly by dimension reduction, and hence require a high computation cost. Despite many improvements in scatterplot visual effects, however, when the data volume is large, the data mapped onto scatterplot data points will overlap, resulting a low quality of visualization. In this paper, we propose a novel software tool that ensembles five integrated components for fast multiview visualization of high-dimensional datasets: *sampling, dimension reduction, clustering, multiview collaborative analysis*, and *dimension re-arrangement*. In our tool, while the sampling component reduces the sizes of the datasets applying the random sampling technique to gain a high visualization efficiency, dimension reduction reduces the dimensions of the datasets applying principal-component analysis to improve the visualization quality. Next, clustering discovers hidden information in the reduced dataset applying fuzzy c-mean clustering to display hidden patterns of the original datasets. Finally, multiview collaborative analysis enables users to analyse multidimensional datasets from different aspects at the same time by combining scatterplot and scatterplot matrices. To optimize the visualization effects, in the scatterplot matrices, we re-arrange their dimensions and adjust the positions of scatterplots so that similar scatterplot points are adjacent in positions. As the result, in comparison with the existing visualization tools that apply some of these techniques, our tool not only improves the efficiency of dimension reduction but also enhances the quality of visualization and enables more comprehensive analysis. We test our tool on different real datasets to demonstrate its effectiveness. The experimental results validate that our method is effective in both efficiency and quality of visualization.

Keywords: Data sampling · dimension reduction · data clustering · multiview visualization · software tool

© The Author(s), under exclusive license to Springer Nature Switzerland AG 2023
N. T. Nguyen et al. (Eds.): ACIIDS 2023, CCIS 1863, pp. 303–316, 2023.
https://doi.org/10.1007/978-3-031-42430-4_25

1 Introduction

For massive volume of high dimensional data generated in various applications, particularly from big data analytics, data visualization is an effective way to display datasets and reveal the relationships among data for users to get useful hidden information. Among various visualization techniques available currently, scatterplot is one of the most popular visualization tool which maps high dimensional datasets into 2D or 3D space in either linear or nonlinear ways. To use this tool effectively, we must first reduce the dimensionality of the dataset by transforming datasets from the original high dimension to a low dimension. In recent years, many dimension reduction methods have been proposed to resolve the difficulties of the high dimensional data analysis and visualization.

Dimension reduction can be divided into linear and nonlinear methods. Linear methods use axes reduction methods, such as Principal component analysis (PCA) [28], to transfer datasets with the purpose of minimizing errors. This transform will produce a new coordinate system, such that the first large variance is in the first coordinate (known as the first principal component), second large variance is in second coordinate and so on, to retain almost all import information of the dataset. Nonlinear methods, such as Locally Linear Embedding (LLE) [23] and ISOMAP [15], can better maintain the original manifold structure by dimension reduction.

However, when the amount of high dimensional data is excessively large, visualization using data reduction methods will produce significant data overlap representing data points coincidence at the same coordinate. Besides, the time of data dimension reduction is also relatively long. Existing visual improvement methods did not address these issues sufficiently. Hence, in this paper, we propose a novel software tool for fast visualization of high dimensional datasets by combining dimension reduction and sampling techniques. The core idea of our method is to first apply random sampling technique to reduce the dataset size before proceeding with linear dimension reduction to reduce dataset dimensionality. By this method, we can get a desirable representation of the dataset that will enable us to have better results of visualization.

In addition, our visualization tool also ensembles a data clustering component deploying fuzzy c-mean clustering method [4,11] to help users perform data mining tasks and analyse the reduced data.

With the above functions of the tool, we can get an overall visualization to perform data analysis on the visualization from a single aspect, which can not meet the needs of many applications. Therefore, as another important improvement in our tool over the existing work, we integrate scatterplot with scatterplot matrices to provide multiview collaborative analysis that enables users to analyze datasets from different aspects.

Furthermore, in order to further optimize the effect of visualization, our tool applies a rearrangement algorithm in the scatterplot matrices to make the similar scatterplot points adjacent in positions.

The rest of the paper is organized as follows: in Sect. 2, we introduce the related work on high dimensional data visualization. Section 3 shows the proposed visualization method. The corresponding experimental results are given in Sect. 4. Section 5 concludes the paper with future work directions.

2   Related Work

In this section we will review the relevant work on data visualization. Most visualization methods apply dimension reduce and clustering to deal with high dimensional datasets and show the results in the scatterplot.

Dash et al. [9] proposed a method for analysing the high dimensional data by the combination of PCA and k-means clustering algorithm. In this method, the author first reduced dimension into 2D space using PCA. The results are then shown by scatterplot. Rajput et al. [22] realized high dimensional data analysis through feature selection and clustering algorithm. It used median absolute deviation which is an attribute extraction method to reduce attributes and it could transform the high dimensional datasets into low dimensional datasets. Musdholifah et al. [19] and Tajunisha et al. [25] also used dimension reduction and clustering algorithm to deal with high dimensional datasets. As visualization of high-dimensional datasets is particularly important for science and engineering applications, Probst et al. presented a web-portal enabled interactive visualization framework for biological datasets [20] and a visualization tool that displays chemi-biological datasets though construction of minimum spanning trees [21]. But in these methods, there is no pre-processing on the high dimensional datasets before realizing dimension reduction, which resulted in not only time wastage but also significant overlapping of data samples in the process of visualization. This motivates us to apply datasets sampling before performing dimension reduction.

Besides, most existing visualization methods are for single view visualization. Zhou et al. [30] proposed an improved visualization method based on Radviz. In this method, high dimensional datasets are mapped into a planar graph. Zheng et al. [29] used scatterplot matrices to visualize high dimensional datasets. In this method, they selected the meaningful scatterplots to be displayed and showed that the visualization results of scatterplot matrices are more effective and clearer. Tatu et al. [26] and Assent et al. [3] presented subspace clustering followed by scatterplots. Instead of applying dimension reduction to deal with high dimensional datasets, they directly used subspace clustering to handle the dataset and then displayed the results. But the time complexity of this method is excessively high and display is in a single aspect. Almir et al. [2] proposed a method to uncover the clustering in parallel coordinates visualization. It used density and frequency to deal with the high dimensional datasets to get the useful data samples. Zhou et al. [31] presented a labeled visualization method in parallel coordinates that enables users to easily get poly-line information. Recently, Wang et al. [27] carried out experimental studies on the effect of data size and pattern salience on visualization comprehension of scatterplot, Deng et al. [10] addressed the problem of causal analysis on urban time series datasets, Zhu et al. [33] proposed a multi-level visualization algorithm through embedding a high-dimensional KNN graph into a low-dimensional space. Although the above visualization methods have been improved, but they all display the results in one aspect and can not meet the needs for many applications.

At last, there are visualization methods that incorporate reordering algorithms to select the better dimension position. Ameur et al. [1] enhanced the parallel coordinates visualization by reordering dimensions to improve the visual results. Iton et al. [14] showed a hierarchical visualization method. Lu et al. [17] proposed a new non-linear dimension reordering method and showed that it not only could get a better visualization results and reduce the poly-lines, but also could reduce time complexity. Bin et al. [6] used dimension reordering algorithm in the Radial visualization to get a better display. Recently, to support structural visualization of high-dimensional datasets with complex topologies, Megill et al. [18] proposed visualization platform that is performant and scalable for high dimensional sparse matrices, Zhou et al. [32] presented an interactive tool for visual exploration supporting topological data analysis. Inspired by the these reordering methods, in our proposed visualization tool, we also ensemble a reordering component with scatterplot matrices visualization.

As shown above, though various improved visualization methods have been proposed recently, but they are unable to meet different needs simultaneously. To enhance the validity of visualization, we combine dimension reduction and sampling technique to preprocess high dimensional datasets. In order to get better visualization results, we use multiview collaborative analysis that integrates scatterplot with scatterplot matrices to display data samples in different aspects. At last, we apply a reordering algorithm to update the scatterplot matrices to improve the visualization effect by rearranging the similarity scatter plots to be adjacent.

3   Our Method

In this section, we present our high dimensional data visualization method which can yield better visualization results. Our method achieves visualization in six steps: sampling, principal component analysis, clustering, scatterplot generation, multiview analysis and reordering of dimensions. It is able to not only improve the efficiency of the reduction and visualization, but also provide more useful information for various analyses of the relationships among dimensions.

3.1   Sampling

Derived from statistics, sampling techniques have the advantages of saving time, saving space, high efficiency. They are widely used in scientific experiments, quality inspection, social investigation, data mining and so on. The goal of sampling is to use a small-size representative dataset to analyse and estimate characteristics of a mass volume of high dimensional data points. While sampling techniques have been widely used in various applications, they are seldom applied in the application of data visualization. In this paper, we apply sampling for data preprocessing to eliminate data overlap in the process of high dimensional data visualization when the amount of data points is large so as to obtain a better visualization effect. By applying sampling, high-dimensional datasets are reduced to improve the speed of visualization of large scale data and get a clear display. An appropriate sampling algorithm not only can maintain information integrity but also can improve efficiency of data visualization, enabling the result of data visualization clearer.

The most popular sampling technique is random sampling [16] that selects data at the equal probability. Its advantages are simple and convenient, we do not need to set assumptions and conditions on the process of random sampling. In our paper, we also use random sampling to select the high dimensional datasets which we want to reduce dimensions for visualization. Another sampling technique is systematic sampling [13], also called equal distance sampling, that samples data points at an equal distance. It has the advantage that when data points are uniformly distributed, the selected samples are less than the random sampling data. The third popular techniques a stratified sampling [5] that stratifies the data by dividing them into different layers and then randomly selects samples from different layers according to their size proportion. This technique provides sampling error is relatively small, however, it is so hard to realize it. It is also a commonly used sampling method. There are other sampling techniques such as repeated sampling [24], area sampling [12] and so on.

3.2   Principal Component Analysis

After the preprocessing of data sampling, we then carry out the dimension reduction in order to realize the scatterplot visualization of high dimensional datasets. In the real application, we can not directly analyse high dimensional data because we live in the 3D space, and are unable to have direct perception for objects beyond three dimensions. In order to handle and analyse high dimensional data, we apply a feature reduction method which is called Principal Component Analysis (PCA) [25]. It is a dimensional reduction method to transform high dimensional data set into a new low dimension space in order to extract key information from high dimensional data. The goal is to eliminate redundant information in high dimensional data, so as to simplify the analysis and visualize the data without much loss of data set information.

PCA is the process of forming PCs as a linear combinations of the measured variables as we have done with our other techniques. All variance is extracted and each variable is given equal weight. The first component is a linear combination of variables that maximizes component score variance for the cases. Second represents the factor that accounts for the most of what is left and so on until there is no left to account.

PCA not only can reduce the dimensionality of high-dimensional datasets, more importantly, but also can remove noise data and find a neat data structure model. In this paper, we apply PCA to transform the original high-dimension datasets to new low-dimension datasets that are uncorrelated with each principal component before applying clustering and visualization algorithms. As most principal components can reflect the original variables, PCA represents the new dataset (Y_i) as linear combinations of the original variables (X_i) given by the following model:

$$Y_1 = t_{11}X_1 + t_{12}X_2 + \cdots + t_{1p}X_p = T_1'X$$
$$Y_2 = t_{21}X_1 + t_{22}X_2 + \cdots + t_{2p}X_p = T_2'X$$
$$\cdots \cdots$$
$$Y_p = t_{p1}X_1 + t_{p2}X_2 + \cdots + t_{pp}X_p = T_p'X$$

which is equivalent to:

$$\begin{bmatrix} Y_1 \\ Y_2 \\ \vdots \\ Y_p \end{bmatrix} = \begin{bmatrix} t_{11} & t_{12} & \cdots & t_{1p} \\ t_{21} & t_{22} & \cdots & t_{2p} \\ \vdots & \vdots & \vdots & \vdots \\ t_{p1} & t_{p2} & \cdots & t_{pp} \end{bmatrix} \begin{bmatrix} X_1 \\ X_2 \\ \vdots \\ X_p \end{bmatrix}$$

In the above model, each component of Y is unrelated to others and the variance of the first component is the largest.

If we want to use PCA to reduce the dimensionality of high-dimensional datasets, we must calculate the covariance matrix of the sample matrix. The covariance between vector X and vector Y is defined as:

$$cov(X,Y) = \frac{\sum_{j=1}^{n}(X_j - \bar{X})(Y_j - \bar{Y})}{n-1} \tag{1}$$

When the sample is n-dimensional data, their covariance is the covariance matrix.

$$C = \begin{bmatrix} c_{11} & c_{12} & \cdots & c_{1n} \\ c_{21} & c_{22} & \cdots & c_{2n} \\ \vdots & \vdots & \vdots & \vdots \\ c_{m1} & c_{m2} & \cdots & c_{mn} \end{bmatrix}$$

where c_{ij} is the covariance between X_i and X_j.

Principal component analysis is the simplest and most commonly used linear process which transforms high dimensional data sets into the new reduced and low dimensional data sets. It can make visualization of high-dimension datasets to proceed more effectively and produce a clearer results.

3.3   Clustering

The third component of our visualization software tool applies data mining technique on the reduced datasets in both size and dimensionality by sampling and PCA in order to reveal the hidden and useful information in the high dimensional data. We use the Fuzzy c-means (FCM) clustering algorithm originally proposed in [11] and improved in [4] for this purpose. As a popular clustering algorithm in data mining field, FCM is an unsupervised machine learning method for clustering analysis of static datasets and divides the datasets into clusters based on their similarity in such a way that data objects are similar within the same cluster and dissimilar across different clusters.

Fuzzy c-means clustering algorithm works on the datasets by repeatedly partitioning the datasets toward the goal of minimizing the following formula:

$$J_m = \sum_{i=1}^{N} \sum_{j=1}^{C} u_{ij}^m \left\| x - c_j \right\|^2 \tag{2}$$

where m is any real number greater than 1, u_{ij} is the degree of membership of x_i in the cluster j, c_j is the center of the cluster.

As an improvement of the traditional K-means clustering algorithm, in each iteration of partitioning FCM clustering updates the value of u_{ij} and c_j in (2) by the following formulae:

$$u_{ij} = \frac{1}{\sum_{k=1}^{C} \left(\frac{\left\| x_i - c_j \right\|}{\left\| x_i - c_k \right\|} \right)^{\frac{2}{m-1}}} \tag{3}$$

$$c_j = \frac{\sum_{i=1}^{N} u_{ij}^m x_i}{\sum_{i=1}^{N} u_{ij}^m} \tag{4}$$

The framework of the FCM clustering algorithm can be described as:

(1) Initializing the matrix U which determine the degree of membership;
(2) Calculating the initial centroid of this clustering algorithm;
(3) Iterating until the objective function converges to the minimum;
(4) Updating the value of u_{ij} and c_j.

3.4   Scatterplot Generation

A scatterplot contains the data points in the rectangular coordinate system on the plane distribution map. In the two-dimension or three-dimension space to show the dataset, we generally use scatterplot visualization [8]. As a useful technology for showing data association, scatterplot is a widely used visualization tool. Hence, after we have reduced the high dimensional datasets into the 3D space by dimension reduction and clustering, we apply scatterplot visualization to see the results of our analysis.

In the scatterplot generation, the locations of the data are collected as a representation of the values of the corresponding dimension. Such simple single scatterplot can give a general presentation, so the data can only be analyzed in general. But the disadvantage of this visualization method is that when the data collected is too large, in the process of drawing, the data points will coincide, resulting in data points overlap and displayed unclearly. In our tool, we use sampling to preprocess datasets in order to get better visualization results. In Fig. 1, we show a simple scatterplot visualization example.

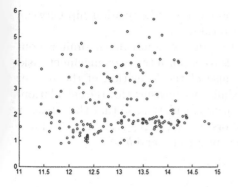

Fig. 1. Scatterplot visualization

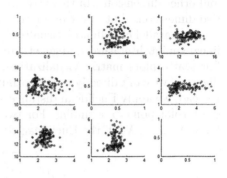

Fig. 2. Scatterplot matrices

3.5 Multiview Collaborative Analysis

In the above simple scatterplot visualization example, we can not obtain the relationship among data points across different dimensions. Hence, we ensemble a multiview collaborative analysis component into our tool to support analysis of the high dimensional datasets through their visualized data samples. We achieve this by integrating scatterplot visualization and scatterplot matrix visualization simultaneously to enable visualization of both the overall information about the high dimensional datasets and their relationships across different dimensions. This allows users to have a better understanding of these high dimensional datasets.

Scatterplot matrices [7] have been widely used in visualization of high dimensional data. A scatter matrix represents the relationship between each pair of dimensions in visualization. As an extension of scatterplot visualization, scatterplot matrix visualization is composed of scatterplots and can overcome the difficulty of displaying high dimensional data on the plane to a certain extent. The advantage of scatterplot matrix visualization is clear, simple and easy to look at all pairwise correlations in the same window.

An example of scatterplot matrices is given in Fig. 2, where the scatterplots on the diagonal are blank. Using this component we can clearly see the relationship of high dimensional datasets between any two dimensions.

3.6 Reordering of Dimensions

As the final tuning to our visualization tool, we optimize the design process of the scatterplot matrix visualization. Although our tool can produce a good visual effect with the above components, there is still a room for improvement. In our tool we improve the generation of scatterplot matrices based on the idea of the rearrangement of axis, which makes the similar scatterplots to be adjacent in the display. The main step of this approach is the rearrangement of the dimensions in each row, and the relationships between the current dimension and other dimensions. In this way, we not only can see the relationship between two dimensions, but also can analyze the overall effect.

For parallel coordinates visualization literature, we apply linear similar, nonlinear similar literature, and genetic methods to perform the rearrangement task. For scatterplots matrix visualization, because of the formation of the scatter diagram, we can't directly use the original similarity measures for the calculation. Instead, we apply Euclidean distance similarity calculation, so that the adjacent scatterplot points are similar. For two vectors $a = (X_{11}, X_{12}, \ldots, X_{1n})$ and $b = (X_{21}, X_{22}, \ldots, X_{2n})$, the Euclidean distance between a and b is:

$$d = \sqrt{\sum_{i=1}^{n}(x_{1i} - x_{2i})^2} \tag{5}$$

The above are the main components that have been assembled into our proposed visualization tool. In next section, we will conduct experiments to verify the effectiveness of our tool.

4   Experimental Results

To illustrate the effectiveness of our proposed visualization tool, we implement it and test its performance on the datasets available in UCI machine learning repository. The experimental results are shown in the following tables and figures. The goal of our proposed tool is to obtain a clearer and more intuitive understanding of the high dimensional data through visualization.

We illustrate the effectiveness of our proposed visualization tool from several aspects. At first, we use time characteristics to verify the efficiency of visualization. Then we use the effect diagram to illustrate the intuitive nature of our approach. The experiment results are shown below.

In our tool, we first use sampling to select a small set of data samples of high dimensional datasets. Then we use dimension reduction to process the selected data samples. In order to demonstrate the efficiency of our sampling technique, we reduce the original datasets and sample datasets separately. As shown in Table 1, the time to realize dimension reduction on the sampled datasets is significantly less than on the original datasets.

Table 1. Results of reduction time

Dataset	Original datasets	Sampled datasets
	Reduction time	Reduction time
CMC	0.001513	0.000984
Liver	0.000884	0.000488

Next, we apply fuzzy-c mean clustering algorithm to process the reduced datasets and display them in the 3D space using scatterplot visualization. Table 2

Table 2. Results of clustering time

Dataset	Original datasets	Sampled datasets
	Clustering time	Clustering time
CMC	0.083611	0.044445
Liver	0.031941	0.028088

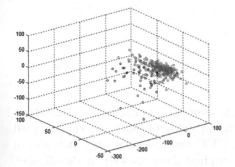

Fig. 3. Liver scatterplot visualization

Fig. 4. CMC scatterplot visualization

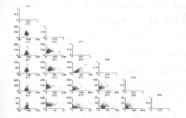

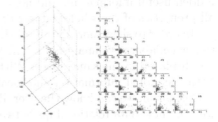

Fig. 5. Multiview visualization

shows the execution time of clustering from which we can see that the clustering time is significantly shorter on the sampled datasets than on the original datasets. The above experiment results have validated the effectiveness of the sampling component in our tool for processing high dimensional datasets.

We now demonstrate the effectiveness of our clustering component by showing the results of applying scatterplot visualization on the sampled dataset clusters and original dataset clusters. Table 3 shows the execution time comparison

Table 3. Results of visualization time

Dataset	Original datasets	Sampled datasets
	Visualization time	Visualization time
CMC	5.374819	3.265279
Liver	0.787527	0.709133

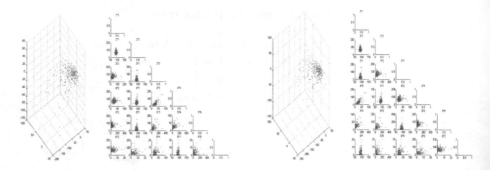

Fig. 6. Reordering visualization   **Fig. 7.** Matrix reordering

of visualization. Figure 3 and Fig. 4 shows the comparison of clarity and intuitiveness of scatterplot visualization on the original datasets (left) and the sampled visualization (right) after clustering using CMC and Liver datasets. It is shown that the sampled datasets represent the original datasets well in the display. In our experiments, we select 90 percent data samples to be displayed, these figures show that we can still clearly see data clustering information and other hidden useful information, and hence illustrate that our sampled data preserve all properties of the whole dataset of the original high dimensions.

In order to show more details of the high dimensional data, we conduct a multiview collaborative analysis, in which the scatterplots and scatterplot matrices are displayed in the same space. With this component in our tool, we can know both the global information and local information of the dataset. In the global visualization, we can know the overall clustering information. In the local views, we can know data relationships between any two dimensions. Figure 5 shows the experiment results. The left side represents the scatterplots matrix visualization of liver dataset which provides the local information. The multiview visualization is displayed on the right side. The advantage of our multiview visualization can be easily seen by comparing these figures on the two sides.

Next, we improve the results of multiview collaborative visualization by rearranging the scatterplot matrices for parallel coordinates visualization. We achieve this in two steps:

First, we fix one dimension which represents the current number of rows, and calculate the correlation between the other correlation dimensions. Figure 6 shows the results of the experiment in which we calculate the relationships between the fifth dimension and other dimensions and rearrange them according to decreasing order of their correlations, i.e., 2, 1, 3, 4.

Then we calculate the similarity between scatterplot matrices. Following the sequence of dimensions produced in the first step, we can calculate the similarity between each other dimension and the current dimension in the similarity decreasing order. Our experimental results as shown in Fig. 7.

The above experiments demonstrate the advantages of our proposed visualization tool which can be summarised in four aspects: First, we improve the efficiency by sampling technology to enhance the visual effect. Secondly, we apply data mining to enhance the user's awareness. Thirdly, we apply multiview collaborative visualization to enable multi-aspect data analysis. At last, we apply dimension rearrangement to display the relationships between dimensions and scatterplot matrices.

5   Conclusion

In this paper, we introduced a novel software tool for visualizing high-dimensional data by combing sampling technique with dimension reduction. Our tool also ensembles the techniques of clustering, multiview collaborative analysis and re-arrangement of dimensions in the scatterplot matrices, to maximizes its visualization effectiveness. In comparison with the existing visualization tools that apply some of these techniques, but not all, the proposed tool not only improves the efficiency and quality of visualization of high-dimensional datasets, but also enables a greater variety of data analysis tasks.

In the future, we intend to add interactive techniques to enhance the interactions between the user and the visual graph. Besides, we will also incorporate more data mining and rearrangement functions into the tool to optimize our visualization results.

Acknowledgement. This work is supported by Macao Polytechnic University Research Grant RP/FCA-13/2022. The corresponding author is Hong Shen.

References

1. Ameur, K., Benblidia, N., Oukid-Khouas, S.: Enhanced visual clustering by reordering of dimensions in parallel coordinates. In: 2013 International Conference on IT Convergence and Security (ICITCS), pp. 1–4. IEEE (2013)
2. Artero, A.O., de Oliveira, M.C.F., Levkowitz, H.: Uncovering clusters in crowded parallel coordinates visualizations. In: INFOVIS 2004. IEEE Symposium on Information Visualization 2004, pp. 81–88. IEEE (2004)
3. Assent, I., Krieger, R., Müller, E., Seidl, T.: VISA: visual subspace clustering analysis. ACM SIGKDD Explor. Newsl. **9**(2), 5–12 (2007)
4. Bezdek, J.C.: Models for pattern recognition. In: Bezdek, J.C. (ed.) Pattern Recognition with Fuzzy Objective Function Algorithms, pp. 1–13. Springer, Boston (1981). https://doi.org/10.1007/978-1-4757-0450-1_1
5. Bickel, P.J., Freedman, D.A.: Asymptotic normality and the bootstrap in stratified sampling. Ann. Stat. **12**(2), 470–482 (1984)
6. Binh, H.T.T., Van Long, T., Hoai, N.X., Anh, N.D., Truong, P.M.: Reordering dimensions for radial visualization of multidimensional data-a genetic algorithms approach. In: 2014 IEEE Congress on Evolutionary Computation (CEC), pp. 951–958. IEEE (2014)
7. Carr, D.B., Littlefield, R.J., Nicholson, W.L., Littlefield, J.S.: Scatterplot matrix techniques for large N. J. Am. Stat. Assoc. **82**(398), 424–436 (1987)
8. Chambers, J.M.: Graphical Methods for Data Analysis (1983)

9. Dash, B., Mishra, D., Rath, A., Acharya, M.: A hybridized K-means clustering approach for high dimensional dataset. Int. J. Eng. Sci. Technol. **2**(2), 59–66 (2010)
10. Deng, Z., et al.: Compass: towards better causal analysis of urban time series. IEEE Trans. Vis. Comput. Graph. **28**(1), 1051–1061 (2022)
11. Dunn, J.C.: A fuzzy relative of the ISODATA process and its use in detecting compact well-separated clusters. J. Cybern. **3**(3), 32–57 (1973)
12. Errington, J.R., Kofke, D.A.: Calculation of surface tension via area sampling. J. Chem. Phys. **127**(17), 174709 (2007)
13. Gundersen, H.J.G., Jensen, E.B.V., Kieu, K., Nielsen, J.: The efficiency of systematic sampling in stereology-reconsidered. J. Microsc. **193**(3), 199–211 (1999)
14. Itoh, T., Takakura, H., Sawada, A., Koyamada, K.: Hierarchical visualization of network intrusion detection data. IEEE Comput. Graph. Appl. **26**(2), 40–47 (2006)
15. Law, M.H.C., Zhang, N., Jain, A.K.: Nonlinear manifold learning for data stream. In: SDM, pp. 33–44. SIAM (2004)
16. Liu, H., Sadygov, R.G., Yates, J.R.: A model for random sampling and estimation of relative protein abundance in shotgun proteomics. Anal. Chem. **76**(14), 4193–4201 (2004)
17. Lu, L.F., Huang, M.L., Huang, T.-H.: A new axes re-ordering method in parallel coordinates visualization. In: 2012 11th International Conference on Machine Learning and Applications (ICMLA), vol. 2, pp. 252–257. IEEE (2012)
18. Megill, C., et al.: Cellxgene: a performant, scalable exploration platform for high dimensional sparse matrices. bioRxiv (2021)
19. Musdholifah, A., Hashim, S.Z.M., Ngah, R.: Hybrid PCA-ILGC clustering approach for high dimensional data. In: 2012 IEEE International Conference on Systems, Man, and Cybernetics (SMC), pp. 420–424 (2012)
20. Probst, D., Reymond, J.-L.: FUn: a framework for interactive visualizations of large, high-dimensional datasets on the web. Bioinformatics **34**(8), 1433–1435 (2017)
21. Probst, D., Reymond, J.-L.: Visualization of very large high-dimensional data sets as minimum spanning trees. J. Cheminformatics **12**(1), 1–13 (2020). https://doi.org/10.1186/s13321-020-0416-x
22. Rajput, D.S., Singh, P.K., Bhattacharya, M.: Feature selection with efficient initialization of clusters centers for high dimensional data clustering. In: 2011 International Conference on Communication Systems and Network Technologies (CSNT), pp. 293–297 (2011)
23. Roweis, S.T., Saul, L.K.: Nonlinear dimensionality reduction by locally linear embedding. Science **290**(5500), 2323–2326 (2000)
24. Soivio, A., Nynolm, K., Westman, K.: A technique for repeated sampling of the blood of individual resting fish. J. Exp. Biol. **63**(1), 207–217 (1975)
25. Tajunisha, N., Saravanan, V.: An increased performance of clustering high dimensional data using Principal Component Analysis. In: 2010 First International Conference on Integrated Intelligent Computing (ICIIC), pp. 17–21 (2010)
26. Tatu, A., et al.: Subspace search and visualization to make sense of alternative clusterings in high-dimensional data. In: 2012 IEEE Conference on Visual Analytics Science and Technology (VAST), pp. 63–72. IEEE (2012)
27. Wang, J., Cai, X., Jiajie, S., Liao, Yu., Yingcai, W.: What makes a scatterplot hard to comprehend: data size and pattern salience matter. J. Vis. **25**(1), 59–75 (2022). https://doi.org/10.1007/s12650-021-00778-8
28. Wold, S., Esbensen, K., Geladi, P.: Principal component analysis. Chemom. Intell. Lab. Syst. **2**(1), 37–52 (1987)

29. Zheng, Y., Suematsu, H., Itoh, T., Fujimaki, R., Morinaga, S., Kawahara, Y.: Scatterplot layout for high-dimensional data visualization. J. Vis. **18**(1), 111–119 (2015). https://doi.org/10.1007/s12650-014-0230-5

30. Zhou, F., Huang, W., Li, J., Huang, Y., Shi, Y., Zhao, Y.: Extending dimensions in Radviz based on mean shift. In: 2015 IEEE Pacific Visualization Symposium (PacificVis), pp. 111–115. IEEE (2015)

31. Zhou, H., Xu, P., Ming, Z., Qu, H.: Parallel coordinates with data labels. In: Proceedings of the 7th International Symposium on Visual Information Communication and Interaction, p. 49. ACM (2014)

32. Zhou, Y., Chalapathi, N., Rathore, A., Zhao, Y., Wang, B.: Mapper interactive: a scalable, extendable, and interactive toolbox for the visual exploration of high-dimensional data. In: 2021 IEEE 14th Pacific Visualization Symposium (PacificVis), pp. 101–110 (2021)

33. Zhu, H., et al.: Visualizing large-scale high-dimensional data via hierarchical embedding of KNN graphs. Vis. Inform. **5**(2), 51–59 (2021)

A Distilled 2D CNN-LSTM Framework with Temporal Attention Mechanism for Action Recognition

Shi-Jie Zhu, Cheng-Rong Lin, Wei-Ting Lin, and Ju-Chin Chen[✉]

Department of Computer Science and Information Engineering, National Kaohsiung University of Science and Technology, Kaohsiung, Republic of China
jc.chen@nkust.edu.tw

Abstract. Action Recognition has been studied for many years. In recent years, there are some methods using 3D-CNN (C3D, I3D, R2 + 1D), which have high accuracy, but it is hard to train and quite time-consuming due to the network architecture of extracting spatial–temporal features and the huge action dataset. Since 2D-CNN has a pre-trained model with high accuracy and speed in object recognition, there is also a method of fine-tune it on Recurrent neural network (RNN), Long Short-Term Memory (LSTM) network and other network that can extract temporal features, but due to the poor performance of fine-tune, although the speed is increased, the accuracy has dropped significantly. Therefore, this research wants to use the high accuracy of 3D-CNN to distill 2D-CNN produce a great pre-trained model for action recognition and combine it with Attention Mechanism LSTM to make model on fine-tune on other action dataset can accelerate and achieve the accuracy of approximating 3D-CNN.

Keywords: Action Recognition · Distilled Framework · LSTM

1 Introduction

Action videos will be converted into continuous pictures as training materials. Spatial factors in the pictures, such as resolution, brightness, characters, angles, distances, etc., will have a preliminary impact on the classification accuracy. Another important factor is the picture the order of time, good spatial features need to be matched with corresponding timing features, in order to distinguish the difference of actions. As can be seen in object classification, the diversity and amount of good category data will affect the accuracy, and the same is true for action classification, but the amount of data required will be several times that of object recognition, which will inevitably lengthen the training time. In order to develop in a usable direction in the future, it is still necessary to find a good balance between accuracy and speed.

This study proposes a method that uses 3D-CNN to motivate 2D-CNN to produce action category pre-training models and supplements the long-short-term memory network of attention mechanism to obtain temporal features for action recognition, so that

N. T. Nguyen et al. (Eds.): ACIIDS 2023, CCIS 1863, pp. 317–324, 2023.
https://doi.org/10.1007/978-3-031-42430-4_26

it can be applied to new actions Data set, by readjusting the network weight (fine-tune) to achieve the accuracy close to 3D-CNN, and because it is not necessary to use all the data sets to retrain the network, the performance of network training is improved.

2 Related Work

The purpose of Action Recognition is to input an action segment and determine the category of the action. This topic has been studied for more than 20 years. In recent years, many deep learning models have also been applied to behavior recognition problems. The mainstream network architecture can be divided into the following three types.

2.1 2D-CNN + LSTM Model

In view of the fact that the 2D-CNN model provides extremely high accuracy in image object recognition, there have been studies in the past [1–4] trying to apply the well-trained model to the Action Recognition problem. Just like training a 2D-CNN network, after extracting the features of each picture, the recognition result of the action of the picture is obtained, and finally the recognition results of each picture are fused to obtain the result of the action classification of the video clip. Compared with the 3D-CNN model, the advantage of this architecture is that the overall training time and implementation are faster. However, its disadvantage is that it ignores the temporal structure characteristics of the film and cannot distinguish the sequence of actions.

Later, some scholars proposed to add a recurrent layer (ex. RNN, LSTM [5]) behind the 2D-CNN to extract the structural features of time series. This is helpful for learning the timing of actions, but this architecture cannot extract shallow networks. The behavioral characteristics of the network will increase the training time of the network.

2.2 3D-CNN Model

In order to obtain more accurate spatio-temporal features, some scholars have studied how to use spatio-temporal filters to apply to the traditional 2D-CNN architecture [6–9]. The 3D-CNN [7] architecture proposed by Ji et al., compared with the traditional 2D-CNN, requires an extremely large amount of parameters for training, which is difficult to train and takes a long time. In addition, because of the difference in kernel size, the imagenet pre-trained model is lost, so it must be retrained from scratch. Later, Tran et al. [7] proposed a new model C3D with general simplicity and improved computational efficiency. Carreira et al. [6] proposed a two-stream model I3D that uses ImageNet's well-trained and trained model and uses 3D-CNN to extract spatio-temporal features, and finally uses optical flow to improve network performance. Among the above-mentioned 3D-CNN-based literature, I3D is the leader, and its ultra-high accuracy has set a benchmark in the field of behavioral tasks. However, there is still no improvement in the training time, and I3D has made the training time longer in pursuit of accuracy. Afterwards, R2 + 1D [9] proposed by Tran et al., the author of C3D, can disassemble 3D-CNN and optimize them separately. Purely improving the network problem will bring the accuracy rate close to I3D.

2.3 Two-Streams-Networks

Simonyan et al. [10] proposed to use a single RGB-frame and ten Multi-Optical-frames obtained through external calculations to obtain spatial and spatio-temporal features through two 2D-CNNs respectively, and finally to the two networks The classification scores are fused to obtain the final video clip classification results. The experimental results also prove that the Two-Streams method does obtain spatio-temporal features, the accuracy is much higher than that of pure 2D-CNN, and it is easier to train than 3D-CNN.

Afterwards, many scholars have improved the dual-stream network architecture. For example, Feichtenhofer et al. [11] proposed to improve the fusion of the final spatiotemporal features to the middle layer of the network. Their experiments have proved that the accuracy of early fusion is higher. Wang et al. [12] proposed an improved Two-Stream input, network structure and training strategy, and proposed the Temporal-Segment-Networks Model (TSN), which provides a good idea for the network model.

I3D author Carreira et al. [6] also improved the Two-Stream Network architecture, adding a time dimension to the 2D-Inception-module of Inception-v1 and expanding it into a 3D-Inception-module to replace the 2D-CNN in Two-Streams, Calling this architecture Two-Stream Inflated 3D ConvNets, experiments have confirmed that this architecture will perform better than 2D-CNN's Two-Streams when the data set is larger.

3 Temporal-Attention LSTM Framework

Figure 1 shows the Temporal-Attention LSTM Framework proposed in this study. The system input is continuous motion images. Through the Distilled 2D-CNN model, the feature map before the fc layer is used as the image feature matrix. There are three layers of LSTM, and the inputs of each layer are 512 dimensions, the hidden layer is 256 dimensions. The hidden layer information (layer 3) output by the third layer LSTM will be multiplied with the current output, and then passed through SoftMax Get the attention-weight and then multiply it with the current LSTM outputs matrix for weighting, and then pull the result to the next stage of LSTM Hidden State (C + 1). Through LSTM learning, Attention will also follow the auxiliary learning. In the last LSTM After the stage output passes through two layers of fc, the action prediction result will be output, and after iterative training, a pretrained model with the ability to deal with action timing problems will be produced.

3.1 2D-CNN

The part of 2D-CNN uses Resnet proposed by He et al. [13]. In order to align the parameters with the output matrix of R2 + 1D-resnet18. ResNet-18 is selected, where the feature matrix output by each layer of Convolution W and H are the width and height of the input image respectively. Conv1 to Conv5_x are composed of Res Block with residual learning mechanism plus fc layer for classification with a total of 18 layers.

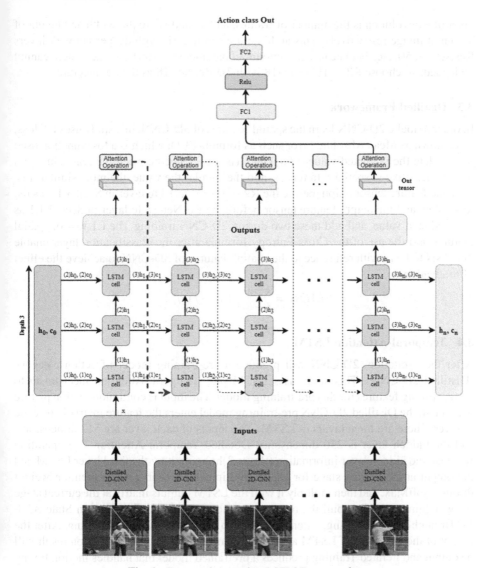

Fig. 1. Temporal-Attention LSTM Framework

3.2 3D-CNN

This study uses R2 + 1D [9]. R2 + 1D disassembles the time and space of traditional 3D Convolution and calculates it, making it approach the best I3D [6] on the data set used in this study. The time taken is almost half of that of I3D. The R2 + 1D implementation uses the 3D ResNet architecture, which changes the original 3D Convolution with a kernel size of $3 \times 7 \times 7$, and splits it into a $7 \times 7 \times 1$ kernel size first. Spatial Convolution, then do Temporal Convolution with a kernel size of $1 \times 1 \times 3$, and optimize them separately. The input is L RGB frames to represent a clip. Therefore, L in the Output size of each layer of Convolution is the number of frames, and W and H are the width and height of the input image respectively. This architecture can use 3D with deeper network layers ResNet-34, 50, etc., but because the amount of parameters is too high, the system cannot be loaded, so choose R2 + 1D-resnet18 with 3D ResNet-18 as the architecture.

3.3 Distilled Framework

In order to make 2D-CNN learn the spatial features of 3D-CNN, this study uses L1-loss, also known as Mean Absolute Error such as formula (3.1), which is a loss function used to calculate the predicted value ($f(x_i)$) and The difference between the real values (y_i) is more sensitive to spatial differences, and the smaller the value, the more similar it is. Take the feature tensor output before the R2 + 1D-resnet18 fc layer in Sect. 3.1.2 as the real value, and the output feature tensor before the ResNet-18 fc layer in Sect. 3.1.1 as the predicted value, and add these two during 2D-CNN training The L1-loss of spatial features and the use of the Cross-Entropy formula after the classification layer enable 2D-CNN to learn with reference to the spatial features of 3D-CNN to achieve the effect of motivation.

$$L1loss = \sum\nolimits_{i=1}^{n} \mid y_i - f(x_i) \mid$$

3.4 Temporal-Attention LSTM

After the excitation, 2D-CNN will produce a pre-training model of action category (Distilled 2D-CNN). This study uses LSTM plus Temporal-Attention mechanism to extract timing features for this pre-training model. The input is continuous action picture data. First, the Distilled 2D-CNN pre-training model enters the feature matrix before the fc layer. There are three layers of LSTM. The inputs of each layer are 512 dimensions, and the hidden layer is 256 dimensions. Detailed Temporal Attention The operation will take the hidden layer information ((layer 3)hn) output by the third layer LSTM and the output at the current stage for matrix multiplication, then get the attention-weight through SoftMax, and then multiply it with the LSTM outputs matrix at the current stage for weighting, and then pull the result to the next stage of LSTM Hidden State (C + 1). Through LSTM learning, Attention will also follow the auxiliary learning. After the output of the last stage of LSTM after two layers of fc, the action prediction result will be output and iterated Training produces a pretrained model that handles motion timing issues.

4 Experimental Results

In order to ensure the maximum performance of the equipment and the stability of the training, the operating system of this research uses the Ubuntu 16.04 system of Debian base. The overall model network architecture is implemented using Python and its open source deep learning library Pytorch. The version of Python is 3.6.13, and the version of Pytorch is 1.8.1. The hardware device uses a CPU of i7-7700 4 cores and 8 threads with a frequency of 3.6G Hz, a RAM of DDR4 2400 MHz 16 GB, a GPU of NVIDIA GeForece 1080 Ti with 12G DDR5x VRAM and 3584 CUDA units to achieve multi-core CPU and Pytorch calls GPU (CUDA10.0) to accelerate model calculation speed.

4.1 Data Set

There are two data sets used in this research experiment, UCF101 [14] used to generate 2D-Distilled-model, and HMDB51 [15] used to finetune test the performance of the pretrained model produced. HMDB51 has a total of 51 Various action categories. The quality of each video is also 320p. There are a total of 6766 videos. The video frames are taken at intervals of 320 × 240 each, and a total of 639,431 pictures are divided into 447,601 training data and test data. There are 191,829 pieces, which is the same as UCF101 data, and the ratio is about 7:3.

4.2 UCF101 Accuracy

This research will use UCF101 to produce an available pre-training model. Table 1 shows the accuracy comparison of each model on UCF101. The accuracy of the stimulated Distilled-ResNet-18 will be 15% higher than that of the unmotivated ResNet18. Percentage points (top-1), compared with R2 + 1D-resnet18, it is an average of 10 percentage points (top-1).

It is difficult to present the LSTM with or without the Temporal-attention mechanism in a table. As the training cycle increases, the LSTM with the attention mechanism will increase the lower limit of accuracy when the training converges, and steadily increase the overall average by 1 to 2 percentile (top-1).

Adding Temporal-Attention LSTM is 3 to 4 percentage points (top-1) higher than R2 + 1D-resnet18, and 10 percentage points (top-1) higher than ResNet18 that also added Temporal-Attention LSTM.

Table 1. UCF101 model top-1top-5 accuracy comparison

Classification	Instructions	Pre-trained model	Top1 acc	Top5 acc
3D-CNN	R2 + 1D-resnet18	Kinetics	**81.94%**	95.43%
2D-CNN	ResNet18	ImageNet	52.46%	53.40%
2D-CNN	Distilled-ResNet-18	ImageNet	70.83%	92.11%
2D-CNN + LSTM	ResNet18 + Temporal-Attention LSTM	ImageNet	73.14%	81.37%
2D-CNN + LSTM	Dsistilled-ResNet18 + Temporal-Attention LSTM	Distilled-ResNet-18	**85.26%**	94.72%

4.3 HMDB51 Accuracy

The comparison in Table 2. Distilled-ResNet-18 is inspired by R2 + 1D-resnet18. In order to verify the pros and cons of the output Distilled-ResNet-18, R2 + 1D-resnet18 and Distilled-ResNet-18 after the excitation, The comparison of fine-tune on HMDB51 is shown in Table 5. The accuracy of Dsistilled-ResNet18 is 10 percentage points (top-1) lower than that of R2 + 1D-resnet18, and the accuracy of Dsistilled-ResNet18 +

Temporal-Attention LSTM is higher than that of R2 + 1D-resnet18. 2 to 3 percentage points lower (its best value is comparable to R2 + 1D-resnet18).

Table 2. HMDB51 model top-1top-5 accuracy comparison table

Classification	Instructions	Pre-trained model	Top1 acc	Top5 acc
3D-CNN	R2 + 1D-resnet18	Kinetics + UCF101 fine-tune	**47.39%**	93.98%
2D-CNN	Dsistilled-ResNet18	Distilled-ResNet-18 (UCF101 fine-tune)	37.18%	90.44%
2DCNN + LSTM	Dsistilled-ResNet18 + Temporal-Attention LSTM	Distilled-ResNet-18 (UCF101 fine-tune)	**45.93%**	90.16%

5 Conclusion

This study proposes a 2D-CNN + Temporal-Attention LSTM action classification pre-training model that can be trained on general hardware equipment, saves time and maintains accuracy. The actual recognition speed is slightly faster than 3DCNN, and the accuracy is comparable. But the misjudgment rate is also high. The two methods proposed in this paper, one is the incentive framework, and the other is the LSTM of the temporal attention mechanism. I think that the incentive framework has a significant effect on improving the accuracy.

And at the present stage, this research finds that 3D-CNN and 2D-CNN have a matching incentive structure, and the number of network layers used by 2D-CNN is still shallow, and its performance is less than half of that of 3D-CNN. If the network depth can be deepened Obtaining better 3D-CNN pre-training models such as R2 + 1D-resnet 34, 50 has the opportunity to enable 2D-CNN to use full performance in general computer training, provide the same depth, and can be quickly trained on ordinary equipment, and There are better equal performance 2D-CNN motivated pre-trained models.

References

1. Donahue, J., et al.: Long-term recurrent convolutional networks for visual recognition and description. In: CVPR (2017)
2. Yue-Hei Ng, J., Hausknecht, M., Vijayanarasimhan, S., Vinyals, O., Monga, R., Toderici, G.: Beyond short snippets: deep networks for video classification. In: CVPR (2015)
3. Qiu, Z., Yao, T., Mei, T.: Learning spatio temporal representation with pseudo3d residual networks. In: ICCV, pp. 5534–5542 (2017)
4. Thung, G., Jiang, H.: A torch library for action recognition and detection using CNNs and LSTMs (2016)
5. Hochreiter, S., Schmidhuber, J.: Long short-term memory. Neural Comput. **9**(8), 1735–1780 (1997)

6. Carreira, J., Zisserman, A.: Quo vadis, action recognition? A new model and the kinetics dataset. In: CVPR, pp. 4724–4733 (2017)
7. Tran, D., Bourdev, L., Fergus, R., Torresani, L., Paluri, M.: Learning spatiotemporal features with 3D convolutional networks. In: CVPR, pp. 4489–4497 (2015)
8. Ji, S., Xu, W., Yang, M., Yu, K.: 3D convolutional neural networks for human action recognition. TPAMI 35(1), 221–231 (2012)
9. Tran, D., Wang, H., Torresani, L., Ray, J., LeCun, Y., Paluri, M.: A closer look at spatiotemporal convolutions for action recognition. In: CVPR, pp. 6450–6459 (2018)
10. Simonyan, K., Zisserman, A.: Two-stream convolutional networks for action recognition in videos. In: NIPS (2014)
11. Feichtenhofer, C., Pinz, A., Zisserman, A.: Convolutional two-stream network fusion for video action recognition. In: CVPR, pp. 1933–1941 (2016)
12. Wang, L., et al.: Temporal segment networks: towards good practices for deep action recognition. In: CVPR, pp. 20–36 (2016)
13. He, K., Zhang, X., Ren, S., Sun, J.: Deep residual learning for image recognition. In: CVPR, pp. 770–778 (2016)
14. Soomro, K., Zamir, A.R., Shah, M.: UCF101: a dataset of 101 human actions classes from videos in the wild.arXiv: 1212.0402 (2012)
15. Kuehne, H., Jhuang, H., Garrote, E., Poggio, T., Serre, T.: HMDB: a large video database for human motion recognition. In: ICCV (2011)

Data Mining and Machine Learning

Goal-Oriented Classification Measure Based on the Game Theory Concepts

Przemysław Juszczuk[(✉)] [ID] and Jan Kozak[ID]

Department of Machine Learning, University of Economics in Katowice, 1 Maja,
40-287 Katowice, Poland
{przemyslaw.juszczuk,jan.kozak}@ue.katowice.pl

Abstract. In this paper, we present the novel idea of the classification measure based on the combination of precision and recall. The weights of these measures are calculated based on the game-theoretic concept of equilibrium. The classical C4.5 algorithm calculates measures: precision and recall for binary decision classes.

In such a game, classification results are used to generate the best weights for the precision and recall classification measures. First, we solve the game and obtain the Nash equilibrium to obtain these weights. Next, we calculate the classification measure according to the measure weights estimated using the Nash equilibrium. Eventually, we compare the results with the more realistic example, where the importance of both decision classes is equal, and only the weights of classification measures can be adjusted. All experiments are performed on several binary classification datasets.

Keywords: Classification · Game theory · Precision and Recall

1 Introduction

The classification problem is among modern computer science's most popular and often discussed issues. A robust classification algorithm should be relatively fast and acquire good results in the case of complex data. By the complex, we can understand anything, from a large amount of data to a large number of conditional attributes or numerous decision classes. Despite the problem of acquiring and initially preprocessing such data, we often face some inequality in the number of objects belonging to the decision classes.

These problems were discussed in many papers and led to a situation where the classical accuracy measure needs to be revised. There is a need to introduce a new, more general measure. Conditions allowing for identifying the accuracy as insufficient are well-documented. Real-world data sets often require an approach based on recall or precision measures, which deal with an unbalanced number of objects in the decision class.

However, there are multiple drawbacks to such an approach. First, the single classification measure is selected, and results are obtained according to the

N. T. Nguyen et al. (Eds.): ACIIDS 2023, CCIS 1863, pp. 327–338, 2023.
https://doi.org/10.1007/978-3-031-42430-4_27

precision or recall measure. One solution is offered by the F1 score, which aims to balance the precision and recall measures. However, such an approach must be revised when multiple decision classes are observed in the data. More general measures like macro precision or macro recall were proposed and discussed in such cases.

Unfortunately, the weight of the classification measure in such cases is the same for all decision classes (macro precision and macro recall) or can be set according to the cardinality of the decision class. Some solution was proposed in [12] and [13]. At first, the authors proposed the goal-oriented approach, which indicates the impact of precision and recall measures on the overall results. Such an approach compensates for the observed problems. In the second paper, the authors further indicate the preference vector indicating the impact of the classification measure on the single decision class. This approach is sufficient when the decision-maker is present and his/her preferences can be easily identified.

In this article, we propose a novel approach for estimating the weights of precision and recall independently from the decision-maker. The advantage of such an approach is that weights are calculated based on the analyzed problem, and the result is automatically derived. The main idea is based on the game theory concepts of the game, where the process is presented as a two-stage game, where at the first stage, the overall quality of classification – calculated for all decision classes and selected classification measures is performed. While on the second stage, the classification measure for a specific decision class is calculated.

The main limitation of our approach in the present form is related to the additional computational cost related to solving the game. Moreover, we focus only on binary classification problems.

This article is organized as follows: in the next section, we derive the overall idea of the classification and the classification measures. The third section is focused on the formal definition of a game in normal and extensive form. We also discuss the concept of the payoff in the game. These elements will be crucial in the fourth section when we describe the model based on precision and recall for estimating classification quality. Finally, the fifth section includes the numerical experiments, while the last section concludes.

2   Classification and Measures

The classification problem consists of constructing a suitable classifier which, for new data, based on its features, predicts a decision whose values belong to a specific distribution (range of values – decision classes). The training data set is thus a set of vectors $a_1, \ldots, a_n, y$ (where $a_1, \ldots, a_n$ are the feature values and y is the decision class). In contrast, the problem is to construct a classifier that, for each new vector $a_1, \ldots, a_n$ will predict the value of y with the highest possible quality, which is evaluated with appropriately chosen measures [11].

In solving machine learning problems, an appropriate choice of classifier must be made – depending on the problem domain, the type and amount of data available, etc. At the stage of classifier selection, a research process should be carried out, but in this work, we focus on a measure to evaluate the classifier's quality so that we will carry out our verification on an example classifier. A good example of a classifier could be a decision tree. The simple and intuitive structure of a decision tree means that trees of small size can be analyzed directly by the user, allowing the classification to be explainable. On the other hand, in the case of large tree sizes, classification using them is still much faster than classification using different methods.

In the literature, one can find many algorithms used to build decision trees, where the classical approaches are mainly the CART [1] and C4.5 algorithms. In this work, as an example classifier, we use the C4.5 [16,17] algorithm, where the classifier is built based on multiple decision-making, where during construction, at each decision (at each node), the information gain is maximized (and thus the entropy of the dataset is reduced).

The performance of a classifier is evaluated, among other things, by the quality of its classification. For this purpose, appropriately selected measures of classification evaluation are used. The primary and simultaneously essential measures of classification evaluation are recall and precision. Another popular measure is accuracy, which carries the least information, e.g., in the case of unbalanced data. Measures such as F-score or Balanced Accuracy are also used to present only one measure (instead of recall and precision together) [2,3,6–9,18]. However, all the measures mentioned can be determined from the confusion matrix [13].

Often, the confusion matrix is presented for binary classification problems, but in this work, the confusion matrix for multi-class classification is presented in Table 1. It shows the actual values of the tested objects (in rows), and the prediction made by the classifier (in columns), where TP_i denotes true positive, i.e., correct assignment of an object to class i; TN_i denotes true negative, i.e., correct non-assignment of an object to class i; FP_i denotes false positive, i.e., wrong assignment of an object to class i; FN_i denotes false negative, i.e., wrong non-assignment of an object to class i.

On this basis, the mentioned most important measures can be defined. In this case, *recall*, which is the measure by which the information is determined: how many objects of a class have been correctly classified – is determined by (1), while when assessing the whole set and not a single class, *macro_recall*, which is determined by (2), is used, among others.

$$recall_i = \frac{TP_i}{TP_i + FN_i} \tag{1}$$

$$macro\_recall = \frac{1}{C} \sum_{i=1}^{C} \frac{TP_i}{TP_i + FN_i} \tag{2}$$

We should also pay attention to *precision*, which is the measure by which information is determined: how many objects assigned to a class belong to that class. Precision is determined by (3), and for the whole set, *macro_precision* by (4).

Table 1. Confusion matrix for multiple classes

Actual	Predicted					
	class 1	class 2	$\cdots$	class i	$\cdots$	class C
class 1	TP_1 $TN\backslash\{1\}$	FP_2 $TN\backslash\{1,2\}$ FN_1	$\cdots$	FP_i $TN\backslash\{1,i\}$ FN_1	$\cdots$	FP_C $TN\backslash\{1,C\}$ FN_1
class 2	FP_1 $TN\backslash\{1,2\}$ FN_2	TP_2 $TN\backslash\{2\}$	$\cdots$	FP_i $TN\backslash\{2,i\}$ FN_2	$\cdots$	FP_C $TN\backslash\{2,C\}$ FN_2
$\cdots$	$\cdots$	$\cdots$	$\cdots$	$\cdots$	$\cdots$	
class i	FP_1 $TN\backslash\{1,i\}$ FN_i	FP_2 $TN\backslash\{2,i\}$ FN_i	$\cdots$	TP_i $TN\backslash\{i\}$	$\cdots$	FP_C $TN\backslash\{i,C\}$ FN_i
$\cdots$	$\cdots$	$\cdots$	$\cdots$	$\cdots$	$\cdots$	$\cdots$
class C	FP_1 $TN\backslash\{1,C\}$ FN_C	FP_2 $TN\backslash\{2,C\}$ FN_C	$\cdots$	FP_i $TN\backslash\{i,C\}$ FN_C	$\cdots$	TP_C $TN\backslash\{C\}$

$$precision_i = \frac{TP_i}{TP_i + FP_i} \tag{3}$$

$$macro\_precision = \frac{1}{C} \sum_{i=1}^{C} \frac{TP_i}{TP_i + FP_i} \tag{4}$$

In addition to the measures given, the accuracy is also worth noting. In this case, it is a measure that determines how many objects were classified well in relation to all objects on which the classification was performed. Using a single equation, this measure can be written independently of the number of decision classes (5).

$$accuracy = \frac{\sum_{i=1}^{C} TP_i}{\sum_{i=1}^{C} TP_i + \sum_{i=1}^{C} FP_i} \tag{5}$$

3   Game Theory

Through the game, we understand any conflict situation involving players. Each player in the game gets some theoretical payoff according to the selected behavior (strategy). Thus, any conflict situation, such as estimating weights in some function, can be modeled and described as a conflict situation in which two players (different classification measures) compete for resources. In our particular case, the resources will be the weights of the classification measures used to combine precision and recall in a single, more general classification measure.

Let the game be defined as follows:

$$\Gamma = \langle A, M \rangle, \tag{6}$$

where $A = (A_1, A_2, ... A_n)$ represents the set of n-tuples, where each element includes a set of strategies for a single player involved in the game. By the M we understand n-tuple including n payoff functions for all players: $M = (\mu_1, \mu_2, ..., \mu_n)$. Thus, A_i is the set of strategies for the i-th player, and μ_i is the payoff function for the i-th player. The idea behind the payoff function is assigning the scalar number in the range $\langle 0 : 1 \rangle$ to each element of the A_i outcome.

A set of all strategies for the player m is defined as follows:

$$A_i = (a_{i_1}, ... a_{i_j}, ..., a_{i_m}), \tag{7}$$

where a_{i_j} is the j-th strategy for the i-th player. A player can select a single strategy, or he/she can select the strategy according to the probability distribution over the set of strategies.

We denote the probabilities of selecting strategies from the set for the i-th player as $\boldsymbol{A_i}$. Therefore:

$$\boldsymbol{A_i} = \sum_{j=1}^{m} P(a_{i_j}) = 1. \tag{8}$$

where $P(a_{i_j})$ is the probability of selecting the strategy j for the player i. Probabilities for all players will be presented as follows:

$$a = (\boldsymbol{A_1}, \boldsymbol{A_2}, ..., \boldsymbol{A_n}), \tag{9}$$

while the set excluding the i-th player is denoted as a_{-i}. Moreover, player i can use any of his/her strategies, which will be denoted as $a_{i_j} = 1$. While mixed strategy, which is the probability distribution over the set of strategies for the i–th player, can be presented as:

$$\sum_{j=1}^{m} P(a_{i,j}) = 1, \tag{10}$$

The example game for two players, each having two different strategies, is presented in Fig. 1. One should know that each player has his/her payoff function in such a game. Thus the result of such a game is different for every player. The main goal is to find a strategy, or the probability distribution over the set of strategies, which gives the best payoff for both players. Such an approach is called the Nash equilibrium, and its computation can be a relatively complex problem. However, in the literature, we can find multiple algorithms capable of deriving the game's equilibrium points, like the classical Lemke-Howson algorithm for identifying the equilibria [14]. Modern algorithms for finding the Nash equilibria are related to the idea of using the enumerating supports of the games (strategies with the non-zero probability) [15] or the integer programming approach [4]. While among the best algorithms for finding the approximate equilibria in polynomial time, we can indicate the approach discussed in [5], where the distance from optimum was equal to 38%. The whole idea of using the concept of the game to estimate the best values for classification measures will be discussed in the next section.

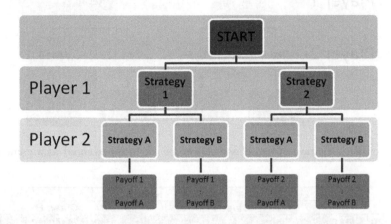

Fig. 1. Example game for two players in tree form

4   Model Formulation

Our primary goal in this approach is to identify the weights of precision and recall measures dependent on the considered problem. To do so, we derive the game-theoretic-based model, which will be used to estimate the difficulty of both decision classes. We use the original formulation of the game, where the player 1 will be identified as the classification measure selection. Thus, its strategies will be as follows $P1 = \{Precision, Recall\}$, while the second player will be identified as the decision class. The set of strategies for the second player is $P2 = \{Class_A, Class_B\}$. Payoff functions in the set M for both players will be defined as follows:

- μ_1 will be identified as the macro precision and the macro recall;
- μ_2 will be recognized as a value for the decision class dependent on the selection of the first player (the precision and the recall).

A game based on the two decision class problem involving precision and recall is presented in Fig. 2.

Any tree-form game can be represented as the normal form game, in which all possible strategy selections are considered jointly. To do so, every path in the tree (please refer to Fig. 2 will be considered, and the payoffs for both players represented by the precision, recall, macro precision, and macro recall will be held in the leaves of the game. Eventually, the tree-form game is transformed into the normal form game (matrix game), presented in Fig. 3.

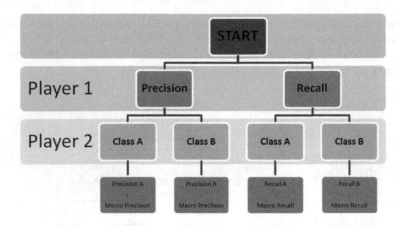

Fig. 2. Conflict situation of two classification measures represented as a game in the tree form

		Recall	
		Class A	Class B
Precision	Class A	Precision A : Macro Precision	Precision B : Macro Precision
	Class B	Recall A : Macro Recall	Recall B : Macro Recall

Fig. 3. Normal form game representation of the situation from the Fig. 2

The final step of the model is the solution of such a game – which will be finding the equilibrium point (Nash equilibrium) to indicate the best possible payoff from the point of view of both players jointly. The Nash equilibrium calculation process is out of this article's scope – for more details, please refer to [10]. A solution will derive the vector of probabilities, which could be as follows:

$$a = \{1, 0 : 0.5, 0.5\}, \tag{11}$$

which can be understood as setting the weight for the precision measure as 1, while the recall is set as 0. For detailed step-by-step example, please refer to the next section.

5   Numerical Experiments

In this section, we perform numerical experiments based on the well-known C4.5 algorithm. As a result, we derive results for two classification measures: precision and recall. Next, we use these results to populate the game matrix and find the equilibrium in the game. Eventually, we estimate the theoretical best classification measure where the weights could be used for both the classification measure and the decision class. The goal of the experiments can be summarized as follows:

– use the C4.5 algorithm for a set of binary classification problems to obtain the classification measure values: precision and recall for both classes, macro precision, macro recall, and accuracy;
– we built the game which allows answering the question, what is the best hypothetical classification value;
– we estimate the real classification value in the situation where both classes are treated equally.

The last point can be used to derive the more general classification measure based on precision and recall, where weights for these measures are calculated according to the game – thus are problem-dependent.

In our experiments, we used five different datasets, for which, initially, the values for precision, recall, and accuracy were obtained. Next, in this section, we present detailed step-by-step examples for calculating the optimal weights for precision and recall, and eventually, we move to experiments covering all datasets.

5.1   Visual Example

We start with the simple step-by-step example calculated with the use of the "Breast Cancer" dataset. The obtained classification results for all considered measures are as follows:

– precision for class A – 0.757;
– precision for class B – 0.742;
– macro precision – 0.749;
– recall for class A – 0.960;
– recall for class B – 0.271;
– macro recall – 0.615.

Accuracy measure is considered globally for all decision classes, thus it is not necessary for our further calculations. The next step is to populate values in the tree-form game (as presented in Fig. 2). Eventually, the tree-form game is presented as normal form game (please refer to Fig. 3). The process and resulting game with populated values is presented in Fig. 4.

To obtain the solution of the game, the Nash equilibrium should be calculated. This can be done by any algorithm from game theory. Here we used the GAMBIT application to obtain the Nash equilibrium, which is equal to:

$$a = \{1, 0 : 0.5, 0.5\}, \tag{12}$$

These values can be understood as: setting the weight of the first measure (Precision) as 1, while the second one should be equal to 0. Next, set the importance of both decision classes equally as the 0.5. Eventually, the payoffs can be calculated:

$$payoff_1 = 1 \cdot (0.5 \cdot 0.757 + 0.5 \cdot 0.742) + 0 \cdot (0.5 \cdot 0.960 + 0.5 \cdot 0.271), \tag{13}$$

$$payoff_2 = 0.5 \cdot (1 \cdot 0.749 + 0 \cdot 0.615) + 0.5 \cdot (1 \cdot 0.749 + 0 \cdot 0.615), \tag{14}$$

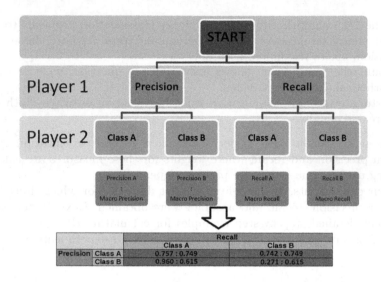

Fig. 4. Tree-form game and its representation in the normal form game

Which gives the $payoff_1 = 0.859$ while $payoff_1 = 0.682$. These are theoretical best values achievable according to the equilibrium concept by both players (game has more than one solution). However, please note, that in such a case the recall is not taken into account. Thus the same payoff calculation can be repeated for the situation, where both measures are equally important:

$$payoff_1 = 0.5 \cdot (0.5 \cdot 0.757 + 0.5 \cdot 0.742) + 0.5 \cdot (0.5 \cdot 0.960 + 0.5 \cdot 0.271), \quad (15)$$

$$payoff_2 = 0.5 \cdot (0.5 \cdot 0.749 + 0.5 \cdot 0.615) + 0.5 \cdot (0.5 \cdot 0.749 + 0.5 \cdot 0.615), \quad (16)$$

Since these probabilities for strategies are not the best (according to the Nash equilibrium concept), with the above values, we end with payoffs equal $payoff_1 = 0.683$ for the first player and 0.682 for the second player. By setting the different weights for precision and recall, we can globally observe how such a change impacts the final result.

5.2 Results

The first part of the experiments is devoted to estimating the classification quality using selected measures and for the set of problems with binary decision class. All results, including the accuracy value, precision, and recall for both classes include the values for the macro precision and macro recall additionally. For these results, please refer to Table 2.

The next step of the experiments involved transforming the obtained results into a conflict situation, which can be solved by estimating the Nash equilibrium

Table 2. Classification results for five selected datasets with binary decision classes (Acc. – accuracy; Prec. A – precision for the first class; Macro Prec. – average precision value; Rec. A – recall for the first class; Macro Rec. – average recall value

Dataset	Acc.	Prec. A	Prec. B	Macro Prec.	Rec. A	Rec. B	Macro Rec.
BreastCancer	0.755	0.757	0.742	0.749	0.960	0.271	0.615
Credit	0.705	0.763	0.511	0.637	0.840	0.390	0.615
Diabets	0.738	0.790	0.632	0.711	0.814	0.597	0.706
Ionosphere	0.915	0.919	0.908	0.918	0.825	0.964	0.895
Vote	0.963	0.970	0.952	0.961	0.970	0.952	0.961

values. Table 3 shows the probabilities for selecting the strategies for both players. These values were calculated according to the Nash equilibrium concept. We selected a single solution (a single Nash equilibrium) for all five datasets. However, there were more equilibria for each game. Please note that these values refer to the probability distribution over the set of strategies, so the first and last values must sum up to 1.

Table 3. Solution (Nash equilibrium) for game build on the basis of classification measures – calculated as in the Visual example

Set	Player 1		Player 2	
	Precision	Recall	Class A	Class B
BreastCancer	1	0	0	1
Credit	1	0	$\frac{11}{18}$	$\frac{7}{18}$
Diabets	1	0	$\frac{35}{59}$	$\frac{24}{59}$
Ionosphere	1	0	1	0
Vote	1	0	1	0

Now, we compare the actual payoff (quality of classification) obtained by using the weights for classes and classification measures according to the Nash equilibrium and the uniform weights. By the uniform weights, we understand the 0.5 weights for both decision classes (the importance of decision classes is equal) and the 0.5 weights for the precision and recall (both measures are equally important). These results are presented in Table 4. First, the left part of the table corresponds to the situation in which a potential decision-maker could focus only on some particular decision class and specific classification measure (like precision). In other words, we can indicate which classification measure gives the best classification quality and which decision class can be considered the easiest to obtain the highest classification results.

Next, we compare these values with the situation where both classification measures and decision classes are considered equally important. For example, taking into account the "BreasCancer" dataset, we can conclude that in the case of the classification according to the Nash equilibrium, we can obtain the best classification equal to 0.742 when focusing on the precision (please see values in the first row for the Table 4). At the same time, the best results are obtained when focusing on the decision class B (classification equal to 0.749). Now, when we assume equal importance of both classification measures and decision classes, these results are equal to 0.683 and 0.682, respectively. Thus we observe a decrease of 5.9% (from 0.742 to 0.683) for the classification measures and by the 6.7% in the case of decision classes.

Table 4. The difference in payoff between the weights based on the Nash equilibrium and uniform weights for both classes and classification measures

Dataset	Payoffs - Nash equilibrium		Payoffs - uniform impact	
	Player 1	Player 2	Player 1	Player 2
BreastCancer	0.742	0.749	0.683	0.682
Credit	0.665	0.637	0.626	0.626
Diabets	0.726	0.711	0.708	0.709
Ionosphere	0.919	0.918	0.904	0.907
Vote	0.970	0.961	0.961	0.961

6   Conclusions and Future Works

In this article, we presented the general idea of adapting the game theory concepts for estimating the weights for different classification measures. We started with the short remainder of the most popular classification measures like precision and recall. Then, we also described the idea of macro precision and macro recall.

To derive the model, we used the basic definitions and concepts from the game theory, particularly in describing the conflict situation presented in the game. Next, we adapted these ideas for the classification process. Finally, the classification results obtained by the classifier were used to populate the game in an extensive form game, which was further transformed into a normal form game.

The next step was to estimate the optimal values of weights for both decision classes and the classification measures. Eventually, we compared the results with the situation where weights for decision classes and classification measures equal 0.5. The difference between these two values indicates the potential achievable classification values if the decision-maker focuses on the particular classification measure and decision classes.

The presented idea suggests the possibility of deriving a procedure capable of estimating the weights for the classification measures. These values are calculated based on the game, which strictly depends on the analyzed problem. Thus we can estimate the precision and recall values independently for the dataset.

References

1. Breiman, L., Friedman, J.H., Olshen, R.A., Stone, C.J.: Classification and Regression Trees, p. 358 (1984)
2. Buckland, M., Gey, F.: The relationship between recall and precision. J. Am. Soc. Inf. Sci. **45**(1), 12–19 (1994)
3. Burduk, R.: Classification performance metric for imbalance data based on recall and selectivity normalized in class labels. arXiv preprint arXiv:2006.13319 (2020)
4. Conitzer, V., Gilpin, A., Sandholm, T.: Mixed-integer programming methods for finding Nash equilibria. In: Proceedings of the 20th National Conference on Artificial Intelligence, vol. 2, pp. 495–501 (2005)
5. Daskalakis, C., Mehta, A., Papadimitriou, C.: Progress in approximate Nash equilibria. In: 8th ACM Conference on Electronic Commerce, pp. 355–358 (2007)
6. Gilli, M., Schumann, E.: Accuracy and precision in finance. Available at SSRN 2698114 (2015)
7. Gösgens, M., Zhiyanov, A., Tikhonov, A., Prokhorenkova, L.: Good classification measures and how to find them. In: Advances in Neural Information Processing Systems, vol. 34 (2021)
8. Grandini, M., Bagli, E., Visani, G.: Metrics for multi-class classification: an overview, pp. 1–17. arXiv preprint arXiv:2008.05756 (2020)
9. Hand, D.J., Christen, P., Kirielle, N.: F*: an interpretable transformation of the F-measure. Mach. Learn. **110**(3), 451–456 (2021). https://doi.org/10.1007/s10994-021-05964-1
10. Juszczuk, P.: A novel approximate method of computing extended Nash equilibria. Appl. Soft Comput. J. **76**, 682–696 (2019)
11. Kozak, J.: Decision Tree and Ensemble Learning Based on Ant Colony Optimization. SCI, vol. 781. Springer, Cham (2019). https://doi.org/10.1007/978-3-319-93752-6
12. Kozak, J., Kania, K., Juszczuk, P., Mitręga, M.: Swarm intelligence goal-oriented approach to data-driven innovation in customer churn management. Int. J. Inf. Manag. **60**, 102357 (2021)
13. Kozak, J., Probierz, B., Kania, K., Juszczuk, P.: Preference-driven classification measure. Entropy **24**(4), 531 (2022)
14. Lemke, C.E., Howson, J.T.: Equilibrium points of bimatrix games. SIAM J. Appl. Math. **12**, 413–423 (1964)
15. Nudelman, E., Porter, R., Shoham, Y.: Simple search methods for finding a Nash equilibrium. In: AAAI-2004, pp. 664–669 (2004)
16. Quinlan, J.R.: Induction of decision trees. Mach. Learn. **1**(1), 81–106 (1986). https://doi.org/10.1007/BF00116251
17. Quinlan, J.R.: C4.5: Programs for Machine Learning. Elsevier, Amsterdam (2014)
18. Saito, T., Rehmsmeier, M.: The precision-recall plot is more informative than the ROC plot when evaluating binary classifiers on imbalanced datasets. PLoS ONE **10**(3), 1–21 (2015). https://doi.org/10.1371/journal.pone.0118432

Comparative Study on Customer Churn Prediction by Using Machine Learning Techniques

Shashikant Kumar and Doina Logofatu[✉][iD]

Frankfurt University of Applied Sciences, Frankfurt am Main, Germany
logofatu@fb2.fra-uas.de

Abstract. Customer churn prediction is crucial for businesses in different industries, such as telecommunications, banking, insurance and e-commerce, because acquiring new customers is often more costly than retaining existing ones. Customer churn prediction (CCP) aims to identify customers who are likely to terminate their relationship with a business, enabling companies to take proactive measures to retain them. Machine learning approaches have emerged as a viable strategy for developing effective churn prediction models, employing past customer data to find churn predictors. A comparative study on the most popular supervised machine learning algorithms, including Logistic Regression, Decision tree and Ensemble approaches such as Bagging, Boosting, Stacking and Voting, was applied to predict customer churn in the telecommunications industry. Since the studied dataset is skewed towards non-churners, we investigated the SMOTE and SMOTEENN sampling strategies to balance the dataset. According to the findings of our study, machine learning is a viable method for predicting customer churn. Furthermore, our results show that ensemble learners outperform single-base learners, and a balanced training dataset is expected to improve the classifiers' performance.

Keywords: Churn Prediction · Machine Learning · Ensemble method · Imbalanced classification

1 Introduction

Telecommunications services have substantially increased their potential usage in a variety of fields, including education, the workplace, and entertainment, over the last few decades. This results in intense competition between telecommunications companies. The Return on Investment (ROI) of customer retention is high for firms since it costs six times more to acquire a new client than it does to keep an existing one who is likely to leave [1], it is crucial to identify customers who are likely to abandon their subscription to the telecommunication service. Determining which clients are dependable and which run the risk of leaving can also help a business address an issue. Companies can gradually lower the amount of churned customers by making focused efforts to prevent churn.

Due to data storage and analytics development, predicting customer churn using data science has grown into one of the most prominent subjects in marketing analytics. Researchers and practitioners attempt to develop accurate churn prediction models [14]. Nevertheless, reliable churn prediction is challenging since numerous variables might influence customer churn. Also, it is challenging for models developed using machine learning to attain high prediction performance due to class imbalances frequently present in customer churn datasets. If a model for predicting customer turnover fails to identify probable churners, the company will lose valued consumers and future income. Furthermore, the company will waste money on client retention if it misidentifies loyal consumers as potential churners.

Customer churn is defined in numerous ways. According to [8], it is defined as the process by which clients move from one phone company to the other. Some refer to it simply as the likelihood that a consumer may discontinue service [14]. Because customer churn incorporates both of these features, this study defines it as "consumer behaviour of discontinuing use of the service, regardless of whether the client switches service providers or simply discontinues consumption."

With a proper machine learning model, telcos can determine which customers will most likely churn based on their consumption patterns. Large data quantities, a vast feature space, and the issue of class imbalance are some difficulties in developing an effective model [11]. Resampling [9] can be employed to enhance the model in order to address the class imbalance issue.

The following contributions are made to the research:

1. Create classification models by combining ensemble classification techniques with hybrid resampling methods.
2. Apply the created models to the data on customer churn, and evaluate the performance of their prediction using a variety of performance indicators.
3. Compare the performance of the generated models in terms of their ability to predict outcomes with that of currently popular models that mix traditional and ensemble approaches with a well-known resampling strategy.

2   Background

Customer churn or attrition is the process of a customer switching from one business service to another. CCP is used to detect potential churners before they leave an organisation. This step helps the company figure out how to keep customers who are likely to leave and keep them as customers. This decreases the financial loss of the company [17].

Predicting customer churn is vital for all businesses since it improves customer knowledge and revenue projections. It may also aid your business in identifying and enhancing areas in which customer service could be enhanced. Several sectors have consumer data that have been and are still being studied. The results are different depending on the type of data collected from each industry.

2.1   Customer Churn

The churn rate indicates the health of every subscription-based business model. The capacity of a telecommunications business to retain its clients is one of the primary issues these firms face in recent times, owing to the flood of rivals within the sector, which essentially provides customers the option to switch from one company to another. Although there is no significant correlation between customer devotion, customer loyalty, trust, and customer churn in the telecommunications business, these factors have a significant association. The primary objectives of a telecom firm have been to develop products and services that meet the needs of its subscribers at reasonable pricing.

The term "customer churn" is frequently heard in the field of customer relationship management. It is a term used to describe clients leaving a company, meaning that the customers entirely cut off their interaction with the organisation [4]. Since acquiring new customers is substantially more expensive than keeping existing ones, it is a crucial business metric in many sectors. This phenomenon is also known by the terms customer attrition and customer churn.

2.2   Related Work

Guo-en et al. (2016) proposed a churn prediction model using the actual Telecom data set from American Duke University. Weighted selected ensembles were used for churn prediction in this study, and these approaches were compared to base classifiers such as Decision Tree, SVM, Naive Bayes and Artificial Neural Network (ANN). The studies are conducted in a MATLAB environment, and the results demonstrate that the suggested technique outperforms the base classifiers [19].

Adbelrahim et al. (2019), the author used tree-based algorithms for CCP with the SyriaTel dataset, including random forest, decision tree, GBM tree, and XGBoost algorithm. Compared to other algorithms, XGBoost outperformed them regarding AUC and accuracy. However, accuracy can be enhanced by using optimization algorithms in the feature selection procedure [2].

Burez et al. (2009) The authors explored the issue of an unbalanced data set in the CCP model. They compared the results with random and advanced under-sampling, the gradient boosting algorithm, and weighted random forests. They evaluated the model using AUC and lift measures. Consequently, it was determined that the under-sampling approach performed better than the other strategies [5].

Verbeke et al. (2012) additionally studied numerous techniques on various datasets to forecast customer churn, including twenty-one algorithms, including Naive Bayes, Random Forest, SVM, Decision Tree, Boosting, and so on. They performed studies with both oversampling and input selection, as well as with and without oversampling. They achieved the maximum AUC of 97.2% on the datasets of operators in East Asia by utilising an alternating decision tree [18].

Shaaban et al. (2012) compared the decision tree, the support vector machine, and the neural networks. The neural network with support vector machine had the highest accuracy at 0.84. With an accuracy of 0.78, the decision tree under-performed [13].

Jain et al. (2020) analysed several uses of machine learning to forecast churn in the banking, telecom and IT sectors. Churn is examined for each sector and the features that contribute to churn in those areas. Comparative analyses of the effectiveness of four different algorithms were carried out for each of these three industries. The banking dataset saw the highest performance with random forest, while the IT and telecom sectors saw better results from logistic regression and XGBoost. This has shown that churn prediction approaches can vary by industry [7].

Shumaly et al. (2020) The data set was balanced using random under-sampling, oversampling, and the Synthetic Minority-Oversampling Technique (SMOTE). In addition, they utilised ensemble approaches like bagging and boosting techniques to increase the accuracy of their predictions and achieved an AUC score of 90.1% using random oversampling and the gradient boost method [16].

Salunkhe et al. utilised a hybrid approach made up of the Tomek Links and SMOTE approaches to deal with the issue of an unbalanced dataset that could have a detrimental impact on performance. Specifically, the SMOTE approach is used to oversample minority samples to produce a balanced distribution, and subsequently, Tomek Links cases from majority classes are identified and elimi-nated. They studied the issue of class imbalance, which is frequent in datasets used for churn prediction because churners are often the minority class [12].

3   Methodology

Customer churn prediction is a binary classification issue; therefore, models must determine whether a given data point has a value of 1 or 0 (i.e., there has been a churn or not). The primary purpose of the research was to develop supervised machine learning algorithms in order to carry out an analysis of comparison models and to identify the model that provided the most accurate predictions. Customer churn was predicted using Logistic Regression and ensemble tech-niques like Bagging, Boosting, Stacking and Voting. Our concepts and strategies are based on the Influence Methods. Figure 1 depicts the steps followed in this work.

In our approach, we select the top 13 features from a total of 21. We use Logistic Regression, Decision tree, and ensemble methods like Bagging, Boosting, Stacking, and Voting classifiers with Imbalanced data and hybrid resampling techniques (SMOTE, SMOTE-ENN).

3.1   Data Overview

It is generally hard to find a dataset with private information because it is often publicly unavailable. The dataset for this paper was collected from the IBM Business Analytics community. The Telecom customer churn data includes

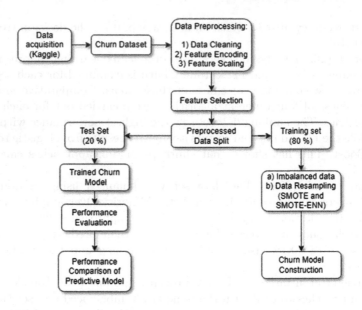

Fig. 1. Churn Classification Methodology

information about a fictional Telco company in California that provided phone and Internet services to 7043 customers in Q3. The dataset comprises 21 columns reflecting the predicted variables and 7043 rows of customer records.

3.2 Data Pre-processing

The raw data were transformed into a final dataset during the data preparation step so that we could feed it into the modelling algorithms and create models. At this phase, many tasks were completed, including data cleansing, handling missing values, selecting features, and data transformation.

3.3 Handling Missing Values

Many machine learning methods do not support data with missing values, so handling missing values is critical. Tenure has some records with Tenure = '0', which means the customer has joined the Telco company recently, and their total charges are NULL. So it will not make much sense to keep these records. Therefore, we will remove these records.

Drop Irrelevant Columns: Customer IDs are removed from the data set as part of the preprocessing step because they are not important to the churn prediction.

3.4   Feature Encoding

Encoding is the process of transforming category data into numerical data. The most frequent type of data in the sample was a categorical data type. Typically, the values for these variables were kept as text. Since machine learning algorithms are built on mathematical equations, they can only be used with numerical data. As a result, leaving the categorical variables in their current state was impossible, and they had to be transformed into a numerical format.

The categorical variables were encoded in this paper using the Label Encoding technique. Each category, in this manner, was assigned a number. This technique does not increase the number of columns; hence it does not slow the learning process. In this paper, Label Encoder was used to encode 16 category variables: 'OnlineBackup', 'gender', 'TechSupport', 'Churn', 'PhoneService', 'StreamingMovies', 'Partner', 'PaperlessBilling', 'InternetService', 'PaymentMethod', 'DeviceProtection', 'MultipleLines', 'Contract', 'StreamingTV', 'OnlineSecurity', 'Dependents'.

3.5   Feature Scaling

This is another stage of the data preparation approach used to normalize the range of independent variables within a dataset. Depending on the scale method used, it is either centred around 0 or between 0 and 1. Large values for input variables may be ignored or skewed by some machine learning algorithms if they apply to additional input variables and have a similar magnitude. The 'MinMaxScaler' approach was used to scale features. We have scaled the numerical value: tenure, MonthlyCharges and TotalCharges.

3.6   Feature Selection

A machine-learning model may not be able to make the required prediction if we use all of the characteristics we find in the dataset. The accuracy of the predictions could be increased by using only more relevant features. Therefore, feature correlation plays a significant role in improving machine learning models. **SelectKBest** is a popular feature selection approach in machine learning. It selects the top K features based on their scores from a specified scoring function. The general idea is that the most informative features are retained, while the less informative ones are discarded. This can help reduce the dimensionality of the data, improve model performance, and speed up training times. In SelectKBest, 'k' represents the number of top features to select based on their scores from a specified scoring function.

3.7   Data Splitting

For each experiment, the complete dataset is divided into an 80% training set and a 20% test set. The training set was used for data resampling, and training the model, whereas the test set was used to evaluate the trained model's performance. For the data split, we used a random seed, which resulted in an identical data split each time the programme was run.

3.8   Data Resampling

The dataset is highly imbalanced. The number of no-churn customers outnumbers the number of churn customers. In this situation, if we use this dataset to build the model, the model tends to be biased toward non-churn customers, resulting in poor performance when evaluated for the Test data set. We utilised resampling methods such as SMOTE [3] and SMOTE-ENN [6] to solve this issue.

3.9   Predictive Churn Modelling

Customer churn prediction is a binary classification issue; therefore, models must determine whether a given data point has a value of 1 or 0 (i.e., there has been a churn or not). In this step, the data that had already been processed was applied to construct the model using machine learning to predict customer churn. The primary purpose of the paper was to develop supervised machine learning algorithms in order to carry out an analysis of comparison models and to identify the model that provided the most accurate predictions. Customer churn was predicted using Logistic Regression and ensemble techniques like Bagging, Boosting, Stacking and Voting.

We trained all models on default parameters to make comparison easy and fair because the hyper-parameter was different for the same algorithm with different data resampling techniques. Firstly we trained all the models without resampling the data, then applied hybrid resampling techniques SMOTE and SMOTE-ENN to train all the models. These are the models:

Logistic Regression: Logistic regression uses the sigmoid function. It generates binary outcomes, such as yes or no. Unlike linear regression, a sigmoid will not appear as a straight line on a graph; instead, it will display a sigmoid. It applies to a categorical variable. A categorical variable denotes a finite collection of values. The output of a logistic model is probability. Recall, precision, accuracy, and confusion matrix are used to evaluate it. Logistic regression is used to solve classification-related topic problems. For solving weather-related issues, logistic regression predicts whether it will rain tomorrow (Yes or no) [15].

Decision Tree: The machine-learning decision tree algorithm begins to develop a tree-like structure. This tree has root, branch nodes, and leaf nodes. A representation of data in the form of a tree that can be navigated and used to provide different options is called a decision tree. The primary terms associated with decision trees are pruning, entropy and information gain. Pruning is the process of eliminating unnecessary branches from a decision tree. Entropy is the measure of contaminants, whereas information gain, or the reduction in entropy, is the measure of purity.

Ensemble Techniques The ensemble method is a typical machine learning approach that combines various learning models, often known as "base learners," and combines their output into a single classifier. Voting is the simplest method for combining classifiers. Bagging, boosting and stacking apply this strategy using a base classifier in various ways. Based on the construction of the model, ensemble can be classified as homogeneous or heterogeneous, as depicted in Fig. 2. Homogeneous ensemble is a group of classifiers of the same type that are generated on a distinct subset of data, similar to how the Random Forest model is built. Heterogeneous ensemble is a collection of different types of classifiers developed on the same data.

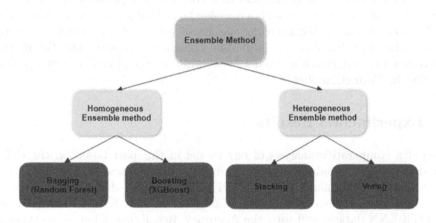

Fig. 2. Ensemble Method

Random Forest: The Random Forest (RF) method is an ensemble learning technique for classification problems. The random forest algorithm builds several decision trees and then calculates the average prediction value for each unique tree. The main distinction between decision trees and random forests is that decision trees utilise the entire dataset to build a single model. In contrast, random forests employ randomly selected variables to build different models.

XGBoost: Another well-known method for enhancing performance is called XGBoost. It is an advanced gradient-boosting algorithm implementation. XGBoost uses the ensemble technique. This technique combines several weak learner sets (decision trees) into a strong model that can make accurate predictions. XGBoost has a lot of benefits, such as the ability to do parallel processing, which speeds up computation, a high degree of freedom in setting objectives, built-in cross-validation, and the ability to avoid splitting when the loss is negative. With these benefits, XGBoost is ideally suited for classification data processing [10].

Stacking: The MLxtend library provides an implementation of the StackingCV-Classifier for scikit-learn estimators. We have used only the default parameter for model training. For constructing the stacking classifier, we have considered logistic regression, Random Forest and XGBoost classifier as stack model and logistic regression as meta classifier, and cross-validation value of 10.

Voting: A voting classifier is a technique for ensemble learning that combines the predictions of numerous machine learning models to provide a final prediction. The VotingClassifier from the sklearn.ensemble package can be used to construct a voting classifier in Python.

We are creating a voting classifier that combines the predictions of four classifiers: a logistic regression model, a decision tree classifier, a random forest, and an XGBoost classifier. We are using the 'hard' voting scheme, which means the final prediction is based on the individual classifiers' majority vote. By altering the constructor's parameters, such as the voting scheme ('hard' or 'soft'), we can modify the VotingClassifier.

4 Experimental Results

We did a comparative analysis of our model in this part based on the different datasets and standards used to gauge the effectiveness of each algorithm. Based on the performance of our model with a different dataset we researched for this paper, we discovered with the original dataset, SMOTE dataset, and SMOTE-ENN dataset and used the Accuracy, Recall, and F1-score to evaluate the performances and chose the best overall model. The ensemble model with hybrid resampling techniques performed very well compared to other models using the accuracy, precision, recall, and F1 score to compare them.

Table 1. Performance comparison chart of the different classifiers before SMOTE is applied

	Accuracy	Recall	Precision	F1-score
Stack_model	**0.790334**	0.475936	**0.642599**	0.546851
Logistic Regression	0.789623	**0.550802**	0.616766	**0.581921**
Voting	0.786780	0.457219	0.638060	0.532710
Random Forest	0.781095	0.483957	0.611486	0.540299
XGBoost	0.776119	0.516043	0.590214	0.550642
Decision Tree	0.724947	0.500000	0.483204	0.491459

Table 1 clearly shows that the Logistic regression as a base model has performed well regarding Recall and F1-score without resampling. However, the stack model has performed well in terms of Accuracy and precision. When the data sampling method was not applied, every model gave a good Accuracy score but failed miserably regarding Recall and F1 scores. While the decision tree performs the lowest out of all the models, Random Forest and XGBoost exhibit acceptable performance.

Table 2. Performance comparison chart of the different classifiers after SMOTE is applied to the data

	Accuracy	Recall	Precision	F1-score
Voting	**0.763326**	0.641711	**0.546697**	0.590406
Random Forest	**0.758351**	0.663102	**0.536797**	0.593301
XGBoost	0.749112	0.660428	0.522199	0.583235
stack_model	0.743426	0.708556	0.512573	0.594837
Logistic Regression	0.724947	**0.775401**	0.489039	**0.599793**
Decision Tree	0.700782	0.588235	0.451745	0.511034

Table 2 shows a performance comparison of the different classifiers after SMOTE is applied to the data. Random forest and Voting classifiers achieve the highest Accuracy and Precision. The Recall and F1-score of all the models have improved compared to the no-resampling data. The Random Forest, voting and XGBoost models have nearly identical performance and performed well.

Table 3. Performance comparison chart of the different classifiers after SMOTE-ENN is applied to the data

	Accuracy	Recall	Precision	F1-score
stack_model	**0.742715**	**0.780749**	**0.510490**	**0.617336**
Voting	**0.742715**	0.778075	**0.510526**	**0.616525**
Random Forest	**0.740583**	**0.786096**	**0.507772**	**0.616999**
XGBoost	0.729211	0.778075	0.494058	0.604361
Decision Tree	0.722104	0.764706	0.485569	0.593977
Logistic Regression	0.700071	**0.815508**	0.463526	0.591085

Table 3 shows a performance comparison of the different classifiers after SMOTE-ENN is applied to the data. Random forest, stacking, and Voting classifiers achieve the highest Accuracy, Precision and F1 scores. The Recall and F1-score of all the models have improved compared to the no-resampling and SMOTE techniques. The Random Forest, stack and voting models performed nearly identically and performed well.

As demonstrated in Table 3, in the heterogeneous ensemble model, Stacking and Voting performed well; in the homogeneous model, Random Forest with

SMOTE ENN has the highest accuracy, precision and F1-score; when comparing all these findings of how each ensemble tree method fared based on the measure. Thus, the Stacking and Voting algorithm could be chosen as the top predictive model for customer churn prediction.

5   Conclusion and Future Work

This paper compared traditional and ensemble machine learning algorithms on their performance in predicting customer churn on a telecom company dataset. Accurately predicting customers that are going to churn helps companies take action and retain their customers, as attracting new customers is very costly. The goal is to identify the machine learning technique that has the best performance. The results show that the Stacking and Voting algorithm achieves the best prediction of customers that will churn.

The results show that the stack model and Logistic Regression achieve the best prediction of customers that will churn with the imbalanced dataset. When we applied SMOTE technique to balance the minority class, the Random Forest and Voting classifier performed well. When we balanced the minority class with SMOTE-ENN, then in the Homogeneous method, Random Forest performed well, and both the Heterogeneous model stacking and Voting classifier outperformed compared to all other algorithms.

The primary goal of churn predictive analytics is to determine customers likely to churn and avoid or reduce the number of churns. Telcos should employ the ensemble technique prediction model to identify customers prone to churn.

Currently, most churn prediction models use structured data such as customer demographics, usage patterns, and billing information. However, a wealth of unstructured data could be used to improve churn prediction, such as customer feedback from social media, call centre transcripts, and online reviews. Future research could focus on developing models that can effectively incorporate these data sources.

References

1. Ahmad, A.K., Jafar, A., Aljoumaa, K.: Customer churn prediction in telecom using machine learning in big data platform. J. Big Data 6(1), 1–24 (2019). https://doi.org/10.1186/s40537-019-0191-6
2. Ahmad, A.K., Jafar, A., Aljoumaa, K.: Customer churn prediction in telecom using machine learning in big data platform. J. Big Data 6(1), 28 (2019). https://doi.org/10.1186/s40537-019-0191-6. https://journalofbigdata.springeropen.com/articles/10.1186/s40537-019-0191-6
3. Batista, G., Prati, R., Monard, M.C.: A study of the behavior of several methods for balancing machine learning training data. SIGKDD Explor. 6, 20–29 (2004). https://doi.org/10.1145/1007730.1007735
4. Buckinx, W., Van den Poel, D.: Customer base analysis: partial defection of behaviourally loyal clients in a non-contractual FMCG retail setting. Eur. J. Oper. Res. 164, 252–268 (2005). https://doi.org/10.1016/j.ejor.2003.12.010

5. Burez, J., Van den Poel, D.: Handling class imbalance in customer churn prediction. Expert Syst. Appl. **36**(3), 4626–4636 (2009)
6. Chawla, N., Bowyer, K., Hall, L.O., Kegelmeyer, W.P.: SMOTE: synthetic minority over-sampling technique. ArXiv abs/1106.1813 (2002)
7. Jain, H., Yadav, G., Manoov, R.: Churn prediction and retention in banking, telecom and IT sectors using machine learning techniques. In: Patnaik, S., Yang, X.-S., Sethi, I.K. (eds.) Advances in Machine Learning and Computational Intelligence. AIS, pp. 137–156. Springer, Singapore (2021). https://doi.org/10.1007/978-981-15-5243-4_12
8. Kumar, S., Kumar, M.: Predicting customer churn using artificial neural network. In: Macintyre, J., Iliadis, L., Maglogiannis, I., Jayne, C. (eds.) EANN 2019. CCIS, vol. 1000, pp. 299–306. Springer, Cham (2019). https://doi.org/10.1007/978-3-030-20257-6_25
9. Andrews, R.: Churn prediction in telecom sector using machine learning. Int. J. Inf. Syst. Comput. Sci. **8**(2), 132–134 (2019). https://doi.org/10.30534/ijiscs/2019/31822019. http://www.warse.org/IJISCS/static/pdf/file/ijiscs31822019.pdf
10. Pebrianti, D., Istinabiyah, D.D., Bayuaji, L., Rusdah: Hybrid method for churn prediction model in the case of telecommunication companies. In: 2022 9th International Conference on Electrical Engineering, Computer Science and Informatics (EECSI), pp. 161–166 (2022). https://doi.org/10.23919/EECSI56542.2022.9946535
11. Qureshi, S.A., Rehman, A.S., Qamar, A.M., Kamal, A., Rehman, A.: Telecommunication subscribers' churn prediction model using machine learning. In: Eighth International Conference on Digital Information Management (ICDIM 2013), pp. 131–136 (2013). https://doi.org/10.1109/ICDIM.2013.6693977
12. Salunkhe, U.R., Mali, S.N.: A hybrid approach for class imbalance problem in customer churn prediction: a novel extension to under-sampling. Int. J. Intell. Syst. Appl. **10**, 71–81 (2018)
13. Shaaban, E., Helmy, Y., Khedr, A., Nasr, M.: A proposed churn prediction model. Int. J. Eng. Res. Appl. (IJERA) **2**, 693–697 (2012)
14. Sharma, T., Gupta, P., Nigam, V., Goel, M.: Customer churn prediction in telecommunications using gradient boosted trees. In: Khanna, A., Gupta, D., Bhattacharyya, S., Snasel, V., Platos, J., Hassanien, A.E. (eds.) International Conference on Innovative Computing and Communications. AISC, vol. 1059, pp. 235–246. Springer, Singapore (2020). https://doi.org/10.1007/978-981-15-0324-5_20
15. Shitole, A., Priyadarshini, I.: Survey of machine learning algorithms & its applications (2021). https://doi.org/10.5281/zenodo.5090570
16. Shumaly, S., Neysaryan, P., Guo, Y.: Handling class imbalance in customer churn prediction in telecom sector using sampling techniques, bagging and boosting trees. In: 2020 10th International Conference on Computer and Knowledge Engineering (ICCKE), pp. 082–087 (2020). https://doi.org/10.1109/ICCKE50421.2020.9303698
17. Umayaparvathi, V., Iyakutti, K.: Applications of data mining techniques in telecom churn prediction. Int. J. Comput. Appl. **42**(20), 5–9 (2012). https://doi.org/10.5120/5814-8122. http://research.ijcaonline.org/volume42/number20/pxc3878122.pdf

18. Verbeke, W., Dejaeger, K., Martens, D., Hur, J., Baesens, B.: New insights into churn prediction in the telecommunication sector: a profit driven data mining approach. Eur. J. Oper. Res. **218**(1), 211–229 (2012). https://doi.org/10.1016/j.ejor.2011.09.031.   https://www.sciencedirect.com/science/article/pii/S0377221711008599

19. Xia, G.E., Wang, H., Jiang, Y.: Application of customer churn prediction based on weighted selective ensembles. In: 2016 3rd International Conference on Systems and Informatics (ICSAI), pp. 513–519 (2016). https://doi.org/10.1109/ICSAI.2016.7811009

Improving the Expected Goal Value in Football Using Multilayer Perceptron Networks

Manuel Méndez, Carlos Montero, and Manuel Núñez$^{(\boxtimes)}$ (iD)

Design and Testing of Reliable Systems research group, Universidad Complutense de Madrid,
Madrid, Spain
{manumend, cmonte09, manuelnu}@ucm.es

Abstract. The development of big data and machine learning is having a special boost in the field of innovation in sports. Football is the most popular sport in Europe with millions of players and billions of euros invested. Currently, machine learning applications in football are focused on video analysis to events detection (tracking of players, statistics matches, scouting, ...), injuries evaluation and prediction, among others. The xG metric (Expected Goals) determines the probability that a shot will result in a goal and is often displayed on screen during the most important football matches in the world. In this paper we present a new model to obtain more accurate predictions of the probability of a shot becoming a goal. The model is based on a multi-layer perceptron neural network (MLP), which allows the interaction of different variables and improves the model's performance. Our proposal includes an evaluation of the quality and a comparison with the xG provided by statsbomb, one of the most important football data providers of the world. The results show that our model outperforms the quality of the expectations provided by statsbomb. Specifically, it is clearly better in their capability to detect actual positive cases (goals).

Keywords: Deep Learning in Sports · Big Data in Football · Expected Goal · Multi-layer Perceptron Networks

1 Introduction

The widespread popularity of big data and machine learning [19, 23, 31] in recent years has led to their extended use in various and heterogeneous fields [12, 13, 18, 20]. One area in which they have driven significant innovation is sports, particularly in football. Currently, it is common for top football teams to employ specialists who analyse a multitude of data variables to identify areas for improvement in upcoming games. Big data is used in several areas of football [3, 11, 28], including player performance analysis, tactical analysis, injury prevention, and scouting. In player performance analysis, big data helps analysts to identify the strengths and weaknesses of individual players, allowing coaches to make informed decisions about including them in the team. In tactical analysis, big data is used to detect patterns in opponents game-play, enabling

This work has been supported by the Spanish MINECO/FEDER project AwESOMe (PID2021-122215NB-C31) and the Region of Madrid project FORTE-CM (S2018/TCS-4314), co-funded by EIE Funds of the European Union.

N. T. Nguyen et al. (Eds.): ACIIDS 2023, CCIS 1863, pp. 352–363, 2023.
https://doi.org/10.1007/978-3-031-42430-4_29

Table 1. xG by metric and threshold above which a shot is considered goal in World Cup 2022.

Threshold	Balanced accuracy	F1-score	Recall	Precision
0.2	0.741	0.517	0.584	0.463
0.5	0.655	0.446	0.333	0.677
0.75	0.617	0.37	0.251	0.7
0.9	0.5	0	0	0

coaches to develop effective strategies to counter them [5]. Big data can also be used to monitor player fitness levels and detect early signs of injury, helping teams take proactive measures to prevent injuries [17]. Finally, big data is used in scouting, allowing teams to identify potential transfer targets based on their performance statistics in other leagues and countries [2].

One of the most popular metrics used to analyse the performance of a football player is the expected goals (xG) generated. This metric aims to determine the probability (between 0 and 1) that a shot will result in a goal. In recent years, the popularity of this metric has increased considerably, to the point that it is now often displayed on-screen during the most important football matches in the world when a shot occurs. In current models, xG is obtained from a logistic regression [24] based on historical records that models the probability that a goal occurs after a shot. This model uses as independent variables the distance to goal, angle to goal, body part of the shot, type of assist, goalkeeper position, position of all attackers and defenders and shot impact height.

However, after an analysis of the quality of the xG model most frequently used[1], we detected some shortcomings. For example, when considering the World Cup 2022 games, we noted that only 6.42% of shots had an xG higher than 0.5. This percentage was reduced to 2.23% if we discard penalty shots. However, the number of goals was 10.63% when discarding penalties and 13.6% when including them. Taking these statistics into account, we concluded that, in general, the xG assigned to any given shot is too low. We continued to analyse the xG in the World Cup 2022 using classical statistical metrics and obtained poor results in most cases, as we can see in Table 1, using different thresholds above which we predict the shot to be a goal (by default, this value is 0.5).

After reviewing the available scientific literature, we realised that deep learning has not been yet used to predict xG; only pure statistical models have been used. Therefore, we decided to explore new alternatives and models to obtain more accurate predictions of the probability of a shot becoming a goal. We believe that one of the reasons for the poor performance of xG models is that while each variable has a determined weight, the relationship between two or more variables is not explored by the model, which is a significant limitation in evaluating a shot. Therefore, we propose a model based on a multi-layer perceptron neural network (MLP), which allows the interaction of different

---

[1] Not all xG models take into account the same factors. We refer in this work to the xG model given by Statsbomb [25], which uses more contextual events and better quality data than any other provider to accurately measure the quality of chances.

variables and improves the model's performance. Our proposed model is trained with data obtained from *statsbomb* [25], which contains many characteristics of more than 16, 000 shots from 19 top-level football competitions played between 2005 and 2022. In order to evaluate the quality of our model, We used five classical statistical metrics for binary classification and a new metric developed by us that directly compares models.

The rest of the paper is organised as follows. In Sect. 2 we review the most relevant and recent contributions related to the topics of the paper. In Sect. 3 we present the evaluation metrics that we will use to compare the quality of the results provided by our proposal with the ones provided by statsbomb. In Sect. 4 we describe the data extraction and preprocessing processes and give the main characteristics of our proposal model, including the hyperparameters fine-tuning. In Sect. 5 we present the results of our experiments. Finally, in Sect. 6 we present our conclusions and some lines for future work.

2 Related Work

xG is a well-known metric that has been used for several years to predict the number of goals in a game. Initially, this metric was calculated based on factors such as goals scored in previous games, average number of goals, average number of goals playing at home or away, first or second half performance, etc. For many years, the Poisson distribution has been the most commonly used model for this purpose. The method was first used to simulate the World Cup 1998 [4]. Over the years, this method has been improved, and it was further refined in 2010 to simulate the World Cup in South Africa [30]. The next major improvement was in the World Cup 2014 [9] where various potentially influential covariates were included. It is important to note that the model predicted the actual world champion, Germany. Other international competitions where the Poisson Distribution (and its improvements) has been employed include the UEFA European Championship 2016 [8], where a bivariate Poisson distribution was used, and the African Championship 2019 [7], where authors employed a nested regression Poisson model.

In recent years, with the significant development of machine learning and real-time technology, the xG metric is no longer calculated solely based on previous goal variables, but also takes into account shots taken during the game. Each shot is assigned a probability between 0 and 1 of being a goal. The prediction of xG has been studied less in the scientific community, mainly due to the difficulty of obtaining data with a high number of shots and enough characteristics of each shot to apply the models. The logistic regression model is the most commonly used model in this case [24]. Although there are not many scientific papers about it, it is widely known that this model is used in the xG metric that appears in the most important football data websites of the world [6, 29], as well as in Statsbomb [25], the site from where we obtain data and use it as a benchmark to compare our proposal.

We would like to mention several studies that have used either statistical machine learning techniques or deep learning models in football video analysis. An extensive survey [1] has reviewed the challenges (e.g. player/ball detection and tracking, event detection, and game analysis) and compared the different deep learning-based methods and their performance. There are methods for the extraction of player's trajectory in a video football game [10]. In this case, the deep learning technology is used for automatic extraction of the features of the players, detection and tracking.

Machine learning methods have been recently used to work with trajectories of the players in the pitch. By comparing actual movements with the reference movements generated via trajectory prediction, it is possible to predict the likelihood of a player without the ball to create a scoring chance for teammates [27]. Another model shows that the first five seconds that a team has possession are fundamental to determine whether the team will be able to create a goal chance [26].

Finally, another line of work focuses on the efficient fatigue monitoring and in maintaining the best performance of players. A deep learning algorithm has been used to predict the Rate of Perceived Exertion (RPE) from players' movement [14]. The model preprocessed the raw GPS data to obtain linear and angular components of velocity, acceleration, and jerk routes. Another proposal uses a multi-dimensional approach to injury forecasting in professional soccer that is based on GPS measurements and machine learning, using GPS tracking technology, and then construct an injury forecaster [22].

3   Evaluation Metrics

In this section, we will describe discuss the performance evaluation metrics, that is, a number of metrics employed to evaluate the quality of a binary classification model.

Let TP be the number of true positives, TN be the number of true negatives, FP be the number of false positives, FN the number of false negatives, and $T = TN + TP + FN + FP$ be the total number of observations. We consider the following metrics to evaluate classification models. *Accuracy* (*Acc*). This is the most typical metric for a classification model. The accuracy measures the proportion of correct predictions made by the model over the total number of predictions. The mathematical formulation of the accuracy is:

$$Acc = \frac{TN + TP}{T}$$

Although accuracy is a commonly used metric for evaluating classification models, it can be misleading in unbalanced problems. When the distribution of classes in the data is imbalanced, accuracy can be biased towards the majority class, leading to misleading results.

Balanced Accuracy (*B_Acc*). This metric addresses the limitations of Accuracy by taking into account the class imbalance in the dataset. It gives equal weight to both classes, regardless of their number of observations, and provides a more accurate measure of the model performance in classifying both classes. The mathematical formulation of the balanced accuracy is:

$$B\_Acc = \frac{\frac{TP}{TP+FN} + \frac{TN}{TN+FP}}{2}$$

Precision (*Prec*). This metric indicates the model ability to accurately identify the positive cases. The mathematical formulation of the precision is:

$$Prec = \frac{TP}{TP + FP}$$

```
def c_met(model1,model2,obs):
    aux1 = []
    aux2 = []
    for i in range(len(obs)):
        if obs[i] == 1:
            if model1[i] > model2[i]:
                aux1.append(True)
            else:
                aux2.append(True)
        if obs[i] == 0:
            if model1[i] < model2[i]:
                aux1.append(True)
            else:
                aux2.append(True)
    if sum(aux1) > sum(aux2):
        print('Model 1 is the best')
    else:
        print('Model 2 is the best')
```

Fig. 1. C_metr implementation in Python.

Recall (*Rec*). This metric indicates the quantity of positive cases that the model can identify. The mathematical formulation of the precision is:

$$Rec = \frac{TP}{TP + FN}$$

F1-score (*F*1). This metric combines recall and precision in only one value. The mathematical formulation of the F1-score is:

$$2 \cdot \frac{\frac{TP}{TP+FP} \cdot \frac{TP}{TP+FN}}{\frac{TP}{TP+FP} + \frac{TP}{TP+FN}} = 2 \cdot \frac{Prec \cdot Rec}{Prec + Rec}$$

Comparison metric (*C_metr*). We developed a metric to facilitate the direct comparison of two models in a binary classification context. The metric operates by assigning a point to the model that assigns a higher probability to an observation that is truly positive and to the model that assigns a lower probability to an observation that is truly negative. Following this process for all observations, the model with the highest number of points is deemed the superior performer. The implementation of this metric in Python is shown in Fig. 1

4   Data Preprocessing, Problem Description and Proposed Model

In this section, we will describe the process of data extraction and preprocessing and the main characteristics of the problem at hand, including the definition of our model. Finally, we present the fine-tuning process applied to obtain the best performance of our model.

4.1   Data Acquisition, Preprocessing and Predictor Variables

Our data was obtained from https://github.com/statsbomb/open-data and downloaded using the *statsbomb* package in Python. The dataset includes a large number of top football games, along with their corresponding events such as shots, passes, and fouls. In this paper, we focus only on shots. We extracted shots performed in nineteen competitions, including the World Cup (2018 and 2022) and the Spanish First Division (from the 2004–2005 to 2020–2021 seasons), resulting in a total of $16,042$ shots. Each shot is associated with 33 variables. Next, we will explain why we decided to discard sixteen of these variables and focus solely on the remaining seventeen for our prediction. We discarded four variables related to the identification of the shot. We also discarded the date, possession, possession team, team name, and player name. Then, we discarded whether the shot was off-camera, as well as the outcome of the shot (because this is the variable we will predict) and whether it was the first shot of the game. We also discarded the variables related to the coordinates that refer to the end location of the shot because our prediction will be given based only on the beginning of the shot, not the end. Finally, we discarded the expected goal according to *statsbomb* because this is the variable against which we will compare our model results.

Therefore, we will use the remaining seventeen variables, which are: *period*, *minute*, and *second*, the *play pattern* (i.e., a regular play, a shot from a free kick, a shot from a throw-in, etc.), the *position* of the player who takes the shot, the *duration* of the ball possession by the player who takes the shot before the play, whether the player who takes the shot is *under pressure* or not, the *body part* that is used to take the shot, the *type* of shot, the *technique* used to take the shot (volley, half-volley, header, back-heel, etc.), whether the shot *is followed by a drive* or not, whether the shot is *redirected* or not, whether the play is a *one-on-one* situation or not, whether the shot is taken on an *open goal* or not, whether the shot is *deflected* or not, and, finally, the coordinates x and y from which the shot is taken. Obviously, the *outcome* of the shot (whether the shot is or not a goal) is the target variable.

Once we have identified the predictor variables and the target variable, we need to describe how we obtained accurate, consistent, and complete data to work with, a process known as *data preprocessing*. First, we take the categorical variables, including the target variable, (they are all except x, y, *second*, *minute*, and *duration*), and apply a technique called *LabelEncoder*. This technique is commonly used to transform a categorical variable into a numerical variable. Then, we apply a *StandardScaler* method to all the variables (except to the continuous, that is just 1 or 0). This method is used to transform numerical data to have a mean of 0 and a standard deviation of 1. It works by subtracting the mean of each variable and then dividing the result by the standard deviation of that variable. Finally, the last step of the preprocessing phase is to ensure that the target variable is properly coded, assigning a value of 1 to the cases where a goal has been scored and a value of 0 to the cases where a goal has not been scored.

In conclusion, our objective is to predict, with an error as small as possible, whether a shot is a goal (y) by using the 17 predictor variables ($X_1, \ldots, X_{17}$) that we described in the previous lines.

4.2 Proposed Model

Our proposal model is a Multi-Layer Perceptron Neural Network (MLP). This is a type of artificial neural network that consists of multiple layers of interconnected nodes, or neurons, which are organised into input, output, and hidden layers. Each neuron

Table 2. Grid of hyperparameters considered in the fine-tuning.

Hyperparameter	Set of values
h	$\{1, 2, 3, 4, 5\}$
h_i	$\{16, 32, 64, 128, 256\}$
lr	$\{0.001, 0.01, 0.1\}$
dr	$\{0.2, 0.3, 0.4\}$
ep	$\{10, 20, 30\}$
bs	$\{32, 64, 128\}$

receives inputs from the previous layer and produces an output that is passed on to the next layer. The neurons in the hidden layers use an activation function to transform the input signals and produce a nonlinear output. The output layer produces the final output of the network, which is typically used to make predictions or classify input data. MLPs are trained using a supervised learning algorithm, such as backpropagation, to adjust the weights and biases of the neurons in the network to minimise the error between the predicted output and the actual output.

The operations occurring in every neuron in the hidden and output layers can be represented by the following equations:

$$H_x = f(b_1 + W_1 \cdot x) \qquad O_x = f'(b_2 + H_x \cdot W_2)$$

being x an input vector, b_1 and b_2 bias vectors, W_1 and W_2 weight matrices and f and f' activation functions. Usual activation functions are the RELU and sigmoid functions.

$$RELU(a) = \max(0, a) \qquad Sig(a) = \frac{1}{1 + e^{-a}},$$

where a is the input data.

Hyperparameters such as the *number of hidden layers* (h), *number of neurons in hidden layer i* (h_i), *learning rate* (lr), *dropout rate* (dr), *number of epochs* (ep), and batch size (bs) will be fine-tuned in order to obtain the optimal performance.

4.3 Hyperparameters Fine-Tuning

In order to perform fine-tuning, we use GridSearch, which is a hyperparameter tuning technique that systematically searches through a specified hyperparameter space to find the optimal combination of hyperparameters that result in the best performance of the model. In GridSearch, a grid of hyperparameter values is defined, and the model is trained and evaluated for each combination of hyperparameters in the grid. The hyperparameters that yield the best performance, as measured by a chosen evaluation metric, are then selected as the optimal hyperparameters for the model. It is usual to improve the quality of the fine-tuning process by combining it with the cross-validation technique. In this case, we develop the grid of hyperparameters shown in Table 2.

We chose this hyperparameter grid, with a low number of layers and epochs, because our dataset has a small number of independent variables. We also used prototypical numbers for the neurons (powers of 2), learning rate (negative powers of 10), epochs (multiples of 10), and batch size (also powers of 2).

Table 3. Metrics comparing our proposal vs. *statsbomb* model.

δ	Acc		B_Acc		Prec		Rec		F1	
Model	Proposal	sts model	Proposal	sts model	Proposal	sts model	Proposal	sts model	Proposal	sts model
0.25	0.868	0.871	0.695	0.707	0.479	0.466	0.463	0.48	0.479	0.492
0.5	0.875	0.871	0.697	0.75	0.443	0.273	0.47	0.79	0.456	0.407
0.75	0.874	0.893	0.712	0.781	0.403	0.174	0.496	0.798	0.445	0.29

We used the *Balanced Accuracy* evaluation metric to determine the best performance, as this metric gives equal weight to both categories and does not discriminate between them. Additionally, we employed a cross-validation method with 3 folds, meaning we split the data into 3 different testing and training sets to prevent over-fitting.

The optimal values obtained according to the best performance in *Balanced Accuracy* are: $h = 4$, $h_1 = 256$, $h_2 = h_3 = h_4 = 64$, $lr = 0.1$, $dr = 0.2$, $ep = 20$ and $bs = 32$. These results show that higher values of the hyperparameters cannot be associated with better performance, as might be expected in cases such as the number of layers, neurons, batch size, or epochs.

5   Experiments

In this section, we compare our (fine-tuned) model with the xG metric provided by *statsbomb*, taking into account all the metrics described in Sect. 3. To conduct the experiments, we randomly divided the dataset into a training set and a testing set with a ratio of $9/10$ and $1/10$, respectively. We then applied our model with the optimal hyperparameters obtained from the fine-tuning process described in the previous section. After running the experiments, we compared and analysed the evaluation metrics applied to the results of our model and the xG metric provided by *statsbomb*.

In order to compare our proposed model and the xG values provided by *statsbomb*, we need to set a threshold. If a model outputs a value above this threshold, δ, for an observation, then the observation will be predicted as a goal. On the contrary, if a model outputs a value below the threshold, then the observation will be predicted as no goal. By default (and logically), the most obvious value of δ is 0.5. However, depending on the context, this value can be higher or lower. In some models, it may be preferred to maximise sensitivity (proportion of true negatives) instead of specificity (proportion of true positives). In other models, depending on the cost of error, it may be more appropriate to increase or decrease the threshold. In order to explore all the options, we will perform the comparison setting different values of δ.

Table 3 shows the evaluation of the performance of our model and the *statsbomb* model according to five metrics and three different thresholds. We can draw several conclusions. Firstly, we can observe that our model performs better than the model provided by *statsbomb* in some cases, while for others the *statsbomb* model is better. Note that when focusing on accuracy and balanced accuracy, both models perform similarly, but our proposed model is slightly worse than the *statsbomb* model regardless of the threshold. However, these metrics do not provide a complete understanding of the model's quality in an unbalanced classification problem and we are working with

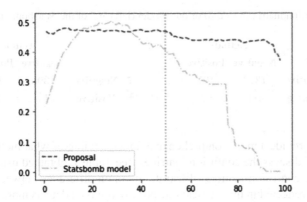

Fig. 2. $F1$ (y axis) by δ value (x axis) in the proposal model and in the model provided by Statsbomb.

a clearly unbalanced one. To gain a better understanding, we need to examine metrics that assess the models' ability to classify negative (no goal) and positive (goal) values. Therefore, we use Precision and Recall, which show very different behaviours of the models. While a better precision denotes a better capability to detect the proportion of true positives among all the positive predicted cases, and is useful when minimising false positives is important, a better recall denotes the capability to detect the proportion of true positives among all the positive cases and is useful when minimising false negatives is important.

The results show that our model clearly outperforms the *statsbomb* model in precision, while the opposite occurs in recall. Because of this, we appeal to F1-Score, a metric that combines both Precision and Recall. By using this metric, the results vary depending on the threshold: with $\delta = 0.25$, the *statsbomb* model is slightly better than our proposal, with $\delta = 0.5$, our proposal is slightly better than the *statsbomb* model, and with $\delta = 0.75$, our proposal clearly outperforms the *statsbomb* model.

Figure 2 illustrates the F1-score as a function of the δ value, ranging from 0 to 0.99. We observe that the F1-score in our model remains constant, while it does not in the model provided by *statsbomb*. Our proposed model outperforms the one provided by *statsbomb* for all δ values except for the range between 0.2 and 0.4, where the F1-score of the *statsbomb* model is slightly higher than our proposal. For the remaining values, our proposal clearly outperforms the *statsbomb* model, including $\delta = 0.5$ (red dotted line), which is the "logical" value that the threshold should receive.

Overall, when using metrics such as Accuracy and Balanced Accuracy, which do not provide a good understanding of unbalanced classification tasks, our proposal performs slightly worse than the model provided by Statsbomb. However, when using specific metrics, our proposal obtains better precision, while the *statsbomb* model obtains better recall. This indicates that our proposal is better at minimising false positive cases (which is a major issue in most xG models), while the *statsbomb* model is better at minimising false negatives. When unifying both metrics, our proposal obtains better results, as can be seen with the F1-Score metric.

Table 4. Confusion matrix ($\delta = 0.5$) of our model (left) and of the Statsbomb model (right).

		Actual					Actual	
		Negative	Positive				Negative	Positive
Pred	Negative	1314	107			Negative	1390	146
	Positive	90	94		Pred	Positive	14	55

In order to provide a more comprehensive understanding of what metrics mean, we will present and discuss the confusion matrices, see Table 4, obtained using a threshold of $\delta = 0.5$. The confusion matrices illustrate the main difference between the models, which was also reflected in the metrics: our proposed model detects more true positives (i.e. goals) at the expense of an increase in false negatives, while the model provided by Statsbomb can only detect a low number of true positives, resulting in an increase in false positives.

Finally, we evaluated the C_{metr} metric as defined in Sect. 3. Our proposed model clearly outperformed the model provided by Statsbomb in 82.5% of the cases, indicating that our model predicted the actual outcome (i.e. goal, represented by 1 or no goal, represented by 0) more accurately.

6 Conclusions and Future Work

In the field of professional football, there is an increasing demand for technical analysis of the teams and players performance. The Expected Goal (xG) is a usual indicator of that performance, which measures the probability of a shot becoming goal. In this paper, we have developed a new method based on a multi-layer perceptron neural network (MLP) to obtain more accurate predictions of the expected goal. The model uses as independent variables the distance to goal, angle to goal, body part of the shot, type of assist, goalkeeper position, position of all attackers and defenders and shot impact height. This work allows the interaction of different variables and improves the model's performance, specially by detecting a higher number of positive cases.

Focusing on the results, we compared our proposal with the *statsbomb* model using several metrics. We addressed some questions, such as the threshold, δ, which represents the probability above which a shot is considered a goal. The accuracy and balanced accuracy metrics do not provide a good understanding of unbalanced classification tasks. Both models obtained similar results regardless of the δ value used. However, the recall metric showed that the *statsbomb* model performed better, while the precision metric indicated that our proposal performed better. We then used the F1-Score metric, which combines precision and recall, to compare the models. Our proposal outperformed the *statsbomb* model according to F1-score. Finally, according to the C_{metr} metric, our proposed model outperformed the model provided by Statsbomb in 82.5% of the cases, indicating that our MLP model more accurately predicted the actual outcome.

We consider some lines of future work. First, since the field is growing, we plan to review the work on machine learning applied to sports. We will follow a methodology similar to the one used in our recent work [16]. Second, due to the high quality and different perspective of the proposed model, we will apply it to more data from professional football leagues to minimise errors by training with a high number of observations (we need to improve/increase the data obtained from *statsbomb*). Third, in addition to the goal, other football plays such as shooting and saving penalties may also be determinants in the match, and similar models to ours can be applied in these cases. Fourth, we rely on a supervised model but it would be interesting to consider an unsupervised approach following recent work on attacks detection [21]. Finally, we would like to implement a model similar to the one described in the introduction that predicts the xG of a team in a match, rather than of a shot. In this case, the model would be based on the team's historical xG in previous games, rather than their historical goals, and might be useful to consider a hybrid approach as we did in our recent work [15].

References

1. Akan, S., Varli, S.: Use of deep learning in soccer videos analysis: survey. Multimed. Syst. **29**(3), 897–915 (2023)
2. Iman Behravan and Seyed Mohammad Razavi: A novel machine learning method for estimating football players' value in the transfer market. Soft. Comput. **25**(3), 2499–2511 (2021)
3. Cacho-Elizondo, S., Álvarez, J.D.L.: Big data in the decision-making processes of football teams. J. Strateg. Innov. Sustain. **15**(2), 21–44 (2020)
4. Dyte, D., Clarke, S.R.: A ratings based poisson model for world cup soccer simulation. J. Oper. Res. Soc. **51**(8), 993–998 (2000)
5. Fang, L., Wei, Q., Cheng, X.: Technical and tactical command decision algorithm of football matches based on big data and neural network. Sci. Program. **1–9**(04), 2021 (2021)
6. Footystats. https://footystats.org/es/spain/la-liga/xg. Accessed 10 Mar 2023
7. Gilch, L.A.: Prediction model for the Africa cup of nations 2019 via nested poisson regression. Afr. J. Appl. Stat. **6**(1), 599–616 (2019)
8. Groll, A., Kneib, T., Mayr, A., Schauberger, G.: On the dependency of soccer scores - a sparse bivariate Poisson model for the UEFA European football championship 2016. J. Quant. Anal. Sports **14**(2), 65–79 (2018)
9. Groll, A., Schauberger, G., Tutz, G.: Prediction of major international soccer tournaments based on team-specific regularized Poisson regression: an application to the FIFA World Cup 2014. J. Quant. Anal. Sports **11**(2), 97–115 (2015)
10. He, X.: Application of deep learning in video target tracking of soccer players. Soft. Comput. **20**(20), 10971–10979 (2022)
11. Herberger, T.A., Litke, C.: The impact of big data and sports analytics on professional football: a systematic literature review. In: Herberger, T.A., Dötsch, J.J. (eds.) Digitalization, Digital Transformation and Sustainability in the Global Economy. SPBE, pp. 147–171. Springer, Cham (2021). https://doi.org/10.1007/978-3-030-77340-3_12
12. Hossain, E., Khan, I., Un-Noor, F., Sikander, S.S., Sunny, M.S.H.: Application of big data and machine learning in smart grid, and associated security concerns: a review. IEEE Access **7**, 13960–13988 (2019)
13. Ip, R.H., Ang, L.M., Seng, K.P., Broster, J.C., Pratley, J.E.: Big data and machine learning for crop protection. Comput. Electr. Agric. **151**, 376–383 (2018)
14. Kim, J., Kim, H., Lee, J., Lee, J., Yoon, J., Ko, S.-K.: A deep learning approach for fatigue prediction in sports using GPS data and rate of perceived exertion. IEEE Access **10**, 103056–103064 (2022)

15. Méndez, M., Merayo, M.G., Núñez, M.: Long-term traffic flow forecasting using a hybrid CNN-BiLSTM model. Eng. Appl. Artif. Intell. **121**, 106041 (2023)
16. Méndez, M., Merayo, M.G., Núñez,M.: Machine learning algorithms to forecast air quality: a survey. Artif. Intell. Rev. (2023)
17. Meng, T., Yang, J.Y.: Intervention of football players' training effect based on machine learning. In: 2nd International Conference on Consumer Electronics and Computer Engineering (ICCECE 2022), pp. 592–595 (2022)
18. Kee Yuan Ngiam and Wei Khor: Big data and machine learning algorithms for health-care delivery. Lancet Oncol. **20**(5), e262–e273 (2019)
19. Qiu, J., Qihui, W., Ding, G., Yuhua, X., Feng, S.: A survey of machine learning for big data processing. EURASIP J. Adv. Signal Process. **1–16**, 2016 (2016)
20. Rodrigues, J.F., Florea, L., de Oliveira, M.C.F., Diamond, D., Oliveira, O.N.: Big data and machine learning for materials science. Discover Mater. **1**(1), 1–27 (2021). https://doi.org/10.1007/s43939-021-00012-0
21. Roldán-Gómez, J., del Rincón, J.M., Boubeta-Puig, J., Martínez, J.L.: An automatic unsupervised complex event processing rules generation architecture for real-time IoT attacks detection. Wireless Netw., 1–18 (2023)
22. Rossi, A., Pappalardo, L., Cintia, P., Iaia, F.M., Fernández, J., Medina, D.: Effective injury forecasting in soccer with GPS training data and machine learning. PLoS ONE **13**, 1–15 (2018)
23. Surender R.S.: A survey of big data and machine learning. Int. J. Electr. Comput. Eng. **10**(1) (2020)
24. Soccermatics. fitting the xg model. https://soccermatics.readthedocs.io/en/latest/gallery/lesson2/plot_xGModelFit.html. Accessed 10 Mar 2023
25. Statsbomb. https://statsbomb.com. Accessed 10 Mar 2023
26. Stival, L., et al.: Using machine learning pipeline to predict entry into the attack zone in football. PLoS ONE **18**, 1–24 (2023)
27. Teranishi, M., Tsutsui, K., Takeda, K., Fujii, K.: Evaluation of creating scoring opportunities for teammates in soccer via trajectory prediction. In: Brefeld, U., Davis, J., Van Haaren, J., Zimmermann, A. (eds.) Machine Learning and Data Mining for Sports Analytics, MLSA 2022. Communications in Computer and Information Science, vol. 1783, pp. 53–73. Springer, Cham (2023). https://doi.org/10.1007/978-3-031-27527-2_5
28. Thakkar, P., Shah, M.: An assessment of football through the lens of data science. Ann. Data Sci. **8**, 823–836 (2021)
29. Understat. https://understat.com/. Accessed 10 Mar 2023
30. Wang,D.: Soccer tournament simulation and analysis for south Africa world cup with Poisson model of goal probability. In: 2010 Chinese Control and Decision Conference, pp. 3654–3659 (2010)
31. Zhou, L., Pan, S., Wang, J., Vasilakos, A.V.: Machine learning on big data: opportunities and challenges. Neurocomputing **237**, 350–361 (2017)

A Projected Upper Bound for Mining High Utility Patterns from Interval-Based Event Sequences

S. Mohammad Mirbagheri[(✉)]

Department of Computer Science, University of Regina, Regina, Canada
Mo.Mirbagheri@uregina.ca

Abstract. High utility pattern mining is an interesting yet challenging problem. The intrinsic computational cost of the problem will impose further challenges if efficiency in addition to the efficacy of a solution is sought. Recently, this problem was studied on interval-based event sequences with a constraint on the length and size of the patterns. However, the proposed solution lacks adequate efficiency. To address this issue, we propose a projected upper bound on the utility of the patterns discovered from sequences of interval-based events. To show its effectiveness, the upper bound is utilized by a pruning strategy employed by the HUIPMiner algorithm. Experimental results show that the new upper bound improves HUIPMiner performance in terms of both execution time and memory usage.

Keywords: Upper bound · high utility · pattern mining · sequential mining · event sequence

1 Introduction

Frequent Pattern Mining (FPM) [1] has been well-studied over the past two decades. The goal of FPM is to discover patterns such that the frequency of their appearances in a dataset is higher than a user-specified threshold. Since the measure of the interestingness of the patterns is frequency, FPM is incapable of addressing problems where the frequency of occurrences of patterns is not of interest.

As a result, High Utility Pattern Mining (HUPM) was proposed for problems where patterns with high utilities, e.g., profits generated by patterns, are of interest, and thus they are measured based on their utilities rather than the frequency of occurrences. In particular, discovering patterns with utilities no less than a minimum utility threshold set by a user is the focus of HUPM. Depending on the domain of the data, and similar to FPM, various types of HUPM have been introduced, e.g., High Utility Itemest Mining [2], High Utility Episode Mining [3], and High Utility Sequential Pattern Mining [4].

Interval-based event sequences (e-sequences) are the sequences in which multiple events can occur coincidentally and persist over varying periods of time.

© The Author(s), under exclusive license to Springer Nature Switzerland AG 2023
N. T. Nguyen et al. (Eds.): ACIIDS 2023, CCIS 1863, pp. 364–375, 2023.
https://doi.org/10.1007/978-3-031-42430-4_30

E-sequences are present in many real-world applications from different domains, such as healthcare [5,6], real-time systems [7], cybersecurity [8], and activity recognition [9].

Table 1 presents four sequences of interval-based events that form a dataset. We will use these sequences as a running example throughout this paper. As shown, each e-sequences contains event intervals with various labels, beginning and finishing times. These e-sequences have been visualized in the furthest right column of the table.

Finding patterns from interval-based event sequences is a relatively new research area. Most prior work [10–13] has been dedicated to finding frequent temporal patterns from event sequences. Other pattern-related problems including mining high utility episodes [3,14] and mining top-k high utility patterns [15] in event sequences have also been studied. However, not much attention has been paid to the HUPM problem in event sequences.

Mirbagheri and Hamilton [16,17] recently conducted a study on HUPM involving e-sequences. They introduced a framework to incorporate the concept of utility into these sequences and proposed an algorithm named HUIPMiner to discover the high utility patterns. They identified an upper bound, namely the L-*sequence-weighted utilization* (LWU$_k$), for the utility of the e-sequences with respect to a maximum length, denoted as k, of the patterns. The upper bound is employed in a pruning strategy in the algorithm to reduce the search space, which results in reducing the execution time and space.

Contributions. In this paper, we improve the previous work [16,17] by deriving a new upper bound on the utility of e-sequences, namely the *Projected utilization* ($\mathcal{P}_k$), and show both theoretically and empirically that if $\mathcal{P}_k$ is employed, the execution of the algorithm will improve compared to when the algorithm utilizes LWU$_k$.

The remainder of this paper is structured as follows. Section 2 provides the background on sequences of interval-based events and relevant preliminaries for high utility pattern mining. Section 3 presents the methodology, reviews the L-sequence-weighted utilization (LWU$_k$), and introduces properties that are used in reducing the search space. It then presents the projected upper bound and the consequential property. Section 4 reports on the empirical results and evaluates the proposed solution. Section 5 concludes the paper.

2 Background

In this section, we review the preliminaries of the HUIPM problem [16,17] that will be used to derive the projected upper bound.

Let $\Sigma = \{A, B, ...\}$ be a set of finite alphabet. An *event-interval* is defined as a triple $e = (l, b, f)$, where $l \in \Sigma$ is the event label, $b, f \in \mathbb{N}$ such that $b < f$, is the beginning and finishing time, respectively. An event-interval sequence or *E-sequence*, denoted by $s = \langle e_1, e_2, ..., e_n \rangle$, is defined as an ordered list of n event intervals which are sorted in ascending order of the beginning times and in case of tie, sorted in the lexicographical order of the event labels. The number of

Table 1. Example of an E-sequence dataset

ID	Event Label	Beginning Time	Finishing Time	Visualized E-sequences
1	A	6	12	A
	B	10	17	B
	C	19	25	C
	E	21	23	E
2	A	2	7	A
	B	5	10	B
	D	5	12	D
	C	16	22	C
	E	18	20	E
3	B	6	12	B
	A	8	14	A
	C	14	20	C
	E	16	18	E
4	B	1	5	B
	C	8	14	C
	E	9	12	E
	F	9	12	F

event-intervals in s determines the *size* of E-sequence s (denoted as $|s| = n$). A set $D = \{s_1, s_2, ..., s_d\}$ containing d E-sequences, where each E-sequence s_i is associated with an unique identifier $1 \leq i \leq d$, is called an *E-sequence dataset*. For example, Table 1 presents an E-sequence dataset that contains four E-sequences with identifiers 1 to 4.

2.1   Representation

Definition 1. *E-sequence unique time points* $T_s = \langle t_1, t_2, ..., t_m \rangle$ is a finite non-empty sequence consisting of the unique time points of s sorted in ascending order such that $t_k < t_{k+1}, 1 \leq k \leq m - 1, t_k \in \{b \vee f \mid b, f \in s\}$.

Definition 2.
Given an E-sequence $s = \langle (l_1, b_1, f_1), ..., (l_j, b_j, f_j), ..., (l_n, b_n, f_n) \rangle$, two consecutive time points $t_k, t_{k+1} \in T_s = \langle t_1, t_2, ..., t_m \rangle, 1 \leq k \leq m - 1$, and a function $\Phi_s : \mathbb{N} \times \mathbb{N} \to 2^\Sigma$, a *coincidence* c_k in s is defined as

$$\Phi_s(t_k, t_{k+1}) = \{l_j \mid (l_j, b_j, f_j) \in s \wedge (b_j \leq t_k) \wedge (t_{k+1} \leq f_j)\} \tag{1}$$

The *size* of coincidence $|c_k|$ is determined by the number of event labels in c_k. The *duration* of the coincidence c_k is defined as $\lambda_k = t_{k+1} - t_k$.

Example 1. The E-sequence unique time points of s_4 in Table 1 is $T_{s_4} = \{1, 5, 8, 9, 12, 14\}$. Coincidence $c_4 = \Phi_{s_4}(9, 12) = \{C, E, F\}$, $\lambda_4 = 12 - 9 = 3$, and $|c_4| = 3$.

Definition 3. We call an ordered list of coincidences $L = \langle c_1 c_2 ... c_g \rangle$ an *L-sequence*. The length of an L-sequence, denoted by K, is defined as the number of coincidences in the L-sequence. The size of an L-sequence, denoted by Z, is determined by the maximum size of the coincidences in the L-sequence.

Example 2. Since $L = \langle \{C\} \{A, B\} \{D\} \rangle$ has 3 coincidences and the maximum size of the coincidences is $max\{1, 2, 1\} = 2$, the length and size of L is 3 and 2, respectively.

Definition 4. Given a coincidence c_k in E-sequence s, a coincidence eventset, or *C-eventset*, denoted by σ_k, is defined as an ordered pair consisting of the coincidence c_k and the corresponding coincidence duration λ_k, i.e., $\sigma_k = (c_k, \lambda_k)$. If c_k in C-eventset σ_k contains only one event label, we will omit the braces for convenience and refer to c_k as a *C-event*. We refer to an ordered list of C-eventsets $C = \langle \sigma_1 \sigma_2 ... \sigma_h \rangle$, where $h = |T_s| - 1$, as *C-sequence*. Consequently, a *C-sequence dataset* δ is defined as a set of C-sequences, where each C is associated with a unique identifier.

Example 3. A C-sequence dataset corresponding to the E-sequences shown in Table 1 is presented in Table 2. C_{s_1} denotes the C-sequence with identifier 1; other C-sequences are denoted correspondingly.

One can notice that in addition to describing E-sequences in a formulated language by transforming them to C-sequences, this representation also captures the durations of the event intervals.

Table 2. C-sequence dataset corresponding to the E-sequences in Table 1

ID	C-sequence
1	$\langle (A, 4)(\{A, B\}, 2)(B, 5)(\varnothing, 2)(C, 2)(\{C, E\}, 2)(C, 2) \rangle$
2	$\langle (A, 3)(\{A, B, D\}, 2)(\{B, D\}, 3)(D, 2)(\varnothing, 4)(C, 2)(\{C, E\}, 2)(C, 2) \rangle$
3	$\langle (B, 2)(\{A, B\}, 4)(A, 2)(C, 2)(\{C, E\}, 2)(C, 2) \rangle$
4	$\langle (B, 4)(\varnothing, 3)(C, 1)(\{C, E, F\}, 3)(C, 2) \rangle$

Definition 5. C-eventset $\sigma_b = (c_b, \lambda_b)$ is said to *contain* C-eventset $\sigma_a = (c_a, \lambda_a)$, denoted as $\sigma_a \subseteq \sigma_b$, iff $c_a \subseteq c_b \wedge \lambda_a = \lambda_b$. C-sequences $C = \langle \sigma_1 \sigma_2 ... \sigma_h \rangle$ is called a *C-subsequence* of $C' = \langle \sigma'_1 \sigma'_2 ... \sigma'_{h'} \rangle$, denoted by $C \subseteq C'$, iff there exist integers $1 \leq j_1 \leq j_2 \leq ... \leq j_h \leq h'$ such that $\sigma_k \subseteq \sigma'_{j_k}$ for $1 \leq k \leq h$. We say a C-sequence $C = \langle \sigma_1 \sigma_2 ... \sigma_h \rangle = \langle (c_1, \lambda_1)(c_2, \lambda_2)...(c_h, \lambda_h) \rangle$ *matches* an L-sequence $L = \langle c'_1 c'_2 ... c'_g \rangle$ and denote it by $C \sim L$, iff $h = g$ and $c_k = c'_k$ for $1 \leq k \leq h$.

Example 4. $\langle (A, 4) \rangle$, $\langle (\{A, B\}, 2)(B, 5) \rangle$, and $\langle (\{A, B\}, 2) \rangle$ are C-subsequences of C-sequence C_{s_1}, while $\langle (\{A, B, D\}, 2) \rangle$ and $\langle (\{A, B\}, 2)(B, 2) \rangle$ are not.

It might be possible that an L-sequence is matched with multiple C-subsequences of a C-sequence. For instance, the L-sequence $\langle B \rangle$ can be matched with both $\langle (B, 2) \rangle$ and $\langle (B, 5) \rangle$ in the second and third C-eventset of C_{s_1}, respectively.

2.2   Utility

We denote the *external utility* of l by $p : \Sigma \to \mathbb{R}_{\geq 0}$. A non-negative real value is assigned to each event label $l \in \Sigma$ to represent its external utility. Any value of interest such as the unit profit can be used to indicate such utility. For instance, the external utilities correspond to event labels from Table 1 are shown in Table 3. We will use these values to refer to the external utilities of event labels in the following examples.

Table 3. External utilities associated with the event labels

Event label	A	B	C	D	E	F	∅
External utility	2	1	1	3	2	5	0

Let the utility of a C-event (l, λ) be $u(l, \lambda) = p(l) \times \lambda$. The utility of a C-eventset $\sigma = (c, \lambda) = (\{l_1, l_2, ..., l_{|c|}\}, \lambda)$ is defined as: $u_e(\sigma) = \sum_{i=1}^{|c|} u(l_i, \lambda)$. The utility of a C-sequence $C = \langle \sigma_1 \sigma_2 ... \sigma_h \rangle$ is defined as: $u_s(C) = \sum_{i=1}^{h} u_e(\sigma_i)$. Therefore, the utility of the C-sequence dataset $\delta = \{C_{s_1}, C_{s_2}, ..., C_{s_r}\}$ is defined as: $u_d(\delta) = \sum_{i=1}^{r} u_s(C_{s_i})$.

Example 5. The utility of C-sequence $C_{s_1} = \langle (A, 4)(\{A, B\}, 2)(B, 5)(\varnothing, 2)(C, 2)(\{C, E\}, 2)(C, 2) \rangle$ is $u_s(C_{s_1}) = 4 \times 2 + 2 \times (2 + 1) + 5 \times 1 + 2 \times 0 + 2 \times 1 + 2 \times (1 + 2) + 2 \times 1 = 29$, and the utility of the C-sequence dataset δ in Table 2 is $u_d(\delta) = u_s(C_{s_1}) + u_s(C_{s_2}) + u_s(C_{s_3}) + u_s(C_{s_4}) = 29 + 46 + 28 + 31 = 134$.

Definition 6. The *maximum utility of k C-eventsets in a C-sequence* is defined as: $u_{max_k}(C, k) = max\{u_s(C') \mid C' \subseteq C \wedge |C'| \leq k\}$.

Example 6. The maximum utility of 2 C-eventsets in C_{s_1} is $u_{max_k}(C_{s_1}, 2) = max\{u_s(\langle (A, 4)(\{A, B\}, 2) \rangle), u_s(\langle (A, 4)(\{C, E\}, 2) \rangle)\} = 14$.

Definition 7. Given a C-sequence dataset δ and an L-sequence $L = \langle c_1 c_2 ... c_g \rangle$, the utility of L in C-sequence $C = \langle \sigma_1 \sigma_2 ... \sigma_h \rangle \in \delta$ is defined as a *utility set*:

$$u_l(L, C) = \bigcup_{C' \sim L \wedge C' \subseteq C} u_s(C') \tag{2}$$

Consequently, the utility of L in δ is defined as:

$$u_l(L) = \bigcup_{C \in \delta} u_l(L, C) \tag{3}$$

Example 7. Given L-sequence $L = \langle\{A\}\{B\}\rangle$, the utility of L in C-sequence C_{s_1} shown in Table 2 is $u_l(L, C_{s_1}) = \{u_s(\langle\langle(A, 4)(B, 2)\rangle\rangle), u_s(\langle\langle(A, 4)(B, 5)\rangle\rangle), u_s(\langle\langle(A, 2)(B, 5)\rangle\rangle)\} = \{10, 13, 9\}$. Also, the utility of L in dataset δ is $u_l(L) = \{u_l(L, C_{s_1}), u_l(L, C_{s_2})\} = \{\{10, 13, 9\}, \{8, 9, 7\}\}$.

As seen from the above example and also in contrast to a sequence in frequent sequential pattern mining, multiple utility values can be associated with an L-sequence. The possibility of having multiple utility values will lead us to the concept of high utility, which is explored briefly in the next section.

2.3   High Utility Interval-Based Pattern Mining

Definition 8. The *maximum utility* of an L-sequence L in C-sequence dataset δ is defined as $u_{max}(L)$:

$$u_{max}(L) = \sum_{C \in \delta} \max(u_l(L, C)) \tag{4}$$

Example 8. The maximum utility of an L-sequence $L = \langle\{A\}\{B\}\rangle$ in C-sequence dataset δ shown in Table 2 is $u_{max}(L) = 13 + 9 + 0 + 0 = 22$.

Problem Statement. Given a user-specified minimum utility threshold ξ, an E-sequence dataset D, and external utilities for event labels, a *high utility interval-based pattern* (HUIP) is an L-sequence L such that $u_{max}(L) \geq \xi$. The problem of mining HUIP is to find all L-sequences such that their utilities are no less than ξ. When the maximum length and size of the patterns are specified, a more specialized problem, which is the focus of our work, is to discover all HUIPs with lengths and sizes of at most K and Z, respectively.

Our goal is not to find a new solution to the above problem, but rather is to improve the solution proposed in [16, 17] with respect to efficiency.

3   Methodology

The *downward closure property* (a.k.a. the Apriori property) [18] is an important property that most algorithms of frequent pattern mining employ to prune the search space and avoid generating infrequent candidates, which results in a more efficient way of pattern discovery. However, this property does not hold among candidates of high utility patterns. Therefore, the main challenge of HUPM is to address the lack of such property. To tackle this problem, a tight upper bound on the utility of the candidates can be used to prune the search space. Here, we review an upper bound on the utility of L-sequences, namely LWU_k, which leads to the L-sequence-weighted Downward Closure (LDC) property (Eq. (8)). This property can be utilized by an algorithm, i.e., it was previously employed by the HUIPMiner algorithm [16,17], to prune redundant (low utility) candidates. We also introduce interesting properties, which are used later to construct and verify the projected upper bound.

Definition 9. (LWU$_k$)   The L-sequence-weighted utilization of an L-sequence w.r.t. a maximum length k is defined as:

$$\text{LWU}_k(L) = \sum_{C' \sim L \wedge C' \subseteq C \wedge C \in \delta} u_{\max_k}(C, k) \tag{5}$$

Example 9. The L-sequence-weighted utilization of $L = \langle\{A\}\{B\}\rangle$ w.r.t. the maximum length $k = 3$ in the C-sequence dataset shown in Table 2 is $\text{LWU}_3(\langle\{A\}\{B\}\rangle) = 20 + 30 + 0 + 0 = 50$.

Lemma 1. *Given a C-sequence C, where $|C| \leq k' \leq k$, then*

$$u_{\max_k}(C, k') \leq u_{\max_k}(C, k) \tag{6}$$

Proof. It follows directly from Definition 6. □

Theorem 1. *Given a C-sequence dataset δ and two L-sequences L and L', where $L \subseteq L'$ and $|L'| \leq k' \leq k$, the following properties hold:*

$$\begin{align}
\text{(i)} \qquad & u_{\max}(L) \leq \text{LWU}_{|L|}(L) \tag{7}\\
\text{(ii)} \qquad & \text{LWU}_k(L') \leq \text{LWU}_k(L) \tag{8}\\
\text{(iii)} \qquad & \text{LWU}_{k'}(L) \leq \text{LWU}_k(L) \tag{9}\\
\text{(iv)} \qquad & \text{LWU}_{k'}(L') \leq \text{LWU}_k(L) \tag{10}
\end{align}$$

Proof. (i) It is inferred from Eq. (4) and Eq. (5).
(ii) The proof of the LDC property in Eq. (8) can be found in [16].
(iii) It trivially follows from Lemma 1.
(iv) It follows immediately from Eq. (8) and Eq. (9).

□

In order to discover high utility patterns, HUIPMiner generates coincidence candidates by concatenating event labels. As the number of candidates can grow exponentially, the algorithm takes advantage of the LDC property in the pruning strategy, to discard unpromising candidates.

Definition 10. A coincidence candidate c is *promising* iff $\text{LWU}_k(c) \geq \xi$. Otherwise it is *unpromising*.

Corollary 1. *Let a be an unpromising coincidence candidate and a' be a coincidence. Any superset produced by concatenating a and a' is of low utility.*

Proof. It follows directly from the LDC property. □

3.1 The Projected Utilization

In this section, we introduce a new upper bound called *projected utilization* of an L-sequence, $\mathcal{P}_k$, and we show that $\mathcal{P}_k$ is a tighter upper bound compared to LWU_k.

Definition 11. ($\mathcal{P}_k$) The projected utilization of L w.r.t. a maximum length k is defined as sum of the maximum utility of L with the L-sequence-weighted utilization of L w.r.t the *remaining length* of k:

$$\mathcal{P}_k(L) = \mathrm{u}_{\max}(L) + \mathrm{LWU}_{k-|L|}(L) \tag{11}$$

where $|L| \leq k$ denote the length of L-sequence L.

Example 10. The projected utilization of $L = \langle\{A\}\{B\}\rangle$ w.r.t. the maximum length $k = 3$ in the C-sequence dataset shown in Table 2 is $\mathcal{P}_3(\langle\{A\}\{B\}\rangle) = \mathrm{u}_{\max}(\langle\{A\}\{B\}\rangle) + \mathrm{LWU}_1(\langle\{A\}\{B\}\rangle) = (13+9+0+0)+(8+12+0+0) = 42$.

In contrast to LWU_k, which remains constant during the process of discovery for an L-sequence, $\mathcal{P}_k$ is dynamically decreasing with respect to the maximum length of the expected patterns. As the length of the pattern gets closer to the maximum length, the maximum utility for the pattern will be projected (decreased), which causes a reduction in the search space for finding the remaining part of the pattern. This will lead us to the following theorem.

Lemma 2. $\mathcal{P}_k(L)$ *is upper bounded by* $\mathrm{LWU}_k(L)$. *More formally,*

$$\mathcal{P}_k(L) \leq \mathrm{LWU}_k(L) \tag{12}$$

Proof. We rewrite Eq. (12) in accordance with Definition 11:

$$\mathcal{P}_k(L) = \mathrm{u}_{\max}(L) + \mathrm{LWU}_{k-|L|}(L) \leq \mathrm{LWU}_k(L)$$
$$\Rightarrow \mathrm{u}_{\max}(L) \leq \mathrm{LWU}_k(L) - \mathrm{LWU}_{k-|L|}(L) = \mathrm{LWU}_{|L|}(L)$$
$$\Rightarrow \mathrm{u}_{\max}(L) \leq \mathrm{LWU}_{|L|}(L).$$

$\square$

Theorem 2 (utility-Projected Downward Closure property). *Given a C-sequence dataset δ and two L-sequences L and L', where $L \subseteq L'$ and $|L'| \leq k$, then*

$$\mathcal{P}_k(L') \leq \mathcal{P}_k(L) \tag{13}$$

Proof.

$$\xrightarrow{\text{Definition 11}} \mathrm{u}_{\max}(L') + \mathrm{LWU}_{k-|L'|}(L') \leq \mathrm{u}_{\max}(L) + \mathrm{LWU}_{k-|L|}(L)$$
$$\xrightarrow{\text{Eq. (7)}} \mathrm{LWU}_{|L'|}(L') + \mathrm{LWU}_{k-|L'|}(L') \leq \mathrm{LWU}_{|L|}(L) + \mathrm{LWU}_{k-|L|}(L)$$
$$\Rightarrow \mathrm{LWU}_k(L') \leq \mathrm{LWU}_k(L).$$

$\square$

We now redefine the promising and unpromising candidates based on the PDC property (Theorem 2).

Definition 12. A coincidence candidate c is *promising* iff $\mathcal{P}_k(c) \geq \xi$. Otherwise it is *unpromising*.

It can be verified that Definition 12 will not affect Corollary 1 as it now holds by the PDC property. In fact, using $\mathcal{P}_k$ will lead to fewer or at most the same number of candidates than applying LWU$_k$. The PDC property of $\mathcal{P}_k$ will especially be beneficial when finding longer patterns, e.g., patterns of lengths $k \geq 2$, since as the length of candidates increases, the upper bound $\mathcal{P}_k$ keeps reducing. That makes the search space keeps shrinking which results in a more efficient approach.

4   Experiments

We evaluate the effectiveness of the new upper bound, $\mathcal{P}_k$, when it is employed by the HUIPMiner algorithm [16] to mine high utility patterns from e-sequences in a real-world dataset. The algorithm was implemented in C++11 and executed on a laptop computer equipped with a 10th Gen Intel Core i7 processor and 16GB of RAM.

4.1   Dataset

We used a publicly available dataset, namely *Blocks* [19], in our experiments. This dataset contains event intervals generated from descriptions of videos of human hands involving colored blocks of objects. For instance, the blue and green blocks are contacted by the hand. Each e-sequences indicates one of eight scenarios, such as stacking the blocks. The dataset has 210 unique e-sequences with a total of 1207 event intervals. The external utilities of event labels were set to 1 as such information is not present in the dataset.

4.2   Evaluation

The experiments were performed to show the impact of the PDC property when it is used by a pruning strategy in the HUIPMiner algorithm. The performance of HUIPMiner is assessed on the execution time and peak memory consumption when the PDC or LDC properties are used on the Blocks dataset while varying the minimum utility threshold ξ and the maximum length of patterns K. Figure 1 and Fig. 2 presents these evaluations on a log-10 scale. In both figures, the execution time in seconds is shown on the left and the peak memory usage in Kilobytes is presented on the right. The maximum size of patterns Z remains constant at 5 in the experiments.

Figure 1 shows the performance of the algorithm on the datasets while varying ξ and keeping K set to 4. As shown, applying the PDC property improves the execution time of the algorithm by an average of 21% compared to when the

LDC property is used. The memory usage is also reduced by an average of 5% with PDC utilization.

Figure 2 depicts the performance of the algorithm on the dataset when K is varied between 1 and 6 and ξ is set to 0.25. The results of these experiments indicate that using the PDC property will improve the running time and memory consumption of the algorithm by an average of 19% and 4%, respectively. Interestingly, when $K = 4$, the algorithm can perform twice as fast by utilizing the projected upper bound.

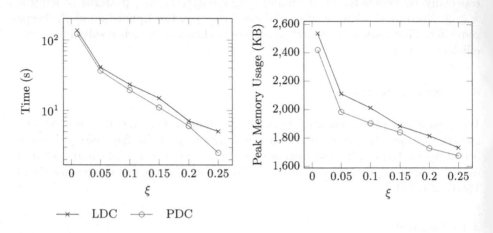

Fig. 1. Performance Comparison of the HUIPMiner algorithm under various ξ

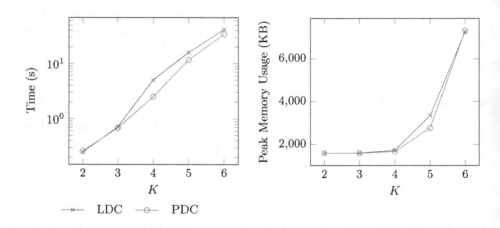

Fig. 2. Performance Comparison of the HUIPMiner algorithm under various K

The number of extracted high utility patterns is also tested to ensure that the projected upper bound does not compromise the completeness of the algorithm.

Figure 3 confirms the integrity of using both upper bounds. As expected, the same number of patterns were discovered from the dataset when any of the two upper bounds are applied.

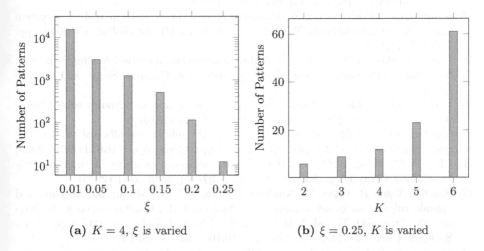

(a) $K = 4$, ξ is varied   (b) $\xi = 0.25$, K is varied

Fig. 3. Number of patterns discovered by the HUIPMiner algorithm when applying the pruning strategy based on either LDC or PDC property

5   Conclusions

We showed that the projected upper bound can improve the efficiency of the HUIPMiner algorithm. By applying the projected upper bound, HUIPMiner can be executed up to two times faster than when LWU is applied. In addition, memory consumption is reduced when the projected upper bound is used.

References

1. Han, J., Cheng, H., Xin, D., Yan, X.: Frequent pattern mining: current status and future directions. Data Min. Knowl. Disc. **15**(1), 55–86 (2007)
2. Fournier-Viger, P., Chun-Wei Lin, J., Truong-Chi, T., Nkambou, R.: A survey of high utility itemset mining. In: Fournier-Viger, P., Lin, J.C.-W., Nkambou, R., Vo, B., Tseng, V.S. (eds.) High-Utility Pattern Mining. SBD, vol. 51, pp. 1–45. Springer, Cham (2019). https://doi.org/10.1007/978-3-030-04921-8_1
3. Wu, C.W., Lin, Y.F., Yu, P.S., Tseng, V.S.: Mining high utility episodes in complex event sequences. In: Proceedings of the 19th ACM SIGKDD International Conference on Knowledge Discovery and Data Mining, PP. 536–544. ACM (2013)
4. Truong-Chi, T., Fournier-Viger, P.: A survey of high utility sequential pattern mining. In: Fournier-Viger, P., Lin, J.C.-W., Nkambou, R., Vo, B., Tseng, V.S. (eds.) High-Utility Pattern Mining. SBD, vol. 51, pp. 97–129. Springer, Cham (2019). https://doi.org/10.1007/978-3-030-04921-8_4

5. Batal, I., Valizadegan, H., Cooper, G.F., Hauskrecht, M.: A temporal pattern mining approach for classifying electronic health record data. ACM Trans. Intell. Syst. Technol. (TIST) **4**(4), 1–22 (2013)
6. Dagliati, A., et al.: Temporal electronic phenotyping by mining careflows of breast cancer patients. J. Biomed. Inf. **66**, 136–147 (2017)
7. Kauffman, S., Fischmeister, S.: Mining temporal intervals from real-time system traces. In: 6th International Workshop on Software Mining (SoftwareMining), pp. 1–8. IEEE (2017)
8. Finder, I., Sheetrit, E., Nissim, N.: A time-interval-based active learning framework for enhanced PE malware acquisition and detection. Comput. Secur. **121**, 102838 (2022)
9. Liu, Y., Nie, L., Liu, L., Rosenblum, D.S.: From action to activity: sensor-based activity recognition. Neurocomputing **181**, 108–115 (2016)
10. Mordvanyuk, N., López, B., Bifet, A.: vertTIRP: robust and efficient vertical frequent time interval-related pattern mining. Expert Syst. Appl. **168**, 114276 (2020)
11. Chen, Y.C., Peng, W.C., Lee, S.Y.: Mining temporal patterns in time interval-based data. IEEE Trans. Knowl. Data Eng. **27**(12), 3318–3331 (2015)
12. Fournier-Viger, P., Chen, Y., Nouioua, F., Lin, J.C.-W.: Mining partially-ordered episode rules in an event sequence. In: Nguyen, N.T., Chittayasothorn, S., Niyato, D., Trawiński, B. (eds.) ACIIDS 2021. LNCS (LNAI), vol. 12672, pp. 3–15. Springer, Cham (2021). https://doi.org/10.1007/978-3-030-73280-6_1
13. Ho, N.T.T., Pedersen, T.B., et al.: Efficient temporal pattern mining in big time series using mutual information. Proc. VLDB Endowment **15**(3), 673–685 (2022)
14. Gan, W., Lin, J.C.W., Chao, H.C., Yu, P.S.: Discovering high utility episodes in sequences. arXiv Preprint arXiv:1912.11670 (2019)
15. Huang, J.-W., Jaysawal, B.P., Chen, K.-Y., Wu, Y.-B.: Mining frequent and top-K high utility time interval-based events with duration patterns. Knowl. Inf. Syst. **61**(3), 1331–1359 (2019). https://doi.org/10.1007/s10115-019-01333-6
16. Mirbagheri, S.M., Hamilton, H.J.: Mining high utility patterns in interval-based event sequences. Data Knowl. Eng. **135**, 101924 (2021)
17. Mirbagheri, S.M., Hamilton, H.J.: High-utility interval-based sequences. In: Song, M., Song, I.-Y., Kotsis, G., Tjoa, A.M., Khalil, I. (eds.) DaWaK 2020. LNCS, vol. 12393, pp. 107–121. Springer, Cham (2020). https://doi.org/10.1007/978-3-030-59065-9_9
18. Agrawal, R., Srikant, R., et al.: Fast algorithms for mining association rules. In: Proceedings of the 20th International Conference Very Large Data Bases, VLDB, vol. 1215, pp. 487–499 (1994)
19. Mörchen, F., Fradkin, D.: Robust mining of time intervals with semi-interval partial order patterns. In: Proceedings of the 2010 SIAM International Conference on Data Mining, SIAM, pp. 315–326 (2010)

Mitigating Catastrophic Forgetting in Neural Machine Translation Through Teacher-Student Distillation with Attention Mechanism

Quynh-Trang Pham Thi, Ngoc-Huyen Ngo, Anh-Duc Nguyen, Duc-Trong Le, Tri-Thanh Nguyen, and Quang-Thuy Ha[⊠]

Vietnam National University, University of Engineering and Technology, Hanoi, Vietnam
{trangptq,19020047,19020004,trongld,ntthanh,thuyhq}@vnu.edu.vn

Abstract. The catastrophic forgetting is a critical problem for deep learning models, where the models learning a sequence of tasks forgets the previously learned knowledge during being trained on new data of the new task. The main reason is that a new task may likely override the weights that have been learned in the past. In this research, we propose a novel approach to address this issue for the neural machine translation model based on improving the COKD model proposed by S. Shao and Y. Feng (2022). The main idea is to divide the training data into $n+1$ parts, train n teacher models into the first n parts, and let the student model learn from the remaining part. We propose ModifiedCOKD, a method to initialize the effective teacher model parameters and use an attention mechanism to distil knowledge from the teacher models to the student models. Experimental results on the task of English-to-Vietnamese translation demonstrate that ModifiedCOKD outperforms the baseline method in mitigating catastrophic forgetting.

Keywords: Neural machine translation · Catastrophic forgetting · Attention · Online knowledge distillation

1 Introduction

Neural network models used to learn a sequence of tasks can suffer from catastrophic forgetting due to the use of mini-batch gradient descent [1], which divides the training samples into mini-batches, leading to imbalanced training where some samples are not sufficiently trained. While some tasks are less affected by this problem, *neural machine translation* (NMT) is particularly susceptible.

Recent efforts in group-based online knowledge distillation have focused on developing cost-effective and unified models to remove the need for pre-training a larger teacher model. [2,3]. The primary concept is to train multiple student models concurrently by acquiring the knowledge from both the ground-truth

© The Author(s), under exclusive license to Springer Nature Switzerland AG 2023
N. T. Nguyen et al. (Eds.): ACIIDS 2023, CCIS 1863, pp. 376–386, 2023.
https://doi.org/10.1007/978-3-031-42430-4_31

labels and the group-derived soft targets, which is a particular type of aggregation of intermediate peer predictions.

Complementary Online Knowledge Distillation (COKD) [4] is a method to address the problem of imbalanced training. The aim of COKD is to create complementary teacher models that can help the student models retain the knowledge from early samples [5]. The primary objective of COKD is to mitigate the issue of the model forgetting the knowledge it has learned from early samples. Using the teacher model to help the student model both have a better initialization of the weights and help the student model retain the knowledge learned from previous data points. This is achieved by dividing the training set into mutually exclusive subsets and organizing them in a specific order for the training of both the student and teachers. COKD is executed in an online manner where the teachers are updated on-the-fly to suit the student's needs. During the training of the student on a particular subset, the teachers can provide complementary knowledge on the other subsets, thus preventing the occurrence of catastrophic forgetting. By using COKD, the negative effects of imbalanced training data can be mitigated as the approach helps the student model to capture the knowledge of different teacher models better and improve overall performance.

Actually, COKD was developed to improve machine translation performance from English to Vietnamese. We propose an efficient model initialization by reusing the knowledge learned from previous teacher models and the weighting method for teacher models by using the attention mechanism.

COKD initializes all teacher models simultaneously, hindering subsequent models from benefiting from the knowledge learned by their predecessors. Our proposed approach initializes the ith teacher model using the models learned from the $(i-1)^{th}$ teacher model, allowing for a sequential learning process that promotes knowledge sharing among the teacher models. This allows the teacher models to progressively learn from one another and provide more comprehensive knowledge to the student model. In addition, each teacher model contributes to the training of the student model with varying levels of significance. We determine the contribution weights using the attention mechanism.

The paper has two contributions: i) Propose ModifiedCOKD built upon COKD using an attention mechanism to leverage the importance of teacher models and an effective way to initialize model parameters; ii) Conduct various experiments to validate the effectiveness of ModifiedCOKD on mitigating catastrophic forgetting and improving machine translation performance compared against the COKD model.

2   Background

2.1   Knowledge Distillation

Knowledge distillation [6] is a class of methods that transfers knowledge from a pre-trained teacher network to a student network by matching the student's predictions to the teacher's predictions. J. Gou et al. [7] provide a framework overview of knowledge distillation that involves a teacher model, a student model, and the transfer of knowledge (distillation) from the teacher to the student. Furthermore, data is shared between both models. Knowledge distillation is a highly effective technique for addressing multilingual problems, neural machine translation [8], and classification models with numerous layers. This method is particularly advantageous for compressing models that have access to a sizable quantity of unlabeled data. There are three main categories of knowledge distillation techniques: cooperative learning, multi-teacher (particularly beneficial in neural translation environments), and converter distillation. Offline knowledge distillation includes two stages, training a large teacher model and transferring knowledge from the teacher model to the student model. Assume that we are training a classifier $p(y|x,\theta)$ with $|V|$ classes, and we can access the pre-trained teacher $q(y|x)$. Instead of minimizing the cross-entropy loss between the ground-truth label and the model output probability, knowledge distillation uses the teacher model prediction $q(y|x)$ as a soft target and minimizes the loss:

$$\mathcal{L}_{KD}(\theta) = -\sum_{k=1}^{|V|} q(y=k|x) \times \log p(y=k|x;\theta) \tag{1}$$

In neural machine translation, the standard training objective is the cross-entropy loss, which minimizes the negative log-likelihood as follows:

$$\mathcal{L}_{NLL}(\theta) = -\sum_{t=1}^{T} \log(p(y_t|y_{<t}, \mathbf{X}, \theta)) \tag{2}$$

where $X = \{x_1, \cdots, x_N\}$ and $Y = \{y_1, \cdots, y_T\}$ are the source sentence and the target sentence, respectively. Kim and Rush [9] proposed to train the student model to mimic the teacher's prediction at each decoding step, which is called Word-level Knowledge Distillation (Word-KD) and its loss is calculated as follows:

$$\mathcal{L}_{Word-KD}(\theta) = -\sum_{t=1}^{T}\sum_{k=1}^{|V|} q(y_t=k|y_{<t}, \mathbf{X}) \times \log p(y_t=k|y_{<t}, \mathbf{X}, \theta). \tag{3}$$

Instead of offline knowledge distillation, recent work focuses on more economic online knowledge distillation without a pre-trained teacher model. Online distillation is proposed to further improve the performance of the student model, especially when a large-capacity high-performance teacher model is not available. In online distillation, both the teacher model and the student model are updated simultaneously, and the whole knowledge distillation framework is end-to-end trainable. Zhang et al. [10] first overcame the offline limitation by training peer models simultaneously and conducted an online distillation in one-phase training between peer models. Since mutual learning requires training multiple networks,

[3,5] proposed to use a single multi-branch network for online knowledge distillation, which treats each branch as a student and the ensemble of branches as a teacher. The multi-branch architecture subsequently became the mainstream for online knowledge distillation [11,12]. Besides, Furlanello et al. [13] performed iterative self-distillation where the student network is identical to the teacher in terms of the network graph. In each new iteration, under the supervision of the earlier iteration, a new identical model is trained from scratch. In NMT, [14] on-the-fly selected the best checkpoint from the training path as the teacher to guide the training process.

2.2   Imbalanced Training

Catastrophic forgetting is a problem faced by many machine learning models during continual learning, as models tend to forget previously learned knowledge when being trained on new tasks. Shao et al. [4] observe that catastrophic forgetting not only occurs in continual learning but also affects traditional static training, which is called imbalanced training. To be specific, the final model pays imbalanced attention to training samples. The model partially forgets about earlier samples, which results in higher losses at the end of the training, whereas more recently exposed samples tend to draw more attention and have lower losses. In short, training samples receive imbalanced attention from the model, which mainly depends on the time when the model last saw the training sample (i.e., the data order of the latest training epoch). The underlying cause of this phenomenon is mini-batch gradient descent, that is, we do not simultaneously use all training samples to train the model but divide them into mini-batches. Therefore, training samples do not get balanced training in each update step.

They also find that NMT, especially low-resource translation tasks, is seriously affected by imbalanced training. To alleviate this problem, they propose COKD, which uses dynamically updated teacher models trained on specific data orders to iteratively provide complementary knowledge to the student model.

2.3   Attention-Based Weights

Attention was first introduced in natural language processing as a means of encoding each word with its most relevant counterparts for a given task [15]. This approach has since been extended to other types of data, such as images and graphs, with impressive results. In particular, self-attention, or intra-attention, involves capturing global dependencies by attending to all neighbouring positions in order to calculate the response at a given position. To achieve this, the input representation of a position is linearly mapped into three vectors (query, key, and value), which are used to calculate the weights for the contributions of neighbouring positions. The output of the position is then obtained by taking a weighted average of the values of its neighbours, based on these calculated weights. Self-attention has been successfully applied to various domains, including natural language processing, computer vision, and graph analysis.

In online learning, when using peer models to derive soft target distributions for a distilled model, the quality of intermediate predictions may vary depending on different initializations. Therefore, it is not appropriate to treat all peer models equally because this could negatively impact the distilled model's performance by including low-quality predictions. Instead, the weights assigned to each peer should reflect their relative importance in contributing to the distilled model. To calculate the soft target from peer models, Chen et al. [11] utilized the attention mechanism.

3   Method

For each student model, we acquire the knowledge from teacher models using the weights derived from the attention mechanism. The teacher models undergo parametric initialization based on the previously acquired knowledge, producing superior teacher models. Figure 1 illustrates the overall architecture of our method. The detailed components are presented below:

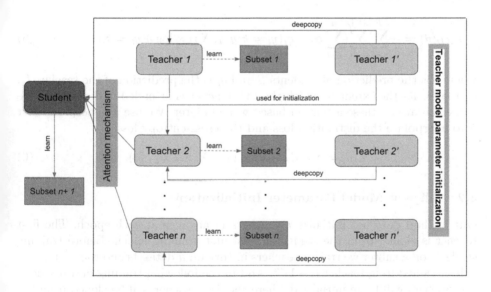

Fig. 1. An overview of our method to learn student model

3.1   Online Knowledge Distillation

COKD [4] resolves imbalanced training by splitting the training set into separate sets and training teachers firstly with subsets then training the student with both ground-truth labels and the distillation from teachers at the same time.

Students gain the knowledge from the current subset while also improving their understanding of other subsets by teachers and distillation by matching the prediction of the student with the average of teachers' prediction simply. In our work, we also divide the data into subsets and train with the same scheme as COKD however instead of using the teacher's predicted mean, we factor in the output of each teacher before combining them. We also change the way of initiation teachers' parameters at each epoch.

Given n teacher models $T_{1:n}$ and a student model S, both teacher- and student models are randomly initialized. In each epoch, we divide the training dataset D into $n+1$ mutually exclusive splits $(D_1, D_2, \cdots, D_{n+1})$. The student model sequentially learns from D_1 to D_{n+1}, where the data order is different for teaching models. We use an ordering function $\mathcal{O}(i, t)$ to denote the training data for teacher T_i at time t, we use $\mathcal{O}(i, t)$ similar to COKD.

$$\mathcal{O}(i, t) = \begin{cases} i + t & i + t <= n + 1 \\ i + t - n - 1 & i + 1 > n + 1 \end{cases} \tag{4}$$

where $i \in \{1, 2, \cdots, n\}$ and $t \in 1, 2, \cdots, n + 1$.

The knowledge from teachers is transferred to students through word-level knowledge distillation:

$$L_{KD}(\theta) = -\sum_{t=1}^{T}\sum_{k=1}^{|V|}(\sum_{i=1}^{n}\alpha_i \times q_i(y_t = k|y_{<t}, X)) \times \log p(y_t = k|y_{<t}, X, \theta) \tag{5}$$

where p is the prediction of students S and q_i is the prediction of the teacher T_i, α_i represents the extent to which the i-th teacher is attended in derivation. We will elaborate on these attention-based weights later. We use a hyperparameter λ to interpolate the distillation loss and the cross-entropy loss:

$$\mathcal{L}(\theta) = \lambda \times \mathcal{L}_{KD}(\theta) + (1 - \lambda) \times \mathcal{L}_{NLL}(\theta) \tag{6}$$

3.2   Efficient Model Parameter Initialization

Our method does not initialize n teachers in advance at each epoch. The first teacher is cloned from the student in the first training epoch. Before training students on a subset we train n teachers in turn on n datasets and the ith teacher will be cloned from teacher $(i-1)^{th}$. And in the following training of n teachers, the teachers will be re-initialized where the first teacher will be cloned from the last teacher of the previous training.

The purpose of this method is to help students learn from good teachers, inheriting teachers from the previous step helps teachers later to learn better.

Algorithm 1: ModifiedCOKD

Input: training set $\mathcal{D}$, the number of teacher n
Output: student model $\mathcal{S}$
1 Randomly initialize student $\mathcal{S}$
2 **while** *not converge* **do**
3   randomly divide $\mathcal{D}$ into $n+1$ subsets $(\mathcal{D}_1, \mathcal{D}_2, \cdots, \mathcal{D}_{n+1})$, $\mathcal{T} \leftarrow [\mathcal{S}]$
4   **for** *t=1* **to** *n+1* **do**
5   **for** *i=1* **to** *n* **do**
6   **if** $i > 1$ **then**
7              $\mathcal{T}.append(\mathcal{T}[i-1])$
8   train $\mathcal{T}_i$ on $\mathcal{D}_{\mathcal{O}(i,t)}$
9   train $\mathcal{S}$ on $\mathcal{D}_t$ according to equation 6
10       $\mathcal{T} \leftarrow [\mathcal{T}[len(\mathcal{T})-1]]$

11 **return** student model $\mathcal{S}$

3.3 Attention

Inspired by Chen et al. [11], we use a linear transformation to project the extracted features from the student and the teacher model into two distinct subspaces.

$$L(\mathbf{h}_a) = \mathbf{W}_L^T \mathbf{h}_s \tag{7}$$

$$E(\mathbf{h}_t) = \mathbf{W}_E^T \mathbf{h}_t \tag{8}$$

where W_L and W_E are the learned projection matrices during student training.

The coefficient α_i is calculated as Embedded Gaussian distance with normalization:

$$\alpha_i = \frac{e^{L(h_s)^T E(h_t)}}{\sum_{f=1}^n e^{L(h_s)^T E(h_f)}} \tag{9}$$

α_i represents the contribution of the $i-th$ teacher's prediction to soft target so $\sum_{i=1}^n a_i = 1$

4 Experimental Results

4.1 Setup

Here, we present experimental results that assess the effectiveness of our proposed approach for the neural machine translation task on the IWSLT15 English-Vietnamese dataset (En-Vi, 133K sentence pairs) with the pre-processed data used in [16]. We utilize case-sensitive SacreBLEU [17] to report reproducible BLEU scores. Models are optimized with Adam [18] with the optimizer settings in [19]. For inference, we used beam search with the beam size 5. The checkpoint interval is 1000. The number of teachers is 3.

4.2   Results

With the objective of validating the effectiveness of ModifiedCOKD in alleviating the problem of imbalanced training, we take the final model and measure the correlation between the batch-id and the loss in the last epoch. Figure 2 shows a downward trend of loss is successfully alleviated on ModifiedCOKD while its efficiency is improved and approximates to the COKD model. Apparently, a model with less fluctuation in the loss function across batches will perform better and be less affected by the phenomenon of catastrophic forgetting.

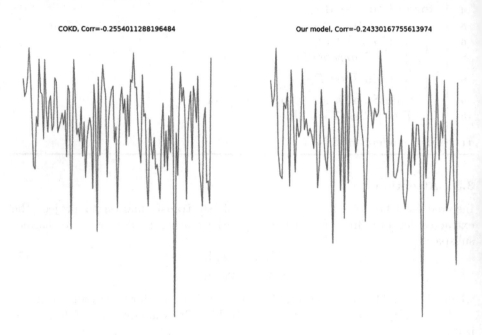

Fig. 2. The relationship between the batch-id and loss.

According to Table 1, the performance of our model increases slightly compared to the COKD model. This result demonstrates the advantage of our model Modifed COKD, where allows students to learn more from the trained teachers in the end as well as maintaining the ability to synthesize soft targets from them effectively for the imbalanced training problem.

Table 1. Model performance on the test sets(Sacre Bleu score)

COKD	ModifiedCOKD		
	Without Attention	Without initialization	With all
35.92±0.05	36.10±0.03	36.12±0.03	36.24±0.05

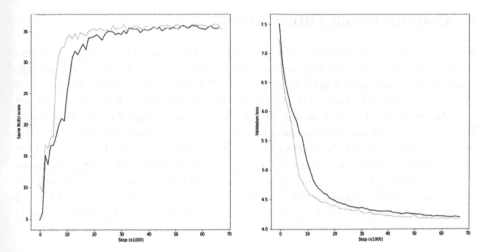

Fig. 3. Model performance on the validation set (left) and validation loss (right), the red line is our model and the blue is COKD (Color figure online)

Via the validation result, we found that our model converged considerably more quickly in comparison to COKD as Fig. 3. Specifically, our model achieves 36.03 Sacre BLEU score at epoch 38, while COKD achieves 35.32 with the same number of epochs and only reach 36.01 at epoch 60.

5 Related Work

Yung-Sung Chuang et al. [20] proposed a lifelong language knowledge distillation (L2KD) model, where a teacher model is trained for each new task, and then, a lifelong learning model (acting as a student model) receives the knowledge ("mimicking behaviour") from the teacher model. The teacher model is the same size as the student model, is used only once for that specific task, and is discarded afterwards, distinguishing the L2KD model from conventional knowledge distillation models. This study requires the pre-training of teacher models before training specific tasks, which contradicts the principles of continuous learning. Furthermore, the current approach employs a single-teacher model to learn each task, thereby failing to leverage the diverse sources of knowledge available from multiple teachers. This paper follows a similar approach to the L2KD model, however instead of using only one teacher model, multiple teacher models are trained to distil knowledge for the student model. Additionally, these teacher models are acquired through the training process of each particular task. The inspiration for this study is derived from the concept of Complementary Online Knowledge Distillation introduced by Chenze Shao et al. [4]. To account for variations in the amount of knowledge and importance of individual teachers for different students, an attention mechanism is employed. Furthermore, in our study, novel techniques are proposed to enhance the teacher model initialization such that the training process can converge more efficiently.

6   Conclusion and Future Work

This paper proposes ModifiedCOKD to address the issue of catastrophic forgetting in the *neural machine translation* task by investigating imbalanced training, teacher model parameter initialization, and effective transfer of knowledge. The experimental results show that our model not only exhibits faster convergence but also outperforms the baseline method COKD in terms of translation Sacre BLEU score. This observation demonstrates its effectiveness in addressing the problem of catastrophic forgetting for the neural machine translation task. Our future work involves exploring replay-based and meta-learning approaches to mitigate catastrophic forgetting in neural networks. We also plan to investigate the use of generative models and memory networks to improve the quality and diversity of the replayed data and retain the previous knowledge while learning new tasks.

References

1. LeCun, Y., Bottou, L., Orr, G.B., Müller, K.-R.: Efficient BackProp. In: Orr, G.B., Müller, K.-R. (eds.) Neural Networks: Tricks of the Trade. LNCS, vol. 1524, pp. 9–50. Springer, Heidelberg (1998). https://doi.org/10.1007/3-540-49430-8_2
2. Anil, R., Pereyra, G., Passos, A., Ormandi, R., Dahl, G.E., Hinton, G.E.: Large scale distributed neural network training through online distillation. In: 6th International Conference on Learning Representations, ICLR 2018, Vancouver, BC, Canada, April 30 - May 3, 2018, Conference Track Proceedings. OpenReview.net (2018)
3. Xu, L., Zhu, X., Gong, S.: Knowledge distillation by on the-fly native ensemble. In: Bengio, S., Wallach, H., Larochelle, H., Grauman, K., Cesa-Bianchi, N., Garnett, R., (eds.) Advances in Neural Information Processing Systems, vol. 31. Curran Associates Inc (2018)
4. Shao, C., Feng, Y.: Overcoming catastrophic forgetting beyond continual learning: balanced training for neural machine translation. In: Muresan, S., Nakov, P., Villavicencio, A. (eds.) Proceedings of the 60th Annual Meeting of the Association for Computational Linguistics (Volume 1: Long Papers), pp. 2023–2036. ACL 2022, Dublin, Ireland, 22–27 May 2022. Association for Computational Linguistics (2022)
5. Song, G., Chai, W.: Collaborative learning for deep neural networks. In: Bengio, S., Wallach, H., Larochelle, H., Grauman, K., Cesa-Bianchi, N., Garnett, R. (eds.) Advances in Neural Information Processing Systems, vol. 31. Curran Associates Inc (2018)
6. Hinton, G., Vinyals, O., Dean, J.: Distilling the knowledge in a neural network. CoRR abs/1503.02531 (2015)
7. Gou, J., Yu, B., Maybank, S.J., Tao, D.: Knowledge distillation: a survey. Int. J. Comput. Vision 129(6), 1789–1819 (2021). https://doi.org/10.1007/s11263-021-01453-z
8. Gupta, M., Agrawal, P.: Compression of deep learning models for text: a survey. CoRR abs/2008.05221 (2020)
9. Kim, Y., Rush, A.M.: Sequence-level knowledge distillation. CoRR abs/1606.07947 (2016)

10. Zhang, Y., Xiang, T., Hospedales, T.M., Lu, H.: Deep mutual learning. In: 2018 IEEE/CVF Conference on Computer Vision and Pattern Recognition, pp. 4320–4328 (2018)
11. Chen, D., Mei, J.P., Wang, C., Feng, Y., Chen, C.: Online knowledge distillation with diverse peers. CoRR abs/1912.00350 (2019)
12. Wu, G., Gong, S.: Peer collaborative learning for online knowledge distillation. In: Proceedings of the AAAI Conference on Artificial Intelligence, vol. 35, no. 12, pp. 10302–10310 (2021)
13. Furlanello, T., Lipton, Z., Tschannen, M., Itti, L., Anandkumar, A.: Born again neural networks. In: Dy, J., Krause, A. (eds.) Proceedings of the 35th International Conference on Machine Learning, vol. 80, pp. 1607–1616. Proceedings of Machine Learning Research. PMLR (2018)
14. Wei, H R., Huang, S., Wang, R., Dai, X., Chen, J.: Online distilling from checkpoints for neural machine translation. In: Proceedings of the 2019 Conference of the North American Chapter of the Association for Computational Linguistics: Human Language Technologies, Volume 1 (Long and Short Papers), pp. 1932–1941. Minneapolis, Minnesota: Association for Computational Linguistics (2019)
15. Bahdanau, D., Cho, K., Bengio, Y.: Neural machine translation by jointly learning to align and translate. In: Bengio, Y., LeCun, Y. (ed.) 3rd International Conference on Learning Representations, ICLR 2015, San Diego, CA, USA, 7–9 May 2015, Conference Track Proceedings (2015)
16. Luong, M.-T., Manning, C.: Stanford neural machine translation systems for spoken language domains. In: Proceedings of the 12th International Workshop on Spoken Language Translation: Evaluation Campaign. Da Nang, Vietnam (2015)
17. Post, M.: A call for clarity in reporting BLEU scores. In: Proceedings of the Third Conference on Machine Translation: Research Papers. Brussels, Belgium: Association for Computational Linguistics, pp. 186–191 (2018)
18. Kingma, D.P., Ba, J.: Adam: a method for stochastic optimization. In: Bengio, Y., LeCun, Y. (ed.) 3rd International Conference on Learning Representations, ICLR 2015, San Diego, CA, USA, 7–9 May 2015, Conference Track Proceedings (2015)
19. Vaswani, A, et al.: Attention is all you need. In: Guyon, I., et al. (eds.) Advances in Neural Information Processing Systems, vol. 30. Curran Associates Inc (2017)
20. Chuang, Y.-S., Su, S.-Y., Chen, Y.-N.: Lifelong language knowledge distillation. In: Proceedings of the 2020 Conference on Empirical Methods in Natural Language Processing (EMNLP). Association for Computational Linguistics, pp. 2914–2924 (2020)

The Achilles Heel of Artificial Intelligence

Upeka Premaratne[1]([⊠])[iD] and Saman Halgamuge[2][iD]

[1] Department of Electronic and Telecommunication Engineering,
University of Moratuwa, Katubedda, Moratuwa 10400, Sri Lanka
upeka@uom.lk
[2] Department of Mechanical Engineering, University of Melbourne,
Parkville, Victoria 3010, Australia
saman@unimelb.edu.au

Abstract. Since the dawn of its development the computer has been a staple of science fiction and thus mostly due to it humanity has constantly dreaded a day when intelligence stemming from computers commonly known as Artificial Intelligence (AI) would allegedly take over the world. The recent advent of advanced AI chatbot technology has again sparked that fear due to its ability to compose essays similar to that of a human being. This chapter discusses the concept of intelligence in biology and binary digital computing. Based upon the weaknesses of either, especially the hidden vulnerabilities of AI predicted by Gödel's First Incompleteness Theorem and role of humans in programming AI, the question of whether it is likely to happen in the near future is discussed.

Keywords: Artificial Intelligence · Emergence · Gödel's First Incompleteness Theorem · Sorites Paradox · Weak AI

1   Introduction

The phenomenal rise of chatbot technology in the recent past appears to have caused a significant and unprecedented stir in humanity. They have resulted in widespread academic misconduct. Chatbots like ChatGPT [36, 49, 56] and fine art generators appear to have struck the primal fear of artificial intelligence reaching the point of replacing some creative aspects of humanity. At least for now this appears to be by replacing certain categories of jobs but as a result endangering the livelihoods of many [16, 23]. Will AI create a new wave of economic refugees? Or will humans adapt to the changing employment landscape? are questions that may be answered in the near future with anxiety and dejection instead of the welcoming optimism of most previous technological advances in computing. In this paper the authors attempt to answer this question by comparing between the general nature of humans (along with other living organisms) and binary digital computing.

N. T. Nguyen et al. (Eds.): ACIIDS 2023, CCIS 1863, pp. 387–398, 2023.
https://doi.org/10.1007/978-3-031-42430-4_32

1.1 A Brief History

The term Artificial Intelligence (AI) was coined by John McCarthy in 1956 to distinguish between natural intelligence of the biological world and similar behavior in computational machines. The first milestone of AI against a human was in 1978 with the development of Lisp based program Eurisko by Douglas Lanet [34]. It was capable of identifying and adapting its own heuristics which enabled it to win the Traveller TCS strategy game championship against human players in 1981 and 1982. The next major milestone was the 1997 defeat of then reigning world chess champion Gary Kasparov by IBM Deep Blue [27]. Next came the victory of IBM Watson which used natural language processing to win the first prize in the quiz show *Jeopardy!* [19]. The first case of AI winning over a human in a strategy game was by AlphaGo which defeated world Go champion Lee Sedol in 2016 [31]. In 2018, it was reported that a deep learning network developed at Stanford University outperformed board certified radiologists [46] with a subsequent study showing that AI can outperform pulmonologists in their interpretation of lung function tests [57]. The progress of AI in outperforming humans has been phenomenal and with the advent of ChatGPT it appears that humans are likely to have competition in the domain of writing as well [56]. However, aside from the victories are the setbacks AI has had over the years. For example, the Boeing 737 MAX incident [54] and the 2018 Uber incident that killed Elaine Herzberg [35]. A further noteworthy incident was the recent victory of amateur Go player Kellin Pelrine against AI [62] which will be further discussed in Sect. 3.1. Therefore, in order to answer the profound question as to whether AI will outdo a human it is necessary to look into the very concept of intelligence itself.

2 What is Intelligence?

The concept perceived as intelligence is a term that defies definition. Legg and Hutter [33] provide the most comprehensive discussion on this topic so far incorporating definitions in terms of both biology and computer science. In the end the authors informally define it as *"Intelligence measures an agent's ability to achieve goals in a wide range of environments"*. Furthermore, the agent and environment interaction model proposed by the authors (Fig. 1 of [33]) and the standard model of reinforcement learning [29] are also of interest to the discussion of this paper. This is due to the fact that it highlights the stark contrast between what is considered as intelligence in biology and in computing devices. The main discussion point is the aspect of the "reward" and how it is incorporated into the agent model in different types of biological and computing agents.

2.1 Emergence

Consider a single celled biological agent like a bacterium capable of quorum sensing [40]. In such a situation, the concentration of a signaling chemical regulates the expression of a gene in the bacterial cell. When the agent is modeled as in Fig. 1a (extending the model of [33]), it is modeled as an agent which observes and acts upon the environment through its embodiment. The action is brought about by a biological computation which in the case of quorum sensing is equivalent to a decision stump (i.e., a decision tree with only the root that reacts to a single input) detecting a threshold concentration of the signaling chemical. However, it should be noted that this single celled organism without a single nerve cell cannot perceive any "reward". Instead the reward for properly executing the computation is a competitive advantage over its peers. This then manifests itself in the form of natural selection of the most suited trait and survival of the organism with the aforementioned trait.

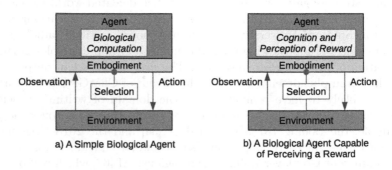

Fig. 1. The Two Types of Biological Agents

For example, consider bacterial specie X that uses quorum sensing to form a biofilm. The strain of X with the decision stump thresholds that suit the optimal conditions will be able to form the biofilm at the optimal place and time to exploit the environmental conditions. Thus, it will be favored for survival.

Organisms of the phylum Cnidaria lack a central nervous system or an organ colloquially known as a "brain". Instead they have an interconnected nerve net [51]. Such organisms exhibit *multiple* behaviors. For example, *Hydra* spp. must capture prey with their tentacles, retract their tentacles when necessary and explore their surroundings once they cleave from the parent as a free swimming bud. These behaviors have to be prioritized depending on the situation [3]. Hence, originates the concept of subsumption coined by Rodney Brooks which allows behaviors to be suppressed according to their priority [9]. For example, a lower priority behavior like foraging will be suppressed by a higher priority behavior such as evading a predator.

By now a reader familiar with gene regulation might wonder why the classic lactose operon (lac operon), the gene that allows *Escherichia coli* to digest lactose has not been discussed so far. It too is a biological computation. The presence of lactose removes the inhibiter of the lac operon allowing it to be expressed. Once the lactose is digested by the expressed enzymes, the inhibitors will again be freed, bind back to the lac operon and inhibit further expression. This is essentially an extended version of the binary on-off control operation [48,58].

In all of the preceding cases the environment will select the organisms that are capable of performing the best assessment of the optimal conditions to exploit the situation. Thus, the observable result such as the formation of a biofilm is an emergence of the combination of simple behaviors of many organisms [21,67]. This emergence goes a step further in the Protist *Physarum polycephalum* [4] which is a coenocyte (cell with multiple nuclii) capable of organizing itself according to a shortest path criterion. According to the definition given by Corning [11] emergence is the unpredictable observable result at a larger (macro) scale of the combined individual elements of a coherent dynamic process. Thus, from this broad definition hurricanes or the resulting pattern of a kaleidoscope can also be considered as an emergence. Therefore, it is necessary to distinguish the types of emergences discussed in this paper as emergences that result from biological computations.

2.2   Cognition

The threshold for determining intelligence in biology can be considered as when the agent can perform a biological computation that selects the *best of many potential options* (Fig. 1b) which can also be broadly defined as cognition [5]. By limiting the discussion from [50] for brevity, the essential elements for cognition can be summarized as

1. Reasoning based upon a value judgment to determine which action is necessary or most suited for a particular observation
2. Learning from past observations and actions to better assess the value of a judgment
3. Compact storage of the learned information as knowledge to efficiently seek and obtain the potential value judgment based upon the available options

In biological agents, the value judgment is based upon a reward which has to be perceived by the agent. This is where biological agents with central nervous systems (i.e., a brain) have a unique method of value judgment, the *mesocorticolimbic circuit* which is also known as the brain reward system. This provides the sensation of *inherent pleasure*. This pleasure drive is most profound when organisms drink, eat, copulate and exhibit parental care which are all primary behaviors essential for the continuation of life [6,42,52,61].

When cognition is involved as in an agent of Fig. 1b, the environmental selection is twofold, first there is the natural selection which also there for a simple biological agent of Fig. 1a. This occurs on a timescale that is in the order of the lifetime of the organism. The other is social or cultural selection which is an adoption or critique of the resulting behavior that can occur at a different timescale [47] which can be shorter than natural selection. For example, a member of a tribe living at a higher latitude can develop a garment to keep warm and the entire tribe can adopt it within days, weeks or months without having to evolve longer body hair to keep warm over many generations.

2.3   Evolutionary Psychology and Function Allocation

Due to the current unknowability and irregularity of how the inherent pleasure from the brain reward system influences a cognitive decision, most explanations offered for behaviors of such organisms are a matter of conjecture from the field known as evolutionary psychology. Evolutionary psychology seeks to answer fundamental questions of behavior through plausible but mostly speculatory empirical and comparative analysis [28]. Using this approach it is possible to speculate about how humans are better at certain things compared to machines.

The practice of *function allocation* to human or machine based upon which was better at the particular task originated out of a comprehensive study by Fitts [14]. Though function allocation has evolved significantly with technological advancements, it can be considered as a truism that at present computing machines are better at crunching numbers, precise operations, consistent operation and deductive analysis of large volumes of data. In the case of humans (and select examples of the animal kingdom), they still excel at detecting subtle differences and anomalies, visual or auditory estimation (in the case of most animals olfactory estimation as well), judgment, induction and innovation (improvisation).

Thus, when it comes to tasks at which humans excel, using evolutionary psychology it is straightforward to explain the fact that such tasks were critical for survival. If an ancestral human failed to detect a well camouflaged predator or venomous creature in time, it would not have survived to pass on its genes [15,30,65]. Similarly when hunting, the predator must determine and target the prey that can be hunted with minimal effort [8,20]. Induction, innovation and improvisation would have been vital when ancient humans developed tools and colonized new territory [32].

2.4   Innovation, Creativity and Embodiment

The basic computing element of the brain is the biological neuron which can be approximated to an adaptable activation function. Estimates for the total number of neurons in the human brain average at around 85 billion [24,59]. When considering the number of neuron connections and ways in which they can be connected, the human brain can be considered as a complex organ of "ordered chaos".

The electrical impulses that result from cultured neuron cells have been shown to exhibit both ordered and random behavior [38,39]. Thus, when millions or billions of similar neurons get together, their combined behavior qualifies as an emergence according to Corning [11]. However, the exact mechanism of the emergence of thoughts in the brain and the contributions from single neurons is still an investigated problem [18]. Studies have also shown that artificial neurons can be used to generate Turing patterns [41]. Thus, emergence according to the definition of Corning [11] from an artificial neural network is possible.

Innovation and creativity are key in allowing humans to solve previously unencountered problems. One necessary factor for innovation is the ability to grasp abstract concepts which primates [17,37,60], the octopus [1] and cetaceans

[13,25] have been demonstrated to be capable of. Empirical studies have also established a correlation with brain size and innovation [32]. This provides a plausible explanation for the higher level of self awareness among great apes compared to smaller basal primates [45]. The ability to abstractly visualize can also be considered necessary for creativity, allowing the problem to be analyzed within the brain. Cetaceans are believed to be capable of this due to their ability to identify shapes with echolocation [13]. Among humans there is the well known phenomenon of brain wandering where a human gets immersed in mental imagery while engaged at a task [43].

Humans have the additional advantage of an embodiment which allows them to realize a new idea. This has endowed humans with versatile tool use which provided a further selective advantage [26] and co-evolution [63] to become the modern organism capable of exploiting quantum mechanics and exploring extra-terrestrial worlds. Such a feat is imperceivable for the great apes who lack the manual dexterity of humans and impossible for cetaceans who lack individual digits whatsoever.

3   Artificial Intelligence

There are tasks at which humans have a significant advantage over computational machines as discussed in Sect. 2.3. Humans on average exhibit a poor aptitude compared to computing devices for arithmetic [14]. The first known mechanical computing device was the abacus which was invented with the expansion of trade and commerce [55]. The modern Von Neumann architecture uses binary logic for logical operations, integer arithmetic and floating point arithmetic. The common objectives of AI can be summarized according to [2,7,50] as

1. Approximate reasoning (also known as reasoning under uncertainty or soft computing) where the computer attempts to reason beyond the false dichotomy of true and false
2. Learning, knowledge representation, classification and prediction
3. Natural language processing
4. Searching, such as when determining the next move by combinatorial search in a game of chess or marble solitaire and optimization as in automated task scheduling or routing on a printed circuit board.

3.1   The Vulnerabilities of Artificial Intelligence

The basic challenges faced by a binary logic computer when attempting to achieve these objectives can be demonstrated using limitations and their associated paradoxes. The first limitation predicted by Gödel's First Incompleteness Theorem [53] which states that a system of logic cannot be both *complete* and *consistent* at the same time. In the simplest of terms, consistency means that the same set of inputs will result in the same output and completeness means all inputs can be evaluated as true or false. However, based on the Self Referential

Lemma there can exist prepositions that refer to oneself to evaluate their truth. Thus, should it be a negation then every evaluation will invert the truth value. An example of such a preposition is that of the Epimenidies (liar) paradox where a Epimenidies being a Cretan himself states that "All Cretans are liars". Within binary logic, no truth can be evaluated. The second is the Sorites paradox which demonstrates the inability of a computer to determine when "a heap" of sand is no longer "a heap" when a grain of sand is removed at a time. It illustrates the fact that the exact thresholds for a decision stump (or any such algorithm trained using data) are approximate and unknowable [64]. This is due to them being derived from subjectively labelled data of an abstract concept (i.e., the heap). Therefore, this results in AI running on a binary computer having three vulnerabilities

1. Predictability due to consistency
2. Incompleteness or the inability to solve all potential problems posed
3. Dependance on limited subjectively labelled data of an abstract concept

The first two vulnerabilities became clear in the recent victory of amateur Go player Kellin Pelrine against AI [62]. The strategy used was based upon the known vulnerability of Go AI to be unable to handle being encircled. However, Pelrine later lost to professional human Go players while using the same strategy.

3.2   Thresholds of Intelligence

It is now possible to discuss the concept of Weak AI [50] where the AI demonstrates superior but not ideal performance compared to a human at a specific task. Chatbots are an example of weak AI [36,49,56] where the fundamental task is word composition. Based on this it is further necessary to distinguish Weak AI from other number crunching operations at which computers are leagues ahead of human beings. This requires an intelligence threshold. When considering biological computations, an intelligence threshold can be defined as an organism capable of adapting its behavior [12]. In other words the merit of its behavior is not determined by natural selection alone.

In the case of a binary computer, the intelligence threshold is less straightforward but can still be considered as any decision that is beyond a trivial decision stump. An example would be in optical character recognition (OCR), when the letter u has to be distinguished from v. It must also consider the letter order. The OCR cannot recognize the word "value" as"ualue","ualve" or "valve". The two former options can be easily dismissed but both "value" and "valve" are valid words in the English language. Therefore, the OCR would have to decide among them and suggest it for a sentence that reads "The value of the antique was estimated to be $3,000". Suggesting the word "valve" still valid being both grammatically and contextually correct albeit less likely to occur. Thus, the OCR must not only be capable of distinguishing the two classes "u" and "v" but be able to statistically place it with the right word order and context as well. All of this will have to be learned by the machine. Thus, for binary computers the

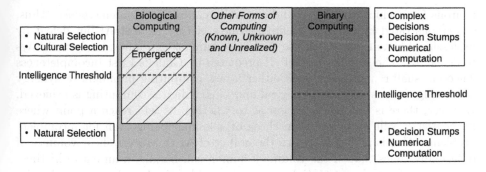

Fig. 2. Intelligence as a Subset of Different Types of Computing that Exist in the Universe

intelligence threshold can be considered as a complex decision that is beyond a mere conditional flow within the program.

Based on these thresholds it is possible to consider intelligence a subset of computing instead of as intelligence alone as in [33,66] or universality [10]. This is to allow flexibility for hybrid forms of computing such as combined analog and digital computing [22] or biological and digital computing [38,44] which may develop in the future with synergic intelligence when combined. Computing as a whole can consist of biological computing, binary computing by electronic circuitry, quantum computing, analog computing and any other form of unknown or unrealized computing at this point of time (Fig. 2). Defining a functional threshold instead of a test like the Turing test has the benefit of being applicable to a wide range of devices such as embedded systems that may be capable of intelligent decisions but not in a manner where they can mimic a human being.

4   Conclusion

Based on the discussion of this paper, it can be concluded that as long as binary numbers are used for digital computing, AI will not be able to completely usurp humanity. Gödel's First Incompleteness Theorem predicts that AI will always be predictable and uninnovative. Thus, the machine will be better than a human in deductive reasoning based on the data it has already learned. Furthermore, human guidance is necessary for programming the necessary abstract concepts and fundamental labelling of data as illustrated by the Sorites paradox. Thus, machines will not be able to invent truly new concepts the same way people do. Also despite technological advances most of the tasks identified in the Fitt's list at which humans excel still remain unchanged. These include detecting subtle differences and anomalies, visual or auditory estimation, judgment, induction and innovation. However, AI chatbots like ChatGPT have also shown that Weak AI can definitely out do humans in specific tasks with large volumes of data available for training. The human brain with its pleasure based reward system is a highly complex and still poorly understood organ. It has billions of neurons from which innovation and creativity can result from emergence. Thus, as demonstrated by amateur Kellin Pelrine's victory against AI but defeat by professional human players in the game Go, humans can innovatively find ways to defeat AI. The Achilles heel of AI predicted by Gödel's First Incompleteness Theorem shall remain valid until either a new computing paradigm or synergy combining the best of both biological and binary digital computing is achieved. However, there is an open question as to whether AI will reach a point where its heuristics will be better than those of a human being even for incomplete problems. This is plausible due to the ability of AI to process shear volumes of data many times that of the volume a human can handle in an entire lifetime. An example for such a potential incomplete problem is the solution of indefinite integrals.

References

1. Adams, S.S., Burbeck, S.: Beyond the octopus: from general intelligence toward a human-like mind. In: Wang, P., Goertzel, B. (eds.) Theoretical Foundations of Artificial General Intelligence. Atlantis Thinking Machines, vol. 4, pp. 49–65. Atlantis Press, Paris (2012). https://doi.org/10.2991/978-94-91216-62-6_4
2. Agrawal, A., Gans, J., Goldfarb, A.: What to expect from artificial intelligence (2017)
3. Aktius, M., Nordahl, M., Ziemke, T.: A behavior-based model of the hydra, phylum cnidaria. In: Almeida e Costa, F., Rocha, L.M., Costa, E., Harvey, I., Coutinho, A. (eds.) ECAL 2007. LNCS (LNAI), vol. 4648, pp. 1024–1033. Springer, Heidelberg (2007). https://doi.org/10.1007/978-3-540-74913-4_103
4. Awad, A., Pang, W., Lusseau, D., Coghill, G.M.: A survey on Physarum polycephalum intelligent foraging behaviour and bio-inspired applications. Artif. Intell. Rev. 56(1), 1–26 (2023)
5. Bayne, T., et al.: What is cognition? Curr. Biol. 29(13), R608–R615 (2019)
6. Berridge, K.C.: From prediction error to incentive salience: mesolimbic computation of reward motivation. Eur. J. Neurosci. 35(7), 1124–1143 (2012)
7. Boden, M.A.: Artificial intelligence. Elsevier (1996)
8. Brodie, E.D., III., Brodie, E.D., Jr.: Predator-prey arms races: asymmetrical selection on predators and prey may be reduced when prey are dangerous. Bioscience 49(7), 557–568 (1999)
9. Brooks, R.A.: New approaches to robotics. Science 253(5025), 1227–1232 (1991)
10. Cook, M., et al.: Universality in elementary cellular automata. Complex Syst. 15(1), 1–40 (2004)
11. Corning, P.A.: The re-emergence of "emergence": a venerable concept in search of a theory. Complexity 7(6), 18–30 (2002)
12. De Houwer, J., Barnes-Holmes, D., Moors, A.: What is learning? on the nature and merits of a functional definition of learning. Psychon. Bull. Rev. 20, 631–642 (2013)
13. Devona, H.: Whales: incredible ocean mammals. J. Geogr. 91(4), 166–170 (1992)
14. Fitts, P.M.: Human engineering for an effective air-navigation and traffic-control system (1951)
15. Galloway, J.A., Green, S.D., Stevens, M., Kelley, L.A.: Finding a signal hidden among noise: how can predators overcome camouflage strategies? Philos. Trans. Royal Soc. B 375(1802), 20190478 (2020)

16. Gauglitz, G.: Artificial vs. human intelligence in analytics: do computers outperform analytical chemists? Anal. Bioanal. Chem. **411**(22), 5631–5632 (2019)
17. Gauker, C.: Visual imagery in the thought of monkeys and apes. In: The Routledge Handbook of Philosophy of Animal Minds, pp. 25–33. Routledge, Milton Park (2017)
18. Gelbard-Sagiv, H., Mudrik, L., Hill, M.R., Koch, C., Fried, I.: Human single neuron activity precedes emergence of conscious perception. Nat. Commun. **9**(1), 2057 (2018)
19. Gliozzo, A., Biran, O., Patwardhan, S., McKeown, K.: Semantic technologies in IBM Watson. In: Proceedings of the Fourth Workshop on Teaching NLP and CL, pp. 85–92 (2013)
20. Greene, C.H.: Patterns of prey selection: implications of predator foraging tactics. Am. Nat. **128**(6), 824–839 (1986)
21. Grobas, I., Bazzoli, D.G., Asally, M.: Biofilm and swarming emergent behaviours controlled through the aid of biophysical understanding and tools. Biochem. Soc. Trans. **48**(6), 2903–2913 (2020)
22. Guo, N., et al.: Continuous-time hybrid computation with programmable nonlinearities. In: ESSCIRC Conference 2015–41st European Solid-State Circuits Conference (ESSCIRC), pp. 279–282. IEEE (2015)
23. Harari, Y.N.: Reboot for the AI revolution. Nature **550**(7676), 324–327 (2017)
24. Herculano-Houzel, S.: The remarkable, yet not extraordinary, human brain as a scaled-up primate brain and its associated cost. Proc. Natl. Acad. Sci. **109**(supplement_1), 10661–10668 (2012)
25. Herman, L.M., Pack, A.A., Wood, A.M.: Bottlenose dolphins can generalize rules and develop abstract concepts. Mar. Mammal Sci. **10**(1), 70–80 (1994)
26. Hirose, N.: An ecological approach to embodiment and cognition. Cogn. Syst. Res. **3**(3), 289–299 (2002)
27. Hsu, F.H.: Behind Deep Blue: Building the Computer that Defeated the World Chess Champion. Princeton University Press, Princeton (2002)
28. Jost, J.T., Sapolsky, R.M., Nam, H.H.: Speculations on the evolutionary origins of system justification. Evol. Psychol. **16**(2), 1474704918765342 (2018)
29. Kaelbling, L.P., Littman, M.L., Moore, A.W.: An introduction to reinforcement learning. In: Steels, L. (ed.) NATO ASI Series, vol. 144, pp. 90–127. Springer, Heidelberg (1995). https://doi.org/10.1007/978-3-642-79629_6_5
30. Kawai, N., He, H.: Breaking snake camouflage: humans detect snakes more accurately than other animals under less discernible visual conditions. PLoS One **11**(10), e0164342 (2016)
31. Koch, C.: How the computer beat the go player. Sci. Am. Mind **27**(4), 20–23 (2016)
32. Lefebvre, L.: Brains, innovations, tools and cultural transmission in birds, non-human primates, and fossil hominins. Front. Hum. Neurosci. **7**, 245 (2013)
33. Legg, S., Hutter, M.: Universal intelligence: a definition of machine intelligence. Minds Mach. **17**, 391–444 (2007)
34. Lenat, D.B.: EURISKO: a program that learns new heuristics and domain concepts: the nature of heuristics iii: program design and results. Artif. Intell **21**(1–2), 61–98 (1983)
35. Liu, P., Du, M., Li, T.: Psychological consequences of legal responsibility misattribution associated with automated vehicles. Ethics Inf. Technol. **23**(4), 763–776 (2021). https://doi.org/10.1007/s10676-021-09613-y
36. Lund, B.D., Wang, T.: Chatting about ChatGPT: how may AI and GPT impact academia and libraries? Libr. Hi Tech News **40**, 26–29 (2023)

37. Mansouri, F.A., Freedman, D.J., Buckley, M.J.: Emergence of abstract rules in the primate brain. Nat. Rev. Neurosci. **21**(11), 595–610 (2020)
38. Mendis, D., Petrou, S., Halgamuge, S.: Neuromechatronics with in-vitro microelectrode arrays. In: Mechatronics, pp. 582–603. CRC Press (2015)
39. Mendis, G., Morrisroe, E., Petrou, S., Halgamuge, S.: Use of adaptive network burst detection methods for multielectrode array data and the generation of artificial spike patterns for method evaluation. J. Neural Eng. **13**(2), 026009 (2016)
40. Miller, M.B., Bassler, B.L.: Quorum sensing in bacteria. Annu. Rev. Microbiol. **55**(1), 165–199 (2001)
41. Mondal, A., Upadhyay, R.K., Mondal, A., Sharma, S.K.: Emergence of Turing patterns and dynamic visualization in excitable neuron model. Appl. Math. Comput. **423**, 127010 (2022)
42. Numan, M.: Motivational systems and the neural circuitry of maternal behavior in the rat. Dev. Psychobiol. J. Int. Soc. Dev. Psychobiol. **49**(1), 12–21 (2007)
43. O'Callaghan, C., Shine, J.M., Lewis, S.J., Andrews-Hanna, J.R., Irish, M.: Shaped by our thoughts-a new task to assess spontaneous cognition and its associated neural correlates in the default network. Brain Cogn. **93**, 1–10 (2015)
44. Pei, J., et al.: Towards artificial general intelligence with hybrid Tianjic chip architecture. Nature **572**(7767), 106–111 (2019)
45. Povinelli, D.J.: Monkeys, apes, mirrors and minds: the evolution of self-awareness in primates. Hum. Evol. **2**, 493–509 (1987)
46. Rajpurkar, P., et al.: Deep learning for chest radiograph diagnosis: a retrospective comparison of the CheXneXt algorithm to practicing radiologists. PLoS Med. **15**(11), e1002686 (2018)
47. Rogers, D.S., Ehrlich, P.R.: Natural selection and cultural rates of change. Proc. Natl. Acad. Sci. **105**(9), 3416–3420 (2008)
48. Romero-Campero, F.J., Pérez-Jiménez, M.J.: Modelling gene expression control using p systems: the lac operon, a case study. BioSystems **91**(3), 438–457 (2008)
49. Rudolph, J., Tan, S., Tan, S.: ChatGPT: bullshit spewer or the end of traditional assessments in higher education? J. Appl. Learn. Teach. **6**(1) (2023)
50. Russel, S., Norvig, P., et al.: Artificial Intelligence: A Modern Approach, vol. 256. Pearson Education Limited, London (2013)
51. Satterlie, R.A.: Cnidarian nerve nets and neuromuscular efficiency. Integr. Comp. Biol. **55**(6), 1050–1057 (2015)
52. Schultz, W.: Neuronal reward and decision signals: from theories to data. Physiol. Rev. **95**(3), 853–951 (2015)
53. Smith, P.: An Introduction to Gödel's Theorems. Cambridge University Press, Cambridge (2013)
54. Spielman, Z., Le Blanc, K.: Boeing 737 MAX: expectation of human capability in highly automated systems. In: Zallio, M. (ed.) AHFE 2020. AISC, vol. 1210, pp. 64–70. Springer, Cham (2021). https://doi.org/10.1007/978-3-030-51758-8_9
55. Sugden, K.F.: A history of the abacus. Account. Historians J. **8**(2), 1–22 (1981)
56. Thorp, H.H.: ChatGPT is fun, but not an author (2023)
57. Topalovic, M., et al.: Artificial intelligence outperforms pulmonologists in the interpretation of pulmonary function tests. Eur. Resp. J. **53**(4) (2019)
58. Veliz-Cuba, A., Stigler, B.: Boolean models can explain bistability in the lac operon. J. Comput. Biol. **18**(6), 783–794 (2011)
59. Von Bartheld, C.S., Bahney, J., Herculano-Houzel, S.: The search for true numbers of neurons and glial cells in the human brain: a review of 150 years of cell counting. J. Comp. Neurol. **524**(18), 3865–3895 (2016)

60. Vonk, J.: Gorilla (Gorilla gorilla gorilla) and orangutan (Pongo abelii) understanding of first-and second-order relations. Anim. Cogn. **6**, 77–86 (2003)
61. Warlow, S.M., Naffziger, E.E., Berridge, K.C.: The central amygdala recruits mesocorticolimbic circuitry for pursuit of reward or pain. Nat. Commun. **11**(1), 2716 (2020)
62. Waters, R.: Man beats machine at go in human victory over AI. Financial Times (2023). https://www.ft.com/content/175e5314-a7f7-4741-a786-273219f433a1
63. Weser, V.U., Proffitt, D.R.: Expertise in tool use promotes tool embodiment. Top. Cogn. Sci. **13**(4), 597–609 (2021)
64. Williamson, T.: Inexact knowledge. Mind **101**(402), 217–242 (1992)
65. Xiao, F., Cuthill, I.C.: Background complexity and the detectability of camouflaged targets by birds and humans. Proc. Royal Soc. B: Biol. Sci. **283**(1838), 20161527 (2016)
66. Yampolskiy, R.V.: Turing test as a defining feature of AI-completeness. In: Yang, X.S. (ed.) Artificial Intelligence, Evolutionary Computing and Metaheuristics. Studies in Computational Intelligence, vol. 427, pp. 3–17. Springer, Heidelberg (2013). https://doi.org/10.1007/978-3-642-29694-9_1
67. Zachreson, C., Wolff, C., Whitchurch, C.B., Toth, M.: Emergent pattern formation in an interstitial biofilm. Phys. Rev. E **95**(1), 012408 (2017)

Using Machine Learning Algorithms to Explore Listeners Musical Tastes

Maciej Walczyński[✉][ID] and Monika Kisz

Wrocław University of Science and Technology,
wybrzeże Stanisława Wyspiańskiego 27, 50-370 Wrocław, Poland
maciej.walczynski@pwr.edu.pl

Abstract. This paper focuses on the possibility of using machine learning to predict song success. The purpose of this paper is to design and implement an application that allows the prediction of the commercial success of a musical piece using machine learning algorithms. The prediction is based on data concerning songs which have been Billboard charts as well as songs that are not on the charts. For the comparison three machine learning algorithms were selected for comparison: random forest, logistic regression and gradient enhancement. Model optimization was also performed using recursive feature elimination and hyperparameters tuning.

Keywords: Machine learning · Digital signal processing · Success prediction

1 Introduction

This paper focuses on determining the predictive feasibility of the success of a piece of music based on an analysis of songs that are on the charts from previous years. Music trends change significantly over short periods of time. The success of any song depends on various factors, a priori and posteriori. The posteriori parameters may include, for example, the number of plays, the number of downloads by users, the appearance in the charts. These parameters are analyzed by systems that recommend the next songs for users to listen to and are used by portals such as YouTube [8, 10]. However, from the perspective of music producers, artists, and music studios, a more important approach would be to analyze a song's potential for success a priori based on song characteristics. For this purpose, the Python programming language was used. The Python programming language was chosen because of the availability of libraries to process acoustic signals [6, 10], the availability of well-described documentation. Machine learning was also used for the analysis as it allows to identify patterns for the analyzed data, which can allow for hit prediction.

The signal considered in this paper is a music signal. A musical signal is a set of sounds that contains a lot of information. It may contain semantic information related to the text of a musical piece or emotional information that allows one to recognize the character of a piece of music. The consequence of the complex structure of a musical signal and the large number of features of such a signal is its complex biological process of music interpretation. For this reason, there are a number of ways to describe and study a music signal.

1.1 Music

Music is most easily defined as a composition of man-organized sounds created from sound and silence. Additionally, music is an intentionally created art. The most important elements of music are [5]:

Most musical instruments, such as those based on the presence of strings or those based on the vibration of air columns, are built to allow the musician to produce sounds with a fundamental period that can be easily controlled. Such a signal is described as a harmonic series of sinusoids with multiple fundamental frequencies. The result of such an action is the perception by the listener of a musical note with a clearly defined tone [2,5].

Sequences of tones create melodies, while another important aspect of music is harmony, which is defined as the simultaneous combination of notes with different tones. This composition of tones is called chords, which can be recognized regardless of the instrument used to generate them. Furthermore, the pleasing sound of chords comes from the ratios of the frequency values of the tones used, which should indicate their many existing common harmonics.

Rhythm is another element of a piece of music that is responsible for organizing the music in a temporal flow. Rhythm is closely related to meter, which organizes tones into metric groups so that accents are regularly spaced.

Musical texture refers to the overall density of layers of sounds, melodies, and rhythms in a work. A distinction is made between monophonic textures with a single layer of sound (e.g., solo voice), homophonic textures, that is, melody with accompaniment, and polyphonic textures with two or more independent voices.

The structure or musical form is responsible for the structure of the piece and is the result of the interaction of the elements of the piece. Form allows the parts of a piece to be organized and defines their relationships to each other and to repetition.

Dynamics is the musical element that regulates the intensity of a sound and determines its loudness.

Tempo is the number of metric units per minute (BPM), or how fast a song should be played.

1.2 Music Signal in Analogue and Digital Form

As a result of the process of musicians producing a musical signal while playing an instrument, the resulting output signal is an analog signal. Such a signal can also be referred to as a continuous-time signal. This means that such a signal takes values from a continuous interval, which may be infinite or limited by an allowed range of variation [3].

Nowadays, digital recorders in particular are used to record music signals, which leads to discrete-time signals. These signals are characterized by the fact that their temporal variable is quantized, i.e. the values of the studied signal at discrete points on the time axis are known. Such a representation results in the signal being presented as a sequence of values instead of a continuous waveform as in the case of analog signals.

The process of digital recording consists, among others, of analog-to-digital processing of the music signal, which is divided into several major stages [7,9]:

- sampling,
- quantization,
- coding.

2   Modeling

This paper focuses on the possibility of using machine learning to predict the success of a song. According to Arthur Samuel's 1959 definition of machine learning, it refers to the ability of computers to learn without programming them explicitly. According to Tom Mitchell's definition, machine learning means learning a task T based on experience E and a measure of quality P if, as experience E increases, the quality of performance on the task T as measured by the measure P improves.

3   Research Object

The songs analyzed were those on the weekly published lists of the best songs according to Billboard magazine from 1960 to 2019.

The existence of APIs allows companies to share data and functionality of a given application with other unrelated developers. An API is a set of rules that define how computers or applications communicate with each other. An API sits between an application and a server and is responsible for mediating the exchange of data between systems [4].

The conditions for classifying a work as not commercially successful are as follows:

- the song did not appear on the charts for that decade,
- the artist performing the song did not appear on the charts for that decade,
- the work belongs to genres that are not mainstream and are classified as more niche,
- the genre of the song has not appeared in the charts.

The database of song features is divided into 6 .csv files, and each file contains information on songs from one of the decades from the 1960s to the 2010s of the current century. The structure of the files belonging to the database is presented in Table 1.

Table 1. Structure of csv files belonging to the works features database.

File name	Number of samples in database	Number of features
dataset-of-60s.csv	8642	17
dataset-of-70s.csv	7766	17
dataset-of-80s.csv	6908	17
dataset-of-90s.csv	5520	17
dataset-of-00s.csv	5872	17
dataset-of-10s.csv	6398	17

3.1   Data Analysis

The data analysis was conducted according to the CRISP-DM standard, which is a diagram illustrating the data mining process. According to the standard, this process consists of 6 phases [1].

1. The phase of understanding the business case, in which it is necessary to formulate the goals and requirements for the project
2. Understanding data, which consists of collecting the needed data and evaluating its usefulness
3. Data preparation, which consists of performing necessary transformations, cleaning data, and removing duplicates and empty values
4. Modeling, which is the selection and implementation of the best modeling technique
5. Evaluation, which involves assessing the effectiveness and quality of the created models
6. Implementation, which uses the created model

Consistent with phase two, elements of descriptive statistics were used to explore the data. Tables 2, 3, and 4 summarized the statistical quantities describing the musical characteristics studied. The tables included statistical quantities such as:

– number of samples,
– average, which is the arithmetic mean,
– standard deviation,
– minimum in the works database for a given feature,
– first quartile (25%),
– second quartile (50%),
– third quartile (75%),
– maximum in the tracks database for a given feature.

The next step focused on preparing the data for further analysis. The database was checked for missing values and duplicates were checked. No empty records appeared in the database, while there were 420 duplicates, which means that some songs appeared in the charts more than once during one year. Due

Table 2. Descriptive statistics

	danceability	energeticity	tone	volume	scale
number of samples	41106	41106	41106	41106	41106
mean	0.54	0.58	5.21	−10.22	0.69
standard deviation	0.18	0.25	3.53	5.31	0.46
minimum	0.00	0.00	0.00	−49.25	0.00
25%	0.42	0.39	2.00	−12.87	0.00
50%	0.55	0.60	5.00	−9.26	1.00
75%	0.67	0.79	8.00	−6.37	1.00
maximum	0.99	1.00	11.00	3.74	1.00

Table 3. Descriptive statistics

	spoken words	acoustically	instrumentality	live rec.	tempo
number of samples	41106	41106	41106	41106	41106
mean	0.07	0.36	0.15	0.20	119.33
standard deviation	0.09	0.34	0.30	0.17	29.09
minimum	0.00	0.00	0.00	0.01	0.00
25%	0.03	0.04	0.00	0.09	97.39
50%	0.04	0.26	0.00	0.13	117.56
75%	0.07	0.68	0.06	0.26	136.49
maximum	0.99	1.00	1.00	0.99	241.42

Table 4. Descriptive statistics

	positivity	duration [ms]	time signature	group
number of samples	0.54	41106	41106	41106
mean	0.54	234877	3.89	0.50
standard deviation	0.27	118967	0.42	0.50
minimum	0.00	15168	0.00	0.00
25%	0.33	172927	4.00	0.00
50%	0.56	217907	4.00	0.50
75%	0.77	266773	4.00	1.00
maximum	0.99	4170227	5.00	1.00

to the fact that the features of a song remain constant for each appearance of a song in the database, the duplicates were removed. After this operation, 40686 rows remained in the database.

The averages of each feature were also compared separately for hit and non-hit songs. The results are summarized in Table 5.

Table 5. Comparison of average features for hit and unsuccessful songs

	average hits	mean non-hit
danceability	0.60	0.48
energeticity	0.62	0.53
tone	5.24	5.17
volume	−8.71	−11.74
scale	0.73	0.66
spoken word	0.07	0.08
acoustics	0.28	0.45
instrumentality	0.03	0.28
live recording	0.19	0.21
positivity	0.61	0.48
tempo	120.27	118.39
duration [ms]	225631	243659
time signature	3.94	3.85

When analyzing the data in Table 5 regarding the mean feature values for the successful and unsuccessful song groups, it was noted that the values of danceability, energeticity, tonality, loudness, positivity, tempo, and time signature are higher for the hit songs. On the other hand, the mean values of spoken word content, acoustic, instrumentality, factor telling whether the song was recorded live, and duration are higher for the unsuccessful songs. Additionally, Fig. 1 summarizes the averages of features that take values between 0 and 1.

Danceability refers to the degree of suitability of a track for dancing, taking into account various musical elements such as tempo, rhythm stability, beat strength, and overall regularity. It is measured on a scale from 0.0 (least danceable) to 1.0 (most danceable).

Energy is a metric ranging from 0.0 to 1.0, which serves as a perceptual measure of intensity and activity in music. Generally, energetic tracks are perceived as fast, loud, and noisy. For instance, genres like death metal tend to exhibit high energy, while a Bach prelude would score low on the energy scale. Perceptual features that contribute to this attribute include dynamic range, perceived loudness, timbre, onset rate, and overall entropy.

3.2   Evaluation of Classifiers with Default Parameter Values

After descriptive statistical analysis, the selected machine learning models were trained. The database samples were split 70 to 30 into a learning string and a test string. Random forest, logistic regression, and gradient boosting algorithms will be compared. Initially, models will be compared with default model parameter values called through the scikit-learn library. The first measure of classifier evaluation presented is the error matrix.

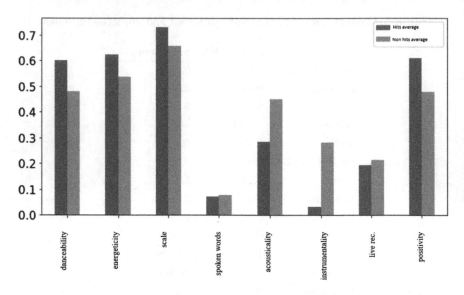

Fig. 1. Average features of successful (blue) and unsuccessful (orange) tracks (Color figure online)

For the default settings of the random forest algorithm, the number of decision trees is 100.

In Fig. 2, which illustrates the error matrix of the random forest algorithm (a), logistic regression algorithm (b) and optimized gradient gain algorithm. For the random forest algorithm, it can be seen that the vast majority of hits are correctly classified as hits. For songs that are not successful the incorrectly classified samples are more than for hits. For logistic regression can be seen that the number of correct predictions is greater than the number of incorrect predictions, but the values are close to each other. The unoptimized logistic regression algorithm is characterized by a large number of incorrect predictions. The most numerous quadrant represents correctly classified works that were successful. Correctly classified songs that were not successful also score high for gradient gain algorithm. As with the random forest algorithm, the incorrectly classified songs that were not successful outnumber the hits.

The obtained results of the classifier evaluation measures for the used default parameters of the models implemented in the scikit-learn library, were found to be insufficient. The next stage of the work proceeded to optimize each model.

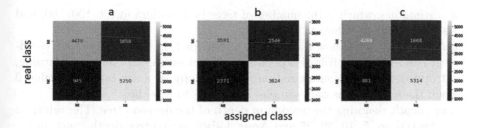

Fig. 2. Error matrices of the studied algorithms before their optimization

3.3 Recursive Feature Elimination (RFE)

Recursive feature elimination is used to reduce irrelevant information. The initial point of analysis is the full set of features in the dataset. In the RFE algorithm, multiple rankings of variables are performed. The model is built and evaluated for the full set of variables and then a ranking of the variables is built. Only the information carried by the model is used to build this ranking. The worst ranked variable is removed and the model is built again for the data set excluding the removed variable. One model is built for each iteration to reduce computational complexity. The procedure is repeated until the variables are exhausted. The result of the completed algorithm is a sequence of optimal subsets from each iteration, from which the most optimal one is selected.

3.4 Hyperparameter Tuning

Hyperparameters are called user-adjustable parameters that control the model training process. The performance of the model depends on the values of the hyperparameters to a large extent.

The process leading to model optimization is based on finding the best configuration of hyperparameters. Such a process is called hyperparameter tuning.

One of the methods for hyperparameter tuning is the grid search method. This method works iteratively by checking all possible combinations of hyperparameters using cross-validation to select optimal hyperparameter values. When there are a large number of hyperparameters and their values to be searched, the grid search method can become computationally very complex.

3.5 Optimization of Tested Models

Recursive feature elimination and grid search method for hyperparameter tuning were used to optimize the random forest model. The feature elimination performed showed that the optimal feature selection was the selection of the full set of 13 input features. None of the features were removed from the input data. The hyperparameters were then selected for tuning:

- *n_estimators*, which is the number of trees in a random forest. 100, 500, and 1000 are given as values to check.
- *criterion*, indicating how the samples are divided. By default, the Gini coefficient is selected, but it is also possible to select entropy. In machine learning, entropy determines contamination. The entropy of a set takes the value 0 when the set contains only samples belonging to one class.
- *max_depth*, denoting the maximum depth of the decision tree. The values to be checked are 5, 10, 20, 25 and *None*, indicating no tree depth constraint.

The hyperparameter values selected as the most optimal by the grid search method were *n_estimators = 500, criterion = 'entropy'* and *max_depth = 20*.

Recursive feature elimination and grid search method were used to optimize the logistic regression model. Feature elimination showed that 11 features were the optimal choice. The features selected as non-significant were *tempo* and *ms duration*. Hyperparameters were selected for tuning:

- *C*, kt that determines the inverse strength of regularization. Regularization means applying a penalty to the estimated parameter values to prevent overfitting the model to the data. 0.01, 0.1, 1.0, 100, 1000, and 10000 were chosen as the values to be checked.
- *penalty*, specifying which type of penalty is imposed during estimation. The l1 and l2 penalties were selected for testing.

The hyperparameter values selected as the most optimal by the grid search method were *C = 100* and *penalty = l1*.

Recursive feature elimination and grid search method were also used to optimize the gradient gain model. Feature elimination showed that the full set of features was the optimal choice. Hyperparameters were selected for tuning:

- *learning_rate*, which is a hyperparameter that controls the training rate of the model. The values chosen for testing were. 0.01, 0.05, 0.1, 0.15, 0.2.
- *max_depth*, denoting the maximum depth of the individual regression estimator. The values chosen were 3, 5, 10, 20, 25.

The hyperparameter values selected by the grid search method as the most optimal were *learning_rate = 0.15* and *max_depth = 5*.

4   Evaluation of Models After Optimization

After the optimization of the tested models, we proceeded with the evaluation of the models conducted analogously to the evaluation conducted for models with default hyperparameter values. The database samples were again split 70 to 30 into a learning string and a test string. Optimized random forest, logistic regression, and gradient enhancement models will be evaluated.

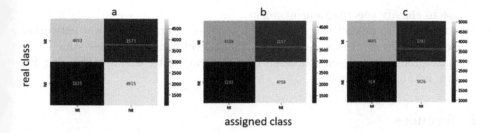

real class

assigned class

Fig. 3. Error matrices of the studied algorithms after their optimization.

In Fig. 3, which illustrates the error matrix of the random forest algorithm (a), logistic regression algorithm (b) and optimized gradient gain algorithm after optimization.

For the optimized random forest model, it can be seen that there was an increase in the number of correct classification of unsuccessful songs from 4479 to 4693 relative to the unoptimized model. At the same time, the amount of correct classification of hits decreased from 5250 to 4915.

For the optimized logistic regression model. Relative to the unoptimized model, the number of correctly classified hits increased from 3591 to 4109 and songs that were not commercially successful from 3824 to 4758.

For the optimized gradient gain model. Relative to the unoptimized model, the number of correct classifications of unsuccessful tracks increased from 4269 to 4485. The number of correct classifications of commercially successful tracks decreased from 5314 to 5026.

5 Summary

The purpose of this paper was to design and implement an application to predict the success of a music piece using machine learning algorithms. The classification algorithms belonging to supervised machine learning algorithms were used in this work. Random forest, logistic regression and gradient boosting algorithms implemented in *scikit-learn* library were selected. Classification was performed based on 13 features of the songs. In this article, we have adopted chart position as a measure of success for songs. We have endeavored to extract those parameters that contribute the most to achieving success. In this study, more complex and subjective parameters describing songs were utilized, such as danceability, alongside other articles that investigated the influence of more fundamental parameters like MFCC.

After comparing the three machine learning models, the gradient gain algorithm model was found to produce the most satisfactory results. Unlike the random forest algorithm, the gradient gain algorithm was not over-trained, and its accuracy for the learning string and the test string was close to 80%. The proposed opportunities for the development of this work are:

- use to classify spectrograms of works,
- attempting to predict the success of a song using artificial neural networks,
- extending the statistical research on the base of works characteristics,
- make predictions of song success for each decade after dividing the song feature database by decade.

References

1. Chapman, P., et al.: CRISP-DM 1.0 step-by-step data mining guide. Technical report, The CRISP-DM consortium (2000). https://maestria-datamining-2010.googlecode.com/svn-history/r282/trunk/dmct-teorica/tp1/CRISPWP-0800.pdf
2. Dowling, W.J.: The perception of interleaved melodies. Cogn. Psychol. **5**(3), 322–337 (1973)
3. Fabbri, R., Junior, V.V.D.S., Pessotti, A.C.S., Corrêa, D.C., Oliveira, O.N.: Musical elements in the discrete-time representation of sound (2014). https://doi.org/10.48550/ARXIV.1412.6853. https://arxiv.org/abs/1412.6853
4. IBM: Application Programming Interface (API). https://www.ibm.com/cloud/learn/api. Accessed 7 Dec 2021
5. Moore, B.C.: An Introduction to the Psychology of Hearing. Brill, Leiden (2012)
6. Sack, S.: acdecom-a python module for acoustic wave decomposition in flow ducts. Softw. Impacts **6**, 100025 (2020). https://doi.org/10.1016/j.simpa.2020.100025. https://www.sciencedirect.com/science/article/pii/S2665963820300166
7. Tsividis, Y.: Digital signal processing in continuous time: a possibility for avoiding aliasing and reducing quantization error. In: 2004 IEEE International Conference on Acoustics, Speech, and Signal Processing. vol. 2, pp. ii-589 (2004). https://doi.org/10.1109/ICASSP.2004.1326326
8. Vall, A., Quadrana, M., Schedl, M., Widmer, G., Cremonesi, P.: The importance of song context in music playlists. In: RecSys Posters (2017)
9. Wu, T.F., Ho, C.R., Chen, M.S.W.: A flash-based non-uniform sampling ADC with hybrid quantization enabling digital anti-aliasing filter. IEEE J. Solid-State Circ. **52**(9), 2335–2349 (2017)
10. Yoshii, K., Goto, M., Komatani, K., Ogata, T., Okuno, H.: Hybrid collaborative and content-based music recommendation using probabilistic model with latent user preferences. In: ISMIR 2006–7th International Conference on Music Information Retrieval, pp. 296–301. ISMIR 2006–7th International Conference on Music Information Retrieval (2006). 7th International Conference on Music Information Retrieval, ISMIR 2006; Conference date: 08–10-2006 Through 12–10-2006

Forecasting and Optimization Techniques

Forecasting Performance of GARCH, EGARCH and SETAR Non-linear Models: An Application on the MASI Index of the Casablanca Stock Exchange

Saoudi Youness[1]([✉]), Moulay el Mehdi Falloul[2], Ouaharahe Smaaine[3], Nader Ahmed[2], and Hachimi Hanaa[1]

[1] Systems Engineering Laboratory Sultan Moulay Slimane University, Beni Mellal, Morocco
saoudiyouness@gmail.com, hanaa.hachimi@usms.ac.ma
[2] Economics and Management Laboratory Sultan Moulay Slimane University, Beni Mellal, Morocco
[3] Organization Economics and Management Laboratory-Ibn Tofail University, Kenitra, Morocco
smaaine.ouaharahe@uit.ac.ma

Abstract. The objective of this paper is to test the forecasting performance of three nonlinear econometric prediction models, namely: Generalized Autoregressive Conditional Heteroskedasticity (GARCH), Exponential Generalized Autoregressive Con- ditional Heteroskedasticity (EGARCH), and the Smooth Transition Autoregressive (SETAR) model applied to the MASI index of the Casablanca Stock Exchange the period studied is from January 01, 2002 to September 20, 2018. Non-linearity tests are used to confirm the study's hypotheses. The optimal delay was also chosen using Schwartz selection criteria. The Mean Absolute Error (MAE) criterion, the Root Mean Square Error (RMSE) criterion, and the Mean Absolute Percentage Error (MAPE) criterion were used to select the best prediction model. The results of using the GARCH, EGARCH and SETAR models revealed that the SETAR model is the best. These results can be beneficial for financial market traders to make good decisions regarding allocative portfolio and asset management strategies.

Keywords: GARCH · EGARCH · SETAR · MASI Index · Forecast

1 Introduction

In the modeling of economic and financial data, non-linear time series have received more attention from researchers in recent years than linear time series. This is primarily due to the inability of linear time series to describe the dynamics of financial time series. Ac- cording to Maponga [1] linear time series are models that describe the behavior of time series in terms of past values.

Dynamic nonlinear equations yield nonlinear time series (Xaba, [2]). These equations represent properties that linear time series cannot represent. These characteristics include time-varying variance, skewed cycles, high moment structures, and data thresholds. As alternatives to the usual linear models, other models have been considered. Examples include the Autoregressive Conditional Heteroscedastic (ARCH) model proposed by Engel [3], the General Autoregressive Conditional Heteroscedastic (GARCH) model proposed by Bollerslev [4], and its exponential extension (EGARCH) proposed by Nelson [5] , are examples.

In contrast, the scientific community has paid particular attention to regime-switching models (Franses and Dijk, [6]). In the econometric literature, this family of nonlinear models has been proposed to capture nonlinearities in economic and financial data. Tong's Treshold Autoregressive (TAR) model, as well as the Self Exciting Trashold Autoregressive (SETAR) model, Teräsvirta and Anderson's Smooth Transition Autoregressive (STAR) model, and Hamilton's Markovian Autoregressive Regime Shift (MS-AR) model, are among the most widely used models in this class [10].

In contrast to traditional linear econometric models, the GARCH, EGARCH, and SETAR models assume the existence of different regimes in which time series can behave differently. The goal of this paper is to look into the feasibility of developing empirical models that can describe and forecast the evolution of the MASI, the Casablanca Stock Exchange's main index.

Furthermore, the aim of this paper is to compare the predictive abilities of three nonlinear regime management models, namely GARCH, EGARCH, and SETAR. The findings may help financial market participants make sound decisions about portfolio and asset allocation strategies. To choose the best efficiency prediction model between these three non-linear econometric models, we use 03 error criteria namely MAE, RMSE, and MAPE [11–13].

This paper is organized as follows: Beginning with an introduction and the methodology of the paper, the properties and econometric tests are studied in the second section, the third section explained the estimation of models such as GARCH, EGARCH and SETAR. The last section is devoted to a comparative approach between these three models in order to select the best model for forecasting.

2 Methodology

The purpose is to study the methods and tests used to test and model the series of the MASI index following the GARCH, EGARCH and SETAR models and choose the most optimal forecasting model.

3 Nonlinear Model Estimates

The objective of this section is to present the descriptive statistics and the econometric tests applied to the MASI for daily data ranging from January 1, 2002 to September 20, 2018.

RETURN MASI INDEX

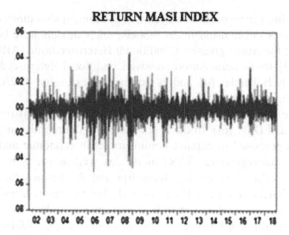

Fig. 1. Logarithmic MASI daily (In level and yields)

3.1   Statistical Properties

The data used is the daily MASI index, which was downloaded from the Casablanca stock exchange website and spans a period of 4176 observations.

The evolution of the MASI series on a sample of 4167 observations is depicted in Figure 1. To account for non-stationarity in variance, this series is transformed into logarithmic difference.

Table 1. Descriptive Statistics on the Yield Series

Series	T	Average	Standard deviation
MASI	4176	0,000,272	0,000,282
Skewness	Kurtosis	J.B	
–0,414,859	9,809,579	8186, 271	

The number of observations is denoted by T, J.B is the statistic of Jarque and Bera

Table 1 shows the log-differentiated series' descriptive statistics (number of observations, standard deviation, mean kurtosis and skewness) as well as the Jarque and Bera normality statistic value. The J.B. statistic rejects the null hypothesis of normality, and the MASI yield series is leptokurtic. The yield series is skewed to the left, as indicated by the negative skew- ness coefficient. This asymmetry suggests that the series is nonlinear. Because the P-value relative to the Jarque and Bera statistic is less than 5%, the Jarque and Bera test confirms the non-normality of the MASI yield distribution (Table 2).

Table 2. ADF Test

Series	ADF test statistic	t-statistic	Prob
MASI		**−48.40257**	0.0001
Level	1%	−3.431732	–
	5%	−2.862036	–
	10%	−2.567077	–
Integration order		I (0)	–

3.2 Statistical Tests: Stationarity, Homoscedasticity and Non Linearity

3.2.1 Stationarity Test: Augmented Dickey Fuller-ADF

The probability associated with the value of t-statistic (−48.40257) is lower than 5%, then the MASI series is stationary, with an integration order of value 0 [14].

3.2.2 Homoscedasticity Test: Breush Pagan and De White

Table 3 shows the results of the estimates obtained by applying the Breush Pagan and White homoscedasticity tests to the MASI yield series.

Table 3. Homoscedasticity Test

TR^2	Q
465,83**	39,38***

TR^2 of White's test is the Breush Pagan statistic, and Q is the Breush Pagan statistic. *** and ** At the respective thresholds of 1% and 5%, the null hypothesis of homoscedasticity is rejected.

The Breush-Pagan and White tests produce similar results in that they both reject the null hypothesis of homoscedasticity. It should be highlighted that the rejection of the homoscedasticity null hypothesis is probably certainly owing to the presence of an ARCH effect, which is prevalent in financial time series.

3.2.3 Non Linearity Test: ARCH

Engel's (1982) conditional heteroscedasticity test has as its null hypothesis the absence of an ARCH effect, i.e. the series does not exhibit conditional heteroscedasticity. According to the alternative hypothesis, the series has an ARCH effect. Table 4 summarizes the esti- mation results.

The ARCH test allowed us to conclude that the MASI return series contains conditional heteroscedasticity (ARCH effect). It should be noted at this point that the presence of conditional heteroscedasticity indicating that the return series is not iid does not

Table 4. Heteroscedasticity test: ARCH

Series	ARCH test statistic	F-statistic	Prob
MASI	F-statistic	**322.2311**	0.0000
	Obs*R- squared	299.2658	0.0000

imply market inefficiency. This case corresponds to Alexandre's (1992) random walk: the unconditional moments of the residuals are the same as those of white noise, but the moments conditional on the set of available information differ.

4 Estimation of Nonlinear Models: GARCH, EGARCH, SETAR Model

4.1 GARCH Model

4.1.1 Presentation of GARCH Model

In 1986, Bollerslev created the GARCH model (generalized autoregressive conditional heteroscedasticity model). Based on the ARCH model, this model evolved through time. In the limited sample condition, the GARCH model tackles the issue of insufficient calculation efficiency and accuracy induced by too many lags in the model. It can be used to create financial data regression models, analyze volatility, and forecast.

The GARCH (p, q) model is a time series variance ARMA (p, q). The AR(p) model represents the residual variance (squared errors) of our time series. The MA(q) portion simulates the process's variation. The GARCH model is simplified to the ARCH model when $p = 0$. The present conditional variance is affected by its lag and residual lag, whereas the current variance is affected by the constant term c, the preceding period's residual varepsilon t, and the forecast variance, according to the GARCH model.

The GARCH (p, q) can be written as follows: [15]

$$\vartheta_t^2 = \alpha_1 \vartheta_{t-1}^2 + \cdots + \alpha_p \vartheta_{t-p}^2 + \beta_1 \varepsilon_{t-1}^2 + \cdots + \beta_q \varepsilon_{t-q}^2 + c$$

$$\vartheta_t^2 = \sum_{i=1}^{p} \alpha_i \vartheta_{t-i}^2 + \sum_{j=1}^{q} \beta_j \varepsilon_{t-j}^2 + c \tag{1}$$

The GARCH (1, 1) Model is:

$$\vartheta_t^2 = \alpha \vartheta_{t-1}^2 + \beta \varepsilon_{t-1}^2 + c \tag{2}$$

where:

ϑ_t^2: The conditional volatility.

ε_{t-1}^2: Squared unexpected returns for the previous period conditional volatility.

α, β, c: Positive constants (Table 5).

4.1.2 Estimation of GARCH Model

The results of this test show that it is a GARCH (1.3)

GARCH = C(4) + C(5) * RESID(−1)^{2}GARCH(−1) + C(6) * GARCH(−1) + C(7) *) * GARCH(−2) + C(8) * GARCH(−3)

Table 5. Coefficients of GARCH model

Variable	Coefficient	Std-Error	z-Statistic	Prob
C	0.000212	0.000106	2.003068	0.0452
AR (2)	0.062214	0.015737	3.953252	0.0001
MA (1)	0.182057	0.017982	10.12457	0.0000
Variance Equation				
C	4.04E-06	3.64E-07	11.10060	0.0000
RESID (-1)^2	0.275708	0.011936	23.09890	0.0000
GARCH (-1)	0.376343	0.050377	7.470467	0.0000
GARCH (-2)	0.016578	0.056897	0.291374	0.7708
GARCH (-3)	0.265998	0.037958	7.007665	0.0000

All coefficients are significant since their p-value is less than 5% except for the variable C.

4.2 EGARCH Model

4.2.1 Presentation of EGARCH Model

Nelson (1991) proposed the Exponential GARCH (EGARCH) model as the first variant of the GARCH model that allows for asymmetric effect

The EGARCH (1, 1) model is written as follows: [16]

$$Ln(h_t) = c + x_{t-1}\alpha_1 + \delta_1[|x_{t-1}| - E|x_{t-1}| + \beta_1 Ln(h_{t-1})] \tag{3}$$

where:

h_t: The conditional variability
x_t: the news's content (positive/small/negative/large).

The EGARCH model (3) describes the relationship between previous shocks and the logarithm of the conditional variance; no parameter (α, δ and β) constraints must be imposed to ensure that h_t is nonnegative.

Utilizing x_t properties, it follows that:

$$f(x_t) = x_t\alpha_1 + \delta_1[|x_t| - E|x_t|] \tag{4}$$

x_t) is piecewise linear in x_t is uncorrelated and has a mean of zero. The function f(,, as shown by:

$$f(x_t) = I(x_t > 0). \, x_t(\alpha_1 + \delta_1) + I(x_t < 0). \, x_t(\alpha_1 - \delta_1) - \delta_1[E|x_t|] \qquad (5)$$

Thus, negative shocks have an effect on the log of conditional variance of $(\alpha_1 - \delta_1)$, whereas positive shocks have an effect of $(\alpha_1 + \delta_1)$.. This property of the function f(xt) results in an asymmetric NIC (Fig. 2).

The NIC for the EGARCH (1,1) model (3), in particular, is given by (Table 6):

$$NIC\left(\varepsilon_t | h_t = \sigma^2\right) = \begin{cases} C.exp^{\left(\varepsilon_t \frac{(\alpha_1 + \delta_1)}{\sigma}\right)} \varepsilon_t > 0 \\ C.exp^{\left(\varepsilon_t \frac{(\alpha_1 - \delta_1)}{\sigma}\right)} \varepsilon_t < 0 \end{cases}$$

With:

NIC: New impact Curve

$$C = e^{(-\delta_1 \sqrt{\frac{2}{\pi}} + c)} \sigma^{2\beta_1} \qquad (7)$$

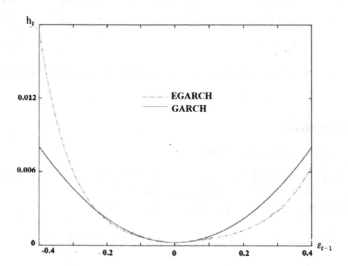

Fig. 2. NIC of The EGARCH /GARCH applied on the MASI

4.2.2 Estimation of EGARCH Model

The results of this test show that it is a EGARCH (1.3)

Log(GARCH) = C(4) + C(5) * |RESID(−1)²|(GARCH(−1))) + C(6) * |RESID(−2)²|(GARCH(−2))) + C(7) * |RESID(−3)²| (GARCH(−3)))+C(8) * Log(GARCH(−1))

All coefficients are significant since their p-value is less than 5% except for the variable C.

Table 6. Coefficients of EGARCH model

Variable	Coefficient	Std-Error	z-Statistic	Prob
C	0.000154	9.72E-05	1.581728	0.1137
AR (2)	0.056105	0.015518	3.615489	0.0003
MA (1)	0.182685	0.017219	10.60950	0.0000
Variance Equation				
C (4)	−0.370176	0.036354	−10.18264	0.0000
C (5)	−0.370176	0.036354	−10.18264	0.0000
C (6)	−0.370176	0.036354	−10.18264	0.0000
C (7)	−0.370176	0.036354	−10.18264	0.0000
C (8)	−0.370176	0.036354	−10.18264	0.0000

4.3 Setar Model

4.3.1 Presentation of SETAR Model

A SETAR (2,1,1) with 2 regimes and an autoregressive process AR (1) with (d = 1) in each regime is as follows: [17]

$$\vartheta t = (\mu_{1,0} + \vartheta_{t-1}\mu_{1,1})(-I[\vartheta_{t-1} > c + 1]) + (\vartheta_{t-1}\mu_{2,1} + \mu_{2,0})(I[\vartheta_{t-1} > c]) + \varepsilon_t$$

$$q_t = \vartheta_{t-d} \tag{8}$$

I(.) Denotes the indicator function, qt is threshold variable $\mu_{1,0}$, $\mu_{1,1}$, $\mu_{2,0}$, $\mu_{2,1}$ are the coefficients represents the coefficients of the AR (1) process.

In the equation, the TAR model allows for different variances for all n segments (regimes). A restriction of the following form is used to stabilize the variance for the different regimes:

$$Y_t = I_1\left[\alpha_{1,0} + \sum_{i=1}^{P_1} Y_{1,t-i}\mu_{1,i}\right] + I_2\left[\alpha_{2,0} + \sum_{i=1}^{P_2} Y_{2,t-i}\mu_{2,i}\right] + \dots + I_w\left[\alpha_{w,0} + \sum_{i=1}^{P_w} Y_{w,t-i}\mu_{w,i}\right] + e_t \tag{9}$$

When it corresponds to the segment j, it is equal to 1, otherwise it is equal to 0. The Ordinary Least Squares (OLS) method can easily estimate each of the m segments, whereas the nonlinear least squares method can estimate the TAR model in equation; however, the boundaries between the segments must be determined. One method for determining segment boundaries is through the localization of structural ruptures. The presence of at least one breaking point in a time series indicates that the data are non-linear.

The threshold change variable qt is now assumed to be any delay qt = ϑ t-d. We used d = 1 in this case. The delayed values of the series determine the regime change. We use the same method as before to find the order p that reduce the BIC and AIC criteria. The delay p = 2 minimizes both the AIC and the BIC criterion (Table 7).

4.3.2 Estimation of SETAR Model

Table 7. Threshold Variable: MASI (–2)

Variable	Coefficient	Std Error	t-Statistic	Prob
MASI (−2) < 0.001053596 − 2353 obs				
C	−0.000144	0.000150	−0.959378	0.3374
MASI (−1)	0.246287	0.019941	12.35062	0.0000
0.001053596 < = MASI (−2) − 1820 obs				
C	0.000540	0.000174	3.095417	0.0020
MASI (−1)	0.306889	0.023134	13.26568	0.0000
R-squared	0.082033	Mean dependent var	0.000270	
Adjusted R-squared	0.081373	S.D. dependent var	0.007520	

5   The Comparative Between GARCH, EGARCH and SETAR Models

We can use model comparison criteria to select the best model; these criteria are numerous and play an important role in econometrics. These criteria are based on forecast error and are intended to be minimized. These are the criteria: MAPE, RMSE, and MAE. Table 8 shows the outcomes of the comparison of the three models.

$$MAE = \frac{1}{n} \sum_{k=1}^{n} |\varphi_k| \tag{10}$$

$$RMSE = \sqrt{MSE} = \sqrt{\frac{1}{n} \sum_{k=1}^{n} \varphi_k{}^2} \tag{11}$$

$$MAPE = \frac{1}{n} \sum_{k=1}^{n} \frac{|\alpha_k - \widehat{\alpha_k}|}{\varphi_k} .100\% \tag{12}$$

where:
  φ_k: The error factor.
  α_k: The actual value.
  $\widehat{\alpha_k}$: The forecast value.
  The above table shows that forecasting the MASI stock market index using the GARCH model is the most optimal because it has the lowest error criteria.

Table 8. Comparison between GARCH, EGARCH and SETAR

Measure	Method	MASI Index
RMSE	GARCH	**0.007520**
	EGARCH	**0.007520**
	SETAR	0.007526
MAE	GARCH	**0.005073**
	EGARCH	0.005074
	SETAR	0.005079
MAPE	GARCH	**182.8022**
	EGARCH	184.7029
	SETAR	175.0816

6 Conclusion

The study examined at how the GARCH, EGARCH, and SETAR models performed in modeling and forecasting the MASI Index from 2002 to 2018. One of the study's goals was to demonstrate that the MASI index used in the study was nonlinear. The assumption of return independence is clearly rejected, according to two tests. In other words, according to financial market theory, the series is nonlinear, and Casablanca's financial market is inefficient. The MAE), RMSE, and MAPE criterion were used in the study to select the best performing model (MAPE). Overall, the results demonstrated that the GARCH modeling technique outperformed the EGARCH and SETAR models in the vast majority of cases.

The results discussion leads to the following conclusions:

– The MASI index's closing price is non-linear and does not change structurally
– The almost non-existent error measures indicate that the various MASI closing price predictive models are robust, efficient, and reliable for forecasting.

When compared to the other 03 non-linear models, the GARCH model performed well.

The paper's future research will compare forecasting between the ANN model and genetic algorithms including the use of deep learning algorithms in order to test prediction efficiency.

References

1. Maponga, L.L., Matarise, F.: Modelling non-linear time series, a dissertation submitted in partial fulfilment of the requirements for the M.Sc. In: Statistics in the Faculty of Science, University of Zimbabwe.
2. Xaba, D., Moroke, N.D., Arkaah, J., Pooe, C.: A comparative study of stock price forecasting using nonlinear models. Risk Gov. Control: Finan. Markets Inst. 7(2), 7–18. https://doi.org/10.22495/rgcv7i2art1

3. Engle, R.F.: Autoregressive conditional heteroskedasticity with estimates of the variance of U.K. Inflation. Econometrica, 55, 987–1008
4. Bollerslev, T.: Generalized autoregressive conditional heteroskedasticity. J. Econometrics, **31**(3), 307–327
5. Nilson, B.: conditional heteroskedasticity in asset returns: a new approach 'econometrica, vol. 59, no. 2, pp. 347–370 (1991)
6. Franses, P.H., Dijk, D.: Non-Linear Time Series Models in Empirical Finance, Cambridge University Press, Cambridge
7. Tong, H.: On a Threshold Model in Pattern Recognition and Signal processing, ed. C. H. Chen, Amsterdam: Sijhoff & Noordhoff
8. Kassam, S., Lim, A.: An improved phase modulator with low nonlinear distortion. In: IEEE Transactions on Communications, vol. 28, no. 1, pp. 111–115 (1980). https://doi.org/10.1109/TCOM.1980.1094581
9. Teräsvirta, T., Anderson, H.M.: Characterizing non-linearities in business cycles using smooth transition autoregressive models. J. Appl. Econ. **7**, 119–136
10. Hamilton, J.D.: A new approach to the economic analysis of nonstationary time series and the business cycle. Econometrica **57**, 357–384
11. Tiwari, S.,Sabzehgar, R., Rasouli, M.: Short term solar irradiance forecast using numerical weather prediction (NWP) with gradient boost regression. In: 2018 9th IEEE International Symposium on Power Electronics for Distributed Generation Systems (PEDG), Charlotte, NC, USA, pp. 1–8 (2018). https://doi.org/10.1109/PEDG.2018.8447751
12. Ahmad, S., Latif, H.A.:Forecasting on the crude palm oil and kernel palm production: seasonal ARIMA approach. In: 2011 IEEE Colloquium on Humanities, Science and Engineering, Penang, Malaysia, pp. 939–944 (2011). https://doi.org/10.1109/CHUSER.2011.6163876
13. Todorova,M.: Application of machine learning methods for determining the stage of cancer. In: 2020 International Conference Automatics and Informatics (ICAI), Varna, Bulgaria, pp. 1–4 (2020). https://doi.org/10.1109/ICAI50593.2020.9311355
14. Zhang, F., Zhao, Y., Zhang, S., Wu, W., Tan, C.: Spacecraft equipment health condition monitoring based on augmented dickey-fuller test and gaussian mixture model. In: 2021 IEEE International Conference on Mechatronics and Automation (ICMA), Takamatsu, Japan, pp. 1379–1384 (2021). https://doi.org/10.1109/ICMA52036.2021.9512583.
15. Christian, F., Jean-Michel, Z.: GARCH Models (Structure, Statistical Inference and Financial Applications) GARCH (p, q) Processes.,(), pp. 17–61 (2010). https://doi.org/10.1002/978047 0670057.ch2
16. Günay, G., Haque, M.: The effect of futures trading on spot market volatility: evidence from turkish derivative exchange. Int. J. Bus. Emerg. Markets **7**(3) (2015). https://doi.org/10.1504/IJBEM.2015.070333
17. Laurence Watier and Sylvia Richardson Modelling of an Epidemiological Time Series by a Threshold Autoregressive Model Journal of the Royal Statistical Society. Series D (The Statisti- cian) vol. 44, no. 3, pp. 353–364 (1995)

Forecasting of Energy Consumption in the Philippines Using Machine Learning Algorithms

Erru Torculas[✉], Earl James Rentillo, and Ara Abigail Ambita

Division of Physical Sciences and Mathematics, University of the Philippines Visayas, Miagao, Iloilo, Philippines
{egtorculas,eqrentillo,aeambita}@up.edu.ph

Abstract. In the Philippines, usage of energy has been steadily increasing over the years, however, the advent of the COVID-19 pandemic brought about unforeseen changes to these parameters. By using machine learning algorithms, energy predictions can be more properly assessed, and corresponding measures can be put into place. The Monthly and Quarterly Market Assessment Report of Wholesale Electricity Spot Market (WESM), governed by Philippines Electricity Market Corporation (PEMC)'s data was analyzed using four machine learning algorithms, namely, Random Forest, XGBoost, Linear Regression, and Support Vector Regression (SVR) to determine the best algorithm in predicting energy consumption within the pre-pandemic and pandemic periods. It was found that the Pre-pandemic (Period 1) data was most accurately predicted by the XGBoost model, having a Root Mean Square Error (RMSE) of 366.691 and Mean Percentage Error (MAPE) of 0.044, while the Pandemic (Period 2) data was most accurately predicted by the Random Forest Model from its RMSE of 687.665 and MAPE of 0.061. While the poorest performing model for both these periods was the SVR, getting an RMSE of 431.366 and 982.202 to the respective periods. The results show how developing tree-based predictive models, XGBoost and Random Forest Models, are significant in forecasting energy consumption in the Philippines, and is therefore also beneficial for future studies that aim to engage in crafting energy conservation and efficiency policies for economic growth.

Keywords: Energy consumption · Forecast · Machine learning

1 Introduction

Energy has always played a vital part in modern society. In fact, consumption of such a resource exhibits a continuous rise to developing economies [1]. It performs as a societal backbone in that its utilization is deemed essential from fueling activities, from mundane ones up to crucial operations. Exemplified by sectors such as residential, commercial, and industrial using electricity as a primary

N. T. Nguyen et al. (Eds.): ACIIDS 2023, CCIS 1863, pp. 424–435, 2023.
https://doi.org/10.1007/978-3-031-42430-4_35

source for operation, energy consumption is thus generally regarded as an index of standard of living [2].

In the Philippines, the average energy consumption per person reached a peak of 5,205 kWh in 2019 and has been relatively increasing in each year prior. Some notable trends which follow this annual increase include country energy consumption (peaked at 563 TWh in 2019), country electricity generation (peaked at 108.27 TWh in 2021), and average electricity generation per person (peaked at 961 KWh in 2019) [3,4].

These statistics, as authored by Ritchie et al., go to show how studying energy consumption in the Philippines proves to be relevant, especially that the population's access to electricity is at an all-time high at 96.84% [3]. Furthermore, there is a lack of datasets in developing economies to be able to predict future demands in electricity [1]. This is where tools such as regression analysis become useful to bridge the gap of such data deficiency [5]. It can be used to generate predicted data and thus arrive at a plausible conclusion if energy demands would still be met in the years to come [4]. More importantly, knowing the pattern of consumption and predicting the trend of energy consumption can work to determine priorities in the process of taking decisions on a sustainable urban environment for the energy sector in the Philippines, and therefore be a reasonable metric to improve energy efficiency of industrial and commercial industries for better policy-making and economic growth.

This paper will assess different machine learning algorithms in forecasting time series of energy consumption in the Philippines and compare the accuracy of each forecasting. Through this, allowing the researchers to investigate on which approach is likely to be accurate for future implementation of energy consumption prediction. It would be beneficial to concretizing findings established in relevant studies, as well as exploring how these build on in more specific contexts such as that of the Philippines.

2 Literature Review

In a study by Shin and Woo [6], For estimating energy usage in Korea, three machine learning methods were compared: Random Forest (RF), XGBoost (XGB), and Long Short-Term Memory (LSTM). The researchers concluded that machine learning can be used to anticipate energy use, albeit classic econometric methods beat machine learning in some circumstances. Machine learning demonstrated advantages in dealing with unexpectedly irregular time series data [6].

Similarly, Rambabu et al. [7] exhaustively delved into the prediction and analysis of household energy consumption through machine learning algorithms for energy management. Their paper focused on predicting household energy consumption where models are trained by using various machine learning algorithms such as Linear Regression, Lasso Regression, Random Forest, Extra Tree Regressor, XG Boost, etc. It must be noted that patterns of household energy consumption are observed by the constant changing of different factors namely, temperature, humidity, an hour of the day, etc. The researchers' findings suggested that tree-based models give the best results among the rest of the machine-learning approaches used [7]. The evaluation metric used was R square which can be utilized to gauge how much variance in the dependent variable can be predicted.

A case study in Malaysia also discussed energy consumption prediction by using three methodologies of machine learning, specifically, Support Vector Machine, Artificial Neural Network, and k-Nearest Neighbor [8]. These approaches were proposed for the algorithm of the predictive model. The paper explored a great insight into real-life applications where the researchers used two tenants from a commercial building as proponents of their case study. The metrics of evaluation used in the paper are compared based on RMSE, NRMSE, and MAPE metrics [8].

These studies show how machine learning algorithms can be an indispensable tool for forecasting power consumption to be able to achieve sustainable and effective systems in their respective contexts. However, testing the predictive models they have created into the context of the Philippines may not show consistent results due to the disparity and nature of the data available for analysis. For Shin and Woo [6], three machine learning algorithms were more extensive, being modeled from January 1997 to June 2021. Rambabu et al. [7], on the other hand, utilized a more continuous dataset on power consumption for analysis, that being measured at 10-min intervals over 4.5 months in terms of house temperatures and humidity. Similarly, the dataset of Salam et al. [9] for machine learning algorithms for power consumption prediction in Tetouan, Morocco followed the same interval collection from January 1, 2017 to December 31, 2017, measured in KW.

Thus, it is important to note that data limitations arise as an additional limitation to model energy demand of developing countries, one of which is the Philippines. In fact, aside from data limitations, Bhattacharyya and Timilsina [10] posited that these countries face such a challenge due to institutional capacity and the specific characteristics of their energy systems as well. In their study, they have compared different energy demand forecasting models and their criteria, including type, purpose, approach, and geographical coverage, among many others. These models varied in their capabilities and coverage, where some were more suitable for general analysis while others were more complex and specific.

These go to show that failure to address these challenges can yield inaccurate results, ultimately misguiding policy recommendations. Therefore, there is a need to improve energy demand modeling tools and institutional capacities in developing countries, one that is tailor-made to address the consumption behavior of a country given its income group, location, and more importantly, the data available to analyze and model energy consumption. Hence, closing the energy consumption gap through effective policies is critical for a sustainable and successful future. Policymakers may minimize climate change, reduce environmental impact, and promote sustainable development by prioritizing energy efficiency and renewable sources. Diversifying the energy mix and investing in resilient infrastructure improves energy security by reducing risks and assuring a consistent supply especially in developing countries like the Philippines.

3   Data and Methodology

3.1   Data

The data used throughout this project is consolidated data from 2014 to the second quarter of 2022 of the Monthly and Quarterly Market Assessment Report of the Wholesale Electricity Spot Market (WESM) governed by the Philippine Electricity Market Corporation (PEMC) [11].

Considering the caveats, the dataset was mostly curated from the summary reports of WESM. So, the total energy consumption data for 2016 is only available through a bar graph without any numeric label accompanying the bar in each month. The dataset also utilized two features which are the *Date*, specified by month and year, and *Total Energy Consumption (in GWh)*.

3.2   Methodology

Time Period Analysis. The analysis is divided into two, namely: Pre-pandemic and Pandemic periods, additionally labeled as Period 1 and Period 2, respectively. The separation of time periods serves as the basis of the efficiency of the models when practiced on a sudden shift of regulations brought by the height of the pandemic [6].

The pre-pandemic period is composed of a rather linear growth in terms of energy consumption and saw a rise from a starting point of 4422 GWh (Jan 2014) to an endpoint of 6224 GWh (Mar 2020) and a peak point of 7697 GWh (Jun 2019). Following this, Figure Period 1 training and test data where it made use of "January 2014 to March 2020" in which the training data started from "January 2014 to June 2018", while the rest was the testing data "July 2018 to March 2020".

Furthermore, it is evident that the data from April 2020, which was the first month of lockdown and in turn, led to a staggering decrease in energy consumption (3760 GWh from the previous month's 6224 GWh) as non-essential buildings were cut off to minimize losses, amongst other reasons. Power generation was drastically reduced due to slowdown in terms of economical manufacturing production, and the energy consumption both in commercial and infrastructure sector by 2.0% [6]. Hence, Period 2 or the Pandemic period used data spanning from "January 2014 to June 2022", with "January 2014 to March 2020" data being used as training data, the period wherein it witnessed the drastic change in energy consumption. Meanwhile, the testing data used "April 2020 to June 2022".

Machine Learning Models. To evaluate the data concerning the scope of the project, four machine learning algorithms were run and compared with each other for accuracy. The models that were implemented in this paper are: Random Forest (RF) Model, XGBoost, Linear Regression, and lastly, Support Vector Regression (SVR).

Random Forest (RF) can be applied to time series forecasting by converting the time series data into a format suitable for supervised learning and using a specific method called walk-forward validation to evaluate the model. This is necessary because using k-fold cross validation on the model would produce overly optimistic results [6,7]. In fact, RF has already been utilized by facility managers for further monitoring and improving of their respective buildings' energy efficiency [12].

Meanwhile, XGBoost has been shown to be effective in a variety of tasks, including time series forecasting. Due to its popularity in regression problems, it is said to hasten performance in which it utilizes parallel processing. Not only that, but it also performs well in small datasets and averts overfitting [6,7].

Linear regression is a simple but powerful technique for forecasting. It is effective because it makes a strong assumption about the relationship between the input variables and the output variable, which allows it to make reliable predictions even when the data is noisy or there are missing values. In fact, linear regression is fast and easy to implement, making it a popular choice for many forecasting tasks [7,14].

Lastly, Support Vector Regression (SVR) is a type of support vector machine (SVM) that is often used for forecasting because it can handle data with multiple features and can make predictions for continuous target variables [8,12,14]. In the case of regression, the classes are continuous, and the goal is to find the hyperplane that best fits the data. Not only that, SVR models can also be trained relatively quickly, making them efficient for use in forecasting tasks.

These models were selected because they yield a significant analysis and meaningful information in a predictive approach based from the previous published related works [6–8]. Not only that, this paper revolves on finding the accurate model to implement in terms of forecasting energy consumption, therefore regression is advantageous in capturing associations and relationships between forecast variable of interest and predictor variables [13,14].

3.3   Evaluating Forecast Accuracy

Since the result of the focus of the project is regression analysis, in the context of prediction driven models, the most widely adopted reliability analysis indicators are Root Mean Square Error (RMSE) and Mean Absolute Percentage Error (MAPE). RMSE measures the differences between the predicted and actual values and therefore a means to measure the quality of fit between the actual data and predicted model. It is preferred over the standard Mean Square Error (MSE) since it is a smaller value and can be compared more straightforwardly. Furthermore, MAPE is one of the metrics of evaluation used in this paper since it relatively measures how accurate the forecast system is. RMSE equation is shown in Eq. (1), while the equation of MAPE is shown in Eq. (2)

$$RMSE = \sqrt{\frac{\sum_{i=1}^{n}(x_{1,i} - x_{2,i})^2}{n}} \qquad (1)$$

$$MAPE = \frac{1}{n}\sum_{i=1}^{n}\left|\frac{x_{1,i} - x_{2,i}}{x_{1,i}}\right| \times 100 \qquad (2)$$

4   Results and Discussion

The group utilized the Sci-kit learn package to build Random Forest, XGBoost, Linear Regression, and Support Vector Regression models. With that, the final model was chosen based on the lowest root mean squared error (RMSE) value. Table 1 summarizes the metric of evaluation for the forecasting. It compares the test data RMSE and MAPE values of the machine learning models for two different periods, Period 1 and 2.

Accordingly, the machine learning model that yielded the lowest RMSE for Period 1 is the XGBoost model with a value of 366.691. Whereas, for Period 2, the Random Forest model was regarded as the final model since it has a RMSE of 687.665 and it has the least RMSE among the models implemented. Based on the empirical data that was presented, the Support Vector Regression (SVR) model accumulated the highest RMSE for both periods with values of 431.366 (Period 1) and 982.202 (Period 2) which in this case will not be regarded as the final model because of it overfitting of data.

Table 1. Performance of the models by period

		ML Models			
	Metric	RF	XGBoost	Linear Reg	SVR
Period 1	RMSE	422.737	366.691	411.578	431.366
	MAPE	0.050	0.044	0.047	0.050
Period 2	RMSE	687.665	692.077	935.880	982.202
	MAPE	0.061	0.061	0.123	0.131

Lewis [15] categorized the accuracy of the forecast based on the predictive models' MAPE values. Through this, the paper utilized Table 2 interpretation of forecasting accuracy. In Period 1, all the models showed a high accurate forecast with their MAPE values of 0.05 (5%), 0.044 (4.4%), 0.047 (4.7%), and 0.05 (5%), for RF, XGBoost, Linear Regression, and SVR, respectively. Comparatively, the Period 2 models forecast returned only good accuracy for both Linear Regression and SVR interpreting that both models were not as high as RF and XGBoost's with 0.061 (6.1%). This goes to show that the latter models can be identified as more accurate models for Period 2 than the former with 0.123 (12.3%) and 0.131 (13.1%) Linear Regression and SVR, respectively.

Table 2. Interpretation of MAPE Results for Forecasting Accuracy.

MAPE-value	Accuracy of Forecast
Less than 10%	Highly Accurate Forecast
11% to 20%	Good Forecast
21% to 50%	Reasonable Forecast
More than 51%	Inaccurate Forecast

Overall, the metrics of evaluation showed the machine learning models that yielded the least RMSE value are the XGBoost and Random Forest model, Period 1 and 2, respectively. Both of these models were deemed *Highly Accurate* in terms of their forecasting ability. On the other hand, Linear Regression and Support Vector Regression (SVR) gained the highest RMSE amongst the models in Period 1 and 2. Not only that, but both of these models forecasting accuracy are simply *Good Forecast* as opposed to the aforementioned models with high accuracy.

4.1   Philippine Energy Consumption Model Forecasts

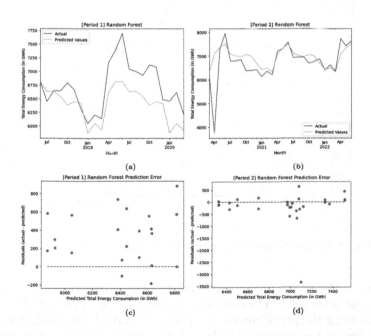

Fig. 1. Random forest model comparison by period with prediction error.

As shown in Fig. 1, both periods were compared in the Random Forest model in which they are accompanied by their respective prediction errors. Figures 1a and

1b show actual values forecasted against the predicted values. Period 1 depicts that the predicted values were much lower than the actual values from April 2019 to March 2020.

Whereas, the prediction in Period 2 slightly forecasted the actual values between January 2021 until March 2022. April 2021 to September 2021 were accurately predicted. The data of the Random Forest model can further be observed through the prediction errors wherein the residual were quite loose for Period 1 as compared to Period 2 which are compact given that there is one outlier due to sudden decrease of energy consumption during the start of lockdowns.

Figure 2 illustrates the XGBoost model comparison of Period 1 and 2 with their respective prediction errors. Figures 2a and 2b show the actual values forecasted against the predicted values in which Period 1 depicts that the predicted values were much lower than the actual values from April 2019 to October 2020.

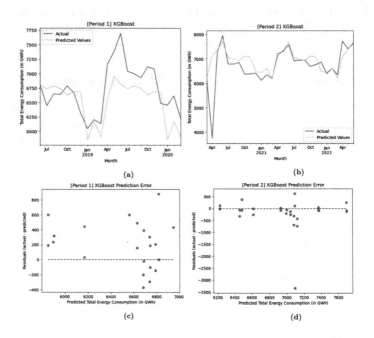

Fig. 2. XGBoost model comparison by period with prediction error.

However, Period 2's prediction forecasted the actual values between April 2021 to September 2021. The data were closely tight from June 2019 until June 2022. Observing the prediction errors, in Figs. 2c and 2d, the residual were quite loose for Period 1 as compared to Period 2 which are more compact given that there is one outlier due to sudden decrease of energy consumption during the start of lockdowns.

Figure 3 illustrates the Linear Regression model comparison of Period 1 and 2 with their respective prediction errors. Based on the graph, Figs. 2a and 2b, it showed a great disparity between the actual values and the predicted values in Period 1. The start of pre-pandemic, August 2018 to November 2018, it was fairly forecasted. However, it took a great turn on the following months wherein the prediction were incongruent to the actual. The analysis can also extend to Period 2's forecast since the graph showed no similarities to the actual values. Importantly, Figs. 3c and 3d showed the prediction of error relatively affected the forecast since the predicted values were not consistent with the actual values.

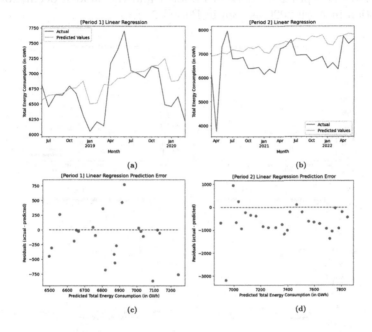

Fig. 3. Linear Regression model comparison by period with prediction error.

Fig. 4 illustrates the Support Vector Regression model comparison of Period 1 and 2 with their respective prediction errors. Figures 4a and 4b, same with the previous model, Linear Regression, it also showed a great disparity between the actual values and the predicted values in Period 1. The forecasting was incongruent with the actual wherein there is somewhat a disconnect using the model in terms of actualizing the predicted values with the actual. The analysis can also extend to Period 2's forecast since the graph showed no similarities to the actual values. With that, comparing the SVR and Linear Regression models, both were quite similar in their forecast.

Figures 1, 2, 3 and 4 compare the predicted values from machine learning models with the actual values and the predicted values from the optimal model for each time period.

Figures 5a and 5b summarize the featured machine learning models forecast using the predicted values against the actual values for Period 1 and Period 2. It can be seen that the forecasting ability of the models varied and there was a noticeable difference in the predicted values when tracking the post-rebound rise. In the first period, the XGBoost model performed the best by following similar trend intervals. In the second period, the optimal model, which was the Random Forest (RF) model, produced predictions that were almost the same as the actual values by only a margin with XGBoost. In their respective cases, both the XGBoost and Random Forest (RF) models show high adaptability to forecasting values given the nonlinearity of the dataset, as modeled by the January 2019 to April 2019 data in Period 1 and the sudden decline of energy consumption in April 2020 as seen in Period 2.

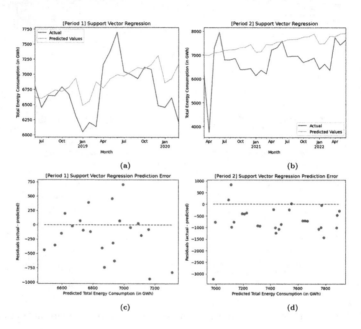

Fig. 4. SVR model comparison by period with prediction error.

The two weakest predictive models, the Linear Regression Model and Support Vector Regression, demonstrate comparable patterns in Periods 1 and 2. Despite the fact that their projected values are closely clustered, they do not perform as well as the XGBoost and RF models.

In time-series problem-solving, tree-based predictive models such as RF and XGBoost outperform other models. Tree-based models, as opposed to linear regression and SVR (linear), may successfully capture non-linear correlations between variables. While SVR can include nonlinearity through the use of kernel functions, it frequently involves a tradeoff between efficiency and complexity, leading in longer training times and possibly overfitting. XGBoost and RF, on the other hand, provide quick training, precise results, and scalability, making them ideal for the task at hand. Furthermore, tree-based approaches have the advantage of being able to handle missing data, with XGBoost automatically inputting missing values using defaults or column means/medians.

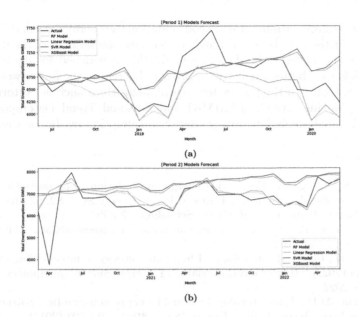

Fig. 5. Machine learning models forecast in Pre-pandemic and Pandemic Period

5 Conclusion

The paper introduced different machine learning algorithms in forecasting time series of energy consumption and compared the viability of these models on which approach has high accuracy to predict these patterns or trends surrounding energy consumption. Two periods were used in the analysis, pre-pandemic and pandemic, Period 1 and 2, respectively.

To summarize, this study explored the use of machine learning to forecast energy consumption and determined the viable model that can be implemented in analyzing energy forecast in the Philippines. In particular, the XGBoost model was the most accurate in predicting the first period, while the RF model had the lowest RMSE in the second period. Thus, these convincingly demonstrate that tree-based predictive models have a superior advantage over other models in solving time-series problems. Knowing this, the study also verified the predictive power of machine learning in the energy market using real data and suggested that this forecasting model could be used by energy companies and governments to respond better to changes in energy consumption and improve the reliability of energy supply and demand data.

There are a few limitations to this research and potential areas for future study. Firstly, the accuracy of the model's prediction and analysis can vary depending on the data and variable settings, making it difficult to determine which approach is superior in all cases. Secondly, the caveats mentioned earlier in the data summarize how the data regarding energy consumption is lacking here in the Philippines. In order to build an effective way for forecasting the consumption of energy, we must start in consolidating the energy data in the country. Thirdly, to further invoke a much higher accuracy, the samples of the data must be increased or at least the data points should be widened for distinguishing more models with better predictive approach. Therefore, the future work should further investigate on time series forecasting algorithms such as Autoregressive Integrated Moving Average (ARIMA) and Seasonal Trend Decomposition to enhance the analysis by integrating energy consumption by day or seasons.

References

1. Barak, S., Sadegh, S.: Forecasting energy consumption using ensemble ARIMA-ANFIS hybrid algorithm. Int. J. Electr. Power Energy Syst. **82**, 92–104 (2016)
2. The National Institute of Open Schooling (NIOS). Importance of Energy in the Society (2012). https://nios.ac.in/media/documents/333courseE/27B.pdf. Accessed 27 Nov 2022
3. Ritchie, H., Roser, M., Rosado, P.: Philippines: energy country profile. Our World in Data (2022). https://ourworldindata.org/energy/country/philippines. Accessed 27 Nov 2022
4. Sahakian, M.D.: Understanding household energy consumption patterns: when "west is best. Metro Manila". Energy Policy **39**(2), 596–602 (2011)
5. García-Martín, E., Lavesson, N., Grahn, H., Casalicchio, E., Boeva, V.: How to measure energy consumption in machine learning algorithms. In: Alzate, C., et al. (eds.) ECML PKDD 2018. LNCS (LNAI), vol. 11329, pp. 243–255. Springer, Cham (2019). https://doi.org/10.1007/978-3-030-13453-2_20
6. Shin, S.Y., Woo, H.G.: Energy consumption forecasting in Korea using machine learning algorithms. Energies **15**(13), 4880 (2022)
7. Rambabu, M., Ramakrishna, N.S.S., Polamarasetty, P.K.: prediction and analysis of household energy consumption by machine learning algorithms in energy management. E3S Web of Conferences (2022)
8. Ali, S.B.M., et al.: Analysis of energy consumption and potential energy savings of an institutional building in Malaysia. Alexandria Eng. J. **60**(1), 805–820 (2021)
9. Salam, A., Hibaoui, A.E.: Comparison of machine learning algorithms for the power consumption prediction: case study of Tetouan city. In: 2018 6th International Renewable and Sustainable Energy Conference (IRSEC) (2018). https://doi.org/10.1109/irsec.2018.8703007
10. Bhattacharyya, S.C., Timilsina, G.R.: Modelling energy demand of developing countries: are the specific features adequately captured? Energy Policy **38**(4), 1979–1990 (2010). https://doi.org/10.1016/j.enpol.2009.11.079
11. Philippine Electricity Market Corporation. Monthly Market Assessment Report (2019). https://www.wesm.ph/market-outcomes/market-assessment-reports/monthly-market-assessment-report. Accessed 27 Nov 2022
12. Li, C., et al.: Building energy consumption prediction: an extreme deep learning approach. Energies **10**(10), 1525 (2017)
13. Mosavi, A., Bahmani, A.: Energy consumption prediction using machine learning; a review (2019). https://www.preprints.org/manuscript/201903.0131/v1. Accessed 27 Nov 2022
14. Garcia-Martin, E., et al.: Estimation of energy consumption in machine learning. J. Parallel Distrib. Comput. **134**, 75–88 (2019)
15. Lewis, C.D.: International and Business Forecasting Methods. Butterworths, London. Scientific Research (1982). Accessed 27 Nov 2022

A Deep Reinforcement Learning-Based Multi-objective Optimization for Crowdsensing-Based Air Quality Monitoring Systems

Nam Duong Tran[1], Manh Cuong Dao[1], Thanh Hung Nguyen[1],
Thi Ha Ly Dinh[1], Kien Nguyen[2,3], and Phi Le Nguyen[1(✉)]

[1] School of Information and Communication Technology,
Hanoi University of Science and Technology, Hanoi, Vietnam
lenp@soict.hust.edu.vn
[2] Institute for Advanced Academic Research, Chiba University, Chiba, Japan
[3] Graduate School of Engineering, Chiba University, Chiba, Japan

Abstract. Global air pollution is becoming increasingly severe. In this context, monitoring air quality at all times and locations is necessary. Traditionally, air quality is monitored using stationary monitoring stations. However, this approach has an inherent shortcoming: limited monitoring locations. Crowdsensing-based air monitoring has recently emerged as a promising alternative that expands monitoring coverage in both temporal and spatial dimensions through the collaboration of numerous participants. Typically, participants in crowdsensing systems are compensated for the data they provide. One of the critical challenges in handling a crowdsensing system is minimizing the cost while guaranteeing the quality of the data collected. For crowdsensing-based air monitoring systems, data quality refers to the temporal and spatial coverage corresponding to the locations and times the data was collected. In this study, we propose a solution based on deep reinforcement learning that simultaneously optimizes two goals: maximizing coverage range and minimizing costs. Our proposed solution is one of the first attempts to optimize both of these objectives for crowdsensing-based air monitoring systems. Compared to other algorithms, experimental results indicate that the proposed solution can increase coverage by more than 30% and reduce cost by more than 70%.

Keywords: Vehicle-based mobile crowdsensing · spatial-temporal coverage · air quality monitoring · cost minimization · deep reinforcement learning

1 Introduction

The urbanization and mechanization processes have exacerbated air pollution worldwide, particularly in developing nations. In Vietnam, the AQI index is

---

N. D. Tran and M. C. Dao—The two authors contributed equally to this paper.

© The Author(s), under exclusive license to Springer Nature Switzerland AG 2023
N. T. Nguyen et al. (Eds.): ACIIDS 2023, CCIS 1863, pp. 436–448, 2023.
https://doi.org/10.1007/978-3-031-42430-4_36

consistently greater than five times the WHO-acceptable threshold for health [6]. Air pollution is the cause of a variety of chronic problems, including respiratory and cardiovascular diseases, as well as imposing serious effects on the immune system, nervous system, etc. . In addition, air pollution is responsible for more than seven million deaths globally each year, according to the WHO report. In such a situation, air quality monitoring is essential for assisting individuals in taking precautions to protect their health and for supporting policymakers in implementing immediate measures to improve air quality.

Monitoring air quality has traditionally been conducted by monitoring stations permanently installed in specified locations. However, this approach suffers from an inherent weakness: the limitation of monitoring coverage, i.e., it can only acquire information from places where the monitoring stations are located. Consequently, the monitoring areas are limited, resulting in the insufficiency of air quality data. For example, there are only less than 50 air monitoring stations in Hanoi, Vietnam, out of a total area of 3300 km^2 [1]. In order to broaden the monitoring area, several mobile air monitoring solutions have recently been proposed. In [8], the mobility of unmanned aerial vehicles (UAVs) is utilized to equip the capability of monitoring air quality in any location. However, the UAV-based paradigm copes with challenges in controlling the UAV's trajectory and guaranteeing the UAV devices' power.

Recently, crowdsensing has emerged as a viable alternative that utilizes the crowd's computing power and sensing abilities to collect data on a phenomenon of interest, e.g., traffic monitoring and prediction, advertisement dissemination [3]. Crowdsensing-based air quality monitoring systems have been introduced in [13]. To encourage users to collect data in a crowdsensing system, users are typically compensated for the data they collect [5]. Consequently, one of the biggest challenges in handling a crowdsensing system is guaranteeing the collected data is of high quality while minimizing the total cost to the participants.

For an air monitoring system, the quality of the data depends on the locations where the data is collected and the time of data collection. More specifically, collecting as much data as possible at as many locations and times as possible is preferable. In the study [4], the authors have introduced two concepts, namely *spatial coverage* and *temporal coverage*, reflecting the quality of data related to the locations where the data was collected and the time of data collection, respectively. In order to reduce expenses, it is necessary to minimize the simultaneous collection of multiple data from the same location. In the literature, there are several efforts have been devoted to maximizing spatial coverage. In [11], the authors studied to determine the optimal set of vehicles to maximize coverage while satisfying the budget constraint. They proved the problem's NP-hardness and then proposed a heuristic approach to solve it. Zhang et al. in [14] addressed the coverage quality maximization problem in mobile crowdsensing. The authors in [2] focused on a crowdsensing network for environmental monitoring applications. They investigated how to choose suitable participants given their traverse path and the rewards. The objective is to maximize the coverage quality while guaranteeing the budget constraints. However, there are few research studies on optimizing temporal coverage and user costs. As far as we know, [4] is one of very few studies to present the first findings on temporal coverage and user cost optimization. This study, however, only considers an ideal mathematical model and thus cannot be implemented in practice.

In this study, we focus on vehicle-based crowdsensing mobile air quality monitoring systems and propose a deep reinforcement learning-based approach to address two objectives simultaneously: maximizing spatial-temporal coverage while minimizing the cost. By exploiting the advantage of reinforcement learning's self-learning and self-adaptation to the environment, our proposal demonstrates the adaptability of different network configurations and the capacity to adapt to shifting network environments.

The main contributions of our paper are as follows.

- We formulate the crowdsensing mobile air quality monitoring system under the reinforcement learning framework and propose a deep reinforcement learning-based approach to solve the multi-objective optimization problem: maximizing spatial-temporal coverage while minimizing the cost. Our originality lies in the design of state representation and the reward function.
- We perform extensive experiments to evaluate the performance of the proposed method and compare it with existing solutions.

The rest of the paper is organized as follows. We formulate the problem in Sect. 2. Section 3 presents the preliminaries and Sect. 4 describes our proposal. We evaluate the performance in Sect. 5 and conclude in Sect. 6.

2 Problem Formulation

In the following, we first present our network model in Sect. 2.1. We then define the terms and formulate our targeted problem in Sect. 2.2.

2.1 Network Model

Figure 1 depicts our network model, which consists of two main components: vehicles and a server. Vehicles are equipped with sensors capable of sensing the air quality indicators and transmitting the collected data to the server via wireless communication channels. We divide the entire timeline into small timeslots. At each time slot, the vehicles decide whether to collect data and send it to the server. Our problem requires vehicles to optimize their data collection (i.e., decide whether to collect data at each timeslot) so that spatial-temporal coverage is maximized while the total cost of data collection paid for all vehicles is minimized.

In the following section, we first present the definitions that quantify the three concepts of spatial coverage, temporal coverage, and total cost, and then formulate our targeted problem.

2.2 Definitions

We have an observation that air quality is frequently constant over a sufficiently short period and in a reasonably small space. We model this observation by the following definitions.

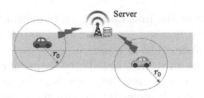

Fig. 1. Network Model

Definition 1 (Spatial-temporal stability).

- With a sufficiently small r_0, data collected concurrently at a point A and a point B, whose distance to point A is within r_0, can be regarded as identical.
- With a sufficiently tiny t_0, the data obtained at location A at time t and at time $t + t_0$ can be regarded as identical.

r_0 and t_0 are named as the *spatial*, and *temporal stable ranges*, respectively.

We inherit the definitions of spatial and temporal coverage from [4], with the spatial coverage representing the monitoring area and the temporal coverage depicting the monitoring time. To be more precise, we divide the region of interest S into sufficiently small grid with each cell denoted by d_S. We denote by $\mathcal{T}(d_S)$ the time over which d_S is monitored; the spatial-temporal coverage is defined as follows.

Definition 2 (Spatial-temporal coverage).
Let S be the region of interest, then the spatial-temporal coverage of the crowdsensing system is defined by

$$\mathcal{Q} = \sum_{d_S \in S} d_S \times \mathcal{T}(d_S). \tag{1}$$

Definition 3 (Cost).
The cost is defined by the total expense paid to all participants. In this study, we assume that all data are compensated equally. Consequently, the cost is proportional to the number of times the participants collect data.

Given the definitions of the spatial-temporal coverage and cost, our problem is formulated as follows.

Definition 4 (Multi-objective optimization problem).
We focus on two optimization objectives: (1) maximizing the spatial-temporal coverage and (2) minimizing the costs. The first seeks to maximize the collected data's quality, as defined by the Formula (1). The second aims to reduce the number of times the vehicles perform monitoring tasks.

3 Preliminaries

This section will present the foundation related to reinforcement learning and deep reinforcement learning, which will be used in our proposal.

3.1   Reinforcement Learning

Reinforcement learning (RL) is the learning technique that enables the agent to acquire behavior in a dynamic environment through trial-and-error interaction [7,10]. A RL framework consists of five main components including environment, agent, action, state, and reward. At each state, the agent selects an action and interacts with the surrounding environment. The environment then responds with a reward signal indicating the effectiveness of the action. Q learning [12] is one of the most popular RL techniques that uses a so-called Q table to represent the actions' value. In Q learning, the agent updates the Q table after every action using the Bellman equation shown below:

$$Q(S_t, A_t) \leftarrow (1 - \alpha)Q(S_t, A_t) + \alpha[\mathcal{R}_t + \gamma \max_a Q(S_{t+1}, a)], \tag{2}$$

where, S_t and S_{t+1} denote the states at time slots t and $t + 1$, respectively; a_t represents the action performed at time slot t, and $\mathcal{R}_t$, $Q(S_t, A_t)$ depict the reward and Q value when performing action A_t at state S_t; $\max_a Q(S_{t+1}, a)$ is the maximum value that may be obtained for all possible actions a at the next state S_{t+1}.

3.2   Deep Q Network

Deep Q-Network (DQN) is the advanced version of vanilla Q-learning, which addresses the challenge of continuous spaces and enormously huge sets of state-action pairings by calculating the Q table with a neural network [9]. The mapping from state space to action-value space is represented as a nonlinear neural network in DQN, enabling the agent to learn extremely complex mapping functions. The DQN architecture includes two structure-identical, function-separated networks: the primary and target networks. The former is used to make decisions and is updated more frequently. The latter network is a reflection of the primary network, which functions as the training reference; therefore, it is updated less frequently and is more stable. In addition, DQN utilizes the experience replay mechanism to retain and sample data from a massive buffer of prior experience. At each time-step, the M-sized buffer stores quartets of $(S_t, A_t, R_t + 1, S_t + 1)$. The data are then selected at random in blocks of size N to train the primary network for minimizing the loss function shown below.

$$\mathcal{L} = \frac{1}{N} \sum_{i=1}^{N} \left[R_t + \gamma \max_{A_{t+1}} Q'(S_{t+1}, A_{t+1}) - Q(S_t, A_t) \right]^2, \tag{3}$$

where $Q'(\cdot)$ and $Q(\cdot)$ denote the Q value determined by the target and primary networks, respectively. The target network replicates the weights of the primary network after m updates, making it the m-update delayed mirror of the primary network.

4   Proposal

In the following, we first model our problem into the RL framework in Sect. 4.1. We then propose the training mechanism in Sect. 4.2.

4.1   Reinforcement Learning Framework Modeling

As stated in the previous section, a RL framework is comprised of five main components: environment, agent, action space, state space and reward function. In this section, we define these components in the context of the problem we are attempting to solve.

Environment, Agents, and Action Space. We consider a multi-agent reinforcement framework, where the network serves as the environment, and each sensor-equipped vehicle behaves as an agent. Every agent will interact with the environment and other agents while driving and decide whether to conduct the monitoring task at every time slot. After performing every action, the agent receives a signal from the environment (via the reward value), which reflects how good the action is. The agent's action space consists of two values, namely *perform monitoring* or *not perform monitoring*.

State. In RL, the state should contain all information that assists the agent in decision-making. As our model consists of multiple agents, a single agent's decision must consider not only its own state but also the states of all other agents. Ideally, the state would include information of all agents. However, this will result in a too large state space, hindering the training process. To solve this problem, we have the following observation (see an illustration in Fig. 2). Given the network's temporal and spatial stable range of t_0 and r_0, respectively, we divide the network into a square grid with the size of each cell being $r \times r$ and assume the air quality measurements at cells separated by less than m cells can be regarded as identical; or in other words, r and m are determined by $r_0 = \sqrt{2}r \times m$. Let A_i be an arbitrary agent who is residing in a cell c_t at time step t, then the air quality information collected by A_i will be applied for all the cells in the square of size $(2m + 1) \times (2m + 1)$ centered at c_t (the ones colored green in Fig. 2). It means that its decision regarding whether or not to perform air quality monitoring at time step t will affect the states of the cells in the square of size $(2m + 1) \times (2m + 1)$ centered at c_t. On the other hand, the information collected by any other vehicles residing in a cell separated by less than m cells from a green cell will be applied to that green cell. It means that the state of the cells belonging to the square of size $(4m + 1) \times (4m + 1)$ centered at c_t may contribute to the decision of A_i. Based on this observation, we define state as follows.

Definition 5 (State). (Figure 2) The state s_t corresponding to A_i at time step t includes information about all the cells within the $(4m + 1) \times (4m + 1)$ square centered at c_t. Precisely, s_t consists of two $(4m + 1) \times (4m + 1)$ matrices, namely the *vehicle position matrix* and the *monitoring status matrix*, whose each item (i, j) representing the status of the cell (i, j) in the $(4m + 1) \times (4m + 1)$ square.

The vehicle position matrix is a binary matrix with 1 representing a cell containing a vehicle and 0 depicting the inverse. The monitoring status matrix indicates when each cell's air quality is measured. To be more specific, the values of each

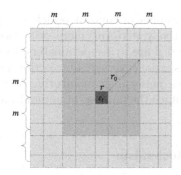

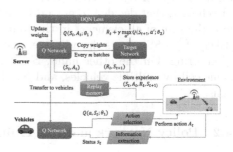

Fig. 2. Illustration of state modeling. The state corresponding to agent A_i staying at cell c_i at time step t conveys information related to all cells in the square of $(4m + 1) \times (4m + 1)$.

Fig. 3. The policy network. The agents use Q network to determine actions, while the server is responsible for training Q network using the DQN architecture.

item (i, j) in the second matrix range from 0 to t_0, where the value of t indicates that the last time the cell (i, j) has been measured is $t_0 - t$ time steps ago (note that if the last time the cell (i, j) is measured is far than t_0, then the value of item (i, j) in the second matrix is set to 0). Intuitively, the vehicle position matrix indicates whether cell c_t can be measured by vehicles other than A_i. Consequently, utilizing this data helps alleviate redundant measurements in spatial space (i.e., measuring the same cell by multiple vehicles). In the meantime, the second matrix tells us how necessary it is to collect data at c_i and its neighboring cells (i.e., if a cell has been measured within t_0 time steps, then it is not necessary to be measured again in the current time step). Accordingly, using this information helps alleviate redundant measurements in temporal space (i.e., measuring the same cell too frequently).

Reward Function. The reward signal in RL quantifies the goodness of actions and is computed by the reward function. Consequently, the goal of the reward function is to encourage desirable behaviors while discouraging undesirable ones. Following the objective described in Sect. 2, we design the reward function to prioritize monitoring cells that have not been measured within the previous t_0 time steps and alleviate measuring the other cells. Our reward function $\mathcal{R}(a_t)$ with respect to action a_t is defined as follows.

$$
\mathcal{R}(a_t) = \begin{cases} \alpha \frac{\Phi(S_u^t - S_c^t + S_{au})}{\Phi(S_r)}, & \text{if } a_t \text{ is to perform monitoring,} \\ \beta \frac{\Phi(S_c^{t+1} - S_u^t + S_{ac})}{\Phi(S_r)}, & \text{otherwise,} \end{cases} \tag{4}
$$

where S_u^t and S_c^t are binary matrices of size $(4m + 1) \times (4m + 1)$, representing the monitoring status of the cells after and before the agent executes action a_t, respectively. Specifically, an item (i, j) of S_u^t (respectively, S_c^t) is assigned the value of 1 if the cell (i, j) is measured after (respectively, before) the agent performs the action. S_{au} and S_{ac} are binary matrices indicating the number of times the cells have not been measured/or measured so far. To be more specific, an item (i, j) of S_{au} (respectively, S_{ac}) is the number of times a vehicle stayed at cell (i, j) that decided to not perform (respectively, perform) monitoring task. Φ is the sum of all elements in the matrix; α and β are hyper parameters. Intuitively, $S_u^t - S_c^t$ reflects the advancement of the spatial coverage after performing monitoring. On the other hand, S_{ac} encourages performing monitoring at the same cell by multiple vehicles, and S_{au} helps reduce the number of unmonitored cells.

4.2 Policy Network and the Training Mechanism

Policy Network. We utilize the DQN architecture for our policy network. The conventional DQN architecture comprises two deep neural networks: the Q Network and the target network. The Q network is trained to make the decision, while the target network acts as the reference for training the Q network. Notably, the efficacy of DQN strongly depends on the amount of training data (i.e., the experience of the agent stored in the experience buffer). Moreover, training a DQN network is a time- and resource-consuming process. Instead of allowing each agent to train its own policy network, we propose the following hybrid paradigm (Fig. 3).

- Each agent (i.e., vehicle) possesses only the Q Network to determine the actions. Upon performing an action, the agent collects its experience and sends it to the server.
- The server holds both the Q network and the target network. After receiving an experience from an agent, the server will store that experience in the experience buffer. The server follows the training mechanism described in Section *Training process* to train the Q network.
- Whenever the Q network on the server is updated, the server will broadcast the updated weights to all agents.

As the agents have to make the decision every time slot, the Q network and target network should be lightweight to ensure quick responses. Accordingly, we design these two networks as Multi-layer Perceptron networks consisting of three light-density layers with total parameters of approximately 120K. **Training Process.** When training a DQN network, the target network is used as a ground truth. The network parameters will be updated by the gradient descent method to minimize the distinction between the predicted Q-values calculated by the main network and the Q-values provided by the target network. To alleviate the exploding gradient phenomenon, we clip the reward value into the range of $[-1, 1]$. To speed up the training process, the model is trained as soon as one batch of experiences is stored in the replay memory. We do not limit the memory capacity but rather adapt the number of training steps to the number of experiences stored. Specifically, when the number of experiences stored in the replay memory is small, we train the model with fewer steps to avoid the overfitting phenomenon. In contrast, as the number of experiences increases, the number of training steps increases proportionally. **Action Selection Strategy.** The ϵ-greedy policy is utilized to strike a balance between exploration and exploitation. In particular,

Table 1. Simulation parameters

Factor	Value
Road length	2km
Road width	250m
Temporal stable range	60 min
Spatial stable range	25m
Car's average velocity	60 km/h
Vehicles produced	8

Table 2. Daily average speed

Average velocity (km/h)	#1	#2	#3	#4	#5	#6
Morning	60	60	90	90	30	10
Afternoon	30	90	10	10	30	60
Evening	10	120	30	90	60	10

the agents will select an action with the highest Q-value by a probability of ϵ and a random action by a probability of $1-\epsilon$. In the early stages, when the Q network has not been adequately trained, its predicted Q value has not yet reflected the quality of the action; therefore, we set ϵ to a small value. In contrast, when the Q network progressively converges, ϵ is increased proportionally.

5   Performance Evaluation

5.1   Simulation Setting

In this section, we conduct experiments to evaluate the performance of the proposed method and compare them with two baselines. In the first baseline, the agents choose the action randomly to meet the predefined average ratio of doing the monitoring task. The second baseline is the *FOPMO* algorithm which is proposed in [4]. In the following, we use terms "Ours", "random", and "FOPMO" to indicate the results concerning our proposal, and the two baselines, respectively. The vehicle generation process is simulated using the Poisson and Uniform distributions. The parameters concerning the road and the vehicles are depicted in Table 1.

As stated in Sect. 1, our objective is to maximize the spatial-temporal coverage and minimize the cost of data collection for all vehicles. To this end, we introduce to metrics of interest, namely the *coverage rate* and *overlap rate* which are defined as follows. Coverage rate is measured by the average ratio of the spatial-temporal coverage (defined by Formula (1)) over the product of the total area and total timeline. Overlap rate is determined by average ratio of the cells that are monitored by more than one vehicle in each time step.

5.2   Experimental Results

Impacts of the Temporal Stable Range. In this experiment, we investigate the effects of the temporal stable range, t_0, on the performance of the algorithm. The value of t_0 is varied from 15 to 90 min. Note that changes in temporal stability will affect the frequency of vehicle delivery and coverage, as the probability of a vehicle appearing in an unmonitored area will decrease. The results

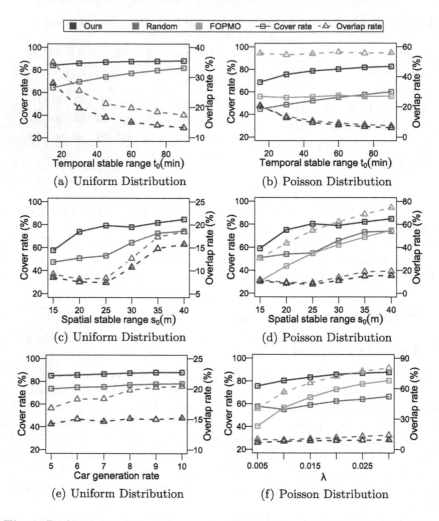

Fig. 4. Performance of algorithms under the Uniform and Poisson distribution.

are shown in Fig. 4(a) and 4(b). As can be observed, the monitoring rate of all algorithms decreases as the temporal stability period increases. Nevertheless, our proposes can maintain a covered area ratio of approximately 85% when the temporal stable period changes but still has a lower overlap rate compared with baselines. Specifically, our proposal improves the coverage rate from 9.09% to 31.44%. Notably, the performance gap between our proposal and the baseline increases when t_0 decreases, indicating that our algorithm has high stability. Concerning the overlap rate, our proposal consistently reduces this metric by about 5% in all settings. The overlap rate caused by our algorithm ranges from 0.87% to 53.74%.

Table 3. Impact of daily changes in velocity on algorithm performance

Scenarios		#1		#2		#3		#4		#5		#6	
Distribution	Methods	Cover	Overlap	Cover	Overlap	Cover	Overlap	Cover	Overlap	Cover	Overlap	Cover	Overlap
Uniform	Ours	**89.68**	**16.83**	**80.68**	**26.3**	**85.26**	**20.48**	**85.26**	**20.48**	**90.31**	**17.36**	**80.28**	**23**
	Random	81.19	27.43	78.34	28.47	80.6	28.65	80.6	28.65	84.16	31.43	75.18	29.18
Poisson	Ours	**82.24**	**19.75**	**84.32**	**25.7**	**82.23**	**26.94**	**85.25**	**21.51**	**72.39**	**19.51**	**76.16**	**19.01**
	Random	76.11	27.79	80.94	32.91	77.21	29.99	80.85	29.91	63.8	24.76	68.37	24.96
	FOPMO	81.7	81.6	80.96	80.86	81.68	81.54	83.86	83.75	70.04	69.94	69.7	69.47

Impacts of the Spatial Stable Range. In this section, we investigate the impacts of the spatial stable range, r_0, on the performance of the algorithms. Figure 4(c) and Fig. 4(d) plot the coverage rate and the overlap rate when we vary the spatial stable range from $15m$ to $40m$. As expected, the coverage rate of all algorithms tends to increase when r_0 increases with the same sending rate. In addition, the overlap rate increases as r_0 rises because, in this scenario, only a small percentage of sensors are needed to monitor a large area, but the proper vehicles must be chosen because the overlap rate between vehicles is incredibly large. In all settings, our proposal improves the coverage rate and reduces the overlap rate significantly compared to the others. Specifically, in the case of Uniform distribution vehicles, our algorithm can enhance the coverage rate from 6.45% to 19.72% and reduce the overlap rate from 4.19% to 6.86% compared to the random strategy. In addition, when the vehicles arrive by the Poisson distribution, our algorithm can enhance the coverage rate from 12.69% to 26.86% and reduce the overlap rate from 0.56% to 49.83% compared to the FOPMO.

Impacts of the Vehicle Generation Rate. In the following, we investigate the impacts of the vehicle generation rate at both experimented distributions. The results are depicted in Fig. 4(e) and Fig. 4(f). In the cases of both the Uniform distribution and the Poisson distribution, it can be observed that the proposed algorithm retains an unchanged overlap rate but increases the coverage ratio compared to baselines. Specifically, our proposed methods can maintain the overlap rate around 15% and 8% in Uniform and Poisson distribution, random method have the overlap rate increase from 16.83% to 20.44% in the Uniform distribution and from 9.92% to 14.04% in Poisson distribution, and the FOPMO has overlap rate increases from 40.19% to 80.35%. The results demonstrate that our proposal can improve the coverage rate from 7.34% to 25.32% compared to the baselines. Regarding the overlap rate, the performance gap between our proposal and the others ranges from 1.31% to 71%.

Impact of Vehicle Velocity. In this experiment, we vary the speed of the vehicles at different periods of a day to evaluate the performance of the algorithms. We use six scenarios with the settings as shown in Table 2. The experiment results are shown in Table 3. It is obvious that when the velocity varies, so also will the number of vehicles on the road. Remarkably, the number of vehicles on the road will increase while the speed is low and decrease as the speed of the vehicle rises. As we can see, our method still produces good results despite the unstable environment. Particularly, in both Poisson distribution and Uniform distribution, our approach reduces the overlap rate from 2.17% to 61.85% and enhances the coverage rate from 0.54% to 8.59% compared to the baselines.

In summary, it can be seen that our proposal could achieve both objectives: maximizing the spatial-temporal coverage and minimizing the cost simultaneously compared to the baseline.

6 Conclusion

In this study, we proposed a deep reinforcement learning-based approach to solving the problem of maximizing temporal-spatial coverage while saving the cost of vehicle-based crowdsensing air quality monitoring systems. We performed experiments with various settings on temporal-spatial stable range, vehicle velocity, and vehicle generation rate. The experiment results show that our proposal increase coverage by more than 30% and reduce cost by more than 70% compared to baselines.

Acknowledgement. This work was supported in part by the Japan Society for the Promotion of Science (JSPS) under Grant 20H0417, 23H03377. This research is also funded by Hanoi University of Science and Technology (HUST) under grant number T2022-PC-049, and partially supported by NAVER Corporation within the framework of collaboration with the International Research Center for Artificial Intelligence (BKAI), School of Information and Communication Technology, HUST under project NAVER.2022.DA07 and by Vingroup Joint Stock Company (Vingroup JSC), Vingroup, Vingroup Innovation Foundation (VINIF) under project code VINIF.2020.DA09.

References

1. Air visual. https://www.airvisual.com/vietnam/hanoi. Accessed Sept. (2021)
2. Chen, J., Yang, J.: Maximizing coverage quality with budget constrained in mobile crowd-sensing network for environmental monitoring applications. Sensors **19**(10), 2399 (2019)
3. Cherian, J., et al.: ParkGauge: gauging the occupancy of parking garages with crowdsensed parking characteristics. In: 2016 17th IEEE International Conference on Mobile Data Management (MDM), vol. 1, pp. 92–101 (2016)
4. Dinh, T.A.N., Nguyen, A.D., Nguyen, T.T., Nguyen, T.H., Le Nguyen, P.: Spatial-temporal coverage maximization in vehicle-based mobile crowdsensing for air quality monitoring. In: 2022 IEEE Wireless Communications and Networking Conference (WCNC), pp. 1449–1454. IEEE (2022)
5. Elhamshary, M., Youssef, M., Uchiyama, A., Yamaguchi, H., Higashino, T.: TransitLabel: a crowd-sensing system for automatic labeling of transit stations semantics. In: Proceedings of the 14th Annual International Conference on Mobile Systems, Applications, and Services, pp. 193–206 (2016)
6. Iqair. https://www.iqair.com/. Accessed Sept (2021)
7. Kaelbling, L.P., Littman, M.L., Moore, A.W.: Reinforcement learning: a survey. J. Artif. Intell. Res. **4**, 237–285 (1996)

8. Lambey, V., Prasad, A.: A review on air quality measurement using an unmanned aerial vehicle. Water Air Soil Pollut. **232**, 1–32 (2021)
9. Mnih, V., et al.: Playing Atari with deep reinforcement learning. arXiv preprint arXiv:1312.5602 (2013)
10. Sutton, R.S., Barto, A.G.: Reinforcement Learning: An Introduction. MIT press, Cambridge (2018)
11. Wang, C., et al.: Maximizing spatial-temporal coverage in mobile crowd-sensing based on public transports with predictable trajectory. Int. J. Distrib. Sens. Netw. **14**(8), 1550147718795351 (2018)
12. Watkins, C.J., Dayan, P.: Q-learning. Mach. Learn. **8**, 279–292 (1992)
13. Wu, D., et al.: When sharing economy meets IoT: towards fine-grained urban air quality monitoring through mobile crowdsensing on bike-share system. Proc. ACM Interact. Mob. Wearable Ubiquitous Technol. **4**(2), 1–26 (2020)
14. Zhang, M., et al.: Quality-aware sensing coverage in budget-constrained mobile crowdsensing networks. IEEE Trans. Veh. Technol. **65**(9), 7698–7707 (2016)

Healthcare and Medical Applications

Crime Scene Detection in Surveillance Videos Using Variational AutoEncoder-Based Support Vector Data Description

Harim Kim[1], Chang Ha Lee[2], and Charmgil Hong[1(✉)]

[1] Department of Computer Science and Electrical Engineering,
Handong Global University, Pohang, South Korea
{hrkim,charmgil}@handong.ac.kr
[2] GMDSOFT, Seongnam, South Korea
yielding@gmdsoft.com

Abstract. With the widespread deployment of surveillance equipment for social security purposes, video data analysis has become increasingly challenging. To address this problem, we study video anomaly detection for automatically identifying crime scenes. Our proposed method adopts an one-class semi-supervised strategy, assuming that the anomalous behaviors that need to be detected make up only a small fraction of the entire video frames. To facilitate effective detection, we adopt a two-step approach that utilizes a 3-dimensional convolutional neural network (3D CNN) and a Variational AutoEncoder-based Support Vector Data Description (VAE-SVDD). To further enhance the performance, we propose to add the Kullback-Leibler divergence loss to the anomaly score. Our method is evaluated on the *Abnormal Behavior CCTV Video Dataset* obtained from AI-Hub and compared to a state-of-the-art supervised approach. The experimental results demonstrate the effectiveness of our proposed method in detecting crime scenes.

Keywords: Video Anomaly Detection · Variational AutoEncoder · Support Vector Data Description · Kullback-Leibler Divergence · Crime Scene Detection · 3D Convolutional Neural Network

1 Introduction

In recent years, the use of surveillance equipment has seen a significant increase worldwide, primarily aimed at identifying criminals and gathering evidence for criminal investigations. As a result, there is a growing volume of video data

This work was supported by Institute of Information & Communications Technology Planning & Evaluation (IITP) grant funded by the Korean government (MSIT) (No. 2014-3-00123, Development of High Performance Visual BigData Discovery Platform for Large-Scale Realtime Data Analysis).

N. T. Nguyen et al. (Eds.): ACIIDS 2023, CCIS 1863, pp. 451–464, 2023.
https://doi.org/10.1007/978-3-031-42430-4_37

that needs to be inspected, presenting a considerable challenge for law enforcement agencies and video analysts. The analysis of video data requires meticulous and objective examination to uncover important details that may help identify suspects, crimes, and evidence. This process is often labor-intensive and time-consuming, requiring the hard work and dedication of video analysts.

To cope with this challenge, there is an increasing interest in developing automated approaches to detect specific patterns in video recordings that may indicate the presence of an accidental event or violent behavior using machine learning techniques. By automating this process, the workload of video analysts can be significantly reduced, allowing them to focus their efforts on the most critical parts of the video data. Furthermore, these approaches have the potential to improve the accuracy and reliability of video analysis, helping law enforcement agencies to solve crimes more efficiently and effectively.

Such machine learning-based video analysis can be divided into two major categories depending on the presence of data labels: **Supervised approach** [2,10,13] includes strategies that analyze and distinguish human behaviors appearing in videos, using a set of pre-defined behavior classes. A limitation of this approach, however, is that it cannot effectively detect unknown behaviors that are not defined during the training. As it is impossible to define all the unusual situations that occur in real life, this approach has difficulty identifying anomalies that were not part of the original training data. On the other hand, **unsupervised approach** [4,16] does not use prior information in the training data. Instead, it only considers the statistical characteristics of the data. These methods detect outliers by comparing various properties of data, such as local densities [4]. Although these approaches offer and implement intuitive definitions of outliers, their performance may become unstable depending on the sample distribution, and making structural modifications to remedy this issue is challenging. Recently, a deep learning-based unsupervised outlier detection approach has been proposed by leveraging data augmentation [16]. While it demonstrated that unsupervised neural architectures can effectively detect outliers by exploiting data imbalance, it is worth mentioning that detection performance tends to deteriorate as the number of outlier data points increases. This inherent limitation can pose challenges in situations with a higher prevalence of outliers, potentially reducing the effectiveness of the approach in identifying and classifying anomalous behavior.

Semi-supervised Approach serves as a middle ground, maximizing the strengths of both ends while compensating for their limitations. One prominent approach is one-class learning, which takes advantage of the relative ease of collecting normal data. This strategy trains a model exclusively using normal data to tightly capture its distribution, identifying outliers based on their deviation from the trained model. Since Schölkopf [12] first proposed this strategy, it has been combined and extended with various machine learning methodologies. In this study, we propose a model that adopts a semi-supervised learning method.

Numerous video anomaly detection methods currently explore the trade-off between low computational cost and generating effective spatio-temporal feature maps by alternating between 2D and 3D convolutional neural networks (CNNs). To address this challenge, we propose a two-step solution that employs a pre-trained 3D CNN model [17] on the large-scale human action dataset, Kinetics-400 [8], along with a Variational AutoEncoder (VAE) [9]. This approach balances computational efficiency and the extraction of informative spatio-temporal features for anomaly detection. The pre-trained 3D CNN generates compact embeddings containing human behavior information from fixed-length videos, reducing the computational burden of existing video processing tasks. By training only the VAE with a linear layer processing the compact embeddings from the 3D CNN, our method is easily adaptable to new domains. The VAE is trained using a one-class semi-supervised method based on Support Vector Data Description (SVDD) [14], allowing it to robustly detect unknown anomalous behaviors compared to supervised methods trained solely on normal behavior data. Additionally, we present a technique to reduce detection noise by refining the SVDD-based approach using the VAE.

The contributions of this paper are as follows:

- Proposing a novel two-step method that employs a 3D CNN and VAE for video anomaly detection tasks.
- Introducing a technique to enhance the detection performance of conventional VAE-based Deep SVDD.
- Demonstrating the robustness of the proposed semi-supervised method in detecting unknown anomalous behaviors compared to supervised methods.

The remainder of the paper is structured as follows: Sect. 2 discusses the research related to our work. Section 3 presents our novel video anomaly detection method. Finally, Sect. 4 presents the experimental results. Our findings demonstrate that the proposed method can effectively detect criminal situations within videos.

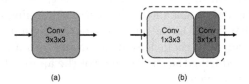

(a)   (b)

Fig. 1. (a) Vanilla 3D CNN block using ($3\times3\times3$) kernel (b) Separable (2D+1D) CNN block using ($1\times3\times3$) and ($3\times1\times1$) kernels

2   Related Works

2.1   Separable 3D CNN (S3D)

3D CNN have been widely used in video analysis tasks because they can extract spatio-temporal features from video data. These networks use 3D convolutional filters to capture both spatial and temporal information from video data. One of the most successful 3D CNN models for video action recognition is Inflated 3D CNN (I3D) [5]. However, I3D has high computational complexity due to the large number of parameters. To address this issue, Separable 3D CNN (S3D) [17] is proposed. S3D improves computational efficiency and achieves better performance than I3D by transforming the 3D convolution operation of I3D into a (2D+1D) convolution operation Fig. 1. In this study, we adopt S3D to process and extract feature maps from video segments. However, we decided not to use the optical flow stream of S3D due to its relatively low impact on performance compared to its higher computational complexity. Therefore, we only use the RGB stream of S3D to obtain feature maps of the video.

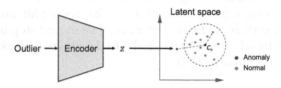

Fig. 2. Anomaly detection using Deep SVDD (**z**: outlier embedding, **c**: centroid of normal embeddings)

2.2 Deep SVDD

Deep SVDD [11] is an extension of the SVDD [14] outlier detection model using an AutoEncoder. The method works by first training the encoder using normal data to generate meaningful features from the input with a reconstruction loss. Then, centroid of the features in the embedding space are calculated, and only the encoder is fine-tuned using the average distance between the centroid and each embedding. Finally, the trained encoder is used for anomaly detection, assuming that abnormal data will produce embeddings far from the centroid as shown in Fig. 2. Recently, there have been notable improvements in anomaly detection performance by incorporating the reconstruction loss into the anomaly score or utilizing a Variational AutoEncoder (VAE) in Deep SVDD-based methods [19]. In this study, we propose an improved scoring method for video anomalies by analyzing Deep SVDD-based methods [7,11,19] for anomaly detection in 2D images.

2.3 Related Supervised Approach

One of the early successes in video anomaly detection was using the Multiple Instance Learning (MIL) [13] strategy that is a supervised approach. By segmenting labeled video data, the authors extracted feature maps from a pretrained 3D CNN [15] and assigned anomaly scores to each segment using the final fully connected layer. However, this approach has limitations as it relies on weakly labeled data, which may not accurately represent the underlying patterns of anomalous behavior in the data. Moreover, the comparison of this method to semi-supervised approaches using AutoEncoder [6,18] in previous studies is imperfect, as it requires additional anomalous behavior data to train the supervised learning model. In this paper, we propose a more convincing evaluation method in Sect. 4.4, assuming that supervised approaches will face challenges in detecting anomalous behaviors that have distinct patterns from those observed in the anomalous behavior videos used for training.

3 Proposed Framework

To perform effective and efficient video anomaly detection, we propose a framework shown in Fig. 3, which comprises two steps. The first step involves acquiring feature maps using a pre-trained S3D on a large-scale human action dataset (Kinetics-400 [8]) without additional training. The second step involves training a one-class, VAE-based Deep SVDD model to detect anomalous behavior using the embeddings generated by S3D.

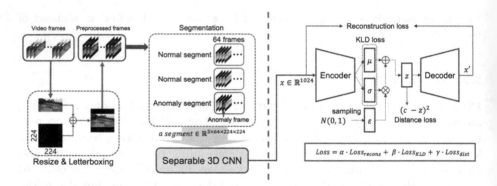

Fig. 3. Proposed framework: a two-step approach performing feature extraction and anomaly detection sequentially. The encoder computes the mean (μ) and standard deviation (σ) for the input embeddings, while ε is sampled from a standard normal distribution. The latent variable $\mathbf{z}$ is reparameterized using the μ, σ, and ε. ($\mathbf{z}$: reparameterized embedding, $\mathbf{c}$: centroid, $\{\alpha, \beta, \gamma\}$: hyperparameters)

We preprocessed the video data to match the input segments of S3D (see Sect. 4.1 for details). Our proposed VAE-based Deep SVDD model is an extension of the conventional VAE-based Deep SVDD [19] model, which calculates anomaly scores only using the distance loss and reconstruction loss. Our approach includes the Kullback-Leibler divergence (KLD) loss that can be obtained before the reparameterization trick to reduce noise in the reparameterization trick sampling process.

The proposed VAE-based Deep SVDD model consists of an encoder and a decoder that map input embeddings to a low-dimensional space and then back to the input dimension. VAE encourages embeddings mapping to the space of the latent variable **z** to follow a standard normal distribution. The difference between the distribution of **z** generated from the input embedding and the standard normal distribution is minimized using the KLD loss. The model is trained to minimize the reconstruction loss by using input embedding in the encoder and output embedding in the decoder. The distance loss between each embedding and the centroid of the normal embeddings mapped to the latent space is also considered. The final objective function is a weighted sum of the three loss values: the reconstruction loss, KLD loss, and distance loss.

For detecting anomalous behaviors, anomaly scores are computed by aggregating the values generated by the trained model depending on the input data. If the computed score exceeds a predetermined threshold, the corresponding input is considered as an anomaly. In Sect. 3.2, our improved anomaly score is proposed that includes the KLD loss in addition to the distance loss and reconstruction loss. A comparative study on the loss values is presented in Sect. 4.2, demonstrating the effectiveness of the proposed anomaly score calculation method compared to the existing method.

3.1   Objective Function

The conventional objective function of VAE is composed of two components: the reconstruction loss and the KLD loss. This objective function is derived through maximum likelihood estimation (MLE) as shown in Eq. (1), where ϕ represents the encoder and θ represents the decoder [9]. Subsequently, VAE is trained by optimizing the evidence lower bound (ELBO), where the first and second terms of ELBO correspond to the reconstruction and KLD loss, respectively.

$$\log p_\theta(\mathbf{x}_i) = \mathbb{E}_{\mathbf{z} \sim q_\phi(\mathbf{z}|\mathbf{x}_i)}[\log p_\theta(\mathbf{x}_i)]$$

$$= \left[\mathbb{E}_{\mathbf{z}}[\log p_\theta(\mathbf{x}_i|\mathbf{z})] - D_{KL}(q_\phi(\mathbf{z}|\mathbf{x}_i)\|p_\theta(\mathbf{z})) \right]^{ELBO}$$

$$+ D_{KL}(q_\phi(\mathbf{z}|\mathbf{x}_i)\|p_\theta(\mathbf{z}|\mathbf{x}_i)) \qquad (1)$$

The reconstruction loss can be approximated as a probability value for a single sample using the Monte Carlo technique, and it can be derived by optimizing the mean squared error (MSE) between the input vector (**x**) and the output vector (**x**′), assuming the output to follow a Gaussian distribution (see Eq. (2)) (D: dimension of **x**) [9]. In order to minimize the reconstruction loss, the model is trained to acquire an embedding with the condensed representation from the input data in the latent space of **z**.

$$\mathbb{E}_{\mathbf{z}}[\log p_\theta(\mathbf{x}_i|\mathbf{z})] \approx \log p_\theta(\mathbf{x}_i|\mathbf{z}_i)$$

$$\implies \underset{\theta,\phi}{\mathrm{argmax}}\left(\log p_\theta(\mathbf{x}_i|\mathbf{z}_i) \right) \propto \underset{\theta,\phi}{\mathrm{argmax}}\left(-\sum_{j=1}^{D}(\mathbf{x}_{i,j} - \mathbf{x}'_{i,j})^2 \right)$$

$$\implies Loss_{recons} = \frac{1}{n}\sum_{i=1}^{n}\sum_{j=1}^{D}(\mathbf{x}_{i,j} - \mathbf{x}'_{i,j})^2 \qquad (2)$$

The KLD loss can be represented as Eq. (3) provided $p_\theta(\mathbf{z})$ and $q_\phi(\mathbf{z}|\mathbf{x}_i)$ are Gaussian, where d represents the dimension of latent space of $\mathbf{z}$ [9]. By this loss, the model is trained to make $q_\phi(\mathbf{z}|\mathbf{x}_i)$ close to $N(0,1)$.

$$Loss_{KLD} = D_{KL}(q_\phi(\mathbf{z}|\mathbf{x}_i)\|p_\theta(\mathbf{z})) = \frac{1}{2}\sum_{j=1}^{d}(\mu_{i,j}^2 + \sigma_{i,j}^2 - \ln(\sigma_{i,j}^2) - 1) \quad (3)$$

VAE-based Deep SVDD [19] introduces the distance loss in addition to the two basic loss values. This loss is calculated as the mean squared error between each training embedding and the centroid $\mathbf{c}$ of all training embeddings that are mapped to the latent space $\mathbf{z}$ (see Eq. (4)). That is, the model is trained to reduce the distance loss by learning weights that bring each normal training embedding closer to the center.

$$Loss_{dist} = \frac{1}{n}\sum_{i=1}^{n}\sum_{j=1}^{d}(\mathbf{c}_j - \mathbf{z}_{i,j})^2 \quad (4)$$

The final objective function, presented in Eq. (5), minimizes the loss values on normal data while encouraging the training data to form a hypersphere in the standard normal distribution space. The objective function is a weighted sum of the three loss values, where the hyperparameters α, β, and γ represent the weighting factors for each loss value.

$$Loss_{total} = \alpha \cdot Loss_{recons} + \beta \cdot Loss_{KLD} + \gamma \cdot Loss_{dist} \quad (5)$$

3.2 Anomaly Score

This work aims to improve the existing VAE-based Deep SVDD [19] that computes the anomaly scores only using the distance loss and reconstruction loss. This, however, could introduce noise during the sampling process using the reparameterization trick [9]. To address this, we incorporate the anomaly score with the KLD loss, which is obtained before the reparameterization. By doing so, the final anomaly score is computed in the same way as the objective function (see Eq. (6)). In Sect. 4.2, we conduct a comparative study on the loss values and demonstrate the effectiveness of our modification compared to the existing anomaly score.

$$Anomaly\ score = \alpha \cdot Loss_{recons} + \beta \cdot Loss_{KLD} + \gamma \cdot Loss_{dist} \quad (6)$$

Fig. 4. Sample frames of the "Abnormal Behavior CCTV Video Dataset"

4 Experiments and Results

4.1 Dataset and Evaluation Metrics

In the evaluation and comparison of our proposed model, we conduct experiments on the *Abnormal Behavior CCTV Video Dataset* obtained from AI-Hub [1], an online service provided by the Korean National Information Society Agency (NIA). The dataset comprises simulated surveillance videos that are 5 to 10 min long, featuring realistic violent / incident scenarios enacted by professional actors. Out of the 12 available scene classes in the dataset, we have selected the 6 cases labeled as fighting, swooning (albeit non-crime related, we chose the visually distinctive swooning class), trespassing, vandalism, robbery, and kidnapping (refer to Fig. 4) for our experiments. We chose these classes due to their distinct visual characteristics.

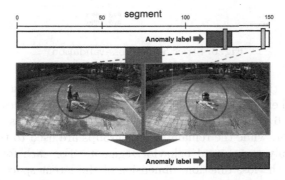

Fig. 5. Re-labeled swooning video

To ensure that our model detects anomalous situations based on videos captured at the same angle, we use only 12 videos recorded during daytime and at the same location for each class. Therefore, a total of (6×12=72) videos are used for model training and validation, including approximately 360 to 720 min of video footage. In the case of the swooning videos provided, the abnormal behavior was originally labeled only at the moment when a person falls to the ground (as depicted in Fig. 5). That is, the footage that followed, depicting an individual after falling and the reactions of the surrounding people, was considered normal behavior. However, we found that these post-fall situations could not be deemed statistically normal due to their uncommon nature. Consequently, we re-labeled the swooning videos to accurately reflect the abnormal behavior throughout the entire scene, as exemplified in Fig. 5.

Each video is pre-processed to align with the input requirements of the S3D model, which requires segments in the format of (channel × time × height × width)=(3 × 64 × 224 × 224). To ensure compatibility with the input frame resolution and maintain a consistent aspect ratio, we apply letterboxing. Letterboxing involves using a 0 intensity image as the background to fit the desired resolution. For validation and testing, segments were labeled as abnormal if they contained at least one abnormal frame, according to segment-level labels (refer to Fig. 3).

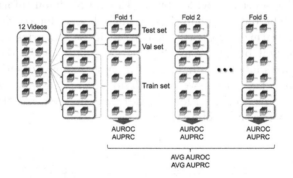

Fig. 6. Strict 5-fold cross-validation

To evaluate the performance of each model, we employ a 5-fold cross-validation for all experiments, as depicted in Fig. 6. In this process, the 12 videos are divided into 6 groups. Two groups are randomly selected as the test set and the validation set, while the remaining four groups are used to train the model, incorporating only the normal behavior segments. For each fold, the learning rate, weights of the loss function, dimension of the latent space (z), and batch size are optimized using the training and validation sets. The performance of the model for each specific fold is evaluated using the test set. Finally, the performance of the model for each class is evaluated by averaging the values obtained from the 5 folds. To measure the performance of the models, we use the area under the receiver operating characteristic curve (AUROC) and the area under the precision-recall curve (AUPRC).

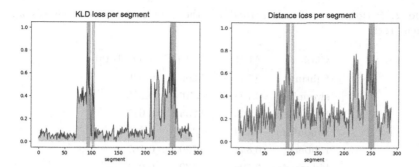

Fig. 7. The KLD and distance loss calculated for the test video segments from the vandalism class, ordered by time axis, with min-max normalized loss on the y-axis and ground truth anomalies marked in red. (Color figure online)

Table 1. Comparative study results (Our method: the KL divergence loss was added in anomaly score, KLD(×): the KL divergence loss was not added in anomaly score)

Comparative study	KLD	VAE	AE	AUROC	AUPRC
Our method	✓	✓		**0.833**	**0.390**
KLD(×) [19]		✓		0.815	0.318
AE Deep SVDD			✓	0.802	0.364

4.2 Effectiveness of the KLD Loss Integration and Performance Across Anomalous Behaviors

In Sect. 3.2, we aimed to enhance the performance of our model by incorporating the KLD loss in the anomaly score, in contrast to existing Deep SVDD-based models. Figure 7 presents the graphs of using the KLD loss and distance loss as anomaly scores for a test video in the vandalism class. The graph shows that the use of the KLD loss could reduce the noise in the anomaly scores compared to using only the distance loss. Table 1 presents a comparison between the inclusion and exclusion of the KLD loss in the anomaly score, as well as the type of AutoEncoder used. The reported AUROC and AUPRC are the average performance across all anomalous behavior classes. Our proposed method achieves the highest performance with an AUROC of 83.3% and an AUPRC of 39%, demonstrating that adding the KLD loss in the anomaly score could improve that of existing approaches.

Table 2 shows the performance of our proposed method for each anomalous behavior class, as well as the prevalence of anomalous segments in the dataset. In particular, our method achieves a maximum AUROC of 93.9% (on trespassing) and an AUPRC of 70.5% (on swooning), demonstrating the efficacy of our approach in detecting anomalous behaviors across various classes.

Table 2. Performance of our method for the abnormal behavior classes and the anomaly ratio

Class	AUROC	AUPRC	True/Total
fighting	0.732	0.269	0.049
swooning	0.793	**0.705**	0.253
trespassing	**0.939**	0.265	0.015
vandalism	0.894	0.413	0.049
robbery	0.841	0.520	0.167
kidnapping	0.796	0.170	0.041
AVG	0.833	0.390	0.096

Table 3. Performance for the influence of the KL divergence loss

KLD * δ	AUROC	AUPRC
$\delta = 1$	0.815	0.348
$\delta = 8$	0.821	**0.398**
$\delta = 64$	0.811	0.366
$\delta = 128$	**0.834**	0.379
$\delta = 256$	0.833	0.390
$\delta = 512$	0.818	0.366

4.3 Performance Analysis with the Kullback-Leibler Divergence Loss Weighting

Table 3 presents the results obtained by incorporating an additional weight (δ) into the KLD loss for both model training and anomaly scoring. As indicated in the table, the proposed model achieves significantly higher performance when the weight is increased compared to the case when no additional weight is applied ($\delta = 1$). This suggests that incorporating the KLD loss into the anomaly score can enhance the model performance, and increasing the weight can lead to even more favorable outcomes. Figure 8 plots the results of Table 3. Based on our experiments, we conclude that the model trained with a weight of ($\delta = 256$) achieves the most stable and highest performance, and we use it for a comparison with a supervised approach.

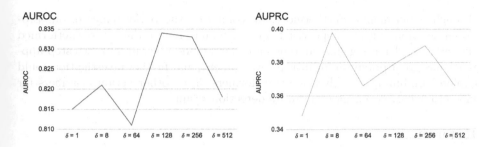

Fig. 8. Performance change graph according to the influence of the KLD loss

4.4   Performance Comparison with Supervised Approaches

To demonstrate the limitations of supervised learning-based methods in detecting anomalous behaviors that are not included in training data, we compare the performance of a well-known MIL-based video anomaly detection method [13] with the proposed method. Since it is challenging to evaluate supervised and semi-supervised methods under the same conditions, we focus on verifying the aforementioned assumption.

For the experiment, the validation set and test set are prepared identically for both models. However, unlike our proposed method, the supervised learning model is trained using both normal and anomalous videos, including the five other anomalous behavior videos that are different from the one to be detected. Consequently, it is trained with more samples than the proposed model's training data. Despite this, the supervised learning-based method does not achieve better performance than our proposed method (see Table 4). This suggests that, compared to the proposed method, supervised methods may face difficulties in detecting anomalous behavior that has not been learned previously.

Table 4. Performance comparison with the supervised method

	AUROC	AUPRC
Our method	**0.833**	**0.390**
MIL-based [13]	0.815	0.384

5   Conclusion

In this study, we presented an enhanced method for detecting anomalous behaviors in videos, such as crime scenes, by combining a pre-trained 3D CNN for extracting spatio-temporal feature maps with a VAE-based SVDD model. Our approach differs from existing VAE-based methods by incorporating the KLD loss in the anomaly score, which was shown to improve performance through experiments. Furthermore, we compared the performance of our proposed method with a supervised approach and found that it outperformed the latter in detecting unseen anomalous behaviors. Overall, our two-step approach has great potential for future development, and further investigation could explore combining it with video transformers [3] or other action classifiers for video to achieve even more accurate detection results.

References

1. Aihub (2019). https://aihub.or.kr/. Accessed 23 Mar 2023
2. Anala, M., Makker, M., Ashok, A.: Anomaly detection in surveillance videos. In: 2019 26th International Conference on High Performance Computing, Data and Analytics Workshop (HiPCW), pp. 93–98. IEEE (2019)
3. Arnab, A., Dehghani, M., Heigold, G., Sun, C., Lučić, M., Schmid, C.: Vivit: A video vision transformer. In: Proceedings of the IEEE/CVF International Conference on Computer Vision, pp. 6836–6846 (2021)
4. Breunig, M.M., Kriegel, H.P., Ng, R.T., Sander, J.: LOF: identifying density-based local outliers. In: Proceedings of the 2000 ACM SIGMOD International Conference on Management of Data, pp. 93–104 (2000)
5. Carreira, J., Zisserman, A.: Quo Vadis, action recognition? A new model and the kinetics dataset. In: proceedings of the IEEE Conference on Computer Vision and Pattern Recognition, pp. 6299–6308 (2017)
6. Hasan, M., Choi, J., Neumann, J., Roy-Chowdhury, A.K., Davis, L.S.: Learning temporal regularity in video sequences. In: Proceedings of the IEEE Conference on Computer Vision and Pattern Recognition, pp. 733–742 (2016)
7. Hojjati, H., Armanfard, N.: DASVDD: deep autoencoding support vector data descriptor for anomaly detection. arXiv preprint arXiv:2106.05410 (2021)
8. Kay, W., et al.: The kinetics human action video dataset. arXiv preprint arXiv:1705.06950 (2017)
9. Kingma, D.P., Welling, M.: Auto-encoding variational Bayes. arXiv preprint arXiv:1312.6114 (2013)
10. Liu, K., Zhu, M., Fu, H., Ma, H., Chua, T.S.: Enhancing anomaly detection in surveillance videos with transfer learning from action recognition. In: Proceedings of the 28th ACM International Conference on Multimedia, pp. 4664–4668 (2020)
11. Ruff, L., et al.: Deep one-class classification. In: International Conference on Machine Learning, pp. 4393–4402. PMLR (2018)
12. Schölkopf, B., Platt, J.C., Shawe-Taylor, J., Smola, A.J., Williamson, R.C.: Estimating the support of a high-dimensional distribution. Neural Comput. **13**(7), 1443–1471 (2001)
13. Sultani, W., Chen, C., Shah, M.: Real-world anomaly detection in surveillance videos. In: Proceedings of the IEEE Conference on Computer Vision and Pattern Recognition, pp. 6479–6488 (2018)
14. Tax, D.M., Duin, R.P.: Support vector data description. Mach. Learn. **54**, 45–66 (2004)
15. Tran, D., Bourdev, L., Fergus, R., Torresani, L., Paluri, M.: Learning spatiotemporal features with 3D convolutional networks. In: Proceedings of the IEEE International Conference on Computer Vision, pp. 4489–4497 (2015)
16. Wang, S., et al.: Effective end-to-end unsupervised outlier detection via inlier priority of discriminative network. In: Advances in Neural Information Processing Systems, vol. 32 (2019)

17. Xie, S., Sun, C., Huang, J., Tu, Z., Murphy, K.: Rethinking spatiotemporal feature learning: speed-accuracy trade-offs in video classification. In: Proceedings of the European Conference on Computer Vision (ECCV), pp. 305–321 (2018)
18. Xu, D., Ricci, E., Yan, Y., Song, J., Sebe, N.: Learning deep representations of appearance and motion for anomalous event detection. arXiv preprint arXiv:1510.01553 (2015)
19. Zhou, Y., Liang, X., Zhang, W., Zhang, L., Song, X.: VAE-based deep SVDD for anomaly detection. Neurocomputing **453**, 131–140 (2021)

Cervical Spine Fracture Detection via Computed Tomography Scan

Le Quang Hung, Tran Duc Tuan, Nguyen Trong Hieu, and Phan Duy Hung[✉]

Computer Science Department, FPT University, Hanoi, Vietnam
{hunglqhe151392,tuantdhe150303,hieunthe151266}@fpt.edu.vn,
hungpd2@fe.edu.vn

Abstract. The application of artificial intelligence in image processing and decision support in the medical field has recently received increasing attention in the community. In this work, we aim to develop machine learning models that match the performance of radiologists in detecting and locating fractures on the seven vertebrae of the cervical spine via Computed Tomography scans. We introduced a two-stage approach using deep convolutional networks with Recurrent Neural Networks and Attention layers to classify whether a patient has a cervical spine fracture. The approach has taken use of the dataset and the metric for evaluation from the Kaggle RSNA 2022 Cervical Spine Fracture Detection contest. Our model achieves acceptable results (equivalent to the top 16 of the contest) but lower inference time with limited training resources (even compared to the top 2).

Keywords: Convolutional Neural Network · Attention · Recurrent Neural Network · Cervical Spine Fracture Detection

1 Introduction and Related Work

Patients with spine fractures often have a lot of difficulties in moving their body, which prevent them from working and daily routines. The cause of spine fractures can be due to accidents or old age. There have been over 1.5 million cases suffered from spine fractures annually in the United States alone, leading to about 18000 spinal cord injuries, and these cases are usually seen in elderly people [1]. The early detection and localization of spine fractures can play an essential role in preventing neurological deterioration and paralysis after trauma. However, it often requires computed tomography (CT) to be performed instead of radiographs (x-rays), which might be more time-consuming and require specialists or experts to carefully examine patients' spine.

Recently, more and more AI-based technologies have emerged to automate various tasks that often require human intelligence to perform. To deal with images, these technologies often use deep learning methods, which perform quite well compared to traditional ones and sometimes even better than what humans could do. However, these methods are not always giving accurate results every time they are in use, which is why there have been many competitions revolving around them in order to find the most accurate method while still achieving the maximum time to be performed. As a result, a competition on Kaggle, namely RSNA 2022 Cervical Spine Fracture Detection [1], was held to find the best AI-based method to support the early detection and localization of cervical spine fracture, which is the most common site of spine fracture.

The application of computer vision in medical image processing has been widely researched in recent years. U-Net [2] was first proposed as an deep learning approach for medical image segmentation, which is the task of classifying each pixel in an image. It outperforms the sliding-window convolutional network which is the prior best method in terms of both score and speed, and from then it becomes a popular approach for image segmentation in general. Along with the strong use of data augmentation, U-Net can produce fine segmentation results while training on a few images and it not only works well with 2D images but also with 3D ones. Convolutional neural network (CNN) serves as backbone in a variety of computer vision tasks such as image classification, detection, segmentation, etc. It has existed from more than decades, starting from the introduction of AlexNet [3] to the more effective architectures namely ResNet [4], EfficientNet [5], ConvNeXt [6], etc. These architectures are well-known in the computer vision community for achieving a lot of great success in terms of both accuracy and speed.

There is some previous research on deep learning models for bone fracture detection. In [7], they proposed a deep convolutional neural network with a bidirectional long-short term memory (BiLSTM) layer for the auto-mated detection of cervical spine fractures in CT axial images. Besides, another work introduced a 3D convolutional sequence to sequence model for vertebral compression fractures identification in CT in [8]. Within the contest, there are several solutions from several top teams of [1] which can detect fractures in cervical spines quite effectively. Most of the top teams in the competition use an architecture that includes at least two models: a segmentation model and a classification model. Qishen Ha in [9] developed a 2-stage method for fracture detection. This method first trained an U-Net model with resnet18d or efficientnet-v2s for 3D semantic segmentation to generate 3D masks for all training data, then a 2D CNN (ConvNeXt) model followed by a LSTM module was trained for final classification. Similarly, Harshit Sheoran's method [10] consists of 2 stages, in which U-Net models were trained for both sagittal and bone segmentation, and EfficientNet CNN with RNN model was trained for classification afterwards. In the classification stage, images were put into 2.5D format, which is concatenating three consecutive slices into a single image, and two bidirectional GRU layers with attention and Conv1D layer were used for RNN model. The authors of [11] (Kaggle Top 2) used an U-Net model for 2.5D segmentation and a CNN with bidirectional GRU layers and attention was trained for classification. In the second stage, a SpatialDropout layer was added to the model; therefore, this gave a slight improvement in the overall classification. However, the architectures mentioned above all take a long time or a large amount of resources for training (or also pretrain).

On the other hand, other approaches are also introduced in the contest's discussion, which require lighter resources for training. The authors of [12] proposed a 3D CNN model for cervical spine fracture detection. They stacked all the slices of a patient into a 3D input, then trained a simple 3D CNN model that includes several 3D CNN blocks, each block consists of a 3D CNN layer, a pooling layer, and a normalization layer.

Their output was an eight-dimension vector, in which seven elements are each type of bones' fracture ratio and the other is patient overall ratio. Besides, in [13], a solution that uses 2D CNN model with EfficientNetV2 as backbone was proposed. The method in [13] optimized two losses simultaneously: one for bone types classification, the other for fracture ratio calculation. The output of the model is a seven-dimension vector that reflects fracture ratio of seven bone types C1–C7. Nevertheless, due to the fact that each patient has a sequence of bone slice images, it can be better if there is a solution that considers the order of images, which was not leveraged by the studies in [12, 13].

The architectures mentioned above all take a long time or a large amount of resources for training (or also pretrain). Therefore, we aim to propose a model that is more timely efficient and still be able to achieve acceptable results. In summary, our contribution in this research paper is as follows: i) We introduce a novel model architecture to detect fractures in cervical vertebrae. Compared to prior research, our approach offers enhanced efficiency by reducing training time and minimizing hardware complexity, while still achieving comparable effectiveness. ii) We conduct experiments to validate the effectiveness and efficiency of our method and provide code for the common good of the community.

2 Dataset

The dataset used for this work is the dataset obtained from RSNA 2022 Cervical Spine Fracture Detection [1] competition at Kaggle (Table 1). This dataset has 3 main folders: *train_images*, *test_images*, and *segmentations*. The *train_images* folder contains training images, and this folder contains 2019 subfolders. Each subfolder is for a specific patient or case study, and it contains multiple slice images of the corresponding case. Therefore, those subfolders were named as the *UID* of their corresponding case study. Every image in those two folders is in the *DICOM* file format, which has slice thickness of under 1 mm, as well as in the axial orientation and bone kernel [1], and has a.*dcm* extension in each one. Meanwhile, the segmentations folder contains annotation masks and those masks are stored in *NIFTI* files (each file for a single patient). Target labels of the training data are given in the *train.csv* file. This file contains a column for case IDs, patient level labels (binary) and labels for a specific vertebra. In addition, this dataset provides a *training_bounding_boxes.csv* file which stores information about bounding boxes, such as anchor coordinates, width and height of bounding boxes.

Table 1. Dataset overview

image_size	# vertebrae	# masks	# training studies	# testing studies
512–768	7	87	2019	1080

In the *train.csv* file, labels for training images are:

- patient_overall: overall target label, when any of the vertebra is fractured.
- C1–C7: seven additional labels, whether a specific vertebra is fractured.

DICOM files, according to [14], in this dataset have 2 uses. One of them relates to the data in each file. After loading images, there are four attributes that can be retrieved: *ImageOrientationPatient, ImagePositionPatient, PatientID, PatientName. PatientID* indicates the ID of the patient, the case study itself. *PatientName* shows the name of the patient; however, in this dataset, the name of the patient is the ID itself. *ImageOrientationPatient* indicates the orientation of the patient, while *ImagePositionPatient* indicates the position itself. *ImagePositionPatient* stores a list of 3 values, which is the position in 3-dimension space (x-axis, y-axis, z-axis). In addition, the authors of [14] revealed that unlike other competitions, z-axis value is the position of the slice image in the sagittal plane, rather than the timestamp. A Sagittal plane is a vertical plane that creates two sections on either side of the body. However, all images in this dataset, according to [14], are in axial orientation, that means there is only one bone to observe for each image. Despite that, the z-axis value can be referenced for position in the sagittal plane.

In order to check which bone the image is corresponding to, we use the data in the segmentation folder. This folder contains 87 files, and each file is for a specific case and named as the UID of that case. Unlike slice images, segmentations are in *NIFTI* format. Moreover, the segmentations loaded are in 3D format (*height, width, num_images*), and *num_images* is the same number of slices of corresponding case study in the *train_images* folder. There are differences in format between *NIFTI* segmentations and DICOM images; while DICOM files are segmented in the axial plane, *NIFTI* files are in the sagittal plane. This allows us to choose the proper orientation so that the *DICOM* pictures and segmentation match each other using the *NIFTI* header information. Besides, segmentation files after being loaded also contain unique values that would indicate which bone on each slice; for example, value 1 is bone C1, value 2 is bone C2, and so on. Therefore, for each slice of 87 patients who have segmentation images, we have its segmentation mask; thus, each of them has information about fractures and bone types (Fig. 1).

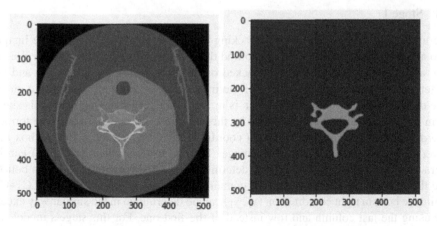

Fig. 1. Example of a slice image and its segmentation mask

3 Methodology

We propose the two-stage pipeline to classify cervical spine fracture as Fig. 2.

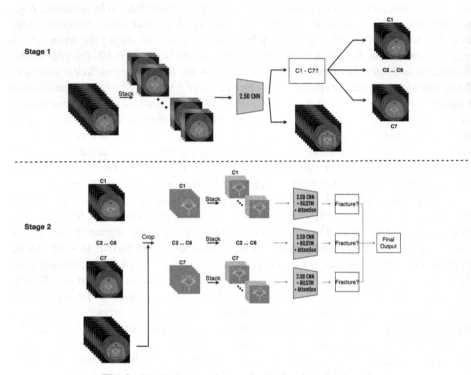

Fig. 2. Block diagram for cervical spine fracture detection

3.1 Stage 1

We used 2.5D images produced by stacking each three consecutive grayscale images into a single 3-channel image. We also find that several images are cropped in a circle (the area outside that the circle is blacked out while the area inside is kept) and the vertebrae tend to exist in the center of the images, so we crop all images in a circle. The detailed data augmentation section is in the Table 2. In preparation for this stage, from the segmentation mask provided by the organizer, we need to determine top left coordination (x_0, y_0) and bottom right coordination (x_1, y_1) of the bounding box that covers all vertebrae C1–C7 in each image. The top left coordination (x_0, y_0) can be extracted from segmentation mask by determining the first column from top to bottom and the first row from left to right that contain the element belong to vertebrae C1–C7, while the bottom right coordination (x_1, y_1) can be determined in the similar way except for using the last column and row instead of the first one. For this stage's model, we used ConvNeXt-Tiny as the backbone of the encoder. In terms of the training process, we used AdamW as the optimizer and CosineAnnealingWarmRestarts as the scheduler. Our model in this stage has two outputs: the bounding box of the vertebra and the ratio of the vertebra's type. Note that the ratio is calculated by dividing the maximum number of pixels belonging to C_k class in all slices by the number of pixels belonging to C_k class in the current slice.

Table 2. Augmentation methods

Augmentation methods
HorizontalFlip
RandomBrightnessContrast
HueSaturationValue
ShiftScaleRotate
Cutout

We split the data into 5 folds using GroupKFold with study id as group and train 5 models, each using 4 folds for training and the remaining fold for evaluation. After the training process, we use these 5 models to infer all 2019 studies and average their predictions to get the final prediction.

3.2 Stage 2

After getting the bounding box for all slices in each study from stage 1, we determine only one bounding box for each study by getting the minimum of (x_0, y_0) and the maximum of (x_1, y_1) across all slices with the ratio of any vertebrae larger than a ratio threshold (i.e. 0.3) in each study. Moreover, for each vertebrae in a study, we gather all slices in that study in which the ratio of that vertebrae is larger than the ratio threshold into a single list under the assumption that fracture is unlikely to exist in the vertebrae when its ratio in a single image is small. We choose 0.3 as the ratio threshold since all the fractured vertebrae in the data have at least one slice larger than that threshold. Each fracture label from train.csv will then be assigned to a list of slices belonging to each vertebrae in each study and a fixed number of slices (i.e. 24) will be chosen from that list of slices using evenly spaced indices (e.g. 47 slices -> 24 slices with index 0, 2, 4, ..., 46). If a list of slices has no slices, the row with that list of slices in the label file will be removed. During the training process, we crop the images using the processed bounding boxes and stack three consecutive slices into one to get the 2.5D inputs, a list of 24 slices chosen as earlier mentioned method turned into a sequence of 8 2.5D images. We used the same augmentation with Stage 1. For the model we also utilized ConvNeXt-Tiny from the *timm* library for backbone model, with the addition of LSTM and Attention layer in order to predict whether a list of slices contains fractured vertebra.

Under assumption of independence of vertebrae fractures we can derive the following simple equation:

$$P_{patient\_overall} = 1 - \prod_{k=1}^{7} \left(1 - P_{C_k}\right)$$

where P_{C_k} is the fracture ratio of vertebrae C_k.

We also split the data into 5 folds using GroupKFold with study id as group and train models in the similar way as the 1st stage. All aforementioned experiments were implemented on resources that are free and available for everyone: Tesla T4 GPU on Google Colab and P100 GPU on Kaggle Notebook. More detail on our experiments can be found at [15]. The parameters of models from both stages are listed in the Table 3.

Table 3. The parameter of models from both stages

Parameter	Stage 1	Stage 2
base lr	1e−4	1e−4
min lr	1e−6	1e−6
batch size	64	8
image size	384	320
seq len	–	24
num epoch	25	20
optimizer	AdamW	AdamW
weight decay	1e−5	1e−5

4 Results

4.1 Evaluation Metric

Model performance is evaluated using a weighted multi-label logarithmic loss. Each fracture sub-type is its own row for every exam, and the model is expected to predict a probability for a fracture at each of the seven cervical vertebrae designated as C1, C2, C3, C4, C5, C6 and C7. There is also an "any label", patient_overall, which indicates that a fracture of any kind described before exists in the examination. Fractures in the skull base, thoracic spine, ribs, and clavicles are ignored. The "any label" is weighted more highly than specific fracture level sub-types.

The binary weighted log loss function for label j on exam i is specified as:

$$L_{ij} = w_{ij} \times [y_{ij} \times log(p_{ij}) + (1 - y_{ij}) \times log(1 - p_{ij})]$$

where the weights given by:

$$w_j = \begin{cases} 1, & \text{if vertebrae negative} \\ 2, & \text{if vertebrae positive} \\ 7, & \text{if patient negative} \\ 14, & \text{if patient positive} \end{cases}$$

Finally, loss is averaged across all rows.

4.2 Results

We compare our solution's score with solutions that use simple 3D CNN and 2D CNN for detecting the cervical spine fracture as mentioned above. Table 4 shows the performance of each approach evaluated on the metric mentioned earlier. Our model's performance has a significant improvement from the other methods.

Table 4. Results on hidden test dataset provided by the organizer (LB: leaderboard). Results are reported on the evaluation metric mentioned in Sect. 4.1.

Model	Public LB	Private LB
3D CNN [12]	0.5399	0.6048
2D CNN [13]	0.4877	0.5268
2.5D CNN + RNN + Attention (ours)	**0.2964**	**0.3302**

Closer to our work, our solution is inspired by the top-2 method [11], which uses a segmentation model along with a classification model. The critical difference in our model is that we use a classification model instead of a segmentation one from the top-2 team; therefore, despite having lower scores, our model has a notably shorter inference and training time and requires fewer resources. Our solution's achievement is equivalent to the score of top 15 and 16 of the contest on the public and private test dataset respectively (Table 5).

Table 5. Comparison with Top-2 solution. Inference time is calculated on full 2019 studies training data.

Model	Public LB	Private LB	Stage-1 inference time (h)
Kaggle Top 2	**0.2115**	**0.2389**	4.6
Our	0.2964	0.3302	**2.2**

5   Conclusion and Future Works

In this work, we propose a solution for Kaggle RSNA 2022 Cervical Spine Fracture Detection that demonstrated higher efficiency in time and resources than the previous methods and achieved a satisfactory result. This model still has various parts that can be optimized for higher performance. With the benefits of Transformer's recently proven string data, such as faster training time due to parallelization and better performance with self-attention techniques, our next steps will be experimenting with Transformer layers instead of LSTM for sequence data processing, training another backbone model, trying models with bigger image size and longer sequence length. The work is also a good reference for image pattern recognition problems [16–20].

References

1. RSNA 2022 Cervical Spine Fracture Detection (2022). https://kaggle.com/competitions/rsna-2022-cervical-spine-fracture-detection
2. Ronneberger, O., Fischer, P., Brox, T.: U-Net: convolutional networks for biomedical image segmentation. arXiv:1505.04597 (2015)
3. Krizhevsky, A., Sutskever, I., Hinton, G.E.: ImageNet classification with deep convolutional neural networks. In: Advances in Neural Information Processing Systems, pp. 1097–1105 (2012)
4. He, K., Zhang, X., Ren, S., Sun, J.: Deep residual learning for image recognition. In: Proceedings of the IEEE Conference on Computer Vision and Pattern Recognition (CVPR), pp. 770–778 (2016)
5. Mozer, M.C.: Induction of multiscale temporal structure. In: Moody, J., Hanson, S., Lippmann, R.P. (eds.) Advances in Neural Information Processing Systems, vol. 4. Morgan-Kaufmann (1991)
6. Liu, Z., Mao, H., Wu, C.-Y., Feichtenhofer, C., Darrell, T., Xie, S.: A ConvNet for the 2020s. arXiv:2201.03545 (2022)
7. Salehinejad, H., et al.: Deep sequential learning for cervical spine fracture detection on computed tomography imaging. arXiv:2010.13336 (2020)
8. Chettrit, D., et al.: 3D convolutional sequence to sequence model for vertebral compression fractures identification in CT. arXiv:2010.03739 (2020)
9. @haqishen. 1st Place Solution (2022). https://www.kaggle.com/competitions/rsna-2022-cervical-spine-fracture-detection/discussion/362607
10. @harshitsheoran. 8th Place Solution (2022). https://www.kaggle.com/competitions/rsna-2022-cervical-spine-fracture-detection/discussion/362669
11. @ryanrong. 2nd Place Solution (2022). https://www.kaggle.com/competitions/rsna-2022-cervical-spine-fracture-detection/discussion/365115
12. @samuelcortinhas. 3D CNN for cervical spine fracture detection (2022). https://www.kaggle.com/code/samuelcortinhas/rnsa-3d-model-train-pytorch
13. @vslaykovsky. 2D CNN for cervical spine fracture detection (2022). https://www.kaggle.com/code/vslaykovsky/train-pytorch-effnetv2-baseline-cv-0-49
14. @harshitsheoran. Explaining Data and Submission in detail (2022). https://www.kaggle.com/competitions/rsna-2022-cervical-spine-fracture-detection/discussion/340612
15. https://github.com/trantuan4132/kaggle-RSNA-Fracture-Detection
16. Hung, P.D., Kien, N.N.: SSD-mobilenet implementation for classifying fish species. In: Vasant, P., Zelinka, I., Weber, G.-W. (eds.) ICO 2019. AISC, vol. 1072, pp. 399–408. Springer, Cham (2020). https://doi.org/10.1007/978-3-030-33585-4_40
17. Hung, P.D., Su, N.T., Diep, V.T.: Surface classification of damaged concrete using deep convolutional neural network. Pattern Recogn. Image Anal. **29**, 676–687 (2019)
18. Hung, P.D., Su, N.T.: Unsafe construction behavior classification using deep convolutional neural network. Pattern Recogn. Image Anal. **31**, 271–284 (2021)

19. Duy, L.D., Hung, P.D.: Adaptive graph attention network in person re-identification. Pattern Recogn. Image Anal. **32**, 384–392 (2022)
20. Su, N.T., Hung, P.D., Vinh, B.T., Diep, V.T.: Rice leaf disease classification using deep learning and target for mobile devices. In: Al-Emran, M., Al-Sharafi, M.A., Al-Kabi, M.N., Shaalan, K. (eds.) ICETIS 2021. LNNS, vol. 299, pp. 136–148. Springer, Cham (2021). https://doi.org/10.1007/978-3-030-82616-1_13

Healthcare 4.0 for the Improvement of the Surgical Monitoring Business Process

Sarra Mejri[1,2(✉)], Sonia Ayachi Ghannouchi[1,3], and Midani Touati[4]

[1] Laboratory RIADI-GDL, ENSI, Manouba 2010, University of Manouba, Manouba, Tunisia
sarra.mejri.fsm@gmail.com
[2] Higher Institute of Computer Science and Communication Technologies of Hammam Sousse, University of Sousse, Sousse, Tunisia
[3] Higher Institute of Management of Sousse, University of Sousse, Sousse, Tunisia
[4] Department of Visceral and Digestive Surgery, University of Medicine of Monastir, University of Monastir, Monastir, Tunisia

Abstract. Post surgical care is an important part of the surgical recovery process. It is a major determinant for recovery and an area that has most benefited from the technological advancements. With the introduction of technologies 4.0, the recovery time of patients is shortened significantly. More precisely, this has led to think of improving the performance criteria (time, cost, flexibility and quality) of the post-operative monitoring process. This paper examines the opportunity to adopt Healthcare 4.0 technologies to improve the performance criteria of the post-operative monitoring process through a questionnaire sent to different physicians in CHU Fattouma Bourguiba hospital. Moreover, a tool named BPIGuide is developed to implement our guidance approach which has been constructed on the basis of the IBPM Ontology and also the decision rules extracted from literature.

Keywords: Healthcare 4.0 · Performance criteria · Business Process Improvement

1 Introduction

Healthcare 4.0 (H4.0) trends include industry 4.0 processes such as the internet of things (IoT), industrial IoT (IIoT), cognitive computing, artificial intelligence, cloud computing, edge computing, etc. [1]. It adapts principles and applications from the Industry 4.0 movement to healthcare, enabling real-time customization of care to patients and professionals. As such, H4.0 can potentially support resilient performance in healthcare systems, which refers to their adaptive capacity to cope with complexity [2].

The monitoring following surgery is a key component in clinical governance [3]. It is a major determinant for recovery and an area that has most benefited from the technological advancements [4]. It contributes to assess the clinical situation of the patient and to recognize those whose health status deteriorates clinically [4]. The management of post-operative recovery is a major concern for patients undergoing surgical procedures

N. T. Nguyen et al. (Eds.): ACIIDS 2023, CCIS 1863, pp. 475–486, 2023.
https://doi.org/10.1007/978-3-031-42430-4_39

and for the care organizations [4]. The ability to provide feedback on performance levels is important to improve healthcare and saves lives [3].

Due to recent technological advancements and innovations in healthcare systems, it is becoming easier to monitor patients in the post-operative and this in turn serves to optimize patient satisfaction and overall outcomes.

A number of H4.0 technologies and eventually IoT, big data, cloud computing, robots, blockchain, SOA and machine/deep learning have been used to improve the Post-Operative Monitoring of surgical patients process (POM). Our aim, in this article, is:

- To describe and highlight the applicability of the H4.0 technologies in postoperative recovery and to provide a comprehensive synthesis of their positive impacts.
- To optimize the performance criteria of the process of the post-operative monitoring of the surgical department of CHU Fattouma Bourguiba (FB) hospital;
- To select the most adequate technology 4.0 that best suits the needs in terms of the improvement of POM process: to achieve this, we used the BPIGuide tool, which is able to take inputs from users regarding the BP modeling or execution language, the application fields and the performance criteria that they desire for their business processes, and then provide them guidance in order to choose the most suitable H4.0 technology.

The remainder of this paper is organized as follows. Section 2 presents related work on improving the post-operative monitoring surgical processes. Our case study related to the POM process and its users performance criteria needs is then presented in Sect. 3. Next, in Sect. 4, we illustrate the main results regarding our guidance tool for this paper related to the POM process. In Sect. 5, we conclude this chapter.

2   Related Work on Improving the Post-Operative Monitoring Surgical (Care) Processes

Improving healthcare process has retained great attention in the last decade. In fact, [5] proposed a cognitive smart healthcare monitoring framework based on the integration of IoT and the cloud computing. They highlighted the challenges of improving quality and flexibility, reducing time and having low-cost of healthcare services using the H4.0 technologies IoT (smart sensors) and cloud at Hospital Boston. On the other hand, [6] suggested a cyber-physical system for patient-centric healthcare applications and services, called Health-CPS, based on cloud and big data analytics technologies, which could enhance the performance of the healthcare system. They proposed a cyber-physical system for patient-centric healthcare applications and services, called Health-CPS, based on cloud and big data analytics technologies. In [7], authors Highlighted the potential impact of the technologies 4.0 big data and cloud computing on healthcare quality with lower time. They propose a novel healthcare system based on a 5G Cognitive System using Big data and cloud computing. [8] proposed a smart healthcare system, based on IoT technology using five sensors to capture the data from hospital environment (named heart beat sensor, body temperature sensor, room temperature sensor, CO sensor, and CO_2 sensor), that can monitor a patient's basic health signs as well as the room condition where the patients are now in real-time. They indicate that the adoption of IoT identified in this research improves hospital performance with reducing the cost of the care process and reducing the need for further hospital admission.

In addition, improving the post-operative monitoring process has recently gained much attention because of the tremendous advantages that it can bring to the patients and the medical staff. In [9], authors evaluated the application of the SPHERE (a Sensor Platform for HealthCare in a Residential Environment) IoT sensor network to produce informative trends of patient behavior during recovery from total hip replacement surgery, using statistical analysis and machine learning techniques. This work's objective was to increase the cost of the system in terms of human resource, reduce time and to maintain the quality of healthcare process. In order to improve the "Surgery" process, [10] presented the utilization of a simulation technique in the field of business process improvement, which is invaluable in developing an efficient, competitive and successful organization. Their aim was to show a great improvement to business process performance by reducing time, increasing the quality of the process and reducing the cost of the surgery carried out. A new solution for post-operative monitoring of surgical patients in [11] was described, which is the Mobile apps using the cloud technology. This work reported on the ability of the technology to improve time efficiency. Besides, [12] authors proposed a robust health monitoring system based on IoT. This work's objective was to enable users to improve health related risks and reduce healthcare costs by collecting, recording, analyzing and sharing large data streams in real time and efficiently.

Table 1 presents a synthesis of the aforementioned works. The various approaches outlined above offer the improving of healthcare processes, seeking to provide relevant information about them. By significantly analyzing the aforementioned contributions, we noticed that none of them offer how H4.0 technologies were selected for improving the post-operative monitoring process, despite performance criteria are often crucial in this respect.

3   Post-Operative Monitoring Process - Eliciting Performance Criteria Needs

In this section, we provide a description of the POM process and present its corresponding process model using BPMN 2.0.

3.1   Description of the Post-Operative Monitoring Process

In this work, we are going to consider the post-operative monitoring of surgical patients process, which initiates with the measurement of the vital parameters and ends with her/his discharge of the surgical department of CHU Fattouma Bourguiba hospital. It passes through three main phases: Long-term, middle-term and early post-operative outcomes.

The main actors in this process are: surgeons, anesthetists, nurses and patients. Tasks of the post-operative monitoring of surgical patients process include:

Table 1. Synthesis of the care processes in Literature.

Emergency care related works	Hospital	Goal	Considered model (language)	Considered H4.0 technology	Type of care process
[5]	Children's Hospital Boston	-Timely, - low-cost, -high-quality, -high efficiency of healthcare services -reduced hospital and medical staff member visits	Not mentioned	IoT Deep learning Cloud computing	Epileptic seizure detection and monitoring
[10]	Not mentioned	-reduce time -high quality of the process -low-cost	Not mentioned	Simulation	Surgery
[9]	Not mentioned	-increase the cost -reduce time - high-quality of healthcare process	Not mentioned	IoT Machine learning	Passive monitoring of outcome and recovery Total Hip Replacement post-surgery
[12]	Not mentioned	-save the time of both patients and doctors -reduce healthcare costs	Not mentioned	IoT	Monitoring patients for emergency medical services
[6]	Not mentioned	-enhance the performance of the healthcare system	Not mentioned	Big data Cloud computing	Monitoring for patient-centric healthcare applications and services
[7]	Not mentioned	-timely -high quality	Not mentioned	Big data Cloud computing	Remote surgery
[8]	Not mentioned	-low-cost -reduce time	Not mentioned	IoT	Monitoring patient's basic health signs

- Measuring the most common vital parameters: heart rate, blood pressure, respiratory frequency, oxygen saturation in the blood and pulse with the pulse oximeter (Fréquence cardiaque, Pression artérielle, fréquence respiratoire, SatO2 température)

- Other measures: diuresis, drainage
- Examination of the operative wound
- Checking the state of the abdomen
- Checking the transit
- Examination of the calves
- Request for the post-operative examination (assessment)
- The surveillance of the post-operative symptoms (agitation, pains…)
- The surveillance of the infusions and treatments
- Access to the results of radiological examinations

Figure 1 shows the process of the post-operative monitoring of surgical patients in BPMN language. We would to improve this post-operative process in our current case study, using observations and interviews with the main actors of the process.

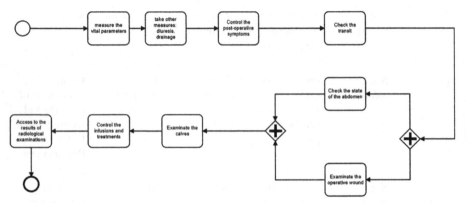

Fig. 1. The adopted process for post-operative monitoring of surgical patients in BPMN language.

3.2 Performance Criteria Needs of the Process

The main technique used to elicit performance criteria needs of the post-operative monitoring process was interviews. The target group of the respondents of these interviews was professionals who are working in the post operative monitoring process.

Interviews. The interview was grouped into the following two sections:

1. Improvement that can occur in the post-operative monitoring process: roles and causes;
2. Performance criteria needs to be considered for the choice of H4.0 technologies.

The first section was designed to get information about the roles responsible for improvement in the post-operative monitoring process and the causes of these ameliorations. The aim of the interview was planned to collect data from the respondents about their needs in terms of the performance criteria (time, cost, quality and flexibility), in order to guide decision makers to choose the best suited H 4.0 technologies to improve the post-operative monitoring process.

POM Process Performance Criteria. POM process performance criteria are defined according to different points of view which are the following:

- According to roles: We have investigated which roles are most commonly seen as responsible for implementing improvements in the POM process. According to respondents and using observations, we have deduced that the surgeon role is the most responsible for enforcing improvements in the post-operative monitoring process. Surgeons, while performing various tasks, are quite independent decision-makers. In very rare cases, nurses may also be responsible for improving the post-operative monitoring process. Concerning the patients, the patient may be involved in choosing treatment options, and may be treated by different POM process participants. They can also be responsible for improving the post-operative monitoring process when signing their discharge. Secretary and other administrative personnel cannot enforce ameliorations. As physicians play the most critical role in implementing improvements, the majority of the following part of our interviews (causes) were tailored to elicit their responses. For these reasons, the performance criteria of the POM process must be strongly enhanced in order to cope with healthcare 4.0 delivery needs.
- According to causes: While physicians are highly motivated to minimize their patients' recovery time, other factors can lead to a delay. We started by presenting the explicit causes mentioned by the interviewed physicians. When asked «Why do you aim to improve the time of the POM monitoring process for surgical patients?», physicians emphasized the importance of timely monitoring to reduce diagnostic errors, prevent postoperative complications in real-time, facilitate prompt decision-making, and ultimately improve the chances of successful treatment for patients. This implies a decrease in the overall cost of the surgical POM process. We identified several factors that could contribute to the complexity of the POM process. These include poor communication between doctors and patients, inadequate availability of resources, and patient dissatisfaction. Despite their efforts to listen attentively and provide clear explanations, physicians may not be able to fully involve patients in the decision-making process. To address these issues, hospitals must be capable of accommodating more patients for surgical treatments and making informed decisions based on each patient's condition. Neglecting these points could lead to delayed post-operative monitoring, which may compromise patient safety and result in suboptimal outcomes.
- Performance criteria needs of the POM process: We resume the answers of the respondents towards the improvement of performance criteria of the post-operative process within the department of the general surgery of CHU FB. Regarding the performance criteria, our study focused on the four known dimensions of process performance defined in the work of [13] which are the time, cost, quality and flexibility dimensions.

Concerning the time dimension, interviewees emphasized the need for timely post-operative monitoring. Generally, surgeons and nurses must be available to perform each step in real time and are trained to do so because the patient's health status can change rapidly after the surgery. To overcome this challenge, the interviewees expressed a desire to minimize the duration of each activity and reduce the time between activities.

Concerning the quality dimension, the interviewees also asserted that the POM process could be of high quality when it is safe (i.e. It avoids injuries to patients through care intended to help them.), effective (i.e. It provides services based on scientific knowledge), patient-centered (i.e. It provides care that is respectful and responsive to the specific preferences, needs, and values of each patient), timely (i.e. It decreases wait times and potentially harmful delays for both care givers and patients), efficient (i.e. It avoids waste, including waste of equipment, supplies, ideas, and energy.) and equitable (i.e. it provides care that is consistent in quality regardless of gender, ethnicity, geographic location, or socio-economic status.).

Concerning the flexibility dimension, the need to provide high-flexibility to POM is valuable. The interviewees considered that the process is flexible when it is possible to change activities to be carried out, the order of these activities and their frequency.

Concerning the cost dimension, making the activities of the post-operative monitoring process less costly is a common problem in the CHU FB. In fact, interviewees believe that the process must be cost-effective by minimizing expenses related to hospital beds and rooms, medical personnel, and equipment.

When physicians were asked, which performance criteria (time, quality, flexibility and cost) they deemed most important for the POM process, they held that time was the most crucial factor for enhancing the POM process. They also stressed the significance of prioritizing quality to enhance the POM. While respondents recognize the importance of cost for process improvement, they consider flexibility to be the least significant factor.

4   Applying Our Guidance Approach to the POM Process

After eliciting the roles and causes for improvements in the POM process, and deriving the associated performance criteria needs based on the questionnaire results, we used this information to advise on a possible technology 4.0 to be used. We have used the decision rules that correspond to decision trees and association rules extracted by the data mining techniques.

4.1   Guidance Approach Based on BP Improvement

Our guidance approach is based on a two-step methodology, as shown in the Fig. 2. Regarding the first step, a set of optimization rules for Business Process performance were defined using Semantic Web Rule Language (SWRL) after developing our IBPM Ontology, in order to successfully redesign the new business process model (optimized BP 4.0). Regarding the second step, we have proposed a guidance approach that is meant to guide users to choose technologies 4.0 that best fit users' needs in terms of different criteria of their BPs. The method consists of several steps. It has been implemented as an application. This BPIGuide application takes as input the users' needs in terms of performance criteria, BP language and the application field. It then provides as output the corresponding technologies 4.0 according to the user's needs in terms of performance criteria, namely regarding the performance dimensions identified in the work of [13].

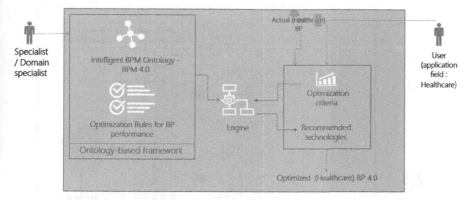

Fig. 2. Our framework for BP Performance improvement.

4.2   Implementation of the BPIGuide Tool

The approach conducted in our research work is supported and tested by an implemented corresponding tool named BPIGuide tool. We will first give an overview of the BPIGuide tool, and then we will describe its features.

BPIGuide Tool Architecture. When starting the use of BPIGuide, the user can pick, from a list, the different criteria of their BP which best fit her/his needs on performance criteria, BP language and the application fields. For each attribute, the user will be required at the provided input interface to choose between yes, no and probably, which means respectively: he/she is interested in the value presented, he/she is not interested in it and it might fit his/her interest. The provided user interface allows choosing user needs related to selection criteria. Her/his choices are then stored. In order to provide an easy means to configure each criterion, three User Interface (UI) components can be used, which allow modifying criteria configurations. The UI components concern the performance criteria, the BP languages and the application fields.

It is important to mention this architectural aspect, which allows the separation between user interface (view) components and the extraction of the optimization rules for Business Process performance. The most important step consists in inferring rules from the IBPM Ontology. To do that, we have implemented the decision rules that correspond to decision trees and association rules by using Semantic Web Rule Language (SWRL). These decision rules are presented in the IBPM Ontology developed in our recent research work for defining means of Healthcare 4.0 adoption and healthcare processes optimization. The IBPM Ontology is an important part of our approach, which ensures the selection of the most suitable technologies 4.0 for BPs. It included the most important concepts of both BPM and Industry 4.0.

Using the ontology-based engine, the result of the execution of these rules is the ranking of the recommended technologies 4.0, which will be presented to users and could be used to redesign and implement optimized BPs 4.0. Finally, these results are shown to the user. Figure 3 depicts this user interface flow with screen captures of our BPIGuide tool.

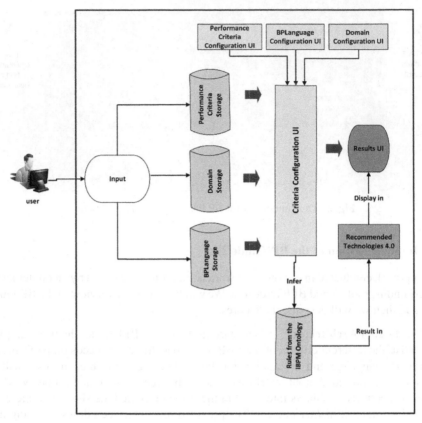

Fig. 3. BPIGuide architecture.

BPIGuide Tool Features. In order to describe our BPIGuide tool features, we have used the use case diagram (UML notation). Overall, a use case aims mainly to describe a specific usage of the system by one or more actors. An actor is a role that a user or another system has [14].

The actors that are involved in this application are the user. For its users, our BPIGuide provides four main features. In fact, it first allows users to select their different criteria needs (performance criteria, BP language and application field). As a result, users obtain the adequate technologies 4.0. They also can select each technology 4.0 in order to get more information about it. Figure 4 illustrates the aforementioned functionalities, using screen captures of our BPIGuide application. The main interfaces are consequently: the performance criteria interface, the BP language interface, the application field interface and the technologies 4.0 specific classification.

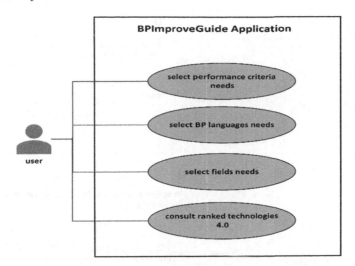

Fig. 4. Use case: Main functionalities provided by the BPIGuide.

4.3 Implementation of Our Guidance Approach and Its Application to the POM Process

To support our guidance approach, we developed the BPIGuide tool implemented by Java and we integrated SWRL Rules for inferring the decision rules. Using the BPIGuide tool, we have entered the needs of the healthcare professionals. This section shows the result of the application of our guidance approach to the POM process. The goal of the case study was to help users to choose (select) the most suitable and adequate H4.0 technologies in order to optimize their BPs. The tool gives as output the most suitable H4.0 technologies. Professionals of healthcare have to specify the different criteria of their POM process in order to allow the selection of specific intelligent technologies to be integrated to their BP. As a result, professionals were guided to use BPIGuide tool. Using the results presented in the previous Sect. 3.2, we deduced that the performance criteria, which are mostly considered as important by our interviewees, are time and quality. Figure 5.a presents the choices of performance criteria. As output, the recommended technology for optimizing the POM process is Blockchain, shown in Fig. 5.b.

The choice of BP language was based on opinions given by BP modelling experts and also on the literature, which is BPMN. Figure 5.c presents the choices of the application domain. As output, the recommended technologies for optimizing the POM process are big data and SOA, as shown in Fig. 5.d.

The recommended technologies 4.0 in both cases (Blockchain, Big data and SOA) were automatically obtained based on the decision rules corresponding to decision trees and association rules extracted by the data mining techniques.

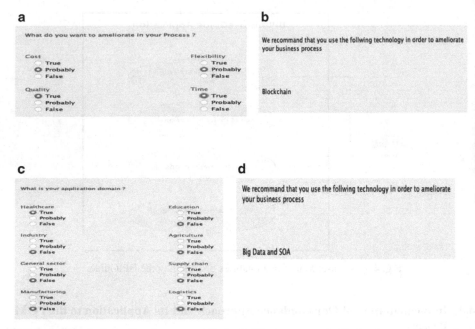

Fig. 5. a. The choices of performance criteria. **b.** The recommended technology. **c.** The choices of the application domain. **d.** The recommended technologies.

5   Conclusion

Nowadays, the adoption of the H4.0 technologies in the domain of healthcare may positively impact the hospitals' performance. This case study aims to contribute with an understanding of the performance criteria needs of a POM process and by guiding POM process participants to choose the most appropriate H4.0 technologies which fits best their needs in terms of performance criteria. Importantly, this study was conducted using observations and interviews related to the POM of surgical patients of the department of the general surgery of Fattouma Bourguiba CHU Hospital in Tunisia. First, we have considered the POM process and modelled it using BPMN language (and specifically by the use of the BPMN 2.0). We have then conducted interviews to elicit the performance criteria needs of the POM process. Using our developed tool "BPIGuide", we have deduced the most recommended H4.0 technologies, which best meet the POM process criteria needs. We consider that the obtained application offer in fact an intelligent POM process. This takes into account the different criteria needs expressed by the POM process professionals. Despite the fact that our guidance approach was well implemented and we have applied it to a case study in the healthcare field, there are still many opportunities for future improvements. We are going to apply our guidance approach in different domains (such as supply chain, agriculture, industry, logistics, education, etc.) to help decision-makers make smart decisions.

Nevertheless, we have only based on the choices of the modeler to only one criteria at the same time and this becomes a constraint since our modelers might be interested in different criteria simultaneously. Thus, in our future work, we will simultaneously deal with all our criteria.

References

1. Kumar, A., Krishnamurthi, R., Nayyar, A., Sharma, K., Grover, V., Hossain, E.: A novel smart healthcare design, simulation, and implementation using healthcare 4.0 processes. IEEE Access **8**, 118433–118471 (2020)
2. Tortorella, G.L., Saurin, T.A., Fogliatto, F.S., Rosa, V.M., Tonetto, L.M., Magrabi, F.: Impacts of healthcare 4.0 digital technologies on the resilience of hospitals. Technol. Forecast. Soc. Change **166**, 120666 (2021)
3. Collins, G.S., Jibawi, A., McCulloch, P.: Control chart methods for monitoring surgical performance: a case study from gastro-oesophageal surgery. Eur. J. Surg. Oncol. (EJSO) **37**, 473–480 (2011). https://doi.org/10.1016/j.ejso.2010.10.008
4. Petros Kolovos, R.N.: Wearable technologies in post-operative recovery: clinical applications and positive impacts. Int. J. Caring Sci. **13**, 1474–1479 (2020)
5. Alhussein, M., Muhammad, G., Hossain, M.S., Amin, S.U.: Cognitive IoT-cloud integration for smart healthcare: case study for epileptic seizure detection and monitoring. Mob. Netw. Appl. **23**, 1624–1635 (2018). https://doi.org/10.1007/s11036-018-1113-0
6. Zhang, Y., Qiu, M., Tsai, C.-W., Hassan, M., Alamri, A.: Health-CPS: healthcare cyber-physical system assisted by cloud and big data. IEEE Syst. J. **11**, 1–8 (2015). https://doi.org/10.1109/JSYST.2015.2460747
7. Chen, M., Yang, J., Hao, Y., Mao, S., Hwang, K.: A 5G cognitive system for healthcare. Big Data Cogn. Comput. **1**, 2 (2017). https://doi.org/10.3390/bdcc1010002
8. Islam, M., Rahaman, A.: Development of smart healthcare monitoring system in IoT environment. SN Comput. Sci. **1**, 1–11 (2020)
9. Holmes, M., Nieto, M.P., Song, H., Tonkin, E., Grant, S., Flach, P.: Modelling patient behaviour using IoT sensor data: a case study to evaluate techniques for modelling domestic behaviour in recovery from total hip replacement surgery. J. Healthc. Inform. Res. **4**, 238–260 (2020). https://doi.org/10.1007/s41666-020-00072-6
10. Damij, N., Damij, T.: Healthcare process improvement using simulation. In: Proceedings of the Third International Conference on Health Informatics, Valencia, Spain: SciTePress - Science and and Technology Publications, pp. 422–427 (2010). https://doi.org/10.5220/0002717504220427
11. Semple, J.L., Sharpe, S., Murnaghan, M.L., Theodoropoulos, J., Metcalfe, K.A.: Using a mobile app for monitoring post-operative quality of recovery of patients at home: a feasibility study. JMIR Mhealth Uhealth **3**, e3929 (2015). https://doi.org/10.2196/mhealth.3929
12. Gupta, P., Agrawal, D., Chhabra, J., Dhir, P.K.: IoT based smart healthcare kit. In: 2016 International Conference on Computational Techniques in Information and Communication Technologies (ICCTICT), New Delhi, India, pp. 237–242. IEEE (2016). https://doi.org/10.1109/ICCTICT.2016.7514585
13. Dumas, M., La Rosa, M., Mendling, J., Reijers, H.A.: Business Process Management. Springer, Berlin, Heidelberg (2013). https://doi.org/10.1007/978-3-662-56509-4
14. Eriksson, H.-E., Penker, M.: Business modeling with UML, p. 12. New York (2000)

Improvement of the Process of Diagnosing Patient's Condition via Computer Tomography Lung Scans Using Neural Networks

Marcin Nahajowski, Michal Kedziora[(✉)] [iD], and Ireneusz Jozwiak[iD]

Wroclaw University of Science and Technology, Wroclaw, Poland
`michal.kedziora@pwr.edu.pl`

Abstract. The aim of the research paper is improvement of the process of diagnosing patient's condition via Computer Tomography lung scans using Neural Networks. The concept is to implement an IT solution that will accelerate the process of verifying the condition of a patient with COVID-19 in a medical facility using AI and to carry out research to improve the accuracy of the diagnosis. Experiments were carried out on two different databases of lung scans with Computer Tomography.

Keywords: COVID-19 · AI · Neural Network

1 Introduction

Artificial Intelligence becomes more important part of the process of diagnosing patient's condition, year after year [1,4]. It guarantees efficient processing of information with a limited level of difficulty. AI provides a highly reliable data analysis on a limited level of abstraction, designed to solve basic issues related to the diagnosis process automatically or semiautomatically [9]. There can be quoted several examples of such processes: determination of imaging modality designation, general characteristics of image data, segmentation dominant structures with the calculation of their parameters, numerical evaluation of the progression of the analyzed changes in subsequent research, detection of changes or easier objects in recognition, etc. The result is the reduction of simple natural human errors, resulting from natural restrictions as well as the lack of automatism and precise repeatability of the diagnostician's actions [3,7]. Stress factors that affect doctors during this pandemic with respect to the increase in the number of patients in hospitals have a significant impact on their work and performance [6]. Actually, such computer-aided diagnosis (CAD) systems are a complement to doctor interpretations [4], on the basis of synergy radiologists' competences and algorithmic computing computers [2]. Even with limited efficiency of the algorithms, positive support effects can be obtained [13].

The aim of the research is to improve the process of diagnosing patient's condition via Computer Tomography lung scans using Artificial Intelligence.

N. T. Nguyen et al. (Eds.): ACIIDS 2023, CCIS 1863, pp. 487–497, 2023.
https://doi.org/10.1007/978-3-031-42430-4_40

The concept is to implement an IT solution that will accelerate the process of verifying the condition of a patient with COVID-19 in a medical facility using AI and to carry out research to improve the accuracy of the diagnosis. Experiments will be carried out in two different databases of lung CT scans.

Convolutional neural networks are widely used in image classification tasks and have achieved significant performance since 2012 [15]. This article also contains research carried out after implementing an IT solution that accelerates the process of verifying the condition of a patient with COVID-19 in a medical facility thanks to the use of artificial intelligence. It emphasizes the role of AI in medicine and presents articles related to this topic. The crucial purpose of experiments is to provide a deep convolutional neural network that works with high efficiency and accuracy. During the research part, multiple experiments were carried out in order to find optimal optimizer and activation functions on layers. All experiments were carried out in two different databases and all results were compared. The summary and discussion of the results with tables helping to interpret the results and possible directions for further research were also performed.

The research problem of this paper is to determine the influence of particular configurable parameters of the neural network. The main parameters that will be analyzed are the influence of optimization selection and the influence of selection of the activation function. Although it is very difficult to collect medical image datasets (due to the need for professional labeling expertise) [10], all results will be compared between two different databases. The differences between databases have been described precisely in the Experiments section. The research carried out as part of this work may help determine the impact of these parameters on the optimal efficiency and precision of the network.

2   Related Works

The most typical use of AI systems in medicine is closely related to chest radiography, especially chest computed tomography (CT) [17]. Most of the techniques created are based on the retrieval of information from various types of medical images [18].

The article entitled "Deep Convolutional Neural Network-Based Computer-Aided Detection System for COVID-19 Using Multiple Lung Scans: Design and Implementation Study" is focused on creating computer-aided detection (CAD) by using a neural search architecture network (NASNet) based algorithm. The authors tried to classify COVID-19 and non-COVID-19 images using a large database containing more than 10000 samples. The authors used convolutional layers in the feature extraction block. The authors presented the results of work with multiple metrics like sensitivity, specificity, and accuracy. Furthermore, the authors showed a high percentage of effectiveness of the neural network in the example of detection of 25 random samples from the test set [8].

In the article "Development and evaluation of an artificial intelligence system for COVID-19 diagnosis", the authors concentrated on creating their own deep convolutional neural network-based system. The authors focused on the fact that a good understanding of computer tomography (CT) and chest radiography is crucial during the process of detecting COVID-19 infection. The authors emphasized that CT can give a lot of information in the early stage of infection. The authors proposed a voluminous database consisting of multiple different symptoms of diseases such as nonviral community acquired pneumonia (CAP) and nonpneumonia. The authors proved that their algorithm works more efficiently than five well-qualified radiologists at the same time. During studies, authors have analyzed ways of selecting phenotype features and modified multiple hyperparameters. The article can be useful for specifying hyperparameters during experiments. [11]

The article "The potential for artificial intelligence in healthcare" this authors considers the influence of artificial intelligence on modern medicine. The authors emphasized that an important aspect of efforts to increase the amount of AI in medicine is still an opinion about the advantage of humans performing healthcare tasks. The authors presented both the profits that AI offers and barriers, which can be crucial problems in such quite dramatic direction change. Authors described most popular types of AI techniques used such as neural networks, deep learning, natural language processing (NLP), rule-based expert systems, physical robots, and robotic process automation. In addition, they marked out the applications used by patients and administrative applications. [5]

The authors of the article "Effective Diagnosis and Treatment Through Content-Based Medical Image Retrieval (CBMIR) by Using Artificial Intelligence" focused on the fact that medicine is mostly based on interpretation of medical images. The authors' whole idea is pretty similar to well-known approaches which concentrate on correct medical image classification. They proposed another system of enhanced residual network named ResNet which generated much better accuracies than the previous idea of CBMIR (content-based image retrieval). The authors have tried to meet all the possible configurations of given images. The authors noticed that many previous approaches created features manually by themselves, which makes the number of possible classes really unsatisfying. In their opinion, that was the reason why the scores made by their predecessors were so disappointing. [12]

The article "The Prospective of Artificial Intelligence in COVID-19 Pandemic" focused on the advantages Artificial Intelligence offers during the COVID-19 Pandemic. The authors described the general procedure to identify COVID-19 symptoms and listed the most possible scenarios of using AI during diagnosis. Moreover, they analyzed the advantages of detecting COVID-19 with AI in various fields of "fight" against disease. Moreover, they raised a topic of future AI in medicine. They agreed that AI can help radiologists in analyzing symptoms more rapidly and with higher accuracy. [16]

The article entitled "The Role of Artificial Intelligence in Fighting the COVID-19 Pandemic" is focused on the way how Artificial Intelligence can support the whole world in fight against pandemic. Here, the authors analyze and discuss how AI can support people in facing the ongoing pandemic. The authors listed several AI achievements present in people's everyday life. Furthermore, the authors noticed the problem of a higher percentage of sickening in countries with a lack of efficient health care system and monitoring actions. In addition, the article consists of an analysis in which regions the highest number of publications and research related to the COVID-19 pandemic are observed. Authors have discussed the ethical aspects of Artificial Intelligence in medicine and proposed to use well-known AI solutions (like image diagnostics) more often and on a much bigger scale. In their opinion, AI can easily contribute to victory over the COVID-19 pandemic. [14]

3 Experiments

We decided to use the two data sources, the first is the database from Tehran, Iran mentioned above and used in one of the cited articles [8]. In the first experiments, it was decided to examine how important is the selection of an optimizer. As a default, the Adam optimizer was chosen (the optimizer that implements Adam algorithm). To start with, ADAM is one of the most popular optimization algorithms used in deep learning. It can be used in place of the classical stochastic gradient decent procedure to iteratively update network weights based on training data. It is a combine of two other extensions of stochastic gradient descent: AdaGrad and RMSProp. The test set is 20% of all data sets, the validation set is 20% of the rest which is 16% and the training set is 64% of all data. The model using ADAM had a very low error rate and high accuracy for the default data from Tehran, Iran was improving as well. It suggests that the model has great potential to detect new cases of COVID-19 from CT scans. The precision and sensitivity in this experiment are also very high, which is a very satisfying result. Next, we used Stochastic Gradient Descent (SGD) algorithm. SGD optimizer made quite good results but not as good as Adam. The problem we can find is the fact that the false positive rate for COVID-19 samples is higher than that for non-COVID. This is probably the main reason why the accuracy is lower. Next, we used the Adadelta algorithm, which did not manage well with this task. The results are definitely worse than when using other optimizers. There is clearly a problem with diagnosing images with COVID-19. Almost 27% of them were wrongly diagnosed as non-COVID. Next, we use Adagrad. The results are not excellent. It did not reach 95% of precision. However, it is definitely better than the previous optimizer in diagnosing non-COVID-19 samples. It still has problems in false-positive rate in COVID-19 cases. Next, we used the RMAprop algorithm.

Here is what confusion matrixes look like. Same as in all the previous experiments, the second one presents the first's data normalized.

RMSprop optimizer achieved great results, almost as good as Adam (more than 99% accuracy). It also has great precision, sensitivity and specificity. This is also one of the best choices of optimizers, it did not have many problems in correct decision.

As was said before, after the feature extraction block, the weights are transferred to 3 dense layers which can be easily modified. Each of these layers has its

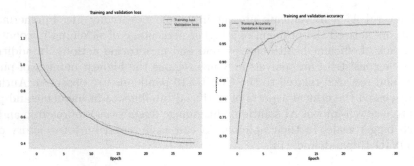

Fig. 1. Training and validation accuracy and loss before fine tuning (RMSprop optimizer — Tehran, Iran database

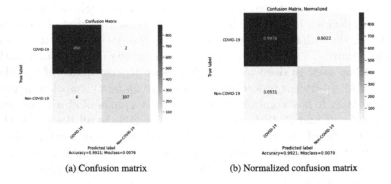

(a) Confusion matrix   (b) Normalized confusion matrix

Fig. 2. Confusion matrixes (RMSprop optimizer — Tehran, Iran database)

own activation function (similar to the typical neural network layer). The activation function must be a differentiable function. As the default, in each of these layers the Relu activation function was used. In this part of the experiments, the default parameters will be used, and the only one to change is the activation function. First, we used the Sigmoid function which achieved very good results (more than 98%). It had a small problem with false positive decisions for COVID-19 samples (more than 11%), but it still worked pretty well. Next, we used the Tanh activation function, which provided even better results than the Sigmoid. It reached a level of accuracy exceeding 99% with great results in sensitivity and specificity as well. We cannot find any crucial problem in making correct decisions on images. Also in these experiments, graphs were presented on how the training and validation accuracy looked before and after fine tuning. It can be clearly seen how accuracy was gained from about 84% before fine-tuning to more than 95% afterwards. The loss function also decreased (Figs. 1 and 2).

Last, we used the Softplus activation function which achieved the worst results among the activation functions so far - only about 95% accuracy. It reached only 74% in negative predictive value, and this is the most possible reason (Fig. 3).

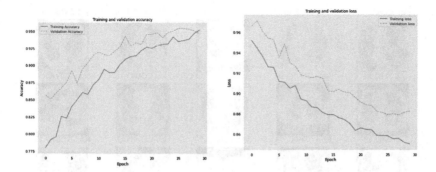

Fig. 3. Training and validation accuracy and loss after fine tuning (Softplus activation — Tehran, Iran database

3.1   COVID CT Images Collected from COVID-19 Related Papers Database

It was decided to check the results achieved in the other database than the default from Tehran, Iran. During all of the experiments in the following section, the database published in the other article was used [19]. This database also contains multiple CT images, divided into COVID and non-COVID classes. It contains data from 216 patients. The database consists of images with degraded quality of images, such as the number of bits per pixel is reduced or the resolution of images is reduced. This data set was confirmed by a senior radiologist at Tongji Hospital, Wuhan, China. In the following experiments, similar tests were performed in order to verify accuracy and other mentioned metrics. This database is a little smaller than the default one, so it was decided to use all of their samples during experiments. Here, we present what data in this custom dataset look like. As can be seen, it contains pretty similar photos to the previous one. Here, the first 25 samples from the training set are presented.

Moving forward, here is what the accuracy and loss of the training and validation before fine-tuning looked like. This experiment was carried out for default parameters with Adam optimizer and was made to the second database.

The results achieved for this optimizer are much lower than those for the Tehran database, Iran. Anyway, it is still a very good result, because of the quality of images and their ambiguity. In such a situation, the result over 82% of accuracy is a great one. Next, we use SGD optimizer which did not achieve an impressing result on the images collected from the articles database. It had a lot of problems in false positive rate, for example. There are other optimizers that achieved much better results. The next optimizer to test is the one with the Adadelta algorithm. This is what accuracy and loss of training and validation looked like.

The Adadelta algorithm again gained really unsatisfactory results. Only 58% of accuracy is only slightly better than a random diagnosis. Looking at this table, Adadelta should not be used as an optimizer in problem such as this. Next we

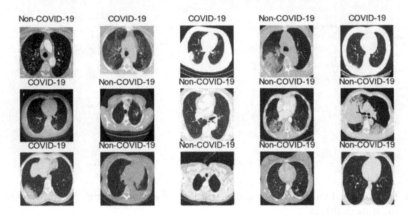

Fig. 4. Second database examples from training set

Table 1. Metrics (Adam optimizer — Images collected from articles database)

	COVID-19	NON-COVID-19
Mean Squared Error	0.17333	
Accuracy	0.82666	
Precision	0.89552	0.77108
Sensitivity	0.75949	0.90140
Specificity	0.90140	0.75949
Negative Predictive Value	0.77108	0.89552
Fall out (false positive rate)	0.09859	0.24050
False Negative Rate	0.24050	0.09859
False discovery rate	0.10447	0.22891

used Adagrad algorithm which made quite good results, but not impressive ones. Training did not go very well, fine tuning helped a little bit and provided such a result. Finally we used RMSprop which achieved the second best results after Adam optimizer. It crossed the barrier of 75% of accuracy. It had problem with false positive for non-COVID-19 samples, but it went really good in false positive for COVID-19 ones (Fig. 4 and Table 1).

3.2 Discussion of the Results

In conclusion, to determine the best parameters of the neural network, several experiments have been carried out. They included selection of the optimizer, influence of activation function, etc. Each of those sections will be summarized with a table colored in a helpful way to interpret the most important results. There are two tables (one for each database) which consist of ranges for different colors because of the difference in difficulty as well as accuracy among both databases.

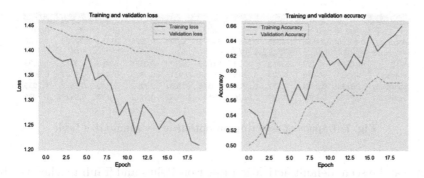

Fig. 5. Training and validation accuracy and loss before fine tuning (Adadelta optimizer — Images collected from articles database)

Color	Range
	(0,988;1)
	(0,97;0,988]
	(0,95;0,97)
	(0,92;0,95)
	(0,85;0,92)
	(0,65;0,85)
	(0;0,65)

(a) Tehran,Iran database

Color	Range
	(0,80;1)
	(0,75;0,80)
	(0,71;0,75)
	(0,66;0,71)
	(0,62;0,66)
	(0,58;0,62)
	(0;0,58)

(b) Images collected from articles database

Fig. 6. Color interpretation tables for Tehran, Iran database and Images collected from articles database

The following table shows what the most important statistics were like for each optimizer in every database. As in "Db 1", we understand "COVID-19 Lung CT Scans from Tehran, Iran database" and as in "Db 2", we understand "COVID CT images collected from COVID-19 related papers database" (Figs. 5 and 6).

As can be seen, Adam optimizer gave the best results on both of the databases. It reached almost 100% of accuracy in the first database and over 82% in the second one. It definitely shows that it is the best optimizer to choose for such a task. RMSprop took the second place with a result almost as good as Adam on a Tehran, Iran database, but a lower one on the Images collected from articles database. Adagrad and SGD made similar results but Adagrad did not produce such a difference between databases as the SGD had. Adagrad has only around 14% of difference and SGD almost 18%. Adadelta definitely made the worst result on both databases. On the Images collected from articles one it has only about 58% (just little more than random would have) and only about 74% on the Tehran, Iran.

The following table shows what the most important statistics were like for each activation function in every database. The same as in the previous summarizing table, we understand here "Db 1" as "COVID-19 Lung CT Scans from Tehran,Iran database" and as "Db 2" we understand "COVID CT images collected from COVID-19 related papers database" (Fig. 7).

	Adam		Adadelta		Adagrad		RMSProp		SGD	
	Db 1	Db 2	Db 1	Db 2	Db 1	Db 2	Db 1	Db 2	Db 1	Db 2
Accuracy	0,99506	0,82666	0,74136	0,5866	0,94471	0,726	0,9921	0,753	0,97729	0,7066
Acc. result										
MSE	0,0049	0,173	0,25863	0,413	0,055	0,273	0,0078	0,2466	0,0227	0,293
Precision	0,9936	0,833	0,624	0,5845	0,848	0,7375	0,9875	0,778	0,9361	0,7067
Specificity	0,9834	0,8304	0,777	0,5826	0,89536	0,7042	0,9272	0,76	0,9527	0,7036
Sensitivity	0,9834	0,8304	0,777	0,5826	0,89536	0,7042	0,9272	0,76	0,9527	0,7036

Fig. 7. Impact of selecting an optimizer — summarize table

As can be seen, default activation function Relu - and Tanh reached the best results on the Tehran, Iran database. On the images collected from articles, one softmax is slightly better than Tanh and achieved almost 80% accuracy. However, softmax made really low result on the Tehran, Iran database. It is also the worst result among all of activation functions. Sigmoid performed quite well on the Tehran, Iran one, but was the worst on the Images collected from articles. To sum up, Relu function should be the best choice to create the most effective neural network which would learn on the mentioned databases.

4   Conclusion and Future Work

The purpose of the research was to improve the process of diagnosing the disease of patients by computer tomography lung scans using Artificial Intelligence. The assumed goal of the work has been achieved. The work was prepared within the scope defined at the beginning. The proposed system reached 99,506% accuracy in its best evaluation for the "Tehran, Iran database" and 82,666% for the "COVID CT images collected from the COVID-19 related papers database". The use of CAD systems like this during the pandemic can minimize the amount of natural human errors, reduce the time needed to interpret images, which can also affect the reduction of the number of patients waiting for diagnosis.

In summary, Adam was definitely the best optimizer to choose. It achieved the best results for the Iran database - about 99,5%. Moreover, it also managed pretty well on the more difficult database (images collected from COVID-19 related papers) - it has also made the best results, almost 83%. RMSProp is also a good option, but it had some difficulties with the second database. The worst choice was Adadelta, whose results were significantly lower than those of the other optimizers. Going to the activation functions, Relu and Tanh reached approximately the best results, so probably one of them should be used on dense layers. Sigmoid produced quite good results on the Iranian database, but it definitely wasn't satisfactory on the second one. The results for Softmax were the least split compared to other activation functions. Although the result on the first database was really low (only about 95%), the result on the second was the second best. Relu guaranteed the best results on both databases.

In future research, a useful idea would be to investigate the impact of a few other configurable parameters and try to reach even higher accuracy. Moreover, if we provide more computer-tomography images, we should expect better results in differentiating positive and negative cases. One of the ideas could be to carry out similar experiments for other databases. Another idea would be to mix two different databases, one with photos with lower resolution, as, for example, the "COVID CT images collected from COVID-19 related papers database" and verify whether we achieved better results, especially in correct detection of photos with lower resolution.

References

1. Abidin, Z.Z., et al.: Crypt-tag authentication in NFC implementation for medicine data management. Int. J. Adv. Comput. Sci. Appl. **9**, 9 (2018)
2. Agbo, C.C., Mahmoud, Q.H., Eklund, J.M.: Blockchain technology in healthcare: a systematic review. Healthcare **7**(2), 56 (2019)
3. Başaran, E., Cömert, Z., Çelik, Y.: Convolutional neural network approach for automatic tympanic membrane detection and classification. Biomed. Signal Process. Control **56**, 101734 (2020)
4. Buch, V.H., Ahmed, I., Maruthappu, M.: Artificial intelligence in medicine: current trends and future possibilities. Br. J. Gen. Pract. **68**, 143–144 (2018)
5. Davenport, T., Kalakota, R.: The potential for artificial intelligence in healthcare. Future Healthc. J. **6**(2), 94–98 (2019). 403–406
6. Debnath, S., et al.: Machine learning to assist clinical decision-making during the COVID-19 pandemic. Bioelectron. Med. **6**(14), 14 (2020). The Northwell COVID-19 Research Consortium
7. Deng, J., Dong, W., Socher, R., Li, L.J., Li, K., Fei-Fei, L.: Deep convolutional neural networks for image classification: a comprehensive review. In: 2009 IEEE Conference on Computer Vision and Pattern Recognition, vol. 29, no 9, pp. 248–255 (2017)
8. Ghaderzadeh, M., Asadi, F., Jafari, J.R., Bashash, D., Abolghasemi, H., Aria, M.: Deep convolutional neural network-based computer-aided detection system for COVID-19 using multiple lung scans: design and implementation study. J. Med. Internet Res. **23**(4), e27468 (2021)
9. Gruda, M., Kedziora, M.: Analyzing and improving tools for supporting fighting against COVID-19 based on prediction models and contact tracing. Bull. Polish Acad. Sci.: Tech. Sci. e137414–e137414 (2021)
10. Yadav, Samir S.., Jadhav, Shivajirao M..: Deep convolutional neural network based medical image classification for disease diagnosis. J. Big Data **6**(113) (2019)
11. Jin, C., et al.: Development and evaluation of an artificial intelligence system for COVID-19 diagnosis. Nat. Commun. **5088** (2020)
12. Owais, M., Arsalan, M., Choi, J., Park, K.R.: Effective diagnosis and treatment through content-based medical image retrieval (CBMIR) by using artificial intelligence. J. Clin. Med. **8**(4), 462 (2019)
13. Ozturk, T., Talo, M., Yildirim, E.A., Baloglu, U.B., Yildirim, O., Acharya, U.: Automated detection of COVID-19 cases using deep neural networks with x-ray images. Comput. Biol. Med. **121** (2020)
14. Piccialli, F., di Cola, V.S., Giampaolo, F., Cuomo, S.: The role of artificial intelligence in fighting the COVID-19 pandemic. Inf. Syst. Front. **121**, 103792 (2021)
15. Rawat, W., Wang, Z.: Deep convolutional neural networks for image classification: a comprehensive review. Neural Comput. **29**(9), 2352–2449 (2017)

16. Swayamsiddha, S., Prashant, K., Shaw, D., Mohanty, C.: The prospective of artificial intelligence in COVID-19 pandemic. Health Technol. **11**(6), 1311–1320 (2021). https://doi.org/10.1007/s12553-021-00601-2
17. Toğaçar, M., Ergen, B., Cömert, Z.: COVID-19 detection using deep learning models to exploit social mimic optimization and structured chest x-ray images using fuzzy color and stacking approaches. Comput. Biol. Med. **121**, 103805 (2020)
18. Ucar, F., Korkmaz, D.: COVIDiagnosis-Net: deep Bayes-SqueezeNet based diagnosis of the coronavirus disease 2019 (COVID-19) from x-ray images. Comput. Biol. Med. 140, 109761 (2020)
19. Zhao, J., Zhang, Y., He, X., Xie, P.: COVID-CT-dataset: a CT Scan dataset about COVID-19. arXiv preprint arXiv:2003.13865 (2020)

Novel Machine Learning Pipeline for Real-Time Oculometry

Albert Śledzianowski[(✉)], Jerzy P. Nowacki, Konrad Sitarz,
and Andrzej W. Przybyszewski

The Faculty of Information Technology, Polish-Japanese Academy of Information
Technology, 02-008 Warsaw, Poland
s13531@pjwstk.edu.pl

Abstract. In modern medicine, there is a need for widely available and efficient oculometric systems. This is because oculometry provides a simple insight into the general motor status of the patient. A good example are neurodegenerative diseases (ND) such as Parkinson's disease (PD) with bradykinesia as one of the effects causing a general slowing of movements, also visible in eye movements. PD develops secretly for many years before showing visible effects, but eye-tracking tests can reveal it sooner. That is why we decided to create a modern system for performing this type of tests based on neural network models, modern inference approach and algorithms of various types to help obtain reliable results. Our idea was to disconnect the software from the hardware and base the hardware requirements on consumer grade equipment, such as a web-camera. This step is necessary because modern telemedicine must necessarily be based on basic equipment available to patients in their households. Our results showed that even with 30 Hz frequency and standard reflexive-saccade (RS) test, our system was able to distinguish the results of healthy person from PD patient or young from old person This solution brings the ability to receive quantitative online data, in opposition to standard telemedicine allowing only for verbal and/or visual interactions with the patient. We hope that low hardware requirements will popularize automated oculometric tests in the context of age-related complications and ND diseases, which may contribute to earlier diagnoses and the collection of the appropriate amount of data to develop new means of preventing different diseases.

Keywords: machine learning · deep learning · eye moves · eye tracking · oculometry · reflexive saccades · saccade detections · neurodegenerative diseases · Parkinson's disease

1 Introduction

The video-oculography is the non-invasive, video-based method of eye tracking allowing for measuring all components of the eye movements. It gives hope for the creation of publicly available systems in the future to support the detection

N. T. Nguyen et al. (Eds.): ACIIDS 2023, CCIS 1863, pp. 498–509, 2023.
https://doi.org/10.1007/978-3-031-42430-4_41

of ND and measure its progress. Many researchers recently showed very good results of video-oculography and oculometric tests in classification or prediction of different ND.

Semmelmann et al. showed good example of JavaScript algorithms for eye tracking with standard webcams to study fixation, pursuit, and free viewing to analyze the spatial precision in the first two, and repeatability of well-known gazing patterns in the third task [1]. The main focus of the study was to test the potential and possible limitations of webcam in terms of noise and accuracy to find differences between laboratory-grade equipment and webcam results [1]. They concluded that web-based eye tracking is suitable to conduct all three tests with little less accuracy and higher variance of the data [1].

Lin et al. developed a real-time eye-tracking system based on a webcam and machine learning models, combining a position criterion, gaze direction detection and lightning filtering [2]. The gaze direction estimation was based on appearance-features of eyes, Fourier Descriptor and the Support Vector Machine [2]. Authors concluded that their webcam solution brought quality results with feasibility of the solution [2].

Meng et al. investigated Convolutional Neural Network models (CNN) with webcams with very promising results for this type of eye-tracking method by detecting 6 eye features to gather more exact eye movement data [3].

Aljaafreh et al. [4] created an oculometric system based on webcam and application projecting dynamic stimulus. It was tested in research on 10 Multiple Sclerosis (MS) patients. The system calculated multiple parameters of saccades and both latency and amplitude gave sufficient results that allowed for diagnosis for MS disorder making this system sensible for clinical diagnosis and identification of neurological disorders [4].

The RS are a very good example of coulometric tests that give good results in the diagnosis of ND. The RS are rapid, ballistic eye movement of the eyes triggered by the influence of an emerging stimulus, with the purpose to direct the gaze focus to interesting element of the environment. Because different regions of the brain are involved in this process, therefore RS are very sensitive to degenerative changes caused by ND and also by human aging. The analysis of the RS parameters, mainly the latency showed in many cases correlation with development the PD [5–8].

Our idea was to build an advanced pipeline that would allow for eye-tracking based on CNN and video stream from a webcam, while controlling the information about the surrounding conditions, because a webcam can provide poor quality and frequency, and hardly depends on the lighting environment. Additionally we equipped our system with the ability to filter and smooth the signal to balance fluctuations, as well as the ability to detect saccades in the movements of the eye and calculate its parameters in an acceptable error range. Therefore, in addition to surroundings validation and signal smoothing, the saccade detection algorithms are oriented towards a lower sampling rate, with assumption that some of the information may be lost between consecutive frames.

Our general purpose was to create a system that would be able to show the differences in saccade parameters between different groups of disease severity of ND. Here we wanted to use the data and experience from previous studies, where we managed to successfully classify PD patients, healthy controls or people in different ages, based on results of their oculometric results.

2 Methods

2.1 The Conduction of Oculometric Tests

We have created a pipeline for real-time oculometric tests, which can be used in both, web browser-server solutions and in local implementations of desktop applications. Our idea was to enable all variants of measurements by using the computer of the examined person. We tested this solution for the capabilities with the RS. Our pipeline is based on a video stream from a web camera, and can be hosted in any application written in Python. The pipeline asynchronously processes images from the camera and for each video frame returning various information including position of the subject face, head position angles, position of the eyes center and current gaze direction. In addition, for each frame, information on the level of lighting is returned with a warning if it is not sufficient. Additionally, during calibration, the signal noise level is checked, which can be caused by various factors and which can also significantly affect the readings of eye movements and other parameters. The pipeline also enables the detection and calculation of saccade parameters in 2 modes: real-time and post-processing. In the real-time mode, the current coordinates are buffered to a window whose size can be set depending on the desired calculation delay and the expected length of the saccade (depending on the distance between the fixation-point and the target). This mode can be useful for trial evaluation of patient saccades, calibration, or setting the distance between markers. In the post-process mode the entire record is subjected to the estimation of the components and the calculation of their parameters, which is usually more practical in the context of the analysis of the patient's results.

In current application, each test starts from head positioning when application shows a stream from a web camera with applied facial landmarks overlaid on the face and information for correction of head adjustments. In this regard, two parameters are calculated:

1. The distance between a head and the camera based on the distance between both eyes
2. The perpendicular head position determined by landmarks positions in the y-axis of the face bounding box.

The optimal distance from the camera was determined experimentally to be between 55 and 80 cm and. It allows the subject to sit close enough to be able to control the computer and not too far as an image of a face must be large enough. Then the next step was the calibration. We decided on a very basic 3-point calibration, because we found out during previous experiments that calibration is a problematic process especially for PD patients. On the other hand, we don't need to cast the entire screen in the physical space as the only purpose is to find fixation and the peripheral targets necessary for saccade stimulations. The Fig. 1 shows subject during calibration process (A) and the calibration schema (B).

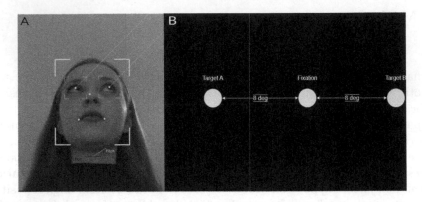

Fig. 1. Subject during calibration process (A) and the calibration process schema (B).

As mentioned before we used calibration to evaluate the noise of the signal and its frequency - thus its quality. The external factors such as insufficient lighting, reflections on the subject's glasses or poor concentration on stimulus can lead to low quality of the registration. We decided to use 2 parameters for noise level measurement: Signal to Noise Ratio (SNR) showing a relationship between means and statistical deviation (SD) in the signal and Periodogram of a signal as parameters, supporting judgment of signal noise level. During previous experiments, we established threshold values for acceptable noise level to be $\leq$ 3.5 for SNR and $\geq$ 0.02 average from the Periodogram with small tolerance for signals slightly different from both thresholds. Additionally we set frequency level to be >23 FPS (ideally 30 FPS, as stated in [9]) as in the course of our experimental work, we found that lower frequencies due to the increasing temporal sample error make impossible to calculate i.e. the saccade latency value within the acceptable error range, which is described in the next part of this text. The lightning condition is determined by calculating dominant color in a gray-scale image from the webcam with k-means clustering. We have experimentally determined that the average value obtained from the RGB of the dominant color indicating acceptable lightning conditions cannot be lower than 90. The complete schema of quality estimation process is presented in Fig. 2.

After successful calibration and checking the quality of the signal, the actual oculometric test is performed. Application displays the green ellipse in different locations dependently for fixation and peripheral targets. The fixation point shows up on the screen in a random interval between 1000 and 2000 ms, then

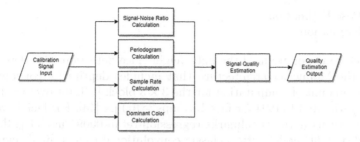

Fig. 2. Schema of a quality estimation process.

disappears in the same moment as the peripheral target appears on the left or right side of the fixation point in the same random time range. We set up the distance between fixation and peripheral markers for ∼8° (fast, regular saccade). This sequence was conducted 10x during the whole test.

We used this "step model" of the measurement ($\Delta t = 0$) as the one in which differences in latency values between healthy controls and PD are the greatest, assuming that it would strengthen the differences between PD and healthy subjects. Prolonged latency in PD is related to both motor and cognitive impairment of the brain, but mostly related to bradykinesia [10] and is the main property differentiating saccades between healthy people and people suffering from the ND.

2.2   Pipeline Estimations and Calculations

We used modern approach of the inference provided by frameworks like Intel OpenVINO™ [11], an open-source toolkit for optimizing and boosting deep learning performance in computer vision [11]. In this approach Deep Learning models are deconstructed into hyper recursive functions (graphs) which allows to obtain results of neural network estimations with almost no delay for light architecture models like Single Shot Detector (SSD). We also took advantage from Intel OpenVINO™ API and used asynchronous pipeline for parallel processing of the image frames. In this type of pipeline, images are received via an asynchronous queue, from where they are retrieved for processing by a parallel thread events, which allows for processing several frames at one time without blocking the main thread by waiting for synchronous results. We also used the OpenCV [12], the open-source library for image manipulations, for operations in image preprocessing (resizing, transpositions and reshaping into neural model input). For webcam video classifications and gaze predictions we used the pre-trained models [13] delivered with the Intel's OpenVINO™ Toolkit framework [11]. In order to estimate the gaze position, in our pipeline we connected 4 pre-trained models, thus our estimation process consists of following 4 steps:

1. Face detection.
2. Facial Landmarks Estimation

3. Head Pose Estimation
4. Gaze Estimation

For face detection we used the lightweight "face-detection-adas-0001" model, based on the MobileNet architecture that includes depth-wise convolutions to reduce the amount of computation for the 3×3 block [14]. Its Average Precision (AP) was estimated to 0.94 for face bitmaps ≥ 100 px [14]. For facial landmarks estimation we used the "landmarks-regression-retail-0009" model [14]. This is a very lightweight model with a classic convolutional design, final regression is done by the global depthwise pooling head and fully connected layers with Mean Normed Error of 0.07 [14]. The model predicts only five facial landmarks: two eyes, nose, and two lip corners, which is enough for estimating eye's bounding box coordinates. For head pose estimation we used the "head-pose-estimation-adas-0001" model [14], an estimation network based on simple, CNN architecture with angle regression layers as convolutions, ReLU, batch normalization, fully connected with one output that represents value in Tait-Bryan angles (used to describe a general rotation in three-dimensional Euclidean space) with accuracy of: yaw 5.4 ± 4.4, pitch 5.5 ± 5.3 and roll 4.6 ± 5.6 [14]. For gaze estimation we used the "gaze-estimation-adas-0002" model, a custom VGG-like CNN for gaze direction estimation, which takes left and right eye images and head pose as an input [14]. It outputs a gaze directions prediction as 3-D vector in a Cartesian coordinate system in which the z-axis is directed from the mid-point between left and right eyes' centers to the camera center with Mean Absolute Error of 6.95 ± 3.58 of angle in degrees [14].

The full gaze estimation process starts from the classification of the Face Estimation model and if a face is detected, the image processing continues in the pipeline. In current approach we took into account only the largest face bounding box, assuming that the face located closest to the screen is the examined subject. The image of the detected face is processed by the Facial Landmarks model to estimate positions of the eye sub-images. Simultaneously, the detected face image is processed by the Head Pose model to estimate Tait-Bryan angles of the head position. Results from both classifiers including the head "roll" angle are transferred to the model estimating gaze vectors. Finally, the gaze X,Y coordinates are calculated on the basis of the gaze vectors and the "roll" angle using trigonometric functions. Next we smoothed the signal using the low-pass butterworth 2nd order filter method implemented in the Scipy library with the cutoff=3.5 [15]. Smoothing was performed by omitting the data containing saccade peaks, pre-detected on the raw data. We just wanted to smooth out fragments of the signal from raw eye fluctuations without changing the shapes of the saccade amplitudes.

For saccade estimations we implemented an incremental rolling method that estimates the execution of the saccades in time series of gaze coordinates basing on stabilization, dispersion and changes in the amplitude. Algorithm first calculates eye fluctuation in the fixation state in the control window, which is set to around 300 ms experimentally by analyzing the registrations. The mean shift of the eye is then calculated from the difference in the x-axis coordinates of the control window. The start of the saccade search window is calculated from the moment when the peripheral target appears with the period of the possible minimal saccade latency assumed as 40 ms. From this starting point, the window end is set to around 500 ms, which covers the maximum saccade length for ~8°. Then the window is searched for a movement of at least 50 ms (possible minimal duration for longer saccade) in the direction of the target direction. We assumed that if shift point between frames is greater than the mean shift in the control window (fixation state) and if the shift between the first and last frame of this sequence is ≥30% of the distance between fixation and the peripheral target, the sequence meets our conditions and first frame can be set as the starting point of the saccade. We assumed the minimal saccade duration of 50 ms. After this interval algorithm looks for minimal inhibition of the eye movement and the frame in which shift relative to the previous will be <30% is considered as the saccade end point. If no starting or ending point was found during those sequences, we treated a trail as a failed or without saccade registration. For each detected saccade, we calculated its Latency, Duration, Amplitude, Average and Maximum Velocity and Gain (the ratio of saccade amplitude and fixation-target distance). Simplified schema of the process is presented in Fig. 3.

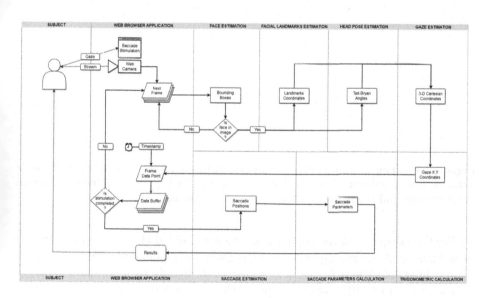

Fig. 3. Schema of a saccade estimation process.

3   Results

We compared the detection results of the implemented system with results obtained from infrared consumer-grade eye-tracker The Eye Tribe ETI1000 60 Hz [16] also used in our previous experiments [17,18]. For this purpose, we simultaneously registered saccadic tests with our pipeline using the webcam placed on top of the monitor and the ET placed on its bottom. The web camera used for this experiment was the Logitech C922 Pro Stream in Full HD and 30 Hz mode and the ET was running in 60 Hz mode. We conducted the experiment in non-perfect lighting conditions, simulating non-laboratory environment. We obtained a recording from The Eye Tribe with actual frequency of 43 Hz, and from the webcam with frequency of 24 Hz.

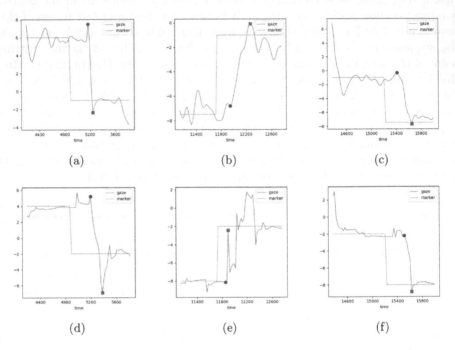

Fig. 4. The examples of horizontal 8°RS registrations from our pipeline with 30 Hz webcam (a,b,c) and from The Eye Tribe ETI1000 60 Hz (d,e,f). The blue circle marks the beginning and the red square marks the end of the RS.

For the adequacy of the comparison, we first unified the time series between recordings, next, we resampled recordings from our pipeline to 43 Hz with band-limited interpolation [19]. We also scaled both signals to a common range of values from −10 to 10°, corresponding with an appropriate margin to distances between both peripheral targets. Then we used both signals as an input for our saccade detection and parameters calculations algorithms. Figure 4 presents the example of these recordings obtained simultaneously from The Eye Tribe and our pipeline. In this example the subject was a middle-aged man.

From these graphs we can see that the signal from our system shows a smaller number of artifacts. We also detected a greater number of saccades (all 20 attempts were found). In case of saccade parameters, the mean latency obtained from the The Eye Tribe was 255.75 ± 60.74 and from our pipeline 245 ± 44.24 (∼10 ms, p value = 0.20). Statistically insignificant differences was also found for mean gain (The Eye Tribe = 1.04 ± 0.14, our pipeline = 1.15 ± 0.20, p value = 0.09) and for mean average velocity (The Eye Tribe = 70 deg/s $\pm$ 36, our pipeline = 59 deg/s $\pm$ 23, p value = 11.35).

As we see, for these parameters we have obtained confirmation of no significant differences between our pipeline and standard infrared eye-tracker with 2x higher frequency, unlike to the maximum velocity (approx. 71 ms difference, p value ≤ 0.05) which seems to be more sensitive to frequency changes in terms of the error rate, due to the temporal sampling error. Additionally, we also compared our results with laboratory measurements for horizontal $8°RS$ tested with 28 subjects done by using infrared eye tracker, The Eyelink 1000 Plus with frequency of 1000 Hz and published in [20] (table "Descriptive and reproducibility results of the pro-saccadic task", first measurements). For our comparison data, the group was 8 people, in range of 23–45 years old and different gender (158 RS samples). The average age of the subjects in both examples was 40–41. Our goal was to gather data from sample equipment and external conditions for the study, rather than to create a large population of diverse individuals.

The comparison brought satisfactory results. In case of latency from our pipeline we obtained the mean of 192 ms $\pm$ 45, while in the reference data mean was 176 ± 21 and even these results are statistically significant (p value $\leq$ 0.05) the nominal difference between results was only 16 ms. In case of mean gain it was 1.12 ± 0.18, while in the reference data it was 0.98 ± 0.05 [20], however in case of both types of velocity parameters we received differences between the reference data around 200 ms, far beyond the acceptable range, which confirms the impossibility of obtaining reliable results for these parameters in the case of lower frequencies. This inability comes directly from the bell-shaped characteristics of the velocity in ballistic type of movements, where the velocity increases and decreases linearly. In this characteristic the lower the sampling rate, the more information is lost about changes in velocity occurring between sampling points, so when eye increases velocity after the first sampling point (n) it results in change not being observed until another sample (n+1) [21]. The bar charts on Fig. 5 presents statistical comparison for both acceptable results of latency and gain as well as for maximum velocity.

4   Discussions

Anderson et al. showed that one-point measures (which include RS) at low frequencies are burdened with a temporal sampling error derived from the fact that data for calculations are collected at a certain, finite frequency [21]. If frequency is lower than 1000 Hz speed or direction are not registered between two consecutive measurements (n, n+1) and this error can affects also calculations of latency or duration. The size of the sampling error determines the difference between the time of the actual event (i.e. start of the saccade) and the time when the system actually registers the event occurrence. It makes actual oculomotor events uniformly distributed between sampling data points and the expected mean of the

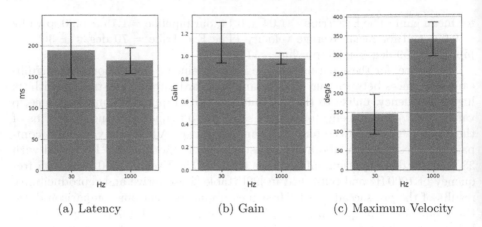

(a) Latency   (b) Gain   (c) Maximum Velocity

Fig. 5. The comparison of horizontal 8°RS between 30 Hz registrations from our pipeline and 1000 Hz from the laboratory reference statistics [20]

sampling error i.e. at 50 Hz is 10 ms (1 ms error is the maximal one-point temporal sampling at 1000 Hz Hz, increasing as the sampling frequency decreases) [21].

However, temporal sampling error has a different effect on different parameters, also depending on the type of the research. For example, for saccades smaller than 10° and the velocity parameters, sampling frequency should be >300 Hz to calculate it accurately [21]. But in the case of the latency (most important parameter for ND estimations) and in context of our research on ∼8°'fast regular' [22] saccades registered at 30 Hz the difference in the result compared to the reference data of 1000 Hz [20] was only 16 ms (20% of latency range 120–200 ms of healthy person). We expected this output because on average the sampling error will be in the middle of the sample interval, thus : $(1000/30)/2 = 16.6$ [21]. Interestingly, the outputs obtained from the ET showed similar difference between 10–20 ms and basing on results of those two experiments, we concluded the mean latency error to be inside this range. Such an error for analysis on difference between healthy subjects and PD patients has an marginal importance. Our previous studies on RS task with the 1000 Hz eye-tracker, patients with PD showed latency ranges of (260.0, Inf) and (308.5, Inf) varying for specific disease stages [18,23]. The healthy subjects for the same task show upper latency limit at around 190–200 ms [22]. In the context of such large differences, sampling error of 10–20 ms is unlikely to substantially affect the results of an overall data classifications.

We think that it is important to understand whether obtained sampling error magnitude brings problem in adequate scale to the research results. In case of this research, we assumed that our pipeline due to the limitations of consumer-grade equipment, will never compete in accuracy with laboratory equipment. However, it can provide reliable results for screening test that could allow specialist in specific cases to determine whether a more thorough examination is needed, this time by using professional equipment such as a 1000 Hz eye-tracker in the laboratory conditions.

5   Conclusions

We propose to use web cameras and oculometric pipelines, such as the one presented in this text, where high frequency is not required and approximate results are sufficient to make assumptions. Using latency as an example we showed that inaccuracy of calculations in low frequencies like 30 Hz can be estimated at approx. 10–20 ms which gives minimal error rate in oculometric classifications of PD. If this rate is acceptable for your type of research, such machine learning solution based on neural networks and supporting algorithms can open possibilities to conduct tests without the need for expensive laboratory equipment.

Acknowledgements. Software frameworks and libraries: OpenVino, Tensorflow, OpenCV, SciPy, Numpy, Pandas, contributed to the development of the software methods presented in this article.

Declaration of Competing Interest. The authors declare no conflict of interests.

References

1. Semmelmann, K., Weigelt, S.: Online webcam-based eye tracking in cognitive science: a first look. Behav. Res. Meth. **50**, 06 (2017)
2. Lin, Y.-T., Lin, R.-Y., Lin, Y.-C., Lee, G.C.: Real-time eye-gaze estimation using a low-resolution webcam. Multimedia Tools Appl. **65**, 543–568 (2012)
3. Meng, C., Zhao, X.: Webcam-based eye movement analysis using CNN. IEEE Access **5**, 19581–19587 (2017)
4. Aljaafreh, A., Alaqtash, M., Al-Oudat, N., Abukhait, J., Saleh, M.E.: A low-cost webcam-based eye tracker and saccade measurement system. **14** (2020)
5. Śledzianowski, A., Szymanski, A., Drabik, A., Szlufik, S., Koziorowski, D.M., Przybyszewski, A.W.: Combining Results of different oculometric tests improved prediction of Parkinson's disease development. In: Nguyen, N.T., Jearanaitanakij, K., Selamat, A., Trawiński, B., Chittayasothorn, S. (eds.) ACIIDS 2020. LNCS (LNAI), vol. 12034, pp. 517–526. Springer, Cham (2020). https://doi.org/10.1007/978-3-030-42058-1_43
6. Sledzianowski, A., Szymanski, A., Drabik, A., Szlufik, S., Koziorowski, D.M., Przybyszewski, A.W.: Measurements of antisaccades parameters can improve the prediction of Parkinson's disease progression. In: Nguyen, N.T., Gaol, F.L., Hong, T.-P., Trawiński, B. (eds.) ACIIDS 2019. LNCS (LNAI), vol. 11432, pp. 602–614. Springer, Cham (2019). https://doi.org/10.1007/978-3-030-14802-7_52
7. Śledzianowski, A., Szymański, A., Szlufik, S., Koziorowski, D.: Rough set data mining algorithms and pursuit eye movement measurements help to predict symptom development in Parkinson's disease. In: Nguyen, N.T., Hoang, D.H., Hong, T.-P., Pham, H., Trawiński, B. (eds.) ACIIDS 2018. LNCS (LNAI), vol. 10752, pp. 428–435. Springer, Cham (2018). https://doi.org/10.1007/978-3-319-75420-8_41

8. Przybyszewski, A.W., Szlufik, S., Dutkiewicz, J., Habela, P., Koziorowski, D.M.: Machine learning on the video basis of slow pursuit eye movements can predict symptom development in Parkinson's patients. In: Nguyen, N.T., Trawiński, B., Kosala, R. (eds.) ACIIDS 2015. LNCS (LNAI), vol. 9012, pp. 268–276. Springer, Cham (2015). https://doi.org/10.1007/978-3-319-15705-4_26

9. Naruniec, J., et al.: Webcam-based system for video-oculography. IET Comput. Vis. **11**(2), 173–180 (2017)

10. MacAskill, M.R., et al.: The influence of motor and cognitive impairment upon visually-guided saccades in Parkinson's disease. Neuropsychologia **50**(14), 3338–3347 (2012)

11. Intel®. Intel® distribution of openvino™ toolkit (2022)

12. Bradski, G.: The OpenCV library. Dr. Dobb's Journal of Software Tools (2000)

13. Intel®. Openvino™ toolkit - open model zoo repository, intel's pre-trained models (2022). https://github.com/openvinotoolkit/open_model_zoo

14. Intel®. Openvino™ toolkit - open model zoo repository (2022)

15. Fundamental Algorithms for Scientific Computing in Python: SciPy 1.0 Contributors. SciPy 1.0. Nat. Meth. **17**, 261–272 (2020)

16. The EyeTribe. The EyeTribe documentation and API reference (2022). https://github.com/eyetribe/documentation

17. Sledzianowski, A.: Predictions of age and mood based on changes in saccades parameters. In: Gruca, A., Czachórski, T., Deorowicz, S., Harężlak, K., Piotrowska, A. (eds.) ICMMI 2019. AISC, vol. 1061, pp. 196–205. Springer, Cham (2020). https://doi.org/10.1007/978-3-030-31964-9_19

18. Szymański, A., Szlufik, S., Koziorowski, D.M., Przybyszewski, A.W.: Building classifiers for Parkinson's disease using new eye tribe tracking method. In: Nguyen, N.T., Tojo, S., Nguyen, L.M., Trawiński, B. (eds.) ACIIDS 2017. LNCS (LNAI), vol. 10192, pp. 351–358. Springer, Cham (2017). https://doi.org/10.1007/978-3-319-54430-4_34

19. Smith, J.O.: Digital audio resampling home page (2002). https://ccrma.stanford.edu/~jos/resample/

20. Nij Bijvank, J., et al.: A standardized protocol for quantification of saccadic eye movements: Demons. PLOS ONE **13**, e0200695 (2018)

21. Andersson, R., Nyström, M., Holmqvist, K.: Sampling frequency and eye-tracking measures: how speed affects durations, latencies, and more. J. Eye Mov. Res. **3**, 1–12 (2010)

22. Ramsperger, E., Fischer, B.: Human express saccades: extremely short reaction times of goal directed eye movements. Exp. Brain Res. **57**(1), 191–5 (1984)

23. Przybyszewski, A.W., Kon, M., Szlufik, S., Szymański, A., Habela, P., Koziorowski, D.: Multimodal learning and intelligent prediction of symptom development in individual Parkinson's patients. Sensors **16**, 1498 (2016)

Elitism-Based Genetic Algorithm Hyper-heuristic for Solving Real-Life Surgical Scheduling Problem

Masri Ayob and Dewan Mahmuda Zaman[✉]

Center for Artificial Intelligent (CAIT), Faculty of Information Science and Technology,
Universiti Kebangsaan Malaysia, Bangi, Selangor, Malaysia
masri@ukm.edu.my, mahmudazaman0509@gmail.com

Abstract. Hyper-heuristic was designed to automate the development of computational search methodologies. Although it has effectively handled a variety of optimisation problems, the surgical scheduling problem (SSP) has not yet been solved by hyper-heuristic. Therefore, we aim to investigate the effectiveness of applying hyper-heuristics to solve a real-world SSP at Hospital Canselor Tuanku Muhriz UKM (HCTM), one of Malaysia's largest public hospitals. We dealt with daily SSP for block scheduling strategy. The daily SSP arranges the sequence of surgical cases in each operating room (OR) for each day, considering the material and human resource availability. In this work, we aim to maximise the number of surgeries and OR utilisation for a given time horizon while solving SSP. In hyper-heuristic, high-level strategy is heuristic selection mechanism where we applied elitism-based genetic algorithm (E-GAHH). Low level heuristics are problem-specific heuristics where we applied simple move operators. Experimental result demonstrate that E-GAHH approach can provide a more practical and effective schedule with more OR utilisation than HCTM's solution and traditional genetic algorithm hyper-heuristic (GAHH) approach.

Keywords: Hyper-heuristic · genetic algorithm hyper-heuristic · elitism · surgical scheduling problem · block-scheduling

1 Introduction

Optimisation problem concerns finding the best or optimal solution within all feasible solutions that can maximise or minimise objectives such as minimising the cost or maximising the efficiency [1]. Real optimisation problems are challenging to solve, and several techniques have been developed to address various optimisation problems. Although meta-heuristics can find the optimal solution within an acceptable timeframe, it provides good results only on specific problem instances because these approaches strongly depend on domain-specific knowledge [2]. So, these approaches cannot be directly applied to other optimisation problems because they are able to obtain high quality results for just a few problem instances [3]. Hyper-heuristics are designed in order to get over the limitations of meta-heuristics and to have a reusable and effective technique that can combine the power of several heuristics into a single framework [2].

© The Author(s), under exclusive license to Springer Nature Switzerland AG 2023
N. T. Nguyen et al. (Eds.): ACIIDS 2023, CCIS 1863, pp. 510–523, 2023.
https://doi.org/10.1007/978-3-031-42430-4_42

Hyper-heuristic framework consists of two levels, which are high level heuristic and low-level heuristic. The decision of which low-level heuristic to use and whether to accept it is made by a high-level, problem-independent heuristic. Low-level heuristics, on the other hand, are a collection of problem-specific heuristics that vary from problem to problem [4]. Single-solution based methods are ineffective when the search space is large and severely confined, however the majority of hyper-heuristic research have a single solution based approach [5]. Therefore, in this study, we focused on the multi-point perturbative heuristic selection, more precisely, automatic heuristic sequencing, which is a genetic algorithm hyper-heuristic (GAHH). In GAHH, it is possible to destroy an individual's chromosome after performing genetic procedures. To solve this problem, we implemented an elite retention strategy, which involves retaining the top individuals across each iteration. After assessing the individuals, GAHH updates the solution. As a result, we identified elite individuals for the updated solution in the suggested elitism-based genetic algorithm hyper-heuristic (E-GAHH) after analysing the population of each generation. Hyper-heuristic has been successfully applied in solving many combinatorial optimisation problems such as nurse rostering problems [2], educational timetabling [6, 7], trainer scheduling problem [8], traveling salesman problems [9] and vehicle routing problems [10]. Nevertheless, it has not yet been applied to address the issue of surgical scheduling (SSP). SSP is a combinatorial optimisation problem that seeks to specify the amount of time and space required by the resources at hand to carry out a series of operations over the course of a day or a week [11]. SSP involves a wide range of parties, including patients, surgeons, and operating rooms (OR). More than 60% of hospital admissions are for surgical procedures, therefore the OR's high output rate is crucial for improving the hospital's services [12].

In this study, we address real-world SSP at one of Malaysia's largest public hospitals, Hospital Canselor Tuanku Muhriz UKM (HCTM). Despite the fact that the HCTM admits a large number of patients each day for surgery, each surgeon team creates the daily surgical schedule by hand. The block scheduling method used by HCTM designates each OR to a different speciality for each day. Pre-surgery, surgery, and post-surgery are the three stages of surgery included in SSP. Various human and material resources were needed for each level. In addition to integrating three operation stages for block scheduling, real-world HCTM constraints are taken into account when solving SSP. Block scheduling considerations with regard to all stages have not yet been disclosed. Thus, in this study, elitism-based GAHH is used to address and optimise a real-world SSP. This work is organised as follows. A survey of related literature on hyper-heuristics and SSP is presented in Sect. 2. The problem description is described in Sect. 3. The approach is then presented in Sect. 4. Section 5 describes the findings and discussion. The perspectives of future research are finally summarised in Sect. 6 as the conclusion.

2 Related Works

2.1 Hyper-heuristics

The nature of the hyper-heuristic search space is classified into two types which are heuristic selection and heuristic generation [2]. The aim of the hyper-heuristic selection framework is to intelligently choose a low-level heuristic and apply it at that decision point. Heuristic generation focuses on generating new heuristics from components of existing heuristics [2]. The performance of an individual heuristic differs from one instance to another and depends on the current stage of solving process. So, it is difficult to determine which heuristic is performing best. The automatic heuristic selection process can overcome this issue. It can help the search process in achieving reasonable quality solutions that can outperform a single heuristic. Both of selection and generation hyper-heuristic can be classified into constructive and perturbative heuristic. This study focused on perturbative heuristic. The main goal of perturbative based hyper-heuristics is to improve the given solution via the selection and application of a set of perturbative low-level heuristics.

Many works reported on hyper-heuristics which are based on metaheuristic approaches auch as [8, 17, 32] etc. The study in [8] applied GAHH for solving a trainer scheduling problem where each individual in the population provides a sequence of integer values and each one represents one low-level heuristic. The GAHH achieved significantly better results than each low-level heuristic applied separately. This hyper-heuristic approach is extended by [17] using an adaptive chromosome length. This hyper-heuristic also outperformed individual low-level heuristics and got better results on the trainer scheduling problem than a standard GA. The study in [17] proposed a guided GAHH to make the dynamic removal and insertion of heuristics and evolve sequences of heuristics in order to produce promising solutions more effectively. GAHH also applied in the study [7], and demonstrated a reasonable performance in solving strip packing problems.

During the search process, GAHH used different types of operators and these operators are named selection, crossover and mutation. The majority of investigations on GAHH that have been published so far only used conventional GA selection operators. For example, GAHH is used in conjunction with a roulette wheel selection to maximise the probability of choosing an individual with low height values [7]. In [8], only elite chromosomes are chosen to address the trainer scheduling issue. They combined the four crossover and four mutation operators to create a sequence of low-level heuristics to solve the job shop scheduling problems [18] by GAHH. For selection operators in GA, they employed the roulette wheel selection. Additionally, it is evident that elitism improves the optimisation process [19]. Elitism is an operational characteristic of GA. It is a strategy that enables individuals to naturally evolve in almost all generations and continuously improve the entire population's quality [20]. Thus, in this study, we integrated elitism with GAHH.

2.2 Surgical Scheduling Problem

The surgical case planning and scheduling problem is a vast area to explore and it is one of the costly functional fields of the hospital worldwide. Several studies tackled this problem with different perspectives such as different solution approaches, decision levels, mathematical models, efficiency of the technique and scheduling strategies. The SSP is a complex problem to solve because it involves many resources and stages. This problem can be classified into three levels: strategic level which is long term planning, tactical level which is medium term planning and operational level which is short-term. In this work, we focus on operational level scheduling for elective scheduling.Furthermore, scheduling approaches can be divided into three categories: block, modified block, and open strategies. Block scheduling refers to the pre-allocation of each operating room to a specific specialty with various operation groups, such as surgeons [15]. Block scheduling is utilised more commonly in many hospitals since it is less complicated to use than the open technique [15]. However, only a small number of research have focused on block scheduling method, whereas the majority have focused on open scheduling approach. Although considering all the stages is important to obtain a good schedule, most of the work reported did not considered all the stages for block scheduling. This study integrates all stages and resources on block scheduling strategy while integrating real-life constraints.

Heuristics and meta-heuristic algorithms are commonly developed to deal with the complexity of operating room scheduling challenges such as constructive heuristics [21], improvement heuristics [22], metaheuristics [23], linear-programming based heuristics [24]. A bi-objective mathematical model is presented for block scheduling in [25] for elective patient surgery planning and scheduling while two stages are considered. However, in this study, no-waiting constraint was not tackled. Which indicates that the patient should wait in the OR unless any post-operative care unit (PACU) bed is available. In the proposed approach, we integrated no-waiting constraint so that the patient can be immediately transferred from OR after surgery and made available for the next patient.

The study [26] focused on bicriteria elective SSP, which involves planning elective procedures for a day, an operating room, and a starting time within a weekly planning horizon with the goal of boosting the OR occupancy and number of scheduled surgeries. They construct the initial solution with the integration of patient priority, OR, and surgeon availability, but they don't consider other stages of surgery or other required resources. The study [27] covered all three stages as well as resource availability, although the constraints were not the same as this study. Therefore, different from previous studies, this study attempts to take into account real-life constraints, three stages for block scheduling strategy and optimise SSP to obtain good solutions by GAHH.

3 Problem Description

3.1 Suegical Scheduling Flow

At HCTM, a surgery must go through three stages: pre-surgery, surgery and post-surgery stages. Different human and material resources are required in each stage. The patient is called from the ward 30 min before the surgery time for pre-surgery stage to be prepared for the surgery. When both the OR and the patient are ready, the patient is moved to that specific OR based on sub-specialty, surgeon and availability of other resoueces. Then the patient is transferred to the recovery stage or PACU after the surgery is done. Below is a description of each stage:

Pre-surgery Stage: This is the initial stage of the surgery scheduling process. Nurses and PHU beds are essential resources for this stage. The properties of this stage for HCTM are:

- Required resources are pre operative holding unit (PHU) beds and nurses.

- Number of available PHU beds:16.
- Pre-surgery duration is 30 min.
- This stage is required for all patients.
- Nurses are always available in pre-surgery stage.

Surgery Stage: This stage starts after the pre-surgery stage and at this stage surgeries are performed. For this stage, several material and human resources are required. The properties for this stage of HCTM are:

- Number of OR for elective patients: 14 and 26 types of sub-specialty.
- Some surgery duration provided in booking data and some are obtained from historical data.
- Cleaning time duration is 10 minutes to clean OR after surgery.
- This stage is required for all patients.
- Patients are assigned to OR based on sub-specialty and availability of human resources and material resources.
- Surgery teams (surgeon, nurses, anesthetists) are available all day long.
- Major surgeries are performed by the specific surgeon who booked the surgery.
- If the surgery is not booked by any specific surgeron then major surgeries are performed by senior surgeon and minor surgeries are performed by junior surgeon of same sub-specialty.
- Some ORs are open for 7 h and some are open for 10 h based on the hospital's schedule.
- 5 working days (Monday-Friday) in each week.

Post-surgery Stage: After surgery, patients go to the recovery stage where resources involved are the post-surgery beds or PACU beds. If the patient requirs PACU bed, then the patient is moved to PACU. Otherwise the patient is moved to post-operative bed. The properties for this stage of HCTM are:

- Number of available post-operative beds: 12 and PACU beds: 4.
- PACU is not required for all patients. PACU requirement depends on patient's age, surgery duration and surgery type (major/minor).
- Patients who don't need a PACU are moved to a post-operative bed.
- Post-surgery duration is 30 min.
- PACU duration varies between 6–24 h depending on patient's condition.
- Nurses are always available in post-surgery stage.

    Since currently, the HCTM employs a block scheduling method, patients are assigned to an OR based on sub-specialty for elective patients. Depending on the day of the week, ORs are open for 7 or 10 h. At HCTM, each surgeon has a fixed day to operate for surgery, such as on Monday, OR-1 will be dedicated only for vascular type patients and surgeons required for vascular surgery are available for that day. Some sub-specialty allocation is also based on week-ID, for example, OR-10 is exclusively assigned to orthopedics during weeks 2 and 4.

Constraints: To generate a feasible solution, several hard constraints (HC) are followed mentioned in Table 1.

Table 1. Hard Constraints for solving SSP in this study

HC	Description
HC1	Every surgery must be assigned to one and only one spot in available material resources for each stage based on requirements
HC2	Every surgery must be assigned to the specific OR based on the surgery requirements
HC3	The operating sequence of three stages must be followed completely and in sequence without any waiting time between two consecutive stages
HC4	All resources must be available at each stage of surgery
HC5	All assigned surgeries must be done within the opening time for each operation room
HC6	Cleaning time must be assigned between each two surgeries

3.2 Multi-objective and Fitness Function

Finding solutions to an optimisation problem where more than one objective has to be minimised or maximised is known as the multi-objective optimisation problem [19]. Among several approaches to solve multi-objective problems, we choose to apply weighted sum approach in this study. The motivation behind this is the high search efficiency of the weighted sum method [28]. In this approach weights are assigned to each objective function by which a multi-objective problem turns into a single-objective problem [5]. We aim to choose the solution with maximum fitness value. The objectives are:

$$F1 = \textit{Maximise the number of surgeries} \tag{1}$$

$$F2 = \textit{Maximise OR utilization} \tag{2}$$

Let the weight value of the parameters be $\beta1$, $\beta2$, respectively, where $\sum_{j=1}^{2} \beta j = 1$ the aggregate objective function for this problem is obtained as:

$$Fitness = \beta1 * F1 + \beta2 * F2 \tag{3}$$

The decision about which objective has to be given how much importance is made before searching for the optimal solutions [5]. For this study, we considered equal weight for both objective functions which are $\beta1 = \beta2 = 0.5$.

4   Proposed Method

4.1 Select Candidate Surgery Pool

The surgical information gathered from the HCTM is used to establish a candidate pool of surgeries. Since one of the objectives for solving SSP is maximising the number of surgeries, we have to select a candidate pool from where new solutions can be generated after applying the LLHs of E-GAHH chromosomes. During the optimisation process, surgeries of initial solution can be scheduled earlier than the end time of time horizon. Thus we have to identify the candidate surgery pool from where new surgeries can be included in the schedule (Fig. 1).

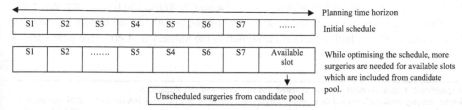

Fig. 1. The process of including new surgeries from candidate pool during optimisation process

Without this candidate surgery pool, it may possible that a surgery from end of booking list will be scheduled instead of recent surgeries. Additionally, there should be enough surgeries in the candidate surgical pool to fill the specified time horizon. To tackle this issue, we created candidate pool where we ensure to take the recent surgeries to create schedule.

Algorithm 1: Create candidate pool of surgeries
Input: Surgery list (sorted by date) with all information (MRN, surgery type, procedure, age, surgery duration, sub-specialty, required surgeon), start and end time for schedule time horizon
Output: Candidate pool of surgery list
- -
1: set *candidate_surgery_pool* ← Ø
2: group surgeries from surgery booking list based on their subspecialty
3: **For** each sub-specialty group
4:      set *total_surgery_duration* ← 0
5:      *total_available_duration* ← Calculate the available time duration for sub-specialty for the given time window
6:      **While** *total_surgery_duration* < *total_available_duration*
7:          take surgeries one by one and increase total_*surgery_duration* by each surgery duration
8:          insert the surgery into *candidate_surgery_pool*
9:      **End while**
10: **End for**
11: **Return** *candidate_surgery_pool*

4.2 Constructive Heuristic

A constructive heuristic is a form of heuristic method that starts with an empty solution and gradually expands it until a complete solution is found [29]. We used First-Come-First-Serve (FCFS) based on the booking date to construct the initial solution while following all the constraints. While solving SSP, each surgery must pass through several processes to complete the flow. When the procedure starts, multiple resources are required throughout the surgical process. In the FCFS approach, the current surgery must first be scheduled before the subsequent surgery can be scheduled. The surgery booking list consists of different sub-specialty. Since the surgery must be assigned to OR based on sub-specialty, it may happen that the current surgery sub-specialty is not available current day. So, any other surgery after current surgery cannot be assigned current day. Thus, to construct the solution, first we group surgeries from the candidate surgery list based on their sub-specialty. Then for each group, surgery is taken from the list one by one, and check if at current time all the required resources (PHU bed, OR, surgeon, anesthetists, post-operative bed, PACU bed) for that surgery are available or not. If all the necessary resources are available, then we assign resources to the current surgery. If not, then wait for the next available slot when all the resources are available and when the resources are available, these are assigned to the surgery and go to the next surgery.

Algorithm-2: Calculate total number of scheduled surgeries and OR utilisation

Input: Surgery booking list (candidate pool of surgery and sorted by date) with all information (MRN, surgery type, procedure, age, surgery duration, sub-specialty, required surgeon), number of available resources (PHU beds, ORs, PACU beds, post-op beds), surgeons with sub-specialty, surgeon type (senior/junior), start time and end time for schedule time horizon

Output: Total number of scheduled surgery planning horizon and average OR utilisation with all details

- -

```
1:  set total_scheduled_surgeries ← 0
2:  set total_or_utilisation ← 0
3:  group surgeries from surgery booking list based on their subspecialty
4:  For each group of surgeries
5:  |    set current_time ← starting time of planning horizon
6:  |    set end_time ← ending time of planning horizon
7:  |    set scheculed_surgeries ← 0
8:  |    set current_surgery ← first surgery of the sub-specialty group
9:  |    Repeat:
10: |    |    take current_surgery from the surgery list and check if all the required
         |    |    resources for the surgery are available or not :(PHU bed at current_time - pre-surgery duration),
         |    |    (OR,surgeon at current_time based on weekday, week-ID, sub-specialty and anesthetist
         |    |    requirement), (PACU/post-op bed at current_time + surgery duration)
11: |    |    If all the required resources for the surgery are available then
12: |    |    |    allocate all those selected resources for the surgery
13: |    |    |    make all resources available after that surgery is completed
14: |    |    |    increment scheculed_surgeries by 1
15: |    |    |    increment current_surgery and go to step-10
16: |    |    Else
17: |    |    |    increment the current_time and go to step-10
18: |    |    End If
19: |    Until surgery list is not empty and current_time < end_time
20: |    increment total_scheduled_surgeries by the number of scheculed_surgeries for sub-specialty group
21: |    increment total_or_utilisation by sub-specialty group or_utilisation
22: |    calculate or_utilisation for each sub-specialty group
23: End For
24: calculate avg_or_utilisation from total_or_utilisation
25: Return total_scheduled_surgeries, avg_or_utilisation
```

4.3 Elitism-Based Genetic Algorithm Hyper-Heuristic

In GAHH, each individual in GA's population consists of a sequence of integer numbers. Each number is an LLH choice which tells us which LLH must be applied, and each individual tells us in which order to apply LLHs. We designed a fixed length chromosome where each LLH repeats several times and stores some additional information such as the number of LLH, swapping positions, meta-heuristic parameters etc. In this study, E-GAHH is applied to solve a real-world SSP. Initial individuals are generated randomly where each individual represents a sequence of LLHs. After generating the population, fitness is calculated for each individual. Individual of GAHH is consist of integer numbers where each integer represents an LLH. To evaluate the individual, we must apply each LLH exists in an individual. After applying the sequence of LLH every time from chromosome, the new domain solution in compared with the current domain solution. If the new domain solution is better than the current one, then the old domain solution is replaced by the new domain solution (Algorithm-3: step 10–12).

Elitism concept is integrated to select the best individual to the next generation directly without performing operations such as crossover and mutation. Using elitism avoids the loss of the best individual after crossover and mutation operations and speeds up the Genetic Algorithm's (GA) performance. These elite solutions are selected as the population of next generation. The rest of the population of the next generation are derived from GA operators. After the chromosome evaluation, the previous domain solution is replaced by the updated domain solution. Thus, I our approach, to get the elite individuals, we identified elite individuals for the updated domain solution after evaluating the population of each generation and rest of the population of next generation derived from all of the current population.

Algorithm 3: E-GAHH (High level strategy)
Input: All the inputs of Algorithm-2 and an initial surgery schedule
Output: Optimal surgery schedule

- -

1: **Initialize parameters:** *max_generation, population_size, elitism_rate, tournament_size, crosssover_probability*
  (Pc), mutation_rate (Pm),
2: set *generation ← 0*
3: set *population ←* Generate initial population randomly where each individual represents a sequence of LLHs
4: set *ssp_solution ←* initial surgery schedule by FCFS within time horizon
5: **While** *generation < max_generation* do
6:     **For each** individual k
7:         apply LLHs in the order given in individual to the candidate surgery pool
8:         record the solution *ssp_solution$_k$* after applying LLH in candidate pool by calling Algorithm-2
9:         record the change each single gene makes to objective function
10:         If *ssp_solution$_k$ > ssp_solution*
11:             *ssp_solution = ssp_solution$_k$*
12:         **End if**
13:     **End for**
14:     *elite_individuals ←* get elite individuals from current population for the updated solution *ssp_solution*
15:     Insert *elite_individuals* into next generation's population
16:     **For** *i* from *elite_individuals* to *population_size*
17:         *first_parent, second_parent ←* perform tournament selection operation (population, tournament
          size)
18:         *child ←* perform single point crossover operation (first_parent, second_parent, Pc)
19:         *newchild ←* perform exchange mutation operation (child, Pm)
20:         **Insert** *newchild* into next generation's population
21:     **End for**
22:     **Update** current population with next generation's population
23:     *generation ← generation + 1*
24: **End while**
25: *optimal_surgery_schedule ←* find best individual and surgery schedule
26: **Return** *optimal_surgery_schedule*

The first operator in the reproduction phase of GA is selection criteria. The selection operator aims to select an individual from the population that will produce offspring for the next generation. For selecting parents, we used tournament selection. The most effective selection method is tournament selection [30]. In this strategy, a competition is held amongst a select group of individuals which are picked randomly from the overall population. The winner joins the mating pool and is selected based on fitness. This procedure is repeated until all the parents have been selected. After selecting parents, crossover operator is performed. Crossover operators are used to generate the offspring. The offspring is generated by combining the genetic information of two or more parents. We applied single point crossover in this study. A random crossover point is chosen in a single point crossover. Beyond that point, two parents' genetic information will be exchanged with one another.

Mutation is the last evolutionary operator. It altered one or multiple genes after creating children solutions. The purpose of this operator is to maintain the diversity of population. The exchange mutation operator is applied in this study which randomly selects two genes in the individual and exchanges them. The selection, crossover, and mutation operations will be repeated on current population until the new population is complete. By repeating this process, the best individual is obtained from the last generation of E-GAHH. The optimal surgery schedule is generated by applying this LLH sequence of the best individual of last generation.

4.4 Low Level Heuristics

The aim of LLH is to explore the neighborhoods of the current solution by altering the current solution. The set of LLH should enable the search over the whole search space [31]. We have designed problem-specific low-level heuristics that take the current solution and then modify the solution to provide improved solution. Since one of the objectives is to maximize the number of surgeries, we swap surgeries among candidate surgery pool and evaluate the result.

LLH-SSP-1: Two surgeries are selected randomly from same sub-specialty group or any two surgeries and swap them.

LLH-SSP-2: Two surgeries are selected randomly from the same sub-specialty group or any two surgeries sequence and reverse between these two selected surgeries.

LLH-SSP-3: Three surgeries are selected from the surgery sequence and reverse between these selected surgeries.

LLH-SSP-4: Two pairs of surgeries are selected from the surgery sequence and reverse in between them.

LLH-SSP-5: Hill-climb meta-heuristic.

5   Experimental Results

In this section we present a performance comparison between the results obtained with E-GAHH, GAHH and HCTM's generated schedule. The GAHH and E-GAHH method is implemented on real-data for year 2019 collected from HCTM. The data contains all the required information such as sub-specialty, surgery duration, surgery type, required surgeon, the requirement of PACU beds, surgery booking date etc. (Figs. 2 and 3).

We generated schedule for different planning time horizon such as schedule is generated for 7 days, 15 days and 30 days for different problem instances. Table 2 compares the surgery schedule manually created by HCTM, surgery scheduled by GAHH and surgery scheduled by elitism-based GAHH. In Table 2 we presented the number of scheduled surgeries (best) and average of 14 OR utilisation (best). The experimental results show that for all instances and for all time horizon, E-GAHH can produce better results than both GAHH and the schedule created by HCTM. In real-life at HCTM's schedule, they scheduled surgeries after the closing time of OR. However, in the comparison we ignored those surgeries. While generating the schedule, all the details related to surgery such as resources allocated for each surgery (PHU bed number, OR number, post-op bed number, PACU number, surgeon) are also created as excel format so that it can be useful at real-life.

Table 2. Comparison between the results obtained with HCTM's schedule, GAHH and E-GAHH

Insta-nces	Planning horizon	No. of Scheduled surgeries by HCTM	OR utilisat-ion by HCTM	No. of Scheduled surgeries by GAHH (Best)	Avg. OR utilisation by GAHH (Best)	No. of Scheduled surgeries by E-GAHH (Best)	Avg. OR utilisation by E-GAHH (Best)	St dev of no. of surgery for E-GAHH	St dev of Avg. OR utilisation for E-GAHH
1	7 days	181	34%	325	79%	337	81%	5.209	2.387
2	15 days	328	37%	601	78%	618	80%	5.513	1.923
3	30 days	694	40%	1215	79%	1236	83%	10.779	1.632
4	7 days	160	42%	313	78%	333	80%	12.22	1.303
5	15 days	264	33%	597	79%	615	81%	8.074	1.341
6	30 days	605	41%	1178	77%	1195	80%	9.948	3.962
7	7 days	172	45%	331	80%	345	83%	6.22	1.224
8	15 days	354	49%	612	77%	623	78%	9.939	1.169
9	30 days	721	50%	1288	78%	1304	82%	8.074	1.112
10	7 days	198	55%	327	77%	349	81%	10.908	1.224
11	15 days	293	34%	664	78%	687	80%	11.205	2.097
12	30 days	580	37%	1137	71%	1166	75%	11.773	2.115
13	7 days	65	10%	316	81%	331	84%	7.765	0.899
14	15 days	135	10%	687	77%	701	80%	8.421	1.14
15	30 days	465	29%	1282	74%	1309	77%	13.152	1.366

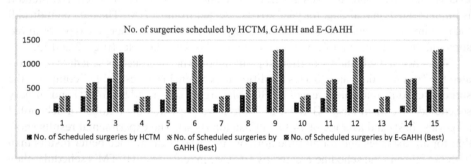

Fig. 2. Comparison of no. of surgeries scheduled by HCTM, GAHH and E-GAHH

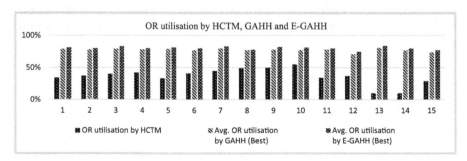

Fig. 3. Comparison of OR utilisation by HCTM, GAHH and E-GAHH

6 Conclusion

This study tackled a real world multi-objective SSP that is not been solved yet by hyper-heuristic. We applied E-GAHH that provides the schedule. We tested our approach for different problem instances collected from HCTM and the results shows that our approach can generate optimal schedule better than the current HCTM generated schedule. The future work will focus on the parameter control of E-GAHH parameters and work with the weight of the objectives for solving SSP. Moreover, the components of E-GAHH needs further improvements to obtain more optimised results as well as need to work with more LLHs. In addition, the generality of this approach is yet to test for different problem domain. Thus, we will extend our approach by tackling all these issues while testing with different problem domains and compare with existing methods.

Acknowledgments. The authors wish to thank the Universiti Kebangsaan Malaysia and the Ministry of Higher Education Malaysia for supporting and funding this work (grant ID: TRGS/1/2019/UKM/01/4/1).

References

1. Sanchez, M., et al.: A systematic review of hyper-heuristics on combinatorial optimization problems. IEEE Access **8**, 128068–128095 (2020). https://doi.org/10.1109/ACCESS.2020.3009318
2. Burke, E.K., Kendall, G., Soubeiga, E.: A tabu-search hyperheuristic for timetabling and rostering. J. Heuristics **9**, 451–470 (2003)
3. Burke, E.K., et al.: Hyper-heuristics: a survey of the state of the art. J. Oper. Res. Soc. **64**, 1695–1724 (2013). https://doi.org/10.1057/jors.2013.71
4. Sabar, N.R., et al.: A dynamic multi-armed bandit-gene expression programming hyper-heuristic for combinatorial optimization problems (2014)
5. Turky, A., Sabar, N.R., Dunstall, S., Song, A.: Hyper-heuristic local search for combinatorial optimisation problems. Knowl.-Based Syst. **205**, 106264 (2020)
6. Raghavjee, R., Pillay, N.: A genetic algorithm selection perturbative hyper-heuristic for solving the school timetabling problem. ORiON **31**, 39 (2015)
7. Garrido, P., Riff, M.-C.: An evolutionary hyperheuristic to solve strip-packing problems. In: Yin, H., Tino, P., Corchado, E., Byrne, W., Yao, X. (eds.) IDEAL 2007. LNCS, vol. 4881, pp. 406–415. Springer, Heidelberg (2007). https://doi.org/10.1007/978-3-540-77226-2_42
8. Cowling, P., Kendall, G., Han, L.: An investigation of a hyperheuristic genetic algorithm applied to a trainer scheduling problem. In: Proceedings of the 2002 Congress on Evolutionary Computation, CEC 2002, vol. 2, pp. 1185–1190 (2002)
9. Kheiri, A., Keedwell, E.: A sequence-based selection hyper-heuristic utilising a hidden markov model. In: GECCO 2015 – Proceedings of the 2015 Genetic Evolutionary Computation Conference, pp. 417–424 (2015)
10. Sim, K., Hart, E.: A combined generative and selective hyper-heuristic for the vehicle routing problem. In: GECCO 2016 – Proceedings of the 2016 Genetic Evolutionary Computation Conference, pp. 1093–1100 (2016)
11. Belkhamsa, M., Jarboui, B., Masmoudi, M.: Two metaheuristics for solving no-wait operating room surgery scheduling problem under various resource constraints. Comput. Ind. Eng. **126**, 494–506 (2018)

12. Denton, B., Viapiano, J., Vogl, A.: Optimization of surgery sequencing and scheduling decisions under uncertainty. Health Care Manag. Sci. **10**, 13–24 (2007)

13. Gür, Ş., Eren, T.: Application of operational research techniques in operating room scheduling problems: literature overview. J. Healthc. Eng. **2018** (2018)

14. Vancroonenburg, W., Smet, P., Vanden Berghe, G.: A two-phase heuristic approach to multi-day surgical case scheduling considering generalized resource constraints. Oper. Res. Heal. Care **7**, 27–39 (2015)

15. Zhu, S., Fan, W., Yang, S., Pei, J., Pardalos, P.M.: Operating room planning and surgical case scheduling: a review of literature. J. Combin. Optim. **37**, 757–805 (2019). https://doi.org/10.1007/s10878-018-0322-6

16. Cowling, P., Kendall, G., Soubeiga, E.: A hyperheuristic approach to scheduling a sales summit. In: Burke, E., Erben, W. (eds.) PATAT 2000. LNCS, vol. 2079, pp. 176–190. Springer, Heidelberg (2001). https://doi.org/10.1007/3-540-44629-X_11

17. Han, L., Kendall, G.: An investigation of a tabu assisted hyper-heuristic genetic algorithm, pp. 2230–2237 (2003)

18. Yan, J., Wu, X.: A genetic based hyper-heuristic algorithm for the job shop scheduling problem. In: Proceedings - 2015 7th International Conference on Intelligent Human-Machine Systems and Cybernetics, IHMSC 2015, vol. 1, pp. 161–164 (2015)

19. Pillai, A.S., et al.: A genetic algorithm-based method for optimizing the energy consumption and performance of multiprocessor systems. Soft Comput. **22**, 3271–3285 (2017)

20. Chen, R., Yang, B., Li, S., Wang, S.: A self-learning genetic algorithm based on reinforcement learning for flexible job-shop scheduling problem. Comput. Ind. Eng. **149**, 106778 (2020)

21. Fügener, A., Hans, E.W., Kolisch, R., Kortbeek, N., Vanberkel, P.T.: Master surgery scheduling with consideration of multiple downstream units (2014)

22. Marques, I., Captivo, M.E., Vaz, M.: Operations research for health care scheduling elective surgeries in a Portuguese hospital using a genetic heuristic. Oper. Res. Heal. Care **3**, 59–72 (2014)

23. Beliën, J., Demeulemeester, E.: A branch-and-price approach for integrating nurse and surgery scheduling. Eur. J. Oper. Res. **189**, 652–668 (2008)

24. Cardoen, B., Demeulemeester, E., Beliën, J.: Sequencing surgical cases in a day-care environment: an exact branch-and-price approach. Comput. Oper. Res. **36**, 2660–2669 (2009)

25. Maha, T., Achchab, S., Omar, S.: The two phases method for operating rooms planning and scheduling. In: 2020 IEEE International Conference on Technology Management, Operations and Decisions, ICTMOD 2020 (2020)

26. Marques, I., Captivo, M.E.: Bicriteria elective surgery scheduling using an evolutionary algorithm. Oper. Res. Heal. Care **7**, 14–26 (2015)

27. Ansarifar, J., Tavakkoli-moghaddam, R.: Multi-objective integrated planning and scheduling model for operating rooms under uncertainty, vol. 232, pp. 930–948 (2018)

28. Wang, R., Zhou, Z., Ishibuchi, H., Liao, T., Zhang, T.: Localized weighted sum method for many-objective optimization, vol. X, pp. 1–16 (2016)

29. Rahimi, I., Gandomi, A.H.: A comprehensive review and analysis of operating room and surgery scheduling. Arch. Comput. Methods Eng. **28**, 1667–1688 (2021)

30. Anand, S., Afreen, N., Yazdani, S.: A novel and efficient selection method in genetic algorithm, vol. 129, pp. 7–12 (2015)

31. Swiercz, A., et al.: Unified encoding for hyper-heuristics with application to bioinformatics, pp. 567–589 (2014)

32. Zhang, S., Xu, Y., Zhang, W.: Multitask-oriented manufacturing service composition in an uncertain environment using a hyper-heuristic algorithm. J. Manuf. Syst. **60**, 138–151 (2021)

Speech and Text Processing

Generation of Arabic Commonsense Explanations

Mohamed El Ghaly Beheitt[1]([⊠])(ID) and Moez Ben HajHmida[2](ID)

[1] LIPAH-FST Laboratory, Faculty of Sciences of Tunis,
University of Tunis El Manar, Tunis, Tunisia
`medghaly.beheitt@fst.utm.tn`
[2] National Engineering School of Tunis, University of Tunis El Manar, Tunis, Tunisia
`moez.benhajhmida@enit.utm.tn`

Abstract. Generating natural language explanations is a challenging task in natural language processing (NLP). With recent advancements in deep learning and language modeling techniques increased attention toward explanation generation. However, generating explanations based on commonsense reasoning remains a distinct and challenging problem. While many researchers have explored automatic explanation generation using deep learning approaches, no work has been done on generating Arabic explanations. This paper addresses this issue by presenting the Arabic machine translation of the Explanations for CommonsenseQA (Arabic-ECQA) and Open Mind Common Sense (Arabic-OMCS) datasets and fine-tuning the pre-trained AraGPT-2 model to automatically generate Arabic explanations. The performance of the fine-tunes AraGPT-2 models is evaluated using STS, METEOR, and ROUGE scores. To the best of the authors knowledge, this work is the first of its kind to generate Arabic explanations. To accelerate research on Arabic NLP, we make the datasets code publicly available (https://github.com/MohamedELGhaly/Arabic-ECQA).

Keywords: Natural language processing (NLP) · Natural language generation (NLG) · Deep learning · AraGPT-2 · Arabic explanations

1 Introduction

The emergence of pretrained large language models (LLMs), such as BERT [7] and GPT [14], changed the natural language processing (NLP) landscape. LLMs significantly improved performance over prior state-of-the-art (SOTA) on most NLP tasks. Based on the Transformer architecture LLMs are able to perform commonsense reasoning by answering questions without accessing external data. With the growing popularity of LLMs comes a need for explainable NLP systems [10]. A model producing explanations of its own answers will help quantify bias and fairness, understand model behavior, and ascertain robustness and privacy [23].

© The Author(s), under exclusive license to Springer Nature Switzerland AG 2023
N. T. Nguyen et al. (Eds.): ACIIDS 2023, CCIS 1863, pp. 527–537, 2023.
https://doi.org/10.1007/978-3-031-42430-4_43

Commonsense reasoning task requires making plausible and reasonable assumptions about everyday scenarios [6]. Recently efforts have been invested in selecting the correct answer from a set of options based on the provided context [17,18,20,25]. While selecting the correct answer is a discriminative task, explanation generation based on commonsense reasoning presents a distinct and complementary difficulty. Therefore, it is crucial to build NLP models with good commonsense reasoning capabilities to be able to provide explanations that express the logic behind the selected answer.

Natural language explanations are categorized in three types: highlights, structured, and free-text explanations. Highlights can be words, phrases, or sentences extracted from the input text to explain the right answer. Structured explanations are written in natural language constrained by specific inference engine format. Free-text explanations are natural communication without any restriction or format [23]. Explainable NLP datasets cover the three explanation types and span a wide range of tasks, including natural language inference [8], relation extraction [9], and common sense reasoning [25]. As noticed in [23] and as far as we know, except SCAT [24], all existing explanation datasets concentrate on the English language [23]. To the extent of our knowledge, no work has been done in explainable NLP for Arabic language, emphasizing the necessity for such study in this field.

In this work, we present Arabic-ECQA and Arabic-OMCS, two new datasets focusing on NLP explanation for Arabic language. Which are machine translations of the ECQA [1] and OMCS [19] datasets, respectively. We propose a method to control the quality of explanation dataset when translating from English to another language. We fine-tuned the pre-trained AraGPT-2 model [4] on new Arabic-ECQA and Arabic-OMCS datasets and evaluated the generated Arabic explanations to proof the effectiveness of the proposed translation method.

This paper's sections are organized as follows. Section 2 examines some recent related works. Section 3 describes the dataset construction pipeline. Section 4 describes the build of Arabic explanation model, the experiments, and the obtained results. Section 5 concludes the paper and proposes future work.

2   Related Work

Dataset collection for commonsense reasoning remains a difficult challenge. Data quality is crucial for making plausible and reasonable explanations. Early research have focused on creating datasets for question answering that utilizes common sense. The Choice of Plausible Alternatives (COPA) dataset [16] focuses on events and consequences. COPA dataset is used for testing the capacity of a system to detect the right cause or effect of a given premise. COPA's premises and alternatives are simple statements, and the correct answer is the one regarded as most probable.

The JHU Ordinal Commonsense Inference (JOCI) dataset [26] is constructed to measure the plausibility of a human response to a situation. The dataset assigns a label from 1 to 5, with 5 indicating a very likely response and 1 indicating an impossible response. In [13], Ostermann et al. proposed a machine-comprehension dataset focusing on commonsense knowledge. This dataset includes queries regarding narrative texts grounded in real-world occurrences that must be addressed using script knowledge. The dataset was gathered through crowdsourcing, producing many inference questions that pose difficulties for the field of natural language understanding.

Recently, efforts have been invested in constructing common sense explanation datasets. Rajani et al. in [15] presented the Common Sense Explanations (CoS-E) dataset and the Commonsense Auto-Generated Explanations (CAGE) framework for commonsense reasoning. The CoS-E dataset consists of human explanations in natural language sequences and highlighted annotations. At the same time, the CAGE framework trains a language model to generate explanations based on input and human explanations.

Similarly, Wang et al. [22] introduced the Commonsense Validation and Explanation (ComVE) task. ComVE task evaluates a system's ability to identify a natural language statement that contradicts Commonsense and explains its decision. The task consists of three subtasks; in the first subtask, the systems must choose the statement that makes sense among two similar statements. The second subtask adds the requirement for the system to select the key reason from three options for why a statement does not make sense, and the third subtask requires the system to generate the explanation. Despite promising results from top-performing models in the first two subtasks, there still needs to be a large gap between system and human performance in the third subtask.

Recently Aggarwal et al. (2021) [1] have aimed to obtain and produce explanations for a given question-and-answer combination from the CommonsenseQA (CQA) dataset [20]. The researchers define what constitutes an explanation and create a first-of-its-kind explanation dataset (ECQA) for 11K question-and-answer pairings from the CQA dataset. They also suggested methods for retrieving and producing common-sense facts to validate the response choice, such as a latent representation-based property retrieval model, a GPT-2-based property generation approach, and a free-flow explanation generation model. The researchers demonstrate that the property generation model has an F1 score of 36.4, and the free-flow generation model has a similarity score of 61.9. The ECQA dataset has been made available to the public [1].

While much work in the field of commonsense understanding has been performed in the English language. However, only a few studies focus on this in Arabic. Inspired by the ComVE task, Tawalbeh et al. [21] translated the English ComVE dataset to Arabic language. This dataset serves as a benchmark for Arabic commonsense and validation. A more recent work [3] addressed Arabic commonsense and validation. To identify commonsense sentences in Arabic authors propose a dataset of 12K sentence pairs. Each pair consists of two similar sentences where one sentence is logical and the other one is illogical.

To the best of our knowledge, however, no work on generating Arabic commonsense explanation has been done, which drove the current effort.

3   Dataset Construction

Inspired by the work of Aggarwal et al. (2021) in [1], we have decided to translate the ECQA(Explanations for CommonsenseQA) dataset to construct an Arabic commonsense explanation dataset. The ECQA dataset is an important step forward in Natural Language Explanations since it contains a detailed explanation of 10,962 question-answer pairs from the CommonsenseQA dataset [20]. The ECQA dataset was developed through crowdsourcing, with annotators required to explain the correct option (answer), why the other options were wrong, and a free-flow of natural language explanations based on the facts explaining the correct and wrong answers. In addition to the ECQA dataset, we also translated the Open Mind Common Sense (OMCS) corpus [19]. This corpus consisted of approximately 800k common-sense facts and was used to build ConceptNet.

The quality of the translated text highly depends on the quality of the source text. So, we started by checking the source datasets where we noticed multiple misspelled words. We were also aware that we must ensure the machine translation's reliability to guarantee the translation's accuracy. Therefore, we developed a three-step pipeline:

- First, we correct the misspelled words taking the context into account.
- Second, we utilize two translation models to ensure translation reliability.
- Third, we control the quality of the translated data by contrasting the results of the two translation models.

Figure 1 illustrates the three steps of the proposed pipeline.

3.1   Spell Check

We have decided to correct the misspelled words in the datasets before proceeding with the translation. We opted for LLM for the misspelling correction task instead of traditional n-gram models. BERT-based models showed their ability to predict correct words given the masked spelling errors. We utilized HuggingFace model[1] for English misspelling correction, which is a fine-tuned model based on the pre-trained BART model [11]. By improving the source datasets quality, we aim to provide a high-quality Arabic translation of the datasets.

3.2   Translation

In this phase, we opted to use two tools Microsoft Bing Translator and the NLLB-200 model[2]. Microsoft Bing Translator is a machine translation service that offers translations in over 60 languages. In addition, the NLLB-200 model is a machine translation model open-sourced by Facebook, explicitly built for machine translation research, particularly for low-resource languages.

---

[1] https://huggingface.co/oliverguhr/spelling-correction-english-base.
[2] https://huggingface.co/facebook/nllb-200-1.3B.

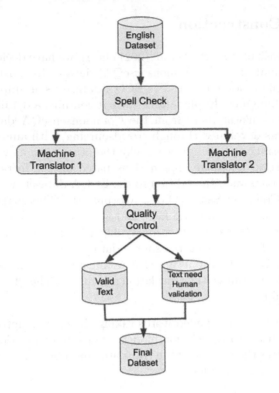

Fig. 1. Proposed pipeline.

3.3 Quality Control

Once we utilized translation tools, we measured the level of resemblance between translations produced by Microsoft Bing Translator and the NLLB-200 model. We accomplished this by utilizing a sentence similarity model[3] that transforms the input texts into vectors (embeddings) that capture semantic information and measure their similarity, resulting in a score between 0 and 1. We set a threshold of 0.8 to determine the closeness between the translations. Our results indicate that around 9.8% of the translations were exact matches, 62.79% were above the threshold, and 27.41% were below the threshold. Next, we selected a sample of divergent translations that were below the threshold and manually compared them with the help of two Arabic annotators. According to their findings, the translations produced by the NLLB-200 model were more accurate than those produced by Microsoft Bing Translator.

3.4 Constructed Datastes

We fed the pipeline ECQA and OMCS datastes to construct the Arabic-ECQA and Arabic-OMCS datasets. Table 1 provides an example of Arabic-ECQA,

---

[3] https://huggingface.co/sentence-transformers/all-MiniLM-L6-v2.

showcasing the concept to which the question pertains, the question itself, the answer choices, the correct answer, an explanation for each answer, and a free-flow explanation.

Table 1. Example of Arabic-ECQA.

Arabic text	Original text
Concept	
الناس	people
Question	
سامي أراد الذهاب إلى حيث كان الناس. أين قد يذهب؟	Sammy wanted to go to where the people were. Where might he go?
Answer choices	
سباقات، المناطق المأهولة بالسكان، الصحراء، شقة، حواجز الطريق	race track, populated areas, the desert, apartment, roadblock
Correct answer	
المناطق المأهولة بالسكان	populated areas
Correct answer explanation	
المناطق المأهولة هي حيث يوجد الكثير من الناس	Populated areas are where there are a lot of people
Wrong answers explanations	
مسار السباق ليس دائماً مليئاً بالناس	Race track does not always have a lot of people
الصحراء غير مأهولة على الإطلاق	The desert is not populated at all
الشقة لا تملك عادة الكثير من الناس	Apartment does not usually have a lot of people
حواجز الطرق لا تملك الكثير من الناس	Roadblock does not generally have a lot of people
Free-flow explanation	
المناطق المأهولة هي حيث يوجد عدد كبير من الناس. مسار السباق ليس لديه الكثير من الناس الصحراء غير مأهولة على الإطلاق. الشقة لا تملك عادة الكثير من الناس. حواجز الطرق لا تملك الكثير من الناس	Populated areas are where there are a lot of number of people. Race track does not have a lot of people. The desert is not populated at all. Apartment does not usually have a lot of people. Roadblock does not generally have a lot of people.

Table 2 displays the total number of words and the number of unique words for translated datasets. To train the proposed models, we divided the Arabic-ECQA dataset into training, validation, and testing sets with a 70%, 10%, and 20% split, respectively.

Table 2. Constructed datasets statistics.

Dataset	#Words	#Unique Words
Arabic-ECQA	1.257K	92K
Arabic-OMCS	5.826K	130K

4 Experiments and Evaluation

Our goal is to construct a high-quality datasets for Arabic commonsense explanation. To evaluate this, we experiment with GPT-2 (Generative Pre-trained Transformer 2) model on two explanation tasks: answer explanation and free-flow explanation. Each task requires a specific fine-tuning objective.

Given that GPT-2 was not pre-trained on the Arabic language, we chose to employ the Arabic variant of GPT-2 known as AraGPT-2 [4]. AraGPT2 is a variant of the original GPT2 model [14], which is trained on a large corpus (77 GB) of Arabic text from the internet and news articles. This advanced Arabic language generation model is based on the GPT-2 architecture and comes in four variants: base (135 million parameters), medium (370 million parameters), large (792 million parameters), and mega (1,46 billion parameters). The evaluation of the model showed success in tasks such as synthetic news generation and zero-shot question answering, with a perplexity of 29,8 [4].

4.1 Answer eXplanation (AX)

For this task, we need to build a model that will be asked to generate explanations for both correct and wrong answers. We perform two-step fine-tuning of the AraGPT-2 base model inspired by the work in [1]. In the first step, we fine-tuned the model to generate sentences with common-sense properties. For this purpose, we fine-tuned AraGPT-2 on a language modeling task using a corpus of common-sense properties, including the Arabic-ECQA train set and Arabic-OMCS corpus. This model is fine-tuned for 5 epochs. In the second step, we fine-tune the model to generate correct and wrong answers explanations given a tuple of (q, a, c). Where q is the question, a is the answer, and c is a boolean that determines whether the answer is correct or not. Again, we use the Arabic-ECQA train set for this fine-tuning process, which lasts for 5 epochs. The model was fine-tuned using an NVIDIA Tesla P100 (16 GB) GPU, which took 10 h to complete. We name this model Ara-AX for Arabic Answer eXplanation.

4.2 Free-Flow eXplanation (FX)

In order to achieve the second task of generating free-flow natural language explanations, we fine-tune the pre-trained AraGPT-2 model. The proposed model provides a free-flow explanation given a question, the set of all answer choices, and the correct answer. To do this, we used the Arabic-ECQA train set to fine-tune AraGPT-2 model over 10 epochs. This model was fine-tuned using the same GPU in task1 and took about 40 min. We name this model Ara-FX for Arabic Free-flow eXplanation. In Table 3 we summarize the fine-tuning hyperparameters used for the two tasks.

Table 3. Hyperparameters used to fine-tune the proposed models.

Hyperparameter	Value
Max seq len	1024
Batch size	20
Learning rate	$5e^{-5}$
# Epochs	10
Model size	135M

4.3   Evaluation

We use STS, METEOR, and ROUGE metrics to evaluate the explanations generated by each model. In the following, we introduce the used evaluation metrics.

Semantic Textual Similarity (STS) is an NLP measure for determining the degree of semantic similarity between two text sequences [2]. It assumes that two text sequences are semantically comparable if they convey similar meanings or communicate similar concepts. STS is widely utilized in applications such as text categorization, paraphrase detection, and machine translation. It is compared to human assessments using the Pearson correlation coefficient and has become an essential method for evaluating the effectiveness of NLP and IR (Information Retrieval) algorithms.

Furthermore, with the introduction of deep learning models such as BERT, STS models may be generated utilizing Transfer Learning without the need to train a model from the start. The fundamental idea of this job is to comprehend word or phrase embeddings and utilize them as features to calculate semantic metrics like cosine similarity and angular distance similarity. We use STS-BERT[4] to compute the STS score.

METEOR (Metric for Evaluation of Translation with Explicit ORdering) [5] is a machine translation evaluation metric. It assesses translation output quality by comparing it to a reference translation and taking into account the sequence of words and phrases in the translations. METEOR may also be tailored to specific language pairings and domains by altering the weights allocated to certain elements in the scoring system.

In addition to its application in machine translation, METEOR can also be utilized to evaluate text generation systems quality. In such cases, a human-generated text serves as the reference that the system is meant to reproduce, and the METEOR metric is employed to compare the generated text to the reference.

The **ROUGE** (Recall-Oriented Understudy for Gisting Evaluation) metric [12] is commonly used to assess the text quality generated by machine learning models. ROUGE is primarily used in summarization tasks because it measures recall, which is important in evaluating the number of words the model can recall in these tasks. The basic idea behind ROUGE is to assign a single numerical score to a summary that indicates its quality compared to one or more reference summaries. In addition, ROUGE is sensitive to N-gram overlap, making it a useful tool for comparing the similarity of the reference summary and system-generated summary.

This study compares the results of the proposed models to those of Aggarwal et al. [1] for the English language on two tasks: answers explanation and free-flow explanation. Tables 4 and 5 illustrate the results; both tasks are evaluated on three metrics. The results show that for both tasks our models maintain high STS scores. This exhibits the semantic closeness between the generated explanations and the explanations contained in the training dataset without

---

[4] https://pypi.org/project/semantic-text-similarity/.

Table 4. Metrics scores comparison for answer explanation (AX) task.

Models	STS	METEOR	ROUGE
Aggarwal et al. [1]	36.4	13.7	25.7
Ara-AX	79.0	12.6	14.7

Table 5. Metrics scores comparison for free-flow explanation (FX) task.

Models	STS	METEOR	ROUGE
Aggarwal et al. [1]	62.5	17.5	12.2
Ara-FX	69.1	8.6	4.9

repeating the same sentences. We also notice from the results low METEOR and ROUGE scores for both tasks. As explanations usually paraphrase the original question text it results in low scores. This behavior can be positively perceived because the models try to generate explanations with words not contained in the question. The study finds that the proposed models generate promising Arabic commonsense explanation outcomes.

5   Conclusion

We introduce Arabic-ECQA and Arabic-OMCS, two new datasets automatically translated from ECQA [1] and OMCS [19] datasets. We propose a pipeline to control the quality of dataset translation and the fine-tuning of the pre-trained AraGPT-2 model [4] to automatically generate Arabic commonsense explanations. This work is the first work in Arabic natural language explanation generation, to the best of our knowledge. Our proposed approach includes fine-tuning AraGPT-2 in two tasks: generating explanations for correct and wrong answers (AX) and generating free-flow explanations (FX). We evaluated the text generated in both tasks using STS, METEOR, and ROUGE metrics. In future work, we plan to explore reinforcement learning models to improve the quality of the generated Arabic explanations. Furthermore, we intend to propose a new dataset for Arabic natural language explanation using crowdsourcing.

References

1. Aggarwal, S., Mandowara, D., Agrawal, V., Khandelwal, D., Singla, P., Garg, D.: Explanations for commonsenseQA: new dataset and models. In: Proceedings of the 59th Annual Meeting of the Association for Computational Linguistics and the 11th International Joint Conference on Natural Language Processing (Volume 1: Long Papers), pp. 3050–3065 (2021)
2. Agirre, E., Cer, D., Diab, M., Gonzalez-Agirre, A.: SemEval-2012 task 6: a pilot on semantic textual similarity. In: * SEM 2012: The First Joint Conference on Lexical

and Computational Semantics-Volume 1: Proceedings of the main conference and the shared task, and Volume 2: Proceedings of the Sixth International Workshop on Semantic Evaluation (SemEval 2012), pp. 385 393 (2012)

3. Al-Bashabsheh, E., Al-Khazaleh, H., Elayan, O., Duwairi, R.: Commonsense validation for Arabic sentences using deep learning. In: 2021 22nd International Arab Conference on Information Technology (ACIT), pp. 1–7. IEEE (2021)

4. Antoun, W., Baly, F., Hajj, H.: AraGPT2: pre-trained transformer for Arabic language generation. arXiv preprint arXiv:2012.15520 (2020)

5. Banerjee, S., Lavie, A.: METEOR: An automatic metric for MT evaluation with improved correlation with human judgments. In: Proceedings of the ACL Workshop on Intrinsic and Extrinsic Evaluation Measures for Machine Translation AND/OR Summarization, pp. 65–72 (2005)

6. Davis, E., Marcus, G.: Commonsense reasoning and commonsense knowledge in artificial intelligence. Commun. ACM **58**(9), 92–103 (2015)

7. Devlin, J., Chang, M.W., Lee, K., Toutanova, K.: BERT: pre-training of deep bidirectional transformers for language understanding. arXiv preprint arXiv:1810.04805 (2018)

8. Do, V., Camburu, O.M., Akata, Z., Lukasiewicz, T.: e-SNLI-VE: corrected visual-textual entailment with natural language explanations. arXiv preprint arXiv:2004.03744 (2020)

9. Hancock, B., Bringmann, M., Varma, P., Liang, P., Wang, S., Ré, C.: Training classifiers with natural language explanations. In: Proceedings of the Conference on Association for Computational Linguistics Meeting, vol. 2018, p. 1884. NIH Public Access (2018)

10. Jacovi, A., Goldberg, Y.: Towards faithfully interpretable NLP systems: how should we define and evaluate faithfulness? In: Proceedings of the 58th Annual Meeting of the Association for Computational Linguistics, pp. 4198–4205. Association for Computational Linguistics, Online (2020). https://doi.org/10.18653/v1/2020.acl-main.386, https://aclanthology.org/2020.acl-main.386

11. Lewis, M., et al.: BART: denoising sequence-to-sequence pre-training for natural language generation, translation, and comprehension. CoRR abs/1910.13461 (2019). http://arxiv.org/abs/1910.13461

12. Lin, C.Y.: ROUGE: a package for automatic evaluation of summaries. In: Text Summarization Branches Out, pp. 74–81 (2004)

13. Ostermann, S., Modi, A., Roth, M., Thater, S., Pinkal, M.: MCScript: a novel dataset for assessing machine comprehension using script knowledge. arXiv preprint arXiv:1803.05223 (2018)

14. Radford, A., Wu, J., Child, R., Luan, D., Amodei, D., Sutskever, I.: Language models are unsupervised multitask learners. OpenAI Blog **1**(8), 9 (2019)

15. Rajani, N.F., McCann, B., Xiong, C., Socher, R.: Explain yourself! leveraging language models for commonsense reasoning. arXiv preprint arXiv:1906.02361 (2019)

16. Roemmele, M., Bejan, C.A., Gordon, A.S.: Choice of plausible alternatives: an evaluation of commonsense causal reasoning. In: AAAI Spring Symposium: Logical Formalizations of Commonsense Reasoning, pp. 90–95 (2011)

17. Sakaguchi, K., Bras, R.L., Bhagavatula, C., Choi, Y.: WinoGrande: an adversarial winograd schema challenge at scale. Commun. ACM **64**(9), 99–106 (2021)

18. Sap, M., Rashkin, H., Chen, D., LeBras, R., Choi, Y.: SocialIQa: commonsense reasoning about social interactions. arXiv preprint arXiv:1904.09728 (2019)

19. Singh, P., et al.: The public acquisition of commonsense knowledge. In: Proceedings of AAAI Spring Symposium: Acquiring (and Using) Linguistic (and World) Knowledge for Information Access, vol. 3 (2002)

20. Talmor, A., Herzig, J., Lourie, N., Berant, J.: CommonsenseQA: a question answering challenge targeting commonsense knowledge. In: Proceedings of the 2019 Conference of the North American Chapter of the Association for Computational Linguistics: Human Language Technologies, Volume 1 (Long and Short Papers), pp. 4149–4158. Association for Computational Linguistics, Minneapolis (2019). https://doi.org/10.18653/v1/N19-1421, https://aclanthology.org/N19-1421

21. Tawalbeh, S., Al-Smadi, M.: Is this sentence valid? An Arabic dataset for commonsense validation. arXiv preprint arXiv:2008.10873 (2020)

22. Wang, C., Liang, S., Jin, Y., Wang, Y., Zhu, X., Zhang, Y.: SemEval-2020 task 4: commonsense validation and explanation. arXiv preprint arXiv:2007.00236 (2020)

23. Wiegreffe, S., Marasovic, A.: Teach me to explain: a review of datasets for explainable natural language processing. In: Vanschoren, J., Yeung, S. (eds.) Proceedings of the Neural Information Processing Systems Track on Datasets and Benchmarks. vol. 1 (2021). https://datasets-benchmarks-proceedings.neurips.cc/paper/2021/file/698d51a19d8a121ce581499d7b701668-Paper-round1.pdf

24. Yin, K., Fernandes, P., Pruthi, D., Chaudhary, A., Martins, A.F.T., Neubig, G.: Do context-aware translation models pay the right attention? In: Proceedings of the 59th Annual Meeting of the Association for Computational Linguistics (2021). https://arxiv.org/abs/2105.06977

25. Zellers, R., Holtzman, A., Bisk, Y., Farhadi, A., Choi, Y.: HellaSwag: can a machine really finish your sentence? arXiv preprint arXiv:1905.07830 (2019)

26. Zhang, S., Rudinger, R., Duh, K., Van Durme, B.: Ordinal common-sense inference. Trans. Assoc. Comput. Linguist. **5**, 379–395 (2017)

Automatic Speech Recognition Improvement for Kazakh Language with Enhanced Language Model

Akbayan Bekarystankyzy[1]([envelope]) [iD], Orken Mamyrbayev[2] [iD], Mateus Mendes[3,4] [iD],
Dina Oralbekova[5] [iD], Bagashar Zhumazhanov[2] [iD], and Anar Fazylzhanova[6] [iD]

[1] Satbayev University, Satbayev Str. 22, Almaty, Kazakhstan
[2] Institute of Information and Computational Technologies CS MES RK, Shevchenko Str. 28, Almaty, Kazakhstan
[3] Polytechnic Institute of Coimbra, ISEC, Coimbra, Portugal
[4] University of Coimbra, ISR, Coimbra, Portugal
[5] Almaty University of Power Engineering and Telecomminucations, Almaty, Kazakhstan
[6] Committee of Science of the Ministry of Science and Higher Education of the RK, Institute of Linguistics and named after Akhmet Baitursynuly, Almaty, Kazakhstan

Abstract. Last time there are unbelievable results in Natural Language Processing(NLP) and Automatic Speech Recognition(ASR). As a result, everybody can use smart search engines such as ChatGPT, smart voice assistants such as Siri, Alexa and more. But these opportunities are available only to the people who can use English or other common languages. For people who use low-resource languages these products are not available. As collection of transcribed data is time consuming and expensive process, scientists search ways of implementing reliable ASR models for low-resource languages. One of ASR improving methods in the case of lack of data is the use of external language model built on text larger than text in the entire dataset. And use this language model in the decoding process. As Kazakh language is also one of low-resource languages it is was decided to test this approach for kazakh language with different language models like Sequential RNNLM and Transformer LM. Inclusion of language model trained on bigger dataset allowed to decrease error values especially for Word Error Rate (WER). The best result was obtained with Transformer LM, WER was decreased to 7.2%.

Keywords: ASR · Language Model · Sequential RNNLM · Transformer · Kazakh Language

1 Introduction

Improving Automatic Speech Recognition (ASR) for low-resource languages is currently one of the main challenges in speech recognition. Kazakh language is one of many low-resource languages, which suffer from lack of transcribed data. Different research works were performed and provided for Kazakh language, in order to make it possible to get reliable ASR for this language, using different well-known Recurrent Neural Networks (RNN) and architectures [1, 2]. Despite improving methods and

© The Author(s), under exclusive license to Springer Nature Switzerland AG 2023
N. T. Nguyen et al. (Eds.): ACIIDS 2023, CCIS 1863, pp. 538–545, 2023.
https://doi.org/10.1007/978-3-031-42430-4_44

advanced popular ASR architectures, achieving high performance is still an open problem for Kazakh language, as it is also for other low-resource languages. Researchers started to apply approaches of pooling the data of different languages to one corpus, in order to get multilingual models and made attempts of transferring knowledge from models trained for other large-resource languages [3]. Other authors studied the impact of languages to each other, from one language group - for agglutinative languages of the Altaic family, for example [4, 5]. Both methods, multilingual training and transfer learning, have their advantages and disadvantages for Kazakh language. In [4], a multilingual model showed promising results for all languages included in the experiment, but in the process of recognition it can mix up characters from different languages in short contexts, because in languages like Kazakh and Kyrgyz the same phrases have similar spellings and different writings. Transfer learning usually can be used only to improve acoustic feature extraction, due to the differences in trained languages' alphabets.

Results close to the state of the art for Kazakh language were reached in experiments which applied Transformer architectures [6]. But all of these methods would not train a reliable ASR model without a large amount of transcribed audio data.

One of the methods of improving correct word recognition in ASR is to get a rich set of parameters describing relations among words. Some researchers study improvements of language models and apply them in ASR by introducing distinct language models trained on enhanced text data [7–10]. This approach also can make the process of ASR development comparatively cheaper, because it is much easier to collect raw text data in comparison with transcribed audio data.

The present work investigates ASR model improvement methods. We propose the enhancement of the text corpus with extra texts for improving the decoding process and transferring knowledge from the model of large models in order to improve the decoding process for Kazakh language.

Section 2 describes related work. Section 3 describes methodology and experiments. Section 4 is about discussions and conclusions.

2 Related Works

2.1 ASR Improvement Ways for Kazakh Language

Some authors specially for agglutinative languages [1] propose contribution to end-to-end CTC/attention architecture by adding new feature extracting approach called Multi-Scale Parallel Convolution and combined it with Bi-LSTM(bidierctional long short-term memory). This contribution improves recognition rate of the end-to-end model. In order check the performance and increase the amount of trained data authors added noises to initial data corpus of Turkish and Uzbek languages from Common Voice. The mentioned approach in combination with language model and increased beam width (=16) decreased WER and CER for trained languages.

Authors of [4] developed 22 different models for agglutinative languages learning the impact of combining languages from one language family and discovered that this type of multilingual learning gives more robust model. But multilingual models can not be used in real applications, because they have problems with transcript meshing in short contexts, due to the issue that in real applications users will not guarantee to use long contexts. It could be proved on the example of several agglutinative languages of altaic family. [11] also presents inclusion of external data to improve ASR, here authors present the idea of including external enhanced text data, but they omit the idea of using words in the context natural to human usage.

2.2 ASR Improvement Practices by Text Corpus Enhancement

In [7] authors propose use of improved word embeddings into speech models in order to decrease WER and improve the predictions of a model for speech translation, moreover authors highlighted that this approach can be applied also in ASR tasks [8]. Also highlights the role of improving word embedding vectors. These vectors can decrease word error rate being integrated to the process of decoding. Because language model built on large-scale data can make possible to recognize rare words in speech recognition [9]. Some studies dedicated to converting text data into the format suitable for ASR: authors of [10] explore techniques and methods of converting written language text into the form which can be used to build better LM for ASR improvement.

3 Methodology

This research proposes the improvement of decoding by using a distinct language model, trained on an enlarged text corpus, which also includes the text corpus of the entire dataset. The architecture of the decoder proposed is given in Fig. 1. As shown in the figure, the decoder has a transformer architecture, which consists of multi headed attention unit, Connectionist Temporal Classification (CTC) loss function and LM of enhanced text corpus. Decoder gives the sequence of words performing joint decoding on high-level features, passing them through all listed parts of the decoder.

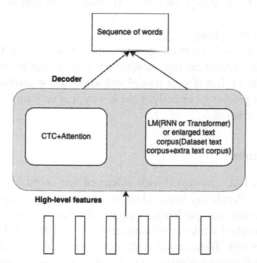

Fig. 1. Improved decoder with the LM of enlarged raw text

3.1 LM Enhancing

ESPnet was chosen as a tool for experiments, because it supports novel architectures for ASR: transformer and conformer, branchformer which use Convolutional Neural Networks (CNNs) for processing input raw signals and apply joint decoding (CTC + attention mechanism) for output. Moreover, it allows to train distinct Language Model (LM) [12, 13] and use it in decoding process to predict the next word (1):

$$\log p(y_n|y_{1:n-1}, h_{1:T}) = \log p^{hyp}(y_n|y_{1:n-1}, h_{1:T}) + \beta \log p^{lm}(y_n|y_{1:n-1}, h_{1:T}) \quad (1)$$

where p is the probability of the next word, p^{hyp} is the probability of word given as hypothesis calculated by entire ASR model, p^{lm} is the next word probability calculated by the external language model, β is the LM coefficient (floating point value between 0 and 1).

Inclusion of extra text corpus can improve featurized representations of words, using different variations of words' usage in an enormous number of contexts. This improves hot vectors (E) and increases the number of word features.

3.2 Featurized Representation

Featurized representation of words is the probability of the words' relations to different features. Features extracted during the training process by calculating relations among words in sentences and phrases. These representations could be used in sequence generation processes like NLP and speech recognition processes to predict the next element of a sentence.

For example, there is a sentence in a dataset:

I like the process of picking apples.

If the trained model have to predict the next word in new sentence which is not from a known dataset:

I like the process of picking _____?

What word will it choose from the given example table? Most likely, it will choose the word "cherry". Because its hot representation is very similar to the hot representation of "apple" (see Table 1). But if your model would not know anything about the word "cherry" it could not predict it correctly. That is why it is very important for a model to know more and more words.

3.3 LM Architectures

Two architectures of LM were tested with enhanced text corpus: Sequential RNN [14] and Transformer[17]. Perplexity value taken in the result of training enlarged data with transformer architecture was the lowest among all other results taken during current experiment: 2.99. Perplexity taken with Sequential RNN LM was 3.99, which is worse than the result taken with Transformer architecture (see Table 2). Also, Table 2 shows that transformer architecture can extract much more trainable parameters in comparison with Sequential RNN LM (50.54 M).

Table 1. Example of featurized representation for some words of Kazakh Language

Words Features	Ep (man)	Әйел (woman)	Әке (father)	Ана (mother)	Алма (apple)	Шие (cherry)
Gender	-1	1	-0.97	0.96	0.00	0.02
Parenthood	-0.25	0.32	-0.99	0.99	-0.03	0.04
Food	0.00	0.00	0.02	0.03	0.92	0.93
Age	0.43	0.38	0.72	0.78	0.04	-0.08
Size	0.05	0.04	0.08	0.09	0.25	0.12
Pet	0.07	0.08	0.01	-0.02	0.00	-0.03
Fruit	0.00	0.00	0.03	-0.01	0.98	0.94

Table 2. Perplexity values of different language models

LM type	Perplexity	Number of trainable parameters	Number of sentences
RNN LM (text of entire dataset)	9.09	6.83 M	5774
RNN LM (enlarged text corpus)	3.99	6.84 M	139810
Transformer LM(enlarged text corpus)	2.99	50.54 M	139810

3.4 Sequential RNNLM

Both of the tested LM architecture types use statistical probability to sequences. This approach was firstly proposed in 1980's [14]. Here, the probability of the final sentence is the product of the probability of each word depending on the previous sequence of words.

$$P(s) = P(w_i w_{i+1} \ldots w_n) = P(w_i|w_{i+1}) \ldots P(w_n|w_i w_{i+1} \ldots w_{n-1}) \qquad (2)$$

In (2) s-is a sentence, i-th word is denoted by w_i. In order to make proper calculation for longer contexts RNNLM was used [15]. As Kazakh language can have very long sentences, which can obtain half of a page or more, simple RNN LM is not sufficient. Because of this reason LM architecture with LSTM RNN type is used in the current study. According to previous suggestions, the first architecture tested with enhanced raw text was Sequential RNNLM. This LM architecture uses 2 layers with 650 units of LSTM cells. Decoder is linear with 650 input features and 48 output features. The number of epochs was 20 and batch size was chosen as 64.

3.5 Transformer LM

Transformer architecture is one of the state of the art architectures [16]. This method basically uses an attention mechanism which initially was proposed for text translation

[17]. Because in translation word sequences in the destination language can differ from the order of words in the source language. In the current study, the transformer language model has embedded a sequential layer with dropout value 0.1 and uses activation function ReLU. Moreover, it has 16 multi sequential encoder layers. Each layer has 8 heads and 512 head units followed by position-wise feed-forward, 2 normalization layers and dropout equal to 0.1. Learning rate is 0.001 and number of epochs is 25.

3.6 ASR Architecture and Training Results with Enhanced LM

Architecture with conformer encoder and transformer was chosen for ASR. Input layer is a two dimensional convolution layer, its activation function is ReLU. Encoder is multi sequential with 12 layers. Each layer of encoder has 4 attention heads with relational positioning. Multihead module followed by 2 layers of position-wise feed-forward and convolution module. Feed-forward layers and convolution modules use activation type swish. Each layer of encoder is finished by normalization layer.

Transformer decoder has an embedded input layer with positional encoding. After the sequential embedding layer, decoder has 6 multi headed attention layers. CTC loss function with coefficient 0.3 is included in joint decoding. Learning rate is 2, as transcribed data amount in the experiment is critically low.

All types of language models were estimated with this ASR architecture. Results of experiments on 15 h of transcribed data for Kazakh language are given in Table 3. LM weight for decoding was chosen as 0.3.

Table 3. WER (validation/test) and CER (validation/test) of ASR with 15 h of Kazakh Language with Sequential RNNLM and Transformer LM, Transformer LM + transferred cross-lingual Encoder.

LM type	WER/val. (%)	WER/test (%)	CER/val. (%)	CER/test (%)
Sequential RNN LM with entire dataset text	53.1	54.0	19.1	20.1
Sequential RNN LM with enhanced raw text	48.7	49.1	18.3	18.9
TransformerLM with enhanced raw text	46.2	46.8	17.7	18.2
TransformerLM with enhanced raw text + cross lingual transfer learning with Encoder	45.5	46.3	17.3	18.3

4 Discussions and Conclusion

Inclusion of LM, trained on the big raw text decreases both types of error rates: WER and CER. Especially it has a significant impact on WER. Sequential RNNLM of big text decreased WER by 5%, transformer LM of the same text data decreased WER by

7.2%. Results of experiments showed that Transformer LM is more effective, as it can decrease perplexity and increase the number of trainable parameters.

The result of cross-lingual transfer learning from the ASR model for English language in joint usage with Enhanced Transformer LM could further decrease ASR error rates. The result of this study shows that inclusion of Enhanced LM to the decoding process for ASR is applicable for Kazakh language. Moreover, it is empirically proved that Transformer LM is more effective in comparison with sequential RNNLM.

Acknowledgement. This research has is funded by the Science Committee of the Ministry of Science and Higher Education of the Republic of Kazakhstan (Grant No. BR11765619).

References

1. Ren, Z., Yolwas, N., Slamu, W., Cao, R., Wang, H.: Improving hybrid CTC/attention architecture for agglutinative language speech recognition. Sensors **22**, 7319 (2022)
2. Mamyrbayev, O., Oralbekova, D., Alimhan, K., Nuranbayeva, B.: Hybrid end-to-end model for Kazakh speech recognition. Int. J. Speech Technol. **08**, 1–10 (2022)
3. Kuanyshbay, D., Amirgaliyev, Y., Baimuratov, O.: Development of automatic speech recognition for kazakh language using transfer learning. Int. J. Adv. Trends Comput. Sci. Eng. **9**, 5880–5886 (2020)
4. Mussakhojayeva, S., Dauletbek, K., Yeshpanov, R., Varol, H.A.: Multilingual speech recognition for turkic languages. Information **14**(2), 74 (2023). https://doi.org/10.3390/info14020074
5. Orken, M., Alimhan, K., Oralbekova, D., Bekarystankyzy, A., Zhumazhanov, B.: Identifying the influence of transfer learning method in developing an end-to-end automatic speech recognition system with a low data level. Eastern-Eur. J. Enterp. Technol. **1**, 84–92 (2022)
6. Orken, M., Oralbekova, D., Alimhan, K., Tolganay, T., Othman, M.: A study of transformer-based end-to-end speech recognition system for Kazakh language. Sci. Rep. **12**(1), 8337 (2022)
7. Chuang, S.-P., Liu, A.H., Sung, T.-W., Lee, H.: Improving automatic speech recognition and speech translation via word embedding prediction. IEEE/ACM Trans. Audio Speech Lang. Process. **29**, 93–105 (2021). https://doi.org/10.1109/TASLP.2020.3037543
8. Kubo, Y., Karita, S., Bacchiani, M.: Knowledge transfer from large-scale pretrained language models to end-to-end speech recognizers (2022). https://www.researchgate.net/publication/358655492_Knowledge_Transfer_from_Large-scale_Pretrained_Language_Models_to_End-to-end_Speech_Recognizers
9. Huang, W.R., Peyser, C., Sainath, T.N., Pang, R., Strohman, T., Kumar, S.: Sentence-select: large-scale language model data selection for rare-word speech recognition. In: Interspeech (2022)
10. Mukherji, K., Pandharipande, M., Kopparapu, S.K.: Improved language models for ASR using written language text. In: 2022 National Conference on Communications (NCC), Mumbai, India, pp. 362–366 (2022). https://doi.org/10.1109/NCC55593.2022.9806803
11. Amirgaliyev, Y., Kuanyshbay, D., Yedilkhan, D.: Automatic speech recognition system for Kazakh language using connectionist temporal classifier (2020)
12. Watanabe, S., et al.: ESPnet: end-to-end speech processing toolkit. In: Proceedings of the Interspeech 2018, pp. 2207–2211 (2018). https://doi.org/10.21437/Interspeech.2018-1456

13. Watanabe, S., et al.: The 2020 ESPnet Update: new features, broadened applications, performance improvements, and future plans. In: Proceedings of the 2021 IEEE Data Science and Learning Workshop (DSLW) (2021)
14. Jing, K., Xu, J.: A survey on neural network language models (2019). https://doi.org/10.48550/arXiv.1906.03591
15. Bengio, Y., Senecal, J.: Quick training of probabilistic neural nets by importance sampling. In: Bishop, Christopher M. and Frey, Brendan J. (eds.) International Conference on Artificial Intelligence and Statistics, Proceedings of the Ninth International Workshop on Artificial Intelligence and Statistics, vol. R4, pp. 17–24 (2003)
16. Guo, P., et al.: Recent developments on ESPnet toolkit boosted by conformer. In: ICASSP 2021 - 2021 IEEE International Conference on Acoustics, Speech and Signal Processing (ICASSP), Toronto, ON, Canada, pp. 5874–5878 (2021). https://doi.org/10.1109/ICASSP 39728.2021.9414858
17. Bahdanau, D., Cho, K., Bengio, Y.: Neural machine translation by jointly learning to align and translate. ArXiv arXiv:1409.0473 (2014)

Relationship Between Linguistic Complexity and MT Errors in the Context of Inflectional Languages

Ľubomír Benko$^{(\boxtimes)}$ ⓘ, Dasa Munková ⓘ, and Michal Munk ⓘ

Department of Informatics, Constantine the Philosopher University in Nitra, 949 01 Nitra, Slovakia
{lbenko,dmunkova,mmunk}@ukf.sk

Abstract. The quality produced by the MT tool varies, from very high to very low, depending on the intrinsic linguistic features of the source and target languages. The more lexical words the text content, the more information contains. Lexical richness is a multidimensional construct for assessing language development. In our study, we apply this concept for assessing the quality of machine translation. We attempt to link lexical richness with types of errors occurring in machine translation. We focus on the identification of the relationship between five types of MT errors and examined measures of language complexity. We used Goodman and Kruskal's gamma to determine which measures of language complexity are associated with the MT error types. The results revealed that not all measures of lexical richness are associated with the MT errors in each examined error category. We showed that readability does not associate with an error rate, namely with error categories used in the present study.

Keywords: Machine Translation · Lexical Complexity · Text Readability · Error Classes · Natural Language Processing

1 Introduction

The last decade has brought many advances in the field of language that are mainly related to artificial intelligence and machine translation. With artificial intelligence, translation is faster not only for professional translators but also for people like tourists or businessmen. Artificial intelligence (AI) is developing extremely fast and is bringing a revolution in the language and translation industries. Machine translation (MT), as one of the applications of natural language processing, as well as natural language processing itself, has become an integral part of the global technological competition for primacy in the field of artificial intelligence [1]. This rapidly developing technology field changes not only the way people work but also how they understand textual data. Understanding a language in its written form is related to internal text properties such as text readability or text diversity (granularity). MT depends on computer language, i.e. on binary language, which distinguishes only 0 and 1, but by applying AI to translation, MT becomes more similar to human translation in terms of fluency and accuracy [2]. Under the assumption of a sufficient training corpus, the performance of an MT model with integrated AI was higher than a statistical MT model, therefore more researchers began to conduct more experiments with AI in machine translation [3].

MT is the automatic conversion of text from one natural language to another natural language. The quality produced by MT tools varies, ranging from very high to very low, depending on the intrinsic properties of the given text and language pair. Its accuracy depends on the source and target languages, industry (domain), source text quality, training corpus, and other factors [2]. Nowadays, the most widely used freely available MT tool is Google Translate [4], which we also used in our study. Google Neural MT is an AI technology that uses deep learning to produce a translation.

MT tools, which are currently used, are based on neural networks. Neural MT offers better results in product quality, especially in terms of text readability, than its predecessor statistical MT. For example, Pangeanic's neural MT tools guarantee very high parity with a human translator (90 - 95%) and this is one of the reasons why many companies and government institutions in the EU have decided to use neural MT tools for translation [5]. MT is also increasingly being applied outside the translation industry. According to Lihua [2: 7] especially in healthcare, the automotive industry, and the IT industry.

Quality assessment plays a key role in optimizing MT tool or engine performance. Based on the results of the manual or automatic evaluation, MT tools are optimized. The biggest disadvantage of manual evaluation is its subjectivity and is labour- and time-consuming. On the other hand, manual evaluation is highly desirable and is considered very reliable. The advantage of automatic evaluation is speed, objectivity, and reusability, but it does not provide detailed information about the translation error rate or its accuracy. The result of the automatic evaluation is a score between 0 and 1, which is calculated based on a lexical comparison of the MT output with a human translation (reference). Despite the fact that results of manual or automatic evaluation provide very valuable information and help to improve MT systems, developers and researchers often look for additional information which could affect the performance of a given system or engine and help them to answer questions such as: What are the biggest problems of MT systems? What are the strengths and weaknesses of the given system? Finding the relationship between the strengths or weaknesses of the system and the result of manual or automatic evaluation is not easy [6]. It motivated us to implement error analysis to create an error profile of MT output. However, during error identification and classification, we encountered the same problems as during manual evaluation, which is mainly associated with time and labour. So besides error annotation, we decided to apply measures of language complexity, characterizing text complexity and examine the relationship between these measures and individual MT error types (categories).

The aim of the study is to determine the relationship between individual types of MT errors and selected measures of text complexity. We attempt to characterize MT errors using the internal properties of the text, i.e., to determine which properties of the text are associated with the error rate of the given category.

The remaining part of this paper is organized as follows: Sect. 2 briefly reviews the research background, Sect. 3 provides information about our data, Sect. 4 demonstrates our results, as well as the analysis and finally Sect. 5 concludes our work.

2 Research Background

The complexity of natural language is one of the current topics that is discussed not only in natural language processing and AI but also in linguistic research. Language complexity is considered a suitable measurable approach that describes performance, indicates proficiency, and measures an individual's development in language [7]. This approach is based on a theoretical framework considering language as a complex adaptive system [8], recognizing the relationship between the target language and its use as a double system, in which linear and non-linear links between several factors are formed by predicative, but also non-predicative tasks of contextual and linguistic elements [9]. Linguistic complexity represents an inherent property of a system by which languages can be compared according to several formal properties, such as the number of rules to obtain a certain output, the number of exceptions to the rules, or the size of the lexicon differing at different levels of representation [10]. It is a property of language that can be measured in several language subsystems [11].

Text Complexity is an internal characteristic of a written text affecting the performance of computer applications which process the text [12]. Text complexity is independent either from the reader of the text or the environmental conditions, i.e. it is an independent typographic representation of the text, which can manifest itself at all three levels - lexical, syntactic, and discourse. At the lexical level, the factors affecting lexical complexity (the meaning of words, or the lexical choice used in the text) mainly consist of rich vocabulary, long words, infrequent and technical terms, ambiguous words, vague quantifiers, inconsistent terminology, and figurative language. Several formulas are applied to calculate the frequencies of individual linguistic units. This approach is based on the premise that the more lexically rich and diverse the text is, the more complex it is. Lexical complexity deals with lexical density, diversity, and rareness [13]. Kalantari and Gholami [13: 3] define lexical density as the proportion of lexical (content) words to the total number of words in a text while lexical diversity measures the number of different words and specific word types used in a text. According to Mat Daud et al. [14], lexical density is inversely proportional to readability, and therefore readability formulas could be applied to lexical density. Modern approaches in natural language processing such as machine learning techniques are applied to automate the process of the assessment of readability [15].

At the syntactic level, the main factors [16] that affect the length and syntactic structure of the sentence are long sentences, complicated syntax, passive voice, and negative constructions. Formulas for measuring syntactic complexity are generally based on quantifying linguistic units [17]. Syntactic complexity is a quality of sentence construction and its underlying principles [11: 456].

In the context of translation quality evaluation, readability measures are often used to assess or determine the complexity of the source and target text [18]. Currently, there are more than 200 readability formulas [19] that are used for different types of documents or for various industries. Even military and governmental agencies develop formulas themselves, as they consider them a very good quality indicator when writing technical manuals. Belonging to the most used formulas are the Automated Readability Index (for technical documents and manuals), Flesch Reading Ease (any kind of text), and Flesch-Kincaid (manuals, forms, and other technical documents).

For the publishing industry, which deals with newspapers, journals, online media etc., it is suitable to use Flesch Reading Ease (any kind of text), SMOG (text aimed at secondary-age readers) or Gunning Fog (business publications and journals).

3 Research Method

We were inspired by the previous research [20–24], who investigated the relationship between automatic MT evaluation metrics and the types of errors that occurred in neural MT. In this research, we focus on the internal characteristics of a complex adaptive system, in our case an MT system, and attempt to determine the relationship between measures of text complexity and distribution of errors over the defined error classes. We attempt to determine which of the examined measures of lexical and syntactic complexity (30 measures) associate the best with individual error classes of a categorical framework for error analysis [25: 100]. The examined texts (1903 sentences/66 texts) were taken from the British online newspaper The Guardian. In 2021, the texts were translated by the freely available Neural Google Translate (NGT) engine. The dataset (Table 1) consists of neural MT texts translated from English into Slovak (NMTs).

Table 1. Dataset composition

Feature type	Feature name	NMTs_SK
Readability	Average sentence length	17.12034
	Average word length	5.696361
	#short sentences ($n < 10$)	469
	#long sentences ($n \geq 10$)	1434
Lexico-grammatical	Frequency of proper nouns	1501
	Frequency of nouns	10070
	Frequency of adjectives	3324
	Frequency of adverbs	933
	Frequency of verbs	5198
	Frequency of pronominals	2371
	Frequency of particles	592
	Frequency of foreign words	841
	Frequency of numerals	617
	Frequency of prepositions & conjunctions	6028
	Frequency of interpunction	5958

Subsequently, the NMTs were manually annotated according to the framework for error analysis [25: 100] by three Slovak linguists. The categorical framework consists of five error classes (categories):

1. Predication,
2. Modal and communication sentence framework,
3. Syntactic-semantic correlativeness,
4. Compound/complex sentences,
5. Lexical semantics.

After manual error classification, we identified 3081 error segments in our corpus. Specifically, we identified 686 errors in the category of Prediction, 52 errors in the category of Modal and communication sentence framework, 1486 errors in Syntactic-semantic correlativeness, 671 errors in Compound/complex sentences, and 2778 errors in the category of Lexical semantics (Table 2).

3.1 Hypothesis

Based on the descriptive statistics we assume that there is a statistically significant difference between the error categories of the framework. We state the following hypothesis:

H0: Between the error categories, there are no differences in the frequency of errors obtained from the examined neural MT texts.

3.2 Methods

For the metrics of lexical and syntactic complexity, the Python Natural Language Toolkit (NLTK) library was used. To calculate the score of lexical diversity of texts [26] we applied the Type-Token Ratio (TTR), Herdan's lexical diversity measure (Herdan's C), Guiraud's Root TTR (Guiraud's R), Carroll's Corrected TTR (CTTR), Summer's lexical diversity measure (Summer's index S), Dugast's lexical diversity measure (Dugast's Uber Index U), Maas's lexical diversity measure (Maas's indices (a, $\log V_0$ & $\log_e V_0$)), Mean Segmental Type-token Ratio (MSTTR), Moving Average Type-token Ratio (MATTR), Measure of Textual Lexical Diversity (MTLD), Hypergeometric distribution diversity measure (HD-D), and Hapax legomenon ratio (Hapax). To calculate the score of lexical density, we applied the following readability formulas: Flesch reading ease (FRE), Flesch-Kincaid Grade Level (FKG), Fog Scale (Gunning FOG Formula) (FOG), SMOG Index (SMOG), Automated Readability Index (ARI), Coleman-Liau Index (CLI), McAlpine EFLAW Readability Score (MAR), and Reading Time (RT). To calculate syntactic complexity, we applied Sentence Count (SenC) and Word count (WordC). We also applied traditional features such as Syllable Count (SC), Character Count (CharC), Letter Count (LetC), Polysyllable Count (PolyC), Monosyllable Count (MonoC), and Lexicon Count (LC), which may contribute to the complexity of a text.

4 Results

Based on the Friedman ANOVA test ($ChiSqr = 246.584, N = 66, df = 4, p < 0.001$) we proved statistically significant differences between the categories (Predication, Modal and communication sentence, framework, Syntactic-semantic correlativeness, Compound/complex sentences, and Lexical semantics) in the frequency of errors found in neural MT texts.

Table 2. Descriptive Statistics

	N	Mean	Median	Sum	Min	Maxi	Lower Q	Upper Q	Quartile R
Error_segments	66	46.68	41.00	3081.00	7.00	141.00	26.00	61.00	35.00
Correct_segments	66	2.88	2.00	190.00	0.00	13.00	1.00	4.00	3.00
Predication	66	10.39	9.00	686.00	1.00	36.00	6.00	14.00	8.00
Modal and communication framework	66	0.79	0.00	52.00	0.00	4.00	0.00	2.00	2.00
Syntactic-semantic correlativeness	66	22.52	19.50	1486.00	4.00	65.00	12.00	30.00	18.00
Compound/complex sentences	66	10.17	9.00	671.00	0.00	32.00	6.00	12.00	6.00
Lexical semantics	66	42.09	37.00	2778.00	6.00	125.00	23.00	54.00	31.00

After rejecting the global null hypothesis, we are interested in the relationship between error categories that have a statistically significant difference. We identified ($p > 0.05$) only one homogeneous group (Compound/complex sentences and Predication). For both categories, the frequency of errors was approximately equal. A statistically significant difference ($p < 0.05$) was identified between the remaining error categories, whereby the lowest frequency of errors was obtained for the Modal and communication framework and the highest for Syntactic-semantic correlativeness and Lexical semantics.

Based on the results of multiple comparisons (Table 3), we showed statistically significant differences between Syntactic-semantic correlativeness/Lexical semantics/Modal and communication framework and other categories, but there is no statistically significant difference between Compound/complex sentences and Predication. This is also confirmed by the median (9), which is the same for both error categories.

We were also interested in how the measures of lexical and syntactic complexity explain the frequency of errors for individual categories, i.e., which of the automatic measures was the best, or conversely, the worst associated with the frequency of found errors for each category. For this purpose, we applied 30 measures of text complexity (including traditional linguistic features) and through Goodman and Kruskal's gamma, we determine the rank associations between error categories and measures of text complexity.

Table 3. Multiple comparisons

	Median	Mean	1	2	3	4
Modal and communication framework	0	0.79		****		
Compound/complex sentences	9	10.17	****			
Predication	9	10.39	****			
Syntactic-semantic correlativeness	19.5	22.52			****	
Lexical semantics	37	42.09				****

Note: *** * p > 0.05

Gamma represents the probability (Table 4) of whether two variables are in the same or opposite order. It represents the degree of association between two variables.

The errors in the category of Prediction (Table 4) are partially identified by measures UniWC, RTTR, CTTR, WordC LC, MonoC, LetC, CharC, SC, RT, PolyC, and SenC, where were achieved low to moderate measures of positive and statistically significant association ($Gamma > 0.27/0.302, p < 0.01/0.001$). Similarly, it achieved a low measure of association, but a statistically significant negative association between Prediction and Hapax and/or TTR ($Gamma < -0.190, p < 0.05/0.01$).

The error rate in the Prediction category is best explained by the metric of syntactic complexity (SenC) and traditional linguistic features that are based on the count, i.e., the higher the score of these metrics and linguistic features, the higher the error rate in the category of Prediction. And vice versa, measures of lexical diversity such as Hapax or TTR are negatively associated with error rate in the category of Prediction, i.e., the greater the score of the total number of unique words (types) divided by the total number of words, the lower the association with the given category.

We proceeded in the same way with the other categories. For the category of Modal and communication framework, a low positive measure of association with measures such as SenC, MonoC or MTLD ($Gamma > 0.244, p < 0.05/0.01$) was achieved. For this category, we also showed a small, but statistically significant association between traditional linguistic features and the occurrence of MT errors as well as between lexical diversity and MT errors in the given category.

For the category of Syntactic-semantic correlativeness (Table 5), we have achieved a low to a high positive measure of association between measures SenC, MonoC (*Gamma* > 0.505, *p* < 0.001), WordC, RT, CharC, LC, SC, LetC, UniWC, RTTR, CTTR, PolyC (*Gamma* > 0.400, *p* < 0.001), HD-D (*Gamma* = 0.178, *p* < 0.05) and error rate of neural MT within this category. Besides the positive measure of association, we also achieved a low to moderate negative, but also a statistically significant measure of association between Herdan, Hapax, TTR, and occurrence of MT errors in this category (*Gamma* < −0.247/−0.319, *p* < 0.01/0.001).

Table 4. Goodman and Kruskal's gamma – Prediction

	Valid N	Gamma	Z	p-value
predication & SenC_NMT	66	**0.334***	3.832	**0.0001**
predication & PolyC_NMT	66	**0.308***	3.555	**0.0004**
predication & RT_NMT	66	**0.302***	3.502	**0.0005**
predication & SC_NMT	66	**0.302***	3.501	**0.0005**
predication & CharC_NMT	66	**0.302***	3.502	**0.0005**
predication & LetC_NMT	66	**0.297***	3.450	**0.0006**
predication & MonoC_NMT	66	**0.296***	3.432	**0.0006**
predication & LC_NMT	66	**0.288***	3.350	**0.0008**
predication & WordC_NMT	66	**0.286***	3.312	**0.0009**
predication & UniWC_NMT	66	**0.285***	3.302	**0.0010**
predication & RTTR_NMT	66	**0.270***	3.133	**0.0017**
predication & CTTR_NMT	66	**0.270***	3.133	**0.0017**
predication & MTLD_NMT	66	0.132	1.538	0.1240
predication & HD-D_NMT	66	0.123	1.425	0.1541
predication & FRE_NMT	66	0.061	0.709	0.4782
predication & MSTTR_NMT	66	0.034	0.397	0.6914
predication & Maas_NMT	66	0.032	0.373	0.7090
predication & MATTR_NMT	66	0.016	0.181	0.8564
predication & Dugast_NMT	66	-0.032	-0.373	0.7090
predication & SMOG_NMT	66	-0.056	-0.645	0.5191
predication & MAR_NMT	66	-0.076	-0.879	0.3795
predication & FKG_NMT	66	-0.077	-0.885	0.3762
predication & CLI_NMT	66	-0.078	-0.902	0.3673
predication & Summer_NMT	66	-0.078	-0.905	0.3655
predication & ARI_NMT	66	-0.103	-1.194	0.2326
predication & FOG_NMT	66	-0.108	-1.257	0.2089
predication & Herdan_NMT	66	-0.161	-1.866	0.0620
predication & Hapax_NMT	66	**-0.190***	-2.206	**0.0274**
predication & TTR_NMT	66	**-0.231****	-2.681	**0.0073**

Note: 0.00 to 0.10 (0.00 to −0.10) – a trivial positive (negative) measure of association; 0.10–0.30 (−0.10 to −0.30) – a low positive (negative) measure of association; 0.30–0.50 (−0.30 to −0.50) – a moderate positive (negative) measure of association; 0.50–0.70 (−0.50 to −0.70) – a high positive (negative) measure of association; 0.70–1.00 (−0.70 to −1.00) – a very high positive (negative) measure of association; ***$p < 0.001$, **$p < 0.01$, *$p < 0.05$

For the category compound/complex sentences, we obtained similar results as for syntactic-semantic correlativeness. We have achieved a low to moderate positive measure of association between measures UniWC, SenC, RT, CharC, WordC, SC, LC, MonoC, LetC, RTTR, CTTR, PolyC (*Gamma* > 0.398, *p* < 0.001), MTLD, HD-D (*Gamma* > 0.193, *p* < 0.05) and occurrence of MT errors within this category. On

Table 5. Goodman and Kruskal's gamma - Syntactic-semantic correlativeness

	Valid N	Gamma	Z	p-value
syn-sem corr & SenC_NMT	66	0.507***	5.876	0.0000
syn-sem corr & MonoC_NMT	66	0.505***	5.916	0.0000
syn-sem corr & WordC_NMT	66	0.496***	5.808	0.0000
syn-sem corr & RT_NMT	66	0.494***	5.787	0.0000
syn-sem corr & CharC_NMT	66	0.494***	5.787	0.0000
syn-sem corr & LC_NMT	66	0.490***	5.742	0.0000
syn-sem corr & SC_NMT	66	0.489***	5.735	0.0000
syn-sem corr & LetC_NMT	66	0.486***	5.706	0.0000
syn-sem corr & UniWC_NMT	66	0.483***	5.658	0.0000
syn-sem corr & RTTR_NMT	66	0.449***	5.269	0.0000
syn-sem corr & CTTR_NMT	66	0.449***	5.269	0.0000
syn-sem corr & PolyC_NMT	66	0.400***	4.669	0.0000
syn-sem corr & HD-D_NMT	66	0.178*	2.089	0.0367
syn-sem corr & FRE_NMT	66	0.142	1.657	0.0975
syn-sem corr & MTLD_NMT	66	0.124	1.450	0.1470
syn-sem corr & Maas_NMT	66	0.038	0.442	0.6582
syn-sem corr & MAR_NMT	66	-0.022	-0.258	0.7962
syn-sem corr & Dugast_NMT	66	-0.038	-0.442	0.6582
syn-sem corr & MSTTR_NMT	66	-0.075	-0.876	0.3810
syn-sem corr & MATTR_NMT	66	-0.079	-0.924	0.3555
syn-sem corr & FKG_NMT	66	-0.117	-1.362	0.1731
syn-sem corr & ARI_NMT	66	-0.128	-1.492	0.1358
syn-sem corr & Summer_NMT	66	-0.141	-1.652	0.0985
syn-sem corr & CLI_NMT	66	-0.147	-1.724	0.0848
syn-sem corr & FOG_NMT	66	-0.154	-1.799	0.0720
syn-sem corr & SMOG_NMT	66	-0.160	-1.865	0.0623
syn-sem corr & Herdan_NMT	66	-0.247**	-2.895	0.0038
syn-sem corr & Hapax_NMT	66	-0.319***	-3.746	0.0002
syn-sem corr & TTR_NMT	66	-0.389***	-4.564	0.0000

Note: 0.00 to 0.10 (0.00 to −0.10) – a trivial positive (negative) measure of association; 0.10–0.30 (−0.10 to −0.30) – a low positive (negative) measure of association; 0.30–0.50 (−0.30 to −0.50) – a moderate positive (negative) measure of association; 0.50–0.70 (−0.50 to −0.70) – a high positive (negative) measure of association; 0.70–1.00 (−0.70 to −1.00) – a very high positive (negative) measure of association; ***$p < 0.001$, **$p < 0.01$, *$p < 0.05$

the other hand, we also achieved a negative low to a moderate measure of association between measures Herdan, Hapax, TTR and error rate for this category (*Gamma* < − 0.184/−0.305, $p < 0.05/0.01/0.001$).

For the category of Lexical semantics (Table 6), we have achieved a moderate to high positive measure of association between measures SenC, MonoC, SC, RT, CharC, WordC, LC, LetC, UniWC, RTTR, CTTR, PolyC (*Gamma* > 0.430/0.529, $p < 0.001$) and occurrence of the error rate of neural MT within this category. Besides the positive measure of association, we also achieved a low to moderate negative, but also a statistically significant measure of association between Summer, Herdan, Hapax, TTR, and occurrence of MT errors in this category (*Gamma* < −0.188/−0.338, $p < 0.05/0.001$).

Table 6. Goodman and Kruskal's gamma – Lexical semantics

	Valid N	Gamma	Z	p-value
lexical sem & SenC_NMT	66	0.529***	6.161	0.0000
lexical sem & MonoC_NMT	66	0.497***	5.852	0.0000
lexical sem & SC_NMT	66	0.496***	5.850	0.0000
lexical sem & RT_NMT	66	0.489***	5.768	0.0000
lexical sem & CharC_NMT	66	0.489***	5.768	0.0000
lexical sem & WordC_NMT	66	0.489***	5.756	0.0000
lexical sem & LC_NMT	66	0.487***	5.746	0.0000
lexical sem & LetC_NMT	66	0.482***	5.688	0.0000
lexical sem & UniWC_NMT	66	0.482***	5.673	0.0000
lexical sem & RTTR_NMT	66	0.440***	5.186	0.0000
lexical sem & CTTR_NMT	66	0.440***	5.186	0.0000
lexical sem & PolyC_NMT	66	0.430***	5.043	0.0000
lexical semas & FRE_NMT	66	0.155	1.828	0.0676
lexical sem & HD-D_NMT	66	0.124	1.465	0.1429
lexical sem & MTLD_NMT	66	0.103	1.209	0.2267
lexical sem & Maas_NMT	66	0.090	1.064	0.2873
lexical sem & MAR_NMT	66	-0.043	-0.503	0.6152
lexical sem & MSTTR_NMT	66	-0.073	-0.855	0.3927
lexical sem & Dugast_NMT	66	-0.090	-1.064	0.2873
lexical sem & MATTR_NMT	66	-0.123	-1.454	0.1460
lexical sem & FKG_NMT	66	-0.130	-1.513	0.1304
lexical sem & SMOG_NMT	66	-0.131	-1.529	0.1263
lexical sem & ARI_NMT	66	-0.141	-1.652	0.0986
lexical sem & FOG_NMT	66	-0.154	-1.812	0.0700
lexical sem & CLI_NMT	66	-0.157	-1.843	0.0653
lexical sem & Summer_NMT	66	-0.188*	-2.223	0.0262
lexical sem & Herdan_NMT	66	-0.291***	-3.437	0.0006
lexical sem & Hapax_NMT	66	-0.338***	-3.983	0.0001
lexical sem & TTR_NMT	66	-0.421***	-4.963	0.0000

Note: 0.00 to 0.10 (0.00 to −0.10) – a trivial positive (negative) measure of association; 0.10–0.30 (−0.10 to −0.30) – a low positive (negative) measure of association; 0.30–0.50 (−0.30 to −0.50) – a moderate positive (negative) measure of association; 0.50–0.70 (−0.50 to −0.70) – a high positive (negative) measure of association; 0.70–1.00 (−0.70 to −1.00) – a very high positive (negative) measure of association; ***$p < 0.001$, **$p < 0.01$, *$p < 0.05$

5   Conclusion

Our study brings two insights into the evaluation of MT quality and into the complexity of language as a system. We find that errors that arise in neural MT of journalistic texts associate the best with linguistic properties which are based on countability. This is mainly the sentence count property. The identified association is logical in terms of a larger number of sentences so that the frequency of error categories will also increase. Other properties that showed strong associations with error categories were based on the count or frequency, such as monosyllabic or polysyllabic words.

A notable finding is that not all examined measures of lexical diversity are associated with the frequency of errors in each category. We found only two measures out of all twelve examined measures, RTTR and CTTR, which show a moderate positive statistically significant association with error frequency in the categories of Syntactic-semantic correlativity, Compound/complex sentences, and Lexical semantics.

Another notable finding is that readability scores do not associate with error categories. We explain this by the fact that our corpus consists of journalistic texts, which themselves are easily readable and therefore we found no correlations. The second explanation is that the neural MT tool is much more fluent than its predecessor and does not produce a large number of MT errors that affect readability. An interesting finding is related only to the RTTR and CTTR measures, despite the fact that both are derived from the TTR measure, but the TTR measure is negatively moderately associated with the three error categories mentioned above, but this association is statistically significant. Here, further research is called for to investigate the reasons for this paradox. Besides the TTR measure, the lexical diversity measures Hapax and Herdan are also negatively associated with the occurrence of MT errors within these categories.

Acknowledgement. This work was supported by the Slovak Research and Development Agency under contract No. APVV-18-0473 and Scientific Grant Agency of the Ministry of Education of the Slovak Republic (ME SR) and of Slovak Academy of Sciences (SAS) under the contract No. VEGA-1/0821/21. This research was funded by the European Commission under the ERASMUS+ Programme 2021, KA2, grant number: 2021-1-SK01-KA220-HED-000032095 "Future IT Professionals EDucation in Artificial Intelligence".

References

1. Koehn, P.: Machine Translation Overview. https://omniscien.com/machine-translation/
2. Lihua, Z.: The relationship between machine translation and human translation under the influence of artificial intelligence machine translation. Mob. Inf. Syst. **2022**, 1–8 (2022). https://doi.org/10.1155/2022/9121636
3. Wang, Y., Wang, Y., Wang, Y.: A new approach to machine translation and human translation in the Era of Artificial Intelligence. Overseas Engl. **7**, 179–180 (2021)
4. GreatContent: The 11 Best Machine (AI) Translation Tools in 2022. https://greatcontent.com/machine-ai-translation-tools/#introduction
5. Virino, V.: Artificial Intelligence applied to Machine Translation at FITUR 2021. https://blog.pangeanic.com/ai-applied-to-mt-at-fitur-2021
6. Popović, M.: Error classification and analysis for machine translation quality assessment. In: Moorkens, J., Castilho, S., Gaspari, F., Doherty, S. (eds.) Translation Quality Assessment. MTTA, vol. 1, pp. 129–158. Springer, Cham (2018). https://doi.org/10.1007/978-3-319-912 41-7_7
7. Bulté, B., Housen, A.: Evaluating short-term changes in L2 complexity development. Círculo de lingüística aplicada a la comunicación **63** (2015). https://doi.org/10.5209/rev_CLAC.2015.v63.50169
8. De Bot, K.: A History of Applied Linguistics. Routledge, New York (2015)
9. Kovačević, E.: The relationship between lexical complexity measures and language learning beliefs <b/>. Jezikoslovlje **20**, 555–582 (2019). https://doi.org/10.29162/jez.2019.20
10. Brunato, D.: A study on linguistic complexity from a computational linguistics perspective. A corpus-based investigation of Italian bureaucratic texts (2015)
11. Kovačević, E.: The relationship between language learning beliefs and syntactic complexity. In: Gudurić, S., Radić-Bojanić, B. (eds.) Jezici i Kulture u Vremenu i Prostoru 6, pp. 455–464. University of Novi Sad, Novi Sad (2017)
12. Temnikova, I.: Text Complexity and Text Simplification in the Crisis Management Domain (2012)

13. Kalantari, R., Gholami, J.: Lexical complexity development from dynamic systems theory perspective: lexical density, diversity, and sophistication. Int. J. Instr. **10**, 1–18 (2017). https://doi.org/10.12973/iji.2017.1041a
14. Mat Daud, N., Hassan, H., El-Tingari, S., Abdul Aziz, N.: Web-based Arabic text readability index. In: 8th International Technology, Education and Development Conference, Valencia, Spain, pp. 1574–1581. IATED Academy (2014)
15. Imperial, J.M., Ong, E.: Application of Lexical Features Towards Improvement of Filipino Readability Identification of Children's Literature. arXiv 7 (2021)
16. Jurafsky, D., Martin, J.: Speech and Language Processing (2020)
17. Lu, X.: Automatic analysis of syntactic complexity in second language writing. Int. J. Corpus Linguist. **15**, 474–496 (2010)
18. Doherty, S.: Investigating the Effects of Controlled Language on the Reading and Comprehension of Machine Translated Texts: A Mixed-Methods Approach (2012)
19. ReadabilityFormulas: How Do I Decide Which Readability Formula Or Formulas To Use On My Document? https://readabilityformulas.com/search/pages/Readability_Formulas/
20. Benko, L., Benkova, L., Munkova, D., Munk, M., Shulzenko, D.: Error classification using automatic measures based on n-grams and edit distance. In: Guarda, T., Portela, F., Augusto, M.F. (eds.) ARTIIS 2022. CCIS, vol. 1675, pp. 345–356. Springer, Cham (2022). https://doi.org/10.1007/978-3-031-20319-0_26
21. Munkova, D., Munk, M., Benko, Ľ., Stastny, J.: MT evaluation in the context of language complexity. Complexity **2021**, 1–15 (2021).https://doi.org/10.1155/2021/2806108
22. Munkova, D., Munk, M., Welnitzova, K., Jakabovicova, J.: Product and process analysis of machine translation into the inflectional language. Sage Open **11**, 215824402110545 (2021). https://doi.org/10.1177/21582440211054501
23. Munkova, D., Munk, M., Benko, Ľ, Hajek, P.: The role of automated evaluation techniques in online professional translator training. PeerJ Comput Sci. **7**, e706 (2021). https://doi.org/10.7717/peerj-cs.706
24. Kapusta, J., Benko, Ľ, Munkova, D., Munk, M.: Analysis of edit operations for post-editing systems. Int. J. Comput. Intell. Syst. **14**, 197 (2021). https://doi.org/10.1007/s44196-021-00048-3
25. Vaňko, J.: Kategoriálny rámec pre analýzu chýb strojového prekladu. In: Munkova, D., Vaňko, J. (eds.) Mýliť sa je ľudské (ale aj strojové), pp. 83–100. UKF v Nitre, Nitra (2017)
26. Zhang, Y., Lin, N., Jiang, S.: A study on syntactic complexity and text readability of ASEAN English news. In: 2019 International Conference on Asian Language Processing (IALP), pp. 313–318. IEEE (2019). https://doi.org/10.1109/IALP48816.2019.9037695

Differential-Privacy Preserving Trajectory Data Publishing for Road Networks

Songyuan Li[1], Hui Tian[2], Hong Shen[1,3]([✉]), and Yingpeng Sang[1]

[1] School of Computer Science and Engineering, Sun Yat-sen University,
Guangzhou, China
[2] School of Information and Communication Technology, Griffith University,
Nathan, Australia
[3] School of Applied Sciences, Macao Polytechnic University, Macao, China
hshen@mpu.edu.mo

Abstract. In the sharing of user trajectory data of road networks, privacy leakage emerges to be a major concern because attackers may make aggressive reasoning and analysis based on the published trajectory data with certain background knowledge to obtain the privacy information (e.g. location) associated with individuals. Most existing trajectory privacy-preserving methods require special assumptions about the types of attacks and their associated background knowledge, are therefore unable to achieve the required strength for privacy protection. This paper proposes a novel algorithm of differential privacy preserving trajectory data publishing for road networks by spatial coupling of ambiguity using a noisy R-tree ($Cons\text{-}XRT$), which can resist attacks with arbitrary background knowledge even in the case of sparse trajectories. Our algorithm first blurs the spatial trajectory locations using an R-tree index of the trajectory data to form a noisy R-tree of the trajectory that satisfies the differential privacy preserving condition. It then generates trajectory count values to hide the relative changes of the statistical data of adjacent sections in adjacent periods, and eliminate the fluctuations of statistical data. Finally, it deploys a fast query algorithm for spatial range count query which uses the noise counts in the noisy R-tree index nodes to quickly return the number of moving objects satisfying differential privacy. Extensive experiments on real public transport vehicle trajectory datasets of Guangdong Province show that our $Cons\text{-}XRT$ method achieves differential privacy trajectory protection which can resist the attacks with maximum background knowledge.

Keywords: Trajectory Data Publishing · Privacy-preserving Computing · Differential Privacy

1 Introduction

In recent years, with the development of mobile Internet, Internet of Things and spatial positioning technology, a large number of trajectory data of people and mobile objects have been generated, which provides a great value for data

© The Author(s), under exclusive license to Springer Nature Switzerland AG 2023
N. T. Nguyen et al. (Eds.): ACIIDS 2023, CCIS 1863, pp. 558–571, 2023.
https://doi.org/10.1007/978-3-031-42430-4_46

analysis and mining. For example, through the analysis and processing of trajectory data, monitoring the traffic status of the road network for people to plan travel paths, query the crowd density for early warning and evacuation, mine the user travel model to provide personalized services, etc. However, as trajectory data usually contains sensitive information of moving objects, improper use of trajectory data can easily lead to the disclosure of sensitive information such as user's habits, health status and social status. For example, the feature of a mobile object visiting a specific bank location and staying for a specific time can expose the identity of cash carrying vehicle. Hence, how to make a trade-off between the degree of privacy protection and data utility such that we can utilize the great value of trajectory data without exposing user privacy maximize the value of data mining while protecting user's privacy becomes an urgent task to accomplish.

Extensive research has been done on trajectory data publishing with user privacy preservation. There is a rich literature on privacy-preserving techniques such as data anonymity [17,30], data perturbation [24] and differential privacy [3,29]. Differential privacy is known as the strongest privacy protection scheme to resist attacks with maximum background knowledge. Trajectory data privacy protection based on differential privacy, which overcomes the shortcomings of traditional privacy protection schemes, has thus become a hot spot of research.

For the problem of privacy-preserving publishing of user trajectory data on a road network, we proposes a novel algorithm deploying a noisy R-tree to achieve differential privacy preserving, which can resist attacks with maximum background knowledge even in the case of sparse trajectories. Experimental results show that the proposed algorithm has good performance in preventing privacy leakage.

2   Related Work

The existing trajectory privacy-preserving methods can be classified into the following three categories:

2.1   Anonymity Based

Most existing privacy-preserving trajectory data publishing techniques use generalization or disruption methods to deal with the published trajectory to conform to the k-anonymity model.

Machanavajjhala et al. [2,20] proposed an enhanced k-anonymity model, l-diversity model. The l-diversity principle requires that each k-anonymity group in a data table contain at least l different sensitive attribute values. The attacker infers that the probability of a recorded privacy message would be less than $1/l$.

Abul et al. [1,4] proposed (k, δ)-anonymity model based on the uncertainty of moving trajectory data. On the basis of the model, the problem of trajectory anonymity was treated by clustering. However, by analyzing the protection degree of (k, δ)-anonymity model, the model can only realize the k-anonymity of the trajectory just under the condition of $\delta = 0$.

Li et al. [16,17] proposed a privacy-preserving publishing method for trajectory data based on data partitioning. With the passage of time, the algorithm can effectively process the trajectories in each data partition without recalculating the published trajectories, thus effectively reducing the computational cost. It has efficient trajectory scanning, clustering and privacy-preserving functions.

2.2 Disturbance Based

Many existing techniques are based on independent and identically distributed (*i.i.d.*) position sampling from random walks on grids, road networks or between points of interests.

Shokri et al. [25,26] proposed a uniform independent identical distribution method, which generates each false location independently from the uniform probability distribution and makes it have an identical distribution. Therefore, the false trajectory is a series of unrelated false positions.

The methods proposed by Chow et al. and Krumm et al. [7,15] can be summarized as follows: giving the probability distribution p of crowd movement, randomly walk on a series of positions with the probability distribution p, and finally generate a false trajectory with the selected positions.

Kato et al. [14] proposed a method to predict the random walk on the user's mobile trajectory, and then to predict the probability distribution $p(u)$ of the user's subsequent mobile trajectory. The probability distribution $p(u)$ was used to walk randomly on a series of positions. Finally, a false trajectory was generated from the selected positions.

2.3 Differential Privacy Based

Differential privacy is the strongest known unconditional privacy protection technique that can resist the privacy attacks with maximum background knowledge.

Gursoy et al. [11,27] proposed a differentially private and utility preserving publication method for trajectory data. The method presents *DP-Star*, a methodical framework for publishing trajectory data with differential privacy guarantee as well as high utility preservation. From comparisons, the *DP-Star* significantly outperforms existing approaches in terms of trajectory utility and accuracy.

Luo et al. [19] proposed an enhancing frequent location privacy-preserving strategy based on geo-Indistinguishability. The method have a three-step framework. First, the location set is classified by the density-based clustering algorithm, and the privacy budget allocation function is used to allocate the corresponding budget for each cluster. Then, the real location is disturbed according to geo-indistinguishability. Finally, this method present a privacy metric approach derived from the information entropy to quantify the information leakage by the mechanism.

Darakhshan et al. [22] introduced *DP*-Where method, which called detailed records (*CDRs*) database to generate different private composite databases, and its distribution was close to real *CDRs*. However, *CDRs* are not equivalent to full position trajectories because the position is known only when called.

Proserpio et al. [23] introduced the $wPINQ$ method, which achieves different privacy by calibrating the weight of some data records. $wPINQ$ method further proposes a method of generating synthetic datasets by using Markov chain Monte Carlo method, which focuses on the graph of noisy measure with a given number of triangles.

Zhao et al. [18,29] proposed a trajectory privacy-preserving method based on clustering using differential privacy. In these method, radius-constrained Laplacian noise is added to the trajectory location data in the cluster to avoid too much noise affecting the clustering effect, and they considered that the attacker can associate the user trajectory with other information to form secret reasoning attack, and proposed a secret reasoning attack model.

For privacy protection of spatial data including trajectories, in comparison with private spatial decomposition (PSD) method [13,28], differential privacy is especially good for resisting active inference attacks based on statistical queries of location data.

3   The Attack Model

3.1   Notations

We define the basic terminologies used in this paper below, and the mathematical symbols in Table 1.

Table 1. Important Notations in This Work

Notations	Description
tr	trajectory
(x, y)	two spatial dimensions
p_k	position of tr at time t_k
$Dist(tr_1[t_k], tr_2[t_k])$	distance between tr_1 and tr_2 at the time t_k
ID	identity of tr
$[t_{start}, t_{end}]$	time interval of trajectory
$tr[t_{start}, t_{end}]$	trajectory segment in $[t_{start}, t_{end}]$
$D(tr)$	trajectory database
$D_t(tr)$	database snapshot of $D(tr)$ at time t
$D_s(tr)$	trajectory sampling database
$D_p(tr)$	protected database of $D(tr)$ for publishing
$G(E, V)$	undirected Graph
MBR	minimum Bounding Rectangle
ε	differential privacy budget
RE	relative Error
rs	road link
t	time

Definition 1. *Trajectory (tr). A trajectory is a path in the three-dimensional space (two spatial dimensions and one temporal dimension), represented by* $tr = \{p_1, p_2, \ldots, p_m\}$*. A point (position) of tr* $p_k = (x_k, y_k, t_k)$*, where* x_k, y_k *are longitude and latitude,* t_k *is time,* $t_1 < t_2 < \ldots < t_k \cdots < t_m$*, and* m *is the number of sampling points.*

A trajectory is identified by a unique number ID *(identity).*

We use $D(tr)$ for the database of trajectories: $D(tr) = \{(ID, tr_i)\}$, $|D| = n$, $1 \le i \le n$, $D_s(tr) \subseteq D(tr)$ for the trajectory sampling database, and $D_p(tr)$ for the protected $D(tr)$ for publishing.

Definition 2. *Spatial range query (Query). Given the spatial range* R *and the snapshot* $D_t(tr)$ *of the trajectory database, the spatial range query* $Query()$ *on the dataset can be expressed as:*

$$Query(D_t(tr), R) = \{x | x \in D_t(tr), x \in range(R)\}. \tag{1}$$

Definition 3. Partition publishing of the road network spatial trajectory data $(D_p(tr))$**.** *The partition publishing of trajectory data in a road network is to establish the road section index tree and publish the counting data of moving objects in the road network based on the road sections in the road network space, where the published snapshot of the trajectory database* $D(tr)$ *is recorded as* $D_p(tr)$*.*

3.2   Attack Model

If the attacker has the complete knowledge of the moving object, road network space and privacy-preserving algorithm, the attacker can use the background knowledge to attack the trajectory of the moving object and restore the original trajectory information of the moving object. This process is called the Strongest Background Knowledge Attack.

We assume that the attacker has the following background knowledge:

1. Links of the published trajectory data $D_p(tr)$ to the moving objects.
2. Attributes and related domain knowledge of the moving objects.
3. Locations of some moving objects at some specific time.

When the attacker identifies the position of the moving object at a certain time, he can infer the trajectory of the moving object by using the fluctuation of the link count. As shown in Fig. 1, through the background knowledge, the attacker can know that the moving object $User$ is in the segment $rs1$ at time t; through the fluctuation of statistical data at time t and $t + 1$, the attacker can infer that a moving object of segment $rs1$ at time t moves to segment $rs2$ at time $t + 1$, thus can infer the trajectory of $User$ from $rs1$ to $rs2$.

Fig. 1. Strongest BK Attack   **Fig. 2.** Outline of the *Cons-XRT* Method

When the attacker identifies the position of the moving object at some time, he can infer the trajectory information of the moving object by using the fluctuation of the link count. As shown in Fig. 1, through the background knowledge, the attacker can know that the moving object $User$ is in the road section $rs1$ at time t; and through the fluctuation of statistical data at time t and $t + 1$, he can infer that a moving object of road section $rs1$ at time t moves to road section $rs2$ at time $t + 1$, thus inferring the trajectory of $User$ from $rs1$ to $rs2$.

4   The Proposed Algorithm

The purpose of differential privacy preserving publishing for trajectory data is to satisfy differential privacy and improve data utility as much as possible. Therefore, we proposes a differential privacy preserving framework which couples spatial ambiguity and noisy R-tree (*Cons-XRT*).

4.1   Algorithm Outline

The framework of our *Cons-XRT* algorithm is depicted in Fig. 2, where $f(T)$ is the query function of the original data table T, F represents the set of $f(T)$ functions, and $S(f)$ is the Laplace sensitivity of function set F.

Our algorithm contains three key components:

1. Noisy R-tree construction to construct the noisy R-tree, establish query index, and implement differential privacy protection in the index.
2. Trajectory data consistency processing to hide the relative changes of statistical data of adjacent sections in adjacent periods, and eliminate the statistical data fluctuations.
3. Spatial range query processing to query the number of moving objects (c) in the given rectangular area based on the noisy R-tree, and return the number of moving objects meeting the requirements of differential privacy protection.

4.2   Construction of the Noisy R-tree

R-tree is a spatial index structure proposed by Guttman [23] that uses the Minimum Bounding Rectangle (MBR) to approximate the spatial objects. Given a road network $G(V, E)$ with road intersections V and roads V, we use R-tree to index the location data of road network information. The leaf node of R-tree corresponds to the MBR of each rs link, and the middle node of R-tree is the MBR that can cover the range of nodes. A count value attribute is added to each node of the R-tree to represent the number of moving objects in MBR.

The detailed algorithm of noisy R-tree construction is given in Algorithm 1.

Algorithm 1. Construct Noise R-tree algorithm ($ConRT$)

1: Input: $D_t(tr)$, ε, $G(E, V)$;
2: Output: return the $D_p(tr)$
3: //compute the node mbr of RT.
4:     for (*each leaf node in RT*) do
5:         $c_{rs_i} \leftarrow$ the user number in mbr_i;
6:     for (*each intermediate node in RT*) do
7:         $c_{mbr_i} \leftarrow$ the user number in mbr_i;
8:     $\bar{\varepsilon} = \frac{\varepsilon}{h}$;
9:     for (*each leaf node in RT*) do
10:         $\bar{c}_{rs_i} \leftarrow c_{rs_i} + Noisy(\bar{\varepsilon})$;
11:     for (*each intermediate node in RT*) do
12:         $\bar{c}_{mbr_i} \leftarrow c_{mbr_i} + Noisy(\bar{\varepsilon})$;
13:     $D_p(tr) \leftarrow$ data consistency processing (RT, G);
14:     Return $D_p(tr)$;

According to the sensitivity of Laplace mechanism, given the query function set F, if $f(T)\epsilon R$, $f\epsilon F$, the sensitivity of F is:

$$S(F) = \max_{T_1, T_2}(\sum_{f\epsilon F}|f(T_1) - f(T_2)|), \tag{2}$$

where T_1 and T_2 are any subsets of $D(TR)$.

We adopt the non-interactive differential privacy mechanism [8,9], which obtains the noisy data by adding Laplace noise to the original trajectory data in advance, and returns the noisy results directly to the user query. Because the noise is added in the preprocessing stage, the output results of the differential privacy algorithm are the same for the same query.

According to the properties of differential privacy [10,21] the composition of different differential privacy algorithms has the differential privacy characteristics of sequential composition and parallel composition theorems. In Algorithm 1, the privacy budget is divided into several parts of equal size $\bar{\varepsilon} = \frac{\varepsilon}{h}$, where h is the depth of R-tree.

According to the property of Laplace distribution, the expected value and variance of the noisy function $Noisy(\varepsilon)$ are respectively 0 and $\frac{2}{\varepsilon^2}$.

According to the requirements of differential privacy technique, noise is added to the statistical value of each road section. That is, the original count value of c is changed into a random number within the range of $[c - 1, c + 1]$. Therefore, the original value of c can not be inferred.

4.3 Consistency Processing

The purpose of trajectory data consistency processing is to resist the attack of trajectory data count value fluctuations under the strongest background knowledge. That is, to hide the relative changes of the statistical values of adjacent sections in adjacent periods and eliminate large fluctuations.

Through consistency processing, the count value $c_{rs_i}^-$ with added noise is transformed into $c_{rs_i}^{\wedge}$ that meets the consistency constraint, and the deviation between them. The deviation is expressed by Euclidean distance as $F(\bar{c}, \hat{c}) = \sqrt{\sum(c_{rs_i}^- - c_{rs_i}^{\wedge})^2}$.

The consistency processing is implemented by Algorithm 2.

Algorithm 2. Consistency Processing of Trajectory Count Value ($Consist$)

1: Input: RT, $G(E, V)$
2:
3: Output: return the noisy consist RT;
4:     //Detect whether there is 1 unit count fluctuation in adjacent road sections.
5:     for $(each\ rs\ in\ E)$ do
6:         for $(each\ rs'\ in\ Neighboour(rs))$ do
7:             if $c_{rs} - c_{rs}(t-1) == 1\ \&\&\ c_{rs'} - c_{rs'}(t-1) == -1$
8:                 if $(\bar{c}_{rs}\ not\ in\ [c_{rs}(t-1), c_{rs}])$
9:                 $(\bar{c}_{rs} \leftarrow c_{rs} - (\bar{c}_{rs} - c_{rs})$;
10:                 if $(\bar{c}_{rs}(t-1)\ not\ in\ [c_{rs}(t-1), c_{rs}])$
11:                 $(\bar{c}_{rs}(t-1) \leftarrow c_{rs}(t-1) + ((c_{rs}(t-1) - \bar{c}_{rs}(t-1))$;
12:                 if $(\bar{c}_{rs}\ not\ in\ [c_{rs'}, c_{rs}(t-1)])$
13:                 $(\bar{c}_{rs} \leftarrow c_{rs'} - (\bar{c}_{rs'} - c_{rs'})$;
14:                 if $(\bar{c}_{rs}(t-1)\ not\ in\ [c_{rs}(t-1), c_{rs}])$
15:                 $(\bar{c}_{rs'}(t-1) \leftarrow c_{rs'}(t-1) + ((c_{rs'}(t-1) - \bar{c}_{rs'}(t-1))$;
16:     Return RT.

4.4 Spatial Range Query

Spatial range query is to query the number of moving objects (c) in a given rectangular area satisfying differential privacy of noised R-tree index nodes by applying noise count values. It is implemented by Algorithm 3.

Algorithm 3. Spatial Range Query $(Query)$

1: Input: RT, n(node number of RT-tree), R (Spatial Range)
2: Output: return the user number c
3:    //Detect whether there is 1 unit count fluctuation in adjacent road sections.
4:    if R covers the MBR of the current node
5:        Return $\bar{c}$ of current node;
6:    if R intersect the MBR of the current node
7:      if current node is not the leaf
8:          for each child node in n do
9:              $c+ = Query(D_p(tr), n, R)$;
10:          Return c;
11:      else Return $(\bar{c} \times \frac{intersection\ area}{area\ of\ current\ node\ MBR})$;
12:    if R not intersect the MBR of the current node
13:      Return 0.

Spatial range query algorithm $(Query)$ uses the structural characteristics of R-tree to traverse and calculate. Each node in R-tree has its corresponding MBR, which can be used to quickly judge the relationship between the node and the query area. By judging the relationship of covering, intersecting or disjoint, the current node noise count value or child node noise count value can be used for fast calculation, which reduces the number of accesses to leaf nodes.

Depending on the relationship between the query area and a MBR, the judgment rules of query result on a node are as follows:

- Case 1. If the query area of $Query$ covers MBR, the query result is the MBR count value.
- Case 2. If there is no intersection between the query area $Query$ and MBR, the query result is 0.
- Case 3 If $Query$ does not cover MBR but intersects with MBR, the query result is the sum of sub MBR query results.
- Case 4. If the query region $Query$ does not cover MBR, but intersects with MBR, and MBR is leaf node. The query result is the MBR count value × proportion of the intersection region.

5   Performance Evaluation

We show that the noisy R-tree algorithm (Algorithm 1 and Algorithm 2) presented in the previous section preserves both good data privacy and utility. Proof is omitted due to space limitation.

Theorem 1. *Algorithm 1 and Algorithm 2 both satisfy the ε-differential privacy property. The data generated by them satisfies (ε, δ)-utility in spatial range query.*

6   Experiments and Evaluations

In this section, we compare our algorithm $(Cons\text{-}XRT)$ on the above metrics with the existing algorithms $Cons\text{-}RT$ [12] and $Cons\text{-}SRT$ [29] that use R-tree and SR-tree as the index storage structure respectively.

6.1 Experiment Environment

We use Python 3.6.6 to implement the proposed method. The experimental hardware environment is an Intel Xeon CPU E7-4807@1.87GHz×2, 64G memory.

The dataset used in this paper is the trajectory data generated by public driving with GPS equipment in Guangdong Province in November 2016, covering an area of about $1000\,km^2$ in Guangdong Province. The sampling interval of GPS trajectory point data is 15 seconds, and the data of all sampling points is about 68.51 million.

6.2 Evaluation of Data Utility

Denoting the snapshot location dataset of the moving object in the given space range R subject to z by $D_z(tr)$, we define the spatial range query $Query()$ on the dataset to be the number of elements of $D_z(tr)$ in R at time t:

$$Query(D_z(tr), R) = \{x | x \in D_z(tr), x \in range(R), \} \qquad (3)$$

where $z \in \{t, p\}$, t stands for time and p for public (published).

We use the Relative Error (RE) which is widely used in the literature [5,6] to measure the utility of published data:

$$RE = \frac{|Query(D_p(tr), R) - Query(D_t(tr), R)|}{max(Query(D_t(tr), s))}. \qquad (4)$$

Data Utility Analysis of Location Count Query: We change the privacy budget ε to construct different published datasets, randomly select 10000 locations in the road network to query on the published dataset and the original dataset respectively, and calculate the average Relative Error (RE). Privacy budget ε range from 0.5 to 1.5 with an interval of 0.25. The experimental results are shown in Fig. 3.

From the experimental results, it can be seen that the RE of the $Cons\text{-}XRT$ algorithm in this chapter is very close to that of the $Cons\text{-}RT$ and the $Cons\text{-}SRT$, and the RE is within 0.3. And the RE increases with the privacy budget ε decreases.

In the scene of location count query, the three algorithms all use the count values of leaf nodes to get the returned

Fig. 3. RE of Location Count Query

results, the RE only comes from the count values of leaf nodes, and the count values of non-leaf nodes do not participate in the calculation, so the results of the three algorithms are relatively close.

Data Utility Analysis of Spatial Range Count Query
The data utility analysis of range count query is to select a spatial range according to the random radius r to evaluate the utility of the count values of moving

objects on the location. The evaluation is done by measuring the value of RE and results are displayed in Fig. 4.

According to the radius of different spatial range, the experiment was divided into four groups with radius of 0.5 km, 1 km, 2 km and 3 km. Each group randomly selected 10, 000 points as the central establishment area, and evaluated the RE of each area. The experimental results are shown in Fig. 4.

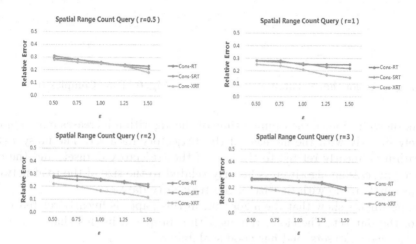

Fig. 4. RE of Spatial Range Count Query

From the above experimental results, we can observe:

- The RE of our $Cons\text{-}XRT$ algorithm is controlled below 0.3, and the trajectory count values with noise are available.
- Compared with $Cons\text{-}RT$ and $Cons\text{-}SRT$, with the increase of spatial range query, $Cons\text{-}XRT$ works more effectively because it can use the intermediate node count values of the index tree. This is because the REs of the count values of the intermediate nodes in the index tree are smaller than that of the leaf node count values, and the RE of the query result decreases with the increase of the query range.

6.3   Evaluation of Algorithm Scalability

This experiment verifies the scalability of the noisy R-tree construction algorithm. The running time of the algorithm is related to the size of trajectory dataset $|D|$ and the growth of the algorithm running time with the increase of different datasets.

As shown in Fig. 5, the X-axis and Y-axis respectively represent the size of the dataset and running time of the algorithm. Data set $D(tr)$ is the trajectory data. Because the format of each trajectory is consistent, the size of trajectory file is proportional to the number of trajectories. In this experiment, 100MB to 900MB trajectory data is selected as the experimental data of operation efficiency. The privacy budget selects the value in the middle range, $\varepsilon = 1.0$.

The experimental results are shown in Fig. 5. Each experimental result is the average running time obtained by running the algorithm several times.

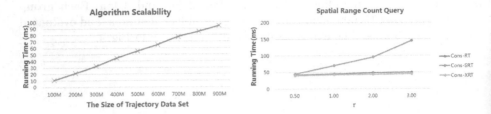

Fig. 5. Algorithm Scalability   **Fig. 6.** Time Complexity

As shown in Fig. 5, the running time of the algorithm increases more approximately linearly with the increase of the trajectory data set. The noisy R-tree algorithm is linearly related to the size of the trajectory dataset, and the consistency processing algorithm is linearly related to the size of the road network, and has little to do with the size of the trajectory dataset.

Experiments show that the algorithm in this paper is linearly related to the size of the dataset. Therefore, the algorithm proposed in this chapter can run on large-scale datasets, and has good scalability.

6.4 Evaluation of Time Complexity

This experiment verifies the efficiency of the spatial range query algorithm. According to the different radius of spatial range, the experiment is divided into four groups with radius of 0.5 km, 1 km, 2 km and 3 km. Each group randomly selects 10, 000 points as the center to establish a continuous query area, and finally gets the average running time of each group of spatial range query. The experimental results are shown in Fig. 6.

Experiments show that the single query time of $Cons\text{-}XRT$ algorithm is within 50 ms, and it increases slowly with the increase of query radius. The performance will be better on a spatial query range. and. The indexes of $Cons\text{-}XRT$ and $Cons\text{-}RT$ both adopt R-tree structure, so the spatial index efficiency is high. The index of $Cons\text{-}SRT$ uses SR-tree structure, and the efficiency of spatial index is not high in range query scenario.

7 Conclusion

This paper proposed novel algorithm for differential privacy preserving trajectory publication of road networks by combining spatial ambiguity and noisy R-tree ($Cons\text{-}XRT$), which can resist attacks with maximum background knowledge even when the trajectory is sparse. Our method applies consistency processing ($Consist$) to deal with bidirectional hidden fluctuations of the statistical count values of the trajectory, which can resist the attacks with maximum background knowledge by inference on fluctuations of statistical results. In addition, it deploys a fast query method for spatial range counts, which uses noise counts on the noisy R-tree index nodes to quickly return the number of moving objects satisfying differential privacy.

Our experimental performance evaluation and comparisons with the existing methods show that our $Cons\text{-}XRT$ algorithm can resist trajectory privacy attacks with maximum background knowledge. It has the advantages of low relative query error rate and good scalability, and is applicable for privacy preserving publishing of large-scale trajectory data for geo-spatial data analysis and management.

Acknowledgement. This work is supported by Macao Polytechnic University Research Grant RP/FCA-14/2022.

References

1. Abul, O., Bonchi, F., Nanni, M.: Never walk alone: uncertainty for anonymity in moving objects databases. In: IEEE International Conference on Data Engineering, pp. 376–385 (2008)
2. Beresford, A.R., Stajano, F.: Mix zones: user privacy in location aware services. In: Proceedings of the Second IEEE Conference on Pervasive Computing and Communications Workshops, pp. 127–131 (2004)
3. Bindschaedler, V., Shokri, R.: Synthesizing plausible privacy-preserving location traces. In: 2016 IEEE Symposium on Security and Privacy, pp. 546–563. IEEE (2016)
4. Bonchi, F., Lakshmanan, L.V.S., Wang, H.: Trajectory anonymity in publishing personal mobility data. ACM SIGKDD Explor. Newsl. **13**(1), 30–42 (2011)
5. Chen, R., Fung, B.C.M., Desai, B.C., Sossou, N.M.: Differentially private transit data publication: a case study on the montreal transportation system. In: Proceedings of the 18th ACM SIGKDD International Conference on Knowledge Discovery and Data Mining, pp. 213–221 (2012)
6. Chen, R., Mohammed, N., Fung, B.C.M., Desai, B.C., Xiong, L.: Publishing set-valued data via differential privacy. Proc. VLDB Endow. **4**(11), 1087–1098 (2011)
7. Chow, R., Golle, P.: Faking contextual data for fun, profit, and privacy. In: ACM Workshop on Privacy in the Electronic Society (2009)
8. Dwork, C., McSherry, F., Nissim, K., Smith, A.: Calibrating noise to sensitivity in private data analysis. In: Halevi, S., Rabin, T. (eds.) TCC 2006. LNCS, vol. 3876, pp. 265–284. Springer, Heidelberg (2006). https://doi.org/10.1007/11681878_14
9. Dwork, C., Jing, L.: Differential privacy and robust statistics. In: ACM Symposium on Theory of Computing (2009)
10. Esmerdag, E., Gursoy, M.E., Inan, A., Saygin, Y.: Explode: an extensible platform for differentially private data analysis. In: IEEE International Conference on Data Mining Workshops (2016)
11. Gursoy, M.E., Liu, L., Truex, S., Yu, L.: Differentially private and utility preserving publication of trajectory data. IEEE Trans. Mob. Comput. **18**(10), 2315–2329 (2018)
12. Huo, Z., Meng, X.: A trajectory data publishing method satisfying differential privacy. Chin. J. Comput. **041**(002), 400–412 (2018)
13. Jin, K., Zhang, X., Peng, H.: KD-TSS: accurate method for private spatial decomposition. J. Front. Comput. Sci. Technol. (2017)

14. Kato, R., Iwata, M., Hara, T., Suzuki, A., Nishio, S.: A dummy-based anonymization method based on user trajectory with pauses. In: International Conference on Advances in Geographic Information Systems (2012)
15. Kumari, V., Chakravarthy, S.: Cooperative privacy game: a novel strategy for preserving privacy in data publishing. HCIS **6**(1), 1–20 (2016). https://doi.org/10.1186/s13673-016-0069-y
16. Li, S., Shen, H., Sang, Y.: An efficient model and algorithm for privacy-preserving trajectory data publishing. In: Park, J.H., Shen, H., Sung, Y., Tian, H. (eds.) PDCAT 2018. CCIS, vol. 931, pp. 240–249. Springer, Singapore (2019). https://doi.org/10.1007/978-981-13-5907-1_25
17. Li, S., Shen, H., Sang, Y., Tian, H.: An efficient method for privacy-preserving trajectory data publishing based on data partitioning. J. Supercomput. **76**(7), 5276–5300 (2019). https://doi.org/10.1007/s11227-019-02906-6
18. Li, Y., Yang, D., Xianbiao, H.: A differential privacy-based privacy-preserving data publishing algorithm for transit smart card data. Transp. Res. Part C: Emerg. Technol. **115**, 102634 (2020)
19. Luo, H., Zhang, H., Long, S., Lin, Y.: Enhancing frequent location privacy-preserving strategy based on geo-indistinguishability. Multimed. Tools Appl. **80**(1) (2021)
20. Machanavajjhala, A., Gehrke, J., Kifer, D., Venkitasubramaniam, M.: L diversity: privacy beyond k anonymity. In: International Conference on Data Engineering, p. 24 (2006)
21. Mcsherry, F.: Privacy integrated queries: an extensible platform for privacy-preserving data analysis. Commun. ACM **53**(9), 89–97 (2010)
22. Mir, D.J., Isaacman, S., Caceres, R., Martonosi, M., Wright, R.N.: DP-where: differentially private modeling of human mobility. In: IEEE International Conference on Big Data (2013)
23. Proserpio, D., Goldberg, S., McSherry, F.: Calibrating data to sensitivity in private data analysis: a platform for differentially-private analysis of weighted datasets. Proc. VLDB Endow. **7**(8), 637–648 (2014)
24. Sheng, G., Ma, J., Shi, W., Zhan, G., Cong, S.: TRPF a trajectory privacy preserving framework for participatory sensing. IEEE Trans. Inf. Forensics Secur. **8**(2), 874–887 (2013)
25. Shokri, R., Theodorakopoulos, G., Danezis, G., Hubaux, J.-P., Le Boudec, J.-Y.: Quantifying location privacy: the case of sporadic location exposure. In: Fischer-Hübner, S., Hopper, N. (eds.) PETS 2011. LNCS, vol. 6794, pp. 57–76. Springer, Heidelberg (2011). https://doi.org/10.1007/978-3-642-22263-4_4
26. Shokri, R., Theodorakopoulos, G., Troncoso, C., Hubaux, J.P., Boudec, J.Y.L.: Protecting location privacy: optimal strategy against localization attacks. In: ACM Conference on Computer and Communications Security, pp. 617–627 (2012)
27. Yuan, S., Pi, D., Zhao, X., Xu, M.: Differential privacy trajectory data protection scheme based on R-tree. Expert Syst. Appl. (2021)
28. Zhang, X., Jin, K., Meng, X.: Private spatial decomposition with adaptive grid. J. Comput. Res. Dev. **55**, 1143–1156 (2018)
29. Zhao, X., Pi, D., Chen, J.: Novel trajectory privacy-preserving method based on clustering using differential privacy. Expert Syst. Appl. **149**, 113241 (2020)
30. ZhaoWei, H.U., Yang, J.: Survey of trajectory privacy preserving techniques. Comput. Sci. (1) (2016)

Using Text Mining and Tokenization Analysis to Identify Job Performance for Human Resource Management at the University of Phayao

Wongpanya S. Nuankaew[1] , Ronnachai Thipmontha[1] , Phaisarn Jeefoo[1] ,
Patchara Nasa-ngium[2] , and Pratya Nuankaew[1(✉)]

[1] University of Phayao, Phayao 56000, Thailand
pratya.nu@up.ac.th

[2] Rajabhat Maha Sarakham University, Maha Sarakham 44000, Thailand

Abstract. A significant problem in many Thai university organizations is the inability to effectively identify employees' roles and functions. This research aims to study the workload management of university personnel by text mining techniques. There are two main research objectives. The first objective is to manipulate highly complex Thai word segmentation. The second objective is to produce a predictive model for identifying job performance for human resource management of university personnel. Research tools are machine learning algorithms and word segmentation analysis, including Decision Tree (DT), Generalized Linear Model (GLM), K-Nearest Neighbors (K-NN), Naïve Bayes (NB), Support Vector Machine (SVM), Term Frequency-Inverse Document Frequency (TF-IDF), Term Frequency (TF), Term Occurrences (TO), and Binary Term Occurrences (BTO) techniques. The research data is compiled from job descriptions for three positions from the School of Information and Communication Technology at the University of Phayao. The results show that the best predictive model is developed with the Generalized Linear Model (GLM). It has a high accuracy value of 89.80%, with Binary Term Occurrences (BTO) technique. Research operational plan for future work, researchers plan to develop an information system to support work within the School of Information and Communication Technology, University of Phayao to support further work.

Keywords: Job description analysis · Human resource strategies · Human resource mining · HR Text Mining · HR Tokenize Analysis

1 Introduction

In a formal organization, there are often many departments. Each department is involved in specific business processes within the company. Additionally, each department's duties and responsibilities are unique and complex, and verbal explanations must be more comprehensive to convey them clearly to employees. Therefore, a written document called a job description is typically produced, which provides a clear and concise summary of the duties and responsibilities of each department. The job description helps employees understand their organizational roles. However, validating that the work being done by an employee matches or fits the job description is an important task for human resource management [1]. Job Analysis is a process for conducting a job that can help to ensure that the job description accurately reflects the work being done. This involves observing and analyzing the tasks, duties, and responsibilities associated with the job [2, 3].

In the context of job analysis, text mining can be used to identify key job duties [2, 4], responsibilities, and required skills and qualifications from job postings and descriptions [5]. By analyzing large volumes of job-related text data, organizations can gain a more comprehensive understanding of the job requirements and develop more accurate and detailed job descriptions [6]. The process of text mining and tokenization analysis involves examining unstructured text data to uncover valuable insights and information. In the field of human resource management, these techniques can be applied to study different types of textual data, such as job descriptions, resumes, and employee performance evaluations [2]. In addition, the increased use of digital technology in businesses means that a large volume of data is generated, including semi-structured and unstructured text data. This data can be challenging to analyze using traditional methods like manual categorization and reading. Moreover, text mining [2, 4, 7] and tokenization analysis techniques offer HR professionals a way to extract meaningful insights from this data, providing a more comprehensive understanding of HR-related concerns.

By utilizing these techniques, HR managers can leverage these methods to uncover insights and trends that may be challenging to spot otherwise. One such method is to scrutinize employee feedback to identify areas of discontent shared by many. Another technique is to analyze job postings to understand the skills and qualifications that recruiters seek most frequently. The primary objective of utilizing text mining and tokenization analysis in HRM is to enhance decision-making, streamline processes, and boost organizational performance.

Finally, the importance of the problem and literature review influences and drives researchers to develop this research with the hope that it will create future value for the University of Phayao.

2   Materials and Methods

2.1   Population and Sample

This research identifies the population as support personnel from the School of Information and Communication Technology at the University of Phayao, Phayao Province, Thailand.

The research sampling was a purposive sampling from three job positions that had worked in the School of Information and Communication Technology for over five years. The three positions consist of Educator, General Administration Officer, and Human Resource Officer, as detailed in Table 1.

Table 1. Population and Sample.

Name of the job positions	Number of employees for each job	Number of job descriptions in each job
Educator (EDU)	6 (50.00%)	113 (46.89%)
General Administration Officer (GAO)	5 (41.67%)	68 (28.22%)
Human Resource Officer (HRO)	1 (8.33%)	60 (24.90%)
Total:	12 (100%)	241 (100%)

Table 1 presents the population and sample defined in the study, where the sample consisted of 12 employees and a total of 241 job descriptions. This gathered information led to a management process comprising four essential phases: data cleaning, data transformation, data integration, and data reduction, as presented in the next section.

2.2 Data Collection and Data Management

The researchers valued and raised awareness of the data acquisition for this research. Therefore, researchers have applied for research ethics approval from the University of Phayao (UP-HEC-1.2/034/66). The researchers then followed the University of Phayao process to request information from relevant parties. Once the data were received, the researchers processed the data in four phases:

Data Cleaning
Data cleaning is the process of detecting and correcting entries for inaccurate data. This research was carried out in four parts: parsing data, correcting data, standardizing data, and duplicating elimination data. The data received and collected for each job position is in hard copy. Researchers discovered that there were redundant and unanalyzable workload issues, that researchers had to collect data in the form of a database for preliminary analysis. Furthermore, duplicate words and phrases were used in each job title, and the researchers removed the same data.

Data Transformation
Data transformation is the manipulation of continuous data into discrete data to manage and interpret the data. It can significantly reduce the space of words and decrease information value. In this process, the researchers applied the tokenization for natural language processing approach to feature manipulation to organize and classify the developmental factors of the data characterization. This process can be divided into several processes to accomplish text preprocessing [8]: (1) the tokenization is the process to split the text from a sentence into tokens and replace each word with a number that calls as tokenization. Word Tokenization for the Thai language named "Attacut" was applied for this research, (2) noise removal of unnecessary characters such as numbers and special symbols, (3) normalization is a process that transforms the words for making

equivalency classes of terms and uniform sequences better., (4) removing stop words by Thai stop words dictionary [9], and (5) stemming.

At this stage, feature extraction (FE) was used to find an efficient Thai word segmentation process. Feature extraction is the process of data conversion to feature extraction for obtaining a representative feature that can be used. It will be represented by the word vectors. The word vectors are representations of tokens in a document. It is significant to fetch the feature values for each instance correct for the problem being regarded because modifications in these be able to change performance. This research applies text vectorization using different methods in a Rapid Miner application which has four primary plans [10, 11]: Term Frequency-Inverse Document Frequency (TF-IDF), Term Frequency (TF), Term Occurrences (TO), and Binary Term Occurrences (BTO).

Data Integration

As data plays a more significant role in the organization's work, it is necessary to use the data available in various ways for maximum benefit. Problems arise when large organizations are made up of many departments. Each department stores information related to its department, which may use different database management systems. The data structure may differ, so it is necessary to manage data availability similarly.

The School of Information and Communication Technology, University of Phayao, although they have the same positions but perform different tasks. This research aims to give importance to job characteristics consistent with job titles. Therefore, developing a prediction model based on job characteristics is essential. Therefore, collecting data is a combination of job characteristics in the same job position that will be used to develop a forecasting model further.

Data Reduction

Data reduction aims to reduce data duplication by employing experts acting as organizational managers to select job descriptions unrelated to the job positions used in this research.

2.3 Model Analysis and Model Development

The model analysis aims to compare models that have been developed with various methods. Research modeling concepts use machine learning to complete the most perfect and predictable model. The techniques used are machine learning with unsupervised learning consisting of five techniques: Decision Tree (DT), Generalized Linear Model (GLM), K-Nearest Neighbors (KNN), Naïve Bayes (NB), and Support Vector Machine (SVM). Each technique has different advantages and disadvantages, as follows:

The decision tree technique is prevalent [12] because it is easy to understand. The model structure is an inverted tree with the most important attributes at the top called the "root node". Out of each node are the branches that create the conditions for making decisions. Finally, the part that serves as the answer to the prediction model is the leaf node. Although decision tree techniques are popular, a major problem is that models with high accuracy are often not practical, which is called "over fitting". Therefore, when choosing a decision tree technique, other components of validity may be considered.

Generalized Linear Model (GLM) [13] is an umbrella term encompassing many other models, allowing the response variable y to have an error distribution other than a normal one. The models include Linear Regression, Logistic Regression, and Poisson Regression. The advantages of GLM make the model effective because it uses many techniques to help each other to learn.

K-Nearest Neighbors (KNN) [14] is a classification method for classifying data (Classification) using the principle of comparing the data of interest with other data to see how similar they are. If the data of interest is closest to any data, the system will answer the answer to the nearest data. The advantage of K-NN is that the distance calculation method can be used to find the answer, but in some cases, the nature of the data set will be distorted—for example, spiral data series, circular data, and so on.

Naïve Bayes (NB) is a probabilistic forecasting model [15]. The advantage of NB is the ease of training, especially with many features (variables) and extensive data. In addition, it can be used to classify many classes. However, there may be a disadvantage in accuracy, or performance may not be able to compete with other types of training algorithms.

Support Vector Machine (SVM) [16] is one of the most popular techniques for pattern recognition and classification problems. SVM relies on the principle of coefficient equations to create the optimal separating hyperplane. The method used to find the best midline is to add a border to both sides of the midline and create a border tangent to the dataset value in the feature space.

2.4 Evaluation of the Model Performance

Model performance evaluation is intended to compare model performance from each technique. By testing the performance of this model, the data splitting method is used to create the model and to test the model called "Split Validation (SV)". The SV has been designed in four characteristics: 50:50, 60:40, 70:30, and 80:20.

In addition, the tool used to measure model performance is the Confusion Matrix process, which has four metrics: accuracy, precision, recall, and f1-score. Accuracy is the value that the model can correctly predict from all response classes. Precision is the value that the model can predict by class. Recall is the actual value that the model can accurately predict by class. Lastly, f1-score is the average of Precision and Recall. The f1-score is a single metric measuring a model's performance.

In this paper, the researchers used all five techniques and the model performance testing process to generate the best model of each method and compare them to select the most appropriate model for further application development. The results of the model development are presented in the next section.

3 Results and Discussion

3.1 Research Results

The job descriptions classified by job position are presented in Table 1 and have already passed the data preparation process to prepare the data. It was then analyzed to construct a classification model from all five classifiers. The accuracy of model development results classified by the five classifiers is demonstrated in Table 2. A comparison of each technique by text vectorization methods and split validation ratio is presented in Fig. 1, 2, 3, 4 and Fig. 5.

Table 2. The model development results classified by five classifiers.

Text Vectorization Methods/Classifier	Split Validation Ratio/Accuracy			
	50:50	60:40	70:30	80:20
Term Frequency-Inverse Document Frequency (TF-IDF)				
Decision Tree	57.50	62.50	59.72	55.10
Generalized Linear Model	83.33	**84.38***	83.33	83.67
K-Nearest Neighbors	73.33	73.97	70.83	69.39
Naïve Bayes	71.67	80.21	84.72	81.63
Support Vector Machine	80.00	82.29	79.17	85.71*
Term Frequency (TF)				
Decision Tree	58.33	62.50	56.95	55.10
Generalized Linear Model	76.67	83.33	87.50	89.79*
K-Nearest Neighbors	76.67	73.96	75.00	69.39
Naïve Bayes	83.33	79.17	80.56	83.67
Support Vector Machine	**86.67***	80.21	80.56	83.67
Term Occurrences (TO)				
Decision Tree	60.83	64.58	63.89	59.18
Generalized Linear Model	78.33	83.33	80.56	85.71*
K-Nearest Neighbors	63.33	72.92	73.61	71.43
Naïve Bayes	77.78	81.25	83.33	77.55
Support Vector Machine	85.00	81.25	76.39	83.67
Binary Term Occurrences (BTO)				
Decision Tree	54.17	62.50	61.11	55.10
Generalized Linear Model	83.33	**84.38***	**88.89***	**89.80***
K-Nearest Neighbors	67.50	70.83	73.61	67.35
Naïve Bayes	75.00	79.17	81.94	77.55
Support Vector Machine	84.17	80.21	79.17	83.67

Table 1 presents the model performance analysis by five classifiers in which the overall developed model is effective with a high degree of accuracy. Researchers subdivided the findings according to the 4-split validation ratio, as reported in Fig. 1, 2, 3 and Fig. 4.

Figure 1(A) presents a comparison histogram of the accuracy by the split validation ratio 50:50. It was found that the Decision Tree (DT) technique had the lowest overall accuracy value. However, it was found that the Support Vector Machine (SVM) technique

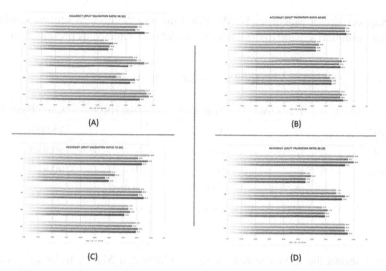

Fig. 1. Accuracy (Split Validation Ratio by 50:50, 60:40, 70:30, 80:20)

had the highest overall accuracy, with the highest accuracy of 86.67 from the Term Frequency (TF) technique.

Figure 1(B) presents a comparison histogram of the accuracy by the split validation ratio 60:40. It was found that the Decision Tree (DT) technique had the lowest overall accuracy value. However, it was found that the Generalized Linear Model (GLM) technique had the highest overall accuracy, with the highest accuracy of 84.38 from the Term Frequency-Inverse Document Frequency (TF-IDF) and the Binary Term Occurrences (BTO) techniques.

Figure 1(C) presents a comparison histogram of the accuracy by the split validation ratio 70:30. It was found that the Decision Tree (DT) technique had the lowest overall accuracy value. However, it was found that the Generalized Linear Model (GLM) technique had the highest overall accuracy, with the highest accuracy of 88.89 from the Term Frequency-Inverse Document Frequency (TF-IDF) technique.

Figure 1(D) presents a comparison histogram of the accuracy by the split validation ratio 80:20. It was found that the Decision Tree (DT) technique had the lowest overall accuracy value. However, it was found that the Generalized Linear Model (GLM) technique had the highest overall accuracy, with the highest accuracy of 89.80 from the Term Frequency-Inverse Document Frequency (TF-IDF) and the Term Occurrences (TO) techniques.

After presenting details classified by classifiers and split validation techniques, the next part was to report the selection of the most influential models classified by test characteristics.

Influential Model by Term Frequency-Inverse Document Frequency Technique
From Table 2, when categorizing considerations by the Term Frequency-Inverse Document Frequency Technique (TF-IDF) technique, it was found that the model developed

by the Support Vector Machine (SVM) technique had the highest accuracy, which the researchers summarized and distributed the model performance as presented in Table 3.

Table 3. SVM model performance with TF-IDF technique.

Accuracy = 85.71	True GAO	True EDU	True HRO	Class Precision
Pred. GAO	12	3	1	75.00%
Pred. EDU	1	20	1	90.91%
Pred. HRO	1	0	10	90.91%
Class Recall	85.71%	86.96%	83.33%	
F1-score	80.00	88.89	86.96	

Table 3 shows the model tested using the Confusion Matrix technique and using four indicators: accuracy, precision, recall, and f1-score. It was found that the Support Vector Machine (SVM) model had the highest accuracy, with an accuracy of 85.71 for the TF-IDF technique.

Influential Model by Term Frequency Technique
From Table 2, when categorizing considerations by the Term Frequency (TF) technique, it was found that the model developed by the Generalized Linear Model (GLM) technique had the highest accuracy, which the researchers summarized and distributed the model performance as presented in Table 4.

Table 4. GLM model performance with TF technique.

Accuracy = 89.79	True GAO	True EDU	True HRO	Class Precision
Pred. GAO	10	0	1	90.91%
Pred. EDU	4	23	0	85.19%
Pred. HRO	0	0	11	100.00%
Class Recall	71.43%	100.00%	91.67%	
F1-score	80.00	92.00	95.65	

Table 4 shows the model tested using the Confusion Matrix technique and using four indicators: accuracy, precision, recall, and f1-score. It was found that the Generalized Linear Model (GLM) model had the highest accuracy, with an accuracy of 89.79 for the Term Frequency (TF) technique.

Influential Model by Term Occurrences Technique
From Table 2, when categorizing considerations by the Term Occurrences (TO) technique, it was found that the model developed by the Generalized Linear Model (GLM)

Table 5. GLM model performance with TO technique.

Accuracy = 85.71	True GAO	True EDU	True HRO	Class Precision
Pred. GAO	10	1	1	83.33%
Pred. EDU	4	21	0	84.00%
Pred. HRO	0	1	11	91.67%
Class Recall	71.43%	91.30%	91.67%	
F1-score	76.92	87.50	91.67	

technique had the highest accuracy, which the researchers summarized and distributed the model performance as presented in Table 5.

Table 5 shows the model tested using the Confusion Matrix technique and using four indicators: accuracy, precision, recall, and f1-score. It was found that the Generalized Linear Model (GLM) model had the highest accuracy, with an accuracy of 85.71 for the Term Occurrences (TO) technique.

Influential Model by Binary Term Occurrences Technique

From Table 2, when categorizing considerations by the Binary Term Occurrences (BTO) technique, it was found that the model developed by the Generalized Linear Model (GLM) techniques had the highest accuracy. The researchers summarized and distributed the model performance as presented in Table 6.

Table 6. GLM model performance with BTO technique.

Accuracy = 89.80	True GAO	True EDU	True HRO	Class Precision
Pred. GAO	11	0	1	91.67%
Pred. EDU	3	23	1	85.19%
Pred. HRO	0	0	10	100.00%
Class Recall	78.57%	100.00%	83.33%	
F1-score	84.62	92.00	90.91	

Table 6 shows the model tested using the Confusion Matrix technique and using four indicators: accuracy, precision, recall, and f1-score. It was found that the Generalized Linear Model (GLM) model had the highest accuracy, with an accuracy of 89.80 for the Binary Term Occurrences (BTO) technique.

3.2 Research Discussion

The research discussion section is aimed at the purpose of the research. It consists of two key points: The first objective is to manipulate highly complex Thai word segmentation.

The second is to produce a predictive model for identifying job performance for human resource management of university personnel. Discussions are broken down as follows:

Thai Word Segmentation Management

Thai word segmentation is an original and persistent problem [9, 17]. The characteristics and writing of sentences in the Thai language without punctuation which is difficult for unfamiliar people. In addition, some words have different meanings and implications depending on the context of the surrounding words and the various user characteristics of the region of the country. Such problems have created space and competition for many researchers to develop effective processes and techniques for Thai word segmentation techniques [18].

This research aims to apply artificial intelligence technology and text mining management by applying four types of word-wrapping techniques to manage word-wrapping: Term Frequency-Inverse Document Frequency (TF-IDF), Term Frequency (TF), Term Occurrences (TO), Binary Term Occurrences (BTO). The Thai word segmentation process used by the researchers was applied to the job descriptions of three positions at the School of Information and Communication Technology, University of Phayao.

The results indicated that researchers existed to apply all four types of Thai word segmentation techniques to achieve their research objectives. The results indicated that researchers existed to apply all four types of Thai word segmentation techniques to achieve their research objectives. The results of this study are relevant and linked to extensive research[9, 18] in which they applied text mining and Thai word segmentation techniques to improve staff performance in university organizations.

Prediction Models to Identify Job Performance

The second theme of this research is to develop a predictive model for the job description of the University of Phayao employees. The researchers applied analytical techniques using machine learning to achieve research outcomes, including Decision Tree (DT), Generalized Linear Model (GLM), K-Nearest Neighbors (KNN), Naïve Bayes (NB), and Support Vector Machine (SVM) techniques. Five techniques were used to develop the model and analyze the model performance. An overview of the analysis is presented in Table 2. In addition, the researchers discussed the details as shown in Fig. 1(A) to Fig. 1(D) and Table 3, 4, 5 and Table 6. This section discusses the results of model development to analyze and select the most efficient and reasonable model for future application development.

The researchers found from the four types of split validation summarized in Fig. 1(A) to Fig. 1(D) that the decision tree technique was effective at all low levels—inappropriate for this research. However, Table 2 shows that correspondingly greater accuracy is achieved with an increasing proportion of modeling. The technique likely to be accepted due to its proportional accuracy is the Generalized Linear Model (GLM) technique which has the highest accuracy in many proportions, i.e., the split validation ratio 60:40, the split validation ratio 70:30, and the split validation ratio 80:20, as detailed in Fig. 1(A) to Fig. 1(D).

The second part of the analysis of discriminant model performance by the four types of word segmentation techniques is summarized and presented in Table 3, 4, 5 and Table 6. The researchers found that the model that achieves the highest accuracy among all three types of word segmentation is the Generalized Linear Model (GLM) technique, as details are as follows; the Generalized Linear Model (GLM) with the Term Frequency (TF) technique has an accuracy of 89.79%, the Generalized Linear Model (GLM) with the Term Occurrences (TO) technique has an accuracy of 85.71%, and the Generalized Linear Model (GLM) with the Binary Term Occurrences (BTO) technique has an accuracy of 89.80%. Only the Term Frequency-Inverse Document Frequency (TF-IDF) technique has the highest accuracy Support Vector Machine (SVM) model with an accuracy of 85.71%.

Based on the results and rationale discussed, the researchers concluded that an efficient and commendable model for application development is the Generalized Linear Model (GLM) with the Binary Term Occurrences (BTO) technique, as shown in Table 6. With all these achievements, the researchers will continue to present this work to the public.

4 Conclusion

This research contributes to human resource management by demonstrating the potential of text-mining techniques in improving workload management and job performance identification in Thai university organizations. Our study utilized machine learning algorithms and word segmentation analysis to analyze job descriptions for three positions at the School of Information and Communication Technology at the University of Phayao. Through this approach, we developed a predictive model for identifying job performance with a high accuracy value of 89.80%.

Furthermore, among the techniques we used, the Generalized Linear Model (GLM) with Binary Term Occurrences (BTO) technique was found to be the most effective. These findings suggest that text mining techniques can provide valuable insights for human resource management, particularly in organizations facing challenges in identifying employees' roles and functions. In future work, we plan to develop an information system to support the work of the School of Information and Communication Technology at the University of Phayao.

Overall, this research provides a promising foundation for improving workload management and job performance identification in Thai university organizations and supporting their ongoing efforts to enhance employee productivity and effectiveness.

5 Research Limitations

This research's findings and limitations were that the research scope and collaboration were low. The root cause, researchers suspect, is a lack of emphasis and awareness of workload in line with the job positions of employees in the organization. The past problem of the organization is the use of imprudence and subjectivity in consideration and the decision to promote employees in the organization. Therefore, the results of this research appear to narrow the gap in artificial intelligence technology to address inequality in the organization.

Acknowledgements. This research project was supported by the Thailand Science Research and Innovation Fund and the University of Phayao (Grant No. FF66-UoE002). In addition, this research was supported by many advisors, academics, researchers, students, and staff. The authors would like to thank all of them for their support and collaboration in making this research possible.

Conflict of Interest. The authors declare no conflict of interest.

References

1. Opatha, H.H.D.P.J.: HR analytics: a literature review and new conceptual model. Int. J. Sci. Res. Publ. **10**, 130–141 (2020). https://doi.org/10.29322/IJSRP.10.06.2020.p10217
2. Feng, S.: Job satisfaction, management sentiment, and financial performance: text analysis with job reviews from indeed.com. Int. J. Inf. Manag. Data Insights **3**, 100155 (2023). https://doi.org/10.1016/j.jjimei.2023.100155
3. Gazit, N., Ben-Gal, G., Eliashar, R.: Using job analysis for identifying the desired competencies of 21st-century surgeons for improving trainees selection. J. Surg. Educ. **80**, 81–92 (2023). https://doi.org/10.1016/j.jsurg.2022.08.015
4. Jung, Y., Suh, Y.: Mining the voice of employees: a text mining approach to identifying and analyzing job satisfaction factors from online employee reviews. Decis. Support Syst. **123**, 113074 (2019). https://doi.org/10.1016/j.dss.2019.113074
5. Hoff, K.A., Song, Q.C., Wee, C.J.M., Phan, W.M.J., Rounds, J.: Interest fit and job satisfaction: a systematic review and meta-analysis. J. Vocat. Behav. **123**, 103503 (2020). https://doi.org/10.1016/j.jvb.2020.103503
6. Chen, H., Zhang, Y.: Educating data management professionals: a content analysis of job descriptions. J. Acad. Librariansh. **43**, 18–24 (2017). https://doi.org/10.1016/j.acalib.2016.11.002
7. Zarindast, A., Sharma, A., Wood, J.: Application of text mining in smart lighting literature - an analysis of existing literature and a research agenda. Int. J. Inf. Manag. Data Insights **1**, 100032 (2021). https://doi.org/10.1016/j.jjimei.2021.100032
8. Albalawi, Y., Buckley, J., Nikolov, N.S.: Investigating the impact of pre-processing techniques and pre-trained word embeddings in detecting Arabic health information on social media. J. Big Data. **8**, 95 (2021). https://doi.org/10.1186/s40537-021-00488-w
9. Ousirimaneechai, N., Sinthupinyo, S.: Extraction of trend keywords and stop words from Thai Facebook pages using character n-grams. Int. J. Mach. Learn. **8**, 589–594 (2018). https://doi.org/10.18178/ijmlc.2018.8.6.750
10. Tripathi, G., Naganna, S.: Feature selection and classification approach for sentiment analysis. Mach. Learn. Appl. Int. J. **2**, 1–16 (2015). https://doi.org/10.5121/mlaij.2015.2201
11. Kompan, M., Bieliková, M.: News article classification based on a vector representation including words' collocations. In: Dicheva, D., Markov, Z., Stefanova, E. (eds.) Third International Conference on Software, Services and Semantic Technologies S3T 2011, pp. 1–8. Springer, Heidelberg (2011). https://doi.org/10.1007/978-3-642-23163-6_1
12. Nasa-Ngium, P., Nuankaew, W.S., Nuankaew, P.: Analyzing and tracking student educational program interests on social media with chatbots platform and text analytics. Int. J. Interact. Mob. Technol. **17**, 4–21 (2023). https://doi.org/10.3991/ijim.v17i05.31593
13. Yang, Y., Yu, C., Zhong, R.Y.: Generalized linear model-based data analytic approach for construction equipment management. Adv. Eng. Inform. **55**, 101884 (2023). https://doi.org/10.1016/j.aei.2023.101884

14. Rico-Juan, J.R., Valero-Mas, J.J., Calvo-Zaragoza, J.: Extensions to rank-based prototype selection in k-nearest neighbour classification. Appl. Soft Comput. **85**, 105803 (2019). https://doi.org/10.1016/j.asoc.2019.105803

15. Chen, J., Huang, H., Tian, S., Qu, Y.: Feature selection for text classification with Naïve Bayes. Expert Syst. Appl. **36**, 5432–5435 (2009). https://doi.org/10.1016/j.eswa.2008.06.054

16. Hearst, M.A., Dumais, S.T., Osuna, E., Platt, J., Scholkopf, B.: Support vector machines. IEEE Intell. Syst. Appl. **13**, 18–28 (1998). https://doi.org/10.1109/5254.708428

17. TeCho, J., Nattee, C., Theeramunkong, T.: Boosting-based ensemble learning with penalty profiles for automatic Thai unknown word recognition. Comput. Math. Appl. **63**, 1117–1134 (2012). https://doi.org/10.1016/j.camwa.2011.11.062

18. Haruechaiyasak, C., Kongyoung, S., Dailey, M.: A comparative study on Thai word segmentation approaches. In: 2008 5th International Conference on Electrical Engineering/Electronics, Computer, Telecommunications and Information Technology, pp. 125–128 (2008). https://doi.org/10.1109/ECTICON.2008.4600388

The Task of Generating Text Based on a Semantic Approach for a Low-Resource Kazakh Language

Diana Rakhimova[1,2](✉) [iD], Satibaldiev Abilay[2], and Adilbek Kuralay[2]

[1] Institute of Information and Computational Technologies, St. Shevchenko 28, Almaty, Kazakhstan
`di.diva@mail.ru`
[2] Al-Farabi Kazakh National University, Al-Farabi 71, Almaty, Kazakhstan

Abstract. In this article, the authors consider the problem of text generation for low- resource languages, using the Kazakh language as an example, based on semantic analysis. Machine learning method is used in the generation of text documents and sources in the Kazakh language. First, semantic analysisis performed, the number of words in the given text, the number of stop words, the number of symbols, etc. Then the TF-IDF algorithm is used to find the semantically important words of the text. Annotation of the given text by means of semantic analysis. And at the end, generation of text with advanced semantic analysis. A corpus for the Kazakh language was prepared for experiments and research. GPT-3 and NLG are used in the process of generation. Generation by means of semantic analysis of the text gives us some great opportunities. The Recurrent Neural Network (RNN) method is used during generation.Generation gives us a lot of opportunities, including not spending time on unnecessary information. It will provide an article or short text related to the keywords you searched for. The description of the developed approach and practical results of experiments are presented.

Keywords: Semantic analysis · Machine learning · Text generation · RNN · Kazakh language

1 Introduction

The generation system for the Kazakh language developed on the basis of machine learning is one of the current issues. Using the generation system, we quickly and easily solve problems such as chat-bots, auto-abstract, writing poems, mathematical or geometric problems. Natural language processing problems are developing rapidly for the Kazakh language, and it should be said that the generation system in the Kazakh language is almost non-existent in the country at the moment. There are very few organizations working on these natural language processing reports, and those that exist do not publish their data Open Source. Therefore, it is our goal to solve this problem and publish it openly. Because if it is open, it will continue to develop and increase in data. And it will be affordable for small businesses as well, because it is financially inconvenient

N. T. Nguyen et al. (Eds.): ACIIDS 2023, CCIS 1863, pp. 585–595, 2023.
https://doi.org/10.1007/978-3-031-42430-4_48

for small businesses to develop technologies like chatbots. For private enterprises, this project will be of great benefit. Every web optimizer knows that a site must have unique texts in order to be liked by search engines. Not just any set of words, but meaningful sentences on the topic of the site. This is especially a problem for aggregators who receive information from other sites and online stores, where the parameters and data of the goods are usually the same. Therefore, standard practice in this case is to order unique texts from copywriters. Consider the task of automatically generating product descriptions based on reviews. Having multiple product user reviews from different sites, we automatically generate a small unique text that summarizes the information from the reviews. The large flow of information on the Internet has led to the rapid development of the natural language processing industry (NLP). Currently, various research mechanisms are developing their own projects, such as information exchange between users, machine translation of information, spam filters, e-mail verification and processing of question-and-answer systems. However, due to the lack of knowledge of the structure of some languages, there are problems where the research result does not fully meet the needs of the user. Today, one of the problems of search engines is the morphological and morphemic analysis of words encountered while processing user requests. An example of such languages is the Uzbek language, which belongs to the family of Turkic languages. Kazakh is one of the agglutinative languages. That is, in this language, each grammatical meaning is expressed by individual affixes. The term affix in the grammar of the Kazakh language is taken in the same general sense as in the grammar of other Turkic languages. This means prefixes, infixes, suffixes, conjunctions. Nowadays, the structure of the Kazakh language has become more complicated due to the influence of Arabic, Persian and Russian languages. Preprocessing input text data is a key initial step in any natural language processing (NLP) application. Extracting the base of the word, that is, extracting the base or root of the input word, is an important process in the preprocessing stage. That is, depending on the keywords you entered, a short answer or text will be generated. If the hulls have a large structure, the result will be a high structure. It is important to do the generation with high accuracy.

2   Related Works

Natural language processing is a powerful tool for creating a clear vision for the organization [1]. Application analysis of customer experience and activity social network helps the economic growth of the company [2]. However, sentimental analysis can lead to inaccuracies in reviews that include both positive and negative reviews [3]. This document focuses on the fact that the solution to this problem in the Kazakh language is still widely studied [4]. Recently, many researches have been conducted in the field of sentimental analysis in Indian, Arabic, Turkish languages [4–6], however, the number of researches is small for the Kazakh language [4, 13].

A study published in [5] used machine learning techniques for semantic analyses. Natural language support vector by training models with contract matching datasets machine (SVM), Naive Bayes. In addition, linguistic methods, such as the systematic use of special morphological analysis, have compiled sensory dictionaries of words and phrases, as well as a set of linguistic rules [4]. In addition, including pre-processing, morphological analysis techniques such as tokenization, word stopping, stamping and POS tagging in research [7] provide detailed information about the data for high accuracy in the results. Evaluation of reviews using semantic analysis created a pattern of neural bags resulting from negative or positive reviews. Word bag model is a method of performing textual data in the process of text modeling with machine learning algorithms. Bag-of-words model is not complex and advances in problems such as device and seen language modeling and document classification [14]. If we consider the problem of generation after semantics.

Text generation is one of the popular problems in data science and machine learning and is suitable for Recurrent Neural Networks. This report uses TensorFlow to create an RNN text generator and create a high-level API in Python3. The solution to the problem was inspired by the work of Aurelien Heron [8]. This CST463 is a great project at Cal State Monterey Bay's Advanced Machine Learning Program led by Dr. Glenn Bruns [9].

Recurrent Neural Network (RNN). A real limitation of vanilla neural networks (as well as convolutional networks) is that their APIs are limited: they take a fixed-size vector as input (like an image) and produce a fixed-size vector as output (like probabilities of different classes). And not only that: these models perform this comparison using a fixed number of computational steps (such as the number of layers in the model). The main reason recurrent networks are interesting is that they allow us to work with sequences of vectors: sequences in the input, sequences in the output, or, in general, both [10].

Natural language generation (NLG) is a subfield of natural language processing. NLG focuses on some basic semantic representation of information from written text generation in natural languages. NLG is used in many applications: Multilingual reporting, text summarization, machine translation, and dialog applications. Therefore, the automated production of language is associated with a large number of diverse theoretical and practical problems. In NLG systems, problems such as multi-content selection, text-based lexicalization, text integration, and linking expressions are common.

Natural language text generation is a recommended way to introduce communication. Semantic graphs are the most representative systems used as input to NLG [9]. Among them, due to the limitation of the representation of the semantic graph, the traditional type of operational or procedural knowledge is incomplete, so it is necessary to assign more structure to the nodes, as well as links [11]. In natural language text generation, there was a great need for more rich graph detail. A new semantic representation called Rich is a Semantic Graph (RSG) that contains additional information. The main purpose of this stage is to evaluate and then arrange the paragraphs according to two factors: consistency between paragraph sentences and synonyms of the most frequently used paragraph words. After experimental testing, we found that the coherence measure produces very close results, so synonyms of the most frequently used paragraph words are used as an additional evaluation factor. First, text consistency assessment is used to assess whether paragraphs are consistent or not.

Therefore, each paragraph is evaluated and ranked according to the number of coherence between its sentences. Second, the synonyms of the most frequently used paragraph words are collected by entering the WordNet rank. Finally, the last paragraphs can be sorted according to the relevance rating, followed by the most frequently used paragraph word degree of synonyms [5]. After that, it will be more efficient to generate with semantics. Adding semantics will help us get better results as the generation produces words or texts that are semantically relevant to the keywords you are looking for. Extracts matching text from corpora based on semantics.

At the moment, many Turkic languages, like the Kazakh language, are of low resource. Due to the lack of available linguistic resources, it is difficult to apply modern methods and develop high-quality technologies in the field of NLP and artificial intelligence.

3   Description of the Model

We conducted research related to our topic and created a semantic analysis model for the Kazakh language through generation. The semantic model consists of three parts. The first is to produce statistics of the text in the Kazakh language. We have researched all sections and prepared the practical section. We will share the results of the semantic generation model for the Kazakh language below. We took out the statistics of the text presented in the first part, entered a short text. As a result, we calculated the number of words, symbols, punctuation marks, punctuation marks in the text (Figs. 1 and 2).

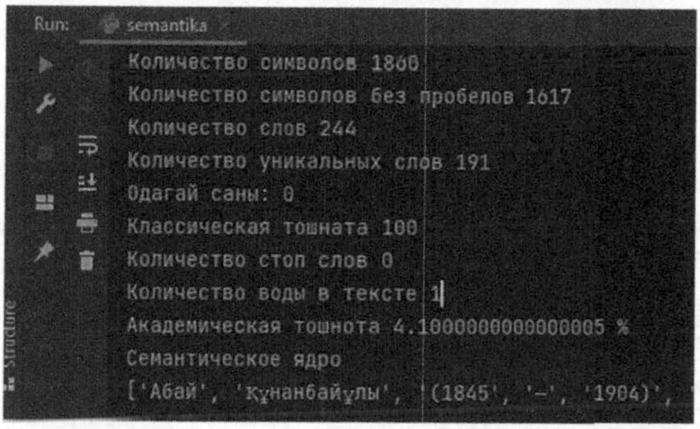

Fig. 1. Example of statistical data of the semantic analysis of the text in the Kazakh language.

Figure 1 shows the total number of words, the number of unique words, classic nausea, academic nausea, semantic core-keywords of the text.

In the second part, we used TF-IDF to extract semantically important sentences for a known Kazakh language text. In this part, we used TF-IDF in order to further improve the semantic analysis [15]. Given a certain text, determine the frequency of each sentence of that given text. Finds the importance of sentences for the text and extracts the most important sentences with their weights (Fig. 3 and 4).

We have generated this pre-text below (Fig. 5 and 6). After testing our model, we gave it the word "science" as an input, and we got the result, which can be seen in (Fig. 5). As a result, we studied only one scientific text, which is not of high quality. But this problem will be solved in the future, because we have a database of more than 35 million

```
{'Құнанбайұлы': 1, '(1845': 1, '1904)': 1, 'бүгінгі': 1,
Слово: Абай | Количество: 10 | Частота: 4.098%
Слово: Абайдың | Количество: 6 | Частота: 2.459%
Слово: және | Количество: 5 | Частота: 2.049%
Слово: мен | Количество: 4 | Частота: 1.639%
Слово: — | Количество: 3 | Частота: 1.23%
Слово: ақындық | Количество: 3 | Частота: 1.23%
Слово: қарасөздері | Количество: 3 | Частота: 1.23%
Слово: жылы | Количество: 2 | Частота: 0.82%
Слово: Шығыс | Количество: 2 | Частота: 0.82%


Process finished with exit code 0
```

Fig. 2. Number and frequency of each word relative to the text.

```
# text = "increase post character limit"
text = "Құралай"
#get_ifidf_for_words(text)
# %%
text = """27 қарашада түнде Шығыс Қазақстан облысының шығысында, оңтүстік-шығысында жаяу бұрқасын, облыстың с

Абай облысының оңтүстік-батысында, оңтүстігінде, шығысында жаяу бұрқасын болады. Түнде облыстың солтүстігінде

Батыс Қазақстан облысында оңтүстік-шығыстан, шығыстан жел соғады, түнде облыстың оңтүстік-батысында екпіні се

27 қарашада Атырау облысының батысында, шығысында, оңтүстігінде шығыстан жел соғады секундына 15-20 метр.

Маңғыстау облысының солтүстік-шығысында көктайғак болады. Шығыстан жел соғады, облыстың батысында, солтүстігі

Алматы облысының солтүстігінде, шығысында және таулы, тау бөктеріндегі аудандарында жолдарда көктайғак, солту

27 қарашада Жетісу облысының солтүстігінде, таулы және тау бөктерінде тұман, көктайғак болады."""
get_ifidf_for_words(text)
```

```
{'15': 0.23192034667290007,
 '18': 0.03313147809612858,
 '20': 0.1987888685767715,
 '23': 0.13252591238451433,
 '27': 0.13252591238451433,
 '28': 0.09939443428838575,
 '30': 0.03313147809612858,
```

Fig. 3. Meaning of words for text according to TF-IDF of semantic analysis.

words collected from Kazakh-language web pages. But first, before using this data, we need to prepare our model for retraining, otherwise we run the risk of memory overflow if we feed all the data to our model [12]. Therefore, we use the Gradient Optimization method to solve this problem (Fig. 5).

In order to test how well our model is learning, we develop the prediction truth and error metrics, which can be seen in Fig. 6 below. As we can see in the figure, the truth prediction metric has a maximum value of 0.5, which means that the sequence of symbols does not have a high probability of placement. To increase the accuracy, we need to retrain the model and train the model by adding new data. The x-axis here is from 0–200, and it is known that our model consists of 4,070,247 parameters, dividing

```
# %%
for s, score in sents_n_scores:
    print(s)
    print(score)
    print()
```

```
Түнде қатты аяз 30-35 градус.
0.5

Өскеменде түнде қатты аяз 33-35 градус болады.
0.447213595499958

Түнде облыстың солтүстігінде тұман болады.
0.447213595499958

Алматы мен Қонаевта жолдарда көктайғақ болады.
0.447213595499958

Семейде 27 қарашада түнде қатты аяз 33-35 градус.
0.4082482904638631

Маңғыстау облысының солтүстік-шығысында көктайғақ болады.
0.4082482904638631

Абай облысының оңтүстік-батысында, оңтүстігінде, шығысында жаяу бұрқасын болады.
0.3333333333333333
```

Fig. 4. Meaningfulness of sentences for text according to TF-IDF of semantic analysis.

```
start = time.time()
states = None
next_char = tf.constant(['Ғылым'])
result = [next_char]

for n in range(1000):
    next_char, states = one_step_model.generate_one_step(next_char, states=states)
    result.append(next_char)

result = tf.strings.join(result)
end = time.time()
print(result[0].numpy().decode('utf-8'), '\n\n' + '_'*80)
print('\nRun time:', end - start)
```

```
Ғылымы жеткен, солына табылмайды.
Мал, мақтан, оған ре емес пе?
Осы екеуі маған қалай табадада саламыз ешнәрсе шықпы, жермеген жерде құмар қылып,
Осының бір фәрдадан жүниеді кәмірет - бәрінің де біліп құрметтейін десең, жатқан т
Құдай тағала әрне жаратты, бір түрлі пайдалы хиямақ үшін кісі шығадам берей қалып,
Осы күнде қазақ ішінде «ісі барамын жемістіген нәрсені хайуандарды асырайтұғын жан
Бұрынғы қазақ жайын жықты.
Еске болы жоқ» деген - өмертің мазааз озі әуелі мал табу к рек, малға мінге қалған
Өл - алла тағаланың фиғыл ғазимларінің аттары, олардың мағынасын біл һәм серіз сиф
Кедей болса, ұрлық хик
```

Fig. 5. The result of text input to the model for generation.

those parameters by 200 and reading it, the prediction probabilities of the symbol at each stage (Fig. 6).

The result of the adjustment model for the generation model of the Kazakh language is as follows (Table 1). Since the model is trained using the recurrent training method, the result of the model does not give significant semantic value, but it has the correct structure of the word. This model has an error rate of 20%, which means that even if the model cannot form a clear idea, it will write words correctly and try not to deviate from the topic.

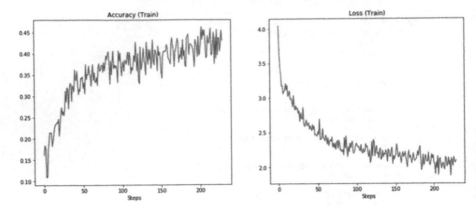

Fig. 6. Metrics indicator of the model.

Table 1. The result of the adjustment model for the generation model of the Kazakh language.

Data type	Example of experimental results
Input text (in Kazakh)	*Қазақстан республикасы*
Output text (in Kazakh)	Қазақстан Республикасы, Шығыс Еуразияда орналасқан елдің өзіндік республикалық жүйесімен басқарылатын мемлекет. Қазақстан Республикасының ең кіші мемлекеттік бірлігін құрастырушы мекеме Парламент, Президент және Ұлттық сәбиекорлық суды. Қазақстан, Қазақстан жерінің шекарасы, Тянь-Шань тасмағының ортақтамасы және Орталық Азияда орналасқаны арқылы бұрынғы шамамен Гүней Еуразияда орналасқан биік алқабылардың бірі. Қазақстан елінің оңтүстігінде, Сырдария және Есіктің кеңістігінде, Каспий теңізінен, Жетісудан және Алтын Емелден бастап, Қарағанды түсіндігіне дейінгі аумақты қамтылады Қазақстан Республикасы, жер орынды дайындық, топографиялық, климаттық, экологиялық, өнеркәсіптік-санақтардың орналасуы және жер-жер аймақтарының жаттығуына көмек көрсету әрекеттерін жүргізеді
Input text (English translation)	*Republic of Kazakhstan*

(*continued*)

Table 1. (*continued*)

Data type	Example of experimental results
Output text (English translation)	The Republic of Kazakhstan is a country in Eastern Eurasia governed by its own republican system. The constituent institutions of the smallest state unit of the Republic of Kazakhstan are the Parliament, the President and the National Child Protection Court. Kazakhstan is one of the high valleys located in South Eurasia, due to the border of the land of Kazakhstan, the border of the Tien-Shan belt and its location in Central Asia. In the south of the country of Kazakhstan, in the space of the Syrdarya and Esik, the territory from the Caspian Sea, Zhetysu and Altyn Emel to Karaganda basin is included The Republic of Kazakhstan conducts activities to assist in the preparation of land, topographical, climatic, environmental, industrial-census location and training of land-regions
Input text (in Kazakh)	*Коронавирус салдары*
Output text (in Kazakh)	Коронавирус салдары дегеніміз, Сарсылмақтан көмекшеленген ауруларды аталады. Коронавирус (COVID-19), Сарсылмақтан қозғалған өзгеріп жататын коронавирустың жаңа түріне байланысты ауру. Осы ауру 2019 жылы Қитайда пайда болған және оның көлігінде жалғасты. COVID-19 оқиғасы ғана Қитайда шығып, кейін сонымен байланысты басқа өлкелерге жетті Коронавирус аурусы тамақ қауіпсіздігін, көтерілген жастарын, диабетпен, асқазан сигаретті қаттылдықпен, бүйір ауруларымен, бет-бетше оралып жатқан жағдайда байланыстырады. Онда көптеген кезде жас, көп адамдар ауру тым өте жасасып, дәрігерлерге медициналық көмек көрсетуі қажет болады Коронавирус салдарының көбіне қанаттар арқылы туындауы, көзқарастар арқылы ауысуы және сауаттылығын қорғау үшін қалаулар қолданылады. Жаттатын гигиена әдістері мен әуелгі ортақ маска носу арқылы жасампаздықты қамтамасыз ету мүмкін. Бірнеше өлкелердегі жергілікті ауружайлары қорына көтерілген COVID-19 вакцинасылары да қолданылады
Input text (English translation)	*Consequences of the coronavirus*
Output text (English translation)	The consequences of the coronavirus are called measles-assisted diseases. Coronavirus (COVID-19), a disease caused by a new type of mutated coronavirus transmitted by Sarsylmak. This disease appeared in China in 2019 and continued in his car. The case of COVID-19 only started in China and then spread to other countries The coronavirus disease is associated with food insecurity, elevated youth, diabetes, stomach stiffness, side effects, and face-to-face contact. In many cases, many young people will become very sick and need medical help from doctors The consequences of the coronavirus are often generated through wings, shifting through attitudes and preferences are used to protect literacy. Creativity can be ensured by practicing hygiene techniques and wearing the first shared mask. In several regions, local hospitals stockpiled COVID-19 vaccines are also used

The table shows fragments of the result of generating text in the Kazakh language. You can see not a bad result. The text is relevant to the topic and has grammatically structured sentences.

4   Evaluation and Discussion

To evaluate the quality of the algorithm for each class, we calculate the Precision and Recall metrics separately. Precision can be interpreted as the proportion of objects called positive by the classifier that are also truly positive, and recall indicates what proportion of objects of the positive class the algorithm found among all objects of the positive class. There are several different ways to combine precision and recall into a summary quality measure. Table 2 presents the results of evaluating the quality of the text generation model on given corpora.

Table 2. The evaluation of the obtained results of the text generation model testing in the Kazakh language

Name of the corpus	Source	Number of characters	Recall	Precision
Health	https://kitaphana.kz	2067887	61.65	69.97
Republic of Kazakhstan	https://bankreferatov.kz	2360983	72.74	75.18
Historical figures	https://bankreferatov.kz	6154140	69.35	73.85

For the experiment, the names of the requests were dependent on the topics and genres of the corpora. Additionally, the requests consisted of 1 to 3 words. The average results obtained from the testing were as follows: Recall = 67.9, Precision = 73. The quality of the results is not satisfactory. During the experiment, the lowest results were observed in text generation for the literary and scientific genres. This was due to the specific themes and structural forms of the texts themselves. For the scientific genre, only scientific articles were considered, which limited the model's learning process. To resolve and improve the quality of the model, future plans involve increasing the quantity and quality of the corpora. However, using all available data for the model without proper cleaning beforehand may lead to overfitting and compromise its performance. To address this issue, future plans involve the utilization of the Gradient Descent method to optimize the cleaning process and enhance the model's overall performance.

5   Conclusion

The developed model of Kazakh language text generation based on semantic analysis presents not bad results. However, it is difficult to achieve such accuracy, which is not 100% accurate. But the more the trained information structure, the higher the result can be achieved. Semantic analysis of the Kazakh language compared to other languages is somewhat difficult. The lack of information and data and the complexity of the morphology of the Kazakh language have a somewhat negative effect. Digital data in the Kazakh language have been collected and supplemented. A prototype of the generation system model for the Kazakh language was created and we trained the model on the collected corpus. The created model was tested and discussed. Recurrent Neural Networks (RNNs) have been studied and discussed. Information about the linguistic resources of the Kazakh language was analyzed. We focused these studies mainly on semantics and generation. Our main task was to generate semantic text. We have developed this model. In the course of this research, corpora in the Kazakh language were collected and models were created. According to the results of the research, search for a text, article or text from the corpus related to the keywords you entered or searched for, and produce the text that is close to the semantics. That is, firstly, it saves time, and secondly, getting rid of unnecessary information. Since generation is important, it is used in various spheres. For example: chatbot, search engines, Q&A in many companies. It allows to save the budget, reduce time, and reduce the number of workers.

Acknowledgments. This research was performed and financed by the grant Project IRN AP 09259556 of Ministry of Science and Higher Education of the Republic of Kazakhstan.

References

1. Yemm, G.: Can NLP help or harm your business? (2006)
2. Ranjan, S., Sood, S., Verma, V.: Twitter sentiment analysis of real-time customer experience feedback for predicting growth of Indian telecom companies. In: 2018 4th International Conference on Computing Sciences (ICCS). IEEE (2018)
3. Liu, B.: Sentiment analysis: a multi-faceted problem. IEEE Intell. Syst. **25**(3), 76–80 (2017)
4. Yergesh, B., Bekmanova, G., Sharipbay, A.: Sentiment analysis on the hotel reviews in the Kazakh language. In: 2017 International Conference on Computer Science and Engineering (UBMK). IEEE (2017)
5. Phani, S., Lahiri, S., Biswas, A.: Sentiment analysis of tweets in three Indian languages. In: Proceedings of the 6th Workshop on South and Southeast Asian Natural Language Processing (WSSANLP 2016) (2016)
6. Baly, R., El-Khoury, G., Moukalled, R., Aoun, R., Hajj, H., Shaban, K.B., El-Hajj, W.: Comparative evaluation of sentiment analysis methods across Arabic dialects. Procedia Comput. Sci. **117**, 266–273 (2017)
7. Yildirim, E., Çetin, F.S., Eryigit, G., Temel, T.: The impact of NLP on Turkish sentiment analysis (2016)
8. Hands-On Machine Learning with Scikit-Learn and TensorFlow: Concepts, Tools, and Techniques to Build Intelligent Systems. CST 463-Advanced Machine Learning. https://catalog. csumb.edu/preview_course_nopop.php?catoid=1&coid=476. Accessed 10 Nov 2022
9. Sherstinsky, A.: Fundamentals of recurrent neural network (RNN) and long short-term memory (LSTM) Network. https://arxiv.org/abs/1808.03314. Accessed 28 Oct 2022
10. Hochreiter, S., Bengio, Y., Frasconi, P., Schmidhuber, J.: Gradient flow in recurrent nets: the difficulty of learning long-term dependencies. In: Kremer, S.C., Kolen, J.F. (eds.) A Field Guide to Dynamical Recurrent Neural Networks. IEEE Press (2001)
11. Haber, E., Ruthotto, L.: Stable architectures for deep neural networks. Inverse Probl. **34**(1), 014004 (2017)
12. Rakhimova, D., Turarbek, A., Kopbosyn, L.: Hybrid approach for the semantic analysis of texts in the Kazakh language. In: Hong, T.-P., Wojtkiewicz, K., Chawuthai, R., Sitek, P. (eds.) ACIIDS 2021. CCIS, vol. 1371, pp. 134–145. Springer, Singapore (2021). https://doi.org/10. 1007/978-981-16-1685-3_12
13. Diana, R., Assem, S.: Problems of semantics of words of the Kazakh language in the information retrieval. In: Nguyen, N.T., Chbeir, R., Exposito, E., Aniorté, P., Trawiński, B. (eds.) ICCCI 2019. LNCS (LNAI), vol. 11684, pp. 70–81. Springer, Cham (2019). https://doi.org/ 10.1007/978-3-030-28374-2_7

14. Rakhimova, D., Turganbayeva, A.: Approach to extract keywords and keyphrases of text resources and documents in the Kazakh language. In: Nguyen, N.T., Hoang, B.H., Huynh, C.P., Hwang, D., Trawiński, B., Vossen, G. (eds.) ICCCI 2020. LNCS (LNAI), vol. 12496, pp. 719–729. Springer, Cham (2020). https://doi.org/10.1007/978-3-030-63007-2_56
15. Rakhimova, D., Turganbayeva, A.: Auto-abstracting of texts in the Kazakh language. In: Proceedings of the 6th International Conference on Engineering & MIS, pp. 1–5 (2020)

Nested Semisupervised Learning for Cross-Note Abbreviation Detection in Vietnamese Clinical Texts

Vo Thi Ngoc Chau[(✉)] [iD] and Nguyen Hua Phung[(✉)] [iD]

Ho Chi Minh City University of Technology, Vietnam National University – Ho Chi Minh City,
Ho Chi Minh City, Vietnam
{chauvtn,nhphung}@hcmut.edu.vn

Abstract. Abbreviation detection in clinical texts is popular and significant due to its contribution to enhancing readability and shareability of electronic medical records (EMRs). Nonetheless, it is limited to low-resource languages like Vietnamese because there is no available labeled dataset for the task. More development is thus needed to handle this task on Vietnamese clinical texts. On the other hand, there are many different note types where abbreviations are generated and used by many various groups of physicians, nurses, and other stakeholders. This fact leads to the necessity of processing a wide diversity of clinical texts for abbreviation detection. At this moment, none of the existing works takes into account the context where abbreviation detection is asked for the clinical texts that belong to one note type, unfortunately with the availability of the labeled clinical texts of another note type. This challenge results in a so-called cross-note abbreviation detection task in our work. In such a context, we address this task on Vietnamese clinical texts by proposing nested semisupervised learning. Our resulting Nested-SSL method is capable of detecting abbreviations in real Vietnamese clinical texts effectively. It is based on an existing semisupervised learning method and then boosts the core semisupervised learning process by a fold-based enhancement scheme in favor of F-measure of the minority class. In the empirical evaluation with real EMRs, Nested-SSL always outperforms its base semisupervised learning method and some existing ones. Its better performance lays the foundations for effectively preprocessing Vietnamese clinical texts in other tasks on EMRs.

Keyword: Electronic Medical Record · Abbreviation Detection · Vietnamese Natural Language Processing · Semisupervised Learning · Data Imbalance

1 Introduction

Electronic medical records (EMRs) are now important in both healthcare activities and their related researches. Among their data types, clinical texts are required in many tasks, especially those with natural language processing. However, due to a generation environment with time shortage and high pressure, clinical texts are normally full of

N. T. Nguyen et al. (Eds.): ACIIDS 2023, CCIS 1863, pp. 596–608, 2023.
https://doi.org/10.1007/978-3-031-42430-4_49

abbreviations and incomplete sentences. The ubiquity of abbreviations in clinical texts might be useful for record simplification but challenging for their processing by both human and machines. Indeed, EMRs get misinterpreted and confused with abbreviations as mentioned in [3, 16]. This is understandable because they are context-dependent as discussed in [12]. As a result, they have a strong impact on the readability and shareability of EMRs. Detecting and replacing them with their long forms thus become important tasks to further make the most of EMRs.

Aware of this abbreviation detection task, many different works and activities were conducted. For example, in [21], a CLEF shared task on clinical acronym/abbreviation normalization was discussed. In addition, [19] considered three natural language processing systems for this task. More recently, [22] introduced the CARD framework for abbreviation detection on English clinical texts.

Besides, many methods were proposed as reviewed below. Unsupervised learning was used in [7] to avoid annotating clinical texts, while [23] discussed the task with word lists and heuristic rules, and [8, 20, 22, 23] used supervised learning. Nowadays, deep learning has been employed in [9, 11, 15] for acronym detection in non-clinical texts while [6] for informal abbreviations in medical notes.

From these related works, it is realized that supervised learning can examine surrounding contexts of abbreviations thoroughly and thus, more generalized than the rule-based approach. Unsupervised learning is promising but not easy to be used for other languages like Vietnamese. As for deep learning with Long Short-Term Memory models in [6] and Transformers and BERT in [9, 11, 15], even more contextual details can be captured. However, they are not straightforwardly applicable to Vietnamese clinical texts. Above all, these works did not consider a diversity of clinical texts. This is a shortage as abbreviations exist in clinical texts of any different note type. Some note types might not have available labeled clinical texts for learning.

On the other hand, most of the existing works like [13, 19, 20, 23] were dedicated to English data, while [4] supported French electronic health records, [7, 8] were proposed for German clinical texts, and [15] conducted the experiments on data in many various languages including Vietnamese but not in the EMR context. Therefore, there are few works on Vietnamese clinical texts. This results in a growing need for preprocessing Vietnamese EMRs with abbreviations as soon as EMRs become widely used in Vietnam. From these perspectives, our work originally defines a cross-note abbreviation detection task on Vietnamese clinical texts to focus on a more practical context where the existing labeled clinical texts of other note types are used.

In order to address the aforementioned task, semisupervised learning is considered so that all the given labeled and unlabeled data can be utilized. Nowadays, several semisupervised learning algorithms in [10, 24, 25] and the others reviewed in [5, 17] are available. Nevertheless, just a few semisupervised learning algorithms are parameter-free. This aspect matters to our work because parameter setting is often non-trivially made for each dataset. For example, as discussed in [17], Self-training is a simpler semisupervised learning framework with high effectiveness, but needs a probability threshold to decide its prediction capability. This parameter-setting is not easy for users to handle the task on new unlabeled data over time. As a result, we take into account

STOPF [10], STDPNaN [24], and Tri-training [25] to formulate our solution in a new semisupervised learning manner.

In particular, we propose a novel nested semisupervised learning method, named Nested-SSL, to detect abbreviations in Vietnamese clinical texts of various note types. It is defined as a nested process with a base semisupervised learning method. It inherits the prediction capability and simplicity of Self-training, but exploits instances in a fold-based selection scheme for enhancing the training dataset. Different from other methods, Nested-SSL can preserve data imbalance in each dataset when selecting and utilizing instances from the unlabeled dataset. This makes Nested-SSL learn with noises for more correct predictions.

Indeed, the experimental results on real Vietnamese clinical texts show that our solution can effectively tackle the cross-note abbreviation detection task on real Vietnamese clinical texts. Moreover, Nested-SSL outperforms its base semisupervised learning method and other existing ones on a consistent basis. With more correctly detected abbreviations, Nested-SSL can support preprocessing Vietnamese clinical texts so that they can be further used in other natural language processing tasks.

2   A Cross-Note Abbreviation Detection Task on Clinical Texts in Vietnamese Electronic Medical Records

In this section, we define a cross-note abbreviation detection task on clinical texts in Vietnamese electronic medical records (EMRs). In particular, given clinical texts in Vietnamese EMRs, the task is to identify all abbreviations in the clinical texts. In the existing works [20, 22, 23], this task was tackled as a binary classification task, using an available labeled dataset of the same note type which the considered clinical texts belong to. By contrast, our task is examined in a more practical context where there is no such an available labeled dataset of the same note type. Instead, there is a labeled dataset of another note type in support of the task. Therefore, our task is called *cross-note*. For example, we want to identify abbreviations in discharge summaries while only labeled data obtained from treatment order notes are now available for the task.

In particular, our cross-note abbreviation detection task is formally defined below.

Given clinical texts in Vietnamese EMRs, a token is identified as a sequence of contiguous characters with no space. Let X_i be a vector representing each token in a vector space where p is the number of the extracted features: $X_i = (x_{i1}, x_{i2}, ..., x_{ip})$.

Given a labeled dataset D_l^{t1} of n tokens extracted and labeled from the clinical texts of note type $t1$ and an unlabeled dataset D_u^{t2} of m tokens extracted from the clinical texts of note type $t2$ in Vietnamese EMRs where $t1 \neq t2$, the task is to assign y_i to each token in D_u^{t2} where $y_i \in \{0, 1\}$, with 0 for a non-abbreviation and 1 for an abbreviation.

The task is now algorithmically detailed with two phases as follows:

(i) Learning: $H = learning(D_l^{t1}, Y_l, D_u^{t2})$ where H is the model obtained from the process of a learning algorithm $learning()$ and Y_l is a label set of the tokens in D_l^{t1}.

(ii) Prediction: $Y_u = H(D_u^{t2})$ such that $Y_u = \{y_i\}$ for each $i = 1..m$, $y_i \in \{0,1\}$.

3 The Proposed Solution

From the task definition, we propose a solution to the cross-note abbreviation detection task on clinical texts in Vietnamese electronic medical records as shown in Fig. 1. Our solution includes three phases: feature extraction, learning phase, and prediction phase. These phases are carried out in sequence. Compared to the existing works, the main contribution of our solution is nested semisupervised learning in the learning phase where Nested-SSL is proposed as a novel method for the task.

3.1 Solution Details

3.1.1 Feature Extraction

As our solution is not end-to-end, feature engineering is needed. In our work, the task is originally defined at this moment and our proposed solution is in its infancy. Therefore, the extracted features are based on those in [20] and then adapted to Vietnamese clinical texts. The following is the final feature list used in our work. More features, e.g. those from word embedding, can be added in our extended work.

i) *Word formation features.* For this category, more special characters such as "&", "%", and "#" are taken into account. In addition, misspelling features are not used in our work because spelling issues belong to another task on Vietnamese clinical texts.
ii) *Features related to vowel and consonant letters.* These features are defined to check if a token contains all/any vowel or consonant letters.
iii) *Features from knowledge bases.* For this category, we use medical terms extracted from EMRs to build a so-called dictionary and further derive their acronyms. Based on those, we define the features to check if a token is a medical term, i.e. in the dictionary and if a token is an acronym.

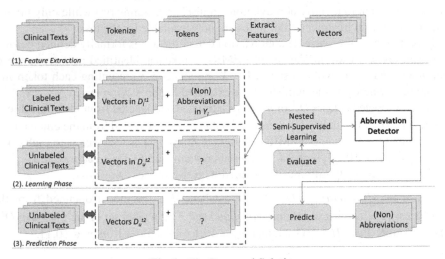

Fig. 1. The Proposed Solution

iv) *Word frequency feature.* This feature is derived from the number of token occurrences in the union of all the datasets we gathered in the work.

v) *Features from the local context.* In this category, the local context of each token is formed by its previous and next ones. So, the features from the previous and next tokens are included. Whether they are at beginning or end of a sentence is also added.

3.1.2   Learning Phase

The learning phase of our solution is based on semisupervised learning to incorporate more characteristics of tokens in D_u^{t2} from unlabeled clinical texts in the learning process. This can be seen as instance-based transfer learning when different note types are considered in the task.

Moreover, our learning phase is different from the existing works as defined in a nested manner, resulting in nested semisupervised learning. This nested fashion aims at boosting the prediction capability of another base semisupervised learning method. The rationale behind nesting is adding one extra learning layer to learn more about unlabeled instances and thus enhance the existing one. The details of nested supervised learning are presented in our proposed Nested-SSL method.

3.1.3   Prediction Phase

In this phase, the resulting nested semisupervised model is used as an abbreviation detector. It is applied on unlabeled clinical texts to return abbreviations in those texts. Post-processing can be further invoked to improve the results before they are utilized.

3.2   The Proposed Nested-SSL Method

A nested semisupervised learning method, Nested-SSL, is proposed in this section. Nested-SSL lays the foundations for our novel solution of the aforementioned task in a more practical context as compared to the existing ones in [4, 7, 8, 11, 15, 20, 22, 23]. Its details and characteristics are presented next to clarify the previous statement.

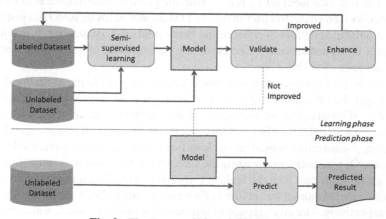

Fig. 2. The Proposed Nested-SSL Method

As sketched in Fig. 2, our method is composed of two phases: Learning and Prediction. In the Learning phase, a semisupervised learning (SSL) framework covers the whole learning process of our method as an outer SSL process in Self-training's manner. In the meantime, there is SSL from an existing SSL method as an inner base learning process. It plays an important role of producing the resulting model. In the Prediction phase, the resulting model is used for predictions like any classifier.

In particular, our Nested-SSL method is formally defined as follows:

Input: D_l^{t1}, Y_l, D_u^{t2}, k which is the number of folds for the enhancement scheme
Output: a model H
Process:

```
1.    lset ← resample_with_weight (D₁ᵗ¹, Y₁);
2.    iH ← base_semisupervised_learning (lset, Dᵤᵗ²);
3.    Yᵤ ← iH(Dᵤᵗ²);
4.    pset ← (Dᵤᵗ², Yᵤ);
5.    repeat
6.        i ← argmaxᵢ₌₁..ₖ { F-measure (iH(foldᵢ(pset.Dᵤᵗ²)),
          foldᵢ(pset.Yᵤ))};
7.        lset ← lset ∪ foldᵢ (pset);
8.        pset ← pset - foldᵢ (pset);
9.        iH ← base_semisupervised_learning (lset, Dᵤᵗ²);
10.   until F-measure (iH(D₁ᵗ¹), Y₁) is not improved;
11.   return H ← argmaxᵢH {F-measure (iH(D₁ᵗ¹), Y₁)};
```

For details, in line 1, we define *lset* as a starting labeled dataset in the learning phase. This dataset is a bootstrap sample of the given labeled dataset. We use a bootstrap sample instead of the original one because we need data for validation. By sampling, some instances are not included in the training set, i.e. *lset*, and thus able to be used for validation. Indeed, validation is done on the original labeled dataset.

After that, in line 2, we obtain *iH* as a model from the employed base semisupervised learning method. In line 3, *iH* is then used to predict each instance in the given unlabeled dataset. The resulting label set Y_u is used with the given unlabeled dataset to form a so-called pseudo-labeled dataset *pset* in line 4. This dataset helps us select the instances in the given unlabeled dataset to enhance the starting labeled dataset *lset*. It is noted that this dataset is dependent on *iH*. Therefore, the performance of our method starts with the performance of the base one.

In lines 5–10, our nested semisupervised learning process happens. In line 6, $fold_i()$ is used to get the i-th fold from the result of stratifying the pseudo-labeled dataset *pset* into k folds. With stratification, the ratio of abbreviations to non-abbreviations in *pset* is preserved in each fold. This can avoid focusing on the instances of just one specific class. In addition, *F-measure()* is used as our loss function to calculate correct abbreviation predictions. Our method is maximizing the value of this function. As a result, line 6 helps us pick a fold from *pset* with the highest F-measure. This fold is then used to enhance the starting labeled dataset *lset* in line 7. *Pset* and *iH* are updated accordingly in lines 8 and 9, respectively. The convergence of our nested semisupervised learning process is shown in line 10 where a termination condition is set with the unchanged performance of iH on the labeled dataset.

Finally, in line 11, H is returned as a model from Nested-SSL on the given labeled and unlabeled datasets after maximizing F-measure in favor of the abbreviation class.

In our method, we used F-measure instead of other performance measures such as Accuracy, Precision, or Recall because it is a harmony mean of Precision and Recall, balancing the correctly retrieved results and returned ones. It also contributes to the data imbalance issue that is faced in the current task.

3.3 Nested-SSL'S Characteristics

In this subsection, the main characteristics of our Nested-SSL method are discussed.

Firstly, it is straightforward to realize the starting performance of Nested-SSL stems from that of its base SSL method in favor of F-measure for the minority class of abbreviations. As a result, the capability of the base SSL method to detect abbreviations is always enhanced, leading to better abbreviation detection of Nested-SSL.

Secondly, Nested-SSL defines an enhancement scheme based on overall predictions of a so-called pseudo-labeled dataset obtained from the given unlabeled one. Its enhancement scheme respects the data imbalance in each dataset to maintain the relative correspondence between the one in the learning phase and the one in the prediction phase. This is important in our context where most of the non-abbreviations are correctly identified with very high confidence.

Nonetheless, our enhancement scheme might include the instances that have been incorrectly detected according to the current model in a round. This is a fact that we accept and then consider those instances as noises. It is noted that the existence of noises helps the resulting model avoid overfitting. The Nested-SSL model thus needs more rounds to get rid of noises and adjust its prediction capability. As a result, the model is more generalized.

Thirdly, the learning process of Nested-SSL converges at the maximum value of F-measure after the limited number of iterations. Its deterministic feature stems from the maximum number of iterations decided by the number of folds in the enhancement scheme. More folds imply less data used for enhancement, leading to more iterations for the outer SSL process. Nevertheless, the convergence of Nested-SSL sometimes needs just a few iterations when several folds have been included. It is obviously dependent on data characteristics. From these perspectives, we decided to generalize it to be one flexible parameter of Nested-SSL.

Last but not least, training time with nested SSL is inevitably higher than that of its base method. However, it is easily affordable with today's computers.

4   An Empirical Evaluation

4.1   Experiment Settings

In order to evaluate our solution with the Nested-SSL method, an empirical study is conducted. The study used four real datasets of Vietnamese EMRs in two hospitals in Vietnam. Due to privacy protection, their details are not disclosed.

The datasets are extracted from clinical texts of four different note types as follows: CPN from care progress notes, TPN from treatment progress notes, DS from discharge summaries, and CON from care order notes. They are also preprocessed with duplicate removal. Details of each dataset before and after duplicate removal are given in Tables 1 and 2, respectively. In both cases, before and after duplicate removal, their sizes are varying from note type to note type. This establishes several various situations for the task in our work.

In addition, these datasets are greatly imbalanced with different ratios of abbreviations to non-abbreviations. Such different imbalances are reasonably different from dataset to dataset. Treatment progress notes were produced by physicians during their treatment process under higher pressure with time limitation. As a result, more abbreviations were used. In contrast, discharge summaries were generated after a treatment process and probably further used by many other stakeholders. Fewer abbreviations were thus included. As compared to those before duplicate removal, the datasets after duplicate removal have data imbalance mitigated.

Furthermore, to demonstrate a cross-note task, we use CON as a labeled dataset while the rest as unlabeled ones. This choice is made for a more practical context where fewer labeled data are available as compared to more required unlabeled data. Regarding the characteristics of each note type, CON is closer to the others.

Table 1. Descriptions of Data Before Duplicate Removal.

Dataset	Total		Non-Abbreviation		Abbreviation	
	#	%	#	%	#	%
CPN	77,875	100.00	73,217	94.02	4,658	5.98
TPN	65,718	100.00	59,927	91.19	5,791	8.81
DS	244,338	100.00	241,816	98.97	2,522	1.03
CON	51,257	100.00	49,321	96.22	1,936	3.78

Table 2. Descriptions of Data After Duplicate Removal.

Dataset	Total		Non-Abbreviation		Abbreviation	
	#	%	#	%	#	%
CPN	11,659	100.00	10,885	93.36	774	6.64
TPN	13,807	100.00	12,572	91.06	1,235	8.94
DS	20,947	100.00	20,404	97.41	543	2.59
CON	6,391	100.00	5,874	91.91	517	8.09

For example, CON and CPN are from their clinical texts, which were all about taking care of patients. On the other hand, CON and TPN are those with the patient treatment process done by physicians. As for CON and DS, some care orders are often included in discharge summaries so that the patient treatment process can be maintained later.

For the implementation, our program was written in Java, utilizing the available source codes of Tri-training [25], Weka [18], and algorithms of STDPNaN [24] and STOPF [10]. C4.5 [14], 1-nearest neighbor (1-NN) [2], and Random Forest (RF) [1] are used as base classifiers. RF has 300 random trees and other default settings according to its popular use in the existing works such as [19]. All the reused algorithms and models were selected according to their free-parameter settings. For Nested-SSL, we use 20, 40, and 60 folds for CPN, TPN, and DS, respectively, according to the grid search results.

For comparison, Accuracy (%) in [0, 100] is used for overall predictions, while Recall, Precision, and F-measure in [0, 1] for correct abbreviation predictions. Their higher values imply the better models. Also, the best results are shown in bold.

For evaluation, we raise three questions in this empirical study as follows:

- Question 1: Is cross-note abbreviation detection a challenging task on clinical texts in Vietnamese EMRs?
- Question 2: Does Nested-SSL outperform some existing semisupervised learning ones for the cross-note abbreviation detection task on Vietnamese clinical texts?
- Question 3: Does Nested-SSL really resolve the aforementioned task?

Question 1 is asked for the significance of our work while Questions 2 and 3 are examined for the contribution of Nested-SSL to the given task. These questions are just discussed in the scope of this work. More issues are considered future works.

4.2 Experimental Results and Discussions

For the first question, we did several experiments with 3 base models: C4.5, 1-Nearest Neighbor (1-NN) using Euclidean distance, and Random Forest using 300 random trees with other default parameter settings. Single-note evaluations were conducted with the 10-fold cross-validation scheme on the same dataset; while cross-note evaluations with the models trained on CON dataset and tested on each dataset in Table 3.

The evaluation results in Table 3 show that if we had enough labeled data of the same note type, abbreviation detection could be handled trivially. This is true for three different note types in our experiments when F-measure values obtained for single-note evaluations on CPN and TPN are very high (> 0.95). By contrast, cross-note abbreviation detection is non-trivial when all the F-measure values for cross-note evaluations are much lower than those for single-note evaluations. A great difference in their evaluation results reflects the necessity for a better method that can support cross-note abbreviation detection when we lack resources for the task. Therefore, Nested-SSL is significantly proposed to resolve this task in such a practical context.

To answer Question 2, the results in Table 4 indicate the appropriateness of Nested-SSL for the aforementioned task in all the cases as Nested-SSL can provide better Accuracy and F-measure values in comparison with the others. For a more particular discussion, there is a little difference in Accuracy between the related methods and ours although our Accuracy is higher. This is because data imbalance is high in the datasets. Therefore, more performance expressed in Accuracy is given to the majority class, i.e. non-abbreviations.

Table 3. Cross-note vs. Single-note Evaluations.

Base Method	Measure	CPN		TPN		DS	
		Single-note	Cross-note	Single-note	Cross-note	Single-note	Cross-note
C4.5	Accuracy	**99.443**	97.341	**99.232**	95.162	**99.375**	98.807
	Recall	**0.952**	0.674	**0.956**	0.553	**0.801**	0.777
	Precision	**0.963**	0.900	**0.958**	0.855	**0.950**	0.766
	F-measure	**0.958**	0.771	**0.957**	0.672	**0.869**	0.771
1-NN	Accuracy	**99.099**	97.736	**99.102**	95.408	**98.916**	98.869
	Recall	**0.926**	0.716	**0.943**	0.555	**0.783**	0.703
	Precision	**0.937**	0.926	**0.956**	0.890	0.796	**0.834**
	F-measure	**0.932**	0.808	**0.949**	0.684	**0.789**	0.763
Random Forest	Accuracy	**99.485**	97.547	**99.515**	95.531	**99.360**	99.045
	Recall	**0.944**	0.687	**0.963**	0.559	**0.814**	0.753
	Precision	**0.977**	0.924	**0.983**	0.906	**0.931**	0.861
	F-measure	**0.961**	0.788	**0.973**	0.691	**0.868**	0.804

Table 4. Cross-note Evaluations with Semisupervised Learning Methods.

Dataset	Measure	STDPNaN	STOPF	Tri-training (C4.5)	Tri-training (1-NN)	Tri-training (RF)	Nested-SSL
CPN	Accuracy	97.341	97.341	97.341	97.470	97.530	**97.847**
	Recall	0.674	0.674	0.674	0.681	0.683	**0.686**
	Precision	0.900	0.900	0.900	0.917	0.925	**0.985**
	F-measure	0.771	0.771	0.771	0.781	0.786	**0.809**
TPN	Accuracy	95.162	95.162	95.162	95.307	95.553	**95.705**
	Recall	0.553	0.553	0.553	0.546	0.557	**0.564**
	Precision	0.855	0.855	0.855	0.886	0.911	**0.928**
	F-measure	0.672	0.672	0.672	0.675	0.691	**0.702**
DS	Accuracy	98.807	98.807	98.807	98.811	99.055	**99.102**
	Recall	**0.777**	**0.777**	**0.777**	0.676	0.751	0.751
	Precision	0.766	0.766	0.766	0.834	0.866	**0.885**
	F-measure	0.771	0.771	0.771	0.747	0.805	**0.813**

Nonetheless, Nested-SSL achieves higher Precision and F-measure particularly for abbreviation detection in all cases while comparable Recall in the case of DS dataset and higher Recall in the remaining cases. It is also worth noting that Nested-SSL can recognize much more true abbreviations than STDPNaN, STOPF, and Tri-training with C4.5. Such a result comes from the nested SSL process in Nested-SSL when it can incorporate more instances from the unlabeled dataset in the learning process. Moreover, it preserves the distribution in the dataset and makes the learning process fit the unlabeled dataset well in a general space. This fact is reflected by a great difference in Precision values, showing the effectiveness of Nested-SSL.

Table 5. Evaluation of Nested-SSL with its Base Methods.

Dataset	Measure	Random Forest	Tri-training (Random Forest)	Nested-SSL (Random Forest)	Nested-SSL
CPN	Accuracy	97.547	97.530	97.547	**97.847**
	Recall	**0.687**	0.683	**0.687**	0.686
	Precision	0.924	0.925	0.924	**0.985**
	F-measure	0.788	0.786	0.788	**0.809**
TPN	Accuracy	95.531	95.553	95.582	**95.705**
	Recall	0.559	0.557	**0.564**	**0.564**
	Precision	0.906	0.911	0.907	**0.928**
	F-measure	0.691	0.691	0.696	**0.702**
DS	Accuracy	99.045	99.055	99.04	**99.102**
	Recall	**0.753**	0.751	0.751	0.751
	Precision	0.861	0.866	0.861	**0.885**
	F-measure	0.804	0.805	0.802	**0.813**

Next, Question 3 is answered with the results in Table 5 which clarify the significant contribution of nested SSL to the cross-note abbreviation detection task. As compared to Random Forest, Tri-training (Random Forest) does not outperform its base model clearly while Nested-SSL (Random Forest) is comparable to Random Forest on CPN and TPN. It seems to contrast with Tri-training (Random Forest). In this case, Nested-SSL (Random Forest) does not exploit the nested SSL process. It works just like any SSL method.

Nevertheless, when Tri-training (Random Forest) is used as a base model of Nested-SSL, the prediction results get improved with Accuracy, Precision, and F-measure. Besides, Nested-SSL sometimes improves on Recall as compared to Tri-training (Random Forest). Generally speaking, Nested-SSL can enhance its base SSL model with better performance in all our experiments.

In short, this evaluation has confirmed that our Nested-SSL method can effectively tackle the cross-note abbreviation detection task on clinical texts in Vietnamese EMRs. Indeed, our method makes more correct predictions than the traditional and base ones on a consistent basis. As a result, our method can identify correct abbreviations in clinical texts of one note type by using the labeled texts of another note type.

5 Conclusions

In this paper, we have defined a cross-note abbreviation detection task on clinical texts in Vietnamese electronic medical records. This task is practical in Vietnamese as there are just a small labeled dataset of one note type and many larger unlabeled datasets of other note types. Such a resource shortage makes the task challenging. To overcome this problem, Nested-SSL has been proposed by utilizing an existing semisupervised learning process inside its semisupervised learning process. The mechanism results in a nested semisupervised learning process to integrate more unlabeled data into the learning process on the small given labeled dataset. Data imbalance is also considered in the enhancement scheme of our Nested-SSL based on k-fold cross validation. As a result, Nested-SSL outperforms some related methods in terms of Accuracy, Precision, and F-measure when resolving the task on several real datasets. In addition, Nested-SSL has preserved and improved the performance of its base semisupervised learning model in all the experiments of our empirical evaluation study. Above all, Nested-SSL has formed an effective solution to our cross-note abbreviation detection task on Vietnamese clinical texts.

In the future, more experiments with more note types are expected so that we can evaluate the generality of Nested-SSL for the task. Abbreviation resolution is also planned for Vietnamese clinical texts. Based on this future task, we can prepare more resources for other research activities on Vietnamese clinical texts.

Acknowledgment. This research is funded by Vietnam National University – Ho Chi Minh City (VNU-HCM) under grant number C2022-20-11.

In addition, our sincere thanks go to Dr. Nguyen Thi Minh Huyen and her team at University of Science, Vietnam National University, Hanoi, Vietnam, for the helpful resources. We also thank the providers of the Vietnamese electronic medical records very much.

References

1. Breiman, L.: Random forests. Mach. Learn. **45**(1), 5–32 (2001). https://doi.org/10.1023/A:1010933404324
2. Cover, T., Hart, P.: Nearest neighbor pattern classification. IEEE Trans. Inf. Theory **13**, 21–27 (1967)
3. Collard, B., Royal, A.: The use of abbreviations in surgical note keeping. Ann. Med. Surg. **4**, 100–102 (2015)
4. Cossin, S., Jolly, M., Larrouture, I., Griffier, R., Jouhet, V.: Semi-automatic extraction of abbreviations and their senses from electronic health records. In: Proceedings of IA & Santé 2021, pp. 1–13 (2021)
5. van Engelen, J.E., Hoos, H.H.: A survey on semi-supervised learning. Mach. Learn. **109**, 373–440 (2020). https://doi.org/10.1007/s10994-019-05855-6
6. Heryawan, L., et al.: A detection of informal abbreviations from free text medical notes using deep learning. EJBI **16**(1), 29–37 (2020). https://doi.org/10.24105/ejbi.2020.16.1.29
7. Kreuzthaler, M., Oleynik, M., Avian, A., Schulz, S.: Unsupervised abbreviation detection in clinical narratives. In: Proceedings of the Clinical Natural Language Processing Workshop, pp. 91–98 (2016)
8. Kreuzthaler, M., Schulz, S.: Detection of sentence boundaries and abbreviations in clinical narratives. BMC Med. Inform. Decis. Making **15**, 1–13 (2015)
9. Kubal, D., Nagvenkar, A.: Effective ensembling of transformer based language models for acronyms identification. In: Proceedings of SDU@ AAAI, pp. 1–6 (2021)
10. Li, J., Zhu, Q.: Semi-supervised self-training method based on an optimum-path forest. IEEE Access **7**, 36388–36399 (2019). https://doi.org/10.1109/ACCESS.2019.2903839

11. Li, S., Yang, C., Liang, T., Zhu, X., Yu, C., Yang, Y.: Acronym extraction with hybrid strategies. In: Proceedings of SDU@ AAAI, pp. 1–7 (2022)
12. Long, W.J.: Parsing free text nursing notes. In: Proceedings of AMIA Annual Symposium, p. 917 (2003)
13. Moon, S., Pakhomov, S., Melton, G.: Clinical Abbreviation Sense Inventory. University of Minnesota Digital Conservancy (2012). http://hdl.handle.net/11299/137703. Accessed 13 Jan 2019
14. Quinlan, J.R.: C4.5: Programs for Machine Learning. Morgan Kaufmann (1993)
15. Sharma, P., Saadany, H., Zilio, L., Kanojia, D., Orăsan, C.: An ensemble approach to acronym extraction using transformers. In: Proceedings of SDU@ AAAI, pp. 1–6 (2022)
16. Shilo, L., Shilo, G.: Analysis of abbreviations used by residents in admission notes and discharge summaries. QJM Int. J. Med. 111(3), 179–183 (2018)
17. Triguero, I., García, S., Herrera, F.: Self-labeled techniques for semi-supervised learning: taxonomy, software and empirical study. Knowl. Inf. Syst. 42(2), 245–284 (2015). https://doi.org/10.1007/s10115-013-0706-y
18. Weka 3. http://www.cs.waikato.ac.nz/ml/weka. Accessed 28 June 2017
19. Wu, Y., Denny, J.C., Rosenbloom, S.T., Miller, R.A., Giuse, D.A., Xu, H.: A comparative study of current clinical natural language processing systems on handling abbreviations in discharge summaries. In: Proceedings of AMIA Annual Symposium, pp. 997–1003 (2012)
20. Wu, Y., et al.: Detecting abbreviations in discharge summaries using machine learning methods. In: Proceedings of AMIA Annual Symposium, pp. 1541–1549 (2011)
21. Wu, Y., Tang, B., Jiang, M., Moon, S., Denny, J.C., Xu, H.: Clinical acronym/abbreviation normalization using a hybrid approach. In: Proceedings of CLEF, pp. 1–9 (2013)
22. Wu, Y., et al.: A long journey to short abbreviations: developing an open-source framework for clinical abbreviation recognition and disambiguation (CARD). J. Am. Med. Inform. Assoc. 24(e1), e79–e86 (2017)
23. Xu, H., Stetson, P.D., Friedman, C.: A study of abbreviations in clinical notes. In: Proceedings of AMIA Annual Symposium, pp. 822–825 (2007)
24. Zhao, S., Li, J.: A semi-supervised self-training method based on density peaks and natural neighbors. J. Ambient Intell. Human. Comput. 1–15 (2020). https://doi.org/10.1007/s12652-020-02451-8
25. Zhou, Z.H., Li, M.: Tri-Training: exploiting unlabeled data using three classifiers. IEEE Trans. Knowl. Data Eng. 17(11), 1529–1541 (2005). https://doi.org/10.1109/TKDE.2005.186

An Effectiveness of Repeating a Spoken Digit for Speaker Verification

Duy Vo[1,2]([⊠]), Si Minh Le[1,2], Hao Duc Do[3], and Son Thai Tran[1,2]

[1] Faculty of Information Technology, University of Science,
Ho Chi Minh City, Vietnam
{vhbduy19,lmsi19}@clc.fitus.edu.vn, ttson@fit.hcmus.edu.vn
[2] Vietnam National University, Ho Chi Minh City, Vietnam
[3] FPT University, Ho Chi Minh City, Vietnam
haodd3@fe.edu.vn

Abstract. In recent years, there has been significant research in speaker verification, and the use of deep neural networks has dramatically enhanced the performance of speaker verification systems. This paper aims to investigate the effect of a predefined passphrase on the system's performance, using the state-of-the-art ECAPA-TDNN model as a speaker modeling technique. Our study focuses on discovering dominant passphrases from spoken digits through text-dependent speaker verification trial types. By comparing the performance of spoken digits and considering their pronunciations, we can analyze the influence of passphrases in the human voice on the speaker verification system. Furthermore, we identify that repeating incrementally up to a certain number of times leads to improvements in the accuracy of the system. Overall, our study has significant implications for advancing speaker authentication systems, especially systems deployed on embedded devices, which require low computation resources and need to be optimized in many aspects.

Keywords: Text-dependent speaker verification · Speaker verification · Speaker recognition · Deep neural networks

1 Introduction

Recently, speaker identification or verification systems have become a popular topic of interest as they provide the possibility of secure and convenient authentication methods. Specifically, speaker verification (SV) is an essential component of these systems as it determines whether two spoken utterances belong to the same person. With rapid advancements in deep learning models across various fields, such as Computer Vision and Natural Language Processing, employing these models in speaker authentication systems can significantly improve their accuracy.

D. Vo and S. M. Le—Equal contribution.

N. T. Nguyen et al. (Eds.): ACIIDS 2023, CCIS 1863, pp. 609–620, 2023.
https://doi.org/10.1007/978-3-031-42430-4_50

SV systems can be classified into two main types: text-independent (TI) and text-dependent (TD). TI does not require the speaker to say a specific phrase or text; instead, the system can analyze the speaker's voice to verify their identity. On the other hand, TD requires the speaker to say the predetermined phrase (passphrase). This type of system is more secure because it ensures that the speaker is who they claim to be by verifying their voice based on a specific phrase or text.

The SV is an essential component of many security and authentication systems. Accurate speaker authentication can provide a convenient and secure method for user identification in various applications, such as banking, home automation, and access control. However, several challenges are associated with speaker authentication, including the influence of human biology (gender, age), interference signals (noise, echo, environmental factors), an extensive requirement for labeled data in a text-dependent system, and the model's effectiveness in capturing the unique characteristics of speakers. Moreover, to facilitate system deployment, especially for embedded systems, which require optimizing time- and space-complexity as well as factors affecting the performance of systems. In addition to the restrictions and affecting factors mentioned above, determining suitable phrases when authenticating may increase efficiency help improve the accuracy of the system and reduce costs for data preparation.

The primary objective of our research is to explore, analyze, and identify phrases that can be effective in the authentication process for a specific dataset of the language by using the state-of-the-art ECAPA-TDNN model in the TI task for extracting embedding features. By discovering these phrases, we can improve the accuracy and effectiveness of speaker authentication systems. In addition, the research has shown that the system's performance depends on the word being emitted. By addressing these challenges and limitations, our research will significantly contribute to the development of more accurate and efficient speaker verification systems, enabling enhanced authentication in various applications.

The paper is organized as follows: Sect. 2 provides a literature review of previous research studies about speaker verification systems. Section 3 will explain components of the structure we used (Fig. 1). The experimental setup and results are outlined in Sect. 4 with the main dataset AudioMNIST [1], and we also define the process of training the speaker model as well as an evaluation protocol. Finally, a summary is presented in Sect. 5.

2   Related Work

Speaker verification is verifying a speaker's identity by analyzing their speech. One aspect of speaker authentication is the analysis and evaluation of phrases or sentences spoken by the speaker. Here is some research works related to this topic.

Speaker recognition has been an active research area for several decades. In particular, Selma Ozaydin at [13] proposed that utilized a combination of Hidden Markov Models (HMMs) and Mel Frequency Cepstral Coefficients (MFCCs)

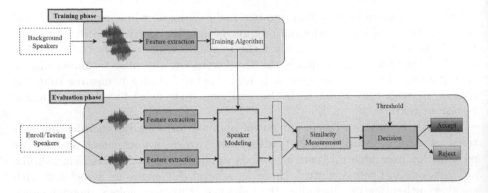

Fig. 1. Basic structure for a speaker verification system. The figure illustrates that the speech inputs are extracted features and generate a speaker model in the training phase. This model is used to extract deep speaker features in the evaluation phase.

as the main feature to extract features from speech signals to identify speakers. The system is trained on a limited dataset of spoken digit utterances with the commonly used techniques. The training data consists of ten people's digit utterances from one to ten. With this constraint, the system is developed to recognize and process such utterances. The system resulted from the recognition accuracy varying depending on the speaker and the specific word. Some speakers and words were recognized more accurately than others. However, this method may not perform well in scenarios where speakers are talking continuously, background noise, or a speaker's voice changes over time due to factors such as age, gender, and emotion.

Deep learning approaches have shown great promise in speaker verification in recent years, with systems such as the end-to-end text-dependent speaker verification system [2,8]. [2] and [8], both developed by Google, present a novel approach to an end-to-end system for text-dependent speaker verification, which means that the system verifies the speaker's identity based on a specific text prompt provided to the speaker. In [8], the system uses a Deep Neural Network architecture (DNN) and Recurrent Neural Network (RNN) while [2] combines attention-based models with deep neural networks to extract features from speech signals and perform speaker verification. The systems are trained on private datasets of speech segments and achieve significant performance on several benchmark datasets.

Most recently, a deep speaker model is a neural network that extracts speaker-specific features by mapping variable-length utterances to fixed-dimensional embeddings. Deep speaker modeling for speaker verification commonly uses Time Delay Neural Network (TDNN) architecture to capture the speech signal's temporal and spectral characteristics [6,16]. X-vector [16] proposed the neural network architecture, selection of training data, and data augmentation techniques to contribute to the robustness of the approach. The x-vector approach has since become a popular method for speaker recognition tasks. In [6], the paper proposed the ECAPA-TDNN architecture and demonstrated improved robustness to noise and reverberation compared to previous TDNN-based speaker verification systems. This architecture consists of multiple TDNN layers, each followed by a channel attention module that learns to emphasize important channels and suppress noise. This architecture is a highly effective approach to noise audio and environmental conditions. ECAPA-TDNN is trained using AAM-softmax [5] and achieves state-of-the-art performance on VoxCeleb1 [12] and VoxSRC [3] dataset.

3   Preliminaries

3.1   Feature Extraction

Feature extraction, a part of the system, aims to extract relevant information from the speech waveform. One of the most commonly used feature extraction techniques in the SV system is Mel-frequency cepstral coefficients (MFCC). The general overview of the steps for extracting MFCC is shown in Fig. 2. This study uses the log mel spectrogram as input for speaker modeling.

Fig. 2. Block diagram of MFCCs based feature extraction algorithm

Pre-emphasis. Due to the structure of the human speech production system, the high-frequency part of the speech signal was repressed. Pre-emphasis aims to increase the magnitude of energy in the high frequencies, which helps improve the system's performance. Widely used pre-emphasis is given by:

$$Y(n) = x(n) - \alpha x(n-1), \tag{1}$$

where α is the pre-emphasis coefficient ($\alpha \in [0.95, 0.97]$), and $x(n)$ is the sample data with $0 \le n \le N - 1$, where N is the sample size of speech signal. The typical value of α is 0.97.

Short-Time Fourier Transform. The valuable speech signal information is represented in the frequency domain instead of the time domain. Fourier Transform (FT) performs the frequency domain signal by summarizing many sinusoidal elements at each frequency. With a discrete signal having N elements, FT of $x(n)$ is formulated by:

$$X(k) = \sum_{n=0}^{N-1} x(n)e^{\frac{-i2\pi kn}{N}} \tag{2}$$

The FT is usually applied to the entire signal at once, so this does not consider any local variations in the signal over time. That leads to the developing of the Short-Time Fourier Transform (STFT) algorithm. The STFT algorithm involves dividing a speech signal into overlapping frames to capture the dynamic characteristics of the speech signal and applying the FT to each frame. Therefore, the amplitude and information of the signal are represented in both time and frequency. The following formula presents the STFT:

$$X(m, k) = \sum_{n=0}^{N-1} x(n)w(n-m)e^{\frac{-i2\pi kn}{N}} \tag{3}$$

where $X(m, k)$ is the amplitude at time m of frequency k, and $w(t)$ is a window function. With speech signal processing, Hamming window is generally preferred. The following formula defines the Hamming window:

$$w(n) = 0.54 - 0.46 \cos \frac{2\pi n}{N-1} \tag{4}$$

where N is the length of the window, and n is the sample index within the window ($0 \le n \le N - 1$).

Mel Filter Bank. The Mel filter bank or Mel scale relates to perceived frequency. The human ear discerns sound, which is different from how machines will perceive sound. Our ears are much better at perceiving small changes at low frequencies than at high ones. Therefore, the Mel scale maps the frequency from the previous step to the frequency humans will discern. The formulas for the mapping between frequency and Mel scale are given by:

$$Mel(f) = 2595 \log_{10}(1 + \frac{f}{700}) \tag{5}$$

$$Mel^{-1}(m) = 700(10^{\frac{m}{2595}} - 1) \tag{6}$$

where f is the actual frequency in Hz and m is the mel scale.

3.2   Speaker Modeling

Based on the recent trends in face verification in computer vision, ECAPA-TDNN [6] uses TDNN architecture and introduces multiple enhancements. The model has implemented Res2Net [7] modules with impactful skip connection and uses Squeeze-and-Excitation (SE) blocks [9] to explicitly model channel interdependencies. Moreover, hierarchical features of each layer operating on a different level are aggregated and propagated in the modules to capture both the shallow and deep feature maps. In ECAPA-TDNN, statistics pooling modules with channel and context-dependent frame attention are improved to focus on speaker-specific properties of vowels rather than consonants. Those improvements allow ECAPA-TDNN to extract speaker characteristics and outperform other models. Figure 3 shows the architecture of ECAPA-TDNN as speaker modeling in our experiment.

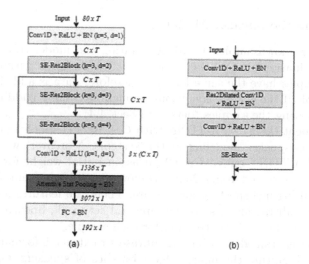

Fig. 3. The illustration of ECAPA-TDNN based speaker modeling. (a) shows the whole architecture of the ECAPA-TDNN network with k standing for kernel size and d for dilation. C and T correspond to the feature map's channel and temporal dimension (b) the detail SE-Res2Block in the ECAPA-TDNN model.

3.3   Similarity Measurement

In the SV system, this is used to determine the degree of similarity between two sets of speaker features. In this study, we use cosine similarity to determine the cosine of the angle between two speaker embeddings. The cosine similarity is defined by:

$$Score(x, y) = \frac{<x, y>}{||x||||y||} \tag{7}$$

where x, y are two vectors, $<\cdot, \cdot>$ represents the inner product of two vectors and $|| \cdot ||$ is Euclidean norm of a vector.

4   Experimental Result

4.1   Dataset Description

We use a public AudioMNIST provided in [1] with 60 different speakers (48 males and 12 females). Due to physiological differences between females and males, gender can impact speaker verification accuracy. Therefore, we split AudioMNIST into the development and evaluation sets based on gender in a 1:1 ratio. Each subset consists of 6 females and 24 males (30 speakers total). We use the development set to train the speaker model for each passphrase and evaluate the accuracy of the system across different gender groups through the evaluation set (in detail in Sect. 4.4). Furthermore, data augmentation, which generates extra samples, brings many benefits to neural networks. Based on the method provided in [16], we combine the MUSAN dataset (noises, music, and babble) [15] and the publicly available RIR dataset (reverberation) [11] for data augmentation.

4.2   Training the Speaker Modeling

All samples are downsampled to 16 kHz during the model training phase as well as the evaluation phase. We consider every word spoken within a second to ensure all samples have the same length. Therefore, data is added zeros to the end of a sample if the sample is not long enough. We apply padding with zeros after concatenating the samples (details in Sect. 4.4).

We implement the ECAPA-TDNN with $C = 1024$ channels in convolutional frame layers as speaker modeling in the systems. Moreover, we use the pre-trained ECAPA-TDNN on VoxCeleb2 [4] as an initial weight for models. The speech signal is extracted from a 25 ms window with a 10 ms frameshift to get an 80-dimensional log mel spectrogram feature. Then, the features are normalized through mean subtraction. As an experimental setup [6], SpecAugment [14] is used to apply the log mel spectrogram for each sample.

One model is trained for each passphrase to extract information from the passphrase and capture the unique characteristics of speakers, and all models are trained with an initial learning rate of 1e−3. During the training model, we use the learning rate decay through StepLR policy along with the Adam optimizer [10] and apply a weight decay of 2e−5 for all weights in the model. All systems use AAM-softmax [5] with a margin of 0.2 and softmax prescaling of 30. The models are trained until convergence with a mini-batch size of 32.

4.3   Speaker Verification

In this study, we use a text-dependent protocol to evaluate the influence of passphrases on the system. In TD-SV, a task involves four types of trials, whether the speaker with the test utterance is the target speaker and whether the test utterance matches the predefined passphrase (Table 1). The system only accepts cases where the target speaker pronounces the correct passphrase (TAR-Correct), while other trials are rejected. Indeed, the target speaker is still rejected by not matching the lexical content, even though the target speaker pronounces the test utterance (TAR-Wrong). In addition, an impostor should be rejected when the impostor pronounces the correct passphrase (IMP-Correct) or a different passphrase (IMP-Wrong).

Table 1. Types of trials defined for text-dependent speaker verification

	Correct pass-phrase	Wrong pass-phrase
Target	TAR-correct	TAR-wrong
Impostor	IMP-correct	IMP-wrong

In the SV system, trial scores are determined using the cosine similarity between two speaker embeddings extracted from the fully-connected layer of the trained models. The system accepts the input when the computed score exceeds the acceptance threshold. Therefore, the rate of impostor acceptance is named the false acceptance rate (FAR), and the rate of target-speaker rejection is named the false rejection rate (FRR). The performance measurement is commonly evaluated based on an equal error rate (EER), where the FAR and FRR are optimal. The smaller the EER is, the better.

4.4 Evaluation Protocol

All utterances pronounced by the target speaker in the evaluation set are used to generate TAR-correct. The other utterances from the other passphrases are used to TAR-wrong, and the other speakers from the dataset (both development and evaluation sets) are used to generate impostor trials. As described in the Sect. 4.1, to ensure accurate speaker verification for both genders, we randomly select impostor trials having the same gender as the target speaker.

In EER measurement, a threshold represents the boundary between positive and negative classifications in a binary classification problem. The threshold is too high, which increases the FRR and decreases the FAR, while setting it too low increases the FAR and decreases the FRR. Therefore, we fine-tune the threshold on the evaluation set to compute the FAR and FRR at different threshold values. The threshold that achieves the EER point is then chosen as the optimal threshold.

4.5 Result and Discussion

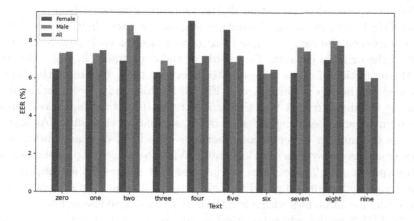

Fig. 4. Comparison of the spoken digits for both genders

We trained a model for three different runs in each passphrase and averaged the results. The result in Fig. 4 shows the difference between females and males due to the unbalanced distribution of gender on the AudioMNIST dataset, so the results on the association of both genders (All) tend to be the distribution of

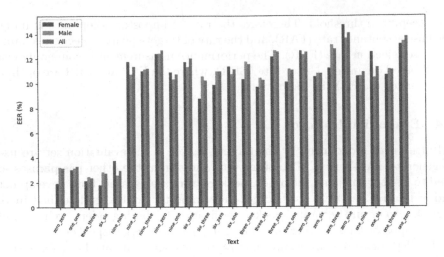

Fig. 5. Comparison between the permutation from the top digits and the repetition of digits.

males that have more samples in the dataset. The accuracy is not too different between spoken digits of each gender except for digits (2, 4, and 5). Overall, some digits, including 9, 6, and 3, reached a higher accuracy than the other digits for both genders. In decreasing order, we selected five digits with the highest average accuracy (nine-six-three-zero-one). The digits are used to generate a new passphrase from a permutation of five digits for two selections, and the results are compared to repeating digits. Data are generated from the original AudioMNIST dataset by concatenating samples of each digit on the different indexes between the samples. The total of samples for each new passphrase is equal to the original dataset. The result of the experiment in Fig. 5 illustrates that the repetition of digits brings better accuracy than combining the digits, as evidenced by the top performance in Fig. 4. In this study, we experiment with repeating the digits from 1 to 5 times. The repetition of digits is based on data generation by concatenating different index samples of each digit. As shown in Fig. 6, as the number of repetitions increases, the EER decrease, indicating an enhancement in the system's performance. With the length of passphrases being 2 s corresponding to 2 repetitions, we can see that the results are improved significantly at each digit compared to digit uttering 1 time. The system produced good results for audio files with a length of 3 s to 5 s due to the architecture of the ECAPA-TDNN model, which is optimized for speech signals having long lengths. However, by combining this model with our protocol, the system has effectively achieved accurate results for audio files with a length of fewer than 3 s. The text discusses the experimental results of the AudioMNIST dataset, emphasizing digit identification. It is observed that the performance system depends on the word being spoken. The recognition rate of the speaker decreases (EER increases) for words with simple pronunciation, clear sounds, and short consonants. However,

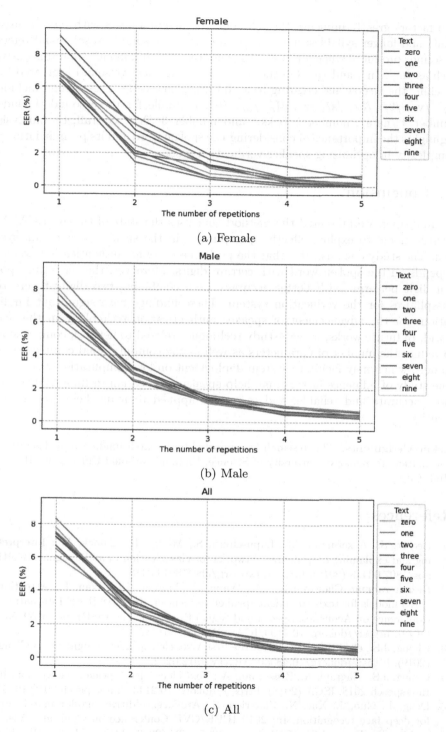

(a) Female

(b) Male

(c) All

Fig. 6. Results of repeating digits with the number of repetitions ranging from 1 to 5 times for each gender. Data are generated from the original AudioMNIST by concatenating digits with different indexes of samples.

two factors greatly influence the difference between numbers with more consonants and longer syllables: nasal sound and fricative sound. Nasal sound refers
to sounds produced when air passes through the nose and mouth simultaneously,
such as /m/, /n/, and /ŋ/. On the other hand, the fricative sound is created by
blocking the airflow and creating friction during an escape. These sound include
/f/, /v/, /θ/, /ð/, /s/, /z/, /ʃ/, /ʒ/, /h/. Example for these sounds include
number 9 /naɪn/, number 6 /sɪks/, and number 3 /θrː/. Overall, the analysis
highlights the importance of considering the spoken word and its pronunciation's
complexity in optimizing speaker verification systems.

5   Conclusion

In this paper, we presented the method that uses the state-of-the-art ECAPA-
TDNN model to explore effective passphrases in the speaker verification system. The study demonstrates that the performance of an authentication system
depends on the spoken word with certain digits. Moreover, the repeating spoken digit performs with better accuracy than combining two digits to create
passphrases for the verification system. These findings have significant implications for the advancement of speaker authentication technology in the real
world. In future works, we can study techniques related to network compression
to reduce the number of parameters as well as the computational complexity of
models, which may facilitate system deployment on low-computation resources.
The study of influence factors may help speaker verification technology become
more accurate and reliable, and it can be applied to many fields related to
security.

Acknowledgments. This research is supported by research funding from Faculty of
Information Technology, University of Science, Vietnam National University - Ho Chi
Minh City.

References

1. Becker, S., Ackermann, M., Lapuschkin, S., Müller, K., Samek, W.: Interpreting and explaining deep neural networks for classification of audio signals. CoRR
   abs/1807.03418 (2018). http://arxiv.org/abs/1807.03418
2. Rezaur rahman Chowdhury, F.A., Wang, Q., Moreno, I.L., Wan, L.: Attention-
   based models for text-dependent speaker verification. In: 2018 IEEE International
   Conference on Acoustics, Speech and Signal Processing (ICASSP), pp. 5359–5363
   (2018). https://doi.org/10.1109/ICASSP.2018.8461587
3. Chung, J.S., et al.: VoxSRC 2019: the first VoxCeleb speaker recognition challenge
   (2019). https://doi.org/10.48550/ARXIV.1912.02522
4. Chung, J.S., Nagrani, A., Zisserman, A.: VoxCeleb2: deep speaker recognition. In:
   Interspeech 2018. ISCA (2018). https://doi.org/10.21437/interspeech.2018-1929
5. Deng, J., Guo, J., Xue, N., Zafeiriou, S.: ArcFace: additive angular margin loss
   for deep face recognition. In: 2019 IEEE/CVF Conference on Computer Vision
   and Pattern Recognition (CVPR), pp. 4685–4694 (2019). https://doi.org/10.1109/
   CVPR.2019.00482

6. Desplanques, B., Thienpondt, J., Demuynck, K.: ECAPA-TDNN: emphasized channel attention, propagation and aggregation in TDNN based speaker verification. In: Interspeech 2020. ISCA (2020). https://doi.org/10.21437/interspeech.2020-2650

7. He, K., Zhang, X., Ren, S., Sun, J.: Deep residual learning for image recognition (2015). https://doi.org/10.48550/ARXIV.1512.03385

8. Heigold, G., Moreno, I., Bengio, S., Shazeer, N.: End-to-end text-dependent speaker verification (2015). https://doi.org/10.48550/ARXIV.1509.08062

9. Hu, J., Shen, L., Sun, G.: Squeeze-and-excitation networks. In: 2018 IEEE/CVF Conference on Computer Vision and Pattern Recognition, pp. 7132–7141 (2018). https://doi.org/10.1109/CVPR.2018.00745

10. Kingma, D.P., Ba, J.: Adam: a method for stochastic optimization (2014). https://doi.org/10.48550/ARXIV.1412.6980

11. Ko, T., Peddinti, V., Povey, D., Seltzer, M.L., Khudanpur, S.: A study on data augmentation of reverberant speech for robust speech recognition. In: 2017 IEEE International Conference on Acoustics, Speech and Signal Processing (ICASSP), pp. 5220–5224 (2017). https://doi.org/10.1109/ICASSP.2017.7953152

12. Nagrani, A., Chung, J.S., Zisserman, A.: VoxCeleb: a large-scale speaker identification dataset. In: Interspeech 2017. ISCA (2017). https://doi.org/10.21437/interspeech.2017-950

13. Ozaydin, S.: An isolated word speaker recognition system. In: 2017 International Conference on Electrical and Computing Technologies and Applications (ICECTA), pp. 1–5 (2017). https://doi.org/10.1109/ICECTA.2017.8251987

14. Park, D.S., et al.: SpecAugment: a simple data augmentation method for automatic speech recognition. In: Interspeech 2019. ISCA (2019). https://doi.org/10.21437/interspeech.2019-2680

15. Snyder, D., Chen, G., Povey, D.: MUSAN: a music, speech, and noise corpus (2015). https://doi.org/10.48550/ARXIV.1510.08484

16. Snyder, D., Garcia-Romero, D., Sell, G., Povey, D., Khudanpur, S.: X-vectors: robust DNN embeddings for speaker recognition. In: 2018 IEEE International Conference on Acoustics, Speech and Signal Processing (ICASSP), pp. 5329–5333 (2018). https://doi.org/10.1109/ICASSP.2018.8461375

Author Index

© The Editor(s) (if applicable) and The Author(s), under exclusive license
to Springer Nature Switzerland AG 2023
N. T. Nguyen et al. (Eds.): ACIIDS 2023, CCIS 1863, pp. 621–623, 2023.
https://doi.org/10.1007/978-3-031-42430-4

Printed in the United States
by Baker & Taylor Publisher Services